5 RESEARCH STRATEGIES   543

6 USING CITATION STYLES   617

7 WRITING STRATEGIES   733

TRACY

MAKE THE CONNECTION

Good writing is all about making connections—and the connection between writer and reader is the most important of all. *The Longman Handbook for Writers and Readers* will help you become a better writer by helping you make this connection in your writing. By focusing on your experience as a reader, and developing your abilities to recognize the expectations of your readers, it can help you learn strategies that will enable you to succeed in a variety of writing situations.

Using the text's unique **"Read, Recognize, Revise"** approach will help you develop an intuitive understanding of grammar conventions. Consulting the **"Strategies"** that appear throughout will help you devise concrete solutions to common problems. Understanding the text's emphasis on writing for **different communities** will help you become more attuned to the needs and requirements of various audiences and assignments—whether you're writing a college paper, composing a résumé, or designing a newsletter.

No matter what context you find yourself writing in, *The Longman Handbook for Writers and Readers* prompts you to attend to your readers' expectations, providing you with the information and strategies you need to become a better writer.

THE "READ RECOGNIZE REVISE" APPROACH TO CORRECTING ERRORS

Consider the contrasts between the following two examples of reasoning, offered in a public context; both are letters to the editor about a controversial proposal to build a greenway between two parks, one of which is in Coolidge (an economically depressed neighborhood) and the other in Lake Stearns (a wealthy, stable neighborhood of fine older homes).

LETTER 1 (LACKS CRITICAL REASONING)

Doesn't consider other points of view

Little evidence

Vague details and ideas

Logical?

Reasonable?

City planners must be out of their minds to cook up this crazy idea. Drug pushers and thieves will have a field day preying on the people who use Lake Stearns Park, and soon the whole neighborhood will be destroyed by crime. We must stop these public officials before they totally destroy our lives with their senseless fantasies.

READER'S RESPONSE: This is just a collection of assertions with little evidence. The writer doesn't try to explain why the assertions are reasonable but feels free to dismiss other perspectives as unreasonable and illogical—without presenting any evidence.

LETTER 2 (DISPLAYS CRITICAL REASONING)

Goes beyond the obvious

Acknowledges other perspectives

Carefully presented evidence and clearly defined ideas

Logical reasoning

Reasonable conclusion

The proposal to create a greenway between Coolidge and Lake Stearns Parks appears to bridge the gap between these two different communities. But the greenway will not solve the existing problems in Coolidge Park. Residents near Lake Stearns are unlikely to ride their bikes or jog into Coolidge, and the presence of Coolidge residents in Stearns will only create a feeling, unjustified though it may be, of defensiveness. City funds could better be used to improve Coolidge Park by adding lighting, a basketball court, and an updated community center.

READER'S RESPONSE: The problem isn't simple, and the writer gives it a careful, balanced treatment. The reasons for both objecting to the proposal and for an alternate solution are supported by specific details.

The lack of critical reasoning displayed in Letter 1 undermines its persuasiveness, except perhaps for those few readers who already agree with its conclusions. In Letter 2, the depth of critical reasoning invites readers to take the writer's thinking seriously, forming their own opinions and agreeing or disagreeing in response.

12b Critical reasoning in academic, public, and work communities

Researchers looking for ways to develop alternative-fuel vehicles will take different paths with their critical reasoning than public officials trying to create (or repeal) regulations, or business executives developing new products. In this case as in many others, though the subject remains the same, the

READER'S REACTION notes help identify potential errors by showing how a reader may react to confusing passages.

12b reason

Also remember that your credibility depends on the credibili community resource you choose to rely on. If you are writing a paper a abetes, citing sources from a collection of official American Diabetes Asse Web pages and a moderated electronic mailing list of endocrinologist more effective (and responsible) than citing email from a local bulletin about a new home remedy. For all information from online sources you w cite, ask yourself, "Where did it come from?" If you are not confident a your answer, your instructor might be able to help you evaluate the credibi of a source. You should also be prepared to find an alternative site.

Cutting and pasting information from Web sites and other Internet sources into a single document for later use is a good way to consolidate ye research. This new form of note taking, however, can lead to accidental p giarism. It is easy to forget where something originally came from and mi takenly convince yourself the writing is your own!

13e plag

STRATEGY

- Always write down the address of any Web site you are using, and clearly label text you copy from that site. For easy reference, print the first page of each Web site you're using in case your later drafts require further documentation. The printout should include the site's URL so you can return to it for future reference and also for citation purposes.
- Always note the date when you found the information. Web sites can be updated daily, and your cited information may disappear. In addition, you will need to provide the access date in your citation if you use the information in your final document.
- If you're citing an email, electronic mailing list, or Web forum message that has not been posted to a publicly accessible location, ask the authors' permission before quoting. It's a good idea to do this even if the posting is public.
- Corroborate your sources. Follow the journalist's rule: If you can't find the same information in at least two credible places on the Internet, don't use the material.

STRATEGY SECTIONS offer practical advice on how to revise and edit.

2 Acting ethically online

When working online, do so ethically and professionally. If you're new to the Internet, it will not take you long to discover paper mills—the electronic equivalent of the infamous fraternity and dormitory "test files." Additionally, many writing classes now post their work to the Web for peer review; and you may find these papers and projects when you use a search engine. You should carefully consider the moral implications of borrowing such Internet resources

Read, Recognize, and Revise
Ten Serious Errors

WHY ARE THESE ERRORS SERIOUS?

These ten errors are identified in our research as among those most likely to confuse or irritate readers in the academic community. Whether errors distort meaning or suggest carelessness, they distract readers from what you want to say. Too many errors can erode your relationship with your readers and diminish the success of your writing.

USING THE "READ, RECOGNIZE, AND REVISE" APPROA

Use the read-recognize-revise pattern to identify and edit errors. First, example provided (column 1). Consider the Reader's Reaction, showin a reader might respond (column 2). Next use the handbook's advice, t Strategies suggested, or your own strategy to help you *recognize* the (column 3). Finally, select a Strategy to revise, or replace the error (co

READ		RECOGNIZE	REVISE
Pay attention to potential problems as you revise and edit	**Consider the possible reactions of your community of readers**	**Try strategies for recognizing problems—or invent your own.**	**Use strategies to edit, repa replace errors or problems**
1. The heavy rain turned the parking are to mud. *And stranded thousands of cars.*	READER'S REACTION: The second part seems detached. Now I've got to stop and figure out how it fits.	**Fragment:** Ask questions. Who (or what) does? Who (or what) is (**21a**)	The heavy rain turned the park mud and stranded thousands c
2. The promoters called *the insurance company they discovered their* coverage for accidents was limited.	READER'S REACTION: I'm confused. Is this about some new insurance company that the promoters discovered?	**Fused Sentence:** Look for a long sentence without internal punctuation; count the separate statements it contains (**22b**)	The promoters called the insura and they discovered their cove accidents was limited. (**22c**)
3. After talking with the groundskeeper, the security chief said *he* would not be responsible for the safety of the crowd.	READER'S REACTION: Who's *he*—the groundskeeper or the security chief?	**Unclear Pronoun Reference:** See whether your sentence contains two or more words to which a pronoun might refer (**22a**)	After talking with the grounds security chief said, "I will not for the safety of the crowd."
4. The local authorities *hadn't scarcely* enough resources to cope with the flooding.	READER'S REACTION: *Hadn't scarcely*— this isn't the way a college graduate or a professional writes.	**Double Negative:** Check for combinations of negative words like no, not, scarcely, or don't (**20b-4**)	The local authorities had scare resources to cope with the fle
5. *After announcing the cancellation from the stage,* the crowd began complaining to the promoters.	READER'S REACTION: I know the crowd didn't announce the cancellation, but that's what this says!	**Dangling Modifier:** When a modifier begins a sentence, consider whether the person or thing modified is the subject of the main clause. (**24a**)	After the promoters announc cancellation from the stage, complaining about the decis
6. Even the *promoters promise* to reschedule and honor tickets did little to stop the *crowds complaints.*	READER'S REACTION: I can't read this without feeling irritated that apostrohes are missing.	**Missing Possessive Apostrophe:** Test for possession by trying to turn a noun ending in -s into an of phrase. (**36a**)	Even the promoters' promise and honor tickets did *little* t complaints. (**36b**)
7. "The grounds are *slippery,* the mayor announced, "so please leave in an orderly manner."	READER'S REACTION: Here are more missing marks! Didn't this writer bother to proofread?	**Missing Marks:** Look for marks often used in pairs such as quotation marks (**32a**) and commas. (**34c, 34e, 34j**)	"The grounds are slippery," announced, "so please leav manner." (**37a**)
8. Away from the microphone the mayor said, "I hope the security chief or the *promoters has* a plan to help everyone leave safely."	READER'S REACTION: Promoters has? This careless writer didn't even make the effort to fit subjects and verbs together.	**Lack of Subject-Verb Agreement:** Find the subject (especially if separated, plural, or compound); match the verb. (**19a–19b**)	Away from the microphon "I hope the security chief have a plan, to help every (**19b**)
9. If *people* left the amphitheater quickly, *you* could get to your car without standing long in the rain.	READER'S REACTION: Why is this sentence mixing people with you? Is *you* suppose to mean *me?*	**Shift:** Hunt for illogical or inconsistent shifts among I, we, you , he, she, it, or they. (**25a**)	If people left the amphith could get to their cars wi in the rain. (**25b**)
10. *Although,* the muddy parking area cause problems, all the cars and people, left the grounds without incident.	READER'S REACTION: It looks as if the writer just tossed in some commas here—and they make the sentence hard to read.	**Unneccasry Commas:** Check for unneeded commas after words like *although* or between subject and verb. (**34a**)	Although the muddy par problems, all the cars and grounds without inciden

"READ, RECOGNIZE, AND REVISE: TEN SERIOUS ERRORS" CHART

Located in the back of the book for *quick reference on the most common problems*, this chart also acts as a guide to using the Read, Recognize, Revise approach.

OTHER USEFUL FEATURES TO LOOK FOR IN THE LONGMAN HANDBOOK

A WORD ABOUT SPEAKING

While Americans tend to "forgive" occasional grammatical lapses or other errors in oral presentations, they also form a negative image of the speaker's credibility if these errors are too frequent or severe. (This is not the case with differences in *accent*.) As you work on your public speaking, transfer your growing knowledge of grammar to your spoken language, but don't become too concerned about your accent unless it affects your audience's ability to understand you.

A WORD ABOUT SPEAKING boxes provide tips and strategies for oral communication and delivering presentations.

DID YOU KNOW?

Language scholars have described several approaches to address the issue of language variation. One approach is *eradication*: try to wipe out all language differences by teaching people to use only the standard. A second approach is *appreciation*: celebrate the diversity of differences in our speech, and accept all dialects as reflections of culture, heritage, and community. A third approach is *biloquialism* or *bidialectalism*: help people to learn more than one variety, so they can express themselves equally well in differing situations and not give up their linguistic identities and ways of relating to their own communities.

DID YOU KNOW? BOXES offer interesting points of fact about the English language. These notes often help students understand how we have come to follow the conventions in use today.

ferent supporting words. Retain the general sense of the passage, but feel free to add your own ideas and perspective.

ESL

16c
gr

ESL ADVICE: ADJECTIVE, ADVERB, AND NOUN CLAUSES

ADJECTIVE CLAUSES

Adjective clauses (also called **relative clauses**) work like adjectives because they modify or add more information to nouns. To form a relative clause, use a relative pronoun: *who, whom, that, which,* or *whose. Who, whom,* and *that,* and *whose* are used to modify people. *That, which,* and *whose* are used to modify animals, places, and things. In spoken American English the use of *whom* generally is optional, but it is always used in formal writing.

Place the relative clause as close as possible to the noun (the antecedent) that it modifies.

ESL ADVICE for non-native speakers is integrated into discussions of grammar and writing, and can be found in contextually relevant areas throughout the text.

USING TECHNOLOGY AS A WRITER AND RESEARCHER

THOROUGH COVERAGE OF WRITING AND TECHNOLOGY

includes in-depth treatment of document design, Internet research, online communities, and more.

THE POWER OF ONE
Alcohol Awareness Week
UNC Charlotte
March 1 – 4, 1999 • UNC Charlotte

SPECIAL EVENTS:

MONDAY, MARCH 1ST
Alcohol Insanity Tour '99
with Wendi Foxx
Nationally renowned comedienne
Wendi Foxx will entertain with Alcohol
Aware Educational Comedy.
McKnight Hall 8pm

TUESDAY, MARCH 2ND
Copacabana Mocktail Bar
Representatives from RSA and SGA
will provide refreshing alcohol-free
"mocktails" in a tropical setting right
here on campus!
After Hours 11:30am-1:30pm

WEDNESDAY, MARCH 3RD
DUI: Decisions
Under the Influence
Campus Police will demonstrate the
hazards of drinking with sobriety
exercises performed on real life
students.
Poplar Hall 2nd floor 8pm

THURSDAY, MARCH 4TH
Pledge Card Drive
Join the campus community in
pledging not to drink and drive.
Belk Tower 11am-3pm

Sponsored by the Department of Housing and
Residence Life, Resident Students

Mine is the Power of One
The power to make my own decisions
The power to achieve all of my goals

Mine is the Power of One
The power to create the life I want
The power to impact the lives of others

Mine is the Power of One
The power to set responsible limits
The power to drink without driving

The Power that is Mine
Comes from within

The Power that is Mine

① Unique font draws attention to headline
② Date and description of the event prominently placed
③ Space directs attention to key elements in poster
④ Scheduling information presented in easy-to-read format
⑤ Original artwork adds visual interest
⑥ Poem uses a more legible font that complements the headline

NUMBERED WEB ICONS

appearing in the margins of the page show where exercises, Web research activities, and more can be found on the Companion Website.

www.ablongman.com/anson

---

1 Redraft unworkable material

When you read and reread your rough draft carefully, thinking critically about its content, structure, tone, style, appeals to audience, and purpose, some parts may seem inappropriate, illogical, or unworkable. You may need to **redraft** these parts entirely.

STRATEGY

Read through your draft as if you were seeing it for the first time. It helps if you have left your draft alone for a short while so that you can see it afresh. As you read, place a question mark next to sections that seem confusing or garbled. Go back to the parts you've marked, and bracket the specific places where your writing seems to lose its vitality, meaning, or style. Ask yourself what you're trying to accomplish in a particular passage. Then, without even looking at the draft, try again on a new sheet of paper to write what you mean.

Jessica White shared with her classmates a draft of her essay reflecting on her cheerleading experiences. They felt the first paragraph didn't capture much tension or excitement, and placed brackets around sentences that seemed particularly weak. After changing a few words, White realized she really needed to redraft the entire paragraph.

ORIGINAL DRAFT WITH BRACKETS FROM PEER GROUP

I was a cheerleading captain and I loved basketball. [I put a lot of work into my cheerleading season.] We had a great team spirit between the cheerleaders and the teammates. [We stood behind our team from the beginning to end.] We led our crowd to great enthusiasm and spirit which I believe had a terrific effect on our team.

REVISED DRAFT

There we were, a bunch of cheerleaders packed into Rebecca's car. Everyone's spirits were soaring; we had won the quarter-final game of the state basketball championship. It was a bitterly cold night, but none of us felt the chill. Surrounded by blaring music, we laughed, joked, and endlessly replayed the highlights of the game. Would the team keep up its level of intensity? What upcoming finals. Talk then turned to the were our chances of winning? What would we do if we lost?

2 Reorganize poorly arranged paragraphs or sections

Structural problems are common in early drafts. Often you find that you've written your way "into" your main point, discovering what you want to say in the process of drafting. It may be more graceful or logical to move that material into your introduction. Or you may recognize that two different paragraphs are making the same point and should be combined.

STRATEGIES FOR FINDING INFORMATION IN THE HANDBOOK

The **Brief Contents**, on the book's inside front cover, provides a quick guide to the handbook's entire contents.

The **Contents** gives a detailed outline of the handbook, with section and page numbers for all topics.

The **Index** provides an alphabetical listing of every key term and topic in the handbook, as well as the precise pages on which it is covered.

The **Usage Glossary** at the back of the book defines key terms, provides capsule usage guidelines, and includes cross-references to text discussions.

The list of **Revision Symbols**, on the inside of the back endpaper, is a guide to the marks that instructors commonly use when they suggest ways to revise essays.

Revision and Editing Symbols

abbrev	incorrect abbreviation, 43	no ¶	no new paragraph, 9
agr	error in subject-verb or pronoun-antecedent agreement, 19	p	error in punctuation, 33–38
		punc	error in punctuation, 33–38
apos	lack of (or incorrect) possessive apostrophe, 35	^	comma, 33a–j
		no ^	no comma, 33j
art	article used incorrectly, 16	;	semicolon, 34a
awk	awkward construction, 10a–b	:	colon, 34b
		∨	apostrophe, 35
cap	capital letter needed, 39	" "	quotation marks, 36
case	incorrect pronoun case, 17	.	period, 37a
clear	clearer sentence needed, 10a	?	question mark, 37b
coh	paragraph or essay coherence needed, 9c	!	exclamation point, 37c
		( ) [ ] —	parentheses, brackets, dashes, 38a–c
cs	comma splice, 22	.../	ellipses, slashes, 38d
coord	faulty coordination, 28a–b	prep	preposition error, 16a
dev	paragraph or essay development needed, 9e	pr ref	pronoun reference error, 23
		ref	pronoun reference error, 23
discrm	sexist or discriminatory language, 32	rep	repetitious, 31
		sent	sentence revision needed, 10
dm	dangling modifier, 24b	shift	shift, 25
dneg	double negative, 20d	sp	word spelled incorrectly, 44
emph	emphasis needed, 10c	spell	word spelled incorrectly, 44
foc	paragraph or essay focus needed, 9a–b	sub	faulty subordination, 28c
		t	wrong verb tense, 18a–c
frag	sentence fragment, 21	tense	wrong verb tense, 18a–c
fs	fused sentence, 22	trans	transition needed, 9c–d
hyph	hyphen (-) needed, 41	und	underlining (italics), 40
inc	incomplete sentence, 26b	us	error in usage, Glossary
ital	italics (underlining), 40	var	sentence variety needed, 10d
lc	lowercase letter needed, 39	verb	incorrect verb form, 18
link	paragraph linkage needed, 9d	wc	faulty word choice, 29a
log	faulty reasoning, 12c–d, 55f	wordy	too many words, 31
	grammatically mixed	ww	wrong word, 29

HOW TO WORK WITH A HANDBOOK PAGE

Look for these elements and reference features to find information in the text.

Running head identifies the chapter topic on the left and the section topic on the right.

Paired examples illustrate draft and edited versions of a sentence.

Reader's Reaction shows how a reader might respond to a problem.

Page tab uses a symbol or abbreviation to identify the section topic.

Web icons indicate interactive activities on the Website

Exercises appear throughout the text offering opportunities for practice.

---

332   Misplaced, Dangling, and Disruptive Modifiers

2. "Non-trads" defer college entry often until after a major life event.
3. Following divorce or job loss, returning to college temporarily provides a boost to self-esteem.
4. Experts report that non-traditional students earn high grade point averages easily exceeding those of traditional students.
5. Nonetheless, failing to take into account the special needs of "non-trads" causes them to drop out frequently.

B. Working with a group of other writers, edit the sentences in Exercise 2A by rewriting each in two different ways.

---

4 Pay attention to clauses beginning with *who, which*, and *that*, or other subordinators

You should generally place a modifying clause beginning with *who, which,* or *that* right after the word(s) it is intended to modify. (See 16c-5 on relative clauses.)

MISPLACED MODIFIER   The environmental engineers discovered another tank behind the building that was leaking toxic wastes.

READER'S REACTION: I know a building can leak, but I'll bet the writer meant to identify the tank as the culprit.

EDITED   Behind the building, the environmental engineers discovered another tank that was leaking toxic wastes.

Modifying clauses that begin with other subordinators, such as *when, although, because,* and *while* (see 16a-7), allow more flexibility in placement. Nonetheless, you still need to check that they convey your intended meaning.

24a
mm/ dm

MISPLACED MODIFIER   The company switched from the old health plan to one offered by a competing insurance company because premiums are rising rapidly.

EDITED   **Because premiums are rising rapidly**, the company switched from the old health plan to one offered by a competing insurance company.

24.1

Exercise 3

A. Revise the following sentences to eliminate any misplaced modifiers.

EXAMPLE
Sliding into second base, ~~my leg~~ broke. _I   my leg_

THE LONGMAN HANDBOOK
COMPANION WEBSITE

Just as the text is meant to be a companion to writers, the Website is a companion to the text, offering a wealth of additional resources designed to help students become better writers and researchers.

The Companion Website includes:

- An easy-access menu to all the interactive exercises and Web research activities that correspond to the Web icons that appear in the text.
- Numerous additional exercises in all areas of grammar, style, punctuation, and mechanics.
- Interactive Tutorials on topics such as incorporating sources, following documentation styles, and other areas of writing.
- Links to a wealth of online resources relating to writing and research.

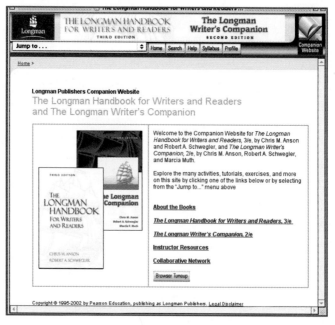

http://www.ablongman.com/anson

THE
Longman
Handbook
FOR
Writers and Readers

THIRD EDITION

CHRIS M. ANSON

North Carolina State University

ROBERT A. SCHWEGLER

University of Rhode Island

Longman

New York   San Francisco   Boston
London   Toronto   Sydney   Tokyo   Singapore   Madrid
Mexico City   Munich   Paris   Cape Town   Hong Kong   Montreal

Senior Vice President and Publisher: Joseph Opiela
Acquisitions Editor: Susan Kunchandy
Development Director: Janet Lanphier
Development Editor: Michael Greer
Supplements Editor: Donna Campion
Media Supplements Editor: Nancy Garcia
Marketing Manager: Christopher Bennem
Senior Production Manager: Bob Ginsberg
Project Coordination, Text Design, and
    Electronic Page Makeup: Nesbitt Graphics, Inc.
Cover Design Manager and Cover Designer: John Callahan
Manufacturing Buyer: Lucy Hebard
Printer and Binder: Quebecor World Taunton
Cover Printer: Coral Graphic Services, Inc.

For permission to use copyrighted material, grateful acknowledgment
is made to the copyright holders on pp. 889–892, which are hereby
made part of this copyright page.

Library of Congress Cataloging-in-Publication Data

Anson, Christopher M.
    The Longman handbook for writers and readers / Chris M. Anson,
  Robert A. Schwegler.—Third ed.
        p. cm.
    Includes index.
    ISBN 0-321-09724-6
    1. English language—Rhetoric—Handbooks, manuals, etc.
2. English language—Grammar—Handbooks, manuals, etc. 3. Reading
comprehension—Handbooks, manuals, etc. 4. Report writing—Handbooks,
manuals, etc. I. Title: Handbook for writers and readers. II. Schwegler,
Robert A. III. Title.

PE1408 .A61844 2002
808'.042—dc21   2002072733

Please visit our website at http://www.ablongman.com/anson

ISBN 0-321-09724-6

12345678910—WCT—05040302

CONTENTS

PART FOUR

Editing and Proofreading:
Meeting Community Expectations   189

PART FIVE

Using Research Strategies: Reading and Writing Within a Research Community   543

PART SIX

Using Citation Styles   617

All writers, whatever their skills and experience, need at least occasional advice. Speakers often need a helping hand, too, whether they are looking for ways to address a large audience or strategies for reporting to a few people. We've designed the third edition of *The Longman Handbook for Writers and Readers* to provide answers to specific questions as well as extended help with larger concerns.

The handbook provides the following in readily accessible form:

- Answers to questions about grammar, punctuation, and style
- Advice on research, analysis, and documentation
- Understanding of the expectations of various communities of writers, readers, and speakers—academic, work, and public
- Descriptions of the various kinds of writing and speaking typical of each community
- Aid for speakers of English as a second language—fully integrated with advice to native speakers, not isolated in a special section of the text.

What makes the *Longman Handbook* unique?

We have written *The Longman Handbook for Writers and Readers* out of a belief that composition instruction will benefit from an innovative approach, one that responds directly to recent theory and practice, but one that addresses traditional concerns as well, always with the aim of providing concrete, helpful advice.

- **Writing as social action.** We emphasize the social nature of writing, especially the way different communities of writers and readers (and speakers)—academic, work, and public—shape texts and the writing process, and offer strategies for responding to these communities.
- **Community of writers.** A more diverse focus on communities for writing relies on examples and strategies illustrating the way writers work in academic, business, and public or civic contexts. While the text recognizes—and highlights—the importance of the academic setting, it also pays attention to the ways writers work in business or in public and civic contexts, drawing examples from these settings and providing strategies for working in them.

- **A fresh approach to correctness.** We believe that correctness in writing—employing the conventions appropriately and effectively—is largely a matter of social awareness. Errors can undermine the writer's relationship with readers or impede effective, persuasive, and imaginative interaction within a community of writers and readers. Using appropriate conventions of grammar, sentence structure, punctuation, and style is an important part of being able to guide the way readers respond to writing.

   The Longman Handbook treats correctness and understanding written conventions as essential to accomplished writing, helping writers recognize the effect of errors on readers as well as the ways conventions may vary from community to community.

- **Recognize and revise.** We believe that just knowing the definition of an error is seldom sufficient. Writers need to be able to recognize errors as they draft, revise, and edit, and then they need to be able to correct mistakes. *The Longman Handbook* helps writers develop the ability to recognize errors in their own writing, an essential step often missing from handbook discussions, and then provides concrete strategies for revision and correction. Each of the chapters in Part 4 of the handbook ("Editing and Proofreading") is built around a **recognize and revise pattern** and offers concrete suggestions for identifying errors and avoiding or revising them.

- **Strategies.** A unique feature of *The Longman Handbook* is its inclusion of concrete advice in the form of highlighted "Strategy" sections, each providing writers (and speakers) with specific steps they can take to accomplish a task; correct an error; or achieve a goal in expression, critical understanding, or style.

- **Reader's reaction**. Another unique feature of this handbook is the reader's reaction to unedited examples, which provides a direct link between writer and reader and shows students how their unedited writing could be perceived.

- **Critical thinking and reading.** We believe that reading, critical thinking, and an awareness of audience expectations and needs are intertwined. For this reason, we emphasize the importance of critical thinking in our discussions of analytical, interpretive, and critical reading—and the roles of reading and readers in our discussions of critical thinking.

- **Research and reading.** Our discussions of research and writing pay considerable attention to critical reading, both analytical techniques such as summary and paraphrase and critical techniques such as synthesis and critical response. We also pay attention to the special roles critical reading needs to play with electronic resources.

- **Language variation.** "Presenting Yourself Through Language Choices" (Chapter 11) focuses on the issue of language variation—home or community language varieties, oral and written dialects, code shifting, the importance of "standard" English in text written for diverse audiences, and the effect that particular choices of personae can have on an audience's reception of a text.

- **Online style.** "Writing in Online Communities" (Chapter 13) treats online communication not simply as a matter of technological awareness but also as a setting with its own unique rhetorical and stylistic demands and strategies.
- **Collaboration.** We treat writing, critical thinking, and research as often enriched through collaboration, either with fellow writers and readers or with potential audiences.

What's New in This Edition?

- New Chapter 49, "Understanding Documentation and Avoiding Plagiarism." Now a separate chapter in the research section, including increased coverage of integrating sources ethically and avoiding plagiarism.
- New Chapter 3, "Strategies for Effective Speaking," in Part One provides advice on oral presentations. New tips and strategies on oral communication are incorporated into chapters on argument, representing the self, and small group interaction and peer response.
- New **A Word About Speaking** boxes provide concrete advice for preparation and delivery throughout the text.
- **Expanded treatment of critical reasoning.** Chapter 12, "Critical Reasoning," has been completely revised to better help students understand how to build a chain of reasoning and how to use supporting evidence.
- Chapter 55, "Writing Argumentative Papers," is fully updated to include current research on persuasion and argumentation. Covers traditional logical appeals and newer approaches to persuasion based in narrative and ethos (persona).
- **Updated and expanded coverage of cross-curricular writing.** The discussion of cross-curricular paper writing has been divided into two separate chapters:

    Chapter 55, "Writing Point-Driven Papers Across the Curriculum," discusses persuasive writing in other disciplines.
    Chapter 58, "Writing Informative Papers Across the Curriculum," discusses informative writing in other disciplines.

- **Recognizing errors.** An increased emphasis on strategies for recognizing errors addresses one of the key problems in writing instruction, going well beyond other handbooks in both coverage and helpfulness.
- **Increased use of the Read, Recognize, Revise approach to editing grammar and style**. Revised chapters have been streamlined to further emphasize the three-step process to editing and proofreading. Key grammar sections are based in current research about patterns of error and the need to understand grammar in use and in context.

- **New marginal Web icons** throughout reference significant new Web content on the text's Companion Website, topically integrating additional coverage not found in the book.
- **Revised Strategy boxes** now include more advice for students which can be applied immediately to help them discover and improve grammar problems.
- **Visuals and visual literacy.** Innovative treatments of visual evidence in argumentative and other forms of writing along with advice on document design, the use of visuals in speaking, and critical "reading" of visual texts are special features of this new edition.

Ancillaries

An extensive package of media and print supplements for both student and instructor is available for *the Longman Handbook*. Please see your representative for details on these and additional supplements.

Student Supplements
Multimedia

- *The Longman Handbook* Companion Website (**www.ablongman.com/anson**) includes practice exercises and writing samples. The Web icons listed in the book indicate supporting material on the Web site. A special ESL Internet Café section offers additional games and links for ESL students.
- *LEZAP* (*Longman Exercise Zone* and *Avoiding Plagiarism Tutorial*) includes over 2,500 exercises in key topic areas, along with a series of tutorials designed to inform students about the issues surrounding plagiarism, and how to avoid it.
- CompSolutions Resources for Course Management [available for *CourseCompass*, *BlackBoard*, and *WebCT*] is a course management option that offer users all the resources of Longman's CompSolutions Website in a format that is integrated into their course management platform, as well as thousands of preloaded exercises and a library of PDF ebooks.
- *iSearch Guide for Composition, 2003 with ContentSelect* is a print guide offering tips, resources, activities, and URLs to help students succeed in college courses. It also includes access to **ContentSelect**—an electronic database offering students access to full-text articles from thousands of print journals and general interest periodicals.
- *Take Note!* Version 2.0 is a complete information management tool for students working on research papers or other projects that require the use of outside sources. This cross-platform CD-ROM integrates note taking, outlining, and bibliography management into one easy-to-use package.
- Longman English Tutor Center is a unique service offering students access to an inhouse writing tutor via phone and/or email. Tutor is available 5 p.m. to 12 a.m. Sunday to Thursday.

Print

- *Researching Online*, Fifth Edition, gives students detailed, step-by-step instructions for performing electronic searches; for researching with email, electronic mailing lists, newsgroups, IRC, and MUDs and MOOs; and for evaluating electronic sources.
- *The New American Webster Handy College Dictionary*, Third Edition, is now available free with any handbook. This superior paperback reference text contains more than 100,000 entries, including clear and concise definitions, selected etymologies, abbreviations, and scientific terms.
- Literacy Library Series: These brief supplements (*Public Literacy*, Second Edition, *Workplace Literacy*, Second Edition, and *Academic Literacy*) offer additional models and guidelines for writing in three different communities. Any one title is free when bundled with the text.
- *iSearch for English* with Content Select provides a thorough introduction to using the Web as a resource for college writing. Comprehensive arrays of useful sites help the composition student begin his or her search, and activities encourage practical hands-on use of the Web. It is free when bundled with the text.
- *The Longman Writer's Journal* provides students with their own personal space for writing, complete with journal writing strategies, sample journal entries by other students, and many more writing prompts and topics to help get students writing. It is free when bundled with the text.
- *The Longman Researcher's Journal* is designed to help students work through the steps involved in writing a research paper. Each section contains record-keeping strategies, checklists, graphic organizers, and pages for taking notes from sources and/or for students' own thoughts and reactions.

Instructor Supplements

Print

- *The Instructor's Resource Manual and Multimedia Guide* includes original course design strategies, sample syllabi, writing assignments, classroom and online activities and resources, and suggestions for integrating the Website into the classroom.
- *Answer Key* prepared by Chris M. Anson and Robert A. Schwegler provides answers to the exercises in this handbook.
- *An Introduction to Teaching Writing in the College Community* offers a wealth of computer-related classroom activities and detailed guidance for both experienced and inexperienced instructors who wish to make creative use of technology in a composition environment.
- *The Allyn & Bacon Sourcebook for College Writing Teachers*, Second Edition. Designed for college writing teachers who are faced with teaching comp for the first time or reexamining their teaching goals and methods, this

collection of writings on important theories and pedagogies in composition studies includes selections written by some of today's foremost scholars and teachers.

- *Diagnostic and Editing Tests and Exercises*, Fifth Edition, includes two diagnostic tests for analyzing common errors, keyed to the relevant handbook sections. The additional exercise sets on grammar, punctuation, and mechanics supplement those found in the handbook. Also available on CD-ROM.

Multimedia

- *The Longman Handbook* Companion Website (www.ablongman.com/anson) includes a password-protected instructor's section containing the full Instructor's Resource Manual, *PowerPoint* presentations, teaching notes, resources on problem-based teaching, and much more.

Acknowledgments

The third edition of *The Longman Handbook for Writers and Readers* represents important improvements in a book that had by its second edition already experienced a decade of development. We are grateful to a number of people for helping us to keep pushing the book forward.

First we wish to thank those who have contributed directly to some chapters in the book in both this and previous editions. A community of special consultants worked closely with us on the development of new chapters and the revision of existing chapters: Victor Villanueva offered us great wisdom as we created our new chapter on language variation. Jim Dubinsky of Virginia Tech contributed Chapter 14 on document design. Mick Doherty and Sandye Thompson, writing, editing, and Internet consultants, authored Chapter 13, "Writing in Online Communities." Christina Haas, Kent State University, has been a thoughtful and generous contributor of workplace-related examples and an excellent reader and reviewer for workplace relevance. Elizabeth Ervin, University of North Carolina, Wilmington, contributed her expertise and creativity in writing for public communities to both the content and the philosophy of past revisions. Gladys Vega Scott, Arizona State University, was a sensitive and creative reviewer of the book's ESL coverage in previous editions.

In addition, many of our colleagues have advised us, reviewed our drafts, and provided general responses to our ideas. Our special thanks go to the following people who reviewed this latest edition of *The Longman Handbook*: Valerie Balester, Texas A&M University; Sue Beebe, Southwest Texas State University; Daniel Bender, Pace University; Nancy Buffington, University of Delaware; Lauren Coulter, Tennessee State; Larnell Dunkley, Benedictine University; Carol Falkenstine de Rosset, Berea College; Christine Farris, Indiana University; Michael C. Flanigan, The University of Oklahoma; James Goldstein,

Auburn University; Laura Gray, University of Arkansas; Sandra Jamieson, Drew University; Michael MacDonald, University of Illinois at Chicago; Tami Penley, Mountain Empire Community College; Linda K. Shamoon, University of Rhode Island; Jean Sorensen, Grayson County College; and Janice R. Walker, Georgia Southern University.

Special thanks to Brad Mehlenbacher, North Carolina State University, and D'Arcy Randall, University of Texas at Austin, for their work on the Companion Website.

We thank especially Marcia Muth, the developmental editor of the first edition and now co-author on another project, who offered constantly sage advice about critical decisions relating to the book.

An extensive team of editors, producers, and managers at Longman were instrumental in the development and publication of the Third Edition: Susan Kunchandy, sponsoring editor; Janet Lanphier, development manager; Donna Campion, supplements editor; Nancy Garcia, media supplements editor; Christopher Bennem, marketing manager; and Bob Ginsberg, production project manager. Susan McIntyre and her team at Nesbitt Graphics did amazing work on a tight schedule to design and typeset the book.

A special word of thanks goes to Michael Greer, our developmental editor, whose professionalism, steadfastness, amazing diligence, and good cheer often helped us to work through the most intense periods of pressure and deadlines.

Chris Anson again expresses his appreciation to his wife Gean for her enduring patience and support for all things handbookish; and to his sons Ian and Graham, the best "test learners" one can imagine. To his longtime mentor, friend, and colleague Michael Flanigan, who passed away just as this book was going to press, Chris dedicates this Third Edition.

Bob Schwegler would like to acknowledge that he couldn't do any of this work without the advice, insight, and support of Nancy Newman Schwegler, who tolerated with grace and wit the far too many years the project has taken—and the sunny days spent worrying about comma splices. This and many other projects are the happy consequence of her understanding of readers, reading, and the creative ways writers can represent themselves. This edition, especially, has benefited from her attention to the ways people learn to recognize tasks and problems—a project she has developed in her work as librarian at Bradley Children's Hospital. "And I'll be sworn upon't that he loves her; / For here's a paper written in his hand, / A halting sonnet. . . ." He would also like to thank Ashley Marie Schwegler for arriving in the middle of the second edition and bounding her way through the third, demonstrating that the writing of books is far from the most important thing in life. Brian and Tara Schwegler (along with Lily)—though far away—added an important anthropological perspective on communities and language. And Christopher added smiles.

CHRIS M. ANSON
ROBERT A. SCHWEGLER

CHAPTER 1

READERS, WRITERS, SPEAKERS, AND COMMUNITY EXPECTATIONS

One or more people created the Web page you browsed yesterday; they wrote the text, designed the layout, and anticipated readers' reactions. Someone else wrote your housing contract, your student loan forms, and the waiver you signed before the technician x-rayed your ankle. Several writers worked together to produce the community newsletter you found in your mailbox last Saturday, and one of them gave a presentation on a community issue to the city council.

In each of these cases, people were fulfilling a need to communicate something. Sometimes this "need" can be quite direct: a psychology professor admonishes you to make sure you include summaries of your interviews in your research paper, or a boss expects that when you give your sales presentation, you'll explain the contradictory figures from the northwest region. On other occasions, your need to write (or speak) will come from the goals of a group you belong to, or it will come from within you, as a desire to be heard on an issue. Your writing and speaking give you voice; they let you do things, express ideas, acquire and share knowledge, and participate in a conversation about issues that matter to you and to our society.

Written and spoken language surrounds us, shaping our lives, choices, responsibilities, and values. This book looks at the roles writers, readers, and speakers play in contemporary culture. It offers concrete strategies for writing, for critical reading and thinking, for oral communication, and for understanding your readers' and listeners' expectations. More broadly, it emphasizes writing and speaking as ways to understand experience and share that understanding with others.

1.1

1a Recognizing academic, work, and public communities

Why would an instructor in a physiology course have little patience with a student paper written in the breezy style typical of a health care column from

2

Cosmopolitan or *Men's Health*? Why would a corporate executive or a city council member frown on a detailed theoretical presentation of a problem but welcome a much shorter report that gets right to the point and proposes a solution?

These audiences' sharply differing needs and expectations are typical of the challenges writers (and speakers) face in knowing what style to use, in deciding what structure their text should have, and in determining what to include or not include in its contents. How can you recognize and respond to these many differences in your own work? First and foremost, you need to envision a *community* of writers, readers, and speakers. A **discourse community** consists of people with shared goals and knowledge, a common setting or context, and similar preferences and uses for verbal and visual texts.

In this book we focus on three broad and important types of communities: academic, work, and public. We suggest ways you can participate in these communities and in other writing and speaking situations you may encounter. We also pay special attention to the way these communities often use electronic communication to carry out their work.

1 Communities in action

What do people in a particular community want? Their preferences and expectations usually reflect their shared goals: to exchange information, to debate an issue, to find a solution to a problem. Communities may overlap as well, which means that you need to be able to participate in more than one community—just as you move from a classroom to a football game or from a book club to a protest rally.

Consider the following example.

> In Greenwood Village, a wealthy suburb of Denver, pets have been disappearing. The culprits are coyotes and other predators, increasingly crowded by new homes and industrial parks. These disappearances are certainly alarming to local residents—will a young child be the next victim? Will the wild animals become even more aggressive?

Much of the real problem solving that takes place in a situation like this starts with the production of written materials and oral presentations. City council members and concerned citizens looking for explanations and solutions turn to discussions produced within the **academic community**: detailed, complex scientific studies and presentations reporting the effects of development on coyotes and other predators. Wildlife experts, for example, prepare reports that show the effects of development on the habitat and feeding habits of coyotes. A line from one of their documents looks like this.

> This report summarizes and compares the data from two studies of the habits of predators in areas that have experienced significant population growth and urbanization over the past ten years.

While such scientific information is useful, it has a focus and a goal (determining how coyotes behave in a shrinking habitat) different from the concerns of parents, pet owners, and others making up the **public community**: How can we protect our children and pets without harming local wildlife? Drawing on scientific detail and knowledge of residents' perspectives, the Colorado Division of Wildlife creates a set of tips directed at a public rather than an academic audience.

If you see a coyote:
- Leave it alone; do not approach it.

If a coyote approaches:
- Use an animal repellent such as pepper spray to ward off the coyote.
- Throw rocks or sticks at the coyote to scare it away.

- Use a loud, authoritative voice to frighten the animal away.

How to coexist with coyotes:
- Keep your pet on a leash.
- Do not let pets out between dusk and dawn, when most predators are active. . . .

(The Denver Post, 30 July 1998, 15A)

A neighborhood action group, which represents a more specific public community, distributes leaflets to residents, urging discussion of the problem, and TV stations turn this material into short oral and visual segments to inform citizens.

COYOTE ALERT!

Are your children safe in their own backyards? Coyotes attacked seven dogs and cats last summer. Find out what we can do. Join the Committee to Safeguard Our Children on Tuesday, October 2, at 7:00 p.m. in the high school gym.

Business leaders, meanwhile, also have views to express. Local officials address the problem with writing directed at several **work communities**, in reports and presentations to the city council, the environmental management department, and municipal development offices. These reports consider options for altering the pace and scope of new developments and for designing educational and management programs to help people, pets, and coyotes live in balance. The Construction Contractors Consortium, for example, sends out a memo to its membership calling attention to the ways that zoning and development restrictions sponsored by environmental groups could hurt their construction businesses.

As you can see from this example, writing and speaking will vary in purpose, organization, and style across these different communities, reflecting the different expectations of the communities' writers, speakers, and audiences. Informed by scientific and analytic work, persuaded by business leaders, and galvanized by concerned citizens, local government officials and the entire community will seek a solution that works for all these communities. They do so by *participating* within and across these communities: talking, reading, and (especially) writing.

THREE MAJOR COMMUNITIES OF READERS, WRITERS, AND SPEAKERS

	ACADEMIC	WORK	PUBLIC
ROLES	Students Teachers Researchers Expert committees Specialized readers	Co-workers Colleagues Supervisors Management Accounting Public relations Clients Government agencies Target public audiences Potential clients or customers	Neighborhood groups Potential supporters Public officials Government agencies Local political groups Issue-oriented readers
GOALS	Create and exchange new knowledge	Provide information Analyze problems Propose solutions Promote organization	Persuade people on issues Provide information Participate in public decision making
FORMS	Analytical report Interpretation of text or event Research proposal or report Lab report Scholarly article Annotated bibliography Grant proposal	Informative memo Factual or descriptive report Proposal Executive summary Letter or memo Guidelines or instructions Promotional material Minutes and notes Formal reports Internal and public Web sites	Guidelines Position paper Informative report Letter or email to agency or group Flyer or brochure Action proposal Grant proposal Charter or mission statement Letter to editor Web announcement
CHARACTERISTICS	Clear reasoning Critical analysis Fresh insight Extensive evidence Accurate detail Balanced treatment Acknowledgment of competing viewpoints Thorough exploration of topic	Focus on tasks and goals Accurate, efficient presentation Promotion of products and services Attention to organizational image and corporate design standards Concise, direct style	Focus on shared values Advocacy of cause or policy Fairness and ethical argument Relevant supporting evidence Action- or solution- oriented Accessible presentation

1.2

2 Recognizing a writing/reading/speaking community

To participate effectively in a community of writers, readers, and speakers, you must recognize the ways it both limits your work and provides choices or possibilities. As you start to compose, and again during the process, stop occasionally to consider the roles, goals, forms, and characteristics that help you recognize the particular community you're addressing and the choices your situation offers (see the chart on p. 5).

- **Roles** that you and your readers or listeners occupy
- **Goals** for communication that you and your audience share
- **Forms** that your audience will look for in writing or speaking directed toward a particular goal
- **Characteristics** typical of communication that fulfills a particular set of goals and meets an audience's expectations

(For further advice, see the discussion of audience in 6b.)

Exercise 1

In groups of four or five, draft a "class charter," that is, a formal statement outlining the principles, purposes, or rules that you think should govern your class. Before you start drafting, discuss the roles, goals, forms, and characteristics of this situation. Which members of the class do you need to address? In what ways might their values or interests be similar or different? What do you hope to accomplish with the document you produce? What does a charter look like? How would you present it orally to the class?

1b The composing process: Realities and myths

Successful writing is almost never a matter of just setting down your thoughts on paper in finished form (or, for a speech, standing up in front of a group and just talking). Instead, it begins with a *response:* to an idea or experience, to reading or an issue, to a problem or a situation. It calls for planning; for definition of purpose and thesis; for awareness of audience; and for careful attention to drafting, revising, editing, and proofreading (and, for a speech, rehearsing). These various elements of the composing processes are explored in the chapters that follow.

Usually, your composing process won't move in a straight line. When you revise, you may need to go back to more planning or reconsider your first response to the task. Or, in some projects, you might need to work collaboratively with others and interact with potential audiences.

Some ways of viewing the composing process can lead to self-defeating habits, especially when it comes to writing. For example, how many of these statements are true?

- People can easily succeed in the "real world" without needing to write.
- Writing is easy for people who have the knack.
- You can be a good writer without doing much reading.
- It's cheating to ask other people to look over your writing before you turn it in.
- Good writing is effective for all readers.

They're all myths. Here's why.

Myth: People can easily succeed in the "real world" without needing to write.

Reality: It's a popular myth that executives don't need to write because their assistants write for them. That's not what the executives themselves say. In Fortune 500 companies, more than half of the employees spend between eight and forty hours writing each week. This shows that the ability to write is crucial for success in the work community. Although the amount of writing on the job varies by type of employment and rank, many workers say that when they were in school, they underestimated the amount of writing they would need to do in their jobs. The same is true in public life and in civic activities.

Myth: Writing is easy for people who have the knack.

Reality: Few of us get to look over the shoulders of good writers. If we did, we would know what researchers know: good writers draft and redraft. They work hard to create effective prose and to consider their work from a reader's perspective. They have become good writers through learning and hard work, not because they were born with a knack for writing.

Myth: You can be a good writer without doing much reading.

Reality: It's not likely. The more you read, the more experience you have with writing. Reading gives you models of writing that work in specific communities; it helps you learn how to adjust your writing to the needs of your readers; and it increases your options for sentence variety and precise words.

Myth: It's cheating to ask other people to look over your writing before you turn it in.

Reality: It certainly is cheating if you have someone else write a paper or parts of it and then claim the work as your own. But successful writers always depend on readers for feedback. Readers' opinions can tell you how an audience will interpret your writing and can help you anticipate responses and concerns. Especially at work and in the community, important documents are likely to be written in groups for this reason.

Myth: Good writing is effective for all readers.

Reality: When it comes to good writing, one size doesn't fit all. While all good writing is clear, coherent, and correct, what works in one community may not work as well in another. The term paper you write for Psychology 265 will have a very different tone, style, and content from the email you write to your cousin or the proposal you write at work.

A WORD ABOUT SPEAKING

Many of the myths of writing have parallels in the domain of speaking: that people have a knack or gift for giving oral presentations; that there is only one kind of public speaking (the formal speech); or that there is only one way to speak effectively in public. Some people, for example, believe they can find jobs in which they will never have to give oral presentations. The reality will shock them. Even people in jobs that don't require them to give speeches must communicate with others constantly. Many of the principles of effective oral presentation are the same for large group presentations and small-group discussions.

Throughout this book, "A Word About Speaking" boxes will help you to apply or adapt the principles of writing in each chapter to the processes and contexts of oral communication.

1C Entering electronic communities

The three general communities illustrated in the coyote example in 1a-1 coexist on the Internet. As you click from Web site to Web site exploring a topic or seeking information, remember that numerous electronic communities, large and small, are organized around a shared interest in a topic, point of view, or issue. Immersed for a while in a highly academic treatise from a university researcher, you can, with a click of the mouse, suddenly find yourself skimming a page at a site sponsored by a major corporation. Many political or nonprofit organizations circulate petitions online. People can register their support of gun control, dolphin-safe tuna, or a favorite TV show simply by typing in their name and email address.

To recognize the electronic community to which a site belongs as well as the conventions and expectations you may need to observe in contributing a Web page or posting of your own, examine one or more sites using the strategy of TASALS.

Topic: On what subject(s) does the site focus? Do contributors belong to any organization or share any other kind of affiliation?

Attitude: Does the site have a clear point of view or set of values? Do contributors have similar perspectives or values?

Strategies: Does the site use particular writing or visual strategies (see Chapter 14 for examples)? Does the writing have a particular tone or style? Does the design of the site have a particular style or emphasis?

Authority: Does the site try to be authoritative, giving support for claims it makes or information it provides? Do contributors reason carefully and offer evidence, or do they give unsupported opinions and supposed "facts"?

Links: Is the site linked to similar sites? Do postings refer to related
online documents, lists, or resources?

Summarize: On the basis of your answers to these questions, summarize the qualities of the electronic community you encountered.

Exercise 2

A. Find the official Web site of your school or city or of an organization
to which you belong. Examine the Web site carefully using the TASALS
strategy. How would you characterize the community that sponsors the
site? What opportunities, if any, are there to participate in the site—to
send comments, to get on a mailing list, or to ask a question of an expert? What kinds of writing or participation would be inappropriate for
this site, and why?

B. Use an Internet search engine to locate several Web sites maintained by or catering to professionals in your future field of work. Evaluate the Web site using TASALS. Compare your results with those of
your classmates.

CHAPTER 2

STRATEGIES FOR CRITICAL READING AND REFLECTION

Reading is almost always responsive. Even when you read a road sign in a split second, you respond: by checking your speedometer, by testing your brakes, or by wondering why you never see the helicopter that's supposed to be monitoring your speed. The way you respond to writing will be shaped by your purposes for reading and by your context—say, whether you're working in a family business or in the office of a busy student organization on campus.

If you respond personally and defensively to a negative sales report or an instructor's critique, you may miss the important information and advice that a more analytical response would allow. **Analytical reading** strategies help you identify information and ideas in a piece of writing. They also direct your attention to how a writer argues for a position or policy, organizes information, or explains a problem and a potential solution.

Analytical reading also involves **interpretive reading**: reading to interpret the meanings and purposes of a piece of writing. Sometimes these meanings and purposes may be clearly and directly stated. More often, you'll need to sift through a text looking for aims and ideas that are presented indirectly, even those that may have escaped the writer's conscious awareness. An interpretive reading is your restatement of the ideas, perspectives, implications, and purposes of a text—but a restatement grounded in the details of the text itself. An interpretive reading is not simple speculation or unfounded opinion. It represents your conclusions about the text and, therefore, must be presented in terms of evidence from the text that supports these conclusions.

Analytical and interpretive reading, in turn, form the basis for critical reading. **Critical reading** helps you to evaluate the ideas and information you encounter and to develop alternative points of view and interpretations (see also Chapter 47).

Reading critically, which puts your mind to work on a text, usually helps you to write and speak more effectively. It gives you new ideas by helping you link what you read to your own experience, to other texts of all kinds, to issues and information, or to a problem or responsibility. Your writing or speaking then *adds* to the discussion of a topic by incorporating insights you've gained from your critical reading. Your words may contribute to the same "conversation" going on in the community that produced the material you read, or you may start or continue a conversation happening in a different community. For example, you might read and critically analyze a dozen statements on an email listserv about the arrest of antipornography protesters and then contribute your own considered response to the list. You could also add some background information to your response and then send it electronically to your local newspaper to be considered for inclusion on the op-ed page. Your letter might even begin a new conversation in the community of newspaper subscribers and readers.

2a Reading analytically

1 Getting ready to read

If you're like most people, you begin reading by opening to the first page of a report, article, or book and plunging into the text. Even when you know something about the text—that a co-worker wrote it, for example, or that it addresses a subject you know well—if you "start cold," you can miss important points or information: What's the problem being described? How valid is the solution? What other issues need to be considered? Is the writer really proposing that . . . ?

Prereading strategies help you "warm up" by previewing the text and any specific situation—academic, work, or public—that it addresses. These strategies also help alert you to the writer's particular purpose(s).

Preview the organization. For books and long articles or reports, preread by skimming the table of contents to see how a work is organized. What appears first, second, third? In magazine articles, essays, scholarly papers, or reports without tables of contents, look first for any headings or subheadings; these road maps tell you where the reading will take you and help you to plan your time. If you have only half an hour to read before you must do something else, knowing that the first section of a scholarly article ends on page nine may help you plan your time accordingly.

Examine the context. Begin by skimming the table of contents and headings in a text or paging quickly through it to get some idea of its subject and focus. Then consider the social setting in which the text was produced and the audience or community it seems to address.

STRATEGY

Use the following questions about context to guide your prereading when you approach a text for the first time.

- Does the text reflect the concerns of a specific academic, work, or public community, or does it appear to address a more general community of readers? (See 6a.)
- Which of the typical forms and characteristics of that community appear in this text? Which do not? (See the chart on p. 5.)
- Does the text appear in a publication (journal, periodical, or Web site) with a particular point of view (conservative or feminist or pro-choice, for example)? Is it associated with a particular industry or political organization? Does it cite or link to other texts endorsing particular perspectives or with common interests?

Sample the content. Your mind will be much more receptive to an unfamiliar reading if you "prepare" yourself for the content of the reading. By scanning the text first, you can activate your knowledge.

STRATEGY

Use the following questions about a text's content and author to focus your scanning as you preread.

- Is the text by a single author or by a group of people representing an organization?
- When was the text published, and how current are the information and ideas?
- Who are the intended readers? Are they identified in the text, and is the purpose clearly stated in the title, in headings, or in highlighted portions of the text?
- Do visuals, graphics, or the text's layout provide obvious cues to the writing's purpose(s), focus, and intended audience? (See Chapter 14 for advice on understanding the visual elements of a text.)
- If the text is in electronic form, do any other texts within the site or linked to it provide any hints about its focus, purpose, and audience?
- Is there any evidence of how popular or well received the text is? Has it appeared in numerous editions? Are there testimonials from authorities on the subject? If the text is on a Web site, does a "hit counter" indicate the number of people who have visited the site?
- What does the back or front of a book tell you? What information can you gather from any abstracts or summaries at the beginning of a report or scholarly article?

Sample key words and specialized terms. If you notice unfamiliar terms, look for patterns of related terms, or consult a dictionary or online glossary. Consider the following excerpt from an internal memo on market competitiveness for an air carrier.

> As per Strategic Plan: Two goals will require further delineation from your group. These are the goals pertaining to fleet types and to industry performance on DOT metrics. The original proposal for fleet type reduction was to reduce from 16 to 6; new proposals, based on year-end figures, suggest that this may need to be revised to 4 fleet types. The key DOT metrics to address include on-time performance and mishandles.

Note how the example uses a number of terms its writers assumed readers would understand: *fleet types, DOT metrics, mishandles.* By glancing through the text first and noting such terms, you'll gain a sense of what the document is about. (Note that for the intended readers of this memo, "insider" terms like these would be common knowledge.)

Make predictions. Sample some paragraphs, sentences, or visuals, and try to predict what the text is about and where it will take you. Do your samples imply a particular direction, focus, or purpose? Jot your predictions down and note which are later confirmed as you read.

Exercise 1

A. Locate a short article, a short electronic document, or a portion of a longer text that has no overt structure—no headings, section divisions, or other organizational signals. Then skim (preread) the material and create headings or divisions for the main parts of the reading.

B. In a small group, compare your structural prereading and organizing with that of several other people. How successful, generally, was this strategy in helping each of you read and understand your chosen texts?

2 During and after reading

You've probably had the experience of reaching the end of a passage in an essay, report, Web site, or book (or the end of the work itself), only to realize that you don't have even the vaguest sense of what you've been reading. To avoid this problem, try the following strategies.

Pause and assess. When you reach a place at which you can stop reading without interrupting a line of reasoning or a crucial narrative, put the reading aside for a moment. Where are you? What have you learned so far? What do you think? What still confuses you? Jot down answers to these questions in your journal or on a piece of paper. Then go back and skim what you've read. If you're uncertain about something, reviewing the text can sometimes clarify it.

Highlight important information. If you've ever bought a used textbook, you've probably seen someone else's bright yellow or pink highlighting. Often there's so much highlighting on each page that you wonder how the person could have separated what was important from what wasn't.

If you're an avid highlighter *while* you read, try to change your style. Don't spend a lot of time attending to tiny details the first time through your reading. Instead, read to capture the essential points of the piece. This will let you see a "bigger picture," a set of organizational or argumentative structures, without getting lost in the little details.

STRATEGY

Do most of your highlighting *after* your first reading. Go back and write notes in the margins of your reading to identify important points and details, or use your highlighter to identify what's *really* important.

Highlighting an electronic document is more of a challenge. Sometimes it helps to print a copy and highlight this paper record of what you've read. You might also find it easier to read analytically when the text is on paper rather than on a screen. If your computer software allows, you may be able to print out selected portions of a document. This can be a form of highlighting, though it detaches the highlighted text from the original, making it more difficult for you to consult the entire document at a later date. You can also try to save electronic documents on a word processor and then add boldfacing, underlining, or font highlighting to especially important sections or passages.

Annotate. At one time, students were punished for writing in books (even their own copies). For some people, this history has turned to habit. If you own the book or document you're reading, go ahead and annotate it using whatever white space is on the page. If you don't own it, consider making a photocopy of relevant material, perhaps reducing it to give you more marginal space for your notes. If you're reading a Web page or other electronic document, consider downloading and printing it so you can make annotations—unless your software allows you to open a note-taking document that you can link to the text you're reading.

After reading, you might also consider taking a file card or creating an electronic file and writing down some of the main ideas from the text. These records are especially useful when you are creating research papers, reports, or documented position papers; they offer a convenient way to review several readings without leafing through dozens of pages of books, articles, or photocopies or having to revisit electronic documents (a time-consuming task even if you have "bookmarked" the various sites).

Read with your audience and purpose in mind. Often we read in order to write: to gather information and ideas or to develop insights and solutions that we plan to share with readers. If this is your goal, highlight or make notes on those sections of a text that are relevant to the community of readers you plan to address, or to your specific purposes for reading.

Reread and review. If you're learning sophisticated concepts, studying complicated issues and problems, or working through difficult arguments, you may need to read material more than once. Every time you read something again, you'll find more information or new ideas.

Rereading doesn't need to take the same shape as the initial reading. Try reviewing, skimming the reading more quickly, and then sampling some of the passages you highlighted on your first pass through the text. The idea is to read from different perspectives—once from afar, once closely. Skim the material quickly once; then study it meticulously.

A WORD ABOUT SPEAKING

Being a careful and critical reader helps you to interpret and recall information produced by writers and shows you effective writing techniques. In the same way, careful, critical listening will give you new insights about how to be an effective speaker. Translate the advice about reading in this chapter into strategies for listening. If you can't employ certain strategies while listening (such as creating critical annotations; see 2b), take the time to do so after the presentation.

Exercise 2

A. Find a relatively challenging article, electronic document, or book chapter, or choose one that you've begun to read for a specific purpose, perhaps as a course assignment or in preparation for a report or other writing task. Then try several of the reading strategies outlined in this section, taking note of which best aided your understanding and which seemed most likely to be useful to you as a writer.

B. Share your observations and readings in a small group. Explain why you think particular strategies aided (or failed to aid) understanding. Tell why you considered specific strategies likely (or not likely) to be useful for your writing.

2b Reading interpretively

What's the central idea a writer is trying to convey? What new insights does a piece of writing offer you? Can you describe the writer's opinions, generalizations, or attitudes toward the subject matter? What underlying themes gradually surface from the text? When you read interpretively, these are some of the questions you try to answer. Clearly, this kind of reading is *active* and *engaged*—you're not ruffling a newspaper; you're focusing energetically on the pages or screen in front of you. It's also obvious that careful reading takes time. Skimming and scanning should give way to focusing, questioning, rereading, and note taking. The following strategies can help you hone your interpretive reading skills.

Make responsive annotations. As you read or reread, it's important for you to keep track of your questions, thoughts, reactions, agreements, and disagreements. You can do this in the margins of a book or article, or on a separate sheet of paper.

STRATEGY

Use the following kinds of annotations and leading questions to arrive at an understanding of a text's meanings and purposes.

- **Interpretations:** What does the author or speaker mean in the text as a whole or in each part?
- **Confusions:** At what points are readers likely to become puzzled, and why?
- **Questions:** What more will readers need to know about the subject, issue, or problem?
- **Communities:** What will different communities of readers perceive as the most important ideas and information in the text? Why might people in two different settings, who may be affected by or interested in the subject, respond in different ways?
- **Restatements:** How can you state the text's key ideas in your own words?
- **Evaluative response:** What do you like or dislike about the text as a whole or about specific parts?
- **Disagreements:** What disagreements does the text (writer) seem to anticipate (or fail to anticipate)?
- **Memories:** What experiences, memories, or related issues/problems come to mind as you read, and is it likely that the writer anticipated such reactions?
- **Retentions:** Which details, insights, or opinions from the text are most likely to stick in readers' minds after they have finished reading, and why?

Clint Graff made some responsive annotations to a passage from a document about the information provided to consumers on food labels.

What were they asked? And do people really read the info? → A recent review on communication of food, nutrition, and health messages did not include dietary supplement labeling specifically but did address consumer understanding of nutrient content and health claims on food labels (80). In an appendix to this report, Levy (83) indicates that <u>consumers in focus groups were interested in having information</u> about the relationship between diet and disease. Some commissioners interpret this study as <u>suggesting that consumer research has not yet established a "mandate"</u> for having health information on food labels as opposed to obtaining such information from health care providers, books, or the print and telecommunications media. Moreover, considering that food labels are viewed by consumers as reflective of the manufacturer's interest in selling the product, <u>consumers are skeptical about the veracity of health messages on food labels.</u>

How does this study lead to this conclusion? →

Points to tension between consumer desire for info & fear that it's just hype. →

Note repetition and emphasis. Words, phrases, ideas, and details that appear repeatedly in a text may shape its meaning and its effect, even if the writer didn't fully intend to provide such emphasis. Devices for creating emphasis—headings, thesis statements, topic sentences, vivid detail, sentence structure, and parallelism or other stylistic strategies—also highlight and create meaning and focus a text's purpose.

Summarize in chunks. Most texts have natural "resting points," often marked with road signs like headings and subheadings, or shifts in focus. These are good places to take stock of what you've learned or how you are reacting to the reading. This can help you to monitor your comprehension and begin interpreting the piece.

2.1

STRATEGY

After reaching a natural stopping point, write an abstract or summary of what you're thinking at that point, glancing back over what you've read if necessary. Ask yourself what the main point or gist is so far. See whether you can guess or predict where the reading will go next.

Share interpretations and insights. Go public with the "conversation" you're having internally with a piece of writing. If other people have read the same piece, their responses can help you to formulate and test your own interpretation. Consider working in a small group to discuss what you noticed about the content, language, or structure of an article, book, or Web site. Compare your responses with those of your fellow readers. Are there differences? Did you miss something? Do any of the other readers' responses puzzle you? Skim back over the reading to see how the others might have arrived at their interpretations.

2.2

Respond in writing. A journal or reading log provides an especially effective method for reading critically (see 2c). If you're keeping a journal, jot down your conclusions about the writer's purpose(s) and key ideas. Be ready to reread the text to check your perceptions and understandings. By struggling to put the text's ideas into your own language, you are already developing your interpretation—and working toward ideas you might develop later in your own writing.

Exercise 3

A. Obtain a copy of the minutes from a recent city council or other public meeting (these may be available online). Read the minutes carefully, making responsive annotations as you read; then, summarize the document for a partner. Once you have done this, speculate about the ways different communities might read this document. Is there any specialized terminology that might be confusing to some audiences? Did any one issue seem like an ongoing problem or controversy? If so, were solutions proposed? Can you tell, from the minutes, who the most influential or powerful participants were?

B. Compare the interpretive reading of an academic text to that of a workplace document. Select a challenging excerpt from some of your course reading, and locate a text from a workplace context. (You might use a document from a current or former job, ask individuals you know in the working world to share a text with you, or locate a relevant document from a work- or profession-related Web site.) Use interpretive reading strategies (making responsive annotations, noting repetition and emphasis, summarizing in chunks, sharing interpretations, and responding in writing) as you actively read the two pieces. Then reflect, in writing, on the differences between your interpretive readings of the two texts: Does one lend itself to this kind of reading more easily? Which strategies were most useful with each text? Which text elicited the strongest response?

2c Journals: Bridging reading and writing

A **working journal** is a place to explore ideas, develop insights, experiment with your prose, write rough drafts, and reflect on your reading. Entries in a working journal may be organized by a particular writing or reading task, or they may be dated and involve sequential observations. A working journal is not a diary. Diaries record people's daily activities, thoughts, and personal lives. Working journals are places where analytical, interpretive, and critical reading take place in the form of written responses. Your journal is also where your own writing begins to murmur and find voice. Unlike a carefully crafted essay or report, a journal is a clearinghouse for ideas, speculations, first starts, notes and jottings, drawings and doodles, plans, occasional insights—anything that helps you to learn more fully and begin writing.

1 How to keep a journal

At first, keeping a journal may feel strange or artificial. After all, you're writing mainly to and for yourself, with no concern about your spelling, no worry that you're using the first person pronoun (*I*) when you're not sure whether this is acceptable. Here are some suggestions for getting started.

What kind of journal should you use? The actual shape and size of your journal is less important to its success than what you do in and with it. It helps to have a journal whose pages can be removed or reorganized. An electronic word-processing document will allow you to do this, as will an inexpensive ring binder.

How much and how often should you write? The more you write, the greater your chances to think about a subject, respond to your reading, and develop interpretations you can use in your own writing. The length of journal entries will (and should) differ. Working half a day in the library or searching the Internet might yield ten or fifteen pages of notes, speculations, quotations, references, and interpretations, but an idea that comes to you late at night might yield just a few lines of drowsy prose sufficient to jog your memory the next morning. Don't hold yourself at gunpoint in order to scratch something out on the page or screen, but at all costs, *write regularly.* Journals abandoned for more than a day or two soon wither and die from lack of nourishment.

DID YOU KNOW?

In a study comparing two groups of students in a high school science course, the group that wrote about their learning remembered more than the group that didn't keep a journal. Similar findings have been reported in several other studies.

Robert Tierney, "Using Expressive Writing to Teach Biology," *The Teacher-Researcher*, ed. Miles Myers (Urbana: NCTE, 1985) 149–99.

2 How to use a journal

Writing in a journal *makes your thoughts visible*. When you use a journal effectively, you create a cycle of connections among thinking, writing, and reading.

Translate new knowledge. After reading or hearing about new ideas or information, imagine one or more people who know little about the topic. Explain your new knowledge to them. You'll find, first, that you'll be forced to *speculate* about the meaning of the information and concepts at places you find difficult to understand. Second, you'll often *clarify and resolve* your confusions in the process of writing.

Brainstorm. Instead of staring at a blank piece of paper or screen, waiting for perfect sentences to roll off your pen or keyboard, use your journal for **brainstorming**. When you brainstorm, you think associatively, letting one idea lead to another or exploring the connections among ideas. You create an exploratory, tentative, and often messy set of responses to reading, issues, and experience that can point the way to a focus and plan for a draft of a paper (see Chapter 4).

Extend your thinking. Imagine that you learn this fact from your reading in a sociology article or textbook: Human aggression increases in hot weather. Recording such an observation in your journal may take a few seconds. But imagine *extending* this idea a little, seeing its implications, wondering about possible solutions and applications. Are people more aggressive in hot regions than in cold regions? If discomfort causes aggression, why aren't people just as aggressive in uncomfortably cold weather? Are workers in hot factories more aggressive than workers in chilly factories? Do Northerners become aggressive on vacations to hot places?

Take issue with ideas. Although your journal may feel comfortably informal, it can also be an excellent place to argue with someone else's point of view or criticize a position. Many writers at first react in a combative way to ideas or beliefs that challenge their own. Journals let them "have it out" with an opponent without risking actual confrontation. The result can be a more balanced view of the controversy.

Exercise 4

A. The following working journal entry was written by Kelly Odeen, a student in a course on literacy in America. Read Odeen's entry, and then identify specific functions for which she is using her journal. What characteristics of her entry suggest these functions?

> Reading on the Amish community left me with very mixed
> feelings--not sure what to make of them yet. I really admired
> the family support of Eli's literacy development. Sounded like

the older family members did just what we've been encouraged to
do as tutors. They gave him positive feedback, etc. Focused on
accomplishments rather than failures. But the setting looked
sort of ideal. Everyone in Eli's family reads and writes, even
more than in my family. I don't think it's possible to make
learning totally individualized in the public school system.
Choices have to be made that are better for some children than
others. I don't have a solution, but I think the author is
being too idealistic to think there can be this match like the
Amish have. I'd like to look into this more for my project,
maybe. Because I do agree that there are many ways of
perceiving literacy, each valid, and we have to be sensitive
to where kids are coming from compared with the school system
they're going into.

B. Should animals be used in laboratory experiments for the advancement of scientific, medical, and behavioral knowledge? Write a page or
two in your journal on this question, considering as many issues and
angles on the topic as you can. Then compare your journal writing in a
small group. What ideas did the writing yield? How helpful was it?
How would you describe the style, organization, and other characteristics of your writing? Which of the purposes described in the preceding
section did your writing serve?

3 How to write in a journal

Like taking a walk alone, you write in a journal mainly for *yourself.*
Your pace can be fast or slow, meandering or purposeful. Here are some tips
for finding a comfortable voice and style in your journal.

Use a personal voice. Use your journal writing to express your beliefs,
opinions, and reactions in personal terms. Speculate. Get to know what
you—personally—think about an issue or subject. Instead of writing in abstract terms and formal language, go ahead and use phrases like "I wonder
if . . . ," "I think it's wonderful that . . . ," or "I can't understand why . . . ." Be
conversational. A sentence like "Hmmmmm . . . I guess I never figured zoning board members would get so ticked off about something so silly" would
cry out for revision in a formal report. In a journal, you can feel safe using
such a casual tone.

Use shortcuts. Try writing quickly. Use abbreviations if you're sure you will
remember what they mean. Don't worry at this point about underlining
titles, correcting commas in a series, or looking up the spelling of every difficult word.

2c
jrnl

Experiment with language. Journals encourage the free play of language and thought. Let the poetry emerge, if you wish, from your writing. Be as expressive as you want. Try out ideas that may at first seem outrageous, or write in a style you've never used before. Try imitating or parodying other writers.

Exercise 5

A. Choose a short reading about a current controversy. First try writing a journal response to the reading, following the suggestions in the preceding section. Next, write a brief letter to the editor of a local, campus, or company newspaper about the same controversy. Try *converting* your journal writing into more formal prose suitable for a general audience.

B. In a small group, discuss your "journal conversions" from Exercise 5A. What information carried over from your journal writing into your letter? On what basis did you select the information? Did you make changes in style, word choice, sentence structure and rhythm, organization, and the use of evidence to support your assertions? What uses can you see for such "conversions" in writing papers for your courses?

CHAPTER 3

STRATEGIES FOR EFFECTIVE SPEAKING

Surveys show that people are more afraid of public speaking than almost anything else they can imagine, including losing a relative or being fired from a job—but why? Like driving a car or playing tennis, public speaking can be learned effectively and performed well. Good presenters will tell you that, with practice and experience, they have come to enjoy the thrill of explaining their ideas, opinions, or information to audiences both large and small. Instead of dreading the moment when they must stand in front of a group of people, they look forward to the challenge. Anxiety about public speaking never goes away; good speakers turn that anxiety into a kind of energy that helps them to present their ideas clearly and enthusiastically.

But effective oral communication is not just about standing up and delivering a carefully scripted address. There are many situations in business, in school, and in public settings when you'll make different kinds of oral contributions that have their own standards of effectiveness. At meetings of city councils or education boards, for example, citizens often express opinions briefly from a place in the audience. In college, you may be asked to explain your response to another student's paper in a small group. In business settings, you may need to give an impromptu report to a dozen people. Like lab reports, meeting minutes, project proposals, or research summaries, these and many other forms of oral communication follow certain conventions of length, style, formality, delivery, and persuasive strategy. Knowing some of these conventions can help you to be effective as a speaker in a range of settings. Knowing how to analyze oral communication events can help you to learn how to do well when it's your turn.

When you know in advance that you'll be speaking, you can greatly improve your performance if you break the presentation down into four stages: *planning*, *practice*, *delivery*, and *reflection*. Fear comes from paying too little attention to the first and second stages; like expecting miracles from a quick rough draft, you'll feel increasingly nervous about your presentation as the date approaches, and your audience will probably know that you haven't prepared well. If you spend time organizing and rehearsing your remarks,

23

3a
speak

you'll feel much more confident about your presentation, and your audience will more easily understand and appreciate what you have to say. If you consider the response to your performance after it's over, and reflect on your own perceptions of the event, you'll be able to improve your presentation skills the next time you speak.

3a Effective oral presentation

3.1

It's Shaun's turn. He gets up from his seat and awkwardly makes his way to the front of the room, saying, as he walks, "OK, I'm gonna talk about, um, my project is, let's see, what I want to tell you about is what I, what my project, what I researched for this unit, the real story of the Exxon Valdez oil spill ten, fifteen, after, um, you know, like what biologists found and stuff when they, like what the data says about it all." He finally reaches the front of the room and turns to face the class. Twenty-three faces are staring at him. He fumbles for some notes he had jotted down the night before, spilling the pages from the folder onto the floor. Picking them up quickly, he notices they're out of order now. Because the pages aren't numbered, he can't remember which one is first. The seconds tick by, an eternity of silence. He flips through the pages; one of them is upside down. The words seem to blur together. "Um, let's see," he continues, still sorting the pages. "Um, like I said, this, my project, what I want to say, to tell you about . . . ." His teacher is writing down notes—about him, maybe? The class looks impatient. He can't recall what he just said. He can feel his body heat rising, sweat forming on his brow, and he wonders whether it shows. He avoids eye contact with his audience, desperately trying to collect his thoughts, find the right words, find his place in his notes, look like he knows what he's talking about, and salvage his presentation, worth 25 percent of his course grade.

Startled awake by his alarm, Shaun is relieved to find that the presentation was just a bad dream. But many of Shaun's problems aren't just the stuff of nightmares; routinely, presenters who haven't planned well may lose their place, avoid making eye contact with the audience, talk on the way to the front of the room, get lost in their notes, or fear judgment. Luckily, Shaun has several more days to prepare for the real thing. Careful planning and rehearsal will eliminate all but the most unforeseen of problems—and his audience will easily forgive him for any problems that he couldn't have anticipated (such as a fire alarm).

1 Planning to speak formally

Before you can begin to draft and practice your presentation, you'll need to make a plan. Keep a list of information about your presentation and let that narrow down and shape the draft or outline of your remarks.

Analyze your situation. To plan effectively, begin by writing down everything you know about your speaking situation.

- What's the occasion?
- How many people will be there?
- How long is the entire gathering, and how long will you speak?
- What sort of place or space will you speak in? Where will you speak from?
- How will you know when to speak?

Having a clear understanding of your speaking situation can help you to plan the content and delivery of your remarks. For example, knowing how much time you have to speak will help you determine how much detail you can provide, how many points you can cover, and what materials (such as handouts) to prepare. If you haven't seen the place where you'll speak, it's always helpful to go there when it's empty and "scope out" the room or area, noting its size, lighting, seating arrangement, speaking location, and so on.

Shaun's planning notes help him to begin visualizing his presentation.

Oral presentation on project: 25% of grade. Purpose is to report main findings of research on topic (Exxon Valdez oil spill a decade and a half later); audience is class (23 students); front of room; teacher announces; total time no more than 15 minutes.

Analyze your purpose and audience. Knowing something about the people you address will help you to make important decisions about the sophistication and style of your presentation. You wouldn't say the same things about your science project to a group of middle-school kids as you would to a group of judges at a college science fair. What do you know about your audience? What do they already know about your subject, if anything? What do they expect to find out or experience from your remarks? What's important to your audience? What can you anticipate about their attitudes toward your subject? (See also Chapter 6.)

In addition to the needs and expectations of your audience, you'll want to ask yourself what *you* hope your presentation will accomplish. Are you trying to persuade people to take action or vote a certain way on an issue? Are you giving them information they can use in their own work or activities? Do you want them to learn something new and come away from your remarks feeling enlightened and interested in a subject? (See also Chapter 5.)

Research your topic. Unless you're already an expert in the topic of your presentation, you'll need to consult various external sources or authorities to plan your remarks, just as you would in a documented paper. (See Chapters 45–50.) Remember that live audiences have even less tolerance than readers for lots of abstract information presented in dull, lifeless language. Choose information that makes your presentation come alive, without distorting accuracy or leaving out essential facts, details, or points.

Organize your content. Instead of trying to write your talk as if it were a paper, begin by creating an outline of your remarks. Usually your talk will consist of three parts:

- **introductory remarks**, in which you introduce yourself and give your audience a preview of what you'll say (or prove, show, cover, etc.);
- **content or substance of the presentation**, which consists of your main ideas, illustrations, and material; and
- **conclusion**, which sums up and restates your purpose, reminding the audience of what you have shown or offered.

Sketching out the first of these three parts will give you a template for the others. For the body of your presentation, consider some of the standard organizational schemes for argumentative and informative writing (see Chapters 55, 56, and 58) as well as advice for developing your point (Chapter 5).

Create talking points. Talking points are key phrases, words, visual cues, or other reminders that guide you through your speech. They include not only your main points, but signals to help you coordinate your talk: "check time," "change overhead," "circulate handout." Most of the time, talking points will be words or short phrases, but you should write out all of your introductory remarks and your conclusion. Doing so will help lead you into your presentation smoothly and allow you to wrap it up cleanly and dramatically. Use typical transitional phrases, such as "next," "now let's consider," "in conclusion," "finally," or "to sum up" (see the chart at 9d-3). Remember that paragraphs or sections of a "paper" are invisible to your audience; you need to signal your intentions and structure verbally or by other means, such as overhead visuals.

Your talking points should include transitions that link one part to the next. These transitions, which you should write out as phrases or full sentences, are important guideposts for your audience. In one of Shaun's transitions, he moved from the immediate impact of the oil spill to the main part of his presentation: "As we've seen, the Valdez oil spill had a devastating short-term effect on the Alaskan shoreline and its ecosystem. I want to turn now to some of the research that has been conducted to assess the long-term environmental impact of the spill."

As you create your talking points, be sure to match the style of your presentation to your situation, audience, and topic. Someone presenting a study of the incidence of rape among teenagers won't tell jokes or treat the topic lightly. Similarly, a medical researcher explaining to a retirement community a new procedure for removing varicose veins will avoid the technical language she might use when addressing other researchers at a national medical conference.

Plan your timing. If your presentation can be no longer than, say, fifteen minutes, begin by estimating the time for each of the components, and then divide the middle part into more specific chunks of time, if that helps.

As Shaun planned his presentation, he created the following outline.

> <u>Introduction</u> (2 minutes): "Have any of you been to Alaska or seen it in films?" (wait . . .) "Someone describe the land for me." (Get 2-3 brief responses.) Unfortunately, all that beauty you describe is seriously threatened by pollution, oil exploration, and development. A case in point is the infamous Exxon Valdez oil spill of 1989. In March of that year, (explain). My purpose is to give a status report, based on secondary research, of the environmental impact of the Exxon Valdez oil spill almost fifteen years later, and to reach a conclusion about the total impact of the spill and whether Exxon met its obligations to restore the environment.
>
> <u>Substance</u>:
>   <u>Background</u> (3 minutes): (Put up Overhead #1.) Remind audience of the original situation and promised restitution. (Pause for effect and check time.)
>   —What I did (2 minutes): (Put up Overhead #2.) Explain how I gathered information and from which sources. Special focus on Valdez Oil Spill Trustee Council. (Check time.)
>   —Major findings (6 minutes): (Put up Overhead #3.) Summary of the most important findings, divided into three categories of assessment (soil/beach, wildlife, long-term ecology). (Be sure to cover statistics.)
>   <u>Conclusion</u> (2 minutes): "In summary. . . ." Explain results of the study and answer question it asked. "As illustrated by this presentation and the evidence I have provided, we must use whatever means—through new legislation, public protest, and private foundations—to safeguard our pristine Alaskan wilderness and shoreline so that we never experience another Exxon Valdez. All of us, no matter what our political leanings, have a fundamental responsibility to protect our environment."

Use note cards. After sketching out your talking points on paper, creating an outline, and working out a time plan, transfer your material to note cards. Use the main categories in your outline to organize your cards. In some cases you may need more than one card for one section of the presentation. Your cards will include major categories of content as well as presentational cues (reminders, transition notes, etc.). Finally, number the cards, so you always know where you are in your presentation.

STRATEGY

To engage your audience, especially in longer presentations, ask them to *do* something (read a handout, talk in pairs about a problem or question, or work on a short activity). Such active moments can be excellent ways to help your audience actually experience your presentation instead of just listen to it.

Don't underestimate the *time* it takes for audience participation. Think about yourself as a member of the audience: how long would it take you to do this activity, write down some ideas, or talk with someone else?

Exercise 1

A. Choose a subject that you know something about and that would make a good informative presentation. First describe a purpose for conveying this information and an audience that might find it useful. Create an outline for a ten-minute oral presentation on this subject to this audience; then sketch out a series of talking points, following the advice in 3a-1, including transitions between points and an estimate of the time for each part of the presentation.

B. In a small group, compare your outlines and talking points. How clearly organized is each presentation? Are the purposes clear, and would the information appeal to the intended audience? Is the timing reasonable? Are the talking points logically arranged? Do the transitions work?

2 Rehearsing your presentation

As you plan your presentation, don't assume you have to "get it right" before you can begin rehearsing. Hearing yourself talking out what you've written down will give you many new ideas that, in turn, will alter your plans.

Stand and deliver. If you recline in a comfortable chair to rehearse your presentation, you won't be building the confidence you need to speak to your audience. Standing up will match the physical and spatial conditions of your talk. Your body, your breathing, the placement of your feet, your eye movements will all be affected by where you're positioned during your rehearsals.

Rehearse alone, then with an audience. If possible, the first few times you rehearse your presentation, do it alone. You won't be embarrassed about stopping and restarting or talking to yourself. As you build confidence and iron out the wrinkles in your talk, it helps to give a "dry run" of your talk to one or more trusted listeners. Work through the entire presentation at once, and then ask them for their suggestions.

Try videotaping or recording your presentation. Shaun had no idea how fast he spoke until he rehearsed with a cassette recorder and then listened to his own words. This awareness helped him to find the right pace for his presentation. If you have access to a camcorder or other video equipment, tape your presentation and then watch it several times to see if you can discern problems, distracting habits, poor transitions, or unclear statements. At first you may be embarrassed or self-conscious to see yourself on tape, but remember that everything you learn about yourself will help you become a more effective presenter.

Rehearse with your visual aids. Visual aids help your audience but they also add a layer of complexity to your presentation. Be sure to include any visual aids in your rehearsal, so you can practice your timing and transitions. If possible, set up the visual-aid equipment that you will use. This will allow you to find out where to stand so you don't block the screen, how to coordinate your visual aids with your remarks, and how to operate the equipment effectively. (Nothing interrupts a presentation more than upside-down or out-of-focus overheads, blocked views, or screens that won't pull down.)

Practice until you know your routine. Don't rehearse once. Keep rehearsing until you know every part of your presentation—its transitions, dramatic pauses, reminders to look around at your audience, and so on. The longer your presentation, the more complex your remarks, and the more formal the occasion, the more you should practice and rehearse.

3 Giving your presentation

Think of an especially effective presentation you attended recently. The speaker probably connected with you in some way, interested you in the subject, and presented his or her information in a lively, engaging manner. He or she probably looked at the audience in strategic ways, modulated his or her voice, and was careful about gesticulation or body movement. Transitions between stages of the remarks were no doubt smooth and effective, and there was a sense of structure to the talk. Such strategies can be learned easily if you plan your presentation carefully and keep yourself focused on a few new techniques at a time.

Avoid reading verbatim. Good public speaking involves more than reading a printed paper aloud, word for word. Although this practice is common in some fields, most audiences prefer speakers to *present* their ideas instead of *reading* them. This kind of speaking is called **extemporaneous speaking** or **conversational speaking**, a mode of delivery that emphasizes greater interaction among the speaker, audience, and ideas. In this kind of speaking, you prepare a set of ideas, not a verbatim text, and you speak from and about those ideas. This is not to say that you don't craft the words for your presentation in advance; you just recall what you want to say from memory and from talking notes rather than reading long, boring sentences out loud.

Speak loudly and clearly. Project your voice out over the entire audience. It's not only important for you to be heard; speaking up will affect your sense of confidence as well. Articulate your words clearly, and monitor your speech rate, being careful not to race through your talk. Much of your pacing will be established in your rehearsals. Vary the pitch and cadence of your voice to accentuate certain points you're making, but don't exaggerate your emotions.

Use purposeful, natural gestures. Standing stock-still will not give your presentation any variety, but be careful not to get carried away with wild hand gestures or body movements. Move around if you wish but don't pace or make repeated motions. Avoid distracting movements (drumming the lectern, jingling change in your pocket, twisting your hair, or shifting your weight). Instead, subtly accentuate your remarks with your gestures and facial expressions.

Maintain eye contact. As you begin your remarks, look out at your audience. Look directly at individuals in the audience, but don't do so for more than two or three seconds unless you are in a question/answer mode, and don't keep returning to the same person. Vary your eye movement so that you don't "favor" one part of the room or one group of people. If it helps, work in a pattern, such as front-left, front-right, center-left, center-right, rear-left, rear-right. Look at members of the audience in a natural way, without expressions that signal to the rest of the audience that you are speaking to one individual. If you're using visual aids, it's appropriate to glance at them from time to time but keep your focus mainly on your audience.

Use visuals effectively. If you use a chalkboard or flip chart to call attention to certain ideas, prepare everything ahead of time. Audiences become impatient if they must wait for you to write something down during your presentation. A more effective way to present information visually is to use a prepared overhead transparency and project it on a screen. If you use transparencies, make sure that anything you project is readable from anywhere in the audience. Nothing frustrates an audience more than an unreadable transparency.

Certain software programs, such as PowerPoint, allow you to create stunning slides that include words, pictures, and other media. If you use such programs, be sure to follow the suggestions that accompany them; learn and practice with the technology before using it "live." Always bring backup overhead transparencies with you whenever you use computer projection devices, in case of equipment failure. Be careful not to make your visual presentation so gimmicky, with motion and sound, that your ideas are lost in the glitz.

3.2

Whatever visual aids you use, they should not control your presentation but supplement and enhance it. Avoid reading every word on your slides: the audience is capable of doing that themselves. Instead, paraphrase or call attention to the material on the slides, or let bullet points summarize points you are making in more detail.

One of Shaun's overhead transparencies contained a bulleted list, created from a pie chart found at an official Valdez environmental impact Web site, of what happened to the oil from the spill. One of the bullet points read, "2% of the oil remains on the beaches." In his presentation, Shaun referred to this statistic by saying, "A 1992 National Oceanic and Atmospheric Administration study showed that as much as two percent of the spill, or approximately 16,000 gallons of oil, remained on the beaches, some of it beneath rocks and within the soil and sand." Notice how Shaun's visual aid called attention to key facts that he could then expand on in his presentation.

Don't panic. If something goes wrong during your presentation—the projector won't turn on, a microphone isn't working, or you lose your place in your talking notes—remain calm. It's better to focus on the source of the problem for a few seconds, even if this is a distraction, than to allow yourself to lose your thoughts or become confused about what to do next. Audiences are more forgiving than you think. Take a deep breath, think about how to get back on track, and try a humorous remark if it occurs to you. If the problem can't be fixed, such as a broken bulb in a projector, move on without it. (This is why it helps to have a backup plan.)

4 Assessing the results

Unless you have outraged your audience, almost no imaginable presentation will fail to end in applause or some sort of positive acknowledgment of your efforts. Although most presenters can tell the difference between a stunning job and a mediocre one by the enthusiasm of the audience, you need a better source of feedback to know what you did well and what you can improve on. Don't be satisfied to step down and put your presentation behind you; actively seek further information so you can improve on your abilities.

Ask a confidante to be in the audience. If possible, ask someone you trust and respect to attend your presentation, and ask them in advance to look for specific areas you're concerned about, such as your body movements or the rate of your speech. Get them to give you an honest appraisal of your strengths and weaknesses.

Carefully study any scoring guides or remarks you may receive from a teacher. Teachers often use sets of criteria to judge the quality of a presentation "live." If these aren't accompanied by explanations, consider asking your teacher for more specific advice and feedback. If you're doing more than one presentation, work on the weakest categories in the assessment of the first one.

Spend some time doing a self-assessment. Although you can't see or know everything about your presentation, you'll probably have some immediate impressions of your performance. Write those down as soon as possible. Then do a mental check on the impressions: Are they accurate? How do you know? Then, after identifying justifiable areas of concern, spend some time thinking of strategies to overcome the problem in the future.

Shaun handed out three documents during his presentation but didn't tell the audience how many were coming around. He made the mistake of starting the batches of handouts circulating all at once, which resulted in confusion when they reached the middle of the room. After reflecting on this problem, he generated two strategies for circulating multiple handouts during a presentation.

Exercise 2

A. Write down what you would consider your two primary delivery difficulties (nervous gestures, filler words, or voice projection). For each, describe (1) when the difficulty usually happens (for example, during transitions or when you look at notes), and (2) something you can do to resolve this difficulty (such as pausing instead of using filler words or placing your hands on the table instead of in your pocket).

B. In a small group, compare your difficulties. Note any similar difficulties and add to your list of possible solutions for each.

3b Managing speech anxiety

Speech anxiety affects people very differently. While no one is entirely immune to the apprehension of public speaking, some people handle the pressure reasonably well, whereas others have intense emotional responses to the prospect of standing in front of an audience, which can cause them to lose entire nights of sleep and, in some cases, become physically sick. Much anxiety comes from lack of experience: like pilots with hundreds of flight hours, experienced speakers have learned to control their apprehension, while most non-pilots are justifiably terrified to sit in a cockpit. Giving oral presentations in college provides you with experience and confidence. To overcome your anxiety about these "flight-school" presentations, try a few common strategies.

1 Analyze the causes of your anxiety

Write down what makes you the most anxious about public speaking. Describe a situation in which you would feel fearful. Does it have something to do with the audience? the subject? your preparation? what you will look like? what people will think? Try to rationalize and compartmentalize your fears, and then work through each one, finding productive, personal strategies for overcoming them. Shaun, for example, had the most fear that he would "sound stupid" in front of his class. After analyzing this fear, he realized it came from how little he felt he knew about his topic. As he began to research the Valdez oil spill, he placed asterisks next to information he found new and interesting, information he was sure his audience wouldn't find "stupid." Focusing on the content of his presentation, in other words, was one answer to his anxiety.

2 Be healthy

Humans are biological organisms. Like any animal, we have automatic physical responses to certain situations (the "fight/flight" reaction, for example). Speech anxiety is part of a cycle: the more afraid we are, the more unpredictable and vulnerable we feel . . . which only generates more fear. We are far more prone to this cycle when we're exhausted or physically deprived (of nutrition, oxygen, or fluids).

Before any presentation—and *especially* before one in which the stakes are high—be sure to rest and eat well, even though you may be anxious. Put your presentation aside for at least an hour before bed, and do something else to take your mind off it, such as reading an unrelated book. On the day of your presentation, eat food with protein, which helps to sustain your energy. Avoid too much caffeine, which can make you more nervous than alert. Instead, drink water or healthy fluids without a high acid content.

3 Control your breathing and calm your body

Public speaking affects every speaker's heart rate, respiration, and other physical properties. The fact that your palms sweat before you speak, or your neck flushes, or your stomach gets butterflies doesn't predict anything about the quality of your presentation; all it means is that you're like most other people, even highly effective speakers. If you let these physical responses control your presentation, they will. You need to control them instead.

Start with your breathing. Discreetly taking long, deep breaths before you talk will help to slow your heart rate, calm your nerves, and provide oxygen to your brain. Think about your entire body from top to bottom, and find the places where you're most tense. Then deliberately relax those tense spots, continuing to breathe slowly and deeply. Keep your focus on your ideas, not on yourself, how you look, or what your audience will think about you.

4 Move confidently and purposefully

When it's your turn to speak, focus first on getting to your speaking position. Move deliberately and carefully; you don't need to rush. Don't begin to speak until you're facing your audience; you can even take a second or two to organize yourself if you have notes or if you need to adjust a microphone. Focus entirely on your opening statement. If you've rehearsed well, your first few remarks shouldn't be difficult, and once you've made it through thirty seconds of your presentation, you'll begin to feel less tense.

5 Practice, practice, practice

Nothing reduces the fear of public speaking more than the confidence that comes from rehearsal. Think of almost any event—a football game, a musical, a parade, a holiday party, a parents' day at a local elementary school, a realtor's open house—none will be successful without some form of rehearsal or practice. The highest-stakes events (the Super Bowl, a space launch, the opening of a Broadway show) will have involved countless hours of practice, sometimes for months or even years in advance. Oral presentations are no different. The more you practice, the less deeply anxious you'll feel. You may still feel a kind of superficial tension, but if you keep reminding yourself that you're thoroughly prepared, that tension will turn into energy and excitement.

6 Remember that you're not on trial

Anxiety often comes from fearing that we'll be "found out," that we're not really experts but frauds. Our audiences seem like examiners or tribunals, ready to pounce on every flaw in our reasoning or demand complicated explanations that we can't provide. Remember that your audience probably knows very little if anything about your topic. You're not the world's expert, but the audience isn't expecting you to be, either. Admit your limitations, stick to what you know, and try to present your ideas in ways that will stimulate and interest your audience.

Exercise 3

A. List and describe your greatest fears about public speaking. Are you afraid you will lose your place? forget your material? say something wrong? Are you fearful that your voice will shake or your hands tremble? For each fear, consider what you can do ahead of time to reduce your anxiety.

B. In a small group, compare fears and strategies. Create a "master list" of ten common sources of anxiety and one or two strategies for reducing each one.

STRATEGY

Expect questions from your audience, and use the following guidelines for responding effectively.

- Anticipate the kinds of questions you may be asked; where necessary, prepare brief answers ahead of time that you can recall during your presentation.
- Ask for clarification if you don't understand a question.
- Respond directly, not evasively. If you don't know the answer, admit it, and don't make one up. Instead, perhaps say that the question suggests a fruitful area for further study or investigation.
- Don't indulge "hostile" questioners. Answer them briefly and diplomatically, with a yes or no, or "I'm not sure," and move to the next questioner.

3c Group presentations and other public forums

Public speaking includes any occasion when one person or a small team addresses people in a public or group setting. The need to be articulate and focused is just as great in these settings as it is in a traditional "speech." If you're being interviewed briefly by the local news media about an event you witnessed, you'll want to be clear and accurate; if you're speaking at a public meeting in order to express your opposition to a proposal, you'll want to persuade with sound reasoning and a balanced perspective. Although not all occasions for public speaking will give you lots of time to plan your remarks, a few strategies can help you to present yourself effectively.

1 Effective group presentations

In many school and workplace settings, you may need to give a presentation with someone else or in a small team. Most of the guidelines for solo public speaking apply in these situations, but collaborative presentations create a need for even greater coordination and planning.

Divide and prepare, unite and practice. Split up the responsibility for researching your presentation, and then come back together to create joint talking points. It's essential that all members of your team participate; don't allow one member to sketch out his or her remarks briefly and tell you it will all work out. Everyone should have a copy of all the talking points for the group.

Behave as a team. During your presentation, an initial lead presenter should introduce the other speaker(s) on the team. Each presenter should create a transition to the next presenter, but these transitions should, whenever possible, be oriented toward your content, not the fact that you're changing speakers. Instead of saying, "Now Ephraim will talk," try something like "The underlying social causes of this phenomenon, to which Ephraim will now turn, help to explain why it became popular in the 1960s." Occasionally, refer backward or forward to the other presenters' remarks during your own: "As Ephraim has explained . . ." or "As Ephraim will show us in more detail shortly . . . ."

Speak to a common theme. Even if members of your team have come up with different information and ideas, don't place yourselves in opposition to each other. Instead, create a single presentation that allows you to reveal differences in your subject matter: "Ephraim has described one way of interpreting this social phenomenon; now I'd like to explain it from another perspective."

Divide your time and stick to the plan. Audiences are aware of imbalances in the time each presenter takes. Don't have someone speak for one minute simply to give them a voice; divide your time evenly among your team. Monitor your own time carefully so that you don't take away from the time of presenters who follow you.

2 Effective speaking in public forums

Every day in your community, people gather to share ideas and opinions about local concerns. Citizen's groups meet with town or city officials to lobby for certain actions. Campus forums bring together students, faculty, and administrators to discuss issues and policies. Open meetings of various organizations share ideas with interested visitors. You can speak effectively in settings like these by using some simple but powerful strategies.

Become informed before voicing an opinion. Don't rush to a meeting of your city council armed with opposition to a proposal until you're well informed. Better still, if you don't know enough about an issue to speak to it, attend the meeting in order to learn. Ask questions first, instead of rushing to judgment.

Bring information. If you feel confident enough about an issue to voice an opinion, it helps to bring information and evidence that supports your points (see 55d on supporting evidence). Opinion alone will help decision makers to know how a community feels, but it may not persuade them as powerfully as will facts and details.

Plan your remarks. In many public forums, you'll have much less time to speak than you would in a traditional presentation—perhaps only a minute or two. Just as you would for a longer speech, plan and rehearse your remarks. Refine what you say to make it as persuasive and balanced as you can. Don't alienate those who might disagree with you; instead, try to strike a balanced, reasonable posture while making your own position clear.

Assess the progress of the meeting. A badly timed comment won't do much to contribute to a forum or discussion. Wait until the focus of the discussion aligns with what you want to say, and then try to make your comments when they will have the most impact. If possible, tie your remarks to the discussion by referring to something someone else has said.

Make your comments clear and persuasive. Although emotional appeals (especially empathy) sometimes help to support a cause, emotion is usually less effective in persuading a diverse audience of a position than careful, balanced reasoning. Fear and nervousness also tend to affect people's demeanor in public settings, causing them to speak angrily, make accusations, or even cry. If you prepare for a tense public meeting by thinking through your ideas carefully and framing a clear, logical argument for your position, you won't fall prey to your emotions, and your audience will be more likely to think about your ideas and modify their positions on an issue.

3 Effective comments on boards and committees

When you play an active role in a business, in school, or in your community, you'll find yourself participating on various boards and committees. These settings have their own "rules" or conventions of successful communication, which, if violated, can lower a member's standing and weaken his or her participation. Because the rules vary from group to group, it's important for you to listen and observe carefully during the first meeting or two, until you have a clear understanding of how people interact. Some boards and committees, for example, are very formal and may use parliamentary procedure for participation or voting. Other boards may be very loosely organized and allow spontaneous comments and informal diversions. Still others may be poorly governed and in need of a few guidelines. As you participate in such groups, a few general strategies may be helpful.

Prepare for the meeting. Boards and committees usually announce an agenda before each meeting. Study the agenda carefully, reading any documents that will be discussed or collecting enough background information to be informed. If you are formally placed on the agenda (to give an update on a project, for example), prepare and rehearse your contribution in the same way that you would an address to a larger audience (see 3a). Carefully prepare any materials that you will hand out to the group.

Choose when and how to participate. During an open discussion on a board or committee, ask yourself whether the comment you want to make will advance the discussion or offer new ideas. Listen carefully to what others say, so that your own contributions aren't thought to be irrelevant. Keep your comments focused and, when appropriate, brief; don't belabor points or ramble. Keep track of your own contributions relative to those of others, so as not to dominate the discussion. When possible, directly link your ideas and remarks to what others have said.

Find an appropriate style for your comments. If you have carefully gauged the level of formality and rules of participation that characterize your board or committee, you'll find you can more easily adjust your language to fit your situation. Of course, you don't want to speak in a way that's unnatural to you, or "put on airs." But if your committee deals with difficult issues and has taken on a somewhat formal nature, don't use casual, slang-ridden language. The kind of discourse used may also change *during* a meeting—with more casual, social discussion before and after the "business" part of the meeting.

Use language sensitively. Consider the makeup of your board or committee. As you frame your remarks, think about how various members may react to any assumptions implied by your words. Keeping your emotions under control will help you to avoid unconsidered, rash, or potentially offensive remarks or terms (see also Chapter 32).

Exercise 4

3.3

A. Watch a brief oral presentation. If you can't find a nonprofessional example and decide to use television, don't choose a news broadcast or other journalistic presentation, but look for a presentation that is given to a live audience, such as a speech in Congress. Local and cable-access stations may broadcast town council meetings, school board meetings, and the like. Choose one that lasts at least five minutes. As you watch, jot down notes about topics discussed in this chapter: the method of delivery, eye contact, the use of notes, body and facial movements, pauses, distracting features, and so on. Write a brief analysis and evaluation of what you saw.

B. Compare your analyses and evaluations in a small group. What principles and strategies can you learn from these analyses? What other issues about public speaking did your analyses raise that were not covered in this chapter?

CHAPTER 4

PLANNING STRATEGIES FOR COLLEGE, WORK, AND PUBLIC WRITING

Imagine trying to build a house without having any plans drawn up beforehand, or going into the playoffs without a team strategy, just to "see what happens." Success would depend on luck, not design. The same is true for writing and speaking. In almost any formal writing (or speaking) project, whether in college, in your community, or on the job, you need to discover and "rough out" your ideas before you can really get started. Planning before you write—often called **prewriting**—helps you to move your project forward more smoothly and confidently by giving you a map of where you want to go. Some planning strategies work well at the earliest stages of writing; others can help you later on as you fill gaps in your knowledge, work out patterns and relationships among ideas, and make tentative decisions about structure.

4a Generating ideas and information

Whatever the writing task, you'll want to ask, "What do I know about what I'm writing? What else do I need to know?" Instead of talking or thinking through these questions, try writing about them quickly and informally. You'll get warmed up for more formal drafting, and you'll generate some crucial ideas and plans for your project.

1 Try informal writing

An ideal place to write quickly and informally is in a journal or planning notebook. Many accomplished writers use a strategy called **freewriting**—fast, highly informal, unselfconscious writing.

> ### STRATEGY
>
> To try freewriting, write quickly for five or ten minutes. Concentrate entirely on *writing without stopping*, even if you think you have nothing to say. Simply writing "I'm stuck, I'm stuck" will at least force you to begin writing. Curiously, such empty or rambling prose will soon begin to bore you, and you'll find yourself almost magically slipping into more interesting ideas.

4.1

Focused freewriting involves writing quickly about an idea or topic you already have in mind, or one that you began developing through freewriting.

> ### STRATEGY
>
> For focused freewriting, continue writing as you freely associate ideas, especially if you start with a general topic. Your first sentence might begin, "Antigambling laws—I guess I'm in favor of them generally." As you continue to write, you'll again find yourself exploring what you know or feel about the topic. Consider stating your topic as an assertion so that you can systematically question that assertion, anticipating a spark that ignites your interest.

2 Use listing

Lists can draw out knowledge already in your mind and *create* new ideas through association.

> ### STRATEGY
>
> Write your topic at the top of a page and then list ten thoughts, facts, or ideas about the subject. Or adapt listing to generate specific ideas. For example, begin with a general impression or idea, and list supporting details and new associations.

As he started working on his proposal requesting permission to allow local bands to perform in the basement of the community center, Morgan Scott listed some of the subjects the report needed to cover.

> *Space isn't used for anything else during the evenings.*
> *Will give teenagers a safe place to go, especially on weekends.*
> *Need plans for cleaning the space up and maintaining it.*
> *Noise wouldn't bother neighbors.*

Plenty of parking for those old enough to drive.
Recreation department and police could easily provide supervision.
Will provide a creative outlet for local residents.
Low cost.
Will have the support of parents.
Add to the city's reputation as a good place to live.

A WORD ABOUT SPEAKING

You can practice all of the prewriting strategies in this chapter when drafting an outline and speaking notes for an oral presentation (see 3b). In planning to address members of the city council about his idea for using the basement of the community center, for example, Morgan Scott might create exactly the same list of points as he would for a written document.

3 Tease out details

Good writing is often detailed. A plea to increase funding in a public school district will be more effective if it includes facts about teachers' low salaries, out-of-date books in the classrooms, and the disrepair of the buildings. Searching for details to particularize general statements can also lead you to new ideas and associations.

STRATEGY

To help you increase the level of detail in your writing, make a **detailing list**. For each general idea, opinion, or impression, list specific examples, features, or facts that particularize it. This will give you a rich resource to draw on as you develop your essay.

Heather Strong began writing an account of her trip to the Grand Canyon for her travel club's newsletter.

When we first looked out over the Grand Canyon, we were just amazed. What a beautiful sight! It was like nothing we had seen before--so impressive and marvelous. It was simply incredible to gaze out over such a spectacle of nature.

This paragraph cries out for specific visual detail. Figure 4.1 on page 42 shows part of a detailing list Strong created to help develop her ideas. These details found their way into her revised draft.

The view from the North Rim was just as breathtaking. From Tiyo Point we could see Shiva Temple. To its east was the flat-topped formation of Buddha Temple, with its red sandstone lit

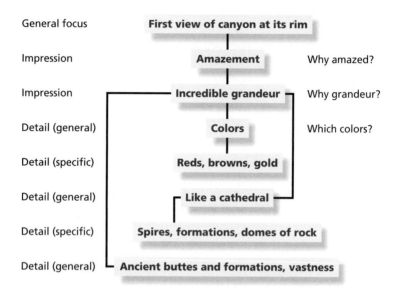

General focus	**First view of canyon at its rim**	
Impression	**Amazement**	Why amazed?
Impression	**Incredible grandeur**	Why grandeur?
Detail (general)	**Colors**	Which colors?
Detail (specific)	**Reds, browns, gold**	
Detail (general)	**Like a cathedral**	
Detail (specific)	**Spires, formations, domes of rock**	
Detail (general)	**Ancient buttes and formations, vastness**	

FIGURE 4.1   Detailing list

up like a flaming torch. The effect of these varied red, brown, and gold formations is almost religious. It felt like we were standing in a cathedral of stone, looking down into a million years of spires, statuary, and domes, all bathed in soft, stained-glass hues of light.

4 Ask strategic questions

You can generate important information for many writing (and speaking) projects, especially proposals and recommendations, if you try answering the questions *what, why,* and *why not* (*where, who,* and *how* may also be important questions, depending on your writing project). Brian Corby used this strategy in prewriting for his report arguing that his city's zoning board should not allow a high-rise apartment to be built adjacent to a public park.

What?
- Proposed high-rise apt.
- 18 stories, 102 units plus 3 penthouses
- Overlooking east side of Piedmont Park between Sunrise Ave. and Claremont St.
- Proposal approved by Feb.; Planning by Feb. next yr.; groundbreaking by June
- Finished structure by Aug. of following year

Why?
- Developers profit
- Brings jobs to Lake Walton
- Raises property tax base—supposed to funnel money back into the city and parks
- Provides medium-cost housing in growing area
- Develops ugly vacant property by park

Why not?
- "Citifies" one of the few green patches in Lake Walton
- Increases traffic, crime rate, park use
- Adds to waste; pollution from proposed garbage incinerator in building
- Opens the door to other high-rise development because of new zoning ordinance
- Blocks sunlight from park
- Raises property taxes for longtime and elderly residents

ESL ADVICE DEVELOPING CLEAR AND FORCEFUL DETAILS

Readers will usually expect your writing to say something *specific* about a topic, problem, or event. If you provide too little detail, your readers may consider your approach too broad, vague, indirect, or poorly supported. You may be accustomed to other expectations, especially ones requiring less detailed support for assertions. If so, examine effective examples of writing addressed to your audience. Also, you may question specific readers about the kind of support they would like you to include in your writing assignment. College instructors, professors, and even supervisors in the workplace

- generally expect writers to request such information,
- find it useful that writers request such information,
- are willing to provide writers with such information, and
- are used to providing writers with such information.

Exercise 1

A. Begin with the topic, issue, or problem for a writing project you are working on, or choose a topic that interests you. Then try the listing procedure with your topic. Begin by listing ten things you know about your chosen topic. Then choose one item and generate another sublist beneath it. If you can, keep going to a third or fourth level.

B. Working in a group of three, exchange topics (issues, problems) with your fellow writers. Try to generate a list of ten ideas for each partner's topic. If you have time, generate sublists of five items from one of the original ten items in each list. Then compare your lists as a group, and see which items overlapped and which were unique.

4b Structuring ideas and information

Ideas and information alone won't lead to successful writing and speaking unless you can find ways to structure them. Some writing tasks, such as business and research reports, need to follow familiar structures. For many other kinds of writing, including essays about personal experience, position papers, critiques, informative pamphlets, and proposals, you'll often need to identify relationships within the information and ideas you've generated.

1 Draw a cluster

A **cluster** is a diagram of interconnected ideas. When you create a cluster, you will find yourself both exploring what you know about a topic and revealing how that knowledge is related.

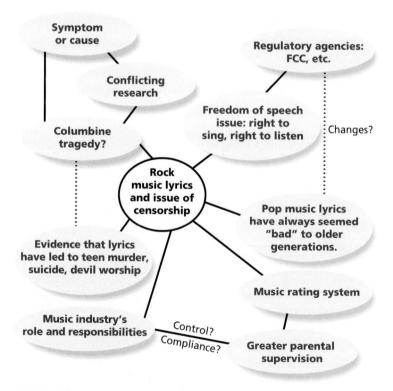

FIGURE 4.2   A simple conceptual cluster

STRATEGY

To create a cluster, begin by writing a concept, idea, or topic in the center of a page, and circle this kernel topic. Then jot down associations linked to this central idea, circling them and connecting them with lines to the kernel topic, like the spokes of a wheel. (See Figure 4.2.) As you continue to generate ideas around the central focus, think about the ways the subsidiary ideas are connected, and draw lines to show those connections. You can also create clusters in cycles; each subsidiary idea becomes the central focus on a new page. The nodes or pieces of the cluster will become a visual representation of how your text might be "chunked" into paragraphs or sections.

2 Create a tree diagram

Tree diagrams resemble clusters, but their branches tend to be more linear and hierarchical, with fewer interconnections. (See Figure 4.3.) Each larger branch can lead to smaller and smaller branches. For this reason, tree diagramming can provide a useful way to visualize the components of your paper.

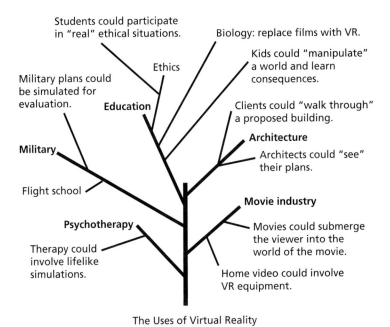

FIGURE 4.3   A simple tree diagram

> ### STRATEGY
>
> Start with your main focus or topic as the "trunk" of the tree. As you work upwards, create primary branches with centrally connected ideas. You can branch off from these with smaller and smaller branches that each relate in a specific way to the main branch. Consider "revising" your tree diagram into a preliminary outline to use when deciding what to place in each paragraph of your paper.

3 Build a time sequence

If you're writing a paper organized chronologically or involving sequences of time, you may find a **time sequence** useful.

> ### STRATEGY
>
> To create a time sequence, begin by framing each event along a time line. Then draw vertical lines of thicker or thinner widths depending on how closely connected one event is to the next.

In planning materials for a self-guided tour of a special museum exhibit on the artist Andy Warhol, James Christenfeld drew a time sequence detailing the history of Warhol's artistic life. With thick connecting lines, he showed how certain pivotal events led to or caused other events or works in Warhol's career. Connections with thin lines were simply chronological.

Exercise 2

A. Choose a simple topic (issue, problem) whose details are familiar to you. Then try creating a cluster or a tree diagram. Does the result suggest a possible structure for a paper or presentation? What problems might arise in "translating" the cluster or diagram into an outline?

B. In a small group, share your cluster or tree diagram and explain its nodes or branches. Then collaboratively try to generate more branches for each writer's diagram.

4c Creating generalization-support patterns

For many writing (and speaking) tasks, you will need to arrive at a **generalization** (an interpretation, conclusion, or thesis) about your subject, identify appropriate **support** for your generalization, and arrange these two elements in a pattern that will help convey their relationship to your audience. The following strategies may prove helpful.

Fact:

Most teenagers who join gangs are from fatherless homes. (Harris, 2001)

Fact:

Joining a gang involves rituals intended to prove manhood or toughness. (*Book of Gangs*)

Fact:

Gangs seek new members in poverty-stricken areas such as ghettos and barrios.

Fact:

Gangs have a hierarchy; new members take risks to impress leaders and gain favor.

Generalization:

Gangs survive by recruiting members who lack strong male role models at home and need ways to build self-esteem. Normal activities that help build self-esteem may not be available in poor and crime-ridden areas, so young recruits look to gang leaders as authorities and protectors.

FIGURE 4.4   Generalizations from particulars

1 Draw principles and look for generalizations

Any writing task that asks you to draw conclusions about (interpret) the meaning of a situation, text, phenomenon, or experience will require arriving at a generalization about the particulars that make up your subject. First, list as many facts or ideas about your subject as possible, using the listing technique described in 4a. Then ask yourself whether you can draw a generalization (conclusion, interpretation) about these facts or ideas. This strategy is illustrated in Tim Pagenhart's planning for a paper on teenage boys' gang membership. Once his list of facts led him to a generalization, he could look for other facts to support it. (See Figure 4.4.)

2 Create a problem-solution grid

In some writing and speaking situations, you may need to focus on a problem and then present an argument for a proposed solution. Proposals, reports, position papers, and other persuasive texts often follow a **problem-solution sequence**. If your writing project calls for this kind of approach, you can use a simple but powerful technique for exploring ideas and information and revealing organizational options for your paper or report: a **problem-solution grid** (see Figure 4.5 on p. 48).

FIGURE 4.5   A problem-solution grid

STRATEGY

Create a problem-solution grid by putting a statement of the main problem at the top of a page. Make a layer of at least two or three possible solutions to the problem. For each, name at least one further problem with that solution. "Solve" each subsidiary problem in turn. You can create as many layers of problems and solutions as you wish, generating many specifics for your paper or presentation.

As Figure 4.5 shows, Paula Masek identified three temporary solutions to the problem of hunger among the homeless. Using a grid to guide her planning and to identify a structure, Masek discussed each boxed item in a separate section of her draft paper.

3 Invent an outline

The best-known traditional prewriting technique is the trusty **outline**, complete with Roman numerals. Unfortunately, the traditional outline doesn't do much to help writers *generate* ideas before they decide how these ideas should be arranged. As a prewriting technique, however, a **working outline** can be useful. The trick is to use the outline to generate new categories of information rather than to label ones you've already discovered.

4c
plan

4.2

Mitch Weber tried this strategy when he began planning the historical section of a report on the nonprofit organization in which he held a summer internship.

III. Creation of the family health center
   A. Founding work of Susan and Roger Ramstadt
      1. The "vision"
      2. Finding the money
      3. The involvement of the Crimp Foundation
   B. The early years (1972–80)
      1. Building momentum
      2. The great financial disaster
      3. Rebirth
   C. Toward maturity
      1. Fund-raising in the 1990s
      2. State recognition and the big award
      3. Health and sustenance
   D. The future
      1. The new board of directors
      2. The new vision

A WORD ABOUT SPEAKING

The traditional outline can be especially useful as you convert your ideas into a structure for your presentation. As you plan, label each part with an estimate of the time it will take you to talk through that part. If you work from an outline, it's also easy to give your audience a preview of your re-marks by referring to the three or four main sections of the outline.

Exercise 3

   A. Create a list of five topics, issues, or problems. Choose the one that most interests you. Then briefly try out three of the planning tech-niques discussed in 4b–c. After experimenting with them, jot down some notes about which one(s) worked worst and best for you. Why do you think this was the case? What sort of topic did you choose, and how did the technique you used affect its development?

B. Compare your general impressions of your three chosen planning techniques in a small group. Which ones seemed to work best for everyone? Were certain strategies more useful for certain topics?

4d Planning in electronic environments

Computer software and the Internet offer many kinds of help to writers exploring ideas and information or planning an essay or report. Using a computer's word-processing or note-taking program to help plan your essay can in itself be a useful strategy, because you can easily save your planning materials for later reference when you're drafting, revising, or re-envisioning your writing. Electronic planning can take other forms as well.

1 Explore question sets and thought collectors

4.3

Sets of questions you can use to explore a topic and identify patterns of ideas and information are available on many Web pages, and as part of some word-processing programs. Such sites and programs provide interactive questions and prompts that help you gather your thoughts and develop plans for organizing a report or essay. One site offers help in planning an argument by asking a writer to type in responses to the following statements.

In my paper I wish to prove that:
I believe my thesis is true because:
Someone who disagrees with me might argue:

The program then lists the responses, allowing the writer to check those she wishes to keep. These lists, in turn, can act as an informal plan for writing a first draft.

2 Try summaries and keywords on search engines

Search engines, such as *Google*, are programs that help you identify Web or Internet sites relevant to a topic or issue. Typically, search engines provide the URLs for Web sites, with or without brief summaries of their contents. Some also provide lists of keywords and key phrases.

Select a word or phrase that identifies the topic or purpose of your writing task or that is related to a subject or issue you wish to explore, such as "sports injuries." When the summaries appear on your screen, read them and list any words, phrases, and sentences that suggest ideas or information you might wish to explore in your writing. Here are some notes that Rick Lopata took from his preliminary survey of links on the controversy about "dirty dancing."

Dirty Dancing

—Also called "freaking," "booty dancing," "grinding," and "the nasty"
—Increasing number of high schools creating policies banning forms of dirty dancing
—Many young people and some parents argue that every generation invents forms of sensual or sexually explicit dancing (e.g., Elvis, 1920s swing dancing)
—Editorials point out that dancing is an art, and consider some kinds of ballet to be highly erotic
—Well-known sociologists disagree about whether such forms of dancing lead to promiscuity or premarital sex

3 Follow links

Web sites contain highlighted words and phrases that provide **links** to sites discussing related issues and ideas. You can use these to survey subjects, develop ideas, and identify possible sources for a report or essay.

STRATEGY

Identify a Web site that discusses ideas and information relevant to your writing task or to a subject you might wish to explore. List any highlighted words or phrases (links) that suggest material worth exploring or possible focuses for your writing. Then click on the links and scan the linked Web sites, writing down words, phrases, and ideas you might develop in your own work. Continue until you have filled a page or two with notes and are ready to look for patterns (see 4b–c) in the material you've gathered.

4e Planning: Paper in progress

Jessica DiGregorio was assigned a paper in a college course focusing on literacy and its consequences for individuals and societies. The task required her to identify a public or official document (such as a charter, certificate, law, set of guidelines, or official publication) and to discuss its consequences for individuals or groups of people. Other people in the class analyzed the effects of documents such as housing contracts, NCAA regulations for college sports, a parent's death certificate, and a "driving while intoxicated" citation. Jessica had always been interested in sports, perhaps because her father was an accomplished basketball player. She decided to do some preliminary listing to see what specific kinds of documents affect participants in sports—amateur, college, and professional (see 4a). Here is a list of questions and ideas she created.

- Injury reports can shape an athlete's participation, the outcome of games, and the emotions of fans and players. Who gives the documents such power?
- Game rules—some rules have serious consequences when broken, but others are less important. Why? Who decides? How do players and fans know?
- Some sports specify the shape, size, weight, etc., of equipment. Does this make a difference? What about the sports that have few regulations on equipment? Do the differences reflect something about the nature of the sports or their roles in society?
- Professional sports contracts seem to be in the news often (Major League Baseball, NBA, NFL). Can they really determine the success or failure of teams? How do they shape the lives of players? My father's contract.
- Following the box scores. What happens when people regard games as box scores?
- Drug regulations. Laws or informal rules. What's the difference?

After deciding on the consequences of professional contracts on players' lives as a focus for her work, Jessica made the following list.

- Contracts in the news—what kinds of things they cover.
- Odd things that some sports stars request.
- My father's NBA contract. What's in it?
- What he had to do as a result of the contract. What the team had to do.
- What it meant for his life. My family. Me?
- Similar to other contracts at the time?
- What if you break a contract?
- What is a contract? Legally. What exactly can contracts do and not do?

Exercise 4

A. Study Jessica DiGregorio's two planning lists. What other topics on the first list do you think would have been worth developing in ways that addressed her assigned task? What questions would you ask her about the topics on the second list? What advice would you give her for either elaborating her second list or choosing specific items on it to include in (or exclude from) her paper?

B. In a small group, compare your responses to Exercise 4A. Work together to generate a list of additional particulars that DiGregorio could use to develop her topic.

CHAPTER 5

DEFINING YOUR PURPOSE AND THESIS

Think about what writing or speaking on the job, in school, and in civic activities actually *does*. It gives you a way to communicate new ideas and information. It helps produce commodities, provide services, make things work well, or streamline the flow of information. It can be coolly informative or passionately persuasive. It can sell, buy, or negotiate things. It can do public good or make private profit. And it can produce new knowledge that will delight and entertain people, lead to personal wisdom, or save lives.

Each time you write, you're also fulfilling specific purposes related to the task at hand. If you're writing to entertain your readers with a rich, interesting description of a personal experience, this purpose will also help you to choose an appropriate style, structure, and content. Thinking about your general and specific purposes can give you a sense of direction for your writing and an organizational plan for carrying it out.

5a Analyzing your purpose

Think about your last substantial piece of writing. No doubt someone else handed you a task or assignment, and it was your job to produce a decent piece of prose. In the business world, almost no one escapes such writing tasks, whether they're actually assigned ("Please reply to this request for information about product X") or you're just expected to do them as part of your job. In most cases, you're writing for several audiences, including co-workers, clients, and others in your organization—not just for your direct supervisor. Likewise, even though a teacher defines your writing assignments in college to get you thinking about a problem or issue or to teach you something, when reading your writing he or she functions as a representative of a subject area or a general community of educated adults. Your purpose is less to "write for the teacher" than to "write for the academic community we share." One of your early steps in planning for any piece of writing, therefore, should be to analyze the task and setting, taking time to figure out what you're being asked (or what you're motivated) to do.

1 Define the focus of the task or assignment

In many writing or speaking tasks, your focus or topic may be defined for you in advance. In a memo to the YMCA volunteer tutoring staff, for example, your topic might be an upcoming training session. In an email message to the members of your ski club, your topic might be the results of a recent fund-raiser. (These topics may be announced in the "subject" line of your memo or email message.) On other occasions, you may need to identify the topic in a task that's given to you, or even come up with a topic on your own. In all these cases, it helps to articulate for yourself just what it is you're writing about.

Look for key noun phrases. When your focus appears in a written assignment or task description, it will inevitably contain nouns that signal the main topics your response needs to focus on or address.

> ## STRATEGY
>
> Look for key nouns or noun phrases in the assignment and underline them. In your planning notes, write these nouns and then, by freewriting or writing conceptual maps (see 4a–c), begin inventing possibilities for your paper's contents.

In analyzing a writing assignment in his child development course, Dennis Buehler underlined three key noun phrases.

> The purpose of this assignment is to integrate what you have learned in the area of cognitive development. Focusing on the second year of life, what are the most important skills that emerge in different domains (attention, language, and perception)? Give specific examples from the studies we have read so far.

The underlined topics can be stated more simply as *cognitive-developmental skills in the second year of life*.

Create a focus statement. When your writing task isn't an assignment given to you by someone else, write your own focus statement to be clear about what you need to do. Include key nouns or noun phrases (as in the preceding example). This can help you to keep your writing from straying from the point. Karla Spellman, for example, was asked to write a page for the Web site of a city project called "Green Chair," explaining how volunteers made green Adirondack chairs that were sold to raise money for creating play spaces in inner-city parks. She wrote the following focus statement and underlined the key noun phrase in it.

In a page for the City Projects Web site, write a <u>description of the Green Chair project</u>, including its goals, how people can volunteer to build the chairs, and where they can buy one.

2 Define the purpose of the task or assignment

Identifying nouns—topics or focuses—gives you a clear sense of what your writing is *about*. But nouns don't act: they're just things that sit, inert, on the page. Your writing doesn't just need to say something; it also needs to *do* something. This "doing" is the rhetorical action—the purpose—of your writing, and it usually appears in a verb or verb phrase.

Look for key verb phrases. In an assignment someone else gives to you, the central purpose of your response will appear in key verbs and verb phrases—statements of action and agency.

> ### STRATEGY
>
> Underline all key verbs or verb phrases that appear in the assignment or task description. Then circle those that appear to be the most important or central—the ones that tell you what to *do* with your writing. Use one or more of the planning techniques (see 4a–c) to generate material for your writing.

In analyzing the second writing assignment in her composition course, Corinth Malletas underlined two key verb phrases.

> *Assignment 2:* Find an advertisement that catches your attention in a popular magazine. Then <u>analyze the ad for its hidden cultural assumptions</u>, being sure to <u>describe exactly what is happening in the ad.</u> Include techniques of camera angle, coloration, and focus.

Create a purpose statement. For self-motivated writing occasions, create your own purpose statement and underline the key verb or verb phrases. In planning an announcement recruiting acoustic bands for a new coffeehouse, Ty Brown wrote the following purpose statement and underlined two key verb phrases.

> Create a flier directed at band members and leaders to <u>encourage their application to audition</u> for the X-Tra Coffee House and <u>explain the process</u> to them as well as details about the coffeehouse.

Notice that these verb phrases contain important assembly instructions for Ty's flier. "Encourage" implies "getting attention," "being positive," and "ad-

5a
thesis

5.1

vertising." "Explain" implies "giving information," "being clear," and "avoiding deception." Here are some of the more common verbs used in writing situations, especially in college writing assignments, along with brief definitions and examples.

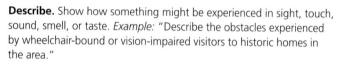

VERBS USED IN WRITING SITUATIONS

Describe. Show how something might be experienced in sight, touch, sound, smell, or taste. *Example:* "Describe the obstacles experienced by wheelchair-bound or vision-impaired visitors to historic homes in the area."

Analyze. Divide or break something into its constituent parts so you can analyze their relationships. Begin with careful description and observation. *Example:* "Analyze the causes of increased wildlife roadkill in a nearby suburb."

Synthesize. Combine separate elements into a synthesis, producing a single or unified entity. *Example*: "Synthesize this list of disparate facts about energy consumption."

Evaluate. Reach conclusions about something's value or worth. Substantiate all evaluations with evidence based on careful observation and analysis. *Example*: "Evaluate the proposals submitted by three different groups who each want to organize this year's charity auction."

Argue. Argue to prove a point or persuade a reader to accept or entertain a particular position (see 55a–d.) *Example*: "Write a letter to the college senate arguing your position on the campus-wide ban on indoor smoking."

Inform. Present facts, views, phenomena, or events to inform your reader. *Example*: "Inform homeowners about the hazards of lead paint in older homes."

Extend. Apply an idea or concept more fully. *Example*: "Extend the production figures to take into account the mechanics' work slowdown."

Trace. Map out a history or chronology, or explain the origins of something. *Example*: "Trace the development of Stalinism."

Discuss. Provide an intelligent, focused commentary on a topic. *Example*: "Discuss citizens' primary objections to the proposed tax hike."

Show. Demonstrate or provide evidence to explain something. *Example*: "Show how specimen transport problems contribute to operating room delays."

Exercise 1

A. Below are two writing tasks, one in the form of a college writing assignment, the other in the form of a work assignment to a writer working in an internship at a local nonprofit agency. Locate the noun(s) that indicate the *focus* of each task, and find the verb(s) that indicate its *purpose*. Restate the focus and purpose in your own words if necessary.

Sample Assignment: At some point, most people recognize in themselves a prejudice against another person or group. These prejudices often come from stereotypes—inaccurate generalizations made on the basis of limited experience, rumor, or what others tell us. Choose some past action in your life that came out of a prejudice. What was the cause of the action? If the same circumstances arose today, would you behave differently?

Sample Task: Draft a proposal to the State Board on Aging for our planned ElderHelp Transport System. Refer to the current guidelines for contents of the proposal, length, and format. It would be useful to include some information on actual beneficiaries of our plan, so you will want to conduct a few informal interviews with some seniors—possibly ones who use our center. Rose has written successful proposals to the state board in the past, so get her input early. Of course, you should also run your draft past Jim.

B. Compare your analyses in a small group. What aspects of the tasks do you agree on? Where do you differ? How might you go about writing each of these texts?

5b Using rhetorical purposes to guide your decisions

Now that you've analyzed the general purpose of a writing task, you can begin to consider more specific effects you want your writing to achieve. These effects are your **rhetorical purposes** for writing: what you want your writing to *do* at each stage. Do you want your first paragraph to grab your reader's attention with something really alarming, or is it more important to begin on a cool note of academic objectivity? Should you use a personal anecdote in the middle of your document to show how you understand a problem, or would it be better to launch into a description of research studies? Do you want to leave your reader hanging at the end by suggesting unexplored questions, or will you wrap everything up with a really strong, opinionated conclusion?

1 Rough out a purpose structure

As you think about how you want to affect your reader, it helps to plan a general **purpose structure** for your paper's contents. This is more primitive, at this early stage, than an outline or detailed description of parts; it's merely a blueprint to help you get started.

STRATEGY

Begin with a few simple categories, such as "beginning, middle, end," or "introduction, body, conclusion." Your categories should correspond to the main parts of your paper or document. Then explain what each of your categories will *accomplish*. Use verbs: "show," "explain," "make the claim that," "create interest," "build up to," "disprove."

In planning to write about housing options for a section of her school's student guide, Carol Stotsky first defined her general purpose (to describe as objectively as possible the benefits and drawbacks of various housing options). But then she needed to get more specific. Did she want to suggest one option over another? For the rhetorical purpose in her beginning, Stotsky decided to *draw her readers in* by *showing them* that it's important to think carefully about where to live while in college.

> **Beginning: Why consider housing options?**
> (*Draw* readers in; *show* that the topic is important to them)

Stotsky decided that after showing why this question is so important, she would discuss each housing option (dorms, fraternities/sororities, off-campus houses and apartments, living at home) in detail, analyzing the advantages and disadvantages of each. For her rhetorical purpose in the middle section, she planned to *explore* the options objectively.

> **Middle: *Explore* housing options in detail.**

She then decided to move her final section toward a *recommendation* by presenting a scheme in which traditional-aged students (seventeen to nineteen years old) start college by living in a dorm or at home and then move toward greater independence in their third or fourth years by considering off-campus housing. Since she'd already analyzed the options, she stood a better chance of demonstrating her point.

> **Ending: *Recommend* that students start secure,
> then move toward independence.**

This informal purpose structure gave Stotsky a tentative order and direction for her contribution to the student brochure.

> ### A WORD ABOUT SPEAKING
>
> Creating a purpose structure will be essential to a well-planned and rhetorically effective presentation. In addition to outlining the main contents of your presentation (see Chapter 4), ask yourself what you want to accomplish in each part—what you want your audience to take away: a changed perspective? some new information? an action plan? the outlines of a problem? the results of a requested study or investigation? a recommendation of some sort? Use your purpose structure to guide the content, language, visual aids, and presentational emphasis of your talk.

2 Particularize your purposes

Rhetorical purposes work at all levels of your writing, from the most global reasons for writing, to the most specific aims you want to achieve by using a particular word or adding a particular sentence. You can further specify each of the rhetorical purposes that have led to a sense of your essay's parts, listing ways to develop those purposes. Carol Stotsky decided, for example, that the beginning of her contribution to the student guide would try to grab the attention of readers who might not understand why housing options are an important topic. She listed three possibilities.

1. I could begin with a true-to-life description of two students who have made different housing options, one wise and one not so wise.
2. I could begin with a string of quotations from parents concerned about their children's well-being while in college.
3. I could begin with the results of a study by Breland on the consequences of housing choices for first-year college students.

As she considered her specific rhetorical purposes for her opening sentences, Stotsky realized that neither research results nor parents' quotations were likely to grab students' attention. She chose her first option and tried some drafting strategies (see Chapter 7), eventually weaving in the research results after she had "hooked" her readers.

Exercise 2

Roz Dane is a nurse practitioner in a family clinic. Clinic physicians have been seeing many patients who have suffered complications from more unusual body piercings, such as tongue studs. In some cases the patients were not aware of the potential complications or dangers. After some discussion, the physicians who own the clinic have asked Roz to produce a short, informative, and unbiased pamphlet on body piercing, which they can make available to patients before they consider various piercings.

Write a purpose statement for Roz's task, and plan a multipart structure for her pamphlet based on that purpose.

5c Defining a main idea or thesis

Most writing has a point, but if that point isn't clear within the first page or so of a text, readers may become frustrated and give up reading. In the work community, for instance, an executive summary might appear first, before a full report, to clarify the main points right away and give readers a sense of what's to follow. In contrast, academic readers may be expected to have more patience as the writer gives background information that leads up to a main point.

One way you can be clear about your purposes and avoid bland, generalized prose is to develop a specific **thesis** for your writing, which you then explore, support, or illustrate using specific examples or arguments. Although you'll hear the term *thesis* almost exclusively in college (with terms like *main idea, message, story,* or *point* being used more often in business and community writing), the principle of the thesis remains the same across contexts: a thesis is the controlling idea of a piece of writing. Many college papers contain a thesis statement, usually a single sentence, that appears somewhere early in the text, most often at the end of the first paragraph. In other writing, the thesis may be more subtle, but it still has the effect of telling the reader what the writing will say and do.

Depending on your writing situation, you can begin a paper with a clear thesis in mind or discover your thesis later and revise accordingly. You can also begin with a clear thesis and then modify it as you look for evidence or **supporting ideas** to back up your assertions.

1 Turn topics into theses

When you begin a piece of writing, do you think about large areas of knowledge or experience that often appear as nouns or noun phrases? These usually take the form of *topics*: "conservation versus jobs in the timber industry," "the use of laser surgery in female infertility treatment," "death penalty by lethal injection in the state of Texas." Developing a thesis means *narrowing* one of these topics into something more specific and verbal, some statement of principle, action, or belief.

STRATEGY

To develop a thesis from a topic, first try **narrowing** the topic to some specific angle or perspective. Then begin turning the topic from a noun (a "thing") into a statement that contains a verb.

Lynn Scattarelli narrowed her topic in an informational pamphlet she designed for a community parenting group.

5c
thesis

VAGUE TOPIC	Ritalin
STILL A TOPIC	The use of Ritalin for kids with attention-deficit disorder
STILL A TOPIC	The problem of Ritalin for kids with attention-deficit disorder
ROUGH THESIS	Parents should be careful about medicines such as Ritalin for kids with attention-deficit disorder.

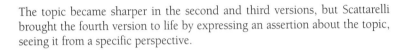

5.2

The topic became sharper in the second and third versions, but Scattarelli brought the fourth version to life by expressing an assertion about the topic, seeing it from a specific perspective.

2 Complicate or extend your rough thesis

Early thesis statements often beg for clarification or elaboration. In Scattarelli's rough thesis, it's not clear what she's suggesting to parents about Ritalin: that it shouldn't be used? that it should be used judiciously? that it's inappropriate for kids with ADD? Answering these questions led her to a more complex and interesting thesis.

FINAL THESIS	Although Ritalin is widely used as a drug treatment for children with attention-deficit disorder, parents should be careful not to overrely on such drugs until they have a complete picture of their child's problem and have explored all the options for its treatment.

Scattarelli complicated her final thesis by accepting Ritalin as a legitimate treatment for ADD. The main point—a caution about overreliance and the exploration of other options—*qualified* or *extended* her rough thesis.

More complex theses often lead to writing that your readers will find interesting and enlightening. In working on a short speech to be delivered at a local PTA meeting, Stephanie Cox turned a vague topic into a complex thesis by connecting the lack of a dress code at her children's school with the concept of social competition.

TOPIC	Lack of a dress code at Morgan County Middle School
ROUGH THESIS	The lack of a dress code at Morgan County Middle School is a problem.
COMPLEX THESIS	The lack of a dress code at Morgan County Middle School has allowed our children to compete over clothing styles and fashions, taking them away from the true social and educational purposes of being in school.

3 Expand your thesis with specifics

Think about how a thesis or main idea helps your reader. Knowing something about what you're going to say, your reader can organize the information that follows in chunks, fitting the ideas communicated by paragraphs and sections into the larger statement of purpose. But you need to decide on these ideas in the first place. Consider using the outlining processes described in Chapter 4 to create a series of points or ideas that extend, support, or illustrate your thesis. Start with a simple list—three items, for example—and then work from there. Joel Kitze, contributing an essay to a special library publication on computer literacy, created the following thesis-governed outline.

THESIS	In spite of advances in new technologies, computers will never take the place of books as the primary medium of written literacy.
SUPPORTING IDEA 1	Books will always be more democratic, since only the middle and upper middle class can afford personal computers.
SUPPORTING IDEA 2	Books can be transported and enjoyed everywhere—on a bus, on a beach, in bed.
SUPPORTING IDEA 3	Children enjoy the physical comfort of reading with adults, a comfort harder to achieve with computers.

Each idea formed a kind of "minithesis" for its paragraph or section, guiding the ideas and focus of that paragraph. At the same time, each idea also provided support for the overall thesis or claim of Kitze's paper.

4 Modify your thesis

Don't force yourself to stick too closely to your original thesis. As you plan, you may find yourself entertaining other ideas, especially those that seem to contradict your main idea or thesis. In such cases, your writing may be more interesting if you can qualify your earlier position or perspective, revising your thesis and its supporting ideas. For example, in searching for good reasons to favor books over computers, Joel Kitze thought of some distinct advantages of computer technology, including ease of storage, huge memory capacity (thousands of book pages can be stored on a disk or hard drive), and the ability of software to search or manipulate texts. A computer can show color and graphics, weakening the argument about the physical appeal of books. After thinking about four or five reasons like these, Kitze went back and modified his thesis, making it more complex and subtle.

ORIGINAL THESIS	In spite of advances in new technologies, computers will never take the place of books as the primary medium of written literacy.

MODIFIED
THESIS
> Although digital technology allows masses of information to be stored easily, it will never replace the bound book as the most convenient, affordable, and magical medium for print.

Kitze's revised thesis acknowledges that computers have certain advantages, yet he still makes a case for books. Readers of this new thesis have more to think about than they would with the earlier version.

Exercise 3

Turn each of the following topics into two different thesis statements or main ideas. Be as inventive as you like.

EXAMPLE

TOPIC
> Saw-blade sabotage in the timber industry

THESIS
> Spiking trees to sabotage the saw blades of timber workers is both illegal and extremely dangerous, but should be understood as a subversive act intended to stop further depletion of virgin forests.

THESIS
> Protests that include the illegal spiking of trees to sabotage the saw blades of timber workers actually help the timber industry, by suggesting to the public that conservationists are less concerned about human safety and human life than about trees.

Topic 1: Grandparents' visitation rights, which allow them to see grandchildren against the parents' will

Topic 2: Gay rights in the Boy Scouts

Topic 3: Metal detectors at public school entrances

Topic 4: Whose fault is air rage?

Topic 5: Laws declaring English the official language of the United States

CHAPTER 6

CONSIDERING YOUR AUDIENCE

Imagine that you're writing a short article for one of the in-flight magazines found in the seat pockets of most commercial airliners. What and how you might write for such a magazine would depend on your knowledge of its readers—people locked into a pressurized cabin 30,000 feet above the earth. What do you know already about such readers, at least generally?

- Your readers are likely to include travel-minded vacationers and businesspeople.
- Your readers' physical circumstances (restrained in a seat, stressed by travel) may make them bored, tired, or uncomfortable.
- Your readers are likely to be impatient to arrive at their destinations.

Potentially bored, tired, and impatient readers will not warm to a deeply theoretical reading. They'll want short, lively pieces they can read in ten or fifteen minutes, preferably on topics of human or geographical interest. They're not likely to enjoy graphic accounts of disasters or articles on the risks of airline travel. Yet they'll certainly want to be informed and entertained, if only as a distraction.

Already you can see how just a few thoughts about your audience can help to limit the infinite choices you face when you write or speak—choices of style, content, and length.

6a Defining your audience

Many writing experts use the term **audience** to refer to actual or implied readers or listeners. An audience may be one person (such as the city official you address in a letter complaining about the poor condition of the neighborhood sidewalks), or it may be dozens, hundreds, or thousands of people (such as the readers of the newspaper that publishes your letter about the same problem).

Your first question in any analysis of audience will be, "Who am I addressing?" Is it a flesh-and-blood person you know intimately? Or is it a shadowy, unknown reader, with only a faint silhouette to guide your thinking? Is your reader a single person or a large group?

To begin answering these questions, study Figure 6.1 on pages 66–67. This illustration shows an audience continuum, beginning with the most intimate reader on one end (yourself), and ending with the remote and amorphous "general community of unknown readers" on the other.

The self. Writing for the self can be an excellent way to learn and to plan for formal writing (see 2c). In more formal writing, the self can also act as a critic or interested reader.

The specific, intimately known reader. *Example*: a close friend, a lover, a family member. Such people make up an audience very different from people you've never met. Letters directed to intimately known readers usually don't have to be very formal, yet you can still carry on an academic conversation with such readers.

The specific, personally known reader. *Example*: A teacher, a supervisor, an acquaintance. Your knowledge of a personally known reader accumulates through a social, scholastic, or occupational relationship. Just as you might talk a little more formally to such a person than you would to a close friend or relative, the style and tone of your writing will also be less casual and chatty.

The specific community of known readers. *Examples*: your writing class, members of a team or club you have joined, a discussion list you're on, your coworkers. Such *groups* of readers often can be characterized socially or geographically. While you can no longer describe this audience's unique personality, you can think of it as a *community* whose members may not all think, act, dress, or live exactly alike but who are bound together by some shared situation.

The specific, publicly known reader. *Examples*: Oprah Winfrey, Britney Spears, your senator or congressperson. You come to know public audiences indirectly through news, gossip and rumor, speeches, interviews, or published works. While you don't personally know someone like Oprah Winfrey, you know *of* her; you may have seen her on her TV talk show, watched her perform in one of her TV or movie roles, or read one of her books. What you know of her largely depends on what's been made available for you to know.

The specific, unknown reader. *Examples*: Mr. Ed Walters, director of personnel at CompuGraphics, Inc.; Sondra Teisch, president, local chapter of Students Against Driving Drunk. Such readers live in the shadows. Often you know only their names and affiliations. Your knowledge usually comes not from any specific actions, words, or direct experience but from what these

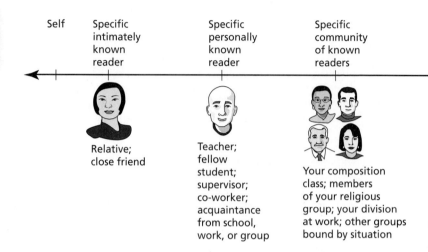

FIGURE 6.1   The audience continuum

people *do,* what *context* they're in when you write to them, and what your relationship is to them. Because you know them neither personally nor publicly, you should usually address such an audience using a formal style.

The specific community of unknown readers. *Examples*: the hundreds or thousands of undergraduates at your college or university, citizens in your hometown, readers of *Mademoiselle* or *Southern Living,* members of a discussion list dedicated to antique furniture, worldwide employees of an international corporation. The larger the group, the less direct knowledge you'll have of its individual members. While it might take only a few weeks to get to know the members of a school club, sorority, or fraternity, it might take months or years (or it might be impossible) to become acquainted with everyone who reads the school paper or alumni magazine. Yet even large communities can still share the same social, academic, or work context, and are tied together by mutual goals, circumstances, and knowledge (or by allegiance to common symbols, mottoes, or slogans).

The general community of unknown readers. *Examples*: Americans, the general public. At this end of the continuum is the most abstract and faceless audience of all. Be careful assuming that you are ever writing for such an amorphous audience. *What* you're writing about already slices away many potential readers; *how* your writing *reaches* your audience slices away many

Specific publicly known reader	Specific unknown reader	Specific community of unknown readers	General community of unknown readers

| Senator Kennedy; Whoopi Goldberg; president of your university; editor of your local newspaper | Personnel director at Inland Chemicals; editor of the *Journal of Economics*; chair of the university committee on animals in research; others known by name and affiliation | Board of directors at Inland Chemicals; members of the local PTA; the choir's electronic mailing list; readers of *Hunting Magazine;* other groups with shared interests | Democrats; educated Americans; readers of popular fiction; concerned citizens; working parents |

more. (Even the medium of communication—written text—already eliminates all nonreaders, most citizens and residents who do not speak or read English, and many people who are homeless or destitute. If you're writing to an electronic audience, the medium eliminates those who don't have access to a computer or the Internet.) When you decide to write for "the general public," think carefully about what this means, and consider the more specific context of your writing.

Audiences themselves can also shift positions over time. A co-worker you might address formally at first can become a friend, then a close friend. Further, workplace texts are often read by very different audiences. A memo requesting personal leave will be read not only by your direct supervisor but by her supervisor as well. Members of your working group will probably receive a copy of the memo, even though they can't make a decision about your request. If your request is approved, the payroll and personnel departments may also see the memo.

Exercise 1

A. Imagine that you're living on Shell Island, located in a small estuary along the coast of Florida. A favorite winter vacation spot, the area boasts some excellent shelling beaches. But now, after years of ravenous beachcombing, fewer shells appear at low tide, and the area is attracting a more limited variety of birds and other wildlife. The local city council has proposed a general ban on beachcombing and plans to pass an ordinance that would require visitors to obtain a beach permit, at a cost of $30, to use the public beaches. The money would be channeled back into the study and preservation of the local environment.

You're planning to write a position statement on the proposed ordinance. Choose one of the three contexts below. Then, referring to the audience continuum, analyze the audience for your position statement. Take a position on the issue, and consider which readers will disagree with your position and why.

Context 1: Surfriders is a small organization for active surfers who visit Shell Island almost daily and are interested in keeping the area clean and safe. Write a letter to Todd Gray, president.

Context 2: *Winter Birds* is a newsletter sent to retired people who live in Northern states but have properties on the island and migrate there for two or three months during the winter. It is published and mailed by a local association for retired people. Write a letter to the editor.

Context 3: Nan Brown is the director of the Shell Island Chamber of Commerce. Business owners, rental agents, and tour operators rely heavily on the Chamber of Commerce for support. Write to Ms. Brown.

B. Compare your letters in a small group. Discuss the ways in which your audience analysis influenced your letters.

6b Characterizing your readers

Although you might identify actual people as readers (your mother, your rabbi, the First Lady, the owner of the gas station down the street), at some level your writing is shaped by how *you* think of your audience. Constructing audiences also draws on your social and cultural knowledge. If you know very little about feminism, for example, and you write to an audience of feminists, you may address them inappropriately. Knowing that there are many varieties of feminism complicates your audience, but the result is a richer and more accurate picture that leads to a better-informed and more incisive piece of writing.

When developing a profile of your audience, be aware that you're dealing with *tendencies*. Ask yourself whether you are unfairly stereotyping your reader(s). Sitting on any given airplane, for example, may be a relaxed person deeply engrossed in a dense philosophical treatise or a complex analysis of trends in computer programming. Are your generalizations accurate and helpful?

6b
reader

6.1

ANALYZING YOUR AUDIENCE

Use the following questions to think critically about the nature of your readers as you plan and revise your writing.

1. **Size and relationship.** How large is your audience, and how generalized? How intimately do you know your audience? What sort of relationship do you have to your audience?

2. **Prior knowledge.** How much does your audience know about the subject of your writing? Are your readers complete novices or just short of being experts? Do they share your prior knowledge of the subject? Are they young or old? Are they wise or inexperienced and naive?

3. **Physical context.** Where are your readers situated geographically? Is it possible to pinpoint their location? If not, can you generalize about it (Florida State University, San Francisco, Capitol Hill)?

4. **Social context.** What characterizes your audience socially and culturally? Are your readers educated? poor? middle class? Do they spend their time watching TV, or reading books? Do they listen to Brahms? Do they go to tractor pulls? Do they spend time at singles bars or PTA meetings?

5. **Intellectual disposition.** How would you characterize your readers' way of thinking? Are they highly conservative? radical? apathetic? Where would they stand on certain major issues? Are they more likely to read and enjoy the *National Enquirer* or the *National Review*? *Science* or the *Christian Science Monitor*?

6. **Conditions of reading.** Under what conditions will your audience be reading your writing? Will readers be at home? at school? at the office? at the breakfast table? Will they be studying your writing closely at a desk or reclining in an easy chair after a good meal? Will they be busy or distracted? Will time be on their side, or will they be wishing they could buy a few extra hours?

7. **Power.** What is your status relative to your reader? Are you expecting the reader to accomplish something? Is your writing accomplishing something for someone else, such a supervisor? Is that person also going to read your writing?

Exercise 2

A. Imagine that your longtime next-door neighbors take a temporary position in another country and rent their house. Soon after the renters move in, they begin piling up their yard and driveway with junk cars, old refrigerators, tires, and other debris. The situation becomes so intolerable that you decide to write to the renters, calling attention to the problem. You also decide to write to the local city inspections office, which is responsible for enforcing various codes on yard debris. Write the two short letters, addressing the first to John and Susan Valentine and the second to Ms. Betsy Lewis, City Inspections Office.

B. In a small group, compare the style, tone, and content of your pairs of letters. In each case, you were writing to a specific audience. How did their positions on the continuum influence your decisions? What general principles can you infer about the relationship of audience analysis to certain choices in your writing?

A WORD ABOUT SPEAKING

You've probably had the experience of being in an audience whose general beliefs or background knowledge a speaker has misjudged. It's painful to be a listener or participant, and the speaker is none too pleased at discovering the mistake, usually after the talk ends. Audience analysis is at the heart of successful oral presentation. Be sure to spend some time considering your audience in both the planning and rehearsal stages of your presentation. Much of your analysis will come from your *context* and *purpose*: Why are people coming to this talk? What do they expect to learn or experience? How did they get there? Who is sponsoring or setting up the talk?

If possible, use strategies during your presentation, such as asking for a show of hands in response to key questions, to gauge your audience with greater specificity. (See Chapter 3.)

6C Adapting your content, structure, and style

Imagining audiences means more than gathering isolated facts about them (average age, occupation, and so on). In analyzing your audience, stopping at facts is like lining up the cumin, coriander, oregano, and basil without knowing how much of which spices you should add to the stew. Analyzing an audience can influence many decisions you make as you plan and revise your writing. In particular, consider how audience influences your *genre*, *content*, *structure*, and *style*.

1. **Genre**. What sort of text you choose for your writing—its **genre**—will depend in part on your audience. Imagine that you are an interior designer commissioned to plan the redecoration of someone's living room. Your reader will be expecting something akin to a proposal, not a poem, an editorial, or a letter. Choices of genre are especially important because they often give you guideposts for other decisions regarding length, style, structure, and purpose.

2. **Content**. What specific information you put into your writing also depends on your audience. Your decorating proposal would probably assess the present design and its limitations; propose a redecorating plan with details about wallpaper, furniture, and lighting; and estimate the work involved and the expense to carry it out. It would be inappropriate to include other kinds of information, such as instructions for hanging wallpaper (since your reader is hiring you to arrange this) or a description of your own living room (since your reader doesn't expect a comparative analysis).

3. **Structure**. How you arrange and organize your ideas will likewise depend your audience. A utilities operations manager proposing an expensive, controversial solution to a water utilities problem might acknowledge the problem itself early but lead gradually to his proposed solution and its benefits. In an essay for a professor who doesn't like unsupported generalizations, it might be wise to establish some points first to lessen the risk of hearing the question, "How do you know this?" In some genres, such as APA-style research reports (see Chapter 52), your structure may be inflexible; you need to know what that structure is and follow it.

4. **Style**. How you think about your audience will influence the style of your writing. How informal or formal should your writing be? how clinical or emotional? how friendly or hostile? how embracing or adversarial? Most teachers of physical anthropology reading a student's formal essay will not accept statements like "Leakey's stuff is awesome," just as most parents reading a strep warning sent from their school wouldn't expect it to begin "It has been determined that the environment of P.S. 46 contains clinical cases of *Streptococcus* bacilli in specific human organisms with whom your offspring may be in routine contact or physical proximity as a consequence of their attendance and participation in academic and extracurricular activities."

6d Addressing communities of readers

6.2

While it may seem as though you've almost always written for a teacher, you actually participate in conversations in many communities through your reading, writing, and speaking. Your college, work, and public communities give you a rich assortment of audiences to address. A campus alone consists of a loose confederation of scholars and teachers, students, administrators, members of teams and clubs, and people serving in many public and private capacities. In some circumstances, you may need to address or think of more than one of these types of readers, which complicates your task. Strategies for addressing different communities of readers depend partly on your relationship to your reader(s).

1 Writing for authorities

Writing for people in positions of authority can be especially challenging; after all, your performance and reputation may be on the line, and the stakes (such as a grade or the renewal of a contract) can be high. In academic settings, for example, a common first-day activity is figuring out the teacher. Is she tough or easy, rigorous or undemanding? Does she expect flawless, highly polished papers, or is she more concerned with the messy, exploratory side of writing? Does she seem to welcome diverse views, even if they don't match her own? In business settings, knowing what a supervisor expects can be just as daunting—and important.

STRATEGY

Always attend to the specific guidelines for completing a writing task (see 5a). If these are provided orally, write them down carefully. Reread all directions several times. Above all, *ask questions*. Most teachers, supervisors, or superiors are willing to elaborate on their expectations. Their answers often tell you how they will evaluate your writing in light of its purposes.

2 Writing for communities of peers

Many public and civic contexts in which you might write or speak are organized democratically. You don't have a supervisor as much as a series of self-appointed roles (such as membership on a committee), so you are on more-or-less equal footing with others in your group. (In other public settings, of course, power takes more complicated forms: a city council member has a certain kind of authority in her work above that of an ordinary citizen, but citizens themselves hold the power to vote such a person out of office.)

Many writing classes today also use peer groups as a way to encourage more diverse responses to your writing than you might get from your teacher alone. Peer groups can give you support during stages when you're uncertain about your writing, and can provide valuable "test runs" of audience response after you've completed a rough draft.

STRATEGY

During the planning stages of your writing, be sure to discuss your ideas and intentions with members of a peer group. Their initial responses (as "themselves") will give you valuable insights from the perspective of a general academic audience. If you have a specific audience you are addressing, ask them to role-play that audience for you so you can test how well you've achieved your purposes. (For more on peer groups during revision, see 8c.)

6d
reader

3 Writing for broad public communities

A murky and ill-defined audience, but one often alluded to in directions for or evaluations of writing assignments, is the "general reader." Although no one yet has defined this audience very clearly, it usually refers to reasonably educated people—for example, most people in your college or university. Many teachers favor the undefined "general academic audience" for classroom writing for the very reason that opinions among this group will vary widely and require of the writer more thought, hence, deeper learning.

Readers in broad public communities are themselves very diverse. Some are well educated, well informed, and interested in the pursuit of knowledge (often for its own sake). Others read very little—just a daily newspaper, for example—in order to keep up on current events. Some readers have incisive, critical minds and like to be entertained with new and stimulating ideas; others read only when they have to and prefer not to spend much time talking about ideas.

In reading your writing, teachers often allude to various public communities with statements like "How would the audience for this piece react to so radical a statement?" or "Are you sure you've considered the opposing views your audience might raise here?" or "How would people opposed to gun control respond to this?" Such statements assume different audiences with different dispositions. Interestingly, academic readers will take you seriously if you can show, through your prose, that you've considered a range of public responses to an issue or idea. That sort of awareness of audiences can also make your writing in work and nonacademic communities stronger and more convincing.

STRATEGY

In your planning notes, circle any assertions or points that readers in various public communities could challenge. Then brainstorm to develop several responses to the challenges. Are the challenges well reasoned? If so, then consider acknowledging or incorporating them in your paper.

4 Writing for yourself and forgetting about audience

Writing for yourself can help you to formulate or explore new knowledge. If you're responding to a task or an assignment given by a teacher or supervisor, ask yourself what the writing process can do for *you*. What sort of learning is implied by the design of the project? How can you maximize your own interest in the subject? What will *you* get from your efforts?

Writing to or for yourself can also help you in the early stages of your writing, when "audience paralysis" can set in. Tough-minded audiences can make you so self-conscious that you can hardly produce a word that will survive your scrutiny. The result is frustration, procrastination, and anxiety.

Audience analysis isn't something you do once, in planning your writing, and then put aside during the later stages. While drafting and revising, keep thinking sharply about your readers. Once you've marked the general outlines in the clay, you can continue to define the features more sharply as you work your way toward the finished sculpture.

Exercise 3

A. Pick a specialized magazine with which you are very familiar (such as *Road & Track, Cooking Light,* or *Wired*). Get a recent copy of the magazine and glance through it, noting the topics, lengths, and formats of its articles; its advertisements; its layout; and its writing style. Then, using the advice outlined in this chapter, select one method for analyzing the magazine's audience. If you can't answer a question definitively, make as educated a guess as possible, and state what further information you'd like to have.

B. Join a group of three or four other students. Briefly describe and compare your magazines, and then discuss your audience analyses. What issues surface about the relationship between the writing and the audience? What problems or questions about audience would you like to discuss?

PART 2

Drafting and Revising: Shaping Your Writing for Your Community

CHAPTER 7

DRAFTING

Drafting means stringing words together into sentences and paragraphs that will begin to make some sense to a reader. All your planning, purpose setting, and audience analysis will prepare you to write. But don't expect to sit down and immediately draft a smooth, coherent paper simply because you've accumulated a lot of material. The process of pulling your information together and *writing* will always be intellectually challenging: drafting is hard work.

When you write a **rough draft**, you create something that begins to resemble a fully elaborated text. If planning can be likened to creating a storyboard for a movie, then drafting means actually filming the movie, always realizing that later you'll reshoot certain scenes, add new material, and let lots of footage fall to the cutting room floor.

7a Moving from planning to drafting

Your use of various planning strategies should produce more than enough material to begin drafting. The problem you face at this stage is knowing how and where to begin writing your draft. You need to assess what you have, and start turning your material into sentences that move your ideas forward.

1 Draft in manageable parts

Conceptual outlines do more than simply help you generate ideas. A good cluster, for example, will also show you relationships among connected ideas and ways you might think about organizing your paper.

7.1

The items in your planning materials will usually suggest chunks of text that you can draft in one sitting. If your fifteen-page paper on the relationship between asthma and ozone levels seems like a daunting task, begin by writing a fairly easy section—for example, two pages summarizing recent research studies.

STRATEGY

In your planning notes, look for specific ideas that suggest paragraphs or sections of your paper. Then choose one idea and write about it, either in draft form or in the form of lists, notes, or sentences.

Albert McCann, a symphony manager in a midsize city, generated the following diagram as he was preparing the planning documents for his symphony's long-range tour schedule. Note how the diagram not only helps Al structure his document but also may help him determine the kind of case to make for including (or excluding) particular destinations.

2002–2003 Schedule

Pittsburgh	St. Louis	San Fran	Salt Lake C.	D.C.
+ Key professional relationship w/Sean T. + short travel – on 00–01 schedule – low profile	+ new venue + fairly cheap travel via Delta – few contacts there	+ group loves it + high profile – cost	+ coordinate with winter sports + new, high-profile location	+ could work on coordinating joint trip w/City Ballet + relatively inexpensive – group won't like this location

2 Develop a general structure

The kind of material you're writing may determine the way you organize it. A narrative, for example, will probably be arranged *chronologically* (each event following the previous event in time); an argument may be organized *logically*, by paragraphs supporting some assertion. Much of the writing done in the workplace or the public arena is highly structured. Whatever you're writing, you need to think about what should come first, second, and third in your paper.

Most academic writing will contain at least three parts: an **introduction**, a **body**, and a **conclusion**. This simple structure can help you to make some preliminary decisions about how to group your ideas.

STRATEGY

Look through the material you have accumulated. Group some of your specific ideas, topics, or terms into one or more of the three categories of introduction, body, and conclusion. Tentatively organizing your ideas in this way will help you to develop a stronger focus when you begin writing.

By thinking about this three-part organizing scheme, Amy Burns was able to generate some ideas for a paper on superstition, and develop a preliminary structure.

INTRODUCTION	Fear; people who believe in superstitions; origins
BODY	Examples of superstitions (black cat, #13, crossing fingers, walking under a ladder, rabbit's foot)
CONCLUSION	Truth and falsity of superstitions; mystery surrounding them; concepts of reality.

7a
draft

When she began drafting her paper, Burns used the ideas from this preliminary plan to write an introduction about how superstitions originate in a fear of the unknown.

> Many people are superstitious or at least practice some of the bizarre rituals of superstition, but very few know why or have thought about the reason. A lot of people practice superstitions without realizing that what they are doing is superstitious. The biggest percentage of people practice superstition because of a fear of the unknown. You might have heard some superstitions from parents or grandparents, been influenced by school or religion, or perhaps even read about them in books. However or wherever you heard of them, you practice superstitions because you are afraid of what will happen if you do not.

Although the introduction-body-conclusion structure can be helpful, much of the material you will write outside the academic community may require another approach. Petitions, newsletters, sales letters, problem descriptions, status reports, and some Web sites, for example, don't follow a rigid structure with set headings; but readers do have expectations about how such pieces should be organized.

A WORD ABOUT SPEAKING

In most presentations, you'll be speaking from notes rather than reading a full written text verbatim. As you draft your talk, you'll want to find the right balance between "imagining" what you'll say and writing down every single word. To draft your presentation, write down key ideas, terms, and reminders in your talking notes. At first, it helps to elaborate on those notes with bullet lists and other points which, after you're rehearsed enough, you can remove from your working notes. (See Chapter 3.)

---

3 Assess your purpose and redraft

Even before you've written a full draft, you may want to stop to think about whether the material is achieving your general purposes for writing (persuading someone of a position, telling a story, explaining how to do something) or your more specific purposes for different parts of your paper (providing information, livening up a paragraph with an anecdote, illustrating a point with an extended example). (See Chapter 5.)

> ## STRATEGY
>
> Read your early material, and extend, cut, or redraft it to more adequately reflect your intended purposes.

7b draft

In her paper on superstition, Burns's broad purpose was to inform her readers about the nature of superstition and to encourage some enjoyable reflection. Her first *specific* purpose statement was "I want to grab my readers' attention and get them thinking about the nature of superstition." From this statement, she realized that her introduction was informative but too dull. She drafted some new sentences and then followed them with her earlier material.

> Do you knock on wood after making a prediction? Shiver when a black cat crosses your path? Consider the number 13 unlucky? If so, then you have already been swept into the fantasy world of superstitions. Many people are superstitious or at least practice some of the bizarre rituals of superstition, but very few know why or have thought about the reason.

Exercise 1

A. Thinking about your experiences as a writer, give some advice about drafting to an imaginary audience of high school students. Feel free to include personal experiences, tips, and specific techniques. When is the best time to write? What are some self-defeating habits? What's the best way to start writing a paper?

B. Share your "advice papers" in a small group. Are any behaviors typical? Is any advice consistent?

7b Using drafting strategies

What makes drafting so challenging? Partly, it's the need to get a complicated job done, finding the right words while you're still figuring out where to begin. It's also dealing with apprehensions, such as feeling the focus slipping away, or thinking your writing isn't working, or revising every sentence instead of moving quickly ahead. You can meet these challenges successfully if you practice some useful techniques for getting words down on the page.

7.2

1 Write about your writing

Worrying about your writing probably won't ever go away—even the pros do it. Worrying yourself into avoidance or confusion, however, won't help you get your draft written.

A very common fear is the deadline. Strangely, many writers react to deadlines by putting off the writing until the specter of doom is practically breathing down their necks (often in the wee hours before the writing is due). For these procrastinators, just about any other task, even the most unpleasant, will be worth doing just to avoid sitting down and actually starting to write.

7b
draft

STRATEGY

Begin drafting not by writing your paper but by writing *about it.* What's foremost in your mind about your paper? What do you hope to do with it? What possible ways might you start it? As you make these notes, you'll soon find yourself a little less anxious about start-ing—after all, you *have* started. As your anxiety lessens, you'll find yourself more willing to take some risks and try out a few lines.

2 Draft quickly

Another source of frustration comes from the struggle to find the right words. Sometimes every sentence seems to tangle you in a mess of contradic-tions, until you're no longer sure what you want to say. In this situation, you want to gain momentum, to feel that your ideas are smoothly giving way to words.

STRATEGY

Draft quickly. As you begin, don't worry about writing perfect sentences and paragraphs. Just aim to get as much material on paper as you can, right from the start. Writers often find that when they write quickly, they feel a momentum developing, a kind of "flow." If you can type faster than you can handwrite, using a computer may encourage this momentum.

3 Semidraft

Writing a first full draft in one sitting, especially of a major document, may be too ambitious, and you'll need to divide the task into several drafting episodes. Some writers, however, can't seem to continue drafting anything for more than a few minutes before they stall out. They can't come up with the words to describe a particular idea, often because they're tired or haven't thoroughly considered their ideas.

STRATEGY

Semidrafting refers to the process of writing full sentences until you feel you're about to stall out. At that point, you simply write the word *etc.* and then continue on to your next point. Or you insert a brief direction to yourself in brackets to remind you what to do when you return to the draft to push that section a little further along.

In a paper on the histories of "wild children" (lost children raised by wolves or other animals in the woods), Kavita Kamal semidrafted the following paragraph.

The first case to be examined was that of Victor, the "Wild Boy of Aveyron." Victor first appeared in a village in southern France in January 1800. His age was estimated to be about eleven or twelve years. [Explain how he was adopted by Jean-Marc Gaspard Itard and Madame Guerin; discuss their subsequent studies.] People assumed that he was a mute when they first dealt with him because he did not speak. Nor did he show any evidence of hearing. [Now go into the stuff from Roger Shattuck's *The Forbidden Experiment* on the fact that he had no malformation of the tongue, mouth, etc., then into Itard's paper in 1801 on Victor.] This selective deafness lasted until January of 1801, when Victor showed the first signs of hearing human voices.

Notice how Kamal suspended what may amount to several paragraphs or even pages while she pushed her draft forward into new areas. This gave her a sense of its form—a kind of flow—without forcing her to flesh out every detail. Later she was able to return to the paragraph and simply add the missing material to an existing structure.

DID YOU KNOW?

In a study of college students with serious writing problems, Mina Shaughnessy found that the more they worried about the correctness of their prose while writing, the more paralyzed they became and the less coherent their drafts turned out to be. "Some writers," Shaughnessy wrote, "inhibited by their fear of error, produce but a few lines an hour or keep trying to begin, crossing out one try after another until the sentence is hopelessly tangled."

Mina P. Shaughnessy, *Errors and Expectations* (New York: Oxford UP, 1977) 7.

4 Talk it out or take a break

Sometimes nothing works. You simply can't, at that moment, put coherent sentences together on the page, and your frustration can cause you to lose interest in the project.

Writing isn't like breathing, something you do as a matter of course. It's more like eating, which depends on your appetite. If you simply can't write, no matter how many techniques you try, then don't. Put off your writing until a little later. Just set a time to return to the task—preferably on the same day, but no later than the same time the next day. In the meantime, try this final Strategy to keep going.

**7c
draft**

> ## STRATEGY
>
> Talk with or send an email about your writing project to someone you know well. Explain what you're trying to do. Expressing your concerns may help you alleviate tension and may even show you some solutions. Your listener may also have suggestions to help you get started.

Exercise 2

A. Try out any one of the Strategies for drafting described in this chapter. Jot down some notes about how well it worked to get you started drafting and keep you moving forward.

B. Compare the results of your experiment in a small group. What worked? What didn't? How could you modify or add to the Strategy to make it work better for you? What other problems did you encounter as you drafted, and how might you solve them in the future?

7C Drafting collaboratively

Different groups work together in different ways depending on the composition and purpose of the group. A committee formed to revise production standards at a manufacturing plant might consist of department managers who each have an area of expertise, whereas a Sunday school parents' committee might include people who have no experience in running a school but share the goal of increasing enrollment. Each group will distribute writing tasks in the way that seems most efficient for its resources and purposes. If your group is uncertain about how to proceed, consider one of the following suggestions.

1 Do parallel drafting

In **parallel drafting**, your group divides the proposed document so that each member is responsible for drafting a particular section. Members can exchange drafts as they revise and edit. This strategy allows writers with different specializations to work comfortably together yet draw on individual expertise, but it may require one person to act as editor, integrating the drafts.

2 Do team drafting

In **team drafting**, the group agrees on first and second authors for each section. The first author begins drafting and continues until he or she gets stuck. Then the draft passes to the second author, who begins where the first writer stopped. This method works well when various writers share similar ideas and approaches. The drafts are recirculated when the group is ready to revise and edit.

7c
draft

3 Do intensive drafting

Intensive drafting is most successful when you are working with a close friend or colleague. You need to find a location where you can assemble your materials and work undisturbed. Decide where each person will start, begin drafting together, and exchange sections at a certain time or as each of you finishes a segment. You continue your intensive, undisturbed work—exchanging drafts and reworking the document—until you are both satisfied with the result.

STRATEGY

Make use of the "track changes" feature in most popular word-processing software to draft collaboratively in an electronic document file. This function allows changes to the original draft to appear in a different color on screen. Drafts can be circulated by disk or email, edited by group members using the tracking feature, and returned to the author. Every member's changes will appear (color-coded by editor in some software) in the draft for review.

Exercise 3

A. Imagine you are part of a student organization that is raising funds for a community project in which volunteers read to children in school libraries. Your organization intends to submit a grant proposal to a local foundation or philanthropic group. Plan how the members might use the following equipment to draft the proposal collaboratively: telephones, email, computers, fax machines. What steps would be involved in your plan?

B. In a small group, compare the plans you developed in Exercise 3A. How comfortable are students in your group with the idea of drafting collaboratively? What are the pros and cons?

7d Drafting: Paper in progress

Recall that Jessica DiGregorio had developed a generalized topic: the consequences of professional contracts on the lives of sports players (see 4e). After listing some possible examples to support this topic, she tried freewriting for a few minutes on selected items in her list. Here is her freewriting passage on the item "What he [her father] had to do as a result of the contract."

- Keep himself fit for five years (meaning?)
- Not indulge in bad habits
- Not stop playing basketball
- Stay clear of ice-skating, skiing, other strenuous activities to avoid injury

Exercise 4

A. Examine DiGregorio's freewriting. At this point she wanted to use some ideas in her freewriting to begin drafting. What advice would you give her about the ideas she has begun to explore? What other details on the subject of the contract requirements could she include in her rough draft? Is there anything in the freewriting that suggests a good place for this passage in her paper (beginning, middle, or end)?

B. In a small group, compare your responses to Exercise 4A. What elements did the members of your group agree could be profitably expanded from the freewriting as DiGregorio drafts her paper? Was there any consensus in your group about where to place this section of the paper?

Because so much of what we read is in a final, published form, we often forget how much work goes into a good piece of writing or successful oral presentation. Invisible to us are the hours the author spent in the process of **revision**—considering and reconsidering content and structure, tearing out whole sections and redrafting them, honing and refining paragraphs, polishing the style, and finding just the right words to express a thought.

Revision is not simply **editing**, a fine tuning for style, grammar, and problems with sentences and wording. Neither is it **proofreading**, a final-stage cleaning up of typographical errors or search for missing commas and apostrophes. When accomplished writers use the word *revision*, they mean the making of principled, effective changes in a draft.

The act of revision involves mentally "stepping outside" your draft, to assess its strengths and weaknesses as if you were reading it for the first time; deciding what parts need to be expanded, clarified, elaborated, illustrated, reworded, restructured, modified, or cut; and then actually making the changes. The kind of work you do during revision takes concentration, determination, and, at times, a sort of ruthlessness with cutting and reworking your prose.

8a Making major revisions

When you begin revising, concentrate on major concerns. A **major revision** is a large-scale change in your draft. For example, if you decide that your paper's tone is too sarcastic, you may end up deleting a negative paragraph or adding several paragraphs exploring more sensibly a position you had earlier trivialized. Or if you've left out a major point, you may need to draft some new material and change your conclusion.

When you make major revisions, you'll perform at least four large-scale operations on your draft: *redrafting, reorganizing, adding,* and *deleting.*

1 Redraft unworkable material

When you read and reread your rough draft carefully, thinking critically about its content, structure, tone, style, appeals to audience, and purpose, some parts may seem inappropriate, illogical, or unworkable. You may need to **redraft** these parts entirely.

8a
revise

STRATEGY

Read through your draft as if you were seeing it for the first time. It helps if you have left your draft alone for a short while so that you can see it afresh. As you read, place a question mark next to sections that seem confusing or garbled. Go back to the parts you've marked, and bracket the specific places where your writing seems to lose its vitality, meaning, or style. Ask yourself what you're trying to accomplish in a particular passage. Then, without even looking at the draft, try again on a new sheet of paper to write what you mean.

8.1

Jessica White shared with her classmates a draft of her essay reflecting on her cheerleading experiences. They felt the first paragraph didn't capture much tension or excitement, and placed brackets around sentences that seemed particularly weak. After changing a few words, White realized she really needed to redraft the entire paragraph.

ORIGINAL DRAFT WITH BRACKETS FROM PEER GROUP

I was a cheerleading captain and I loved basketball. [I put a lot of work into my cheerleading season.] We had a great team spirit between the cheerleaders and the teammates. [We stood behind our team from the beginning to end.] We led our crowd to great enthusiasm and spirit which I believe had a terrific effect on our team.

REVISED DRAFT

There we were, a bunch of cheerleaders packed into Rebecca's car. Everyone's spirits were soaring; we had won the quarter-final game of the state basketball championship. It was a bitterly cold night, but none of us felt the chill. Surrounded by blaring music, we laughed, joked, and endlessly replayed the highlights of the game. Talk then turned to the upcoming finals. Would the team keep up its level of intensity? What were our chances of winning? What would we do if we lost?

2 Reorganize poorly arranged paragraphs or sections

Structural problems are common in early drafts. Often you find that you've written your way "into" your main point, discovering what you want to say in the process of drafting. It may be more graceful or logical to move that material into your introduction. Or you may recognize that two different paragraphs are making the same point and should be consolidated.

STRATEGY

Number each paragraph in your draft. Then, on a clean piece of paper, explain in a phrase or a single sentence what each numbered paragraph says—its main point. When you've finished, look back at your list of statements. Could any paragraphs be consolidated? Are any paragraphs ineffectively ordered? Could you arrange the paragraphs or parts of the paper to yield a clearer, smoother flow of ideas?

Keyshawn Williams drafted a section of his paper on the problems of electronic archives. Reading over his draft, he noticed that the parts seemed out of order and that two short paragraphs said similar things. He began revising by identifying the main points of the paragraphs, and could then arrange the paragraphs in a more logical order. Having done this, he realized that his new paragraphs needed considerable elaboration. He also added a sentence that helped to focus his next two paragraphs.

ORIGINAL

Although most people think that electronic archives can store written documents permanently, they would be surprised to learn that medieval parchment makes a far more lasting medium than computers. In fact, electronic media will begin decaying rapidly.

To create a digital archive that will last without being recopied, you would have to preserve the original system software, hardware, operating manuals, recording devices, and all the other apparatus that did the original archive.

decay

The decay is so rapid that the federal government requires its records to be recopied every ten years and "exercised" once a year. A congressional report notes that there are

obsolescence

now only two machines in the world that can read the electronically stored information from the 1960 U.S. Census. Another problem concerns the fact that some records are written in programs that are obsolete, making it impossible to read the data even if the disk is in good shape.

REVISION

Although most people think that electronic archives can store written documents permanently, they would be surprised to learn that medieval parchment makes a far more lasting medium than computers. **There are two main reasons why electronic document storage is highly questionable even as our society plunges into the electronic age**.

First, electronic media will begin decaying rapidly. [Explain why the magnetic medium decays.] The decay is so rapid that the federal government requires its records to be recopied every ten years and "exercised" once a year.

Another problem concerns the fact that some records are written in programs that are obsolete, making it impossible to read the data even if the disk is in good shape. A congressional report notes that there are now only two machines in the world that can read the electronically stored information from the 1960 U.S. Census. To create a digital archive that will last without being recopied, you would have to preserve the original system software, hardware, operating manuals, recording devices, and all the other apparatus that created the original archive.

3 Add new material

Because you may write your first draft quickly, just to get it down on the page, you may find places where something is missing. Added material can enliven a dull description, clarify or extend a point, or provide essential information that your readers will need in order to make sense of your ideas.

> **STRATEGY**
>
> As you reread your paper, look at how your sentences and paragraphs relate to each other. Mark any cases in which a paragraph doesn't connect clearly enough to the one before it. Also note any gaps (in information or detail) within and between paragraphs. Try making a detailing list if you need to add information to your draft (see 4a-3).

Looking over her draft Web page telling employees how to transfer to a new email system, Gina DiGiacomo noticed some gaps and filled them in.

Your new email address is listed below. It should be easy to remember **because it consists of the first four digits of your name and the last four numbers of your Social Security number**. Our company's address is the same: @Wishfactory.com. You may send your new address to people or discussion groups that send you frequent email, but you don't need to. **Our server will automatically forward any mail directed to your old address**.

DiGiacomo added an explanation of the format of the address as a way of helping people remember it. She included mention of the forwarding process to help ease people's worries about lost mail.

4 Delete unnecessary or redundant material

Too much prose can be just as distracting or frustrating to a reader as too little. But cutting can be hard. Once your words are on the page, they seem almost sacred. Don't be afraid to slash away large portions of your draft if it's clear that they're unnecessary, distracting, illogical, or redundant.

> ## STRATEGY
>
> Reread your draft as if an editor has accepted it for publication in a magazine with the stipulation that you trim at least ten percent. What can you cut? Could some paragraphs be eliminated altogether, perhaps by merging just the essential material from them into another paragraph?

Brian Corby decided to cut two sentences from a petition he was preparing because they didn't add important information or make the petition more persuasive.

> At twenty-four stories and fifteen apartments per floor, Regency Towers will cast a long, wide shadow over Piedmont Park. ~~The building will be quite tall and very wide,~~ For several hours a day, the infant and toddler play area will be darkened, depriving both parents and children of a sun-filled playtime. On summer afternoons, the shadow will cut across the baseball diamond. Players will lose track of swiftly thrown pitches and balls hit directly at them. ~~This could be dangerous.~~ People will not want to spend their leisure time at the park.

Exercise 1

A. Compare the following first-draft and revised versions of Maureen Lagasse's paper on racism. Describe the nature of Lagasse's changes—did she redraft, reorganize, add, or cut? What do you think motivated her revisions?

FIRST DRAFT

In setting out to write this paper my concept to explain was racism, and in doing some reading and thinking, I realized that racism can't be defined or explained in one simple definition. In the dictionary the definition of racism is "the practice of racial discrimination or segregation, etc." Although this is what racism is, this definition doesn't fully explain racism. What exactly are races, and how do people actually develop these discriminations against people of different races?

REVISED DRAFT

Have you ever wondered why people view interracial relationships as unacceptable? Have you wondered whether there really is a difference between you and someone of another race? In the dictionary the definition of racism is "the practice of racial discrimination or segregation." Although this is a legitimate definition, it doesn't fully explain racism.

B. In a small group, compare your responses to Exercise 1A. Were there any revisions you didn't notice? What other major revisions might you suggest for Lagasse's first paragraph?

DID YOU KNOW?

In a study of skilled versus unskilled writers, the skilled writers spent more of their time in various kinds of revision than the unskilled writers, who tended not to look back over their drafts when they had finished writing them. This suggests that, contrary to popular myths about writing, better writers spend *more* of their time, not less, revising.

Nancy Sommers, "Revision Strategies of Student Writers and Experienced Writers," *College Composition and Communication* 31 (1980): 378–88.

8b Making minor revisions

Minor revisions are fairly small changes, mostly in the individual sentences of your prose. Like major revisions, minor revisions involve redrafting, reorganizing, adding, and cutting, but now you have the goal of refining and polishing. Most minor revisions are made for three reasons: *sense* (how clear and understandable is your prose?), *style* (how elegant and smooth is your prose?), and *economy* (how much can you say in the least space?).

1 Revise for sense

Too full an immersion in your writing can sometimes make you forget what your reader *doesn't* know, which can lead to illogical, contradictory, or puzzling statements.

STRATEGY

Read each sentence of your paper individually and test its clarity: does the statement *make sense* in the context of the paper? Don't let your mind float back into your own construction of ideas; instead, imagine yourself as your intended reader. If you have peer readers, ask them to place question marks next to any statement or group of statements they find confusing or garbled.

2 Revise for style

When you revise for style, you're concerned with the way your prose "sounds"—that is, with its rhythm, complexity, and diction or word choice (see 29b). When you read a rough draft, some parts will usually sound better to you than others. Use your intuition as a reader.

Many workplaces have their own stylistic conventions. As a new employee, you will need to learn the "house style" or "company style."

> **STRATEGY**
>
> Place an asterisk in the margin next to any paragraph that seems to need polishing. Then go back to the first paragraph you marked and code each sentence according to what you feel about it: **+** (positive), ✓ (neutral), **–** (negative), **?** (unsure). Now concentrate on revising the sentences you do not like in that paragraph. Move on to revising the questionable sentences. Reread the entire paragraph. When you are satisfied, go to the next paragraph you marked with an asterisk. If you're still uncertain about any sentences, ask peer readers for their impressions. *When in doubt, try an alternative.*

In his report on the environmentally threatened wild mustangs of Nevada, Paul Tichey placed an asterisk next to a paragraph he had already revised for sense. Something still bothered him about the paragraph, so he looked carefully at each sentence. Tichey liked the clarity of his revision, but the end of his new sentence seemed awkward because so many words began with a *d* ("dehydration and death during the duration of the drought"). He also thought that "during the duration" seemed redundant. Here's his further revision.

> The Air Force, which was partly responsible for the demise of the wild mustangs on the Tonopah missile range, has now joined forces with the Bureau of Land Management and a group of wild-horse preservationists to help save the mustangs from **fatal** dehydration and death during the duration of the drought **while the drought persists**.

3 Revise for economy

To revise for economy, read your writing and think about what you can cut from it *without causing it to lose sense or coherence.* In the middle of Tichey's paper, one paragraph included too much material. He decided that half of it could be cut.

SECOND DRAFT

A serious problem confronting groups who want to manage wild mustangs on military sites in Nevada is the relative inaccessibility of the sites, since many require security passes or are fenced off, and environmentalists can't come and go as they please, as they can on public or even some private land. It's simply harder to study or help horses on restricted military installations. Open rangeland has easier access, and inspectors can simply move in and out at will.

THIRD DRAFT

Restricted access to Nevada military sites presents a serious obstacle to successful horse management. In contrast to open rangeland, where inspectors can come and go as they please, military sites are often fenced off and require security clearance.

8b
revise

In the revised paragraph, Tichey said essentially the same thing in thirty-eight words that he had said before in seventy-eight—a cut of over 50 percent! Note, however, that he had to reword the sentences remaining after his cuts.

A WORD ABOUT SPEAKING

Although it's important to revise your talking points before you begin rehearsing your presentation, practicing your delivery will also give you ideas for further revision. Think especially about ways to tighten the oral part of your presentation; consider shifting some of the oral material to visuals such as overhead transparencies, *PowerPoint* slides, or handouts.

Exercise 2

A. Examine the following paragraphs from Anita Jackson's paper on Buddhism. Then characterize the sorts of minor revisions Jackson made. Did she revise for sense, style, or economy? What sorts of changes did she make?

EARLY DRAFT

The man who became the first Buddha was named Siddhartha. Siddhartha was a prince in northern India who lived in a large palace. His father didn't allow him outside the palace because he wanted to spare Siddhartha from the miseries of the world.

Siddhartha became curious and one day he went riding outside the palace. What he saw would forever change his life and influence the lives of many thereafter. That which Siddhartha saw has since been named the Four Sights.

REVISED DRAFT

The man who became the first Buddha was Siddhartha, a pampered prince of northern India who lived in a lavish palace. Yet for all his riches his father would not allow him to venture beyond the castle walls because he wanted to spare Siddhartha the miseries of life. Siddhartha grew extremely curious about the outside world and one day went riding beyond the limits of the palace. What he saw that day would forever change his life and influence the lives of many thereafter.

What Siddhartha saw has since been named the Four Sights.

B. In a small group, compare your analyses of Jackson's revisions. How successful were her changes? Why?

8c Revising collaboratively

Professional writers rarely produce a good piece of writing without getting responses from many readers along the way. Follow their lead: *make sure to ask at least one person you respect to read your papers and give you some honest feedback, and promise you'll do the same in return.* Here are some tips for getting and giving helpful feedback in **collaborative revision**.

1 Respond helpfully

When you're reading someone else's writing in order to offer constructive criticism, remember that your most helpful role is not as proofreader or editor but as real, warm-blooded *reader*. But because you may not be a part of the intended audience for your partner's work, you need to get some background information before you start.

8.2

- Find out the writer's purpose for the paper. What is the writer trying to accomplish? What sort of paper is this?
- Who is the writer's intended reader?
- What are the writer's main concerns at this point? What would the writer most like to learn from you?

Once you have answers to these questions, read the paper through, jotting down some comments in the margins and keeping track of your thoughts and impressions as a reader.

When you convey your responses to your partner, remember that you'll need to balance praise with helpful criticism. Don't just say "I liked it. It was really good," or give directions like "You should move this paragraph up to page 3." Instead, offer diplomatic advice; ask, "What would happen if you moved this paragraph?" or suggest, "I wonder whether that paragraph would fit better on page 3."

2 Make the most of responses

Remember, you're not out to collect a dozen pats on the back for a job well done; you want the most useful, constructive commentary you can get from astute, honest readers. This will mean accepting even hard-hitting reactions and suggestions with grace and diplomacy. If you react defensively to a peer reader's criticism, that person is not likely to keep giving you much feedback. If a reader questions something you especially like in your draft, *remember that no one can force you to make a change*. You have the final say.

Take note of these tips.

- Give your readers a list of specific concerns you have about your draft. Do you want them to comment on tone? style? structure? logic?
- Keep your apologies to a minimum. You may feel anxious about sharing a first draft with your classmates, but as writers you're all facing the same situation.
- If you and your group members are short on time, consider giving them each an inexpensive cassette tape for their reactions. You'll get far more response than if you ask for something in writing. A group meeting, of course, is always preferable. If all of you are working on papers at the same time, forming a writer's group and spending time on each of your drafts can be an especially valuable experience.
- Using your readers' responses, *spend some time planning your changes*. If no one liked the description of your grandmother, do you want to change it? If so, how? Do you want to delete it completely, or find another way to describe her, or show what she's like by portraying her more completely in the action of your narrative? A few minutes planning your revisions may save you lots of time experimenting.

3 Workplace collaboration

Collaborative revision is often the norm outside the school setting. However, workplace collaboration may be somewhat different from sharing your draft with classmates.

- In the workplace, many people will have a stake in your text. They are more likely than fellow students to be willing—even eager—to review it for you.
- Supervisors, in particular, may be direct and insistent about making certain changes.
- It helps to solicit responses from individuals with a range of perspectives and with different kinds of knowledge about your topic or problem.

ESL ADVICE: REVISING WITH A PEER READER

If you are worried about your grammar or spelling, you might want to review these items quickly before sharing your rough draft. Look for a peer reader who is willing to ignore these details. Ask this reader to focus on specific issues (such as the order or development of your ideas) or on problems you often have in your papers (such as weak first paragraphs). Consider sharing your draft with several readers, including native speakers of English, to get a range of responses.

ESL

8d
revise

Exercise 3

A. If you haven't done so, form a small revision group, and circulate rough drafts of your papers in progress. Using the tips in this section as well as the techniques for major and minor revision described in 8a and 8b, comment on your partners' drafts. Then meet in a revision group to discuss your drafts. Keep track of the group's comments on your own paper.

B. Analyze your group experience. What was helpful? What comments will lead (or have led) to specific revisions? What comments did you choose not to act on? Why?

8d Revising: Paper in progress

After semidrafting several paragraphs about items on her list of particulars, Jessica DiGregorio was prepared to write the following full rough draft of her paper about her father's sports contract.

First Draft of Sports Contract Paper

Jessica DiGregorio

A few days ago I decided to go through the musty old cedar chest in my living room and dug up some of the old documents that I had read years earlier. I came across the Contract marked NBA (National Basketball Association) that I had looked at before, but remembered that it was very confusing. It contained words such as: hereunder, however, notwithstanding, and hereof, but when I read this over for the second time it made me realize that my father, for a total of five years was bound to this document, and chose to live his life according to what it had said. This twelve-page "AGREEMENT" caught my attention from the time I was young, but it did not make sense to me until now.

When I was younger I never took interest in my father's past mainly because I was tired of hearing people telling me "Did you know your father was the best basketball player?!" and "If you could have seen him play!" I used to just smile and not say anything because I never thought my father could be an athlete as good as Michael Jordan or Larry Bird. My perspective on his basketball career changed as I got older, I became interested in watching videos of him and asked him questions on what it was like to be a basketball legend.

**8d
revise**

"CLUB DOES HEREBY EMPLOY PLAYER AS
A SKILLED BASKETBALL PLAYER"

This statement which was said on the first page of his contract set the setting for all of the other statements that followed. Since the NBA decided that my father was good enough to play the sport, a contract was made to fit the needs of both the Club (the Buffalo Braves) and the Player (my father). After my father read the first line he was honored and knew that all of his hard work and determination had paid off. The Club which drafted him in 1973 knew that he was a person of great charisma and talent including basketball legend Red Auerbach. This contract was the beginning of a five-year long agreement which was taken very seriously.

"HE WILL TO THE BEST OF HIS ABILITY MAINTAIN HIMSELF IN
PHYSICAL CONDITION SUFFICIENT TO PLAY SKILLED BASKETBALL"

This rule stated in the contract meant that my father had to keep himself fit for the next five years, and not allow himself to overindulge in bad habits. The Club made up this rule to insure themselves that they were signing someone who was serious about the

game. This meant that my father had to stay physically fit and never
stop playing basketball. He was advised to stay clear of skiing, ice-
skating, or any other strenuous activity not related to basketball so
that he would not get injured. If my father, or any other player
disobeyed this part of the contract it stated that, "the club shall
have the right to suspend the player for a period of one week . . .
and will be examined by a physician."

> "IN THE EVENT OF THE DEATH OF THE PLAYER PRIOR
> TO THE TERMINATION OF ANY SEASON . . .
> THE CLUB SHALL PAY TO THE PLAYER'S HEIRS . . ."

8d
revise

This particular part of the contract interested me the most. It
stated that if my father had died, all of the money which was already
promised to my father within the contract went to my mother. This was
very important to my father since my mother was a housewife and
stayed home with my older sisters. The Club added this statement to
the contract to give the player's family the proper amount of
financial help after the loss of their loved one. Basically after the
death of a player the money which was promised throughout the five
year term is terminated and the family only received what the player
lived for. If there was to be a breach in the contract then lawyers
would have had to be appointed to the family of the deceased, and
determining where money goes can be a sticky situation if it is not
written down and documented properly.

> "THE CLUB SHALL HAVE THE OPTION IN ITS SOLE DISCRETION
> TO TERMINATE THIS AGREEMENT AND RENDER IT NULL AND VOID"

This final part in this contract stated that the Club had the
final say in any of the decisions that would have come along. This
meant my father had to follow all of the requirements made within the
document which he had signed. If he or anyone else did not follow any
of the regulations, then they would have no say if their contract was

to be null and void. This left the final power up to the Club and gave them the upper hand in everything that dealt with the players. This was an important part of his contract because it allowed the Club to demonstrate how powerful it really was in the make or break of a person's professional basketball career.

Contracts and legal documents shape our everyday life. Some people underestimate the power of legal documents which bind and connect us to different things. A single piece of paper can determine where we live or how we live our lives. The contract which bound my father to the NBA shaped his life in a major way. For five years he lived by rules and regulations created by the Club to which he belonged. He became a basketball legend and lives in the memories of some people, but to me he is just my dad.

8d
revise

Exercise 4

A. Study DiGregorio's first draft. Assuming that she has drafted with a loose structure in mind, how would you describe that structure? What is your impression of the draft as a whole, and what suggestions would you make for its organization and its supporting points relative to the main goal of examining her father's NBA contract?

B. In a small group, compare your analyses of DiGregorio's first draft, and try to reach some consensus about what she should focus on in her revision.

CHAPTER **9**

FOCUSING, LINKING, AND DEVELOPING PARAGRAPHS

Every time you begin a new **paragraph**, you send a signal to readers: you tell them to watch for a shift in topic, a different perspective, or a special emphasis. You make promises, too: you say that you will develop ideas and details in ways appropriate to your writing task, and that you'll link sentences and ideas in ways that make their relationships clear.

Whether you're writing a short documented essay for a history class, a business letter at work, or a grant proposal for the soccer team you coach, you need to create paragraphs with a clear *focus (unity)*, *coherence* among sentences, and adequate *development* of ideas and content. If you fail to do these things for your readers, they may have trouble deciding what a paragraph is about, and following your reasoning from sentence to sentence, as in this example.

> The caffeine in popular beverages comes from natural sources: coffee beans (coffee), tea leaves (tea), evergreen leaves (maté), and kola nuts (colas). Tea comes from the leaves of bushes native to Asia. Maté comes from a South American shrub similar to holly. More caffeine is found in coffee or tea than in maté. Tea and maté are made in similar ways except that the water for maté is heated in a gourd. People often drink the beverage through a straw stuck into the gourd. In Paraguay, Argentina, Chile, and the southern regions of Brazil, many people find refreshment in a maté-filled gourd.
>
> READER'S REACTION: **What is the topic of this paragraph: tea and coffee? caffeine? caffeinated beverages? maté? Every time one sentence focuses on a topic, the next sentence suddenly changes direction.**

By making the relationship among paragraphs clear, you can help readers keep track of a line of argument or the logic of an explanation.

9a Recognizing and revising paragraph focus

By making a paragraph's topic, main idea, or perspective clear to your reader, and by maintaining this focus throughout, you can create a paragraph that is focused or unified. A **focused paragraph** is effective because it doesn't confuse or mislead readers by straying into unrelated or loosely related details and statements. In a **unified paragraph**, all the sentences are clearly and directly related to the main idea, as in the following selection.

Topic and main idea
> Values are changing, too. Solid majorities of both women *and* men now believe that when a woman works for pay, household responsibilities should be shared. The idea

Definition of *values*
> that a woman's hours of employment are irrelevant for the distribution of household work no longer holds the power it once did. Of course, old habits die hard and many men who "believe" in sharing housework are not actually willing to take

Supporting evidence
> on much of this often-unrewarding work. Twenty-four percent of employed wives are still saddled with *all* the household work, and an additional 42 percent do "the bulk" of it. How-

Look at the future
> ever, things are improving, especially among young people. It is likely that the future holds more, not less, household equality.

—Juliet Schor, *The Overworked American*

Schor unifies this paragraph by making sure all its parts develop and support the main idea: people are beginning to view housework as a responsibility shared by women and men.

STRATEGY

Use the following questions to identify and revise any unfocused paragraphs in your draft. Ask a peer reader to apply them to your draft, or use them as a framework for self-assessment and revision.

- *What is my main point (or topic) in this paragraph?* For a paragraph lacking a central theme, decide on a focus.
- *How many different topics does this paragraph cover?* For a paragraph with many possible centers of interest, decide which one you will emphasize.
- *Have I announced my focus to readers? Where? How?* Look for sentences or phrases announcing the focus or clearly implying it. Add such statements if necessary.
- *Do statements in the paragraph elaborate on the main idea? Do details fit within the topic?* Look for material not directly related to a paragraph's focus, and decide whether it undermines the unity or adds interesting variety.

9b Revising for focus

To bring focus to a paragraph, you need to decide what you want the paragraph to do for readers. Do you want it to announce and explain your conclusion or recommendation? Do you want it to explain a concept or process? Do you want it to support your arguments on an issue?

One way to keep a paragraph focused as you write, and to help readers recognize that focus, is to state your topic and your main idea or perspective in a single sentence, a **topic sentence**. As you write, you can use a topic sentence as the focal point for the other sentences in a paragraph. When you revise, you can often easily improve an unfocused paragraph by adding a topic sentence, placing it in an effective position in the paragraph.

9b
¶ foc

STRATEGY

You can often trace the explanation or argument of a piece quickly by scanning paragraphs and reading just the topic sentences. Look at your own draft essays this way to check for paragraphs with missing, misleading, or inadequate topic sentences. When you find such paragraphs, decide whether they also need revision for focus. In addition, this is a good way to identify paragraphs that take the discussion in misleading or irrelevant directions.

1 Using a topic sentence at the beginning

When you want readers to grasp the point of a paragraph right away, state it in a topic sentence at the beginning. In the following paragraph, the author uses the topic-sentence-first strategy to comment on the art of comedy.

9.1

Topic sentence

Supporting example

When writing jokes, it's a good idea to avoid vague generalizations. Don't just talk about "fruit" when you can talk about "an apple." Strong writing creates a single image for everyone in the crowd, each person imagining the same thing. But when you say "fruit," people are either imagining several different kinds of fruit or they aren't really thinking of anything in particular, and both things can significantly reduce their emotional investment in the joke. But when you say "an apple," everyone has a clear picture, and thus a feeling.

—Jay Sankey, "Zen and the Art of Stand-Up Comedy"

2 Using a topic sentence plus a limiting or clarifying sentence

If you're covering a broad topic or offering much detailed information, you can give a paragraph a sharper focus by creating a **limiting** or **clarifying sentence** (or two) following the topic sentence. The added sentence tells readers which specific aspects of the topic you will discuss or clarifies your point of view.

ESL

9b
¶ foc

Topic sentence	Children on soap operas are secondary. Because they
Clarifying sentence	serve largely as foils for the adult characters, their development

does not follow the slow, steady pattern of the rest of the action. Their growth is marked by a series of sudden and unsettling metamorphoses as new and older juvenile actors assume the role. On Tuesday, little Terence is cooing in his cradle [. . .] then one day he again emerges from the off-camera cocoon transformed into a full-fledged adult, with all the rights, privileges, pain, and perfidy of that elite corps. And so the cycle continues.

—DONNA WOOLFOLK CROSS, *Sin, Suffer, and Repent*

3 Using a topic sentence at the end

A topic sentence at the end of a paragraph can summarize or draw conclusions from the information that comes before. This strategy can show how your perspective grows logically from the evidence, and it can tie together details with a forceful generalization.

A few years ago, at an international conference held in an exotic and luxurious setting, a prestigious professor invited me to his room for what he said would be an intellectual discussion on matters of theoretical importance [. . .] But only minutes into the conversation—held in all-too-adjacent chairs—it emerged that he was interested in something more substantial than a meeting of minds.[. . .] Every time his comments took a lecherous turn, I chattered distractingly; every time his hand found its way to my knee, I returned it as if it were something he had misplaced. This went on for an unconscionable period (as much as 20 minutes); then there was a minor scuffle, a dash for the door, and I was out—with nothing violated but my self-esteem. I, a full-grown feminist,

Topic sentence   conversant with such matters as rape crisis counseling and sexual harassment at the workplace, had behaved like a ninny—or, as I now understand it, like a lady.

—BARBARA EHRENREICH, "What I've Learned from Men"

ESL ADVICE: ADJUSTING TO PARAGRAPH CONVENTIONS

In English, readers expect paragraphs to have a specific focus and often look to a topic sentence for guidance. In other languages, however, paragraph conventions can take quite different forms. For example, Hindi paragraphs need not focus on a sharply defined topic, do not require a clear topic sentence, and often contain discussion of loosely related ideas or information. Paragraphs in other languages, such as Thai, also differ from English paragraphs. Consequently, become familiar with paragraph conventions as you learn to write in a second language.

> —Robert Bickner and Patcharin Peyasantiwong, "Cultural Variation in Reflective Writing," and Yamuna Kachru, "Writers in Hindi and English," *Writing Across Languages and Cultures*, ed. Alan C. Purves (Newbury Park: Sage, 1988) 160–74, 109–37.

4 Implying rather than stating a topic sentence

At times, the main point is so clear that you can rely on readers to recognize it without a topic statement. Omitting a topic statement is useful when you don't want to state a very obvious point or when an explicit statement might distract from examples and details. This strategy is also helpful when a topic clearly continues for more than one paragraph.

> Whenever we went to my grandfather's house, he would lead the three of us to the closet stocked with toys, saying "I bought these especially for you" as his crystal blue eyes twinkled. I can remember playing with the toys outside on the lawn and running through the sprinkler he set up for me and my brothers on sunny days. Just when we started getting tired and hot, he would call us in for a lunch of hot dogs or tuna sandwiches with plenty of potato chips and soda pop. And there were always popsicles for dessert.
>
> —CAREY BRAUN, college student

READER'S REACTION: **Your grandfather seems like a person who understands children and knows how to make them feel cared for and loved.**

Exercise 1 ─────────────────────────────

A. Identify any topic sentence and clarifying or limiting sentence in the following paragraph. Analyze how the paragraph makes use of these sentences to create focus and emphasis.

> Kids are in the mall not only in the passive role of shoppers—they also work there, especially as fast-food outlets infiltrate the mall's enclosure. There they learn how to hold a job and take responsibility, but still within the same value context. When *CBS Reports* went to Oak Park Mall in suburban Kansas City, Kansas, to tape part of the hour-long consideration of the mall, "After the Dream Comes True," they interviewed a teenaged girl who worked in a fast-food outlet there. In a sequence that didn't make the final program, she described the major goal of her present life, which was to perfect the curl on top of the ice-cream cones that were her store's specialty. If she could do

that, she would be moved from the lowly soft-drink dispenser to the more prestigious ice-cream division, the curl on top of the status ladder at her restaurant. These are the achievements that are important at the mall.

—WILLIAM SEVERINI KOWINSKI, "Kids in the Mall: Growing Up Controlled"

B. After you have examined the paragraph in Exercise 1A to see how it uses topic, clarifying, or limiting sentences for focus and emphasis, work in a group to reach consensus on the ways the paragraph employs these strategies.

9c Recognizing and revising paragraph coherence

When your readers can move from sentence to sentence within a paragraph without any trouble following your train of thought or explanation, the paragraph displays **coherence**. Lack of coherence comes from abrupt changes in your topic from sentence to sentence, or from a lack of transitions or other devices to guide readers from statement to statement. A paragraph like the following is hard for readers to understand, because it offers them little guidance.

LACKS COHERENCE

Captain James Cook discovered the island of Hawaii in 1779. Mauna Kea, on Hawaii, is the tallest mountain in the Pacific. Cook might have noticed the many mountains on the island as he sailed into Kealakekua Bay. The island also has five major volcanoes. Mauna Loa, another mountain on the island, is a dormant volcano that last erupted in 1984. Kilauea is the most active volcano on earth. It continues to enlarge the land that makes up this largest island in the Hawaiian chain. The volcano sends forth lava continuously.

READER'S REACTION: This paragraph jumps from sentence to sentence without saying much about the way the ideas and details fit together. It's just hard to read and remember.

STRATEGY

Use the following questions to test your paragraphs for coherence.

- Does the paragraph highlight and repeat words naming the topic and main points?
- Do transition words alert readers to relationships between sentences?
- Do parallel words and structures highlight similar or related ideas?
- Do sentence beginnings identify a topic and stick to it?

9d Revising for coherence

1 Repeating words and phrases

By repeating words and phrases that refer to your topic and main point, you keep readers aware of a paragraph's focus and link one sentence to another. Synonyms and related words can also be part of a pattern of effective repetition, as in the following paragraph.

> **"Childhood is the kingdom where nobody dies"** is a line, from the poem by Edna St. Vincent Millay, that has stuck in my mind ever since I first read it, when I was in fact **a child** and **nobody died**. Of course **people did die**, but **they** were either very old or **died** unusual **deaths**, **died** while rafting on the Stanislaus or loading a shotgun or doing 95 drunk: **death** was construed as either a "blessing" or an exceptional case, the dramatic instance on which **someone else's** (never **our own**) story turned. Illness, in that **kingdom** where I and **most people** I knew lingered long past **childhood**, proved self-limiting. Fever of unknown etiology signaled only the indulgence of a week in bed. Chest pains, investigated, revealed hypochondria.
>
> —JOAN DIDION, "After Henry"

9d
¶ coh

2 Supplying transitions

You can use **transitional expressions**, statements, and paragraphs to alert readers to relationships among sentences and paragraphs and to highlight a paragraph's design and purpose.

STRATEGY

Think about the possible connections among the ideas and information you are discussing; then decide which connections you wish to highlight. Draw on the following techniques to link paragraphs in ways that emphasize connections and that call attention to your line of reasoning.

- Use transitional words and phrases (see the chart on p. 107)
- Announce your purpose
- Provide boundary statements
- Create transition paragraphs

9.2

Note how the use of transitions makes the following paragraph easy to read.

> Many people still consider the choice of college the most important career decision you can make. **These days**, **however**, graduate school is the most important choice **because** the competition for all

kinds of jobs has gotten fiercer. **For example**, business positions at the entry level often go to people with MBAs and law degrees. **In addition**, many good jobs require advanced training and skills. **Moreover**, employers pay attention **not only** to the presence of an advanced degree on your résumé **but also** to the program of study **and** the quality of the school. **Therefore**, think about going to graduate school, **and** choose your school carefully.

You can use a direct or an indirect statement to announce your purpose and organization near the beginning of a new section, and to help readers anticipate the line of reasoning you will use to develop and support ideas.

9d
¶ coh

DIRECT STATEMENT	The next section looks at the new generation of situation comedies that has taken over the top of the ratings chart in the last two years.
INDIRECT STATEMENT	Advertisers have developed sophisticated ways to identify the tastes, purchasing power, and needs of consumers. Each of these tactics needs to be examined in detail.

To help present detailed reasoning or information, consider opening paragraphs with a **boundary statement**—a sentence at the start of a paragraph that acts as a bridge from the paragraph before. A boundary statement begins with a reminder of material covered in the preceding paragraph (or paragraphs). It then presents the topic sentence of the paragraph to come. For example, in the following sentence the writer briefly mentions the subject he has just finished discussing and then highlights the main point of the paragraph itself.

> **The rise of the Sunbelt** in recent years has been accompanied by **the decline of rural America**.
> —BRAD EDMONDSON, "Making Yourself at Home"

In short essays, simple transitions or boundary statements generally provide adequate guidance for readers. In longer essays or complicated discussions, you may need to give readers extra guidance with one- or two-sentence transition paragraphs. Brief transition paragraphs perform the same functions as transitional expressions and statements.

A WORD ABOUT SPEAKING

Transitional words and expressions are extremely important in moving from point to point in a presentation, especially because your audience can't "see" your text. Announce your purpose and use explicit transitions both within and between your main points to clarify your ideas and help lead your audience through your talk.

TRANSITIONAL EXPRESSIONS

TIME AND SEQUENCE	next, later, after, while, meanwhile, immediately, somewhat earlier, first, second, third (firstly, secondly, thirdly), shortly, thereafter, in the future, over the next two days, concurrently, subsequently, as long as, soon, since, finally, last, at that time, as soon as
COMPARISON	likewise, similarly, also, again, in the same manner, in comparison
CONTRAST	in contrast, on one hand . . . on the other hand, however, although, even though, still, yet, but, nevertheless, conversely, at the same time, regardless, despite
EXAMPLES	for example, for instance, such as, specifically, thus, to illustrate, namely
CAUSE AND EFFECT	as a result, consequently, since, accordingly, if . . . then, is due to this, for this reason, as a consequence of
PLACE	next to, above, behind, beyond, near, across from, to the right, here, there, in the foreground, in the background, in between, opposite
ADDITION	and, too, moreover, in addition, besides, furthermore, next, also, finally
CONCESSION	of course, naturally, it may be the case that, granted, it is true that, certainly
CONCLUSION	in conclusion, in short, as a result, as I have demonstrated, as the data show
REPETITION	to repeat, in other words, once again, as I said earlier
SUMMARY	on the whole, to sum up, in short, to summarize, therefore

9d
¶ coh

3 Using parallel structure

You can link elements within a paragraph by using **parallelism**—repeating the same grammatical structures to highlight similar or related ideas (see also 27c). Note how the parallel words and phrases in the following paragraph create coherence.

> I have a place on the West Coast **where** my relatives still farm, **where I heard** the stories of feuds and backbiting, and **where I saw** that people **survived and flourished** because fundamentally they **trusted and relied** upon one another. **A death in the family** is not just **a death in a family**; it is a **death in the community**. **I saw people** help each other with money, materials, labor, attention, and time. **I saw men** gather once a year, without fail, to clean the grounds

of a ninety-year-old woman who had helped the community **before**, **during**, and **after** the war. **I saw her** remembering them with birthday cards sent to each of their children.

—Kesaya E. Noda, "Growing Up Asian in America"

Exercise 2

A. In the following paragraph, increase coherence and readability by repeating words, adding transitions, using parallel structures, and making any other changes necessary.

Heart attacks have many causes. Some heart attacks occur because a blood clot closes a coronary artery. Sometimes a mass of fatty substances (plaque) has the same effect. Heart attacks with these causes are the most frequent. A spasm in an artery may also close it and prevent blood from reaching the heart. Smoking, hypertension, and diabetes can create conditions that keep blood from reaching the heart. The blood-starved tissue may die. This will cause permanent damage to the heart's ability to pump blood. A dead portion of the heart is called a myocardial infarction.

B. Copy a paragraph from one of your own essays, scrambling the order of the sentences, and then exchange scrambled paragraphs with a fellow student. Rewrite and strengthen your partner's paragraph by putting the sentences in the most effective order and revising to increase coherence among sentences.

9e Recognizing and revising paragraph development

Suppose you encountered the following paragraph in an essay on pets. How would you react?

Dogs and cats make wonderful pets, but certainly not trendy ones. Exotic animals of all kinds, including Vietnamese pot-bellied pigs and llamas, have begun appearing in living rooms and backyards.

You would probably respond that the paragraph has a clear main point and a potentially interesting example but seems skimpy and uninteresting. Without supporting details, the paragraph is neither informative nor convincing. **Paragraph development** provides the examples, facts, concrete details, explanatory statements, or supporting arguments that make a paragraph informative and supportive of your ideas and opinions, as in this fully developed version of the paragraph.

Topic sentence Dogs and cats make wonderful pets, but certainly not trendy ones. Exotic animals of all kinds, including Vietnamese pot-bellied pigs and llamas, have begun appearing in living rooms and backyards. About the size of beagles, the pigs are affectionate and easy to care for. Llamas require more room and care, but these gentle animals are now in demand as well—at least among people who can afford the one or two thousand **Brief examples** dollars needed to buy one. Ferrets, Amazon parrots, pygmy goats, and dwarf rabbits have been finding places in fashionable homes as well. People who want to keep well ahead of the crowd might consider Old World chameleons or dart-poison frogs (the source of poison for blowdarts used by jungle hunters).

9e
¶ dev

1 Developing paragraphs with details

The details of how you dangled from the sheer rock face when your climbing equipment failed may thrill the readers of your essay in an outdoor magazine. They'll look for long paragraphs filled with specifics. The equipment recall announcement you write for the Consumer Product Safety Commission will probably offer more compact paragraphs with relevant statistics, specific warnings, and product identifying information. Your memo for the equipment company would probably contain several concise paragraphs, each with the precise information needed to answer some key questions: How did the equipment fail? Why did it fail? How can we correct the problem?

Fully developed paragraphs give readers an in-depth picture of a subject when this is necessary for the purpose and context of the writing. Your readers will usually expect two kinds of statements in a paragraph: those presenting ideas (including your own conclusions) and those presenting information. Beyond this, however, you have many choices, depending on what you want a paragraph to do.

STRATEGY

Use this checklist to remember some of your many options for developing a paragraph's content.

- **Examples.** Use brief, specific examples or an extended, detailed example.
- **Concrete details.** Recreate sights, sounds, tastes, smells, movements, and sensations of touch.
- **Facts and statistics.** Offer precise data from your own field research or from authoritative sources, perhaps in numerical form. Summarize the results or quote your sources. Facts and statistics are the kinds of evidence many readers consider convincing proof of generalizations and opinions. They also help readers understand complicated social and natural phenomena.

- **Summaries.** Summarize other people's opinions, conclusions, or explanations (47c-1). Tell how they agree with and support your conclusions. Or point out their omissions and weaknesses as a way of arguing for your own conclusions or insights.
- **Quotations.** Use statements you have gathered from field, electronic, or library research (48c-1) as ways of supporting your conclusions or as ways of making your discussion more dramatic and memorable.

9e

¶ dev

Rely on examples. Whether brief or extended, examples are effective strategies for paragraph development because they help you clarify difficult concepts, provide good reasons for readers to agree with your opinion, or show how widespread a phenomenon is. Extended examples can draw readers into an event and connect with their emotions. Brief examples can play important roles, especially in work and public settings where readers have little patience for long explanations but still expect you to justify your opinions and recommendations. Brief examples can be particularly effective when blended with facts and statistics, as in this excerpt from a newsletter published by the Consumer Product Safety Commission.

> All kinds of products have been included in the fast-track recalls. For example, a major manufacturer recently recalled tens of thousands of humidifiers that could potentially overheat or catch fire. A leading manufacturer of children's products recalled tens of thousands of baby monitors that could smoke and flame. A prominent clothing retailer recalled more than 100,000 children's jackets with zipper pulls containing unacceptable levels of lead. A well-known company recalled tens of thousands of gas grills because a defective hose could leak gas or cause fires.
>
> —"Fast-Track Recalls," *Consumer Product Safety Review*

A WORD ABOUT SPEAKING

In oral presentations, details are just as important as they are in well-developed paragraphs. In your talking points, add facts, statistics, and examples to make your generalized statements clearer and more engaging to your audience and to provide support for your claims. Be careful, however, not to get carried away with specifics; if time is a concern and you need to trim information from your talk, see whether one or two details will suffice to support or illustrate a point, and eliminate the rest. Alternatively, provide details on a hand-out or an overhead transparency, and call attention to one or two of them orally.

Interpret for your readers. When you use examples, details, facts, and statistics to develop a paragraph, you can make them more persuasive and easier to understand by providing interpretive statements of your own to link them to the paragraph's main point.

> Breakfast cereals can differ radically in serving size even though most cereal boxes define a single serving in the same way, as a one-ounce portion. A one-ounce serving of Cheerios is 1 $\frac{1}{4}$ cup, for example, while a one-ounce serving of Quaker 100% Natural Cereal is $\frac{1}{4}$ cup. Weight measurements can disguise the differences between products; measurement by volume reveals the contrasts. For dieters, volume can be as important a measure as the number of calories per serving because the volume indicates how much cereal you will have to appease your appetite: two bites or a bowlful.
>
> —Sara Brilliant, College Student

Interpretive statement marks the sentences from "is 1 ¼ cup" through "reveals the contrasts."

9e
¶ dev

Exercise 3

A. First, examine the paragraph in Exercise 2A and identify the various strategies of development used by the writer. Which seem particularly effective, and why? Which, if any, seem ineffective?

Next, for each of the following topic sentences, explain which kind or kinds of supporting information (examples, concrete details, facts and statistics, or supporting statements) you believe would create the most effective paragraph.

1. The fall promotional campaign increased sales of our October and November issues.
2. Upgrading our computer software would result in more efficient handling of our customer accounts.
3. Increased funding would enable us to extend our after-school basketball program for preteen boys and girls.
4. Should our budget surplus be used to fund additional hours at the senior center or to assist meal-delivery programs for the homebound?

B. Working in a group, compare your responses to Exercise 3A. Record both agreements and disagreements about the paragraph in Exercise 2A. Then continue to work together to develop one of the topic sentences into a paragraph. Be ready to explain why you chose to develop the paragraph in the way you did. Feel free to revise the topic sentence.

2 Creating paragraph structures

9.3

How will you arrange the content of your paragraphs? **General patterns of development** such as narration, comparison, and cause and effect offer you ways to develop a paragraph's content as well as its arrangement.

Specific patterns of development reflect the outlook of readers and writers in specific settings (academic, work, or public) on useful ways to develop paragraphs.

General patterns of development. Each of the general patterns enables you to accomplish a different writing task, as the following chart indicates.

PATTERNS FOR PARAGRAPH DEVELOPMENT

TASK	DEVELOPMENT STRATEGY
Tell a story; recreate events; present an anecdote	Narrating
Provide detail of a scene or object; portray someone's character; evoke a feeling	Describing
Explore similarities or differences; evaluate alternatives	Comparing and contrasting
Provide directions; explain the operation of a mechanism, procedure, or natural process	Explaining a process
Separate a subject into parts; explore the relationships among parts	Dividing
Sort things or people into groups; explain the relationships among the groups	Classifying
Explain the meaning of a term or concept; explore and illustrate the meaning of a complicated concept or phenomenon	Defining
Consider why something happened or might happen; explore possible causes and consequences	Analyzing causes and effects

Narration presents events in the past, the present, or even the imagined future. In academic writing, for example, narratives can provide historical background, and in public settings, narratives can help readers understand how an issue or disagreement came about. In work settings, narratives can provide information necessary for understanding a problem or challenge, but their focus generally must be limited to details relevant to the current situation.

Description helps you create images of a place or object (often using a spatial organization), sketch a person's character, or evoke feelings. In a technical or business report, however, description can convey important details of a product or physical setting.

You can use paragraphs built around **comparing** and **contrasting** to evaluate alternative policies or products. In arranging comparison paragraphs, you can employ a **point-by-point organization**, examining each comparable feature for first one subject and then the next.

Topic sentence	But biology has a funny way of confounding expectations. Rather than disappear, <u>the evidence for innate sexual</u>
Feature 1	<u>differences only began to mount.</u> In medicine, researchers doc-
Feature 2	umented that <u>heart disease strikes men at a younger age than it does women</u> and that <u>women have a more moderate physi-</u>
Feature 3	<u>ological response to stress.</u> Researchers found <u>subtle neuro-logical differences between the sexes</u> both in the brain's struc-
Feature 4	ture and in its functioning. In addition, another generation of parents discovered that, despite their best efforts to give baseballs to their daughters and sewing kits to their sons, <u>girls still flocked to dollhouses while boys clambered into tree forts.</u> Perhaps nature is more important than nurture after all.

—CHRISTINE GORMAN, "Sizing Up the Sexes"

9e
¶ dev

Or you can use a **subject-by-subject organization**, considering each subject in its entirety, as in the next example.

Topic sentence	For everyone, home is a place to be offstage. But <u>the comfort of home can have opposite and incompatible mean-ings for women and men.</u> For many men, the comfort of
Subject 1	<u>home means freedom from</u> having to prove themselves and impress through verbal display. At last, they are in a situation where talk is not required. They are free to remain silent. But
Subject 2	for women, <u>home is a place where they are free to talk,</u> and where they feel the greatest need for talk, with those they are closest to. For them, the comfort of home means the freedom to talk without worrying about how their talk will be judged.

—DEBORAH TANNEN, "Put Down That Paper and Talk to Me!"

To explain a **process**, you may need to provide readers with a paragraph of **directions** or an **explanation** of how a mechanism or procedure works. You can also divide or classify. When you divide a subject, you split it into parts. A **division** paragraph offers you a chance to explain a subject in detail and to highlight the relationship of its parts. When you classify, you sort several subjects into groups based on their similarities. A **classification** paragraph is an opportunity for you to identify the groups and explore similarities within them or the differences and relationships among them.

When you need to introduce a term or concept to your readers, you may need to write just a phrase or sentence to define it, or you may need to create a **definition** paragraph if the term is complicated.

When you hear the word crystal, many people think of a mineral dug from the ground. But the lead crystal used to make beautiful plates, glasses, and vases does not come from this source. The crystal in these objects—artworks, actually—is glass with a high lead content. The glass is made from a mixture of sand and other ingredients like potash (potassium) or soda that help the mixture melt. The various minerals also affect the color and clarity of the glass. Lead crystal must contain at least 30 percent to 35 percent lead oxide (by weight) in its ingredients. The resulting material is easier for artists to work with as they grind intricate facets into the surface to create designs that sparkle and intrigue like a finely cut diamond.

—ANDREA HERRMANN, College Student

When you wish to explain why something has occurred, you might focus a paragraph on causes; to explore consequences, you might focus on effects. Or you might combine them, to create a **cause-effect** paragraph.

Specific patterns of development. In longer business reports, writers often devote separate paragraphs to problems and recommendations. In shorter documents such as letters and memos, however, writers often turn to **problem-solution** paragraphs like the following, from a memo.

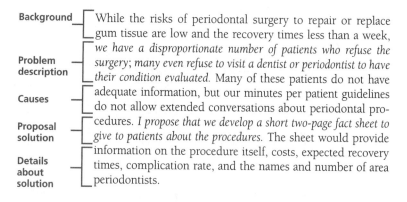

Background — While the risks of periodontal surgery to repair or replace gum tissue are low and the recovery times less than a week,

Problem description — *we have a disproportionate number of patients who refuse the surgery; many even refuse to visit a dentist or periodontist to have their condition evaluated.* Many of these patients do not have

Causes — adequate information, but our minutes per patient guidelines do not allow extended conversations about periodontal pro-

Proposal solution — cedures. *I propose that we develop a short two-page fact sheet to give to patients about the procedures.* The sheet would provide

Details about solution — information on the procedure itself, costs, expected recovery times, complication rate, and the names and number of area periodontists.

Another paragraph structure that addresses problems and recommendations is the **question-and-answer** pattern. This pattern is particularly useful in public settings because the question segment allows writers to raise concerns they share with readers while the answer segment allows writers to explore possible policies or recommendations for dealing with the concerns. The following paragraph from a Web site on athletic nutrition <www.athleticnutrition.com/Stjohns.html> uses the question-and-answer pattern to share research relating the use of St. John's Wort, an herbal antidepressant, to athletic workouts.

What research has been done on St. John's Wort?

The active derivative in St. John's Wort is called hypericin. This active ingredient [. . .] has been shown to increase the half-life of certain neurotransmitters and thus, by extending the time that these neurotransmitters are in the brain, extend and enhance their positive effects. Most studies done on St. John's Wort have explored its possible antidepressant activity. These double-blind studies indicate that indeed, St. John's Wort does possess these antidepressant capabilities and can stave off mild depression. Finally, some studies have shown that St. John's Wort may inhibit cortisol secretion, as well as possibly block the release of other catabolic hormones. This is of particular significance to weight-training athletes as this can lead to better gains and increased strength and size.

9e
¶ dev

Paragraphs in public discourse often begin by stating or summarizing facts or information (such as statistics, quotations, events, or studies) and then moving into interpretation, critique, or application of information; a statement of need; or a plan or request. This is especially true of the first paragraph of a public document, such as this grant application.

Recent research in gerontology suggests that nursing home residents benefit from regular contact with animals. Such benefits include enhanced motor skills, increased interest in physical activities such as walking or dancing, decreased loneliness and stress, and increased appetite. Despite these benefits, no nursing homes in the tri-county area have made "therapeutic animal" programs available to their residents. In the hope of putting our facility at the forefront of senior care in this area, I am requesting $300 to purchase a therapy dog from the local organization Paws with a Cause.

Exercise 4

A. Choose one of the following pairs of topics. Drawing on your own knowledge, develop each topic into a paragraph, using the pattern of development indicated in brackets.

1. A paragraph about finding a part-time or summer job [process] and a paragraph on an unusual or memorable person [description or narration]

2. A paragraph exploring different outlooks on the relationships of parents and children [comparison-contrast] and a paragraph providing advice about dealing with a difficulty in parent-child relationships [question and answer]

3. A paragraph identifying the differences between educational requirements, expected income, and working conditions for two jobs (such as restaurant manager and doctor, or teacher and chemical engineer)

[comparison-contrast] and a paragraph exploring a common work or college problem and offering possible solutions [problem-solution]

4. A paragraph identifying the reasons some students do well (or poorly) on tests [cause-effect] and a paragraph describing a good way to study for tests [process]

5. A paragraph exploring different views people hold about taking buses and driving cars [subject-by-subject comparison] and a paragraph identifying differences between educational requirements, expected income, and working conditions for two jobs [point-by-point comparison]

9f
¶ dev

B. Working in a group, identify the patterns of development in the following paragraph. There may be a single dominant pattern or more than one. Explain how each pattern or combination is used.

> None of the foreign geologists had ever encountered anything quite like the disaster at Lake Nyos. Our earliest hypotheses seemed to be almost as numerous as the scientific teams present. Some workers, impressed by the accounts of survivors who reported smelling rotten eggs or gunpowder and hearing explosions, were convinced that a volcanic eruption beneath the lake had released sulfurous gases. Others, including me, suspected that the gas had come from within the sediments on the lake bed. Eventually, though, geological and chemical investigations made it obvious that the lake had released carbon dioxide from within its own waters—independent apparently of any other process. Like an enormous bottle of soda water, it belched and fizzed gas from its depths.
>
> —Samuel J. Preeth, "Incident at Lake Nyos"

9f Using special-purpose paragraphs in academic, work, and public settings

Beginning and concluding a piece of writing are challenges you can meet with some useful special-purpose paragraphs.

1 Creating introductory paragraphs

In the opening paragraphs of an essay, report, or public document, you create a relationship with your readers, inviting them to learn about a subject, explore ideas, address a problem, or examine a line of argument. Examples of different types of introductory paragraphs follow the chart on page 117.

> ## TWELVE WAYS TO DEVELOP AN EFFECTIVE INTRODUCTORY PARAGRAPH
>
> ### PROVIDE BACKGROUND
> Provide background information on a topic or problem; present an issue in context; give the history of the subject.
>
> ### TELL A STORY
> Open with a brief anecdote or story.
>
> ### OUTLINE A PROBLEM
> Outline a problem, danger, or challenge.
>
> ### EXPLAIN AN ISSUE
> Present the different sides of an issue, along with any particularly well-known or controversial events relevant to the topic.
>
> ### PRESENT A SITUATION
> Describe a situation, a set of relationships, or recent events that require some response from readers or an organization to which they belong.
>
> ### OFFER A DEFINITION
> Define an important concept or term that will recur throughout the piece.
>
> ### ASK A QUESTION
> Present provocative questions or opinions that require further discussion.
>
> ### USE AN EXTENDED EXAMPLE
> Start with an extended example related to the topic and main idea.
>
> ### PRESENT A QUOTATION
> Quote from an authority, or from someone whose opinion leads into the topic or highlights key ideas.
>
> ### MAKE A COMPARISON
> Highlight the importance of a topic or issue by comparing it to another situation, historical period, subject, or issue; offer an intriguing analogy.
>
> ### PROVIDE STATISTICS
> Supply facts and statistics that introduce the topic or that help define an important issue or problem.
>
> ### DESCRIBE A MYSTERY
> Present a mysterious or interesting phenomenon worth exploring or explaining.

9f
¶ dev

ANECDOTE   It was advertised as the biggest non-nuclear explosion in Nevada history. On October 27, 1993, Steve Wynn, the State's official "god of hospitality," flashed his trademark smile and pushed the detonator button. As 200,000 Las Vegans cheered, the 18-story

Dunes sign, once the tallest neon structure in the world, crumbled to the desert floor.

—MIKE DAVIS, "House of Cards"

Davis introduces the environmental threat posed by Las Vegas culture.

DEFINITION

It used to be that a diner was a lowly place to eat. It was known as a greasy spoon, a hash house, or—in trucker lingo—a choke and puke. Diners were where the city's fallen angels went for a cup of mud (coffee) and a sinker (a doughnut) beneath fluorescent lights; where night hawks and wandering hoboes whiled away the wee hours. As for the food at diners, it was strictly for the crude of palate—heavy on the starch, grease, and gristle.

—JANE STERN AND MICHAEL STERN, *Roadfood*

The Sterns are about to review a different kind of diner: clean, with good food and more fashionable customers.

PROBLEM

A candle-lit Christmas tree at Grandmother's house may be a thing of the past, but fire hazards still loom in American homes, ready to turn this season's joy into holiday tragedy.

—"Fire Safety Tips for a Safe Holiday Season,"

<www.sema.state.mo.us/firexmas.htm>

9f
¶ dev

2 Creating concluding paragraphs

Paragraphs that conclude essays should generally remind readers of key ideas, and encourage them to think about information or proposals you have presented. The following paragraph illustrates one strategy used in concluding paragraphs.

SUMMARY OF MAIN POINTS

So if it's any consolation to those of us who just don't manage to fit enough sleep into our packed days, being chronically tired probably won't do us any permanent harm. And if things get desperate enough, we just might have to schedule a nap somewhere on our busy calendars.

—DANIEL GOLEMAN, "Too Little, Too Late"

Exercise 5

A. Revise the following concluding paragraph to make it more effective.

I probably have left out some of the arguments for and against gun control, though I think I have covered the main ones. The point I really want to stress most is that gun control is a difficult question. Simple proposals such as banning all handguns or getting rid of all regulations won't work. We need new ideas that balance the rights of gun owners with the right to be free from violence and crime. Though I have not explained it in detail, we probably need a program like the national registration and education system that has been recently proposed. And we certainly need to do something about the many handguns readily available to teenagers.

B. Have each of the members of a writing group bring in a popular magazine containing relatively long articles. As a group, examine the articles, and choose three openings and three conclusions that you consider successful. Identify the strategies used in each.

9f
¶ dev

EIGHT WAYS TO DEVELOP AN EFFECTIVE CONCLUDING PARAGRAPH

SUMMARIZE MAIN POINTS
Review the main points briefly; a detailed summary will seem repetitive.

RESTATE THE THESIS
Put the thesis in different words to drive home the essay's main point.

RECOMMEND ACTIONS OR SOLUTIONS
Repeat, for emphasis, the specific solutions, policies, recommendations, or actions proposed in the text, perhaps summarizing them in a list.

PREDICT FUTURE EVENTS OR SPECULATE
Look at relatively clear consequences, not those requiring explanation; keep speculations interesting but not so provocative that they require extensive discussion.

USE A QUOTATION
Provide a quotation that makes key ideas memorable or supports your conclusions.

OFFER A STRIKING EXAMPLE, ANECDOTE, OR IMAGE
Supply a mental picture or brief narrative to reinforce an essay's message.

ECHO THE INTRODUCTION
Use this echo to create a sense of completion.

RESTATE IMPLICATIONS
Review the implications of any actions or policies discussed in the text.

CHAPTER 10

CREATING CLEAR, EMPHATIC, AND VARIED SENTENCES

10a
sent

Most people would find the following sentences hard to read and understand.

> Our ski club president did not, because he was embarrassed by his lack of advanced skiing experience, sign us up for the University Ski Clubs Association trip to Utah.

> It is suggested that employee work cooperation encouragement be used for product quality improvement.

You can make sentences like these clearer and easier to read with some simple revision strategies.

SIMPLE AND DIRECT Because he was embarrassed by his lack of advanced skiing experience, our ski club president did not sign us up for the University Ski Clubs Association trip to Utah.

CLEAR We will try to improve the quality of our products by encouraging employees to work cooperatively.

But don't just create sentences that are clear and direct. You can also use a number of strategies to create appropriate emphasis and pleasing variety, and to meet the demands of different writing situations: academic, work, and public.

10a Creating clear sentences

Generally, the clearest sentences answer the question "Who does what (to whom)?"

	subject	verb	object
CLEAR	The research team	investigated	seizure disorders in infants.
	Who?	does what?	to whom?

120

	subject verb
CLEAR	The seizures often become harmful.
	Who? does what?

Of course, many sentences in good writing are more complicated than those that move directly from subject to verb (to object), yet you can still make them clear by helping readers to answer the question "Who does what (to whom)?"

1 Use significant subjects

Sentences with subjects that name important ideas, people, topics, things, or events are generally easy for readers to understand. You can create sentences with significant subjects by asking, as you write, "Who (or what) am I talking about in this sentence?" and "Is this the subject I want to emphasize?" You can also use these questions to identify and revise sentences whose subjects are not significant. Consider this sentence from an essay titled "Should You Try to Get a Tan?"

UNFOCUSED   The greatest risk comes from exposure to a tanning machine as well as the sun because both of them can damage the skin.

READER'S REACTION: I thought this essay was about the dangers posed by sunbathing and tanning salons. Why are these subjects buried in the middle of the sentence?

POSSIBLE REVISION   Either **the sun or a tanning machine** can damage the skin, and the greatest risk comes from exposure to **both** of them.

2 Avoid unnecessary nominalizations

When you create a noun from some other kind of word, the result is a **nominalization**. A verb like *complete* can become a noun like *completion*; an adjective like *happy* turns into a noun like *happiness*. Some nominalizations play important roles in effective sentences; others act as stumbling blocks for readers.

Nominalizations may name ideas and issues essential to a discussion. As subjects, they can serve as focal points for clear sentences.

USEFUL NOMINALIZATION   **Distractions** like television, the VCR, and electric lights (for reading or conversing) keep us up at night, robbing us of the hours of sleep previous generations enjoyed.

Distractions, a nominalization, comes from *distract*, a verb.

VAGUE   Dissatisfaction among employees often leads to shoddiness in products.

Nominalizations created from adjectives may lead to vague statements, as is the case with *dissatisfaction* and *shoddiness* in this sentence.

10a
sent

REVISED   Dissatisfied employees often make shoddy products.
                   The new verb, *make,* specifies the action more clearly.

Used inappropriately, nominalizations may obscure important information from your readers or cause you to omit it entirely.

STRATEGY

As you write or as you review a draft, pay special attention to nominalizations that

- Draw readers' attention away from a sentence's proper focus
- Lead to vague sentence subjects or objects
- Cause you to leave important information out of a sentence

Revise sentences with these nominalization problems by making sure every sentence indicates clearly who did what (to whom). To do this, replace an inappropriate nominalization with a word indicating a clear and significant subject (or object), and name the sentence's action (did what?) in the verb.

COMMON NOMINALIZATIONS

Spotting nominalizations can be difficult at first, but you can quickly turn this search into a useful habit. Words ending in *-tion, -ence, -ance, -ing,* and *-ness* are often nominalizations. Here is a list of some common nominalizations to watch for.

NOUN	VERB	ADJECTIVE
analysis	analyze	
appropriateness		appropriate
beginning	begin	
calculation	calculate	
comparison	compare	
convenience		convenient
delivery	deliver	
denial	deny	
guidance	guide	
investigation	investigate	
opening	open	
openness		open
preference	prefer	
solution	solve	
suggestion	suggest	

3 Consider using *I, we,* and *you* as subjects

Although *I*, *we*, and *you* are often inappropriate in academic and professional writing, there are many settings in which these pronouns can act as clear subjects in effective sentences. Workplace documents such as reports, proposals, and memos; writings in the public sphere, such as election campaign materials, posters, reports, petitions, and magazine articles; and even an occasional academic text—all of these can benefit from careful use of *I*, *we*, and *you*.

Using *I*. When you are the subject of an essay, when you are speaking directly to readers, or when you are reporting on your own investigations or conclusions, *I* is an appropriate subject.

> In designing the survey, **I** avoided questions likely to embarrass respondents.

On the other hand, adding statements like *I think* and *I feel* when you are already clearly stating your point of view makes your writing more wordy but not more effective.

Using *we*. *We* is appropriate when you use it to report the actions of a group or to discuss experiences you as a writer share with most readers.

> **We** [North Americans] consume a large portion of the world's resources.

Using *you*. *You* is appropriate when used to mean "you, the reader." Consider using *people*, *individuals*, or a similar word if your reader will incorrectly assume you are referring to him- or herself and not to people in general.

APPROPRIATE Before asking a large number of people to complete the survey, **you** should test it on a few individuals to identify any major flaws in the design.

INAPPROPRIATE According to an article in *Rolling Stone*, **you** were less drawn to the 1960s British rock invasion if **you** lived in the Midwest than if **you** lived on the East or West Coast.
READER'S REACTION: **I was born in 1984. Is the author writing to my parents?**

REVISED According to an article in *Rolling Stone*, **people** were less drawn to the 1960s British rock invasion if **they** lived in the Midwest than if **they** lived on the East or West Coast.

4 Be careful with strings of nouns

In a **noun string**, one noun modifies another.

10a
sent

NOUN	NOUN	NOUN
hip	joint	replacement
computer	network	server

Or nouns plus adjectives modify other nouns.

ADJECTIVE	NOUN	NOUN	NOUN
triple	bypass	heart	surgery
preliminary	digital	array	radar

10a
sent

Familiar noun strings can help you create concise yet clear sentences. Unfamiliar noun strings, however, can make sentences hard to understand. Readers may have trouble deciding which noun represents the focal point.

CONFUSING   The team did a ceramic valve lining design flaw analysis.

> READER'S REACTION: **Did the team analyze flaws or use a special procedure called flaw analysis? Did they study ceramic valves or valve linings made of ceramic material?**

One solution is to turn the key word in a string (usually the last noun) into a verb. Then form the other nouns into prepositional phrases.

REVISED   The team **analyzed** flaws **in** the lining design **for** ceramic valves.

Another strategy involves turning one noun into the subject.

REVISED   **Flaws** in the lining design for ceramic valves were analyzed by the team.

> **This version highlights the subject being analyzed.**

Exercise 1

A. Revise the following sentences to create clear subjects and make the sentences easier to understand.

EXAMPLE

We expect

~~Our expectation is that~~ athletic shoes, ~~will~~ to look good as well as feel comfortable.

1. Our expectation is that our elected officials will look like the populations of people they represent.
2. Fifty years ago, election of only one gender of people, male, and of only one race, white, was possible.
3. Today, politicians boast of every level of our government's racial and gender diversity.

4. Choice between candidates is on the basis of their stand on the issues, their media savvy, and their ability to communicate.
5. Choice of candidate is not always on the basis of race, in other words.

B. In a group, collaboratively revise each sentence in Exercise 1A in two ways. Then decide which (if either) is better, and why.

---

5 Use clear and specific verbs

Clear, specific verbs can make sentences forceful and easy to understand. Overuse of the verb *be* (*is, are, was, were, will be*) can lead to weak sentences. Always consider replacing forms of *be* with more forceful verbs.

WEAK   Our agency is responsible for all aspects of disaster relief.

STRONGER   Our agency **plans**, **funds**, **delivers**, and **monitors** disaster relief.

10.1

Look for predicate nouns (nominalizations) you can turn into clear, specific verbs (see 10a-2). Eliminate general verbs (*do, give, have, get, provide, shape, make*) linked to nouns by turning the nouns into verbs.

WEAK   Our company **has done a study** of the new design project and **will provide funding** for it.

STRONGER   Our company **has studied** the new design project and **will fund** it.

---

6 Keep subjects and verbs clearly related

Clear subjects and verbs play key roles in effective sentences. When subject and verb are separated by long phrases, readers may have trouble identifying these elements and may find the sentence difficult to understand.

The veterinary association **in response to concern about the costly facilities required by new guidelines for animal care and disposal of medical waste** has created a low-cost loan program for its members.

Separating the parts of a verb phrase (see 16a-3) with a long phrase or other group of words can also make sentences difficult to read.

Manufacturing companies **can** if they wish to improve product quality, cost, and reliability, **contact** the university's Design for Assembly program.

10b Creating direct sentences

A direct sentence structure moves from subject to verb (to object). An indirect sentence structure uses an **expletive construction** (*there is*, *there are*, or *it is*) to control the arrangement of the words. An expletive construction does not name the subject until well into a sentence. Much of the time, expletive constructions make your sentences wordy and hard to understand.

EXPLETIVE   It is important for us to increase community awareness of our services in order to reach target audiences.

REVISED   We should increase community awareness of our services to reach target audiences.

An expletive construction may also enable you to withhold information about the "doer," the person or thing responsible for an action. You need to decide whether this is appropriate, given your context and purpose, or whether you are omitting details important to your readers.

DOER NOT NAMED   There was considerable debate over whether to build a new library or renovate the old one.

DOER NAMED   Members of the fund-raising committee debated whether to build a new library or renovate the old one.

MORE SPECIFIC   Veit, Gould, and Clifford, the three members in charge of studying the issue, debated whether to build a new library or renovate the old one.

In rewriting, you can replace an expletive construction with a significant sentence subject.

You can sometimes use expletive constructions to good effect. By waiting until late in a sentence to name the subject, you can create suspense and surprise. And you can use expletives to introduce topics that will be taken up in following sentences. (See 10d-3.) A sentence with an expletive construction may also be the clearest and most precise way to make a statement.

> Historians used to believe that a sudden invasion by shepherding tribes caused major changes in the region's culture. Now, however, **there is** new archaeological evidence that the "invasion" was actually a gradual resettling that took about a century.

Exercise 2

A. Rewrite the following sentences, using clear verbs to make them easy to understand.

EXAMPLE   *induces stress*
Negotiating, ~~is a stress-inducing experience~~ for many people in business.

1. Negotiating, regarded by many experts as an important element in successful business careers, especially on the executive level, is not offered as a course at many colleges.
2. Included among the programs offered by our consulting company is a course in professional negotiation. It is considered to be very useful.
3. We also give demonstrations of how to prepare effective proposals, counter-offers, and other negotiation-related documents.
4. Our consultants can, if a company wishes, provide training for both small and large groups.
5. It is generally agreed that the training program is a confidence builder for many people.

B. Work with several other writers to turn the sentences in Exercise 2A into a clear, forceful paragraph that a consulting company might include in a pamphlet advertising its services. Add material if necessary to produce an effective paragraph, and combine or rearrange sentences as appropriate.

10c
sent

10c Creating emphasis

You want your readers to notice the most important ideas and information in a sentence. In drafting and revising, you can highlight this material by placing it at the beginning or end of a sentence, by presenting it in a special sentence pattern, or by using the passive voice in a careful manner.

1 Use sentence beginnings and endings

A reader's attention gravitates toward sentence beginnings and endings. You can take advantage of this phenomenon by shifting the material you wish to emphasize to a sentence's opening or closing.

UNEMPHATIC   Gases produced during the cheese-making process by the "eye former," a bacterium, create the holes in Swiss cheese.

REVISED   **The "eyes,"** or the holes in Swiss cheese, are created during the cheese-making process by gases produced by a bacterium, **the "eye former."**
    Words at the beginning and end emphasize the unusual names. The verb shifts from active to passive voice (see 10c-3).

REVISED **Called "eyes" and produced by gases from a bacterium called the "eye former,"** the holes in Swiss cheese are created during the cheese-making process.
Phrases at the beginning emphasize the names.

2 Create emphatic sentence patterns

Inverted sentence order, climactic order, periodic sentences, and cumulative sentences—which you've seen many times before in your reading—all offer ways to create emphasis. During revision, you can use them to add interest or vary emphasis.

10c
sent

Inversion. By inverting the normal subject-verb-object/complement word order, you can shift the focus of a sentence. **Inverted sentence order** often calls attention to the element you have moved to the initial position.

INVERTED **From the darkness near the rear of the auditorium thundered the director's voice** with criticisms of our acting.

NORMAL **The director's voice thundered** from the darkness near the rear of the auditorium with criticisms of our acting.

Because inversion creates emphasis in part by disrupting a reader's expectations for sentence order, overuse of it or other exotic sentence orders will confuse or irritate readers.

Climactic order. Using **climactic sentence order**—in which elements build to a climax—can create powerful emphasis, especially on the last item in a series.

What every truly modern home has, she said, is a dishwasher, a gas grill, a Jacuzzi, **and a divorce**.

Periodic sentences. A **periodic sentence** piles up phrases, clauses, and words at the beginning, delaying the main clause of the sentence. The suspense casts a spotlight on the main clause.

Because she knows that inspired designs often spring from hard work, because she loves perfection yet fears failure, and because she believes that risk-taking does not eliminate attention to detail, Jennifer is working eighteen hours a day on her fall clothing collection.

The risk, of course, lies in delaying so long that the reader loses track of the meaning, as in the following example.

CONFUSING
Having begun the business as much to escape from boredom as to make a profit, and also suffering from a lack of skill in accounting and an unwillingness to listen to the good advice of the professionals they hired to review the management and recordkeeping procedures that

were causing dissension among employees, Sheila and Stefan decided to declare bankruptcy.

Cumulative sentences. To build a **cumulative sentence**, you start with the main clause, then add details and statements in the form of modifying phrases, clauses, and words. The main clause provides a firm base to which you can add details and ideas, bit by bit.

A cumulative sentence allows you first to emphasize the main clause, then the successive words, phrases, and clauses that work cumulatively to build a detailed picture, an intricate explanation, or a cluster of ideas and information.

Main clause	Varna stumbled down the stairs,
Details	the flowerpot falling from her grip,
Details	spilling dirt into the air,
Details	shattering on the linoleum floor just seconds before she landed among the shards of pottery and fragments of geranium,
Details	the loud thud bringing everyone in the house to attention.

**10c
sent**

3 Use the passive voice with care

When a sentence's verb is in the active voice (see 18h), the doer (or agent) is also the subject of the sentence.

> doer   action   goal
> The outfielder caught the towering fly ball.
> subject   verb   object

When you choose the **passive voice** for the verb form, you turn the sentence's goal into the subject and make naming the doer optional.

> goal   action   [doer]
> The towering fly ball was caught [by the outfielder].
> subject   verb   [prepositional phrase]

Using the passive voice, you de-emphasize the doer by placing it in a prepositional phrase or by dropping it altogether (see 16a-7). In addition, you create sentences that are generally wordier than corresponding versions in the active voice. Note how emphasis and length differ in active and passive versions of the following sentence.

> doer (subject)
> ACTIVE VOICE   **The Centers for Disease Control** interviewed three thousand people affected by the toxin.

> subject
> PASSIVE VOICE   **Three thousand people** affected by the toxin were interviewed by **the Centers for Disease Control**.
> doer

10.2

STRATEGY

Review your writing, looking for sentences that use verbs in the passive voice (see 18h). (If you're working on a computer, turn on your software's editing function and look for cases it marks as passive. Alternatively, use the search function to locate the words "is," "was," "were," and "by," which will narrow your search for passive constructions.) Recast in the active voice any sentences that are unnecessarily wordy or that create inappropriate emphasis. Consider naming the doer in any sentences that fail to provide this information.

10c
sent

If you wish to emphasize the *doer*, use the active voice. If you wish to draw readers' attention to the goal or outcome of an action rather than its doer, consider using the passive voice.

ACTIVE   **Poorly trained contract workers** caused the explosion and fire at the refinery.
Subject emphasizes cause.

PASSIVE   **The explosion and fire** at the refinery were caused by poorly trained contract workers.
Subject emphasizes result.

You can also use the passive voice to highlight significant elements in a discussion.

Refineries are potentially dangerous workplaces. **Most accidents** can be prevented, however, by careful training of workers.
Passive voice in the second sentence keeps attention on the dangers.

You can choose whether or not to name the doer in a sentence written in the passive voice.

Requirements for the term paper were distributed in all sections of the psychology course [by the individual instructors].

When the doer is unknown, unimportant, or obvious, you can appropriately omit it.

Federal income tax forms will be mailed on January 1.
By the IRS, of course.

But when leaving out the doer would omit important information or mislead readers, include it.

Consumers were not informed of their right to sue for damages.
The sentence doesn't say who withheld the information.

A WORD ABOUT SPEAKING

Because you are more likely to give extemporaneous or conversational oral presentations (see Chapter 3) than to read verbatim from a prepared script, you'll be creating many of your sentences "live," using your talking points and a sharp memory of your ideas from your rehearsals. To avoid speaking dull, lifeless, unvaried sentences with many passive or expletive constructions, jot down and memorize, or include in your talking points, a few sentences that guarantee some variety or dramatic effect, as Julio Cordoza did in his notes for a presentation on the rise of small American wineries.

Post-1950s—sharp decline # of small family-run wineries; growth of huge, industrial-style winemakers. *But no more. Bloomington, Indiana: The Oliver Winery. Prosser, Washington: Chinook Winery. New Paltz, New York: Adair Vineyards. Sparta, North Carolina: Chateau Laurinda. And yes, Volcano, Hawaii: Volcano Vineyards, the only winery on the Big Island.* These and hundreds of other . . . [show overhead graph with numbers and explain].

10c
sent

DID YOU KNOW?

Advice on using the passive voice has changed radically during the last hundred years. According to Dennis Baron, experts on grammar and writing style during the eighteenth and nineteenth centuries had few objections to sentences using the passive voice. By the middle of the twentieth century, however, they had begun criticizing the passive voice for encouraging wordiness, vagueness, and even deception (by allowing writers to avoid naming the person or group responsible for an action). Now, editors and writing teachers regularly advise writers to eliminate passive voice whenever possible.

Dennis Baron, "The Passive Voice Can Be Your Friend," *Declining Grammar and Other Essays on the English Vocabulary* (Urbana: NCTE, 1989) 17–22.

Exercise 3

A. Revise the following sentences to eliminate passive voice.

EXAMPLE

Grocery stores sell many
~~Many~~ different kinds of ice cream ~~are sold by grocery stores.~~

1. The superpremium ice cream brands are chosen by many people.
2. More butterfat and less air is contained in superpremium ice cream than in regular ice cream.
3. The high fat content ought to be considered before the ice cream is purchased.

4. The rich, tasty ice creams are being challenged by the new frozen dessert products.
5. Frozen yogurts with candy and nuts mixed in have been heavily promoted.

B. Examine the following passage carefully, and identify the strategies the author uses to create emphasis. Then share your responses.

There was a time when people who wanted to keep the peace and keep the crockery intact held to a strict dinner-table rule: Never argue about politics or religion. I don't know how well it worked in American dining rooms, but it worked pretty well in our schools. We dealt with religion by not arguing about it.

Children who came out of diverse homes might carve up the turf of their neighborhood and turn the playgrounds into a religious battlefield, but the public classroom was common ground. Intolerance wasn't tolerated.

In place of teaching one religion or another, the schools held to a common denominator of values. It was, in part, the notion of Horace Mann, the nineteenth-century father of the public-school system. He believed that the way to avoid religious conflicts was to extract what all religions agree upon and allow this "non-religious" belief system into schools.

I wonder what Mann would think of that experiment now. Was it naive or sophisticated? Was it a successful or a failed attempt to avoid conflict in a pluralistic society?

—ELLEN GOODMAN, "Religion in the Textbooks"

Working with a group of fellow writers, try to agree on answers to these questions about the Goodman passage: Which sentence strategies add to the effectiveness of the passage, and why? Which, if any, detract from its effectiveness?

10d Revising for variety

Too many sentences of similar length, type, and structure can create unemphatic writing that bores readers. Variety helps. Many of the strategies that create emphasis (see 10c) can also create variety, and the two qualities often go together.

1 Vary sentence length

Revision is a good opportunity to pay attention to varying the length of sentences. Use short sentences for dramatic contrast and for emphasis. Create longer sentences to explore relationships among ideas and to add rhythmic effects to your prose. Use middle-length sentences as workhorses, carrying the burden of explanation and description.

Note how variety in sentence length helps make this explanation easy to read and interesting.

> The real country ham may or may not be smoked after curing. Smithfield, Virginia, hams are smoked over hardwood or hardwood sawdust. Unscrupulous producers use smoke flavoring. But Mac Pierce, who runs the country's largest retail pork market, Nahunta Pork Center in Pikeville, North Carolina, says less than 1 percent of his hams are smoked, and most of those are bought by northerners. "Smoke masks a good ham's flavor," says Mac.
>
> —BILL NEAL, "How to Cure a Pig"

10d
sent

STRATEGY

Vary sentence length as you revise. (Some computer programs will give you a "mean sentence length" index, or allow you to compare the length of your sentences. If you're working on a computer, you can also "sample" a typical paragraph by marking and counting words in each of its sentences. In the example by Bill Neal above, the four sentences contain twenty-two, five, thirty-six, and fifteen words, respectively, showing a lot of variety.) Combine some of your own draft sentences to highlight relationships; compress others to emphasize ideas.

DRAFT   Political conventions used to be occasions for selecting among rival candidates. They are no longer serious contests. The likely winners are known well in advance. Conventions are now simply places for political strategists and campaign workers to meet. They are also ways of getting attention from the media.

REVISED   Political conventions used to be occasions for selecting among rival candidates, but no longer, for the likely winners are now known well in advance. Conventions are now simply meeting places for political strategists and campaign workers. They are media events.

2 Vary sentence types

It's easy to get into the habit of using only **declarative sentences**, sentences that make statements (see 16e-2 for sentence types). An occasional exclamation (**exclamatory sentence**), a mild order (**imperative sentence**), or a question (**interrogative sentence**) can vary the pace of your prose effectively, making it more lively and memorable.

VARIED

Some of the less familiar sports offer good opportunities for entertainment and exercise. Are you looking for fast-paced, thrilling events? Go see a soccer game, a lacrosse match, or a bicycle race. Do you want strenuous exercise and vigorous competition? Sign up for a rugby team, a badminton class, or a squash league. To benefit from these activities you need only take a simple step: Get involved!

A **rhetorical question** is one that requires no answer or that you plan to answer yourself in the course of an essay.

10d
sent

These are all ways you can get more time for sleep, even in the midst of a busy schedule. **But is it really important for most of us to get more sleep?** It is, and staying healthy and staying alert aren't the only good reasons for doing so.

3 Vary sentence structures and patterns

You can create variety by blending sentence structures in your writing (use simple, compound, and complex sentences; see 16d) and by varying the kinds of coordination and subordination you employ (see Chapter 28). You can also create variety by using periodic and cumulative sentence patterns and inversion (see 10c-2). By trying different sentence openings (see 10c-1), you can make sure your sentences vary in arrangement.

EXPLETIVE	Then there was the time we painted our house.
PHRASE	**To our neighbor's eyes**, the house looked like it belonged somewhere else.
PHRASE	**Looking for a bargain**, we bought paint at a discount store.
PHRASE	**The paint having been cheaply made**, the house began peeling within a year and a half.
DEPENDENT CLAUSE	**If you want to be happy with a paint job**, spend the money for quality materials.
TRANSITIONAL EXPRESSION	**In addition**, choose the color carefully.

Exercise 4

A. Rewrite the following passage to add variety. You may wish to rearrange the order of statements, to cut or add words, or to combine some sentences and divide others.

Psychologists have been studying what events people remember. People from middle age on remember events from their early years more clearly than they remember more recent events. People in their seventies have clear memories of their thirties but less clear memories of their fifties. Most of us remember very little about childhood. Almost no one remembers events from before four years old. Researchers think that we tend to remember events that are new or exciting to us and to forget routine events. Memorable events are most likely to occur early in life. Infants probably have not developed the mental abilities necessary to create memories, however.

B. Compare your rewritten version of the passage in Exercise 4A with those produced by other writers. Working in a group, produce one version of the passage that draws on the best parts of each version.

10d
sent

4 Create surprise

Good writing often employs strategies that intrigue readers. **Summative modifiers**, **resumptive modifiers**, and **antithesis**, which change—or seem to change—the direction of a sentence, are particularly effective at creating surprise and interest.

A **summative modifier** summarizes the preceding part of a sentence and then sends it off in a new direction.

To protect your vegetables against harmful insects, you can use soap sprays, scatter insect-repelling plants among the beds, or introduce "friendly" insects like ladybugs and praying mantises—**three techniques** that will not leave a harmful chemical residue on the food you grow.

A **resumptive modifier** extends a sentence that appears to have ended, adding new information or twists of thought.

People who are careful about what they eat may lead healthier lives—**healthier**, though not necessarily longer.

The advertising campaign is a surprising failure, **surprising** because it worked so well with test audiences.

Antithesis—the use of parallelism to emphasize contrast—can be witty, dramatic, cynical, ironic, or memorable.

To err is human, to forgive divine.   —ALEXANDER POPE

Can an honest politician be smart, or a smart politician honest?

Exercise 5

A. Browse through some current magazines, looking for one that contains relatively long essays with varied and often surprising writing style. You might look at *Vogue*, *The New Yorker*, *Rolling Stone*, *Business Week*, *GQ*, *Vanity Fair*, *Advertising Age*, *Utne Reader*, *Commentary*, *Tikkun*, *Scientific American*, or *Details*. Choose two paragraphs whose style you admire, and identify any of the sentence strategies discussed in this chapter. Be ready to discuss why the sentences can be considered effective in communicating the author's ideas.

B. Although correct, carefully crafted sentences are important for writing in most communities, sometimes complex sentences are unnecessary or even distracting. Make a list of types of writing that don't require complete sentences (for example, classified ads). Then speculate about when sophisticated or complex sentences are necessary and appropriate and when they are not.

PART 3

Representing Yourself: Creating a Place in a Community

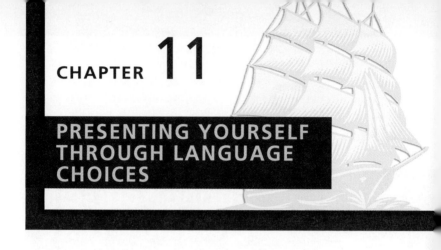

CHAPTER 11

PRESENTING YOURSELF THROUGH LANGUAGE CHOICES

How do you talk at home, at school, at work, or in your neighborhood? Do you find yourself using language differently when you're with friends, teachers, and bosses? Are there groups of people you feel more comfortable speaking with, and do they share your way of speaking?

In an area of Miami, José Barrientes, a college student, notices how he changes his language choices the moment he walks into his physics lab or his Western civilization course. In those settings, he uses a more formal style than he does when he speaks to people in his neighborhood. This academic way of speaking feels a little uncomfortable to him, especially because he has to avoid slipping Spanish words and phrases into his speech that would help him to express himself. But he also knows that there are other students in his classes who unfortunately aren't bilingual, and who may not even understand the variety of English he speaks at home.

José is not alone: his situation is also shared in varying degrees by Solita Johnson, an African American student from Camden, New Jersey; by Karl Buccanan, who comes from a rural farming community in central North Dakota; and by Steve Thibodeaux of Baton Rouge, Louisiana. From the northern tip of Maine to the Mexican border south of San Diego, people speak in hundreds of different ways in their homes and communities. These language differences help define who they are and give them a sense of personal history and group identity.

Every speaker of the English language uses a variety shaped by his or her region, culture, exposure to other languages, and home community. Where they're commonly used, these varieties seem natural; they may even show up in the way members of the community write to each other. Not so, however, in most business, academic, and broader public settings, where the use of such varieties may be seen as "erroneous" or "sloppy." Except for very casual and personal occasions, writers substitute more general standards for their regional, cultural, and home language varieties. (The same is true, to a somewhat lesser degree, for public speaking.) Members of your reading community, even those in your local area, usually expect your writing to conform to these generalized standards, in part because writing can move beyond your own surroundings and into other settings. Becoming a flexible writer means developing an aware-ness of the differences between the habits and standards of your own commu-nity and the biases or expectations of a more general reading public.

11a Understanding home and community language varieties

Every language in the world is spoken in a variety of ways called *dialects*. English has hundreds of dialects, which vary in obvious ways be-tween different countries, like England and the United States, but also within these countries. The American English spoken in Natchez, Mississippi differs considerably from the American English spoken in Bar Harbor, Maine, and speakers in Fort Wayne, Indiana don't, as a group, share the same dialect as Hoosiers who live just a few hours south in Bloomington or Evansville. Dialects can also vary by culture, ethnicity, and nationality. Not only do Cuban Americans and Puerto Rican Americans speak different dialects of American English in New York City, but their dialects may vary between the Bronx and Brooklyn. Similar people may have different dialects even though they live just a few miles from each other—or a few blocks.

11a
lang

1 Learn to see dialect variations as "rules"

Linguists point out that all dialects have rules. What conforms to a rule in one dialect may break a rule in another. This is how all language works— the "rules" are really structures and conventions that people within a group unconsciously agree to use in their speech. Pronouncing the word *pen* to rhyme with *hen* is a rule of Northern and much Midwestern speech, but the rule in large parts of the South is to rhyme *pen* with *tin*. Many British speak-ers pronounce the *t* in the word *butter* but leave off the *r* at the end ("but-tah"), whereas Americans generally turn the *t* into a *d* and pronounce the *r* ("budder")—except in the South and in parts of New England. Who's right? Each group follows the rules of its own community. To break them is to be seen as an outsider.

2 Understand standard English as a function of power and social prestige

If every community has its own language rules, then who's to say that the so-called standard language is the "better" language? Why *should* it be any more correct to say "There isn't anyone who can tell me anything about what I haven't seen" than to say "Ain't no body gon' tell me nuffin' bout what I ain't see"? After all, double negatives are acceptable in hundreds of languages around the world, so there isn't any logical reason why they should be incorrect in English. In fact, they were once perfectly acceptable, and were used by Chaucer and Shakespeare.

The answer to this question doesn't come from something in the nature of the language; it comes from something about the people who speak it. Around the world, each language has a prestige dialect that is thought to be more "correct" or "proper" than other dialects. How this dialect came to be preferred is almost always a matter of historical, political, and social forces. Some group of people came into power. They used language in a certain way. Because they had power, they also controlled things like schools, information, and books. Before long, their language variety became associated with correctness; grammarians then simply described that form of the language *as* correct, and people who wanted to be thought powerful or educated had to learn its rules.

If your home dialect differs from the standard, you may be unfairly stereotyped or discriminated against by people in positions of power. Even unbiased people may not listen to you, because they can't: they aren't part of your dialect group; you're leaving them out of the conversation. Before deciding what, if anything, you want to do about differences between your community dialect and the standard, it's important to reflect on this issue of power. Some people believe that our society must begin accepting more varieties of language. Others believe that if such acceptance occurs, it will happen very slowly, but people will still discriminate against certain language varieties in the meantime. If that's true, people without power will remain powerless if they can't communicate in the language of the powerful. But if they can gain positions of power, maybe they can then help to change public prejudices about language and culture.

11a
lang

DID YOU KNOW?

Language scholars have described several approaches to address the issue of language variation. One approach is *eradication*: try to wipe out all language differences by teaching people to use only the standard. A second approach is *appreciation*: celebrate the diversity of differences in our speech, and accept all dialects as reflections of culture, heritage, and community. A third approach is *biloquialism* or *bidialectalism*: help people to learn more than one variety, so they can express themselves equally well in differing situations and not give up their linguistic identities and ways of relating to their own communities.

Exercise 1

A. Briefly describe any features of your own home or community language that you're aware of in your speech or writing habits. What kinds of features are they: words? accent? grammar? What are their sources? Have you ever felt stereotyped or discriminated against because of your home or community language, or felt awkward in a situation in which your speech differed from that of others? Is there disagreement within your own community about what's correct? How do you feel about the issue of language authority? Do you want to hold on to your community language? Or do you want to get rid of all traces of that language? If you did, how do you think people in your home community would respond?

B. In a group, compare your reflections from Exercise 1A. Focus specifically on the problems of power, prestige, and language prejudice.

3 Recognize the difference between accents and written variations

Different *accents* get stigmatized all the time, yet they're more likely to be accepted than differences in *grammar*. While Americans don't usually mind differences in our leaders' accents, most people would balk at a president who said, "Them senators ain't ready for this-here veto" or "The First Lady, she all d'time be givin' me good advice on foreign policy."

In writing, the most glaring (and least forgiven) variations are *grammatical*, followed by *lexical* differences (word choice, including slang, jargon, and the like). People form unfair stereotypes on the basis of these language features, thinking that they're signs of ignorance or laziness. To avoid such negative stereotypes and to succeed in your most important goal—having your readers listen to and respect your ideas—you'll need to recognize and edit any instances of home or community language variations that may not be shared by a wider reading public. Paying attention to these differences will make you a more flexible communicator, able to move effectively between a home or community dialect and a broader public form of language.

11a
lang

A WORD ABOUT SPEAKING

While Americans tend to "forgive" occasional grammatical lapses or other errors in oral presentations, they also form a negative image of the speaker's credibility if these errors are too frequent or severe. (This is not the case with differences in *accent*.) As you work on your public speaking, transfer your growing knowledge of grammar to your spoken language, but don't become too concerned about your accent unless it affects your audience's ability to understand you.

4 Learn how to code-shift

One way speakers adjust their language to meet the expectations of particular communities is through what's called **code-shifting**. Some situations compel you to talk in ways that meet the expectations of your home or community language variety, while other situations—less personal, or more broadly public—beg for a different kind of speech. In other words, you have to talk the talk and walk the walk.

Code-shifting is also a characteristic of writing. Many people write in a home or community language to their friends, but they shift into formal language in an essay, a letter to an elected official, or a corporate report. University of Pittsburgh assistant dean Barbara Mellix, for example, describes her own code-shifting in an essay, "From Outside, In." Annoyed by her daughter's persistent interruptions while she's writing, she tells her, "Looka here, Allie, you are too old for this kind of carryin' on. I done told you this is important. You wronger than dirt to be in here haggin' me like this and you know it. Now git outta here and leave me off before I put my foot all the way down." Yet, to make her points about language difference, Mellix feels compelled to use a different code in her writing.

11a
lang

> Now that I know that to seek knowledge, freedom, and autonomy means always to be in the concentrated process of becoming—always to be venturing into new territory, feeling one's way at first, then getting one's balance, negotiating, accommodating, discovering one's self in ways that previously defined "others"—I sometimes get tired.
>
> —BARBARA MELLIX, "From Outside, In"

In some formats—such as personal letters, or working journals designed to help you think about course material (see 2c)—you should feel at ease writing in a home or community variety. In other, typically more formal situations, where home or community variations can be stigmatized, most writers play it safe and adopt a style for their writing that will work across many different communities. In the United States, this variety is often called standard edited American English.

STRATEGY

Seek out a member of your home language community who also has good facility with standard edited American English. Ask this person for advice about how to edit one of your papers for readers who expect this standard from what they read. As you work with this reader, see if you can figure out his or her techniques for managing to use several language varieties successfully.

5 Become aware of the grammatical variations in your home dialect

Grammatical variations in your home or community dialect can be tricky to notice in your writing; after all, they may not look the least bit odd or problematic—to you. But someone who isn't a member of your dialect community will see them right away.

11.1

HOME VARIETY	Miss Brill know that the lovers making fun of her, but she act like she don't care.
EDITED	Miss Brill knows that the lovers are making fun of her, but she acts as if she doesn't care.
HOME VARIETY	The FDA guy said to Dougherty could he borrow him the test kit, but Dougherty said he would bring it with.
EDITED	A representative of the FDA asked whether Dougherty could lend him the test kit, but Dougherty said he would bring it with him.
HOME VARIETY	The minutes of the last meeting state that unless if RayCorp had ordered the resistors, the shipment was sent out on accident.
EDITED	The minutes of the last meeting state that unless RayCorp had ordered the resistors, the shipment was sent out accidentally.

11a
lang

STRATEGY

If you can see variations in your home or community language as rules or patterns, it may be easier for you to match them up against the rules of a standard. What are the rules of your community language? Keep a list in a notebook. First, record examples of rules specific to your community language; then write down the corresponding examples in standard English. Then try to write an explanation of the differences in your own terms, as in the following example written by a student from Kentucky.

Rule in my part of Kentucky: The lawn needs mowed.
Rule elsewhere: The lawn needs to be mowed.

Everyone in my part of Kentucky leaves out the *to be* and just puts in the verb after *needs*. It's always seemed natural to me, but I learned that it is only done in certain parts of the United States. I can use the "search" function on my computer to look for the word *needs* and then make sure I fix the mistake.

Exercise 2

A. Consider the following excerpt from *Their Eyes Were Watching God*, a novel by African American author Zora Neale Hurston. This conversation between two characters, Phoeby Watson and Janie Stark, represents the language variety used in the characters' home and community and is therefore the most expressive way for them to relate to each other.

> [Phoeby] found [Janie] sitting on the steps of the back porch with the lamps all filled and the chimneys cleaned.
>
> "Hello, Janie, how you comin'?"
>
> "Aw, pretty good, Ah'm tryin' to soak some uh de tiredness and de dirt outa mah feet." She laughed a little.
>
> "Ah see you is. Gal, you sho looks *good*. You looks like youse yo' own daughter." They both laughed. "Even wid dem overhalls on, you shows yo' womanhood."
>
> "G'wan! G'wan! You must think Ah brought yuh somethin'. When Ah ain't brought home a thing but mahself."
>
> "Dat's a gracious plenty. Yo' friends wouldn't want nothin' better."
>
> —Zora Neal Hurston, *Their Eyes Were Watching God*

The second passage is a letter requesting that a local YWCA suspend the writer's membership until she is able to exercise again. The passage contains features of the writer's home community dialect that are not considered standard. The letter is aimed at a general reading public, because the YWCA may employ people who do not share the writer's language variety.

Dear Mrs. Voit,

Like I explain to you when I call last week, I ain't been use my YWCA membership since November because I am pregnant and my doctor be telling me not to work out. Please stop my membership now and I call you when I want it start up again.

Sincerely,

Loretta Saunders

Edit both passages to make them conform to standard written English. Now reflect on the consequences of your changes. Has anything been lost from either passage? Has anything been gained through editing? How appropriate are the changes made to each passage?

B. In a group, compare your changes and your reflections from Exercise 2A. What does this exercise suggest about the principle of standard English and the idea of flexibility?

11b Understanding how dialects influence writing

Along with dialect differences, all speakers of English also use differences in **register** in both their speaking and their writing. Register is the form that language takes in a particular context. The variations can be in pronunciation, grammar, or word choice. You might use a *formal* register when being interviewed for an important job, an *informal* register at a ball game, a *technical* register when explaining to a colleague how a piece of electronic equipment works, or a *simplified* register when talking with a toddler.

In writing and formal speaking occasions, you want to be sure to use the right register. Your choice of register will depend on your intended audience or readers and their knowledge, your context, and your **persona**, or who you want to "be" in your writing. You may need to shift registers if aspects of your home or community language are generally thought to be too informal for broader or more formal settings. (See also 11a-5.)

1 Become aware of oral language influences

Most of the language we produce is spoken. If you haven't been an avid reader, there may be expressions, terms, and constructions that you've *heard* often but haven't *seen* much in print. Your knowledge of the sound can trick you into making an error when you turn that sound into print.

Consider one of the most common mistakes in writing: spelling the phrase *a lot* as one word (*alot*). Why do so many people do this? Partly because they're smart: spoken, this phrase really does sound like one word, with little or no pause between *a* and *lot*. Or they may not have noticed *a lot* spelled again and again as two words. These sorts of transcription errors show up often in unedited prose.

I should of signed the check	for	*I should have signed the check*
excetera	for	*et cetera*
Atom and Eve	for	*Adam and Eve*
It's a doggy-dog world	for	*It's a dog-eat-dog world*
expresso	for	*espresso*

The way language sounds in your home or community variety can also end up in your writing, and this may unfortunately (and often unfairly) lead your reader to judge you negatively or doubt your credibility or intelligence. In the first example on page 146, the omission of *-ed* from *ask* is clearly an intelligent mistake: the *-ed* of *asked* is pronounced as a *t*, and the *t* of *Trish* swallows it in speech. In the second example, illustrating the influence of Spanish, *this* sounds like *these* to the writer, leading to another intelligent mistake, while the repetition of *either* is a common feature of the Chicano English of Southern California.

DRAFT
The personnel department ask Trish Walters could she expedite the request.

READER'S REACTION: **Why is *ask* in the present tense? Also, when I get to *could,* I'm thrown off track. The writer seems careless.**

EDITED
The personnel department asked Trish Walters whether she could expedite the request.

DRAFT
Either the character cause all this events, or either they are coincidental.

EDITED
Either the characters cause all these events, or they are coincidental.

2 Consider your word choices

Usually, writers consciously choose their words to make them appropriate for the occasion—formal or informal, complex or simple. Sometimes, however, writers unknowingly use words that are part of their home or community language but are not shared by a broader community of readers. In such cases, readers may think the text is too informal because it uses "local" words. These words can usually be spotted with a careful editorial eye and the help of a good dictionary.

11b lang

DRAFT
Our interoffice mail is consistently slow because the mailboy has to schlep the large packages along with the memos and letters.

READER'S REACTION: **"Schlep?" Is that some sort of corporate term?**

EDITED
Our interoffice mail is consistently slow because the mailboy has to carry the large packages along with the memos and letters.

DRAFT
Some of the budget surplus should be used on our public parks, which need new play areas and working bubblers.

READER'S REACTION: **What's a bubbler?**

EDITED
Some of the budget surplus should be used on our public parks, which need new play areas and drinking fountains that work.

STRATEGY

To gauge the appropriateness of your word choices, first consider the intended audience and the occasion of your writing. In something directed to members of a specific community, it may be acceptable to use "local" words such as *homeboy, mazeh,* or *happa.*

If your writing audience and occasion are broader and more formal (for example, a corporate memo or an academic paper), skim through your writing looking for word choices that strike you as questionable or problematic. Circle or underline those words as you encounter them, but keep reading to the end of the paper.

Finally, work back through the text, stopping at each underlined or circled word and listing or trying out alternatives that seem more in keeping with the level of formality, audience, and occasion of your writing.

3 Distinguish between slang and dialect

Words that are part of a dialect have usually been around in that dialect for some time. People of all ages may use them, and they are known by much or most of the dialect community. Sometimes these words even become part of the standard language—for example, the word *jazz*.

When groups within a dialect community (often young people) create new words that aren't shared by the entire community, those words will be considered **slang**. Many older members of a dialect community express negative attitudes toward the use of slang by younger people, even though all of them may be using a language variety considered to be nonstandard. Although slang is an important way to show membership in a group and is often very creative, you should avoid using it in writing (except perhaps in informal journals or learning logs). Some people may not understand it; others may feel alienated from your prose. Still others, both within and beyond your language community, may not trust your ideas or take them seriously.

SLANG   The battle scenes in *The Iliad* are phat. Just when Agamemnon chill, someone diss him or jack something up and he wage another war.

(For more on word usage, see Chapter 29.)

4 Recognize hypercorrection

People who use a nonmainstream or stigmatized dialect may become aware of certain language habits that are not considered the norm. When they shift registers in formal situations, they may consciously or unconsciously try to "repair" their speech. Sometimes they may unwittingly create a new error in trying to be correct. Linguists call this phenomenon **hypercorrection**.

In speech, for example, some New Englanders who don't pronounce their rs at the end of words after vowels (*mothuh, fathuh,* and *cah* for *mother, father,* and *car*) may hypercorrect themselves by putting an *r* at the end of a word where it doesn't belong. Some Cockney speakers in London incorrectly

11b
lang

11.2

put *hs* at the beginning of words with vowels (*howl* for *owl* or *hasked* for *asked*) in formal situations, because they tend to drop the *h* from words that should have it (*'e* for *he*, *'asn't* for *hasn't*, *'ad* for *had*).

Certain kinds of hypercorrection can affect writers, especially in the area of grammar. Writers create hypercorrection because they're *trying* to be formal. In an urge to be correct, the writer guesses that a construction is wrong and ironically substitutes an error for it.

HYPERCORRECT   Stuart will give the petitions to Mary and I.

EDITED   Stuart will give the petitions to Mary and me.

The concept of hypercorrection can also apply to the style and structure of your sentences. If you try too hard to be formal and sophisticated, you may end up writing tangled prose. Don't be fooled into thinking that complex words and sentences alone will create an "impressive" register; your readers won't be impressed, just frustrated.

CONVOLUTED   That the girl walks away, and the showing of the parrot to the restaurant owner who, having closed shop, is not about to let her inside, is indicative of that which characterizes the novel throughout, i.e., denial and deception.

EDITED   The central theme of denial and deception is illustrated when the girl tries to show the parrot to the restaurant owner and is turned away.

Hypercorrection can also affect the use and spelling of words. For example, when a writer spells the phrase *Adam and Eve* as *Atom and Eve*, she's assuming that the *d* in *Adam* works like the *ts* in *writer* or *batter* (which are pronounced like *ds*), so she hypercorrects the word to *Atom*.

STRATEGY

When you are uncertain about a construction or grammatical rule in your formal writing, circle the words in question or put an asterisk in the margin. Then check the rule in this handbook or another grammatical resource, or ask someone for advice. Keep a running list of any cases of hypercorrection you identify, and explain them to yourself in your own words. Do the same for any cases of hypercorrection that are identified for you by a peer reader, teacher, or collaborator.

CHAPTER 12

REPRESENTING YOURSELF THROUGH CRITICAL REASONING

What convinces people to accept your conclusions about a subject? To share your opinion on an issue? To follow your recommendations? Or to trust the explanations you offer? Many things do, of course. Perhaps the most important of these is the quality of your reasoning: the kind of careful, logical, insightful thinking your writing (or speaking) embodies. Thinking that displays these qualities is called **critical reasoning** or **critical thinking**.

Whatever its focus, critical reasoning in general calls for attention to logic, supporting evidence, and accurate detail, as well as awareness of alternative perspectives and opinion. But what constitutes critical thinking may differ markedly depending on the community you are addressing: academic, public, or work (see 12c). What's more, the quality and design of your thinking contribute significantly to the representation of yourself that you create for an audience; that is, your **persona**. Do you present yourself as thoughtful, informed, and fair-minded—hence persuasive? Or do you undermine your effectiveness by coming across as illogical, careless about ideas and information, and uninterested in other points of view?

12a
reason

12a What is critical reasoning?

Critical reasoning is any process of reasoning, inquiring, or explaining that displays the following qualities.

- Attention to the logic or reasonableness of conclusions, and to the evidence supporting them.
- Willingness to question one's own assumptions and consider differing outlooks.
- Concern for precise information and clearly defined ideas.
- Desire to go beyond superficial explanations and opinions to reach fresh insights.

Consider the contrasts between the following two examples of reasoning, offered in a public context; both are letters to the editor about a controversial proposal to build a greenway between two parks, one of which is in Coolidge (an economically depressed neighborhood) and the other in Lake Stearns (a wealthy, stable neighborhood of fine older homes).

LETTER 1 (LACKS CRITICAL REASONING)

Doesn't consider other points of view

Little evidence

Vague details and ideas

Logical?

Reasonable?

City planners must be out of their minds to cook up this crazy idea. Drug pushers and thieves will have a field day preying on the people who use Lake Stearns Park, and soon the whole neighborhood will be destroyed by crime. We must stop these public officials before they totally destroy our lives with their senseless fantasies.

READER'S RESPONSE: This is just a collection of assertions with little evidence. The writer doesn't try to explain why the assertions are reasonable but feels free to dismiss other perspectives as unreasonable and illogical—without presenting any evidence.

LETTER 2 (DISPLAYS CRITICAL REASONING)

Goes beyond the obvious

Acknowledges other perspectives

Carefully presented evidence and clearly defined ideas

Logical reasoning

Reasonable conclusion

The proposal to create a greenway between Coolidge and Lake Stearns Parks appears to bridge the gap between these two different communities. But the greenway will not solve the existing problems in Coolidge Park. Residents near Lake Stearns are unlikely to ride their bikes or jog into Coolidge, and the presence of Coolidge residents in Stearns will only create a feeling, unjustified though it may be, of defensiveness. City funds could better be used to improve Coolidge Park by adding lighting, a basketball court, and an updated community center.

READER'S RESPONSE: The problem isn't simple, and the writer gives it a careful, balanced treatment. The reasons for both objecting to the proposal and for an alternate solution are supported by specific details.

The lack of critical reasoning displayed in Letter 1 undermines its persuasiveness, except perhaps for those few readers who already agree with its conclusions. In Letter 2, the depth of critical reasoning invites readers to take the writer's thinking seriously, forming their own opinions and agreeing or disagreeing in response.

12b Critical reasoning in academic, public, and work communities

12.1

Researchers looking for ways to develop alternative-fuel vehicles will take different paths with their critical reasoning than public officials trying to create (or repeal) regulations, or business executives developing new products. In this case as in many others, though the subject remains the same, the goals and procedures of critical reasoning are likely to differ from setting to setting, according to audience and occasion.

1 Academic contexts

Working in academic communities, researchers and students alike analyze and interpret their subjects (social or natural phenomena, texts, artworks, and so forth). Their critical reasoning aims to offer interpretations, explanations, and insights. The reasoning process (both as an act of discovery, and in the final written product or oral report) has the following characteristics.

- Detailed reasoning and critical analysis, often explained at length, with careful attention to the logic leading up to conclusions
- Special attention to insights and conclusions that go beyond the obvious and beyond common knowledge
- Care in gathering and presenting extensive evidence and accurate detail to support conclusions
- Balanced treatment acknowledging and explaining other viewpoints

12b
reason

Balanced treatment
Goes beyond obvious
Detailed reasoning & analysis

Regardless of whether there has been a shift in attitudes among employers, race is obviously a factor in many of their current decisions; however, the issues are complex and cannot be reduced to the simple notion of employer racism. Let me pursue this point by first focusing on the way in which employers themselves perceive the issues of prejudice and discrimination and, second, examining black employers' perceptions of inner-city workers.

Care in presenting accurate evidence

If discrimination is a significant factor in the employment woes of inner-city blacks, it is not recognized as such by a substantial majority of the employers in this survey. When asked the reason for the high levels of unemployment in Chicago's inner-city neighborhoods, only 4 percent of the 179 employers mentioned discrimination.

—William Julius Wilson, "The Meaning and Significance of Race"

2 Public contexts

In public settings, reasoning often focuses on issues or policies as part of democratic decision making, with the goal of persuading or providing issue-oriented information. As a result, the process of reasoning and its expression in writing or speaking emphasizes the following elements of critical thinking.

- Concentration on author's point of view and provision of plausible, logical reasons for agreeing with this perspective

- Special attention to shared values and goals that support advocacy of a cause or policy, and to the need for specific kinds of information
- Awareness of the importance of relevant evidence in supporting positions or claims
- Fair recognition of others' interests, goals, and points of view

Shared values; concentrates on own point of view

How is health care like going to the grocer? The more you put in the cart, the higher the bill. But unlike your grocery expedition, where all you pay for are the items in your own cart, with health care the other customer's cart is on your tab, too.

Fair recognition of others' outlook

Nor will the tab get any better with the patient protection legislation being considered in Washington. Sure, Americans will get guaranteed access to emergency rooms, medical clinical trials and specialists. Senate legislation even provides the right to sue your insurer and be awarded up to $5 million in punitive damages. [. . .]

Relevant supporting evidence

According to the Employee Policy Foundation, the right to sue in the Senate's so-called Patients' Bill of Rights will add up to $16.3 billion per year to health care costs. The litigation costs, and the efforts by some employers to avoid liability, could lead to an additional 9 million uninsured Americans by 2010.

—"Restrict Right to Sue or We'll Pay in the End,"
Atlanta Journal-Constitution, July 19, 2001

3 Work contexts

Analysis of problems, proposal of solutions, and provision of information are often the focus of critical reasoning, writing, and speaking in work settings. These tasks call for focus on the following elements of critical thinking.

- Accurate analysis of problem or need for information; clear explanation of solution, with special attention to its reasonableness and logic
- Sharp focus on task, problem, or goal
- Attention to evidence that indicates the importance of the problem or task and the appropriateness of the solution
- Awareness of alternative explanations or solutions; concern with the likely consequences of actions

Exercise 1

A. Locate a site where two or more people discuss the same topic in writing or speaking, preferably directly addressing each others' reasoning: an online discussion, a newspaper opinion page with contrasting editorials, a magazine article or interview, or records of a debate. Briefly summarize the position of each participant, and then discuss how each addresses or criticizes flaws or gaps in the reasoning of the other, either directly or by implication.

B. Working with a group in class or online, begin discussion by briefly stating your conclusions on an issue and giving the most important evidence for them. Pass this statement on, asking the next person to add other conclusions, evidence, objections, and counter-arguments. Have the last person summarize conclusions, evidence, and objections and circulate the original document and the summary to the rest of the group. Discuss how your group's reasoning was changed by the serial dialogue.

12c Building a chain of reasoning: Practical suggestions

12c
reason

Critical thinking works toward creating a **chain of reasoning**, the path you take in linking ideas, conclusions, evidence, and alternative perspectives to explore an academic topic, urge people to take a stand, or make a recommendation at work. Some links in a chain may consist of *information*: examples, facts, evidence, details, and scientific or scholarly data. Other links may offer *ideas*: reasons, analysis, logical argument, citations from authorities, or differing points of view. It is crucial to be able to turn your thinking into a chain of critical reasoning that gives shape to your writing and speaking. The following strategies can help you develop this ability.

1 Recognize conclusions

The links in your chain of reasoning may include supporting conclusions and related (though nonessential) observations, interpretations, or recommendations. The end point of the chain—the **main conclusion**—is the most important. In some cases, you may offer more than one conclusion; for example, both adding workstations *and* upgrading software to keep better track of inventory.

STRATEGY

List your conclusions to strengthen your chain of reasoning.

- **List** all your conclusions (interpretations, opinions, and so on), both major and minor. Decide which make up your main area of focus, and which offer support as part of the chain of reasoning. Create two more lists, one for main and another for secondary conclusions.

- **Review** your two lists of conclusions. Do any more come to mind? Are any important assertions missing? If so, do you need to develop them?
- **Consider** the lists as readers might. Will they see any assertions as interpretations or judgments? Will they expect your conclusions?

2 Recognize information and inferences

A chain of reasoning needs both information and inferences. **Information** includes facts of all kinds—examples, data, details, quotations—that you present as reliable, confirmable, or generally undisputed. **Inferences** or **generalizations** are conclusions you reach based on and supported by information. Information turns into **evidence** when it's used to persuade a reader that an idea or proposition is reasonable.

12c
reason

STRATEGY

Distinguish between information and inference.

- **List the key facts** relating to your subject. Which facts will readers regard as undisputed? Which can you confirm with observations, details, or a reliable source? If facts are in dispute, what are the reasons for accepting them as you present them?
- **Next, list your inferences**. What do the facts imply? Which inferences reflect your understanding of the subject? What *might* happen or be true as a result of the facts?

12.2

3 Assess evidence and reasoning

Readers expect you to select evidence carefully, and to link it reasonably with assertions—that is, to proceed logically.

STRATEGY

Use these questions to evaluate evidence as you read and write.

- How *abundant* is the evidence? Is it *sufficient* to support your claim?
- Does it *directly* support the claim?
- How *relevant*, *accurate*, and *well documented* is the evidence?

Proceeding logically is complicated when evidence that would persuade one group of readers would not convince another group. Consider, for example, how two citizens' groups might respond to the proposal to build a greenway between two parks, one in Coolidge (an economically depressed neighborhood) and the other in Lake Stearns (a wealthy, stable neighborhood of fine older homes). Starting from the assumption that the generally law-abiding residents of Coolidge are deprived of shopping and services that have left the area because of a high crime rate, the Coolidge Citizens' Consortium logically supports the greenway because it will give residents access to recreation and shopping in Lake Stearns. In contrast, starting from the assumption that the balance of a peaceful, low-crime neighborhood can easily be upset, another group, Preserve Lake Stearns, argues logically that though most Coolidge residents are law-abiding, the greenway will draw some habitual criminals who will undermine the quality of life in both neighborhoods. Each side reasons logically, but each starts with different assumptions and arrives at different conclusions. (See also Chapter 55.)

STRATEGY

Ask questions to evaluate your assumptions.

- How do I view the groups of people on each side of this issue?
- What will my readers want in a plan that addresses this problem?
- What do specialists in this field see as questions worth investigating?

12c
reason

4 Consider your and your readers' assumptions

Some of your assumptions and values as a writer are easy to identify, but others are unspoken. After hearing a lot of talk at work about efficiency, you might think that your co-workers and readers want only to cut costs. But preserving jobs and offering a quality product are also shared goals. The success of your reasoning may depend on how closely your assumptions correspond to those of your audience.

STRATEGY

Focus on assertions to anticipate how readers may respond to your reasoning.

- List your assertions that identify cause-effect links, classify or compare, connect generalizations and examples, or define. Delete or rethink any that are weak or possibly illogical (see 55d).

- To spot weak reasoning, imagine a skeptical reader's reaction to each assertion.

  WEAK   Violence in schools is rising because of increased violence in movies and on TV.

  READER'S REACTION: **Is this true? My kids watch a lot of TV, but they aren't more violent than I was as a kid, when TV was far less violent.**

Exercise 2

A. Locate a document whose success or failure depends on the quality of its reasoning: a proposal, a position paper, an editorial, an academic article, or a memo on an important issue. Read it carefully, and identify its conclusions and the main kinds of evidence it presents. Next, try to identify any assumptions the writer makes that differ considerably from yours or those of another possible audience. Finally, use the strategy in 12c-3 to assess the quality of the evidence.

B. Share your document with a group of readers, and ask them to analyze it critically as in Exercise 2A. When they have finished, share your critical analyses and account for any differences, if you can. Decide as a group whether you consider the document successful or unsuccessful, and be ready to explain why.

12d
reason

12d Representing yourself through critical reasoning

The way you represent your reasoning in writing or speaking is crucial to the acceptance of your information and ideas. Will your audience know that you have analyzed information and ideas critically? Will they recognize that you are presenting your ideas and those of others in balanced, thoughtful ways?

Look again at the ways the writers of two letters to the editor represent themselves in arguing about the Coolidge/Lake Stearns greenway project.

WRITER 1

City planners must be out of their minds to cook up this crazy idea. Drug pushers and thieves will have a field day preying on the people who use Lake Stearns Park, and soon the whole neighborhood will be destroyed by crime. We must stop these insane public officials before they totally destroy our lives with their senseless fantasies.

WRITER 2

The proposal to create a greenway between Coolidge and Lake Stearns Parks appears to bridge the gap between these two different communities. But the greenway will not solve the existing problems in Coolidge Park. Residents near Lake Stearns are unlikely to ride their bikes or jog into Coolidge, and the presence of Coolidge residents in Stearns will only create a feeling, unjustified though it may be, of defensiveness. City funds could better be used to improve Coolidge Park by adding lighting, a basketball court, and an updated community center.

Both letters argue the same point: the greenway proposal is shortsighted. But think about the way these two writers present themselves.

WRITER 1	**WRITER 2**
Attacks proposers and Coolidge residents	Focuses on the proposal
Uses emotionally charged words (*insane*, *crazy*)	Uses balanced language
Comes up with vague ideas (stopping officials)	Offers specific alternatives
Stereotypes Coolidge residents	Suggests enhancing quality of life in Coolidge
Seems impulsive, shallow, uninformed	Seems balanced and thoughtful

12d
reason

Clearly, the persona created by the first writer is unlikely to lend credibility to what the writer has to say, and may discourage readers from agreeing with the writer's point of view. What can you do to avoid representing yourself in such a negative manner? What can you do to create a representation that encourages an audience to respect and trust what you have to say? The following suggestions may help.

1 Be well informed

Whether you're writing an academic paper or making a public statement, you need to be well informed and to help your audience benefit from your knowledge, through both the quality of your insights and the depth and relevance of the information you present. Information, issues, and ideas are rarely isolated; they're embedded in the social, occupational, historical, or disciplinary contexts that surround a topic.

STRATEGY

Explore what you know, and draw on the insights and perspectives of others. List what you know about your topic and what surrounds it. Identify the most important areas, given your purpose, and try to define what's still unclear and where you might find material to fill the gaps.

- Use face-to-face or electronic discussions (see Chapter 13) to identify issues, conclusions, evidence, and possible objections to your reasoning.
- Put your thoughts on paper tentatively, and then identify gaps in your evidence or logic by reading what others say about the topic or issue.
- Ask others to read your drafts critically and to identify reasonable objections that you can address as you revise.
- Put your work aside for a while; then read it as your readers might, noting any gaps that undermine clarity, persuasiveness, or credibility.

2 Acknowledge other perspectives and anticipate readers' reactions

If you fail to acknowledge other views, contrary arguments, conflicting evidence, or alternative solutions to a hotly contested issue, your readers may find your presentation one-sided and question your credibility. By anticipating such reactions, you can complete your chain of reasoning, building readers' confidence in you and your conclusions.

12d reason

3 Be balanced and reasonable

Emotional language may be appropriate when you're urging a public audience to act on the basis of shared belief. The same language would probably irritate, even offend, co-workers or academic readers, who generally expect critical analysis of information. As you select the words and tone to represent your thinking, you create an image of yourself—a persona—whose qualities may shape readers' responses. Your persona can make your reader trust and respect you, distrust and dislike you, or find you imbalanced and your conclusions ridiculous or unconsidered.

UNCONSIDERED   The greenway will just transport the Coolidge low-lifes into Lake Stearns Park and destroy its peace and quiet.

> READER 1: What's a "low-life"? Is this term based on race? or class? Is everyone in Coolidge a "low-life"?

> READER 2: Why—and how—would people from Coolidge destroy the "peace and quiet" of Lake Stearns?

4 Assess the appropriateness of strong bias to the occasion

To write effectively, you must know when to be cool and logical and when to show emotional commitment. At work, bias is expected when you represent an organization, but you'll need to write objective internal memos and reports. In public, your devotion to a cause generally will be accepted as such. Your academic writing, however, should lean toward unimpassioned, reasoned assessments.

STRATEGY

Adjust your bias to the occasion. Try to judge whether strong opinion is appropriate for your writing situation. Imagine a scale running from biased, opinionated writing to objective, neutral writing. Put an *X* somewhere on the scale to indicate your best assessment of your readers' expectations. Now put an *O* on the scale to indicate your best assessment of where your draft fits. If you find any distance between the *X* and the *O*, rework your word choice, your sentence structures, and the claims you're making until your draft better suits your situation.

<--->
BIASED, OPINIONATED   **OBJECTIVE, NEUTRAL**

A WORD ABOUT SPEAKING

Audiences bring to your presentation both an interest in your ideas and a kind of "critical listening" strategy that helps them to interpret, digest, and contemplate your ideas, sometimes with a healthy skepticism. As you create your talking points, be especially careful to analyze your presentation for excessive or unwarranted bias. Don't mistake interest or enthusiasm for bias; it's one thing to show passion for your subject matter, and another to be unjustifiably passionate about only one view, perspective, or conclusion.

12d
reason

Exercise 3

A. Locate an essay, article, or report on a controversial topic or issue, and analyze the ways in which the writer succeeds or fails to convincingly represent his or her reasoning. Begin by deciding what community or communities of readers the author is addressing. Base your judgments on the presentation's appropriateness for particular readers, and on its purpose. Use the following questions to guide your analysis:

1. Does the writer appear well informed?
2. Does the writer acknowledge other perspectives?
3. Does the writer seem to respect his or her audience?
4. Is the presentation balanced and reasonable?
5. Does the writer anticipate readers' reactions?
6. Is the writer's bias appropriate for the occasion?

B. Share with a group of other readers the document you analyzed in Exercise 3A. As a group, prepare a revision plan addressing ways the writer could improve the presentation of his or her reasoning. Then choose one paragraph from the text and, as a group, revise it according to your plan.

CHAPTER 13

WRITING IN ONLINE COMMUNITIES

Thanks to computer technology and advances in telecommunication, vast amounts of information can be had with a few keystrokes or clicks of a mouse. Easy access to this information has improved the lives of students and researchers, helped civic groups to publicize their efforts, and brought knowledge and information to many ordinary citizens.

But online environments are not just places to get information, like books in a library. Whenever you participate in a course electronic mailing list, chat with friends through an online messaging service, email a question or comment to a nonprofit organization, or read and write in a Web-based forum, you are participating in an **online community**. Each of these communities follows certain standards for membership in the group. As you participate in online communities, you'll need to pay attention to the community's language, customs, and accepted standards, and learn to represent yourself in appropriate ways.

13a Writing online

Whether you are writing an email message to classmates about a collaborative project, building a personal Web site to supplement your résumé, or participating in an online "bulletin board" discussion about a local environmental issue, you need to consider the specific needs of your online audience, your purpose, how you wish to represent yourself to others, and the conventions of online language.

1 Finding your audience online

People usually join online communities because they are interested in a particular topic. Fans of the Dallas Cowboys can chat daily about the latest trade rumor or game story. Students in a course on African American literature and culture might design a Web-based forum to share interviews with local African American artists and activists. Opponents of a bill in Congress can use email to gather "electronic signatures" on petitions to their legislative representatives. In each instance, online writers must tailor their messages to the specific community to achieve their purposes.

As you explore various online resources in your field of interest, pay attention to the **format** of the information. Is it long and technical, brief and informal, argumentative or conversational? Are there many links to other sites and sources, or is the site self-contained? The format reveals the type of writing typically used in an online community as well as the type of writing the community will expect from you. Also be aware of the expected **decorum** (or conduct) of the community's members.

A brief period of "lurking" (reading without participating) is a good opportunity to determine whether the audience for a particular email discussion, Web forum, or other online community is appropriate to your own talents and expectations. It's also a good time to note who else frequently participates, and to learn the rules of participation or pick up any terms or ideas commonly employed.

2 Defining your purpose for writing online

Because it's so easy to send information and messages online, you may be tempted to participate very spontaneously in online communities. Remember that online communication has created so much more information for the average computer user that your audience may be irritated if your message doesn't really contribute anything new or have a clear purpose. If you quickly send an email response to a discussion you've just joined, without taking the time to see what messages have already been sent, you may seem to be "out of the loop" and lose credibility.

13a
online

STRATEGY

Before you commit to publishing your work on the Internet, consider carefully your readers and, above all, what you want to tell them.

- What's the context of my message? How does my information extend, amplify, or clarify prior information?
- Why will readers find my information helpful or interesting?
- What do I want readers to *do* with the information or ideas that I present: respond? take action? think more deeply about the issue?

3 Creating an online persona

When you participate in an online community, your **persona**, or how you represent yourself to others, can be developed in depth, because you can make repeated contributions in response to what others say. Still, this aspect of online communication differs from face-to-face communication in important ways.

- You can remain anonymous.
- You can represent yourself in as many styles or voices as you wish.
- You can use your real name or choose a made-up name.
- You can identify or conceal your gender or ethnicity.
- You can choose to be a "silent" type and contribute rarely, or you can contribute often.
- You can "lurk," in itself a choice of persona.

These choices, when made honestly and ethically, can be useful as you join new online communities. Tailor your persona to suit your purpose. If you're asking for a letter of recommendation, for example, you'll want to do so respectfully and formally. If you're contributing to an online peer review of a classmate's paper or presentation, you'll want to be supportive and friendly— but neither too casual nor too harshly critical.

4 Recognizing community standards: Netiquette

13a online

13.1

Online communities vary widely in the kinds of language and behavior they tolerate and expect from members. It's your responsibility to familiarize yourself with the commonsense guidelines (known as **netiquette**) that apply across nearly all Internet communities and to learn the standards of the specific group you want to address. Otherwise you may unintentionally create a negative persona: brash, hypercritical, bossy, insensitive, or crude. As in any social situation, members will discount or ignore such participants or "expel" them from the group. Here are some guidelines.

- **Think before you act.** You can't take back an email message once it's been sent. Never put anything in an email message you wouldn't want your mother to read in the newspaper. The same goes for Web pages: while you can always take them down, you never know how many people have already seen them—including potential employers.
- **Learn before you act.** Lurk and learn the norms of the community. Don't post to a group to ask what something means if you can find the answer on an FAQ (frequently asked questions) page at the group's site.
- **Act, don't react.** Avoid posting "flames" (personal attacks) to contributors you disagree with.
- **Don't "spam."** Spamming is sending unsolicited email to large groups. The practice is rude and, in some cases, illegal. Avoid sending off-topic messages.
- **Don't use ALL CAPS.** Like shouting, this practice is rude.

- **Attend to grammar.** Even if online messages seem informal, bad grammar, spelling mistakes, and poor word usage still convey a feeling of sloppiness or a lack of concern for readers.
- **Cut the fat.** Include only *relevant* information from previous messages. When you reply to a message, delete everything from the quoted original that's not necessary.
- **The Golden Rule of netiquette.** Don't forget that there are real people behind every computer that receives your email or loads your Web site.

13b Communicating with email

Email is a popular means of communication primarily because it's *fast*. But its speed shouldn't be an excuse to avoid writing carefully and thoughtfully before you send a message.

1 Writing email for different communities

There are two main types of electronic mail: individual mail and list-based mail. When you write individual mail, you decide exactly who will receive your message. When you write list-based mail, you address a predetermined audience of subscribers to a list, all of whom will receive what you write.

Don't assume, however, that individual mail is more "personal" and list mail is more "professional." Many lists are chatty with informal conversation between friends, and individual mail might be written as an introduction to a potential employer or to complain about a rent increase. As in any other type of writing, you must adopt the appropriate tone for your audience. If you don't adjust your persona to suit your purpose for writing, your message will likely not be communicated to your audience in the way you intend.

13b
email

2 Using the elements of email

Every email message has elements that convey a specific kind of information and help you effectively communicate your purpose or create your persona.

> **From.** State your identity in the "from line" of each email message you send. While some email programs show a sender's address in the "from" section, others display a chosen **screen name**, a self-identifier the user chooses. Your screen name creates an important part of your online persona. A screen name like *LeoFan* might entertain your friends, but it will not make a positive impression on a potential employer.

Sent. This line displays the date and time your mail is sent.

To. This line identifies the recipient of your email, either an individual or a group. Two other lines—"Cc:" (carbon copy) and "Bcc:" (blind carbon copy)—enable you to send mail to people who are not part of the primary audience, but who might be interested in the subject matter. With blind carbon copy, you can send copies without the main recipients knowing, because the addresses for the copies will not appear in the message sent to the main recipients.

Subject. Use this line to draw readers into reading the actual message. Short and clear subject lines are best. If you're adding commentary to a continuing "thread" or (discussion), the reply function of your mail program will usually automatically suggest the subject line: "Re: <Original Subject>."

Message body. Long messages are more likely to be deleted, left unread, or only partially read. If you're replying to someone, make clear what it is that you are replying to, but don't include previous messages in their entirety.

Signature or sig file. Sign your email. Differences between email programs mean that your message might not always be easily identified by the recipient. If you have a mail program that allows you to automatically attach a signature file, write out your full name and some contact information. Many people include clever quotations, song lyrics, and jokes in their signature files. Be aware of how such additions affect your online persona.

13b
email

3 Email appearance

Most email systems produce "primitive" text, without the formatting options that you have in word-processing programs. For the purposes of a vast number of daily email messages, it doesn't much matter what your text looks like. But a few considerations can also make your communications more efficient and can show your sensitivity to the needs of your audience.

- Don't let email do the work of full-length documents. If you need to send a paper, report, or other substantive text to someone, send it as an attached document or find some other means to convey it to your reader(s). It's difficult to read long texts sent via the email medium.
- Break up your messages into paragraphs. People become tired and frustrated reading long blocks of email text.
- Use emoticons and acronyms appropriately, based on your audience. **Emoticons** (*emotion* + *icon*) constitute a kind of shorthand code that allows writers to add a jolt of feeling to their text. Emoticons are faces drawn with keyboard characters; tilt your head to the left as you look at these.

:-)	grin	:-/	ambivalent
:-(	frown	:-0	shouting
;-)	wink	8-0	bug-eyed surprise

Internet **acronyms** are abbreviations for common phrases, which are used to speed up communication.

BTW	by the way	FYI	for your information
F2F	face-to-face	HTH	Hope that helps!
FAQ	frequently asked questions	TIA	thanks in advance
		IMHO	in my humble opinion

Emoticons and acronyms are generally considered to be appropriate for casual communication but not for professional or academic writing.

4 Using the functions of email

Just as each email message has certain elements (see 13b-2), every email program has buttons or commands that allow you to manage your correspondence in a variety of ways.

Reply and **Reply-all.** When you respond to a posting or email using the *Reply* function, your message will go to the person who sent you the message. When you use the *Reply-all* function, it will also go to any other people who received the original communication. (To determine who they are, check both the "To:" and "Cc:" lines.) Be careful when you use the *Reply-all* function, so that you don't accidentally post a personal note to a public space.

Forward. It's very easy to forward email; this is one of the reasons that Internet hoaxes are so common. Remember that what you have written can be forwarded to anyone who has an email account. Also, think carefully before forwarding other people's messages. Are you sure that the original author would want his or her message forwarded to someone else? When in doubt, urge the original author to send the message to the person(s) you have in mind.

Attach. Most mail programs allow you to attach and email files such as word-processor documents, spreadsheets, image files, and video clips. Not all mail programs support attachments, so you can't assume your recipients will always be able to read or open your attachments.

13c
online

13c Participating in online communities

The four most common formats for online communities are electronic mailing lists, newsgroups, Web forums, and "real-time" writing. Each format plays host to communities engaged in writing on a variety of topics.

1 Electronic mailing lists

Electronic mailing lists *come* to you. You *go* to newsgroups. The writing format and style concerns of each are similar. To join or subscribe to an **electronic mailing list**, the most common type of subscriber-based mailing list, you send an email message to the service that hosts the list. You then automatically receive all the messages from the list at your email address. When you post a message to an electronic mailing list, usually it's first reviewed by the list moderator (some lists, however, are not moderated). If it passes the moderator's standards, he or she sends it to the personal addresses of all the people subscribed. It's important, then, to adapt to the community's standards, or your messages will never be made available to your peers.

You can access **newsgroups** without having email messages sent to your personal address. You can scan the topics and threads for a subject that interests you and choose the individual posts you wish to read. Messages you send to a newsgroup are immediately posted and available for reading by anyone. Newsgroups are usually not moderated.

In all unmoderated situations, it's easy to become careless, especially because such situations often have an informal tone. But messages sent to electronic mailing lists and newsgroups can be read by anyone, and if the messages are archived, they can be accessed and read for years to come.

13c
online

2 Writing in Web-based forums

Web-based forums allow users to easily access sites where they can participate in conversations with others who share interests. More than a quarter of a million Web forums are already in existence, covering topics that range from current events to entertainment.

These Web forums are a refined version of the early text-only bulletin boards, which required special software. Unlike electronic mailing lists, which are mailed only to those who request to join, anyone with the proper software could read these bulletin boards. Some Web-based forums are moderated. Many, such as the popular CollegeEdge forums, ask you to set up a user name with a password; a few charge a fee for participation.

Writing in Web-based forums has adopted most of the conventions associated with those early bulletin boards: informal language, frequent use of emoticons and abbreviations, and the citing of previously written material to provide context.

3 Real-time writing

The Internet now supports a variety of ways for people to participate in "real-time" electronic discussions and communities. **Real time** means that the discussion takes place without delay; your words appear on the screen of every user involved in the discussion as soon as they are typed. Such conversations can take place between participants who are in the same classroom or scattered around the world.

The most popular real-time communities in current use are **chat rooms** hosted by private Internet services or available via the Internet Relay Chat (IRC) network. Chat rooms are usually quite informal and have become a popular way for celebrities to "meet" their fans online. Chats open to the public, such as interviews with politicians or "town hall" meetings, are almost always moderated, so in those contexts your writing will be controlled by an "editor" who decides whether you may post your questions or comments.

The real-time venue most often used in academic situations and in some corporate settings is called a **MUD**, or multi-user domain. Users learn a series of commands to communicate with each other and to "move" from room to room, or place to place, in a carefully described text environment. They may adopt permanent characters, or "avatars," to regularly interact with other participants. Writing in MUD space, while playful and informal in many cases, requires significantly more practice than chat rooms to attain the comfort level most writers need for effective participation. MUD technology is frequently used to connect classrooms on different campuses, or even in different countries, so that students can discuss a group project and post their work.

13d Writing for the World Wide Web

13d
web

13.2

There are various types of Web pages. The most common is the **personal home page**, an individual author's effort to create a place for herself online. Additionally, you will see commercial sites (including corporate pages, sites sponsored by nonprofit organizations, and online shopping opportunities), educational sites (including school and university pages, scholarly journals, and free informational presentations), and news/entertainment sites (including newspapers, magazines, and other media). **Search engines** are dedicated entirely to indexing and sorting Web pages for user convenience.

1 Establishing a purpose and persona for your Web page

If you're building a personal home page on the Web, consider what you want the general format to be. Are you fulfilling an assignment for a biology class project on coral reef preservation? You might include maps and photographs of reefs to illustrate your research, along with links to sites sponsored by environmental organizations. Are you setting up an "online business card"? Limit the material to very general information and contact listings. Will your site function like a résumé? Provide detailed information about your professional interests and abilities, perhaps with links to volunteer organizations you have worked with and classroom projects you are proud of. Are you designing a resource for people with interests similar to yours? Add links and commentary on sources you find useful. Or are you producing a kind of autobiography, so your friends and family can see what you're up to?

You need to determine your audience and what aspects of yourself you want to present to the online community. If your site is designed for your instructor and your fellow students, will you be surprised or annoyed if someone you do not want to hear from or have never met sends you email commenting on your site? If your autobiographical page shows off your keen sarcastic wit and comments on your political views, are you comfortable knowing that a potential employer may find that site using a simple search engine?

STRATEGY

Before building any Web site, visit sites with similar purposes. Make lists of what you do and do not like about these sites. Consider contacting the authors and designers of those sites to ask for advice before you start, or for feedback after you have begun. Some sites include design rationales or "About This Site" pages that describe the site's design goals and features. (See, for example, <www.ncsu.edu/rationale.html>.) And, just as you would ask for peer feedback on a paper in progress, ask fellow students, colleagues, or friends for comments and suggestions. Be careful in naming your site. Search engines will index it based on the words that appear in the title and in the text of the site. Select your words carefully, and when you're ready to publish, visit the major search engine sites to learn the process of registering and indexing your site and its title. When writing for the Web, effective search engine registration is almost as important as ensuring the accuracy of the information in your site.

13d web

2 Considering your audience

Getting feedback from your intended Web audience is the best way to make sure you are effectively participating in an online community. There are a few simple principles to remember when constructing and maintaining a site.

- **Content is key.** Most Web users are looking for information, not "cool" design and graphics. Make sure any graphics reinforce your topic rather than just take up space.
- **"Cluster" your content.** Users prefer to scan online information when it is organized in simple, functional categories. A long list of topics arranged alphabetically is difficult to scan. Group related topics together in short menus.
- **Update, update, update.** In many ways, outdated content is worse than none at all. Don't leave "under construction" icons all over your site.

- **Count the clicks.** Your users should not have to navigate more than three clicks to find information they need. Users often get lost or discouraged if they have to make four or more clicks to find critical information. Try not to bury content in too many menus and subcategories.
- **Check your links.** If your site includes links to supporting documents and data or to other sites of interest, be sure to check those links from time to time to make sure they are still accurate. Repair or replace broken links often.
- **Allow ample "white space."** Online readers generally find black type on white background the most readable; avoid too many contrasting colors and textures and use a consistent set of colors throughout your site.
- **Test your Web pages on various platforms and browsers.** Something designed using *Internet Explorer* on a PC may look significantly different in *Netscape Navigator* on a Macintosh. Check to see that your images download quickly: most of your users will probably be on 56 Kbps modems, so be sure to test from off-site locations as well as on campus or in your studio.
- **Always include contact information,** preferably in the form of an automatic email link. However, *never* put your full name, address, and phone number (or other vital information) in this space.
- **Build feedback into the process.** Monitor the way visitors access and navigate your site, ask for their feedback, and respond promptly to user suggestions.

13e
plag

(These guidelines are adapted from Kelly Houk and Brad Mehlenbacher, "Design Rationale." 20 Dec. 2001 <http://www.ncsu.edu/rationale.html>.)

13e Avoiding plagiarism when working online

The easy availability of so much content online can challenge the very foundation of what we mean when we talk about plagiarism. Careful documentation of sources in your work is more critical to effective communication than ever before. (For more on plagiarism, see Chapter 49.)

13.3

1 Always document or credit information borrowed from others

It's so easy to forward electronic mail, download software programs and images, create Web pages, and copy material published online that governments worldwide are being forced to reconsider the concept of "intellectual property." Who owns the rights to words, images, or ideas? How can those rights be protected without prohibiting the free flow of information that the Internet makes possible? These issues make it important for you to document every online source you use in developing your writing.

Also remember that your credibility depends on the credibility of the community resource you choose to rely on. If you are writing a paper about diabetes, citing sources from a collection of official American Diabetes Association Web pages and a moderated electronic mailing list of endocrinologists is far more effective (and responsible) than citing email from a local bulletin board about a new home remedy. For all information from online sources you wish to cite, ask yourself, "Where did it come from?" If you are not confident about your answer, your instructor might be able to help you evaluate the credibility of a source. You should also be prepared to find an alternative site.

Cutting and pasting information from Web sites and other Internet resources into a single document for later use is a good way to consolidate your research. This new form of note taking, however, can lead to accidental plagiarism. It is easy to forget where something originally came from and mistakenly convince yourself the writing is your own!

STRATEGY

13e
plag

- Always write down the address of any Web site you are using, and clearly label text you copy from that site. For easy reference, print the first page of each Web site you're using in case your later drafts require further documentation. The printout should include the site's URL so you can return to it for future reference and also for citation purposes.
- Always note the date when you found the information. Web sites can be updated daily, and your cited information may disappear. In addition, you will need to provide the access date in your citation if you use the information in your final document.
- If you're citing an email, electronic mailing list, or Web forum message that has not been posted to a publicly accessible location, ask the author's permission before quoting. It's a good idea to do this even if the posting is public.
- Corroborate your sources. Follow the journalist's rule: If you can't find the same information in at least two credible places on the Internet, don't use the material.

2 Acting ethically online

When working online, do so ethically and professionally. If you're new to the Internet, it will not take you long to discover paper mills—the electronic equivalent of the infamous fraternity and dormitory "test files." Additionally, many writing classes now post their work to the Web for peer review, and you may find these papers and projects when you use a search engine. You should carefully consider the moral implications of borrowing such Internet resources and claiming them as your own. Also keep in mind that your instructor has access to those same sources. A common practice among teachers who suspect plagiarism is to input random phrases from student papers into a search engine and see whether those phrases appear anywhere else on the Web.

Many employers worry that the Internet provides workers with too much opportunity to "surf," to catch up on sports scores, make vacation plans, or download inappropriate material using company equipment on company time. Keep in mind that it is now possible, and legal, for these employers to track and monitor the Web sites and other Internet resources that employees are accessing, and to block out certain kinds of material. If you are using an email account provided by your employer, you should be aware that in most situations you don't have any legal expectation of a right to privacy for anything you write or post from that account.

When you're using an email account provided by a college or university—even when you access it away from campus—you are responsible for adhering to the institution's policies and regulations. If you access the Internet through a service provider, you're obligated to abide by the client rights and responsibilities outlined in your contract.

13e
plag

CHAPTER 14

DESIGNING DOCUMENTS

What makes a research project, an essay, or a report clear? How does a document convey complex information memorably and persuasively? Why do some résumés and letters grab readers' attention? How do they build confidence in the writer's ability and knowledge? Why are some forms hard to read and some instruction manuals difficult to understand?

The answers to such questions often lie in the way a document is designed: how the writer integrates text and graphics, how visual aids (such as photographs, charts, and illustrations) are used, and how the type itself is laid out on the page to engage the reader and convey meaning clearly. Well-designed documents don't just appeal to readers and facilitate communication; they also present a positive image of the person who created the document, making that person's message more persuasive.

14a **design**

14a Goals of document design

By using the principles of good document design, you convey your ideas and information effectively. A well-designed document helps you accomplish the following objectives.

- **Help readers visualize and understand information.** A chart can show readers the relationship between education and income level; a photograph can bring home the terrible effects of tornadoes.
- **Help readers locate the information they want.** Headings signal the parts of a report that contain specific data, provide directions, or outline a problem. A line drawing shows which parts of a reader's community are threatened by toxic waste and which are not.
- **Emphasize key points or ideas.** Boldface or colored type can make your key recommendations stand out. Material set off from the text in a box gets special attention from readers.
- **Send signals to readers about your knowledge of a subject and your perspective.** Detailed but easy-to-read charts and tables show readers you know your subject well and can convey your knowledge simply and

clearly. Well-chosen lists and drawings can help emphasize your interpretation of a subject and add weight to your opinion on an issue.

- **Let readers know that you've carefully considered them as you've planned and created a document.** This consideration for readers creates a positive image of your persona. By following the design conventions of different communities of writers and readers, you show your readers that you understand their expectations and concerns. By putting complicated information in visual form, and by highlighting key statements in complicated explanations or arguments, you project an image of yourself as someone who cares about communicating ideas in ways that readers can understand easily.
- **Make your writing persuasive.** By strategically using images and design as well as words, you show that you're aware of different perspectives on your subject and that you're skilled at the many techniques for conveying meaning. When blended with effective reasoning and clear expression, skillful document design can encourage readers to pay special attention to your conclusions and possibly persuade them to see things from your point of view.

14b Planning your document

Designing effective documents requires planning. There is no substitute for taking the time to consider your writing task and audience before determining format, layout, and what visual aids (if any) you will use to support and enhance your presentation.

14b
design

1 Consider the principles of document design

Designing effective, engaging documents requires an understanding of the nature of the printed page and computer screen, as well as a clear understanding of the abilities and limitations of readers in processing information. Study the following principles of document design.

14.1

- **Presentation matters.** If your document is crowded or difficult to understand, the reader will simply not take the time to read it. On the other hand, if your document is easy to understand because of your effective use of headings, graphics, and other elements of design, your readers will respond positively.
- **First impressions are critical.** Often the first impression you make is based on a document you have created. This is certainly the case when you're applying for a job, turning in your first essay in a class, or sending a letter to a local government official. In each of these cases, your document represents you to your readers.
- **Documents are visual.** All too often people forget that their texts are also pictures. Visual elements include the letters and numbers on the page as well as any photos, charts, or other visual aids. Whether you

are producing traditional paper documents or Web pages, you need to organize graphics and text on the page or computer screen to engage readers, direct their attention, prioritize information, and make the experience of reading enjoyable and efficient. To design effective documents, you must plan ahead (see 14c), and learn to use the various elements of design, such as layout (see 14d), type (see 14e), and visual aids (see 14f). Understanding how all these elements work will help you to create unified, attractive pages that will catch your reader's attention and achieve your intended effect.

2 Consider your rhetorical situation and readers' needs

Your document design choices are affected by the same fundamental considerations that define your writing task: audience, purpose, and context. On the basis of your topic or focus, your understanding of your reader(s), and other considerations such as time and equipment, you must make thoughtful choices about the kind of document you will produce.

Readers need different things from different documents. The same reader approaches an essay about air pollution quite differently than a set of instructions concerning the operation of a chain saw. Equally true is the fact that two people might approach either document differently. An engineer for a chemical plant that is working to comply with EPA guidelines will read the essay about pollution very differently than will a homeowner who lives downwind from the plant.

As you participate in various communities, pay special attention to the way information is presented and received. For example, while your academic readers will expect to read a document from beginning to end, few in the work community will read that way. Eager to get to the point, readers in the work community audience are likely to limit their reading to the introduction and the conclusion. Thus, if you want to communicate effectively in that community, you must ensure that those sections are clear, easy to access, and persuasive.

3 Determine the form and shape of your document

The following questions will help you visualize the big picture (the entire document) and then move to the small but important details (the way you integrate the various design elements).

- What format or document type will you use? How will you lay out the pages? (See 14c.)
- What highlighting devices will you use to make your organization readily visible? For example, will you use a table of contents? color? (See 14c.)
- What kind of font, typeface, and type size will you use? (See 14d.)
- Will you use visual aids? If so, which ones? Why? How will you integrate them with the text? (See 14e.)
- If you use certain aids, such as photographs or drawings, are there any copyright issues or legal concerns you must address first? (See 14e.)

14b
design

Create a mock-up version. After you answer these questions, you should create a mock-up version of your document—a quick sketch that will help with planning. Such quickly sketched versions of a document will help you visualize how the various design elements addressed in Sections 14c–e work together.

14c Laying out your document

Layout refers to the way elements such as words, sentences, lists, tables, graphs, and pictures are arranged on a page or computer screen. Laying out your document effectively involves presenting information in a way that is easy to access, read, understand, and use. Good document design does not apply only to special documents such as letters of application and résumés; every document you write, from the directions to your party to your term paper in history, requires careful and thoughtful attention to layout.

1 Use visual cues

To increase the readability of your document, use visual cues such as boldface text and color. These devices will simplify your readers' task and influence their attitudes. Always use visual cues with your audience and purpose in mind, and be careful to avoid overwhelming your text with visuals. Often, simplicity—a few well-chosen visual cues—will work best.

14c
design

Use highlighting to direct the reader's eye and create emphasis. Typographic devices such as **boldface**, *italics*, shading, underlining, and boxes signal distinctions among items in a text, create impact by emphasizing a specific section, and help the reader locate main sections.

- *Italics* and **boldface type** should be used sparingly to create emphasis. Compare these examples.

  When you want to emphasize something, consider using **bold type**.

  When you want to emphasize something, consider using bold type.

- Use *italics* for emphasis or when irony or humor is intended. (See 40b for more on using italics.)

  His rent was late for the *third* straight month.

- Use capital letters for emphasis only, and infrequently. Using all capital letters in body texts becomes monotonous and hard to read. (See Chapter 39 for more on using capital letters.)

- Don't overuse exclamation marks and <u>underlining</u>. Be **angry**, or perhaps *angry*, but not <u>angry!!!</u> Underlining, particularly on Web pages, can cause confusion because hypertext links are almost always underlined. (For more on exclamation points and underlining, see 37c, 40b.)

Use color to create order in a document. Effectively using color can reveal patterns and relationships (charts and graphs), speed searches, and help readers to identify recurring themes (titles and subtitles). It can aid in decision making. Be aware, however, that colors have different connotations depending on the professional audience (as shown in the following list), and that using color is not appropriate or necessary in all contexts.

COLOR	ENGINEERING	MEDICINE	FINANCE
blue	cold/water	death	reliable/corporate
red	danger	healthy/oxygenated	loss
green	safe/environmental	infection	profit

14c
design

STRATEGY

As you draft and revise your documents, choose color carefully. Follow these basic principles for the use of color in effective document design.

- Use color to accomplish specific goals (to warn or caution, for instance).
- Use color to communicate, not to decorate.
- Use color to prioritize information. Readers will go to bright colors first.
- Use colors to symbolize. Draw on your knowledge of your readers.
- Use color to identify a recurring theme or to sequence information.
- Use color to code different symbols or sections and thus make it easier to search for information.

2 Arrange information effectively

www
14.2

Effective document design enables users to locate important information quickly.

Use white space to organize information into chunks and guide the reader's eye. *White space* is the term that describes open space not filled by other design elements. It can be the spaces between letters, words, or lines, within a paragraph, or between paragraphs. It also includes the margins (top, bottom, and sides) of a page (usually one or one and a half inches), and the space surrounding graphics. Used effectively, white space can guide the reader's eye from one point to another without overwhelming her. Crowded pages are never crowd pleasers; always be sure there is adequate white space on every page of your document.

Use informative headings to help readers find information. Headings are brief phrases that forecast or announce content in upcoming sections. Because they are usually larger and darker than the body text or other content of a document, headings work to catch a reader's eye—as they do in this handbook. Headings also move readers along, helping them to see the visual organization of a document (the big picture) and to find the information they seek at a glance.

14c
design

STRATEGY

Based on the organization of your information and how efficiently readers will be able to make sense of it (see 4b), create appropriate headings for your document. Adhere to the following principles as you create your headings.

- Use consistent font and style for headings.
- Use different sizes of type to indicate different levels of headings.
- Make your headings stand out—use boldface type and/or white space between headings and text.
- Position your headings consistently (for instance, if you center first-level headings, as in the example that follows, do so throughout your document).
- Make headings content-specific and task- or reader-oriented: **Deducting Student Loan Interest** rather than **Student Loan Interest**.
- Make headings parallel in structure (see Chapter 27).
- Use only those headings you need; avoid clutter.

Here is an example of an effective heading structure.

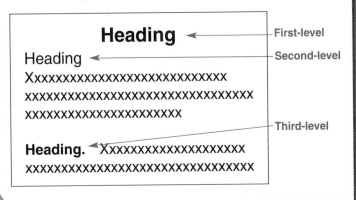

Use lists to highlight important information and to separate or group items. Lists are an effective way to present information concisely, making it easy for readers to get to your major points. They also help to break up dense text and make your document more attractive. Lists help readers complete tasks (a "to do" list, for example), and are useful whenever you need to group related items (a list of healthy food groups versus not-so-healthy food groups). Consider highlighting the items in your lists with visual cues such as bullets or numbers.

Rely on visual conventions. Just as our language has grammatical conventions, there are conventions for document design. Depending on the community you're in and the document you're writing, readers will expect to find certain features. Humanities papers written in MLA style will follow MLA formatting conventions (see Chapter 51); APA papers will follow APA guidelines (see Chapter 52). Letters, memos, reports, and brochures all come with a host of formatting and visual conventions. Your history teacher will expect to see a report that follows certain conventions while your prospective employer will look for others in your résumé. Learn which conventions you must follow in the particular document you're designing, including which ones are essential and which are optional.

14d
design

14d Using type

In designing your document, you can take advantage of the large variety of fonts, typefaces, and type sizes now available. But remember to do so judiciously, always sensitive to your audience and purpose. Most readers would rather see few fonts than many (at most, two or three fonts in a single document). In addition, always select a typeface or font that speaks to the audience in a tone that best reflects the subject matter without sacrificing readability.

- **Use proper type size and weight to influence readers and help them read the text quickly and easily.** Type size affects legibility. Standard text type size is 10 or 12 point because both are easy to read (see the sample font sizes below). Type size also affects how the reader will perceive the information: the larger the type, the more important the information will appear. Twelve-point type is the most common in academic texts.

12 point   10 point
A New Deal.   A New Deal.

Type weight (letter width and stroke thickness) is also important in reinforcing your message levels. Because some fonts have thicker or wider letters, you can use them to highlight messages without relying on changing the type style (boldface, italics, shadow, and so on).

- **Make reading easier by using serif and sans serif typefaces appropriately.** Serif typefaces are those that have "feet" or small perpendicular strokes at the end of each main stroke of the letter. Sans serif fonts lack them.

N   N

Serif   Sans serif

Readers tend to find serif typefaces easier on their eyes in long documents. Sans serif fonts are harder to read in long documents but work well in titles, headings, and labels. They also work well for material that will be presented on a computer screen. Notice how serif and sans serif fonts are used in this handbook, for example. There are many variations of serif typefaces; a few examples include Times New Roman, Courier, Garamond, and **Century Schoolbook**. Sans serif faces include Arial, **Impact**, and Tahoma.

- **Add interesting flourishes with display or decorative fonts** such as *Mistral*, **Sixpack**, **Cooper Black**, or *Emma Script*. Some documents, such as brochures, invitations, or posters, require special touches to catch readers' attention or sway their emotions. Decorative fonts have strong personalities and do this well. However, these fonts are intended to be more ornamental than informative, so they should be used sparingly, and with discretion.

- **Add emphasis or direct attention with symbol fonts.** Used carefully, symbol fonts (such as those you find in Zapf Dingbats, Monotype Sorts, or Wingdings) can direct a reader's attention, emphasize a point, and help you add simple graphic flourishes to your documents. There are many of these special characters, which you'll often find listed under "Symbols" in a pull-down menu in a word-processing program or in a list of fonts. You may find ornamental symbols and icons like these in your font menu.

14e Using visuals

Albert Einstein once said, "I rarely think in words at all." He thought in symbols and pictures; he envisioned concepts and information. This is an essential concept for writers to understand. Sometimes words aren't sufficient, or aren't as efficient as tables, graphs, charts, photographs, maps, and drawings are in making a point. These visual aids, or graphics, are effective in bringing information to life.

14e
design

- Graphics communicate what words cannot.
- Visuals are understood more quickly than words.
- Tables, charts, and other visuals help readers learn and retain information.
- Graphics entice readers.

Consider the needs of readers as well as your context as you decide how to use and choose appropriate graphic and visual aids (if they are needed at all) for a particular project.

1 Use tables to organize information

Tables are useful when you need to present information—usually text or numbers, in columns and rows—in a relatively small space. They're also helpful in depicting complex information. Tables are labeled as such and are numbered and titled, as in the example that follows; all other graphics are called *figures*.

Table 1 Services on the Campus WWW Site (percentages, by sector)				
	PUBLIC UNIVERSITY	PRIVATE UNIVERSITY	PUBLIC 4-YR. COLLEGE	PRIVATE 4-YR. COLLEGE	COMMUNITY COLLEGE
Undergraduate application	76.3	78.8	69.4	54.1	39.1
Course catalog	86.4	91.3	75.7	62.2	54.7
Program/degree requirements	83.1	69.5	73.9	68.4	46.0
Course registration	52.5	39.1	27.0	10.7	16.1
Library catalog	84.4	95.7	83.8	68.4	37.3
Student transcripts	44.1	43.5	22.5	12.2	8.7
Instructional software	57.5	60.9	26.1	26.5	5.0
e-Commerce (new)	18.5	13.0	1.8	4.1	3.1
Bookstore (new)	49.2	52.2	28.8	28.5	9.9

Source: Casey Green, *The Campus Computing Project.*

2 Use graphs and charts to represent relationships among data

If you want to emphasize trends, add credibility, interest the reader in data, or forecast future values, then graphs or charts are very useful. Graphs, like Fig. 1, rely on two labeled axes (vertical and horizontal) to show relationships between two variables.

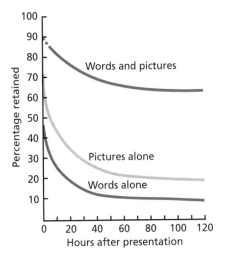

Fig. 1. Audience retention of information.
Source: Maurice Broner, "Stand Up and Be Heard," *IEEE Trans. Eng. Writing Speech* EWS-7 (1964):25–30.

Charts display relationships in other ways. Some, such as pie charts (see Fig. 2), show percentages of a whole; others, such as bar charts, compare items or show correlations (see Fig. 3 on p. 182). Graphs and charts also need to be labeled with brief captions and have a figure number (in MLA style, the word *Figure* is abbreviated *Fig.*, as in all the samples shown here).

14e
design

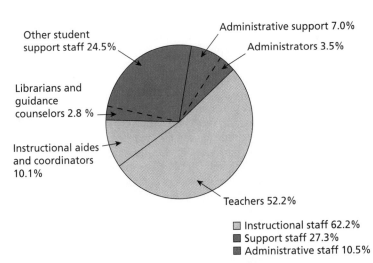

Fig. 2. Distribution of elementary and secondary education staff, by category.
Source: U.S. Department of Education, National Center for Education Statistics, *State Nonfiscal Survey: School Year 1993–94* <http://nces.ed.gov/pubs/96213.html#figure>.

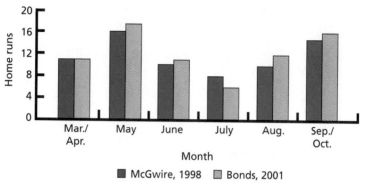

Fig. 3. Bonds versus McGwire: Chasing history.
Source: Based on data provided by ESPN <http://sports.espn.go.com/mlb/chasing>.

3 Use other visual devices

Use drawings and diagrams to present physical appearance, to show connections among parts, and to illustrate spatial relationships. Think of the diagrams you've seen in auto manuals or that you've used to set up a priority schedule for schoolwork. All such diagrams and drawings aid readers by helping them actually *see* how to proceed with a task.

You can also use photographs or illustrations to record reality, to define and provide examples, the way newspapers and magazines do. Photographs and illustrations are useful when you don't have time or expertise to create a drawing, or when the external appearance (rather than the structure) is the focus. But keep in mind the need to credit sources, and consider the appropriateness of such visual devices in various contexts—and avoid overusing them.

Some word-processing programs include a selection of "clip art"—simple drawings that you can easily paste into your document to enhance a point or draw a reader's attention. You can also purchase CDs of clip art and photographs you can use to enhance your documents. Many Web sites also offer clip art and stock photography. In all cases, however, you should be sure that your use of images complies with copyright law. Most disks, publications, and Web sites of clip art and photographs include information on copyright; do not assume that images are available for use without researching the source thoroughly.

STRATEGY

- Choose the appropriate visual aid.
- Use the visual to illustrate one point, and make sure it supports the point or argument. Don't use graphics as decoration or filler.

- Keep graphics as simple as possible.
- Set graphics off with white space. Don't crowd them.
- Use textual cues to guide the reader: label the graphics consistently, number them, and provide accurate, brief captions that explain the relationship of the graphic to the text.
- Help readers make sense of your graphics by positioning them as close to their text references as possible.
- Be sure to credit sources for borrowed graphics.

A WORD ABOUT SPEAKING

Good oral presentations often include handouts or visuals shown to the audience on an overhead or laptop projector. All of the principles of effective document design apply to such written material and visuals, except that in some ways you need to be even more diligent in your sensitivity to the needs of your audience.

- Don't expect your audience to be able to process material too quickly. Either give them the time they need to read the supplementary material or keep it very brief—a few bullet points, for example.
- Look at the layout of your material. Cluttered overhead transparencies won't make your points clear. Avoid hard-to-read fonts and graphics.
- Remember that most charts and graphs take longer for audiences to comprehend than words in short phrases or bullet points. Keep them simple and direct.

14f
models

14f Model documents

The following model documents (on pp. 184–187) show how the principles of document design outlined in this chapter work in action.

14.3

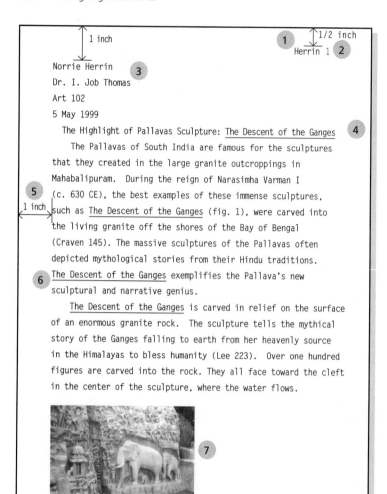

① 1/2 inch

1 inch

Herrin 1 ②

Norrie Herrin ③

Dr. I. Job Thomas

Art 102

5 May 1999

The Highlight of Pallavas Sculpture: The Descent of the Ganges ④

⑤ 1 inch

The Pallavas of South India are famous for the sculptures that they created in the large granite outcroppings in Mahabalipuram. During the reign of Narasimha Varman I (c. 630 CE), the best examples of these immense sculptures, such as The Descent of the Ganges (fig. 1), were carved into the living granite off the shores of the Bay of Bengal (Craven 145). The massive sculptures of the Pallavas often depicted mythological stories from their Hindu traditions.

⑥ The Descent of the Ganges exemplifies the Pallava's new sculptural and narrative genius.

The Descent of the Ganges is carved in relief on the surface of an enormous granite rock. The sculpture tells the mythical story of the Ganges falling to earth from her heavenly source in the Himalayas to bless humanity (Lee 223). Over one hundred figures are carved into the rock. They all face toward the cleft in the center of the sculpture, where the water flows.

⑦

⑧ Fig. 1. The Descent of the Ganges, Mahabalipuram, Tamil Nadu, India, seventh century

① 1/2-inch margin at top

② Author's last name and page number on every page including the first, even if using a separate title page

③ Name, instructor's name, class, and date included

④ Title centered with no extra space before or after

⑤ 1-inch margin at left, right, and bottom

⑥ Text double-spaced throughout, including long quotations and works cited list

⑦ The author decided to include a photocopy of a photo she took of the sculpture. For best quality, she used the "photo" setting on the copier.

⑧ Figures are numbered and give proper credit to the artists. In this case the artist is unknown, so the work's title and location are given.

14f
models

THE POWER OF ONE
Alcohol Awareness Week
March 1 - 4, 1999 • UNC Charlotte

SPECIAL EVENTS

MONDAY, MARCH 1ST
Alcohol Insanity Tour '99
with Wendi Foxx
Nationally renowned comedienne
Wendi Foxx will entertain with Alcohol
Aware Educational Comedy.
McNight Hall 8pm

TUESDAY, MARCH 2ND
Copacabana Mocktail Bar
Representatives from RSA and SGA
will provide refreshing alcohol-free
"mocktails" in a tropical setting right
here on campus!
After Hours 11:30am-1:30pm

WEDNESDAY, MARCH 3RD
DUI: Decisions
Under the Influence
Campus Police will demonstrate the
hazards of drinking with sobriety
exercises performed on real life
students.
Poplar Hall 2nd floor 8pm

THURSDAY, MARCH 4TH
Pledge Card Drive
Join the campus community in
pledging not to drink and drive.
Belk Tower 11am-3pm

Sponsored by the Department of Housing &
Residence Life, Resident Students

Mine is the Power of One
The power to make my own
    decisions
The power to achieve all of my
    goals

Mine is the Power of One
The power to create the life I want
The power to impact the lives of
    others

Mine is the Power of One
The power to set responsible limits
The power to drink without
    driving

The Power that is Mine
Comes from within

The Power that is Mine

14f
models

1. Unique font draws attention to headline
2. Date and description of the event prominently placed
3. Space directs attention to key elements in poster
4. Scheduling information presented in clear format
5. Original artwork adds visual interest
6. Poem uses a more legible font that complements the headline

RELATIVELY SPEAKING

Youth Shelters and
Family Crisis Services

Runaway/Crisis Shelter • Transition House • SafePlace • In-Home Services * Telephone
Information Line • Youth Involvement • Juvenile Restitution & Community Service

① ② Volume 11, No. 2   *A Publication of The Relatives, Inc.*   **Winter, 1998**

③ 1998 ENDS WITH STRONG SUPPORT FOR YOUTH AND THE RELATIVES, INC. ⑥

As we reflect on 1998, the generosity of the community becomes so vivid. All of us at The Relatives, Inc. are thankful for the sincere commitment to helping youth that so many made, especially as the end of the year and Holidays approached. Let us take a look at these last few months.

(Photo by Randall Hitt)
Employees from First Union's Direct Commercial Market Group visited the Runaway/Crisis Shelter to donate holiday gifts and household items. Pictured above are volunteers who made the delivery.

④ FOUNDATION GIFTS LEAD THE WAY

Special gifts from foundations led us into the New Year, beginning with a **$3,000** contribution from the **TJX Foundation, Inc.** (TJ Maxx and Marshalls stores) to support our Runaway/Crisis Shelter. Following this, a **$12,000** contribution was made by the **Mecklenburg County ABC Board** to support an outreach project of The Relatives' Youth Ambassadors—SHOUT! A Month To Be Heard, which will occur in March,1999.

Once again, the **Speedway Children's Charities** was a driving force in supporting youth through a **$6,000** donation while **Winn-Dixie** contributed **$2,000** during its annual awards luncheon from community organizations. Thanks must also go to the **Royal Sun Alliance Insurance Foundation** for their **$3,000** contribution.

Additionally, **The Foundation of the Carolinas and The Duke Endowment** contributed **$5,000** respectively to assist The Relatives, Inc. in strategic planning to ensure the success of the agency in the future. More on this will be revealed in future newsletters.

⑤ A special thank you goes to **The Charlotte Observer**, for its recommendation that a **$15,000** gift be made to The Relatives, Inc. from **The Knight Foundation Endowment Fund** in support of The Relatives' follow-up services. This very important gift will help ensure that after youth leave our Runaway/Crisis Shelter, they will be offered ongoing contact and services with The Relatives, Inc. to help with their continued improvement.

Thank you to all of these wonderful groups for their support. They are helping to keep kids safe and families together, while creating a better future for the entire community. Their philanthropic efforts do not go unnoticed and certainly serve as encouragment for others to give!

WAL-MART-ARBORETUM DONATES PROCEEDS

Shopping experts say that the day after Thanksgiving is the busiest shopping time of the year. For youth and The Relatives, Inc.—we said—shop til you drop! Wal-Mart Associates at the Arboretum chose to donate a portion of their proceeds from the day after Thanksgiving to The Relatives, Inc. Altogether, **$2,795** was contributed. Thank you goes to Manager Todd Taylor, Sherry Hicks, Sue Stegall, and all the Wal-Mart Associates for their ongoing commitment to helping youth.

Continued on page 2

(Photo by Randall Hitt)
⑦ *Volunteers help unload a truck load of christmas gifts donated from employees and patrons of Dilworth Billiards. Altogether, 3 families were sponsored.*

**14f
models**

① Appealing masthead and logo repeated on every issue

② Publication information displayed prominently without distracting from the newsletter's message

③ Large headline directs readers to most important message

④ Subheads help break up a long story

⑤ Two-column format helps break up layout into manageable chunks

⑥ Photos add visual interest

⑦ All photos include a caption and a photo credit

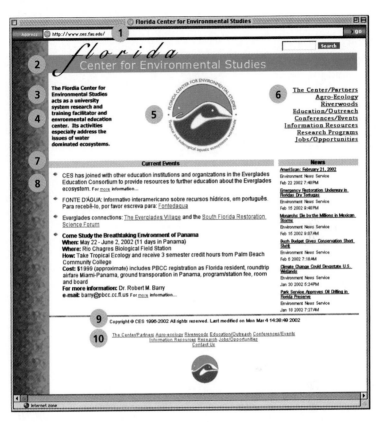

1. Descriptive title in the window frame lets users see if they're in the right place. Search engines index this title, not the one appearing on the page itself.

2. Title repeated on the actual Web page to create a visual tone for the site

3. Textured background adds appeal without diminishing legibility

4. Opening block of text identifies organization and its mission

5. Icon represents organization and reveals illustrations of menu options

6. HTML tables used to create a menu on the side of the page

7. Up-to-date information presented first so users don't have to scroll to see it

8. Textual descriptions offer another method to link to the same pages as the icons

9. Date tells visitors how current the information is

10. Contact information for organization and staff

14f
models

PART 4

Editing and Proofreading: Meeting Community Expectations

CHAPTER 15

THE EDITING AND PROOFREADING PROCESS

After making major and minor revisions in your writing (see Chapter 8), you should turn your attention to editing. **Editing** means fine-tuning your work for a reader—adjusting sentences and words for clarity, for precise meaning and effect, and for correctness. It means identifying problems in grammar and sentence structure as well as glaring omissions or repetitions. And it means looking for consistency in style, punctuation, word usage, and tone.

Recognizing and revising such problems is not the same as proofreading, however. When you proofread a paper, you hunt for distracting or careless typographical errors such as misspelled words, transposed letters, and incorrect hyphenation or word division. Proofreading is your last chance to make sure that errors in presentation don't distract and annoy your reader.

The ability to edit and proofread is a valuable skill—so valuable, in fact, that it serves a professional role in dozens of occupations, such as advertising, journalism, speech writing, public relations, marketing, teaching, publishing, the law, and most scientific and technical fields. Learning how to edit your own and other people's writing can be a powerful asset in your career.

Successful editing also means recognizing and using the conventions of specific communities. Some conventions don't vary much across such communities: a spelling mistake stands out in your document regardless of its intended readers or context. Other conventions, however, may not be so rigid. For example, newspaper or magazine readers wouldn't be surprised to find only one comma in this sentence: *The suspect jumped from the car, evaded the officers and ran into the motel.* In an academic context, though, many readers would argue that a second comma ought to follow *officers*, and for evidence they might cite the well-known guides of the Modern Language Association or the American Psychological Association (see Chapters 51 and 52). Likewise, a scientist would use numerals (such as *12* or *84*) for the numbers in a lab report, while an art historian might spell out *twelve* or *eighty-four* in an interpretive paper. Many workplace communities use particular "local" conventions that you'll need to learn as you adapt your writing to these contexts.

15a Editing your own writing

To edit successfully, you need to read your writing with an editor's eyes, focusing hard on a text and reading carefully and slowly. You can't edit well if you're skimming a paper twenty minutes before class.

Editing for style and correctness calls for a special kind of reading, one that shifts away from content (what's being said) and toward form (how it's being said). Once you've restructured confusing paragraphs or garbled sentences through major and minor revision, you can then take a magnifying glass to each sentence and scrutinize it for smaller stylistic concerns, grammar, and punctuation. Problems, inconsistencies, and errors will emerge, and you *must* fix them before your paper can be considered finished.

Often, editing requires you to keep in mind a certain concern (commas, for example, or sexist language) while you scour your entire text for specific cases. It's hard to look for too many kinds of problems at once. Sometimes you may need to read your text four, five, six, or more times, keeping in mind a different cluster of concerns for each reading.

1 Final editing for economy and style

Even after major and minor revision have tightened the focus and eliminated inessential or repetitive sections (see Chapter 8), most papers can still profit from some final cosmetic surgery. If any part of a sentence adds little or nothing to style or meaning, eliminate it during a final check for redundancy or wordiness.

15.1

NEAR-FINAL DRAFT

In actual fact, the aligned pulleys are lined up so that they are located up above the center core of the machine.

READER'S REACTION: **This seems repetitive and confusing.**

EDITED

The aligned pulleys are **positioned** above the **machine's core**.

STRATEGY

Use the following questions to help you edit your draft for final trimming and styling.

- **Are my sentences reasonably easy to read?**
  Try reading your sentences (especially out loud) from the perspective of a reader unfamiliar with their content and purpose. Whenever you stumble over a phrase or a whole sentence, try rearranging the structure for easier reading.
- **Do any words stand out as odd or inappropriate for my purpose?**
  Try to choose a more appropriate word. Consider turning to a dictionary or thesaurus for help (see Chapter 30).

15a edit

- **Have I used some sentence structures too often?**
  Try varying sentence structures. For example, do almost all sentences begin with nouns or with a pronoun like *I*? Then try starting some sentences with prepositional phrases or subordinate clauses.
- **If I had to cut ten words from each page, which ones could I eliminate?**
  Cut the excess if you can do so without creating new problems in style (for example, short, choppy sentences) or meaning.

Exercise 1

A. In a brochure-writing assignment, Kim Francis wrote the following draft paragraph for a pamphlet describing tourist attractions and accommodations near her Wisconsin home. Read the paragraph once for meaning and then a second time for editing. During the second reading, ask some of the questions listed in the Strategy in 15a-1 (above). Then edit the paragraph to make it more effective.

> After spending a day exploring the countryside, rest and relax at a quaint country inn, relaxing by the fire and sipping on some mulled wine. After spending a quiet night in a room decorated with beautiful old antiques, wake up to a country breakfast. Then after your pleasant stay at the inn, explore the quaint towns and roads that have made Door County, Wisconsin, such an attractive vacation destination for people who like to escape and get away from it all.

B. Meet with some fellow writers and share your edited versions of the paragraph in Exercise 1A. Work as a group to prepare a single edited version of the paragraph. If you wish, make use of the individual versions produced by group members.

15a
edit

2 Editing for grammatical problems

When you edit your writing for grammatical problems, first you need to *identify* or *recognize* the problem, and then you must *edit* your prose to fix the problem. Many writers spend too little time identifying problems and simply correct those few they spot while quickly skimming their drafts. Don't leave it up to your reader to find errors you missed.

You'll be able to identify some problems in your writing immediately because you simply "slipped" while you were more engaged in your thoughts than in your expression. Other problems may be less obvious but still identifiable because you have a "sense" that you've made an error or because you know you have difficulty with that feature. Still others may be errors that you're not conscious of making or that you don't know how to spot. You may need to try different strategies in each of these situations.

Identifying known errors. All writers make identifiable mistakes in grammar, word choice, and other editing concerns while immersed in their thoughts during the writing process. These are the easiest problems to spot because you already know what's wrong.

STRATEGY

Read your paper slowly from start to finish but don't become too immersed in the ideas. Instead, look carefully and deliberately at each paragraph, circling or marking any errors in grammar, punctuation, and sentence logic. If you can quickly correct an error along the way, do so. If you're not certain how to correct the error, wait until you've finished identifying problems; then refer to the appropriate sections in this handbook or other reference tools for advice.

"Before and after" passages from Jim Tollefson's newsletter article on the Endangered Species Act for his local conservancy group show his circled errors (labeled in the margins) and his edited version.

DRAFT WITH ERRORS IDENTIFIED

caps
fragment/
apostrophe
Who?
comma splice

Critics of the endangered species act think it is too broad. Because some specie's may be less vital to environmental balance than others. They want to protect species selectively, however, scientists still do not know which species are more important.

15a
edit

EDITED

Critics of the Endangered Species Act think it is too broad because some species may be less vital to environmental balance than others. These critics want to protect species selectively. However, scientists still do not know which species are more important.

Here is a list of errors that many instructors are likely to consider quite serious because they confuse or irritate readers. Refer to the chapter or section listed in parentheses for more information on these topics.

Sentence fragments (Chapter 21)
Comma splices and fused sentences (Chapter 22)
Pronoun reference (Chapter 23)

Subject-verb agreement (19a–b)
Comma usage (Chapter 33)
Lack of parallelism (Chapter 27)
Misplaced, dangling, and disruptive modifiers (Chapter 24)
Mixed sentence structures (26a)
Problems with verb form and tense (Chapter 18)
Spelling (Chapter 44)

You may wish to begin your editing by focusing on problems like these, and then continue by checking other areas of sentence structure, word choice, spelling, and punctuation that interfere with the relationship between you and your reader.

Identifying suspected errors. Other kinds of problems in your writing that require editing will be somewhat less obvious to you. You may suspect that you've made an error but may not be completely sure. *Don't take a risk.* Check the rule or convention to be sure, and edit accordingly.

STRATEGIES

- **Circle or mark all suspected problems or errors in your paper.** Then check appropriate sections in this handbook or another reference work, and edit those that are, in fact, errors. If any suspected errors are still unresolved after a thorough check, ask a teacher, editor, or knowledgeable peer or friend to help you.
- **Create an editing checklist of problems or errors that you often encounter in your writing.** Apply the checklist to each paper you write. Begin by analyzing your own papers and by giving some samples of your writing to a teacher or expert writer. Ask that person to identify *patterns* of error in your writing, and also look for them on your own. Using this handbook, study the errors and try to identify their causes. Then create your own strategies for recognizing the errors, and turn these into a personalized editing checklist for your papers and other writing. As you get better at recognizing and repairing these problems, you can delete strategies you no longer need and add new ones. This process can be especially useful as you learn to write in more diverse settings.

15a
edit

After thoroughly editing her paper on the effects of loud music, Carrie Brehe put three more items on her editing checklist.

1. A lot—sounds like one word but is actually two. Think of an entire "lot" full of whatever. Think of the opposite of a little. From the noise

paper: "Alot of teenagers have no information about how their hearing works." Search for all cases of alot.

2. Their vs. there. Sound the same. I usually write "there" for "their" when I make this mistake, but not the reverse. "Their" is possessive only, and "there" is location. From the noise paper: "Most people are not even aware that there hearing can be damaged by lawn mowers, chain saws, and even jets taking off." Search for all cases of there/their.

3. If they would have known. I say this a lot (ha!). I'm still not sure what the subjunctive means, but this problem shows up when I write "if." Correct to if they had or if they were. Search for all cases of "if + would." From the noise paper: "If they would have known what the concerts were doing to their eardrums, they might have stopped going."

Identifying unknown errors. A final category of mistakes consists of those you have no idea you're making. These mistakes are especially frustrating because in most cases you need to learn them through experience. Writing courses and tutoring services are designed to help you identify and edit such errors so that you can eventually avoid them in the first place. Studying handbooks and reading as much professional prose as you can may help; but by far the best strategy is to work with your own writing.

STRATEGY

Read your writing, preferably aloud. Sometimes this will help you to locate problems intuitively. Or you may recognize them because you encounter difficulty reading a passage. Circle everything you question; then use the strategy on page 194 to check suspected errors.

Ask someone to read your paper and to mark or circle any problems he or she encounters. Your reader doesn't need to be a grammarian to call attention to problems with sentences, usage, and the like. Good readers will spot errors intuitively. Since they're not as close to the text as you are, these readers may find some problems you have overlooked. (See 15b for more on collaborative editing.)

As you discover them, add *all* previously unknown errors to your editing checklist. Refer to your checklist when you edit all future papers. You can remove these items from the checklist when you are sure you can consistently identify or avoid them.

15a
edit

Exercise 2

A. Working from a paper that your instructor has commented on (or that you have asked another teacher or expert writer to examine), begin creating your own editing checklist.

B. Share checklists with a group of your fellow writers, and create a checklist for the entire group. Do you all have the same problems? Try to explain why particular features cause difficulties for writers in the group, and come up with strategies for identifying and overcoming the problems. Then create an editing checklist for your entire class.

15b Editing collaboratively

When you edit collaboratively, you identify and talk about specific problems in a paper with one or more "consulting readers," usually friends or peers. Your goal is not just to rid your paper of errors but to learn to identify and correct errors on your own. Every time someone points out an error to you, focus on it and its effects on your reader. Identifying problems takes only a few minutes of hard, conscious attention, and the investment in time will pay off for the rest of your writing life.

STRATEGY

When you are the consulting reader in a group *or* the writer, use these suggestions for providing and receiving good advice.

- When someone asks you to read his or her paper for editorial feedback, be sure the paper is finished enough for this kind of work. If the paper still requires attention to matters of content and organization, explain to the writer that until these matters are dealt with, surface editing will be a waste of time. (You can also provide feedback for larger revisions, as explained in Chapter 8.)
- Use familiar language and symbols for your comments so the writer will readily understand them. The terminology used in this handbook is generally accepted in education and business. As you learn to identify errors in your writing, attach the appropriate labels to them.
- If you're uncertain about a feature, such as a possible spelling error, just note your uncertainty. Let the writer use a reference source (a dictionary, a style guide, or this handbook—see Chapter 30) to identify and correct the problem.
- Avoid "taking over" the writer's draft. Identify outright errors, but don't rewrite whole sentences and paragraphs. Rewriting is the author's job.
- If you think that a writer has been unnecessarily sloppy, hoping that you'll clean up the mess, don't spend much time working on the paper. The draft you're editing should be as clean a version as the writer can produce.

- Comments about style are always more helpful when they're specific. Marginal comments like "awkward," "good," or "I like this" won't always help the writer know specifically what works or doesn't work.
- If something is good or bad, explain why. But don't spend time writing long explanations.
- Try to identify patterns of error in the writer's prose. If the writer repeats the same mistakes, point the repetition out.

A WORD ABOUT SPEAKING

An "editorial" level also exists in oral presentations: small details of style and delivery. Many of these will be invisible or unconscious, such as your habit of twisting your hair while you speak, or the way you favor one side of the room when you make eye contact with your audience. The best way to learn about and "edit" these problems is to ask one or more trusted people to give you honest feedback on an oral presentation. Like reading a draft of a paper aloud, videotaping can also help.

Exercise 3

On the day your teacher returns drafts or finished papers with comments, look for any errors he or she has noted or identified. Working in groups of three or four, read each other's papers, looking for patterns of error. Compare these patterns and, as a group, try to write "rules" explaining how to fix them. In creating the rules, feel free to use your own terms and ways of explaining. Add any new cases to your editing checklist.

15c Editing on the computer

15c edit

Editing has its share of "quick fix" remedies. Among the most attractive are computer programs that "read" a piece of prose and then tell you how to correct or improve it. Before buying such a program, learn something about what it can and can't do.

1 What computer editors can do

Each year, programs that claim to identify problems in your writing become more sophisticated. Some can be useful, depending on your goals and your writing situation. Some editing programs, for example, can identify problems common in business writing by giving the average length of sentences or noting instances of the passive voice. They can also provide a "jargon index" of words not in the vocabulary of most readers. You can then use this information to edit your prose.

When examining an editing program, see whether it will meet your specific needs. Use the following questions as a guide.

- Does the program identify errors in spelling, punctuation, capitalization, and usage?
- Does it identify incorrect sentence structure?
- Will it alert you to unclear sentences, problems with subject-verb agreement or modifiers, sexist or discriminatory language, and vague expressions?
- Is it linked to a spelling checker, thesaurus, dictionary, synonym finder, or other utility?
- Will it identify clichéd or vague expressions and commonly misused words?
- Does it allow you to design and add your own rules, tailoring the program to your editorial needs and to meet the conventions of use within your writing community?

2 What computer editors can't do

Although they may claim to answer most of your writing problems, computerized editing programs are no match for human readers and editors. Most programs will alert you to a potential problem but leave you to identify and repair it yourself. Grammar and style checkers also take a lot of time for what they deliver, and they can check only material that has been typed into the computer. The programs provide few options for different kinds of writing or for audiences that differ in sophistication and background knowledge. Beware, therefore, of blanket pronouncements from the program. They may be inappropriate for your writing situation.

Of course, *anything* that responds to your writing can be useful, if only in increasing your awareness of the features in your text. Go ahead and try some programs. If they work for you, so much the better. But remember, computers can't do what human readers can. The challenging work of editing is probably here to stay.

DID YOU KNOW?

The activities of writers, readers, and editors are quite different. Research shows that when you engage in one of the activities, it's very hard to engage in the others, because each requires a certain way of thinking and a different way of perceiving the text. It's important, therefore, to set aside time for each activity.

Karen M. Petit, "Communication as a Function of Writers Writing, Readers Reading, and Editors Editing," diss., U of Rhode Island, 1993.

15d Proofreading

Finally, after you've made as many conscious decisions about your writing as possible and are ready to submit it, it's time for **proofreading**, looking for errors you may have missed during the editing process. No writer produces an absolutely flawless document every single time. This book, for example, has undergone extensive scrutiny to be sure that *every* word is spelled correctly and that *every* punctuation mark is in the right place. And still, after everything the authors did, after every one of the numerous reviewers had spotted mistakes, after every editor worked on the project, there were tiny flaws only an astute proofreader's eye could find. (We hope, of course, that all of them were found, but published books often contain at least one *erratum*, a trivial mistake overlooked by the entire crew working on the project.)

15.2

You may wonder why there is so much fuss about editing. Every time a reader encounters even a tiny error, the author looks slightly less in control. One or two insignificant mistakes have little impact, especially if the work is otherwise powerful. But as the slips accumulate, the author's credibility sinks.

In college, when teachers read your writing, loss of credibility can ruin the effectiveness of your ideas and lead to a poor assessment of your work. The same thing can happen at work, where good communication skills may be essential for advancement. Surprisingly, many people skip proofreading, one of the simplest of all the processes a paper must go through before it's finished. Before you turn in a piece of writing, submit it to a meticulous reading. Use a spelling checker. Focus consciously on every word of your document. Don't let your eyes blur. Instead, move from word to word, fixing your eyes on each word to be sure it doesn't contain transposed letters, typographical errors, and the like. Or try reading your writing out loud. Treat every error you identify as if it were a prize catch, raising the credibility of your ideas.

Exercise 4

A. Two versions of a paragraph follow—one in an unedited form, the other partly edited. Without looking at the edited version, read the unedited draft like an editor. Scrutinize the passage as ruthlessly as you can, making any corrections you wish and explaining these in a notebook. Then compare your editing with the changes made in the second paragraph. What differences do you find between your own editing and the writer's editing?

UNEDITED DRAFT

At the start of her career, historian Barbara Smithey, felt forced to choose between a life of: public service vs. research. As curator of the Westville Museum of New England culture in Westville, Ct, she was passionately devoted to preserving or restoring old houses in disrepair and seeing to it that they were entered if they qualified into the National Register of Historical Places. At the same time, she had a kean interest in research on the town of Westville which had been settled in the early 17th-Century. She manfully seized control of all public documents on the area, that were not already protected and got them housed in the local historical archives. These included, some early notes about the Indian savages that the White men encountered when they settled the land. Also some personal diaries lady settlers kept.

EDITED DRAFT

At the start of her career, historian Barbara Smithey felt forced to choose between a life of public service ~~vs.~~ and research. As curator of the Westville Museum of New England culture in Westville, ~~Ct,~~ Connecticut, she was passionatly devoted to preserving or restoreing old houses in disrepair and seeing to it that they were entered if they qualified into the National Register of Historical Places. At the same time, she had a kean interest in research on the town of Westville, which had been settled in the early ~~17th-Century.~~ seventeenth century. She ~~manfully~~ seized control of all public documents on the area that were not already protected and ~~got~~ had them ~~housed~~ placed in the local historical archives. These included some early settlers notes about ~~the Indian savages that the White men encountered~~ local Native Americans, as well as ~~when they settled the land.~~ Also some personal diaries ~~lady settlers~~ of women settlers. ~~kept.~~

15d proof

B. Compare your editorial changes to those of a small group of your peers. Did you all notice the same things? Did you all make the same changes? Does each member of the group have a different editing style? Prepare a brief report summarizing differences and similarities among the ways members of the group edited the paragraph. Share your report with other groups in class.

Editing Grammar

CHAPTER 16

RECOGNIZING SENTENCE ELEMENTS AND SENTENCE PATTERNS

To create a sentence, you need not be consciously aware of its different parts. Careful revising and editing depend on such awareness, however. Most of the time, you need a basic understanding of grammatical concepts and terms in order to spot difficulties in your writing, to correct them, or to find the information in a handbook that will help you make a correction. Discussions in this handbook generally avoid technical language. Some technical knowledge is essential, however, and this chapter provides a basic introduction to the features of sentence grammar, along with tips for identifying and using them.

16a Using words

At the simplest level, sentences consist of different types of words, often called *parts of speech:* nouns, pronouns, verbs, adjectives, adverbs, prepositions, conjunctions, and interjections.

1 Recognizing nouns and articles

16a
gr

This familiar definition can help you recognize nouns: A **noun** is a word naming a person, place, idea, or thing.

> **Rosemary Wells** employs **humor** in her **books** for **children**.

Nouns often require an **article**: *the, a,* or *an* (*a* before consonants, *an* before vowels).

> **A** report proposes **an** administrative solution to **the** problem.

Most nouns add *-s* to the singular form to make the plural: *cow + s = cows; cake + s = cakes.* Some nouns ending with *s*-like sounds (*s, z, j, x, ch, sh,* for example) add *-es* for the plural: *gas + es = gases; base* (silent *e*) + *es = bases;*

fax + *es* = *faxes*. Some nouns have irregular plurals: child/children, deer/deer, goose/geese, mouse/mice, ox/oxen.

Count nouns indicate individual items that can be *counted* (e.g., two *chairs*, four *cups*). **Mass (noncount) nouns** indicate material that can't be counted (e.g., *flour*, *water*, *steel*). **Collective nouns** generally take singular form but refer to a unit of more than one (e.g., *group*, *board of directors*, or *family*), and may be singular or plural in meaning.

Proper nouns refer to specific people, places, titles, or things. They are capitalized: *Miss America; Tuscaloosa, Alabama; Tierra del Fuego;* and *Microsoft.* All others are **common nouns** and are not capitalized (see 39b). Nouns indicating possession (**possessive nouns**) are easy to identify because they usually add an apostrophe and *-s* (see 35a): school (common); Tollgate High (proper); school's, Tollgate High's (possessive).

ESL ADVICE: THE ARTICLES *A, AN,* AND *THE*

In using the **indefinite articles** *a* and *an* or the **definite article** *the*, you need to follow rules and guidelines but you also need to pay attention to the many exceptions. Remember: the basic meaning of your sentence will still be communicated even if you choose the wrong article or forget to use one.

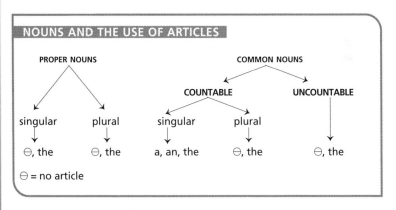

NOUNS AND THE USE OF ARTICLES

PROPER NOUNS / COMMON NOUNS

COUNTABLE / UNCOUNTABLE

singular	plural	singular	plural	
⊖, the	⊖, the	a, an, the	⊖, the	⊖, the

⊖ = no article

ESL

16a
gr

Singular proper nouns generally use no article, and **plural proper nouns** usually use *the*.

SINGULAR   **Rosa Parks** was an important figure in the American civil rights movement.

PLURAL   **The Everglades** have abundant wildlife and tropical plants.

Singular **count nouns** use *a*, *an*, or *the*. They cannot stand alone.

The pig is an intelligent <u>animal</u>.

Plural count nouns use either no article (to present a generalization) or *the* (to refer to something specific).

Books are the best teachers. (generalization)

The books on his desk are from the library. (specific)

Noncount (mass) nouns use either no article or *the*, but never use *a* or *an*.
General noncount (mass) nouns sometimes stand alone. **Specific noncount (mass) nouns** use *the*.

INCORRECT	A laughter is good medicine.
CORRECT	**Laughter** is good medicine. (general)
INCORRECT	Laughter of children is good medicine.
CORRECT	**The laughter** <u>of children</u> is good medicine. (specific) **The prepositional phrase makes the noun specific.**

STRATEGY

- Use *a* or *an* when you are not talking about a specific person or thing (a nonspecific, singular count noun). Use *a* before a consonant sound, *an* before a vowel sound.

  You need **an identification card** to cash a check.
  [nonspecific, *any* identification card]

- Use *the* when you are talking about a specific, singular noun, meaning you know the exact person or thing to which you are referring.

  You need **the university identification card** to borrow books.
  [a specific, known card]

  The beach she visited had unusually white sand.

- Use no article with plural nouns because most plural and mass nouns do not require one.

COUNT	**Airline tickets** to Florida are at half price.
MASS	**Information** about flights to Florida is available.

- Use *the* when a plural noun is followed by a modifier, because all plural count and mass nouns are specific when they are followed by modifiers.

ESL

16a
gr

COUNT	**The** airline <u>tickets</u> <u>that you bought</u> are at half price.
MASS	**The** <u>information</u> <u>that you received</u> about flights to Florida has changed.

In each sentence, <u>the modifying clause</u> makes the <u>noun</u> specific.

2 Recognizing pronouns

A **pronoun** is a word like *them, she, his,* or *it* that takes the place of a noun (or another pronoun) and that can play the same roles in a sentence as the word to which it refers—its **antecedent**.

antecedent   pronoun
Jean presented **her** proposal to the committee.

(For detailed help on making pronoun-antecedent relationships clear, see 19c and 23a–b.)

Pronouns can also modify a noun or another pronoun.

pronoun noun   pronoun pronoun
This <u>part</u> has been on order for a week, **that** <u>one</u> for twenty days.

Pronouns change form to indicate the **number** (singular or plural) or **gender** (masculine, feminine, or neuter) of the noun to which they refer. Pronouns also change form according to their role in a sentence—subject, object, or possessive (see 17a).

Personal pronouns. Personal pronouns designate persons or things and change form (or **case**) according to their role in a sentence (see 17a).

SINGULAR	I, me, you, he, him, she, her, it
PLURAL	we, us, you, they, them

Possessive pronouns. A possessive pronoun shows ownership. (See 17a.)

SINGULAR	my, mine, your, yours, her, hers, his, its
PLURAL	our, ours, your, yours, their, theirs

Relative pronouns. The relative pronouns *who, whom, whose, which,* and *that* introduce subordinate clauses (**relative clauses**) that modify or add information to a main clause (see 16d). They answer the questions "What kind of?" and "Which one?" *Who* takes different forms depending on its role (see 16d).

Interrogative pronouns. The interrogative pronouns *who* and *which* introduce questions.

Intensive and reflexive pronouns. **Intensive pronouns** (*-self*, *-selves*) add emphasis.

> They did all the work on the new barn **themselves**.

Reflexive pronouns enable the subject or doer to also be the receiver of an action.

> He paid **himself** for the work.

Indefinite pronouns. Indefinite pronouns refer to people, things, and ideas in general rather than to specific antecedents. They include *all, any, anybody, anything, anyone, another, both, each, every, everybody, everyone, everything, either, few, fewer, many, neither, nothing, nobody, no one, none, one, several, some, somebody, someone,* and *something*.

Demonstrative and reciprocal pronouns. Demonstrative pronouns or **demonstrative adjectives**—*this, that, these,* or *those*—point out or highlight an antecedent or sum up an entire phrase or clause.

> **That** copier breaks down about once a week.

> She was late for the meeting. **This** surprised me because she is usually punctual.

Reciprocal pronouns (*one another, each other*) refer to individual parts of a plural antecedent.

> The two kinds of birds compete, destroying **each other's** nests.

16a
gr

Exercise 1

A. Underline each noun in the following selection *once* and each pronoun *twice*.

> Seconds later the Help Desk received a call from another user with the same problem. The switchboard lit up. There were callers from all over the company, all with the same complaint: their computers were making odd noises. It might be a tune, one of the callers added helpfully, coming from the computer's small internal speaker. The sixth caller recognized the melody. The computers were all playing tinny renditions of "Yankee Doodle."
>
> —PAUL MUNGO AND BRYAN CLOUGH, "The Bulgarian Connection"

B. Exchange papers in progress with another writer, and identify all the nouns and pronouns in a relatively long paragraph of your partner's work. Then return the essay and point out where you agree or disagree with your partner's identification of nouns and pronouns (or lack of identification).

---

3 Recognizing verbs

Verbs express actions (*jump*, *build*), occurrences (*become*, *happen*), and states of being (*be*, *seem*).

You change a verb's form to signal relationships in time (**tense**), **person**, and **number**.

TENSE	They **prepare** invoices.	They **prepared** invoices.
PERSON	He **restores** antique cars.	They **restore** antique cars.
NUMBER	The copier **makes** noise.	The copiers **make** noise.

Differences in **voice** (active or passive; see 18e) and **mood** (18g) also require changes in form.

ACTIVE VOICE	The pump **cleans** the water.
PASSIVE VOICE	The water **is cleaned** by the pump.
INDICATIVE MOOD	The proposal **was** in the file.
SUBJUNCTIVE MOOD	If the proposal **were** in the file, I would have found it.

You may employ a **main** verb on its own or with one or more **helping** (or **auxiliary**) **verbs**, including forms of *be*, *do*, and *have* (main verb + helping verb = **verb phrase**). You may use **modal auxiliary verbs** (*will/would*, *can/could*, *shall/should*, *may/might*, *must*, and *ought to*) as helping verbs, though never as main verbs. (See 18b.)

       helping main
       verb   verb
The tourist agency **is planning** to make a video of the local attractions.

         main
    modal verb
They **might decide** to include the old courthouse.

A **verb phrase** consists of a main verb plus a helping verb.

  verb phrase   verb phrase
I **am hoping** that the renovations **can be done** in time.

16a
gr

Use **action verbs** to indicate an action or activity, for example, *swim*, *analyze*, *dig*, *turn*, or *negotiate*. Use **linking verbs** (also known as **state-of-being verbs**) to express a state of being or an occurrence: *is*, *seems*, *becomes*, *grows* (see 16b-2). A linking verb links a subject with a complement that renames or describes it.

ACTION   The company and the union **negotiated** a new contract.

LINKING   Flowers **remain** my favorite gift.
                  subject   verb   complement renames subject

                  The flowers **smelled** musky.
                  subject   verb   complement describes subject

Phrasal verbs consist of a verb plus a word that seems like a preposition but is known as a **particle**, as in *run along* (depart), *run down* (exhaust), or *look up* (improve). The meaning of phrasal verbs differs considerably from the meanings of the separate words.

PHRASAL VERB   VERB + PREPOSITION
I **ran** the idea **by** the committee.   I **ran by** the house.
Profits are **falling off**.   My cousin **fell off** the deck.

Exercise 2

A. In the following sentences, underline each main verb once and each helping verb twice.

EXAMPLE
The new construction in Maple Valley has created some problems.

1. The power company's engineers began studying a map of the area.
2. They had thought about using underground cables.
3. A field test revealed a large rock ledge, so the engineers decided that underground lines would be too expensive.
4. They proposed cutting a path through the woods for the power lines, but the contractor claimed that potential homebuyers might not like the effect on the scenery.
5. They strung the power lines on poles along the main road into the development.

B. Exchange papers in progress with a fellow student. Choose a relatively long paragraph, and underline all main verbs once and helping verbs twice.

16a
gr

4 Recognizing adjectives

Adjectives can modify nouns, pronouns, or word groups acting as nouns. They answer questions like "How many?" "What kind?" or "Which one?"

HOW MANY?   The **three** meetings will last all day.

WHICH ONE?   Our report was the **longest** one.

WHAT KIND?   Their proposal was **unacceptable**.

Adjectives come in three degrees of comparison: *high, higher, highest; crooked, more crooked, most crooked* (see 20c).

ESL ADVICE: ADJECTIVE FORMS

Adjectives in English never use a plural form.

NOT APPROPRIATE   Santo Domingo is renowned for beautifuls beaches.

CORRECT   Santo Domingo is renowned for beautiful beaches.

5 Recognizing adverbs

You can use **adverbs** to modify verbs, adjectives, other adverbs, and entire sentences. They enable you to describe or limit your meaning by answering such questions as "When?" "Where?" "Why?" "How often?" "Which direction?" "What conditions?" and "What degree?"

WHEN?   Our committee met **yesterday**. [modifies verb *met*]

WHAT DEGREE?   We had a **very** long meeting. [modifies adjective *long*]

HOW OFTEN?   I attend school board meetings **quite frequently**. [modifies adverb *frequently*, which modifies verb *attend*]

You can recognize many adverbs easily because they consist of an adjective plus -*ly*: *quickly, blindly, frequently, efficiently*. Others do not take this form, including *very, too, tomorrow, not, never, sometimes, well,* and *so*. In addition, some adjectives end in -*ly*, including *neighborly, slovenly,* and *lovely*. The surest way to distinguish an adverb from an adjective, therefore, is to see whether the word modifies a noun or pronoun (it's an adjective) or a verb, adjective, or adverb (it's an adverb). By adding *more, less, most,* or *least* to many adverbs, you can describe three comparative levels: *quickly, more quickly, most quickly; clearly, less clearly, least clearly* (see 20c).

Conjunctive adverbs, such as *however, moreover, thus,* and *therefore,* indicate logical relationships. (See 22b.)

They did not like the new administrative guidelines; **nevertheless**, they promised to implement the policies.

ESL

16a
gr

Exercise 3

A. In the following passage, underline all adjectives once and all adverbs twice.

Back in Chicago, Sereno's analysis of his new dinosaur's skeleton convinces him it is indeed more primitive than *Herrerasaurus*. It lacks a flexible jaw that let *Herrerasaurus* and later carnivores snag and trap struggling prey. Thus Sereno believes this new creature is the closest fossil we have to the first dinosaur.

"I call it 'Eoraptor,'" he says. "Eos was the Greek goddess of dawn. Raptor means thief. It was a light-bodied little rascal. And it may have been a thief, dashing in to grasp scraps of someone else's kill."

—RICK GORE, "Dinosaurs"

B. Expand the following sentences by adding details and information in the form of adjectives and adverbs.

EXAMPLE

generally   deep, extended
The term *coma* refers to a state of unconsciousness.

1. Accidents leave people in comas.
2. Comas are serious medical problems.
3. Newspapers contain reports of people awakening from comas.
4. Long comas are dangerous.
5. They cause irreversible damage.

16a
gr

DID YOU KNOW?

Since the 1700s, **sentence adverbs** like *frankly, strictly, regretfully,* and *basically* have been used to modify entire sentences, for example, "Sadly, they could not raise enough money to keep the bank from repossessing the farm." Nonetheless, some readers may react negatively to *hopefully* (meaning "let us hope" or "I hope") used as a sentence adverb.

QUESTIONABLE   Hopefully, the tests will be finished today.

ACCEPTABLE   I hope the tests will be finished today.

As Robert Burchfield points out, the ban on *hopefully* is recent but quite forceful: "Suddenly, round about 1968, and with unprecedented venom, a dunce's cap was placed on the head of anyone who used just one of the [-*ly* adverbs]—*hopefully*—as a sentence adverb."

Robert Burchfield, *Points of View* (New York: Oxford UP, 1992) 85.

6 Recognizing prepositions

A **preposition** is a word like *on, over, for,* or *with;* followed by a noun or pronoun, it becomes a **prepositional phrase**. Prepositional phrases can add detailed and precise information to sentences.

A faint smell of grilled onions came through the window and
        adjective   **adverb**

mixed with the musty air of the dungeon.
    adverb   **adjective**

—Jimmy Buffett, *Where Is Joe Merchant?*

COMMON PREPOSITIONS

about	at	despite	near	to
above	before	down	of	toward
across	behind	during	off	under
after	below	except	on	until
against	beneath	for	out	up
along	between	from	outside	upon
among	beyond	in	over	with
around	by	into	past	within
as	concerning	like	through	without

Exercise 4

A. Underline all the prepositions in the following sentences. Circle all the prepositional phrases.

EXAMPLE

At eighteen minutes after one o'clock, the emergency number received a call from Mrs. Serena Washington.

1. From its station near city hall, the rescue truck drove to Briar Brook Avenue.
2. Along the way, it narrowly missed colliding with a bread truck that failed to pull to the side of the road.
3. Despite the near accident, the rescue team arrived at the Washingtons' home in less than five minutes.
4. Mr. Washington was complaining of pain in his chest and back and displaying other symptoms of a heart attack.
5. By its quick response to the emergency call, the rescue team may have saved a life.

16a
gr

B. For each of the following word groups, create two sentences, one using the words as a verb plus preposition, the other using the words as a phrasal verb (see 16a-3). Then rewrite the sentence that contains the phrasal verb, substituting another word or words for the phrasal verb.

EXAMPLE: TEAR OUT

Brian tore out the old shelving.

Brian tore out the door.

Brian hurried out the door.

cut down	hang around	run up
fill in	put up with	call up

ESL ADVICE: PREPOSITIONS

PREPOSITIONS OF TIME

Use *at* for a specific time; *on* for days and dates; and *in* for nonspecific times during a day, month, season, or year.

Brandon was born **at** 11:11 a.m., **on** Monday, **in** the morning.

PREPOSITIONS OF PLACE

Use *at* for specific addresses; *on* for the names of streets, avenues, and boulevards; and *in* for large areas of land—counties, states, countries, and continents.

ESL

16a
gr

He works **at** 99 Tinker Street, but his home is **on** Chance Avenue, **in** Evers County, Maine.

Use prepositional phrases in this order: **prepositional phrase of place + prepositional phrase of time**.

                        place   time
The runners will be starting **in the park on Saturday**.

PREPOSITIONS OF PLACE: *IN, AT, ON*, AND NO PREPOSITION

IN	AT	ON	NO PREPOSITION
the bedroom	the bottom of the stairs	a bicycle	downstairs
the car	home	the ceiling	downtown
a mirror	the office	the floor	inside

the newspaper	a party	the horse	outside
a picture	school*	the plane	upstairs
school*	work	the train	uptown

*You may sometimes use different prepositions for these locations.

GOING TO A PLACE, EXPRESSED WITH OR WITHOUT *TO*

In expressing the idea of going to a place, use the preposition *to*.

I am going **to** work; she is going **to** the office.

Use no preposition in the following cases.

I am going home. They are going downstairs (downtown, inside).

FOR AND *SINCE* IN TIME EXPRESSIONS

Use *for* with an amount of time (minutes, hours, days, months, and years); use *since* with a specific date or time.

The housing program has been in operation **for** many years.

The housing program has been in operation **since** 1974.

PREPOSITIONS WITH NOUNS, VERBS, AND ADJECTIVES

Some nouns, verbs, and adjectives are typically associated with specific prepositions.

noun + preposition
He has an **understanding of** global politics.

verb + preposition
Vegetarians often **care about** animal rights.

adjective + preposition
Life in your country is **similar to** life in mine.

ESL

16a
gr

NOUN + PREPOSITION COMBINATIONS

approval of	fondness for	need for
awareness of	grasp of	participation in
belief in	hatred of	reason for
concern for	hope for	respect for
confusion about	interest in	success in
desire for	love of	understanding of

VERB + PREPOSITION COMBINATIONS

apologize for	jump into	step into
ask about	look at	study for

ask for	look for	talk about
belong to	look into	think about
care for	participate in	trust in
come out of	pay for	walk away from
go by	prepare for	work for
grow into	refer to	worry about

ADJECTIVE + PREPOSITION COMBINATIONS

afraid of	fond of	proud of
angry at	happy about	similar to
aware of	interested in	sorry for
capable of	jealous of	sure of
careless about	made of	tired of
familiar with	married to	worried about

7 Recognizing conjunctions

Conjunctions join words and groups of words, enabling you to signal relationships among them.

Coordinating conjunctions. Use the coordinating conjunctions (*and, but, or, nor, for, yet,* and *so*) to link grammatically equal elements.

WORDS   analyze **and** discuss

PHRASES   determined to cut costs **yet** worried about quality of service

CLAUSES   They surveyed the wetland, **and** they prepared a positive report.

ESL

16a
gr

Subordinating conjunctions. Use a subordinating conjunction such as *because, although, while, if,* or *since* to create a subordinate or modifying clause (see 16d; see 28c for a list of subordinating conjunctions). Remember that the clause created by a subordinating conjunction is a modifying clause, so it cannot stand on its own as a sentence; attach it to a **main** (or **independent**) **clause** that it qualifies or limits.

main clause   subordinate clause
The equipment still works, **although** it needs routine maintenance.

Correlative conjunctions. Correlative conjunctions come in pairs, including *not only . . . but also, either . . . or, neither . . . nor, both . . . and, whether . . . or,* and similar combinations. You can use them to join sentence elements that are grammatically equal. (See 27c-2 on parallelism.)

8 Recognizing interjections

You can use an **interjection** to convey a strong reaction or emotion, such as surprise (*Hey!*) or disappointment (*Oh, no!*). Interjections often stand on their own or are loosely linked to the rest of a sentence.

Exercise 5

A. Underline all the conjunctions in the following passage. Indicate whether each is a coordinating, subordinating, or correlative conjunction.

Thirty-five years ago, E. R. Guthrie and G. P. Horton described an experiment in which cats were placed in a glass-fronted puzzle box and trained to find their way out by jostling a slender vertical rod at the front of the box, thereby causing a door to open. What interested these investigators was not so much that the cats could learn to bump into the vertical rod, but that before doing so each animal performed a long ritual of highly stereotyped movements, rubbing their heads and backs against the front of the box, turning in circles, and finally touching the rod. The experiment has ranked as something of a classic in experimental psychology, even raising in some minds the notion of a ceremony of superstition on the part of cats: before the rod will open the door, it is necessary to go through a magical sequence of motions.

—Lewis Thomas, "Clever Animals"

B. Working with a group, rewrite the passage in Exercise 5A by employing different conjunctions (or kinds of conjunctions) than those in the original. Try to retain the general sense of the original, but feel free to add your own emphasis or perspective in the revision. Reword as necessary.

**16b
gr**

16b Recognizing sentence parts: Subjects and predicates

Each sentence you create needs to be built around a subject, which names the doer or the thing talked about, and a predicate, which indicates an action, a relationship, the consequences, and any conditions.

1 Creating sentence subjects

In a sentence **subject** you indicate the doer or the topic being addressed. A **simple subject** consists of one or more nouns (or pronouns) naming the doer or the topic. A **complete subject** consists of the simple subject *plus* all its modifying words or phrases.

> simple subject
> **Cellophane** was originally made from wood fiber.

> complete subject
> **Clear plastic wraps used today** are petroleum products.

A subject may be singular, plural, or compound (linked by *and* or *or*).

SINGULAR SUBJECT   **She** put the monitor on the desk.

PLURAL SUBJECT   These **trucks** cannot carry the load.

COMPOUND SUBJECT   **John and Chifume** are medical students.

In an imperative sentence expressing a request or command, the subject is *you*, generally implied but not stated (see 16d-2).
[You] Put the insulation around the edges of the doorframe.

Subject-verb order. In most sentences, the subject comes before the verb.

> subject   verb
> **Homeless people camped** in this area during the summer.

By beginning a sentence with expletive constructions such as *there is (are)* or *here is (are)*, you can delay the subject until after the verb (see 10a).

> verb   subject
> There **were homeless people** camping in this area during the summer.

By inverting sentence structure for emphasis or dramatic effect, you also alter the position of subject and verb (see 10c).

> verb subject
> In this valley, millions of years ago, **grew plants** whose leaves are recorded in fossils.

Questions frequently place the subject between the helping verb and the main verb (see 16a-3).

> helping   main
> verb   subject   verb
> **Did dinosaurs live** in this valley millions of years ago?

2 Creating sentence predicates

In a sentence **predicate** you indicate the action or relationship expressed in the sentence and may also specify the consequences or conditions. A **simple predicate** consists of a verb or a verb phrase (see 16a-3).

VERB   The engineers **met**.

VERB PHRASE   The engineers **might meet**.

The verb may be single or compound (linked by *and* or *or*).

SINGLE   The customer **slipped**.

COMPOUND   The customer **slipped and fell**.

A **complete predicate** consists of a verb or verb phrase *plus* any modifiers and other words or word groups that receive the action or complete the verb.

Object patterns. With a *transitive verb*, you can include in the predicate a **direct object** that tells *who* or *what* receives the action.

>   subject   predicate
> The bank officer approved the loan application.
>   verb   direct object

A sentence with a transitive verb can also include an indirect object. An **indirect object** (a noun or pronoun) lets readers know *to whom* or *for whom* the action is undertaken.

>   indirect direct
>   subject   verb   object   object
> The Marine Corps Reserve gives needy children toys.
>   to whom?

You can add information to a predicate with an **object complement**, a word (noun or adjective) that renames or describes the direct object.

ADJECTIVE   Critics judged the movie **inferior**.

NOUN   His co-workers elected Jim **project leader**.

Subject complement patterns. When you build a sentence around a linking verb, such as *is*, *seems*, or *feels* (see 16a-3), you can also include a **subject complement**. A subject complement "completes" the linking verb by describing the subject or renaming it.

>   subject
>   subject   verb complement
> The new store seems successful.

>   subject
>   subject verb complement
> The plan is too complicated.

16b
gr

Intransitive verb patterns. An intransitive verb does not take either an object or a complement; the verb's meaning is complete without them.

Our team **lost**.   Last week, the ferryboat **sank**.

16.1

> ## FIVE BASIC PREDICATE STRUCTURES
>
> 1. **Subject + intransitive verb**
>   The bus crashed.
>
> 2. **Subject + transitive verb + direct object**
>   A quick-thinking passenger called the police.
>
> 3. **Subject + transitive verb + indirect object + direct object**
>   The paramedic gave everyone blankets.
>
> 4. **Subject + transitive verb + direct object + object complement**
>   Officials found the driver negligent.
>
> 5. **Subject + linking verb + subject complement**
>   The quick-thinking passenger was a hero.

Exercise 6

A. In each of the following sentences, circle the complete subjects and draw a wavy line under the complete predicates.

EXAMPLE

Stories about Mount Everest often mention people known as Sherpas.

1. The Sherpas are well-known guides for mountain-climbing expeditions in the Himalayas.
2. They are a group of about 35,000 people who live in the country of Nepal.
3. The Sherpas, who are primarily Buddhists, live in a country dominated by Hindus.
4. Before the early 1900s, most Sherpas did not attempt to scale the mountains in their homeland.
5. In the early part of this century, however, Westerners wishing to climb the mountains gave many Sherpas jobs as guides and laborers.

B. Exchange papers in progress with another writer. Choose two paragraphs, and identify which of the five predicate patterns (listed in the chart in 16b-2) the writer uses in each sentence. Then suggest revi-

16b
gr

sions that vary the predicate patterns in order to provide appropriate emphasis and variety. When you are finished, work together to identify those suggested revisions most likely to improve each paper.

16c Recognizing phrases and clauses

A **main clause** (also called an **independent clause**) is a word group that includes a subject and a verb and can act as a complete sentence (see 16b). A **phrase** is a word group that lacks one or more elements needed to make a complete sentence. (For example, the phrase *will be climbing* lacks a subject; *the man running across the field* lacks a predicate; and *under the sink* lacks both.) A **subordinate clause** contains both a subject and a predicate yet cannot stand on its own as a sentence because it begins with a subordinating word such as *because, since, although, which,* or *that* (see 16a-7).

1 Recognizing prepositional phrases

A prepositional phrase has two parts. Look first for a preposition—a word like *at, for, in, to, according to, instead of,* or *under* (see 16a-6). Then identify the **object of the preposition**—the noun, pronoun, or word group that follows the preposition.

> **to** the branch office   **near** her   **after** a city council meeting

You can use a prepositional phrase as an adjective, almost always following the noun or pronoun it modifies.

> The coupons **in the newspaper** offer savings **on groceries**.

When you use a prepositional phrase as an adverb, place it next to the verb being modified or elsewhere in the sentence.

> Her electronic wristwatch started beeping **during the meeting**.

> **During the meeting**, her electronic wristwatch started beeping.

2 Recognizing absolute phrases

An **absolute phrase** includes (1) a noun, a pronoun, or a word group acting as a noun; (2) a present or past participle and any modifiers (*the deadline approaching quickly*). You can use an absolute phrase to modify a sentence as a whole as well as a word or element within the sentence.

> **Their lungs burning from the acrid smoke**, the firefighters pressed ahead into the burning building.

16c
gr

3 Recognizing appositive phrases

You can use an **appositive** to rename a noun in order to add information to a sentence. An **appositive phrase** consists of an appositive (generally a noun) along with its modifiers.

Ken Choi, **my classmate**, won an award for packaging design.

He used "environmentally conscious" materials, **for example, recycled paper and soy-based ink**.

4 Recognizing verbal phrases

Several kinds of phrases are built around the verb parts known as **verbals** (**infinitives**, **present participles**, **past participles**, and **gerunds**). Verbals can act as nouns, adjectives, or adverbs, but cannot act alone as verbs. A **verbal phrase** consists of a verbal plus its modifiers, object, or complements.

present
participle   **object**   **adverb**
sanding the tabletop with care

infinitive   **object**   **modifying (prepositional) phrase**
to bury the roots under an inch of soil

Participial phrases. You build a **participial phrase** around the -ing (present participle) or -ed/-en (past participle) forms of a verbal. You can use it as an adjective to modify a noun or pronoun.

Everyone **watching the show** failed to notice the commotion in the lobby.

The chef chose a cake **flavored with orange peel**.

Gerund phrases. You build a **gerund phrase** around the -ing form of a verbal and can use it as a noun in a subject, object, or subject complement.

                                                         object of
              sentence subject   **preposition**
Closing the landfill will keep it from **polluting the groundwater**.

Infinitive phrases. You can create an **infinitive phrase** using the *to* form of a verbal and use it as an adjective, adverb, or noun.

                 noun (sentence subject)
To live in the mountains of Montana was his goal.

                                                         adverb
He used several books on organic farming **to help plan his garden**.

16c
gr

16.2

Exercise 7

A. First, identify all the phrases in the following passage, and tell whether each is a prepositional, verbal, absolute, or appositive phrase.

Without electricity, we would perish. We could learn to do without the flow of electrons that power VCRs and food processors, but the currents inside our bodies are vital. The brain needs electricity to issue its commands from neuron to neuron. When these signals reach a muscle, they set up a wave of electrical excitation in the fibers, which in turn triggers the chemical reactions that make the fibers contract or relax. The most important muscle is the heart; it shudders under a wave of electricity about once each second.

—CARL ZIMMER, "The Body Electric"

Next, combine the following sentences to create a paragraph that might follow the one above. Try to create a variety of phrases.

The heart has an electric field. The field radiates into the chest cavity. The field sends clues. The clues are about the heart's function. The clues go toward the skin. Cardiologists can get a peek at the heart. They are taping electrodes. The electrodes are taped to a person's torso. Each electrode produces a familiar squiggle. The squiggles are on an electrocardiogram. The electrocardiogram shows how the voltage changes at that single point. The point is on the body. Cardiologists spend years learning. They learn to infer heart function from these signals. They learn to recognize the telltale signs. The signs are in EKG readings. The signs tell of dangerous heart conditions.

B. Share your revised paragraph from Exercise 7A with a group of fellow writers in order to decide which versions are the most effective.

ESL

16c
gr

ESL ADVICE: GERUNDS AND INFINITIVES

Gerunds and infinitives are verbals (see 16c-4).

GERUND	**INFINITIVE**
verb (base form) + *-ing*	*to* + verb (base form)

VERBS FOLLOWED BY EITHER GERUNDS OR INFINITIVES

You can use a gerund or infinitive after some verbs, sometimes changing their meaning slightly.

Developers <u>prefer</u> **working** [gerund]/**to work** [infinitive] with local contractors.

COMMON VERBS TAKING EITHER GERUNDS OR INFINITIVES

begin	intend	regret
can't stand	learn	remember
continue	like	start
forget	love	stop
hate	prefer	try

The meaning of some verbs (such as *remember*, *forget*, and *stop*) will change depending on whether you use a gerund or an infinitive.

GERUND   I **remembered** meeting your friend.
I recall an event in the past.

INFINITIVE   I **remembered** to meet your friend.
I did not forget to do something in the past.

GERUND   I never **forget** visiting the Statue of Liberty.
I recall a past event.

INFINITIVE   I never **forget** to study for exams.
I remember to do something.

GERUND   I **stopped** smoking.
I do not smoke anymore.

INFINITIVE   I **stopped** to smoke.
I paused to smoke.

VERBS FOLLOWED BY GERUNDS

After some verbs you can use only a gerund (and not an infinitive).

subject + verb + gerund
GERUND   Children enjoy **reading** fairy tales.

COMMON VERBS TAKING GERUNDS

admit	deny	mind
anticipate	discuss	miss
appreciate	dismiss	postpone
avoid	enjoy	practice
can't help	finish	quit
consider	imagine	recommend
delay	keep	suggest

ESL

16c
gr

You *must* use gerunds with some idiomatic expressions.

- After the word *go* (in any tense): I **go** shopping. I **went** hiking.
- After the expression *spend time*: Researchers **spend** a lot of **time** preparing reports.
- After the expression *have* + noun: Young children **have difficulty** following directions.
- After a preposition: Physicians' assistants are trained **in** treating routine cases.

In the following examples, the phrase beginning with *to* is not an infinitive. *To* acts like a preposition in each sentence and must be followed by a gerund ending in *-ing*.

I am looking **forward** to living abroad.

Managers are **accustomed** to receiving frequent updates.

Patrons are **used** to viewing complex exhibits.

VERBS FOLLOWED BY INFINITIVES

After some verbs, you must use an infinitive instead of another verb form.

INFINITIVE   Some students need **to work** part time.

COMMON VERBS TAKING INFINITIVES

agree	hope	pretend
ask	intend	promise
choose	manage	refuse
decide	need	seem
expect	offer	venture
fail	plan	want

ESL

16c
gr

You must use an object and then the infinitive to follow some verbs.

subject + verb + object + infinitive
Doctors often **advise** their patients to eat well.

COMMON VERBS TAKING AN OBJECT + INFINITIVE

advise	convince	force	teach
allow	encourage	permit	tell
ask	expect	persuade	urge

When *make*, *let*, and *have* suggest "cause" or "forced," they follow a different model using the infinitive without *to* (the base form).

subject	+	verb	+	object	+	base form
She		**made/let/had**		me		clean my room.

Use infinitives after certain adjectives.

I	**am**	delighted	to meet you.
The report	**is**	easy	to understand.
The volunteers	**are**	pleased	to help.

5 Recognizing subordinate clauses

A **main** clause (or **independent** clause) contains a subject and a verb; it can stand on its own as a complete sentence. While a **subordinate clause** also contains both a subject and a complete verb, it cannot stand on its own as a complete sentence because it begins with a subordinating word. This word (usually a subordinating conjunction like *because*, *although*, or *if*, or a relative pronoun like *who*, *which*, or *that*; see 16a-2 and 16a-7) signals that the clause is merely a sentence element—modifying the main clause to which it is attached. For this reason, subordinate clauses are sometimes called **dependent clauses**; that is, they "depend" on the main clause.

SUBORDINATE CLAUSE   **because** I was very busy

AS PART OF A SENTENCE   **Because I was very busy**, I forgot to call.

Do not punctuate a subordinate clause as a sentence (see 21a-2).

ESL

16c gr

Subordinate clauses as adjectives. You can use a subordinate clause to modify a noun or a pronoun. Use a **relative pronoun** (*who*, *which*, *that*, *whom*, *whose*) or a **relative adverb** (*when*, *where*) as a subordinating word.

Many people **who live in Foxwood Estates** came to the meeting.

They asked about the industrial park **that the county plans to create**.

Subordinate clauses as adverbs. You can use subordinate clauses as adverbs. An adverb clause begins with a subordinating conjunction such as *because*, *although*, *since*, or *while* (see 16a-7) and modifies verbs, adjectives, or adverbs.

As the workshop proceeded, many of Jeanelle's questions were answered.
The clause is an adverb answering the question "When?"

She had registered for the workshop **because she was interested in learning about tax deductions for small businesses**.
The clause is an adverb answering the question "Why?"

Subordinate clauses as nouns. Noun clauses begin with *who, whom, whose, whoever, whomever, what, whatever, when, where, why, whether,* or *how.* They can play the same roles as nouns: subject, object, or complement.

SENTENCE SUBJECT   **Whoever is interested in a career in accounting** ought to attend.

DIRECT OBJECT   You should pack **what you need for the weekend**.

Exercise 8

A. Underline all subordinate clauses in the following passage.

Because the tax laws have gotten more complex recently, we have published a guide to tax preparation that highlights new features of the tax code. In addition, the guide provides step-by-step instruction for tax forms, which should be helpful even if a person has considerable experience filling out the forms. Anyone who plans to file taxes for a small business will be interested in the special section on business tax laws. Although many professionals and businesspeople rely on accountants when tax time arrives, they will nonetheless find that the guide provides money-saving advice.

B. Working with another writer, revise the passage in Exercise 8A by combining ideas and word groups in different ways and by using different supporting words. Retain the general sense of the passage, but feel free to add your own ideas and perspective.

ESL

16c
gr

ESL ADVICE: ADJECTIVE, ADVERB, AND NOUN CLAUSES

ADJECTIVE CLAUSES

Adjective clauses (also called **relative clauses**) work like adjectives because they modify or add more information to nouns. To form a relative clause, use a relative pronoun: *who, whom, that, which,* or *whose. Who, whom, that,* and *whose* are used to modify people. *That, which,* and *whose* are used to modify animals, places, and things. In spoken American English the use of *whom* generally is optional, but it is always used in formal writing.

Place the relative clause as close as possible to the noun (the antecedent) that it modifies.

DRAFT   The <u>attorney</u> is excellent **who advises on product liability**.

REVISED   The <u>attorney</u> **who advises on product liability** is excellent.

You may drop the relative pronoun if it is not the subject of the clause. Either use is correct.

INCLUDED   The apartment **that** we rented was very lovely.

OMITTED   The apartment we rented was very lovely.

When a relative pronoun is the subject of an adjective clause, you can change it to an **adjective phrase**. To change a clause with a *be* verb, omit the relative pronoun and the *be* verb.

CLAUSE   He is the man **who is studying German**.
(WITH *BE*)

PHRASE   He is the man **studying German**.

To change a clause with another verb to a phrase, omit the relative pronoun and change the verb to the present participle form (see Chapter 18).

CLAUSE   He is the man **who wants to study German**.
(WITHOUT *BE*)

PHRASE   He is the man **<u>wanting</u> to study German**.

ADVERB CLAUSES

Adverb clauses give information about time, reason, contrast, and condition, acting like adverbs to modify verbs.

TIME   <u>**When** the season changes</u>, clients want to see new colors.

REASON   Last year's clothes seem dated <u>**because** the color palette has changed</u>.

CONTRAST   <u>**Although** many clients want the new colors</u>, some choose the old palette.

CONDITION   We may have cost overruns **unless** we move the inventory.

ESL

16c
gr

SOME WORDS TO INTRODUCE ADVERB CLAUSES				
TIME		REASON	CONTRAST	CONDITION
while	when	because	although	if
before	whenever	since	though	even if
since	as soon as	as	even though	only if
until	after	now that	while	unless
once	as		whereas	provided that
				as long as

NOUN CLAUSES

Noun clauses work in the same way as nouns in the sentence: subject, object, object of preposition, and complement of an adjective.

SUBJECT   **What she said** was interesting.

OBJECT   We don't know **where the ambassador is going**.

COMPLEMENT
OF PREPOSITION   His parents were concerned about **how safe the car was**.

COMPLEMENT
OF ADJECTIVE   They are confident **that he will pass the test**.

SOME WORDS TO INTRODUCE NOUN CLAUSES

who	where	however
whom	why	how much
whose	whether	how many
what	that	how long
which	which	how often

You may also use noun clauses to report information questions. Word order in *wh-* question noun clauses may vary.

- The word order changes when the question includes a form of *be* and a subject complement.

    QUESTION   Who **are** your friends?

    NOUN CLAUSE   I wonder who your friends **are**.

- The word order changes when the question includes a modal.

    QUESTION   How **can** I meet them?

    NOUN CLAUSE   Please tell me how I **can** meet them.

- The word order changes when the question includes the auxiliary *do, does,* or *did*.

    QUESTION   When **do** you plan to introduce us?

    NOUN CLAUSE   Let me know when you [do] plan to introduce us.

- The word order changes when the question includes the auxiliary *have, has,* or *had*.

    QUESTION   How **have** you met so many people?

    NOUN CLAUSE   I'm interested in how you **have** met so many people.

ESL

16c
gr

Sometimes the word order remains the same as the word order in the original question.

QUESTION	Who discovered the fire?
NOUN CLAUSE	Do you know **who discovered the fire**?

QUESTION	What started the fire?
NOUN CLAUSE	Did anyone see **what started the fire**?

QUESTION	How much damage was caused?
NOUN CLAUSE	The company knows **how much damage was caused**.

QUESTION	Which firefighters came to help?
NOUN CLAUSE	He knows **which firefighters came to help**.

16.3

16d Recognizing different sentence types

You can create **sentences** with a variety of structures and purposes.

1 Recognizing sentence structures

Sentences vary in structure according to the kind and number of clauses they include.

ESL

16d
gr

Simple sentence. A sentence with one main (independent) clause and no subordinate (dependent) clauses is a **simple sentence**.

The community development program sponsors construction projects.

Compound sentence. A sentence with two or more main (independent) clauses and no subordinate (dependent) clauses is a **compound sentence**.

main clause

Most people in the audience seemed pleased with the plans, yet

main clause

some complained about the lack of green space.

Complex sentence. A sentence with one main (independent) clause and one or more subordinate (dependent) clauses is a **complex sentence**.

subordinate clause
Because people complained about the lack of green space,

main clause   **subordinate clause**
the architect revised the plans. When the new plans were ready,

main clause
the director came back to the senior center to discuss them,

subordinate clause   **subordinate clause**
even though she was sure that most people would like the plans.

Compound-complex sentence. A sentence with two or more main (independent) clauses and one or more subordinate (dependent) clauses is a **compound-complex sentence**.

subordinate clause   **subordinate clause**
Because he wanted to make sure that work on the extension did not

                        main clause
damage the existing building, the architect asked the contractor to

                    main clause
test the soil for stability, and he then proceeded with the plans.

2 Recognizing sentence purposes

You can create different kinds of sentences according to the relationship you want to establish with readers. A **declarative sentence** makes a statement. An **interrogative sentence** poses a question. An **imperative sentence** makes a request or command. An **exclamatory sentence** makes an exclamation.

DECLARATIVE   The motor is making a rattling noise.

INTERROGATIVE   Have you checked it for overheating?

IMPERATIVE   Check it again.

EXCLAMATORY   It's on fire!

16d
gr

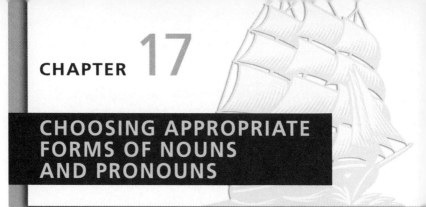

CHAPTER 17

CHOOSING APPROPRIATE FORMS OF NOUNS AND PRONOUNS

As you write and speak, you use changes in pronoun form to guide your audience through sentences and highlight your meaning. In the following sentence, for example, the forms of pronouns change. People can understand what you are saying because they recognize the different forms (and functions) of pronouns.

> Aretha Franklin started making recordings in the 1960s, and **she** has kept on releasing **them** during the five decades of **her** career.

As you read the pronouns in this sentence, you probably noticed, quickly and unconsciously, that *she* indicates the sentence's subject, *them* indicates the object of the action, and *her* indicates possession.

In writing and speaking, for the most part, you choose appropriate pronoun case as quickly and unconsciously as you recognize case forms during reading or listening. At times, however, you may have to struggle with choices between *we* and *us*, *her* and *she*, and *who* and *whom*. The wrong choices can be misleading.

17
pron

CONFUSING   Dr. Landova criticized the report. The other team members liked it better than **her**.

> READER'S REACTION: *Her* makes the sentence say that the team members liked the report more than they liked Dr. Landova. It's possible that the writer means this, but I don't think so.

EDITED   Dr. Landova criticized the report. The other team members liked it better than **she**.

> READER'S REACTION: This sentence makes more sense. They liked the report better than *she* liked it.

Moreover, some errors are likely to irritate your audience and create a negative image of you.

INCORRECT   **Him** and **me** will make a strong management team.

READER'S REACTION: *Him and me* sounds careless and uneducated. It's a lot easier to trust the judgment and leadership of someone who writes more carefully and precisely.

EDITED   **He** and **I** will make a strong management team.

17a Recognizing pronoun forms

Because a pronoun's form can signal its role in a sentence, you need to recognize the different forms so you can choose those that accurately reflect your meaning.

1 Recognizing forms of pronoun case

Pronouns acting as subjects take subjective form (**subjective case**). Those acting as objects take objective form (**objective case**). Those indicating possession or ownership take possessive form (**possessive case**).

SUBJECTIVE CASE   **He** designs furniture for Herman Miller Company.

OBJECTIVE CASE   The modular furniture we are using was designed by **him**.

POSSESSIVE CASE   **His** design team created the work spaces in the sales office.

When your sentences follow a familiar order, such as subject-verb-object (see 16b-1), pronoun case merely highlights roles that will also be obvious to readers from the sentence's arrangement.

> subjective   objective
> case   case
> Tanika helped them.
> subject verb object

When you use complicated sentence structures, your readers will depend even more on pronoun case to grasp your meaning.

17a
pron

With Jim, **her**, and Susan, **you** have hired three people **who** are better able to work together than **we**. In addition, as industrial engineers, **they** always pay attention to a product's ease of assembly as well as **its** appearance.

2 Recognizing forms of personal pronouns

I, we, he, she, it, you, and *they,* the **personal pronouns**, take additional forms to provide readers with other kinds of information, as the following chart indicates. **First person** pronouns (*I*, *we*) tell who is speaking. **Second person** (*you*) tells who is being spoken to. And **third person** pronouns (*he*, *she*, *it*, *they*) tell who or what is being spoken about. Pronouns can also indicate **number** (*I*, *we*, *he*, *she*, *they*) and **gender** (*he*, *she*, *it*).

FORMS OF PRONOUNS

PERSONAL PRONOUNS

	SUBJECTIVE		OBJECTIVE		POSSESSIVE	
	SINGULAR	PLURAL	SINGULAR	PLURAL	SINGULAR	PLURAL
FIRST PERSON	I	we	me	us mine	my ours	our
SECOND PERSON	you	you	you	you yours	your yours	your
THIRD PERSON	he/she/it	they	him/her/it	them	his/her/ hers/its	their/ theirs

RELATIVE AND INTERROGATIVE PRONOUNS

SUBJECTIVE	OBJECTIVE	POSSESSIVE
who	whom	whose
whoever	whomever	whosever
which	which	
that	that	
what	what	

INDEFINITE PRONOUNS

SUBJECTIVE	OBJECTIVE	POSSESSIVE
anybody	anybody	anybody's
everyone	everyone	everyone's

17a
pron

Other kinds of pronouns (**relative**, **interrogative**, and **indefinite** types—see 16a-2) change form only to indicate case. Because nouns in English vary in form only for the possessive case—*the study/the study's conclusions*—the present chapter looks primarily at pronoun variation.

3 Choosing subjective forms

Deciding to use a pronoun's subjective form is relatively easy if the pronoun is the subject of all or part of a sentence.

She <u>wants</u> to know why the orders have not been filled.

Often, however, you need to choose the subjective case for pronouns playing other roles. (See 16b for discussion of subjects, complements, and other sentence parts.)

STRATEGY

As you edit, check whether a pronoun is acting as a subject within some part of a sentence. Check also whether it renames or re-states a subject. If it plays either role, use the word's subjective form.

subject of subordinate clause
Because **they** were unable to get a loan, the business failed.

subject of relative clause
Atco Manufacturers will be hiring people **who** are willing to work the night shift.

subject of implied verb
I attend class more regularly than **he** [does].

complement renames subject
The new auditor is **he**, the person at Sandi's desk.

appositives rename subject
Two of the people in the group, **she** and **I**, have experience with desktop publishing.

4 Choosing objective forms

When you make a pronoun the direct (or indirect) object of an entire sentence, use the word's objective form.

direct object
The police arrested **them** for disturbing the peace.

indirect object
The company bought **her** a spreadsheet program.

In addition, choose the objective form for pronouns playing a number of ob-ject roles in a sentence. (See 16b for definitions of objects and similar ele-ments.)

17a
pron

STRATEGY

As you edit, check whether a pronoun is acting as an object within some part of a sentence. Check also whether it renames or re-states an object. If it plays either role, choose the word's objective form.

object of preposition
The rest of **them** had to wait several months for the software.

object in relative clause
An accountant **whom** the firm hired helped her out.

object in gerund phrase
Mr. Pederson's research for the report included interviewing **them**.

object in participial phrase
Having interviewed **us**, too, Mr. Pederson had a lot of material to summarize.

The report contained interviews with the two dissatisfied workers,
appositive renames object
her and him.

You may find that pronouns used with infinitive phrases are tricky, so keep the following example in mind.

Mr. Pederson asked **us** to read the summaries of the interviews.

You might be tempted to treat *us* as the subject of the phrase *to read the summaries of the interviews. Us* is the direct object of the sentence, however (*Mr. Pederson asked* us), and the objective form is correct.

5 Choosing possessive forms

When you use a pronoun to show possession, choose the possessive case. Remember that the particular form of the possessive you use depends on whether you use the pronoun *before a noun* or *in place of a noun.*

17a
pron

BEFORE NOUN   The Topeka office requested a copy of **her** report.

IN PLACE OF NOUN   **Hers** was the most thorough and up-to-date study available.

You should also use the possessive form before a gerund.

gerund
Their requesting a copy of the report pleased the project supervisor.

CHOOSING POSSESSIVE FORMS		
BEFORE A NOUN		**IN PLACE OF A NOUN**
my problem	=	mine
your problem	=	yours

her problem	=	hers
their problem	=	theirs
our problem	=	ours
BUT		
his problem	=	his
its problem	=	its

Do not use an apostrophe with a possessive pronoun. Readers will notice the error. (See 35a.)

INCORRECT   your's, her's, it's, their's

CORRECT   yours, hers, its, theirs

Use *it's* only as a contraction meaning *it is*.

Form possessive nouns with an apostrophe: *Luis's, cat's, Barbara's, government's*.

DID YOU KNOW?

In the 1300s and 1400s the pronoun *it* (neuter) took these forms: *hit* (subjective), *his* (possessive), and *hit* (objective). By the 1600s, *hit* lost the *h* to become *it*, but *his* remained the possessive form. As a result, one of Shakespeare's characters says, "How far that little candle throws his beams," instead of "throws *its* beams." During the seventeenth century, however, people began using several substitutes for *his* as a neuter possessive, finally accepting *its*, the form we use today.

Albert C. Baugh and Thomas Cable, *A History of the English Language*, 3rd ed. (Englewood Cliffs, NJ: Prentice Hall, 1978) 243.

17a
pron

Exercise 1

A. In each of the following sentences, choose the correct pronoun from the pair within parentheses. Then name the case of the pronoun you have chosen.

EXAMPLE

Ruth and (*I*/me) are planning to open a children's clothing store.
subjective

1. The design for the new store was prepared by (*she/her*).
2. The city requires (*we/us*) to submit plans for remodeling the store we plan to rent.

3. Having interviewed Ruth and (*I/me*) about our marketing plan, the bank's officer approved our loan.
4. The person who will choose the stock for our store is (*she/her*).
5. I will supervise the salespeople (*who/whom*) we hire.

Next, revise the following sentences by correcting any errors in pronoun case.

EXAMPLE

her

The foundation sent copies of the grant proposal to ~~she~~ and me.

1. Her and three other people worked for three weeks preparing the grant proposal.
2. The original grant-writing team included two other people, Kristen and she.
3. Because I spent more time working on the grant, I think I ought to get more credit for its success than him.
4. It is me who will have to supervise research work done under the grant.
5. Responsibility for budgeting the grant money is your's.

B. Working with a group of writers, choose a draft paper one of the group has written, and examine two paragraphs carefully. Identify all pronouns in the subjective, objective, and possessive cases, and check to see that they are used correctly. Then suggest revisions for the paragraphs, drawing on some of the sentence and pronoun patterns illustrated in 17a–b.

17b pron

17b Recognizing common problems with pronoun forms

We all struggle at times with pronoun forms. Many of your troubles are likely to occur at predictable places in a sentence; pay attention, therefore, to the following troublesome sentence constructions.

1 Pay attention to compound subjects and objects

When you use a compound such as *the committee and I* or *Jim and me*, you need to decide on the proper form for the pronoun. The rule is simple enough: Use the same case for pronouns in compounds that you would use for single pronouns playing the same role.

COMPOUND SUBJECT	Denise or (*he/him*) should be responsible for creating the new database.
USE SUBJECTIVE CASE	Denise or **he** should be responsible for creating the new database.
COMPOUND OBJECT	The coach selected (*she and him/her and him*) as team representatives.
USE OBJECTIVE CASE	The coach selected **her and him** as team representatives.

In practice, however, you may often find it difficult to decide on the correct pronoun case. The following strategy may help.

STRATEGY

To choose the correct pronoun form in compound subjects and objects, use the **focus-imagine-choose strategy.**

- **Focus** on the pronoun for which you need to choose the appropriate form.

  UNEDITED   Anne-Marie and **me** will develop videotapes for the sales presentation.
  I or me?

- **Imagine** each possible choice for the pronoun as a singular subject (or object) in a sentence.

  Me will develop videotapes for the sales presentation.

  I will develop videotapes for the sales presentation.

- **Choose** the correct form, and use it in the compound subject (or object). If the correct form is not immediately apparent to you, refer to the chart on page 232. (Choosing the form that "sounds right" can be a misleading strategy with compounds.)

  EDITED   Anne-Marie and **I** will develop videotapes for the sales presentation.

17b
pron

An incorrect pronoun form may pass without much notice in conversation because it "sounds right."

SPOKEN   This is a private agreement between you and **I**.

You need to be alert for problems like this as you edit because readers are more likely than listeners to notice the faulty choice of pronoun form.

EDITED   This is a private agreement between you and **me**.

As you edit, pay special attention to pronoun forms that sound "wrong" or "unusual." Some of them may actually be correct, as in the following instance.

CORRECT   Responsibility for keeping the coffee room clean is shared between **them** and **us**.

2 Watch for *we* or *us* with a noun

When you pair *we*, *us*, or other pronouns with nouns, make sure the pronoun form—*we*, *they* (subjective) or *us*, *them* (objective)—matches the role played by the noun (subject or object).

CORRECT   **We taxpayers** ought to demand that the city fill the potholes on Pine Avenue.

CORRECT   The award went to the coach, but it really belonged to **us team members** who worked so hard during the season.

CORRECT   If a customer returns to our store because of the quality of the service, the credit belongs to **you salespeople**.

17b
pron

STRATEGY

Check for a correct match of pronoun and noun by imagining a sentence in alternative versions without the noun.

SENTENCE   The teaching evaluation should be conducted by (*us?* *we?*) students, not by the faculty or administration.

VERSION 1   The teaching evaluation should be conducted by **we** . . . .
(INCORRECT)

VERSION 2   The teaching evaluation should be conducted by **us** . . . .
(CORRECT)

EDITED   The teaching evaluation should be conducted by **us** students, not by the faculty or administration.
              Us is the object of a preposition and takes the objective form (see 17a-2).

3 Be alert for subject complements

When you follow a form of the verb *be* (*is, am, are, was, were*) with a pronoun renaming the subject, you create a **subject complement** (see 16b-2). Because you are renaming or restating the subject, choose the subjective form of the pronoun.

CORRECT   The last pharmacy graduates to get jobs at Upstate Medical Center were Rebecca Soares and **I**.

In speaking, the objective form is often acceptable. Moreover, in writing, the correct form may seem stilted and call for rewriting.

CONVERSATION   The new traffic reporter is **him**.

STILTED   The new traffic reporter is **he**.

REWRITTEN   **He** is the new traffic reporter.

4 Check appositives

When you rename a preceding noun or pronoun in an appositive phrase (see 16c-3), match the case of the word being renamed.

17.1

CORRECT   As an investment, the two sisters, **she** and her twin, bought a small chain of dry cleaners.

STRATEGY

Check for the correct pronoun form in an appositive by imagining alternative versions in which you leave out the noun (or pronoun) that was renamed in the original sentence.

SENTENCE   The two children's book illustrators on the panel, (*she? her?*) and (*I? me?*), discussed all the questions asked by the audience.

VERSION 1 (INCORRECT)   **Her and me** discussed all the questions asked by the audience.

VERSION 1 (CORRECT)   **She and I** discussed all the questions asked by the audience.

EDITED   The two children's book illustrators on the panel, **she and I**, discussed all the questions asked by the audience.
The pronouns rename the subject, so the subjective forms are correct.

17b
pron

5 Be careful with comparisons using *than* or *as*

When using *than* or *as* followed by a pronoun ("Josie located the resources more quickly *than* **he**"), make sure the pronoun form you choose accurately signals the information left out: "more quickly *than* **he** [did]." A pronoun in the subjective case acts as the subject of the implied statement; a pronoun in the objective case acts as the object.

SUBJECTIVE   Josie located the resources more quickly than **he** [did].

OBJECTIVE   Josie located the resources more quickly than [she located] **him**.

You can leave out part of a sentence containing a comparison with *than* or *as* so long as your readers are able to fill in the missing part easily and accurately.

CLEAR   I earned a better grade in chemistry than she [did].

Rewrite sentences that may be ambiguous or confusing even though they employ correct pronoun forms.

POTENTIALLY AMBIGUOUS   I like working with Aisha better than she.
READER'S REACTION: **Does this mean you prefer to work with Aisha? Or that you like to work with Aisha better than someone else does?**

REWRITTEN   She doesn't like working with Aisha as much as I do.

6 Consider using possessive forms with gerunds

A **gerund** is the *-ing* form of a verb used as a noun (see 16a-4). Choose the possessive case when you put a noun or pronoun before a gerund in order to modify it.

17b pron

CORRECT   **My** skidding across the wet floor frightened me.

CORRECT   **Roseanna's** skidding across the wet floor frightened me.

Why is using the possessive case important? Versions of a sentence with and without the possessive may differ considerably in meaning.

WITH POSSESSIVE   We were surprised by the principal's golfing.
He was golfing, and we were surprised that he had taken up the sport (or that he was so good at it).

WITHOUT POSSESSIVE   We were surprised by the principal golfing.
We were golfing, and he came up to us unexpectedly.

Admittedly, placing a possessive before a gerund can make some sentences hard to read. When this is the case, rewrite the sentence.

INCORRECT   The new store manager was surprised by virtually **everybody** in town showing up for the sale.

> READER'S REACTION: **Does this writer mean that** *virtually everybody* **managed to surprise the new manager? Wasn't it the number of people who showed up that was so surprising?**

AWKWARD   The new store manager was surprised by virtually **everybody's** in town showing up for the sale.

REWRITTEN   The new store manager was surprised **that virtually everybody in town showed up for the sale**.

7 Be cautious when using *myself* and other reflexive pronouns

17.2

People sometimes use *myself*, *yourself*, and other **reflexive pronouns** (see 16a-2) inappropriately as sentence subjects or objects, perhaps because they are not sure which pronoun form is correct and assume that *myself* and the other *-self* pronouns will stretch to fit all cases.

INCORRECT   The Nucor project led to some major disagreements between Stan and myself.

CORRECT   The Nucor project led to some major disagreements between Stan and **me**.

> *Me* **is the object of a preposition, so the objective case is correct; see 17a-2.**

Exercise 2

17b
pron

A. Correct any errors in pronoun case in the following sentences.

EXAMPLE   *she*
Denise and ~~her~~ joined the Disney film group in our class.
                      ∧

1. The rest of us team members decided we should use recent animated movies as the subject of our project.
2. Because their parents own a video store, her brother and her brought in tapes of the movies we planned to study.
3. Bill and I decided to take notes on *Aladdin;* Pat and her chose to study *Beauty and the Beast.*
4. I thought the notes we took were more detailed and better than they.

5. Writing the final paper led to some disagreements between the other members and myself.

B. Working with a group, create a brief story involving three or four characters. Use at least five of the troublesome pronoun case patterns discussed in 17b, avoiding problems in their use.

17c Choosing *who* and *whom*

Many writers and speakers find it hard to choose between *who* and *whom*. They will be inclined to forgive, and even ignore, an occasional misuse of *who*, *whom*, *whoever*, and *whomever*. Nonetheless, the places where you are most likely to have trouble with these pronoun forms, in relative clauses and at the beginning of questions, are also places where the pronouns can affect the meaning of a sentence substantially.

1 Choosing between *who* and *whom in* relative clauses

You probably often use the pronouns *who* and *whom*, *whoever* and *whomever* to begin the subordinate clauses known as **relative clauses** or **adjective clauses** (see 16c-5). Choose *who* and *whomever* when you use the pronouns as subjects; choose *whom* and *whomever* when you use them as objects (see 17a-1 and 2).

SUBJECT   The artist **who creates a painting or sculpture** ought to benefit from its sale.

OBJECT   The proceeds benefit **whomever** the artist designates.

> **STRATEGY**
>
> Deciding between *who* and *whom* can be difficult. You need to choose the appropriate form according to the role the pronoun plays *within the relative clause.* You need to ignore the role the clause plays *within the sentence.*
>
> INCORRECT   The fine must be paid by **whomever** holds the deed to the property.
> Although the whole relative clause is the object of the preposition *by,* within the clause the pronoun acts as a subject, not an object.
>
> EDITED   The fine must be paid by **whoever** holds the deed to the property.

If you are in doubt about either the use of *whom* or its appropriateness to your writing situation, try rewording your sentence to avoid making the choice.

EDITED   The person with the deed to the property must pay the fine.

2 Choosing between *who* and *whom* in questions

You should use *who* at the beginning of a question when the pronoun is the subject of the sentence. You should use *whom* when the pronoun is an object. (See 17a-1 and 2.)

SUBJECT   **Who** is most likely to get the reader's sympathy at this point in the novel, Huck or Jim?

OBJECT   **Whom** can Cordelia trust for counsel about her dilemma?

CASE OF *WHO* AND *WHOEVER*

	SUBJECTIVE	OBJECTIVE	POSSESSIVE
FIRST, SECOND, AND THIRD PERSON	who whoever	whom whomever	whose whosever

Exercise 3

A. Correct any errors in pronoun case in the following sentences.

EXAMPLE

<u>Whomever</u> has taken an IQ test probably remembers the score.
    Whoever

1. In the past, psychologists assumed that whomever scored well on IQ tests was likely to succeed at school and work.
2. Recent studies of IQ tests have produced evidence of them being unable to predict success.
3. A test of constructive thinking skill may tell more about your or mine ability to meet challenges.
4. Reporting on research conducted by he and two of his colleagues, Robert Sternberg points out that "the ability to sell" is an important part of practical intelligence.

17c
pron

5. Other psychologists claim that personal qualities like self-confidence and optimism may by theirselves have as much to do with our mental abilities as IQ does.

B. Working with fellow writers, identify the pronouns in the following passage, and correct any mistakes in case. Keep a record of those identifications and corrections you found most difficult, and be ready to try to explain why you found them difficult.

For we humans, yawning is a familiar activity. You and me probably yawn when we stretch, though not always. Boredom is also a likely cause for us yawning. People often think that no one yawns as much as them, but this is seldom true. We all yawn frequently during a day. We may even start yawning ourselves when we notice someone else whom is yawning.

CHAPTER 18

CHOOSING APPROPRIATE VERB FORMS

Readers may sometimes forgive a spelling mistake or two, but as soon as you write "The Dolphins done real good in the playoffs" or "The polio vaccine could have brang about some forms of cancer," readers are likely to lose confidence in your ideas. Irregular verb forms may be accepted in many communities, especially in speech, yet when they appear in academic, work, or public writing, they undermine a writer's credibility. Being able to identify and edit verb problems in your writing is therefore an important part of being able to communicate effectively with a wide range of readers.

18a Recognizing and editing simple present and past tense verbs

When you use a simple verb in a sentence, you will put that verb into the **present tense** for action occurring now or the **past tense** for action that has already occurred. Most verbs form their past tense by adding -*ed* to the present tense form, also called the **base form**. Depending on the particular verb, this addition can be pronounced as -*t* (*baked*), -*d* (*called*), or -*ed* (*defended*). You need no special ending to mark the present tense *except* in the third person singular form (with *he, she,* or *it* or a singular noun).

The trucks **wait** in line until the border crossing **opens**.

1 Using present and past tense in academic settings

Academic and professional readers may expect you to use the present and past tenses in some special ways. When discussing a piece of literature, a film, an essay, a painting, or a similar creative production, use the present tense. Treat events, ideas, characters, or statements from such works as if they exist in an ongoing present tense.

In Erdrich's *Love Medicine*, Albertine **returns** to the reservation.

In the social and natural sciences, use the present tense to discuss the results and implications of a current study or experiment, but use the past tense to review the findings of earlier researchers.

> Although Maxwell (1991) **identified** three crucial classroom interactions, the current survey **suggests** two others as well.

2 Pay attention to the endings of past tense verbs

When you write the past tense of a regular verb, you usually add -ed to its base form. Sometimes you may incorrectly leave off the -ed because you don't "hear" it, particularly when a word beginning in d or t follows the verb.

DRAFT   The company **use** to provide dental benefits.

EDITED   The company **used** to provide dental benefits.

3 Watch for irregular verbs

About sixty or seventy common English verbs are exceptions to the "add -ed" rule for past tense. Most of these irregular verbs change an internal vowel in the simple past tense, such as *run* (present) and *ran* (past).

STRATEGY

Because the forms of each irregular verb must be learned independently, you may occasionally use a past tense form that is not acceptable in standard written English or in most work, public, and academic communities. Make a list of any verbs that are troublesome for you, and scan your drafts for them when you edit.

DRAFT   The characters in the movie **sweared** at each other constantly.

EDITED   The characters in the movie **swore** at each other constantly.

The following chart of the principle parts of common irregular verbs should help you as you edit. Check a dictionary for verbs not included in the list.

**18a
verb**

COMMON IRREGULAR VERBS

PRESENT	PAST	PAST PARTICIPLE
arise	arose	arisen
am/is/are	was/were	been
bear	bore	borne

PRESENT	PAST	PAST PARTICIPLE
begin	began	begun
bite	bit	bitten/bit
blow	blew	blown
break	broke	broken
bring	brought	brought
buy	bought	bought
catch	caught	caught
choose	chose	chosen
come	came	come
creep	crept	crept
dive	dived/dove	dived
do	did	done
draw	drew	drawn
dream	dreamed/dreamt	dreamt
drink	drank	drunk
drive	drove	driven
eat	ate	eaten
fall	fell	fallen
fight	fought	fought
fly	flew	flown
forget	forgot	forgotten
forgive	forgave	forgiven
freeze	froze	frozen
get	got	got/gotten
give	gave	given
go	went	gone
grow	grew	grown
hang (object)	hung (object)	hung (object)
hang (person)	hanged/hung (person)	hanged/hung (person)
know	knew	known
lay	laid	laid
lead	led	led
lie	lay	lain
light	lit/lighted	lit
lose	lost	lost
pay	paid	paid
prove	proved	proved/proven
ride	rode	ridden
ring	rang	rung
rise	rose	risen
run	ran	run
see	saw	seen
seek	sought	sought
set	set	set

18a
verb

(*continued*)

COMMON IRREGULAR VERBS (*continued*)		
PRESENT	PAST	PAST PARTICIPLE
shake	shook	shaken
sing	sang/sung	sung
sink	sank/sunk	sunk
sit	sat	sat
speak	spoke	spoken
spring	sprang	sprung
steal	stole	stolen
sting	stung	stung
strike	struck	struck
swear	swore	sworn
swim	swam	swum
swing	swung	swung
take	took	taken
tear	tore	torn
throw	threw	thrown
wake	woke/waked	woken/waked/woke
wear	wore	worn

18b Recognizing and editing problems with participles

When you provide the main verb in a sentence with a **helping**, or **auxiliary**, **verb** (such as *is* or *has*) and also change the form of the main verb, you create complex verb forms conveying important aspects of past, present, or future time, as in the following sentences.

After **having eaten** up all the cake, little Jennifer **would have begun** to feel guilty **had it not been** for her father's unexpected treat—a box of delicious parfaits for the family.

Assuming he **would be going** on the trip, Terry **had started** packing when to his surprise the whole apartment **began** to tremble from a small earthquake that **will be remembered** as the July Surprise.

But how can you be sure you are using the correct verb forms when creating sentences like these?

The form a verb takes when it's linked to a helping verb is called a **participle**, which itself can take two forms: **past participle** and **present participle**. When writers have problems with complex tenses, they typically use the wrong participle.

To form the present participle, add *-ing* to the base form of the verb (the form with no endings or markers).

HELPING VERB	PARTICIPLE (MAIN VERB)
He was	loading the truck.
He will be	loading the truck.
He had been	loading the truck.

Chan is **greeting** the jugglers at the airport as we speak.

To form the past participle of most verbs, just use the simple past tense.

HELPING VERB	PAST PARTICIPLE (MAIN VERB)
Mike has	rented the truck
Mike had	rented the truck.

Chan has **greeted** the jugglers every year for the past five years.

Some participial forms are irregular, however, involving an internal vowel change or an *-en* ending. To help recognize and edit them, consult the list of common irregular verbs on pp. 246–248.

INCORRECT	Louise lost the pie-eating contest because she **had drank** three glasses of lemonade just before it began.
EDITED	Louise lost the pie-eating contest because she **had drunk** three glasses of lemonade just before it began.
INCORRECT	By the end of the trial, the lawyers **had went** too far in their defense of the rapist.
EDITED	By the end of the trial, the lawyers **had gone** too far in their defense of the rapist.

Most verbs are formed by combining one or more helping verbs with a main verb (see 16a-3). The main verb plus any helping verb is called a **verb phrase**.

18b
verb

	verb phrase
ONE HELPING VERB	I **was walking** to school during the snowstorm.

	verb phrase
TWO HELPING VERBS	I **have been walking** to school for many years.

Exercise 1

A. In each of the following sentences, a correct or incorrect irregular verb form appears in parentheses. Edit each sentence to make it correct, or indicate that it's already correct. If necessary, consult the list on pp. 246–248 or look in a dictionary for the principal parts of a particular verb.

EXAMPLE

had fallen

The rain (~~had falled~~) all night.
                      ^

1. Jeremy (*had chose*) to work along the levee as part of the volunteer corps.
2. The floodwater (*had rised*) rapidly during the night.
3. The work team (*had heaved*) sandbags on top of the levee for almost twenty-four hours.
4. Jim O'Connor and Rebecca Gomez (*had hung*) plastic sheeting up to plug a leak.
5. By eight o'clock in the morning, people (*had woke*) up to find that the river (*had fell*) by six inches and the town was safe.

B. Review the list of irregular verbs in 18a. Compose five sentences in which you correctly or incorrectly use the past or past participle form of an irregular verb. In a small group, exchange lists and edit your sentences. Discuss the changes you made or did not make.

ESL ADVICE: VERB FORMS

THIRD PERSON -S OR -ES ENDING

Be sure to add an *-s or -es* to verbs that are third person singular

SUBJECT	VERB	SUBJECT	VERB + -S
I/you/we/they	write	he/she/it (animal, thing, concept)	**writes**

ESL

18b verb

SIMPLE PRESENT AND SIMPLE PAST

These are the two tenses that add no helping verbs to form the verb, except for the negative and interrogative forms. No other verb forms can stand alone!

SIMPLE PRESENT   They **live** in the dormitory this semester.

SIMPLE PAST   They **lived** in an apartment last semester.

PRINCIPAL PARTS OF VERBS IN ENGLISH

In English, verbs can have the following forms.

BASE FORM	PAST	PRESENT PARTICIPLE	PAST PARTICIPLE
REGULAR VERBS			
live	lived	living	lived
want	wanted	wanting	wanted

IRREGULAR VERBS

| eat | ate | eating | eaten |
| run | ran | running | run |

HELPING VERBS

Most verbs combine one or more helping verbs (also called auxiliary verbs) with a main verb to form a **verb phrase**. Helping verbs include *am, is, are, will, would, can, could, have, has, had, was, were, should, might, may, must, do, does,* and *did.* Sometimes these words work in combination, as in *have been, has been, had been, will be, will have,* and *will have been.*

VERB FORMS AND HELPING VERBS FOR COMMONLY USED VERB TENSES

The past, present, and future progressive use forms of *be.*

PROGRESSIVE FORM

subject + *was/were* + present participle
PAST   I **was** working in my studio yesterday.

subject + *am/is/are* + present participle
PRESENT   I **am** working in my studio right now.

subject + *will* (modal) + *be* + present participle
FUTURE   I **will be** working in my studio tomorrow.

The past, present, and future perfect use forms of *have.*

PERFECT FORM

subject + *had* + past participle
PAST   I **had** tried to call you all day.

subject + *have/has* + past participle
PRESENT   I **have** tried to call you all day.

subject + *will* (modal) + *have* + past participle
FUTURE   I **will have** called you by midnight.

ESL

18c
verb

18c Editing progressive and perfect tenses

The **present, past,** and **future progressive** allow you to show an action in progress at some point in time. When you attach a helping verb to a main verb in the **progressive tense**, the main verb must take the *-ing* ending. In the future tense, the progressive must also include the verbal element *be.*

PRESENT PROGRESSIVE   Sales **are increasing** this quarter.

PAST PROGRESSIVE   At this time last year, we **were working** for improvement.

FUTURE PROGRESSIVE   I **will be discussing** the results at the meeting.

Note that irregular main verbs are not affected in any unique way by the progressive tense; all consist of the base form plus -*ing*.

> The park ranger **is catching** the injured raccoon.

> The campers **will be hanging** their food from a tree at night.

The **perfect tenses** are used to show the order in which events take place. The **past perfect tense** allows you to indicate that something had already happened before something else happened. The form consists of *had* plus the past participle (see 18b for participle forms).

> The general practitioner **had treated** the patient for six months before the specialist took over the case.

The **present perfect tense** works much like the past perfect, but the action is something that has recurred or that the writer is insisting has already occurred.

> I **have reported** the burglary already.

The present perfect also presents something begun in the past and continuing into the present. It differs from the simple past, which indicates an action already completed or specified in time.

PRESENT PERFECT   I **have lived** in St. Louis for three weeks.

SIMPLE PAST   I **lived** in St. Louis in 2001.

> The **future perfect tense** shows that something will have happened by the time something else will be happening. This form consists of the helping verb *will* plus *have* plus the past participle of the main verb.

> The technician **will have finished** by the time the dentist is ready.

1 Check the helping verb in progressive tenses

Most errors in progressive tense occur when you either use the wrong form of the helping verb or omit part of it. Look over sentences in a progressive tense carefully to see if you have used the correct form of the helping verb or have omitted part of it (as is common in some dialects).

18c
verb

DRAFT	The interview **starting** five minutes late.
EDITED	The interview **is starting** five minutes late.

DRAFT	The employees **was running** for the elevator.
EDITED	The employees **were running** for the elevator.

2 Check the form of the past participle in the past perfect tense

Writers sometimes set out to use the past perfect tense but mistakenly substitute a simple past tense form for the past participle.

DRAFT	Pierre **had rode** for six years before he got injured in a rodeo.
EDITED	Pierre **had ridden** for six years before he got injured in a rodeo.

ESL ADVICE: SIMPLE PRESENT AND PRESENT PROGRESSIVE TENSES

Use the **simple present** tense to describe activities that are factual or habitual. These activities occur in the present, but they are not necessarily activities in progress.

subject + verb (with -s if third person singular)

SHOWS FACT   The planets **revolve** around the sun.

SHOWS HABIT   The museum **offers** summer programs for children.

COMMON TIME EXPRESSIONS FOR PRESENT TENSE HABITUAL ACTIVITIES

all the time	every holiday	every year	rarely
always	every month	frequently	sometimes
every class	every semester	most of the time	usually
every day	every week	often	never

Use the **present progressive** tense to describe activities in progress.

subject + am/is/are + present participle
Santiago **is testing** the revised formula.

Santiago **is testing** the revised formula **this month**.

ESL

18c
verb

COMMON PROGRESSIVE TIME EXPRESSIONS FOR ACTIVITIES IN PROGRESS

at the moment	this afternoon	this month	this year
right now	this evening	this morning	today

CHOOSING BETWEEN SIMPLE PRESENT AND PRESENT PROGRESSIVE

When you choose between the simple present and present progressive tenses, think about which time expression best describes the activity. Is it happening only at the moment (present progressive) or all the time as a fact or habit (simple present)?

NOT APPROPRIATE All people are communicating in some language.

CORRECT All people communicate in some language.
This is a fact, so the correct tense must be simple present tense.

NOT APPROPRIATE The students are speaking their own languages in class.

CORRECT The students speak their own languages in class.
This is a habitual activity that occurs all the time, so the correct tense is simple present.

VERBS THAT CAN BE TROUBLESOME IN PROGRESSIVE TENSES

VERB	EXAMPLE	OTHER USAGES AND MEANINGS
SENSES		
see	I **see** the beauty.	Also: I **am seeing** the consultant. (meeting with, visiting, dating)
hear	I **hear** the birds.	Also: I **have been hearing** about the problem for a while. (receiving information)
smell	The flowers **smell** strong.	Also: I **am smelling** the flowers. (action in progress)
taste	The food **tastes** good.	Also: The cook **is tasting** the soup. (action in progress)
POSSESSION		
have	We **have** many friends.	Also: We **are having** a lot of fun. (experiencing)
own	They **own** many dogs.	
possess	She **possesses** much knowledge.	
belong	The book **belongs** to me.	

VERB	EXAMPLE	OTHER USAGES AND MEANINGS
STATES OF MIND		
be	I **am** tired.	
know	I **know** the city well.	
believe	She **believes** in God.	
think	LaShonda **thinks** it is true. (knows, believes)	Also: LaShonda **is thinking** about relocating. (having thoughts about)
recognize	His dog always **recognizes** him. (knows)	
understand	The social worker **understands** the problem.	
mean	I **don't mean** to pry. (don't want)	Also: I **have been meaning** to visit you. (planning, intending)
WISH OR ATTITUDE		
want	We **want** peace.	
desire	He **desires** his freedom.	
need	We **need** rain.	
love	Children **love** snow.	Also: I **have been loving** this book. (enjoying)
hate	Cats **hate** getting wet.	
like	He **likes** skiing.	
dislike	Patients **dislike** waiting.	
seem	The office **seems** efficient.	
appear	He **appears** tired. (seems to be)	Also: He **is appearing** at the theater. (acting, performing)
look	He **looks** tired. (seems to be)	Also: We **are looking** at the revised maps. (action of using eyes) I **am looking** it up in a dictionary. (consulting, investigating)

ESL

18d
verb

18d Editing troublesome verbs (*lie, lay, sit, set*)

Even for experienced writers, a few verbs can be tricky. Until you can remember their correct forms, you should identify these verbs when you edit your drafts and then check them by reviewing this section. Here are the verbs most often confused.

VERB	PRESENT	PAST	PARTICIPLE
lie (oneself)	lie	lay	lain
lay (an object)	lay	laid	laid
sit (oneself)	sit	sat	sat
set (an object)	set	set	set

1 Check *lie* and *lay*

When you use the verb *lie* to mean "lie down," you may confuse it with the verb *lay*, which means to put something down, as in "Lay the book on the table." *Lie* is an intransitive verb—it can't be used with a **direct object** (see 16b)—whereas *lay* must be used with a direct object.

DRAFT   I **laid** down yesterday afternoon for a nap. I **have laid** down at around 2 p.m. each day for over a year now.

EDITED   I **lay** down yesterday afternoon for a nap. I **have lain** down at around 2 p.m. each day for over a year now.

DRAFT   Dr. Parsons **lay** the cadaver on the table and began the autopsy.

EDITED   Dr. Parsons **laid** the cadaver on the table and began the autopsy.

A third verb, *lie*, meaning "to tell an untruth," is a regular verb whose past tense ends in *-ed* ("I *lied* to my sister"). Don't confuse it with the form for the other verb *lie*.

2 Pay attention to *sit* and *set*

The verb *sit* means to place oneself on or in something, such as a chair. *Set*, however, means to place an object, such as a book, on a surface. You can figure out which form to use by asking yourself whether there is a direct object in your sentence. *Sit* can't be used with a direct object, but *set* must be used with a direct object.

DRAFT   First Erica and Steve **sat** the projector down on the table. Then they **set** down and listened to the chairperson's speech.

EDITED   First Erica and Steve **set** the projector down on the table. Then they **sat** down and listened to the chairperson's speech.

18d verb

Exercise 2

A. For each sentence, circle the appropriate verb from the choices within parentheses.

EXAMPLE
A fire last Saturday (lead/(led))to Sandy's first big assignment as a reporter.

1. Sandy (laid/lay) the article for the newspaper on her editor's desk.
2. To get information for the article, she (sat/set) in the waiting room of the fire commissioner's office for three days.
3. During the interview, she (layed/lay/laid) on his desk a copy of the report criticizing the fire department's performance during the Brocklin Warehouse fire.

4. The commissioner looked the report over and then (*sat/set*) it next to the other report, which praised the department's performance.

5. After she had (*lead/led*) the three-hour discussion with the commissioner, Sandy was convinced that the department had done an adequate job at the fire.

B. Write four or five sentences in which you use *incorrect* forms of *sit*, *set*, *lie*, and *lay*. Exchange your sentences in a small group, edit them, and then discuss your changes.

EXAMPLE

Mrs. Jones sat the tuna salad dangerously close to Puff, her Siamese cat.

18e Recognizing active and passive voice

Verbs in the **active voice** appear in sentences in which the doer of an action is the subject of the sentence.

	DOER (SUBJECT)	ACTION (VERB)	GOAL (OBJECT)
ACTIVE	The car	hit	the lamppost.
ACTIVE	Dana	distributed	the fliers.

18.1

To rewrite an active sentence in the **passive voice**, add a form of *be* as a helping verb, and use the participial form of the verb. Place the subject (or doer) into the object position after the word *by*. (A prepositional phrase states the doer and is optional.)

	GOAL (SUBJECT)	ACTION (VERB)	[AGENT] [PREPOSITIONAL PHRASE]
PASSIVE	The lamppost	**was hit**	[by the car].
PASSIVE	The fliers	**were distributed**	[by Dana].

18e
verb

The active voice and passive voice versions of a sentence create different kinds of emphasis because they use different words as sentence subjects. In addition, a passive sentence that eliminates any mention of the doer can mask responsibility for an action.

ACTIVE VOICE	The city council banned smoking in restaurants.
PASSIVE VOICE	Smoking in restaurants was banned by the city council.
AGENT ELIMINATED	Smoking in restaurants was banned.

(For a discussion of use and misuse of the passive voice, see 10c-3.)

ESL ADVICE: THE PASSIVE VOICE

All transitive verbs in English may be written in the passive voice *except* the progressive forms of the present perfect, past perfect, future, and future perfect. The verb *make* in the passive voice, unlike in the active voice, is followed by the infinitive.

ACTIVE VOICE   The council member made us **wait**.

PASSIVE VOICE   We were made **to wait** by the council member.

Exercise 3

A. Edit the following passage by rewriting unnecessary uses of the passive voice into the active voice. In rewriting passive voice sentences that do not indicate an agent (doer), fill in the names of the person(s) or thing(s) you consider responsible for the action.

Having cash registers full of change was found to increase the likelihood of a late-night robbery. In one example, a store clerk was held up at gunpoint. It was decided by management that requiring full payment for gasoline in advance of a purchase would minimize the risk of further holdups. This course of action had been voted on by the board of directors prior to implementation. The decision was posted at each location. Following implementation, it was discovered that holdups were not minimized unless large signs indicating the clerk's lack of available cash were placed in plain view. Once this was done, fewer holdups were experienced, and the turnover of late-night personnel was decreased.

ESL

18f
verb

B. Compare your rewritten version of the passage in Exercise 3A with those produced by other students. Be sure you explain why you have decided to let any sentences remain in the passive voice. Working with several other students, produce one version of the passage reflecting group agreement on the best way to rewrite the sentences.

18f Creating clear tense sequence

In conversation, we often shift from verb tense to verb tense indiscriminately, sometimes moving from past to present and back again with little warning or planning. In writing, however, such tense shifts can be annoying to readers who expect consistency. Thus you need to maintain a clear **tense sequence** in your writing, making plain the time relationships of events and ideas. In the following passage, the shift from past to present is logical and clear.

LOGICAL In the 1950s, great ocean liners still **offered** an attractive way to travel. Nowadays, people **prefer** jet travel because it is so much faster.

When changes in tense do not reflect clear relationships in time or do so inconsistently, your readers may become confused.

INCONSISTENT The author **begins** by giving a factual account of the storm. He **said** that if people had heeded the warnings, many lives would have been saved.

EDITED The author **begins** by giving a factual account of the storm. He **says** that if people had heeded the warnings, many lives would have been saved.

You can shift tenses inside a sentence without creating confusion as long as you make the tense sequence logical.

                                         past   present
LOGICAL Although my mother and father both **loved** cats, I **dislike** them.

              present   past
LOGICAL People **forget** that four serious candidates **ran** in the 1948 presidential election.

              future   present
LOGICAL I **will accept** your recommendations because they **seem** reasonable.

                    past
LOGICAL The accountant **destroyed** evidence of the embezzlement
                  past perfect
because the police **had forgotten** to warn him of the importance of the records.

                       past perfect
LOGICAL None of the expedition's crew **had recognized** that food stored
                  present
in cans sealed with lead solder **is** poisonous.
      Putting *is poisonous* in the present tense is appropriate because the phrase is a generally true (or widely applicable) statement.

18f
verb

Use the present tense to discuss events, ideas, and statements in a piece of literature, a film, an essay, a painting, or a similar creative production.

INCORRECT   In *The Mating Season*, the main character **described** an unpleasant relative as a person "who chews broken bottles and kills rats
with her teeth."

CORRECT   In *The Mating Season*, the main character **describes** an unpleasant relative as a person "who chews broken bottles and kills rats
with her teeth."

18g Recognizing the subjunctive mood

Sentences can be classified according to **mood**, a term that highlights
the speaker's or writer's attitude as reflected in the statement. Most of your
sentences will be in the **indicative mood** (characterizing statements intended as truthful or factual) or the **imperative mood** (characterizing statements like "Stop!" or "Watch out!" which function as commands). Most of
the information in this chapter focuses on verbs in the indicative mood.

Because it is not used heavily in ordinary speech, you may have trouble with the **subjunctive mood** in your writing. The subjunctive mood is
used to express uncertainty—supposition, prediction, or possibility.

Were the deadline today, our proposal would not be ready.

The subjunctive mood has faded from most casual speech and even
some writing, but it is still used on occasion, particularly in formal writing.
Teachers or highly educated readers may expect you to use the subjunctive.
Whenever you create sentences that express desires or wishes, whether positive or negative, the subjunctive may be required.

DRAFT   Jacqueline wished the news **was** not true.

EDITED   Jacqueline wished the news **were** not true.
(SUBJUNCTIVE)

Many **conditional statements**, expressing the improbable or hypothetical
and often beginning with *if*, require the subjunctive.

DRAFT   If Sandy **was** a person who always wore a helmet, his family
would be much less worried about his riding motorcycles.

EDITED   If Sandy **were** a person who always wore a helmet, his family
(SUBJUNCTIVE)   would be much less worried about his riding motorcycles.

Finally, some clauses with *that* require a subjunctive verb when they follow
certain verbs that make demands or requests. The common error in such
cases is to use the incorrect form of the main verb, which should be the same
as for the past participle (see 18c-2).

18g
verb

DRAFT   Parents desire that their child **shows** respect.

EDITED   Parents desire that their child **show** respect.

DRAFT   The judge asked that the eyewitnesses **be swore** in before tes-
               tifying.

EDITED   The judge asked that the eyewitnesses **be sworn** in before tes-
               tifying.

When you write conditional sentences (with *if*), be careful not to add the
auxiliary *would* to the *had + verb* structure in the conditional clause. This error is common, in part because the clause after the conditional often does
correctly contain that structure.

DRAFT   If Sandy **would have worn** his helmet on the night of the
               party, he **would have hurt** himself less seriously.

EDITED   If Sandy **had worn** his helmet on the night of the party, he
               would have hurt himself less seriously.

Exercise 4

A. Decide whether the complex verb forms highlighted in the following sentences are correct. Edit those that are not; explain why you left
any as they appear.

EXAMPLE

The team leader **is planning** to ask for reports just after the produc-

tion meeting ~~will begin~~. *begins.*

1. Kamal **is finished** testing the circuit board by the time the production meeting **had started**.
2. The team members **will ask** Kamal if he **was planning** to test the
   remainder of the circuit boards.
3. As I prepare this report on the project, Michelle **is assembling** the
   prototype using the circuit boards.
4. The other people **will assemble** the extra machines as soon as the
   delivery van **arrived**.
5. If our customers **will be able** to recognize the advantages of our
   product, they **would order** more of the machines.

B. Compose five sentences with correct and incorrect subjunctive mood
or tense shifts. Edit each other's sentences in a small group; then discuss
the changes you made.

18g
verb

Exercise 5

A. Rewrite each of the following sentences in the tense or mood indicated in brackets by substituting appropriate main verb forms and any necessary helping verbs for the verb in parentheses.

EXAMPLE

The airplane assembly plant *(fail)* ^ *has been failing* for several years. [present perfect progressive]

1. First, the recession (*hurt*) the market for small airplanes. [past perfect]
2. Then a new management team announced, "We (*close*) the plant unless productivity increases." [future]
3. At the same time, the company (*lose*) a product liability lawsuit. [past progressive]
4. This week, the company president (*announce*), "Unless we get some new orders in a few days, we (*declare*) bankruptcy." [simple past; future progressive]
5. If the plant (*be*) closed, three hundred workers would lose their jobs. [past subjunctive]

B. Write five sentences of your own, three using different complex tenses and two employing the subjunctive mood. Exchange sentences with a fellow writer and check that your partner has used the tenses and the subjunctive mood correctly.

ESL

18g
verb

18.2

ESL ADVICE: CONDITIONALS

Three types of **conditional** statements depend on a condition or are imagined. These statements may be (1) *true* in the present, true in the future, or possibly true in the future; (2) *untrue* or contrary to fact in the present; or (3) *untrue* or contrary to fact in the past. Each includes an *if* clause and a result clause that combine different verb tenses.

TYPE I: TRUE IN THE PRESENT

IF CLAUSE	RESULT CLAUSE

- Generally true as a habit or as a fact

if + subject + present tense verb	subject + present tense verb
If Rafi drives to school every day,	he gets to class on time.

- True in the future as a one-time event

if + subject + present tense verb	subject + future tense verb
If Rafi drives to school today,	he will get to class on time.

- Possibly true in the future as a one-time event

if + subject + present tense verb	subject + modal + base form verb
If Rafi drives to school today,	he may/might/could/should get to class on time.

TYPE II: UNTRUE IN THE PRESENT

IF CLAUSE	RESULT CLAUSE
	subject + *would/could/might* + simple form of verb
if + subject + past tense verb	
If Rafi drove to school,	he would/could/might arrive on time.

With Type II statements, the form of *be* in the *if* clause is always *were*.

If she **were** president, she would reform tax laws.

TYPE III: UNTRUE IN THE PAST

IF CLAUSE	RESULT CLAUSE
	subject + *would/could/might* + *have* + past participle
if + subject + past perfect tense	
If Rafi had driven to school,	he would not have been late.

ESL

18g
verb

CHAPTER 19

MAKING SENTENCE PARTS AGREE

What's wrong with the following sentence?

INCORRECT   The Citizenship Institute and the Civic Program focuses on social justice.

> READER'S REACTION: I assumed the sentence was about two things—the Citizenship Institute and the Civic Program—until I came to the word *focuses*. I know *focuses* is *singular* in form, so it can't refer to more than one thing.

EDITED   The Citizenship Institute and the Civic Program **focus** on social justice.

Readers expect you to make the parts of a sentence fit together grammatically. Especially important are **agreement** between a subject and a verb and agreement between a pronoun and the word to which it refers (its **antecedent**). By failing to align the parts of a sentence, you create inconsistency and confusion, as in the case of the misaligned pronoun and antecedent in the following example.

INCONSISTENT   Project status reports should address the needs and values of it audience.

CLEAR   **A project status report** should address the needs and values of **its audience**.

CLEAR   **Project status reports** should address the needs and values of **their audiences**.

19a Creating subject-verb agreement (simple)

To make subjects and verbs agree, you need to make sure that they are aligned in two ways: **number** (singular or plural) and **person** (first, second,

19a
agr

or third). Keeping them aligned helps your sentences convey consistent, clear meaning.

SINGULAR   The **worker** tears down the platform.

NOTE: Present tense verbs add -s when the subject is in the third person even though the subject and verb are both singular.

PLURAL   The **workers** tear down the platform.

FIRST PERSON   **I** operate the air compressor.

We operate the air compressor.

SECOND PERSON   **You** operate the air compressor.

THIRD PERSON   **He** (**she**, **it**) operates the air compressor.

They operate the air compressor.

When the subjects and verbs in your writing take relatively simple forms, recognizing and editing problems with subject-verb agreement can be a straightforward process. (See 19b for recognizing and editing strategies useful with more complex subject-verb patterns.)

STRATEGY

To identify (and edit) **subject-verb agreement**, look for a subject, identify its *number* (singular or plural) and *person* (first, second, or third), and make sure the verb agrees with it in grammatical form.

INCORRECT   The clients is impatient.

CORRECT   The **clients** are impatient.

CORRECT   The **client** is impatient.

(For help in identifying number and person, see the chart on pages 278–279)

19a
agr

Pay special attention to plurals. Subjects plural in both form and meaning need plural verbs, but recognizing and choosing the right verb forms can sometimes be tricky.

STRATEGY

1. **Find the subject.** Look for *-s* or *-es* endings indicating a plural subject. Look for plural pronouns such as *they* and *we*. (*Exceptions:* nouns with irregular plurals such as *person/people*, *child/children*, or *louse/lice* as well as nouns with the same form for singular and plural, such as *moose/moose*.)
2. **Identify the verb.** Locate the verb and check that its form is also plural. Remember, in contrast to subjects, present tense verbs become *singular* with the addition of *-s* or *-es*. (*Exceptions:* Verbs with irregular forms, including *be* and *have*, see 18b.)
3. **Edit.** If the subject is plural but the verb singular (or vice versa), edit to make them agree.

   SINGULAR   The dam prevent**s** flooding.

   PLURAL   The dam**s** prevent flooding.

4. **Check again.** Check if the verb contains more than one word (a verb phrase, see 16a-3). If you find a main verb *plus* a helping verb, remember this: the helping verb *sometimes* changes form for singular and plural, while the main verb remains the same.

	HELPING VERB CHANGES FORM	HELPING VERB DOES NOT CHANGE FORM
SINGULAR	The **park** <u>does</u> <u>seem</u> safer.	The **park** <u>might</u> <u>seem</u> safer.
PLURAL	The **parks** <u>do</u> <u>seem</u> safer.	The **parks** <u>might</u> <u>seem</u> safer.

19a agr

Exercise 1

A. Fill in the blanks in the following sentences with verbs that agree in number and person with their subject.

EXAMPLE
Every day I _walk_ past the Valois Cafeteria.

1. The retired men in the neighborhood _____ lunch at the cafeteria.
2. The cafeteria's motto, "See What You Eat," _____ on the sign above the entrance.
3. The restaurant _____ run down.
4. Nonetheless, it _____ a clean and safe place.
5. A sociologist has studied the ways people of different races and cultures _____ with each other at the cafeteria.

B. Copy a paragraph from one of your papers or a book, but replace the verbs with blanks (as in Exercise 1A). Exchange paragraphs with a partner and fill in the blanks in that paragraph. Work together to check your answers.

ESL ADVICE: SUBJECT-VERB AGREEMENT WITH TROUBLESOME VERBS

Watch for troublesome verbs that change form according to person or tense, and select the correct form so subject and verb agree.

- *Be* (present and past): I **am**, **was**. You (sing., pl.)/We/They **are**, **were**. He/She/It **is**, **was**.
- Helping verb *be* (present progressive and past progressive)

  Present Progressive: I **am** talking. You/We/They **are** talking.

  Past Progressive: He/She/It **is** talking. I/He/She/It **was** talking. We/You/They **were** talking.

- *Have* (present): I/You/We/They **have** a new home. He/She/It **has** a new home.
- Helping verb *have* (present perfect and present perfect progressive)

  Present Perfect: I/You/We/They **have** lived here for years. He/She/It **has lived** here for years.

  Present Perfect Progressive: I/You/We/They **have** been living here since May. He/She/It **has** been living here for a long time.

- *Do* or *Does* to show emphasis: I/You/We/They **do** want the contract! He/She/It **does** want the contract!
- *Doesn't* or *Don't* to show the negative: I/You/We/They **don't** exercise enough. He/She/It **doesn't** exercise enough.

In English, many nouns, called **mass** or **noncount nouns** (see 16a-1), use the singular form and need a singular verb.

Her **clothing** <u>was</u> made by hand.

Rush-hour **traffic** is always heavy.

ESL

19b
agr

19b Creating subject-verb agreement (complex)

The usually simple process of checking for subject-verb agreement sometimes becomes more complex. Certain kinds of words and sentence structures can pose special problems for writers seeking to match subject and verb forms.

Keeping all the "rules" in mind as you write can be distracting. The best solution is to remember the kinds of words and structures likely to cause problems, and then be ready, if necessary, to look up strategies for editing the problems.

- Plural words with singular meanings (for example, *politics*, *statistics*, or *news*)
- Collective nouns (for example, *audience*, *crew*, or *herd*)
- Subjects linked by *and*, *or*, and *nor* (compound and alternative subjects), sometimes accompanied by the word *each*
- Word groups coming between subject and verb (often beginning *as well as* or *along with*)
- Unusual word order (including sentences beginning *There is* or *There are*)
- Words like *all*, *everybody*, *none*, *who*, *which*, *that*, *is*, and *seems*.

1 Watch for plural forms with singular meanings

Subjects plural in form (*shoes*, *filters*, *children*, *mathematics*, *we*, *they*) generally need a plural verb—but not always.

Subjects with plural forms and singular meanings. Words like *politics*, *statistics*, *linguistics*, *news*, *physics*, *mumps*, and *athletics* have the *-s* ending of plural nouns but are singular in meaning—and need singular verbs.

Mathematics is an increasingly popular field of study.

STRATEGY

Try the **pronoun test**.
Choose a pronoun that can accurately replace the subject: *he*, *she*, or *it* (singular); *they* (plural). Read the sentence with the replacement and edit the verb to agree.

DRAFT   The **news** about the job market ___ surprisingly good.
PRONOUN TEST: **Replace "The news" with "it" to read "It is surprisingly good."**

EDITED   The **news** about the job market **is** surprisingly good.

The pronoun test is especially useful for two special kinds of subjects.

- **Measurements or numbers**
  A measurement or figure (even one ending in *-s*) may still be singular if it names a quantity or unit as a whole. When it refers to individual elements, however, treat it as plural.

Four years is the amount of time Dr. Santiago spent studying the effects of stress.
PRONOUN TEST: **"It is the amount of time Dr. Santiago spent . . . ."**

One-third of the job trainees leave the program after three weeks.
PRONOUN TEST: **They [plural] leave the program individually.**

- **Titles and names**
  When the title of a work or a company's name is the subject, choose a singular verb even if the name or title is plural.

  New West Logistics **pays** high wages and **has** excellent benefits.
  PRONOUN TEST: **"It [the company] pays high wages . . . ."**

  The White Roses **is** second on the best-seller list this month.
  PRONOUN TEST: **"It [the book] is second . . . ."**

2 Be alert for collective nouns

A **collective noun** is singular in form yet identifies a group of individuals (*audience, mob, crew, troop, brood, tribe,* or *herd*). When a group acts as a single unit, choose a singular verb; when its members act individually, choose a plural verb.

19.1

The **staff** is hardworking and well trained.

The **staff** have earned the respect of our clients.

If using a plural verb makes a sentence sound awkward, rewrite using a plural subject.

AWKWARD   The congregation react to Reverend Cullen's sermons in different ways.

REWRITTEN   **Members** of the congregation react to Reverend Cullen's sermons in different ways.

19b
agr

3 Check subjects linked by *and, or,* and *nor*

And creates a **compound subject**; *or* and *nor* create **alternative subjects**. As you edit, look for subjects containing these words.

Compound subjects joined by *and*. By joining two or more subjects with *and* or *both,* you create a **compound subject**. Because *and* makes the subject plural even if one or all of the individual parts are singular, you generally need to choose a plural verb.

> **Aaron and the rest of the staff** <u>were</u> responsible for the display.
>
> **Both rain and condensation** <u>cause</u> damage to the frame.

However, if the parts should be taken as a unit or if the parts designate a single person, thing, or idea, you need to choose a singular verb.

UNIT (SINGULAR)	**Ham and eggs** <u>is</u> still my favorite breakfast.
TWO ELEMENTS (PLURAL)	**Ham and eggs** <u>are</u> the main ingredients in this casserole.
ONE PERSON	**My fellow art teacher and friend** also <u>has</u> paintings in the show.
TWO PEOPLE	**My fellow art teacher and my friend** also <u>have</u> paintings in the show.

Depending on where you place the words *each* or *every*, you can give a compound subject a singular or plural meaning.

EACH BEFORE COMPOUND SUBJECT

compound subject   singular verb

Each shift manager and unit manager **reviews** the progress logs daily.

EACH AFTER COMPOUND SUBJECT

compound subject   plural verb

The shift managers and unit managers **each review** the progress logs daily.

Alternative subjects joined by *or*. When you use *or* or *nor* (*either . . . or*, *neither . . . nor*) to link alternative elements of a subject, make the verb agree with the closer part. Putting the plural element closer to the verb generally makes a sentence less awkward.

PLURAL CLOSE TO VERB	The auditor or **the staff accountants** <u>review</u> each report.
SINGULAR CLOSE TO VERB	False records or **late reporting** <u>weakens</u> the review process.

When parts of a subject differ in person and therefore need different verb forms (for example, *I have, he has*), make the verb agree with the part of the subject closer to it. Rewrite if this makes the sentence awkward.

19b
agr

AWKWARD   Either the other new residents or **I** am going to file a complaint.

REWRITTEN   Either the other new **residents** are going to file a complaint or **I** am.

4 Pay attention to separated subjects and verbs

When you insert words or even a whole phrase between the subject and verb of a sentence, you may be tempted to make the verb agree with one of the intervening words (usually the nearest noun) rather than the actual subject.

FAULTY
AGREEMENT   The new trolley system, with its expanded routes and lower fares, are specially popular with senior citizens.
The words *routes* and *fares* are not the subject of the sentence.

EDITED   The new trolley **system**, with its expanded routes and lower fares, **is** especially popular with senior citizens.

STRATEGY

To identify possible problems with subject-verb agreement, be alert for common phrases like *as well as*, *in addition to*, *together with*, and *along with*, or any other clusters of words coming between a subject and a verb.

UNEDITED   A regular tune up, *along with* frequent oil **changes**, prolong the life of your car.

To recognize faulty agreement, identify the real subject by imagining the sentence without the intervening phrase, then check that the subject and verb agree.

FAULTY
AGREEMENT   A regular **tune-up** . . . prolong the life of your car.

EDITED   A regular **tune-up**, along with frequent oil changes, prolongs the life of your car.

Because phrases like *as well as* can be easily mistaken for *and*, you may unintentionally treat a singular subject as a compound (plural) subject.

19b
agr

MISTAKEN	The university's **provost**, as well as the deans, <u>have</u> issued new guidelines emphasizing teaching.
EDITED	The university's **provost**, as well as the deans, <u>has</u> issued new guidelines emphasizing teaching.

If you mean *and*, use the word itself.

REWRITTEN	The university's provost **and** the deans <u>have</u> issued new promotion guidelines emphasizing teaching.

Exercise 2

A. In each of the following sentences, choose the word inside the parentheses that creates subject-verb agreement.

EXAMPLE

The mayor, as well as members of the city council, (*has*/have) been searching for better ways to fund the zoo.

1. Several large lizards and an eight-foot python (*makes/make*) up the main attractions in the reptile building of the tiny zoo.
2. The displays as well as the building itself (*appears/appear*) well designed and well maintained.
3. The animals each (*displays/display*) good health and behavior.
4. Neither the zoo's overseers nor its director (*is/are*) satisfied with the reptile building and the number of animals on display.
5. Of the zoo's visitors, three-quarters (*says/say*) that the collection should be enlarged.
6. This year the Cajun and Bluegrass Festival (*features/feature*) several new bands.
7. The group Beausoleil (*appears/appear*) twice on the program.
8. The Cajun food, along with more familiar snacks, (*does/do*) draw many people to the refreshment tent.
9. The festival staff (*wears/wear*) buttons saying "Ask me for help."
10. Both the dancing lessons and the crafts display (*occupies/occupy*) the same tent.

B. Make up five sentences like those in Exercise 2A on any topic of your choice. Give them to a partner to complete, and work on those your partner has created.

19b
agr

ESL ADVICE: PAIRED CONJUNCTIONS AND SEPARATED SUBJECTS AND VERBS

Both . . . and always needs a plural verb, whether the elements joined are singular or plural.

Both the president **and** her advisor are in Tokyo this week.

Both the president **and** her advisors are in Tokyo this week.

Either . . . or, neither . . . nor, and *not only . . . but also* may take either a singular or plural verb. The subject closer to the verb determines the form of the verb.

Either the president **or** her advisor is in Tokyo.

Neither the president **nor** her advisors are in Tokyo.

Check agreement when phrases or clauses come between a sentence's subject and verb.

PHRASES

NOT APPROPRIATE A person with sensitive eyes have to wear sunglasses.

CORRECT A **person** with sensitive eyes **has** to wear sunglasses.

CLAUSES

NOT APPROPRIATE A person whose eyes are sensitive have to wear sunglasses.

CORRECT A **person** whose eyes are sensitive **has** to wear sunglasses.

ESL

19b
agr

5 Recognize unusual word order

When you invert typical word order to create emphasis or ask a question, make sure the verb still agrees with the subject.

	verb	subject

QUESTION Are **patient satisfaction and increased efficiency** possible at the New Rockville Medical Clinic?

EMPHASIS Following landslide victories comes **overconfidence** for many politicians.

6 Watch for *there is, there are*

There is/are, it is/are, and *here is/are* help you reverse the usual subject-verb sentence order so you can present the subject *after* the verb. As a result, you need to make the verb agree with the subject following it.

19.2

	verb subject
SINGULAR	There **is opportunity** for people starting new service industries.

	verb subject
PLURAL	There **are** many new **opportunities** for service industries.

Although it is strictly grammatical to use *there are* with a compound subject, you may use *there is* if the first part of a compound subject is singular.

> There is **a guard and an alarm system** protecting the warehouse.

7 Pay attention to *is, appears, feels,* and other linking verbs

When you build a sentence around *is, appears, feels,* or another linking verb (see 16a-3), make sure the verb agrees with the subject. You may be tempted to make it agree with the noun or pronoun renaming the subject (the complement—see 16b-2), but edit carefully to avoid this problem.

	subject verb complement
INCORRECT	The chief **obstacle** to change <u>are</u> the **mayor and her political allies**.

EDITED	The chief **obstacle** to change <u>is</u> the mayor and her political allies.

19b
agr

8 *All, everybody, none; who which, that*—using special subjects

All, everybody, none (and other indefinite pronouns) do not refer to specific ideas, people, or things. Most have clearly singular meanings and require singular verbs.

> **Someone** <u>is</u> preparing the pamphlet.

> **Everybody** <u>has</u> the right to appeal a zoning decision.

You can treat a few pronouns, such as *all, any, most, none,* and *some,* as either singular or plural according to meaning.

STRATEGY

To decide whether to choose a singular or plural verb for words like *all*, *any*, or *none*, start by identifying the noun or pronouns to which they refer, then use the following test.

- Does the pronoun refer to something that *cannot be counted*? Choose singular.

  SINGULAR **All** of the food is for the elderly lunch program.
  all = singular noun
  food = food in general (not countable)

- Does the pronoun refer to two or more elements of something that *can be counted*? Choose plural.

  PLURAL **All** of the food supplies are for the elderly lunch program.
  all = plural noun
  supplies = many different kinds of supplies (countables) such as flour, meat, and canned vegetables

Who, which, and *that* (relative pronouns—see 16a-2) do not have singular and plural forms, yet the words to which they refer (antecedents) generally do have separate singular and plural forms. Choose a verb for *who, which,* or *that* so that it matches the number of the antecedent.

SINGULAR He prefers **a program** that awards grants to individuals.

PLURAL I support **programs** that distribute funds to community groups.

19b
agr

Make a habit of noticing the phrases *one of* and *the only one of*. They can create agreement problems when they come before *who, which,* or *that.*

Dr. Gotari is **one** of those professors who help students succeed.
Who refers to the plural *professors;* consequently the verb, *help,* is plural. There are other professors like Dr. Gotari.

Dr. Gotari is **the only one** of the professors who helps students succeed.
Who refers to the singular *Dr. Gotari;* consequently, the verb, *helps,* is singular. Dr. Gotari is the only supportive instructor.

9 Pay special attention to titles and names

When you use the title of a work or the name of a company as a sentence subject, choose a singular verb even if the name or title is plural.

New West Consultants **pays** high wages and **offers** excellent benefits.
Think to yourself: The company <u>pays</u> . . .

The White Roses **is** second on the best-seller list.
Think to yourself: The book <u>is</u> . . .

"Tall ships" **is** the name given to the largest sailing ships.

Exercise 3 ───

A. For each of the following sentences, give the correct present tense form of the infinitive verb indicated in parentheses.

EXAMPLE   *has*
None of the department heads ~~(to have)~~ the same administrative style.

1. Frieda O'Connor is one of those managers who (*to lead*) by example.
2. All the other department heads (*to respect*) her leadership ability.
3. She knows each of the employees who (*to work*) in her department.
4. Each year, Alberti and Campos Design Associates (*to give*) a plaque and a bonus to the employee with the highest rating on a peer survey.
5. The award, both the plaque and the money, (*to be*) given to Frieda almost every other year.

B. Working with another student, correct the errors that have been introduced into the following passage from Thomas R. McDonough's "Is Anyone Out There?" Not all the sentences contain an error, and some may have more than one. If correcting an error results in an awkward sentence, rewrite, but do not do so simply to avoid dealing with an agreement problem. When finished, compare your corrections with those of another pair of students, and explain the differences.

Each of the scientists involved in the search are pretty sure something is out there. A lot of numbers, some high and some low, is thrown around to express the probability of intelligent life somewhere else in the universe. Here is some figures that are middle-of-the-road. There is an estimated four hundred billion stars in the Milky Way. Planets may be fairly common, so you can figure one out of every ten of these stars have planets, which equals forty billions stars with planets. But how many of these places seems suitable for life? Neither too hot nor too cold is the conditions needed for life forms similar to our own. An atmosphere along with some water are also necessary. In our solar system only Earth qualifies, though Mars and Venus each comes close. Let us be conservative and estimate that only one of each solar system's planets fit the pattern. That's still forty billion habitable planets.

ESL ADVICE: WORDS AFFECTING SUBJECT-VERB AGREEMENT

QUANTIFIERS

A quantifier—a word like *each*, *one*, or *many*—indicates the amount or quantity of a subject.

expressions followed by a plural noun   +   **a singular verb**
Each of/Every one of/One of/None of   the ESL **students** <u>lives</u> on campus.

expressions followed by a plural noun   +   **a plural verb**
Several of/Many of/Both of   the **students** <u>live</u> off campus.

In some cases, the noun after the expressions determines the verb form.

expressions followed by either a singular or a plural verb   **noncount noun + singular verb**
Some of/Most of/All of/A lot of the **produce** <u>is</u> fresh.

plural noun + plural verb
Some of/Most of/A lot of/All of the **vegetables** <u>are</u> fresh.

MUCH AND *MOST* (NOT *MUCH OF* OR *MOST OF*) WITH NONCOUNT AND PLURAL NOUNS

NONCOUNT NOUN   **Much traffic** <u>occurs</u> during rush hour.

PLURAL NOUN   **Most Americans** <u>live</u> in the cities or suburbs

OTHER, *OTHERS*, AND *ANOTHER* AS PRONOUNS OR ADJECTIVES

PRONOUNS

Others **+ plural verb:** adds points about a topic; there may be more points.

I enjoy Paris for many reasons. Some reasons are the beautiful architecture and gardens; **others are** the wonderful people, culture, and language.

The others **(plural) + plural verb;** *the other* **(singular) + singular verb:** adds the last point or points about the topic; there are no more.

Some hikers favor Craig's plan; **the others want to follow Tina's**.

ESL

19b
agr

ADJECTIVES

Another + **singular noun:** adds an idea; there may be more ideas.
Other + **plural noun:** adds more ideas; there may be more ideas.

One strength of our engineering team is our knowledge of the problem. **Another strength** is our experience. **Other strengths** include our communication skills, our teamwork, and our energy.

The other + **singular or plural noun:** adds the final point or points to be discussed.

Of the two very important sights to see in Paris, one is the Louvre Museum, and **the other** is the Cathedral of Notre Dame.

One of the major sights in Paris is the Louvre Museum. **The other sights** are the Eiffel Tower, the Champs-Elysees, the Cathedral of Notre Dame, and the Arc de Triomphe.

19c Creating pronoun-antecedent agreement

A pronoun takes its meaning from another word to which it refers (its **antecedent**).

antecedent   pronoun
Campers should treat **their** tents and sleeping bags with a mildew-preventing spray.

pronoun   antecedent
Its preference for damp fabric makes **mildew** a major problem for campers.

ESL

19c agr

Matching pronoun and antecedent (either a noun or another pronoun) in *gender, person,* and *number* helps link the two by creating pronoun-antecedent agreement. **Number** refers to singular or plural forms. **Person** refers to the speaker or the subject spoken to/about. **Gender** refers to masculine, feminine, or neuter qualities generally associated with a noun or pronoun. The chart below provides a detailed explanation of these features.

> ### NUMBER, PERSON, AND GENDER
>
> **NUMBER**
> *Number* shows whether words are singular or plural in meaning.
>
> **SINGULAR**   This **community** needs its own recreation center.
> **PLURAL**   Local **communities** need to share their facilities.

SINGULAR WORDS

1. Nouns naming individual people, animals, ideas, and things
2. *I, you, he, she, it* (personal pronouns referring to individuals)
3. *Each, someone* (indefinite pronouns) or *who, which, that* (relative pronouns) when they refer to singular nouns or pronouns
4. Verbs in their singular forms (I *am*, she *is*; I *analyze*, she *analyzes*)

PLURAL WORDS

1. Nouns naming more than one person, animal, idea, or thing
2. *We, you, they* (personal pronouns referring to more than one individual)
3. *All, none* (indefinite pronouns) or *who, which, that* (relative pronouns) when they refer to plural nouns or pronouns
4. Verbs in their plural forms (we *are*, they *are*; we *analyze*, they *analyze*)

PERSON

Person indicates the speaker or the subject being spoken to or about

First person (speaker): *I, we*

I operate the compressor.   **We** operate the compressor.

Second person (spoken to): *you*

You operate the forklift.

Third person (spoken about): *he, she, it, they*; nouns naming things, people, animals, ideas

He/she/it operates the drill.   **They** operate the drill.

GENDER

Gender refers to the masculine, feminine, or neuter character generally attributed to a noun or pronoun.

MASCULINE/FEMININE

While the father printed the document on **his** computer, his daughter completed the financial report on **hers**.

NEUTER

Despite **its** income from sales, the company has yet to show a profit.

Masculine wording: *he*, nouns indicating males, and pronouns (*everyone, somebody, who, which, that*) when they refer to males
Feminine wording: *she*, nouns indicating females, and pronouns (*everyone, somebody, who, which, that*) when they refer to females
Neuter wording: *it*, nouns indicating places, things, and ideas, and pronouns (*everything, something, which, that*) when they refer to places, things, and ideas

19c
agr

1 Recognize antecedents joined by *and, or,* and *nor*

When you wish to make a pronoun refer to several things (Luis *and* Jennifer, for example, or the other students *and* I), the pronoun form you choose should depend, to a great extent, on the word that links the elements of the antecedent: *and, or,* or *nor.*

STRATEGY

Identify the antecedent and the word used to link its parts: *and, or (either . . . or),* or *nor (neither . . . nor)*

- **And** (compound antecedent)
  Choose a plural pronoun (such as *they*) even if one or more of the antecedent's parts are singular.

  Luis and Jennifer said that the tests <u>they</u> ran on the groundwater were conclusive.

  The other students and I admit that the tests <u>we</u> ran were not conclusive.

EXCEPTIONS

1. A compound antecedent can refer to a single person, thing, or idea. When it does, use a singular pronoun.

   My colleague and coauthor is <u>someone</u> skilled at analyzing soil samples.

2. You can place *each* and *every* before a compound antecedent to single out the individual elements. When you do, use a singular pronoun.

   Each of the soil and water samples <u>is</u> brought to the lab in **its** own sterile container.

   Every soil and water sample brought to the lab <u>undergoes</u> **its** own three tests.

- **Or** and **Nor** (alternative antecedent)
  Choose a pronoun that agrees with the part of the antecedent that is closer to it.

  Neither the project manager **nor** the engineers submitted <u>their</u> accident reports on time.

  Editing advice: If one part of a subject is singular and the other part plural, consider putting the plural element second or rewriting to avoid an awkward or confusing sentence.

19c
agr

CONFUSING	Either Jamal and Alan or **Richard** will include the sales projections in his report.
	READER'S REACTION: **Does this mean that Jamal and Alan may be putting things in Richard's report? Or does it mean that there will be two reports, Richard's plus Jamal and Alan's, one of which will contain the projections?**
EDITED	Either Richard or **Jamal** and **Alan** will include the sales projections in their report.
REWRITTEN	Either Richard will include the sales projections in his report, or Jamal and Alan will include the projections in theirs.

2 Pay attention to *everyone, any, something* (indefinite pronouns) as antecedents

Many words like *somebody* and *each* (indefinite pronouns) are singular. Make sure that the pronouns you use to refer to them are also singular.

Somebody on the staff left confidential data disks in the lunchroom.

Each member of the women's basketball team has her own training regimen.

Sometimes you may use an indefinite pronoun to mean *many* or *all*. In formal writing or speaking, your audience may prefer a plural antecedent.

INFORMAL	Everyone on the research team handed in their sections of the report.
EDITED	**Members** of the research team handed in their sections of the report.

To avoid sexist language (see 32a), many publishers and communities of writers accept a plural pronoun with a singular antecedent; when in doubt, however, use *both* a plural pronoun and a plural antecedent.

SEXIST	Everybody should include charts and slides in his sales talk.
INFORMAL/ SOMETIMES ACCEPTABLE	**Everybody** should include charts and slides in their sales talks.
SAFEST	**All presenters** should include charts and slides in their sales talks.

19c
agr

3 Watch for collective nouns as antecedents

A noun such as *team, group, clan, audience, army,* or *tribe* (collective noun) can act as a singular or plural antecedent, depending on whether it refers to the group as a whole or to the members acting separately.

SINGULAR The **subcommittee** submitted its revised version of the report.

PLURAL The **subcommittee** brought their different suggestions for a revised report to the meeting for discussion.

ESL ADVICE: DEMONSTRATIVE ADJECTIVES

In addition to subjects and verbs, other elements in a sentence must agree. **Demonstrative adjectives** or **pronouns** (*this, that, these,* and *those*) must be either singular or plural, depending on the noun being modified. (See also 16a-2.)

INAPPROPRIATE This agencies conduct outreach programs in local schools.

APPROPRIATE **These agencies** conduct outreach programs in local schools.

INAPPROPRIATE Those agency conducts outreach programs in local schools.

APPROPRIATE **That agency** conducts outreach programs in local schools.

Exercise 4

A. Correct any errors in pronoun-antecedent agreement in the following sentences. You may need to change other parts of a sentence besides the pronoun or the antecedent. Each sentence can be corrected in more than one way.

EXAMPLE

    People   *like*

A person who likes camping should no longer feel they are unusual.

1. In any circle of friends, several are likely to say that he or she enjoys camping.
2. Everyone who goes camping needs to pay attention to their equipment.
3. All hikers should select good shoes and socks to protect your feet.
4. A camper or a hiker needs to choose their clothing carefully, paying attention to comfort, durability, and protection as well as style.

5. Both regular campers and occasional campers should be willing to put his or her money into well-designed tents, sleeping bags, and cooking equipment.

6. Each store or chain of stores in the retail camping industry meets the needs of their customers in a different way.

7. A store catering to campers and the hiker usually offers him or her a wide choice of equipment at different prices.

8. Eddie Bauer or L.L. Bean provides mail-order service to his customers.

9. A camping supplies and athletic equipment store may provide a narrower range of choices to their customers because of the need to stock sporting goods as well as camping equipment.

10. Nonetheless, any of these businesses should be able to provide you and their other customers with good, safe camping equipment.

B. Working with a group of students, compare your corrections for the sentences in Exercise 4A. Make note of any differences, and decide which version (if any) is preferable and why.

CHAPTER 20

USING ADJECTIVES AND ADVERBS

If you use the wrong forms of some familiar words, your readers will be likely to notice the errors.

DRAFT   The new medication acts **quick**.

EDITED   The new medication acts **quickly**.

DRAFT   They **hadn't never** implemented the cost-saving program.

EDITED   They **had never** implemented the cost-saving program.

Admittedly, not all mistaken forms are likely to irritate or confuse your readers. Some readers, for example, may not notice the difference in meaning between the following two sentences.

The fumes from the mixture smelled **bad**.

The fumes from the mixture smelled **badly**.

Others, however, will notice that the second sentence says the fumes themselves have a sense of smell, but one that isn't working well.

20a Recognizing what adjectives and adverbs do

Adjectives and adverbs **modify** other words, adding to, qualifying, focusing, limiting, or extending their meaning. The following table summarizes the features of adjective and adverbs. (See also 16a-4.)

Because the *-ly* ending does not appear on all adverbs, and because some familiar adjectives do end in *-ly* (such as *friendly, lonely*), you may sometimes have to determine whether a word is an adjective or adverb by looking at how it is used in sentences or by looking it up in a dictionary.

20a
adj/adv

FEATURES OF ADJECTIVES AND ADVERBS

ADJECTIVES

- Modify nouns and pronouns
- Answer the questions "How many?" "What kind?" "Which one (or ones)?" and "What size, color, or shape?"
- Include words like *blue, complicated, good,* and *frightening*
- Include words created by adding endings like *-able, -ical, -less, -ful,* and *-ous* to nouns or verbs (such as *controllable, sociological, nervous, seamless, careful*)

ADVERBS

- Modify verbs, adjectives, and other adverbs
- Modify phrases (*almost* beyond the building), clauses (*soon after* I added the last ingredients), and sentences (*Remarkably,* the mechanism was not damaged)
- Answer questions such as "When?" "Where?" "How?" "How often?" "Which direction?" "What degree?"
- Consist mostly of words ending in *-ly,* like *quickly, carefully,* and *smoothly*
- Include some words that do not end in *-ly,* such as *fast, very, well, quite,* and *late*

20b Avoiding confusion between adjectives and adverbs

20.1

20b
adj/adv

Much of the time, you will have little trouble deciding whether to use the adjective or adverb form of a word. Nonetheless, a recent trend in informal speech has been the dropping of *-ly* in the adverb form of some words. In addition, some pairs of words, such as *good/well*, and some common sentence patterns need special attention.

1 Figure out what a modifier does in a sentence

If you can't tell which modifier to use, analyze what the word will do in your sentence. (Check the lists of features of adjectives and adverbs in the chart above.)

DRAFT   Write **careful** so the directions are clear.
     QUESTION: Write *how*? It answers an adverb question.

EDITED   Write **carefully** so the directions are clear.

STRATEGY

Try drawing an arrow to the word that is modified. If this word acts as a noun or pronoun, modify it with an adjective; if it acts as a verb, adjective, or adverb, modify it with an adverb.

DRAFT   The rubber insulation underwent **remarkable** quick deterioration.

> CORRECTION: *Remarkable* modifies *quick* (and answers the adverb question "How quick?"). *Quick* in turn modifies *deterioration* and answers the adjective question "What kind of deterioration?"

EDITED   The rubber insulation experienced **remarkably** quick deterioration.

DID YOU KNOW?

Dictionary entries tell whether a word is an adjective, an adverb, or both. They also indicate the comparative and superlative forms of many adjectives and adverbs.

2 Be alert for verbs like *look, feel, prove,* and *is*

Verbs such as *look, feel,* and *prove* can show both states of being (**linking verbs**) and activities (**action verbs**). The verb *is* always acts as a linking verb. Choose an adjective for a state of being or an adverb for an activity. (The adjective following a linking verb is called a **complement**, see 16b-2.)

SUBJECT	LINKING VERB	COMPLEMENT (ADJECTIVE)
The room	smelled	musty.
The procedure	proved	unreliable.

ADJECTIVE (BEING)   The motor's metal cover turned **hot**.

ADVERB (ACTION)   The large wheel turned **quickly**.

ADJECTIVE   The movement grew **rapid**. [The motion became quick.]

ADVERB   The movement grew **rapidly**. [The group got bigger, and its ideas spread rapidly.]

3 Pay special attention to *real/really, sure/surely, bad/badly,* and *good/well*

Some common uses of words like *bad/badly*—especially *sure* for *surely*— may be acceptable in informal speech or writing, but not in academic, workplace, or public writing. Use the following chart to help you choose the appropriate form.

CHOOSING BETWEEN *BAD/BADLY, GOOD/WELL, REAL/REALLY,* AND *SURE/SURELY*

BAD/BADLY

Use *bad* (adjective) with linking verbs such as *is, seems,* or *appears.*

I feel **bad** that our group isn't working well together. (not *badly*)

Use *badly* (adverb) with action verbs.

The expensive new breathing apparatus works **badly**. (not *bad*)

GOOD/WELL

Use *good* (adjective) with linking verbs.

The chef's new oil and garlic dressing tastes **good**. (not *well*)

Use *well* (adverb) with action verbs, unless it refers to health.

The new pump works **well**. (not *good*)

REAL/REALLY

Use *really* (adverb) to modify an adverb like *fast, efficient,* or *hot.*

Lu Ming is **really** efficient. (not *real*)

SURE/SURELY

Use *surely* (adverb) to modify adjectives like *misleading, outdated,* or *courageous.*

This drawing of the mechanism is **surely** misleading. (not *sure*)

---

4 Check the words that complete direct objects

When you add a word right after or before a direct object to complete (or complement) its meaning, make sure you choose an adjective.

The review panel considered the researcher **objective**.
Objective completes *researcher* by indicating the person's qualities.

You can place an adverb after the object, but it will modify the verb.

The review panel considered the researcher **objectively**.
Objectively describes their manner in evaluating the researcher.

Unlike adjectives completing a direct object, adverbs can usually appear at other places in a sentence.

ADJECTIVE   The agency judged her artwork **competent**.

ADVERB   The agency judged her artwork **competently**.

ADVERB   The agency **competently** judged her artwork.

Exercise 1

A. Rewrite the following sentences to eliminate any problems in adjective or adverb use.

EXAMPLE

I thought the band sounded ~~badly,~~ though many of my friends enjoyed the music.
bad,

1. Many scholars have begun studying some real surprising subjects such as rock music.
2. At first, they had trouble persuading many people to take their work serious.
3. Now they produce careful researched studies of musicians like the Beatles as well as biographies of influential figures like Sid Vicious, Joey Ramone, and Courtney Love.
4. Remember, just because a piece of rock music sounds well does not mean that it is worth careful study.
5. At a time when the careers of many rock musicians are going bad, rock is doing quite good on campus.

B. Working in a group, decide which piece of advice in sections 20a and b applies to the particular problem in adjective or adverb use illustrated by each of the following sentences. Make a note of each relevant section of the discussion, and rewrite the sentence to eliminate the problem.

EXAMPLE

Some dead rock musicians have ~~surprising~~ large and active fan clubs.
surprisingly

1. Over the past year, the number of books devoted to rock groups or rock stars has grown remarkable.
2. The writer Greil Marcus has produced several high-regarded books that praise Elvis Presley as an artist and person.
3. The title of one of Marcus's books, *Dead Elvis: A Chronicle of a Cultural Obsession*, may suggest that he views Elvis "sightings" and memorabilia as humorously.
4. Some of the events he describes are undoubted weird.
5. Nonetheless, he feels surely that Elvis and his music really deserve respect.

20b
adj/adv

ESL ADVICE: ADJECTIVES IN A SERIES

When using two or more adjectives in a series, place them in correct order before the main noun, as illustrated in the following chart.

DETERMINER	QUALITY	PHYSICAL DESCRIPTION	NATIONALITY	MATERIAL	QUALIFYING NOUN	MAIN NOUN
that	expensive	smooth black	German	fiberglass	racing	car
our	friendly	big old	English		hunting	dog
four	little	round white		plastic	Ping-Pong	balls
several	beautiful	young red	Japanese		maple	trees

20c Choosing correct forms for comparatives and superlatives

You can use most adjectives and adverbs in three forms: positive, comparative, and superlative. Choose the form appropriate for your purpose.

POSITIVE (NO COMPARISON)	COMPARATIVE (COMPARE TWO THINGS)	SUPERLATIVE (COMPARE THREE OR MORE THINGS)
quick	quicker	quickest
quickly	more quickly	most quickly
	less quick	least quick
	less quickly	least quickly

POSITIVE   This is a **quick** route.

Rainha drove **quickly** through the circuit.

COMPARATIVE   This is a **quicker** route.

Rainha drove **more quickly** through the circuit.

SUPERLATIVE   This is the **quickest** route.

Rainha drove **most quickly** through the circuit.

(For advice on the specific ways to create comparative and superlative forms of adjectives and adverbs, see 20c-4, below.)

1 Watch out for illogical comparatives

Some adjectives and adverbs cannot logically take comparative or superlative form. These include *unique, impossible, pregnant, infinite, dead, gone, perfectly,* and *entirely.*

ESL

20c
adj/adv

ILLOGICAL   Gottlieb's "Nightscape" is a **most unique** painting.

READER'S REACTION: *Unique* means "one of a kind." How can a thing be *more* or *most* if it is the only one?

LOGICAL   Gottlieb's "Nightscape" is a **unique** painting.

2 Look for imprecise use of comparatives

In conversation, people often use comparative forms loosely, knowing listeners will still grasp the intended meaning of a phrase like "She is my oldest daughter" even though the speaker has only two daughters. In writing, you need to be more precise, especially if you are presenting facts and figures.

INACCURATE   The survey covered four age groups: 20–29, 30–44, 45–59, and 60+. The people in the older group smoked the least.

READER'S REACTION: Did the people in the older *groups* smoke the least or did the people in the *oldest* group smoke the least?

PRECISE   The survey covered four age groups: 20–29, 30–44, 45–59, and 60+. The people in the **oldest group** smoked the least.

3 Check for double comparatives

Most readers will not accept double comparatives or superlatives.

INCORRECT   The temperature dropped, and the weather became **more foggier**.

EDITED   The temperature dropped, and the weather became **foggier**.

INCORRECT   Jorge is the **most agilest** athlete on the team.

EDITED   Jorge is the **most agile** athlete on the team.

4 Check for irregular comparatives and superlatives

Some familiar modifiers have irregular comparatives and superlatives.

20c
adj/adv

20.2

IRREGULAR COMPARATIVES AND SUPERLATIVES		
POSITIVE	COMPARATIVE	SUPERLATIVE
ADJECTIVES		
bad	worse	worst
good	better	best
ill (harsh, unlucky)	worse	worst
a little	less	least

many	more	most
much	more	most
some	more	most
well (healthy)	better	best
ADVERBS		
badly	worse	worst
ill (badly)	worse	worst
well (satisfactorily)	better	best

20d Avoiding double negatives

Negative words include *no, none, not, never, neither, hardly, scarcely, barely*, and words like *haven't* and *don't* (formed with *n't*, the abbreviation for *not*). In general, negative words do not become more forceful when more than one appears in a sentence. Instead of enhancing a statement, a **double negative** often undermines it. Readers may view the negatives as canceling each other out.

DOUBLE NEGATIVE   The highway department hasn't done nothing about the dangerous exit ramp.

READER'S REACTION: **If the department hasn't done nothing, maybe it** *has* **done** *something.*

EDITED   The highway department hasn't done anything about the dangerous exit ramp.

Exercise 2

A. Revise the following sentences to eliminate any incorrect use of adjectives or adverbs.

20d
adj/adv

EXAMPLE

I think the real difference between Necco Wafers and Skittles is that
longer
Necco Wafers last ~~longest~~.

1. Of the three candy bars, Snickers, Three Musketeers, and Baby Ruth, which is older?
2. Which of the two kinds of gummy bears is more sweeter?
3. Broccoli-flavored candy had even badder sales than chocolate-dipped carrots.
4. Trying to create a candy bar that pleases everyone's taste is a most impossible task.
5. Some people can't hardly bear the taste of sour-flavored candy.

B. Working in a group, create two different correct versions of each of the following sentences. Then decide as a group which version of each sentence you prefer and why.

1. Surveys of customers' preferences are the most costliest method of market research.
2. They are not unlikely to be a waste of money.
3. One survey showed that consumers find a blend of hazelnuts and raspberries a most tastier combination.
4. The company wanted a more unique combination, however.
5. By adding marshmallows to the blend, the company eventually turned the bar into a most complete marketing success.

Editing for Sentence Problems

CHAPTER 21

SENTENCE FRAGMENTS

To treat a cluster of words as a sentence, start with a capital letter and put a period at the end, but make sure you include essential elements such as a subject and a verb; otherwise, you may confuse readers by leaving out crucial information.

SUBJECT MISSING   Began pumping water out of the basement.
READER'S REACTION: **Who was pumping, or what was doing the pumping?**

EDITED   **The fire truck** began pumping water out of the basement.

VERB MISSING   The insurance company responsible for the costs.
READER'S REACTION: **What did the company do?**

EDITED   The insurance company **became** responsible for the costs.

A cluster of words punctuated as a sentence but lacking a crucial element that enables it to stand alone as a sentence is called a **sentence fragment**. Another kind of fragment consists of a group of words acting as a modifier but mistakenly asked to stand on its own as a sentence. Such fragments make readers do the writer's job, forcing them to reattach mentally a word group to a nearby sentence.

FRAGMENT   They were able to get the pump started again. **By replacing the gas filter**.
The second statement is a modifying phrase detached from the preceding sentence.

EDITED   They were able to get the pump started again **by replacing the gas filter**.

Fragments that confuse readers or make them do extra, unnecessary work are serious errors. On occasion, an **intentional fragment** (also called a **partial**

sentence, see 21c) may effectively create emphasis or a change of pace; fragments may also be used effectively in lists, as in this book; for the most part, however, academic, business, and professional readers will judge a piece of writing (and its writer) harshly when they encounter a fragment.

21a Recognizing sentence fragments

Some sentence fragments are easy to recognize, others less so. Watch for word groups falling into one of these three general categories.

- Word groups lacking a subject or a verb
- Modifying word groups detached from the sentences to which they belong
- Troublesome constructions, such as *for example* fragments or verbal phrases

1 Look for a subject and a verb

If a word group punctuated as a sentence lacks either a subject or a complete verb, expressed or implied, it is a fragment (see 16b).

STRATEGY

Two strategies for identifying fragments are to ask questions or to create questions.

- **Ask Who (or what) does? or Who (or what) is?** If a word group does not answer "Who?" or "What?" then it lacks a subject and is a sentence fragment.

    FRAGMENT   Yet also needs to establish a family counseling program.
    READER'S REACTION: **This doesn't say who (or what) needs to establish the program.**

    EDITED   Yet **Community Health Clinic** also needs to establish a family counseling program.

    If a word group does not answer "Does?" or "Is?" then it lacks a verb and is a sentence fragment.

    FRAGMENT   The new policy to determine scholarship size on the basis of grades rather than on the basis of need.
    READER'S REACTION: **This doesn't indicate anything about what the new policy *does* or *is*.**

21a
frag

EDITED   The new policy **determines** scholarship size on the basis of grades rather than on the basis of need.

In trying to identify the "Who" in a passage, remember that in commands, the subject *you* is understood: [**You**] Use the spectrometer to test for the unknown chemical ingredient. Some familiar sentence patterns also use a clearly implied verb: John went to Stanford, Regina [**went**] to UCLA.

- **See if you can turn a word group into a question that can be answered *yes* or *no*.** If it can be, it is a sentence.

WORD GROUP   They bought a van to carry the new equipment.

QUESTION: **Did they buy a van to carry the new equipment?**

CONCLUSION   The word group is a sentence.

To decide whether a subject or a verb is missing, see if you need to add or alter an element to create a question.

WORD GROUP   Bought the building to use as a warehouse.

QUESTION: **Did _____ buy the building to use as a warehouse?**

CONCLUSION   The question does not have a subject, so the word group is a fragment lacking a subject.

EDITED   **Johnson Manufacturing** bought the building to use as a warehouse.

WORD GROUP   The company providing repairs for our computers.

QUESTION: **Does the company providing repairs for our computers?**

CAUTION: **Do not begin the questions with *is/are* or *has/have*. In doing so you may unintentionally provide a verb for the word group you are testing.**

CONCLUSION   The word *providing* cannot act as the verb in its present form.

The word group is a fragment lacking a verb.

EDITED   The company **is** providing repairs for our computers.

21a
frag

In checking for fragments, be careful not to mistake a verbal for a verb. Verbals include words like *testing*, *tested* (participles), *to test* (infinitives), and *testing* (gerund). A verbal alone cannot act as the verb in a sentence. (See 21a-3.)

DID YOU KNOW?

In a survey conducted by the authors of this book, college instructors listed sentence fragments as one of the sentence-level errors they considered the most serious. The people surveyed included teachers of chemistry, business, nursing, mathematics, literature, and psychology as well as composition.

Chris M. Anson and Robert A. Schwegler, "A Survey of Attitudes Toward Error Among Instructors at Four Colleges," unpublished ms.

Exercise 1 ————————————————————————————————

Indicate which of the following word groups are sentence fragments and which are complete sentences. Correct sentence fragments by supplying any information necessary to make complete sentences.

EXAMPLE

is
Our job to find a new head for nursing services.
  ^

1. Several people applying for the job.
2. The job description in the newspaper asks for someone who is a good administrator and also an innovator.
3. Is able to convince fellow workers to develop their own innovative staffing plan and present it to the hospital administration.
4. Julie Kim, the prior head of nursing services responsible for so much turmoil during her time in the job and also so many improvements in the way nurses interact with patients and physicians.
5. A study suggesting that nursing administrators develop in-service programs to create improved morale among the professional staff and also better patient care.

21a
frag

---

2 Look for *although, because, that, since*, and other subordinating words

When you look for sentence fragments, pay attention to word groups containing a subject and a verb but beginning with subordinators such as *although, if, because,* or *that.* Subordinators tell readers to regard the word group that follows as part of a larger statement. They signal that the word group is a modifying (subordinate or dependent) clause needing to be attached to the main clause that it modifies.

STRATEGY

Look for a word group beginning with a subordinating conjunction such as *after, although, if, because, unless,* or *since* (see 28c) or with a relative pronoun (*that, what, which,* or *who*). Then check whether this word group is attached to a main clause (see 16c)—a cluster of words that can stand on its own as a sentence. If the word group is unattached, then it is a fragment.

FRAGMENT   Most residents love the friendly, unspoiled nature of the town. **Which has led to rapid population growth and a rise in property values.**

EDITED   Most residents love the friendly, unspoiled nature of the town, which has led to rapid population growth and a rise in property values.

FRAGMENT   Many experts think that the SAT and the ACT are somewhat biased. **Although they also consider most criticism of the tests overblown.**

EDITED   Many experts think that the SAT and the ACT are somewhat biased, although they also consider most criticism of the tests overblown.

EDITED   Many experts think that the SAT and the ACT are somewhat biased yet also consider most criticism of the tests overblown.

Exercise 2

A. Indicate which of the following word groups are sentence fragments and which are complete sentences. Correct all the sentence fragments by supplying any information necessary to make complete sentences or attaching a fragment to an adjacent main clause.

EXAMPLE

Although many people think that afternoon sleepiness is caused by a heavy lunch, Researchers say this is not true.

1. People such as interns and truck drivers often feel drowsy. Even though they are aware of a need to stay awake and alert.
2. Having an afternoon nap can greatly increase your alertness. Whether or not you got enough sleep the night before.
3. Almost accidentally, researchers started becoming aware of the importance of naps while they were mapping cycles of drowsiness and alertness we each go through during an entire day.

4. Almost everyone experiences sleepiness and a decline in mental alertness during the afternoon. Because our internal clocks tell us it is time to nap and get out of the sun's strongest rays.

5. Despite a widespread belief that siestas and naps are cultural customs. They actually have a biological base.

B. Working with a group, look through one or more popular magazines, focusing on either the advertising or the articles. Identify ten sentence fragments and list them. Indicate which fragments lack a subject or a verb (or both), and indicate which fragments are modifying clauses that contain a subject and a verb but are controlled by a subordinating word.

---

3 Look for troublesome constructions

As you edit, watch for three sentence structures that are often incorrectly treated as complete sentences:

21.1

- *For example* fragments
- Split predicates
- Disconnected verbal phrases

***For example* fragments.** Word groups beginning with phrases like *for example, such as,* or *for instance* are sometimes disconnected from sentences and mistakenly made to stand on their own. You can identify such fragments by looking for one of the phrases at the beginning of a word group and then checking whether the word group is either (1) attached to a main clause or (2) contains all the elements needed to act as a complete sentence.

FRAGMENT	We are trying to hire a new staff member who has skills that none of us possess. **For example, knowledge of computer-aided design.**
EDITED (SEPARATE SENTENCE)	We are trying to hire a new staff member who has skills that none of us possess. For example, **we need** someone with knowledge of computer-aided design.
FRAGMENT	Very few people are aware of the familiar species that are suffering from pollution or mismanagement. **Such as the striped bass and the snook.**
EDITED (ATTACHED TO MAIN CLAUSE)	Very few people are aware of the familiar species, **such as the striped bass and the snook**, that are suffering from pollution or mismanagement.

21a
frag

Split predicate. A sentence can contain two or more complete verbs (for example, "I *unfastened* the seat and *removed* it."). Writers sometimes mistakenly split off the second (or last) element as a separate sentence, perhaps unconsciously assuming that the subject in the opening section is still present in the later one. To recognize a fragment of this type, look for a word group whose verb comes near the beginning (often following a word like *and*, *yet*, or *but*) and whose subject is nearby—but in another sentence.

FRAGMENT	Beethoven's work as a composer began in a style similar to that of Mozart. **But soon took on its own unique style.**
CORRECTED (SUBJECT ADDED)	Beethoven's work as a composer began in a style similar to that of Mozart. But **his work** soon took on its own unique style.
CORRECTED (REATTACHED)	Beethoven's work as a composer began in a style similar to that of Mozart **but** soon took on its own unique style.

Disconnected verbal phrases. To identify a disconnected verbal phrase, you need to be aware of the difference between verbs and verbals. Verbals are similar in form to verbs, but play different roles: participles (*analyzing, analyzed*), infinitives (*to analyze*), and gerunds (*analyzing*). (See 16c-4.) When combined with a helping verb (such as *is, has, can,* or *should*—see 16a-3), a verbal can be part of a complete verb (*was analyzing, should analyze*). Often, verbal phrases (verbal plus object and modifiers) are detached from adjacent sentences or related to them as modifiers.

FRAGMENT (PARTICIPIAL PHRASE)	**Frustrated by the meager offerings in journalism.** She decided to transfer to another university.
EDITED (ATTACHED TO MAIN CLAUSE)	Frustrated by the meager offerings in journalism, she decided to transfer to another university.
FRAGMENT (INFINITIVE PHRASE)	Divorcing parents should seek advice from a counselor. **To help lessen emotional problems for their children.**
EDITED (ATTACHED TO MAIN CLAUSE)	Divorcing parents should seek advice from a counselor to help lessen emotional problems for their children.
FRAGMENT (GERUND PHRASE)	**Introducing competing varieties of crabs into the same tank.** He did this in order to study aggression.
EDITED (REWRITTEN)	He **introduced** competing varieties of crabs into the tank in order to study aggression.

21a frag

Exercise 3

A. Correct each of the fragments in the following passages in two different ways.

EXAMPLE

Some innovative rock groups have been touring this year. Drawing large crowds.

Some innovative rock groups have been touring this year. They have been drawing large crowds.

Some innovative rock groups have been touring this year, drawing large crowds.

1. Realizing that musical tastes are probably changing. Many record companies have decided to explore new and newly rediscovered kinds of music.
2. Some formerly popular musical artists no longer have recording contracts. Their sales of CDs having dropped drastically.
3. In recent campus concerts, jazz artists have attracted large and enthusiastic audiences. Because of their innovative melodies and sounds.
4. The rhythm section of one group consists of a single unusual instrument. An electronic instrument making sounds like a drum but looking like a guitar.
5. Undecided about whether to sign new groups to long-term contracts. Some companies agree to produce and sell a single CD with an option for future recordings.

B. Instead of doing Exercise 3A on your own, work with another person and create *three* correct versions of each passage, rewriting extensively if necessary. Note the ways each of you prefers to correct fragments, especially any differences between your choices.

21b Editing sentence fragments

As you edit, correct sentence fragments in the way that best suits your purpose for writing, your meaning, and the stylistic effect you wish to create.

STRATEGY

You can correct sentence fragments in four ways.

1. **Supply** the missing sentence element.

   FRAGMENT (LACKS VERB)   Several arguments favor enabling adopted children to contact their birth parents. **Among the most important the need to find out about any hereditary diseases.**

EDITED
: Several arguments favor enabling adopted children to contact their birth parents. Among the most important is the need to find out about any hereditary diseases.

2. **Attach** the fragment to a nearby main clause. Rewrite if necessary.

FRAGMENT (SUBORDINATE CLAUSE)
: Modern trauma centers are equipped to give prompt care to heart attack victims. **Because rapid treatment can minimize damage to heart muscles.**

EDITED
: Modern trauma centers are equipped to give prompt care to heart attack victims because rapid treatment can minimize damage to heart muscles.

3. **Drop** a subordinating word so the subordinate clause can act as a complete sentence (main clause).

FRAGMENT
: **Although** several people argued strenuously against the motion. It passed by a considerable majority nonetheless.

EDITED
: Several people argued strenuously against the motion. It passed by a considerable majority nonetheless.

4. **Rewrite** a passage to eliminate the fragment.

FRAGMENT
: Some sports attract large numbers of participants in their fifties, sixties, and even seventies. **For example, tennis and bowling.**

EDITED
: Some sports, **such as tennis and bowling**, attract large numbers of participants in their fifties, sixties, and even seventies.

21b frag

Exercise 4

A. Correct each of the fragments in the following passages in two different ways.

EXAMPLE

Living and working in another country creates many challenges for families. For example, arranging for children's schooling.

Living and working in another country creates many challenges for families. Arranging for children's schooling is one such challenge.

1. The armed forces run elementary and secondary schools around the world. To provide education for dependents.
2. Japanese executives working in North America worry about educating their children in the Japanese language. And worry about whether they will fit into Japanese culture when they are adults.
3. Americans and Canadians working outside North America often look for schools conducted in English. To make sure their children will be prepared to attend college when the families return home.
4. The modern world makes many demands on parents. Who must spend considerable time and energy educating their children.
5. Whoever grows up with knowledge of two different cultures. I think that person will have some distinct advantages.

B. Working with a group, identify the fragments in the following word groups. Then combine word groups to form a paragraph consisting of complete sentences. Feel free to alter wording or add information necessary to make the paragraph interesting and clear.

21.2

1. One store chain asks people to provide an address when cashing a check. And uses the information to create a mailing list for its advertising.
2. As a result, people who buy two pairs of pants and a few blouses are going to be receiving something in the mail each week for the next few months. For instance, a colorful flyer about home furnishings or automobile accessories.
3. Some people resent this marketing strategy. And complain to the post office or the company itself.
4. Lots of people consider advertising brochures fun to read. And a way to make shopping easier.
5. I think they are one of the many small irritations we encounter every day. Such as free samples of useless products and computerized telephone calls.

21c
frag

21c Using partial sentences

In writing of all kinds, you are likely to encounter sentence fragments used properly and effectively. Fragments of this kind can be called **partial sentences**. Used sparingly, partial sentences can call attention to details, provide special emphasis for ideas, heighten contrasts, or create powerful images, as in the following passage.

> Our house stood apart. A gaudy yellow in a row of white bungalows. We were the people with the noisy dog.
>
> —RICHARD RODRIGUEZ, "Aria"

Here are some guidelines for creating partial sentences.

1. Have a clear purpose, such as highlighting details and ideas or providing strong emphasis and contrast.
2. Make sure readers will recognize the purpose and not mistake the fragment for a detached modifier or word group missing an important element.
3. Take care that readers will be easily able to understand the fragment and any connections among it and other word groups.

Exercise 5

If you have not already completed Exercise 2B, do so now, making a copy of each fragment you locate. Working with a group, share your different sets of fragments. Identify those fragments you consider effective partial sentences. Explain how each effective fragment fits the criteria in 21c, and tell what purpose each one fulfills.

CHAPTER 22

COMMA SPLICES AND FUSED SENTENCES

You can easily confuse and annoy readers if you inappropriately join two or more sentences using either a comma only (comma splice) or no punctuation at all (fused sentence). Readers may have to look over a sentence containing a comma splice several times to be sure of its meaning, because the sentence does not clearly specify the relationship between the clauses making it up.

COMMA SPLICE   CBS was founded in 1928 by William S. Paley, his uncle and his father sold him a struggling radio network they had bought to advertise their La Palina cigars.

READER'S REACTION: **At first I though CBS had three founders: Paley, his uncle, and his father. Then I realized that the sentence probably means Paley founded CBS after buying the radio network from his relatives.**

EDITED   CBS was founded in 1928 by William S. Paley ; his uncle and his father sold him a struggling radio network they had bought to advertise their La Palina cigars.

Even after a close examination, however, readers may find it difficult to understand a fused sentence, two sentences joined with no punctuation at all.

22a
cs/fs

FUSED SENTENCE   The city had only one swimming pool without an admission fee the pool was poorly maintained.

READER'S REACTION: **I can't decide if the *single* swimming pool in the town is poorly maintained or if the only swimming pool that does not charge a fee is in bad shape.**

EDITED   The city had only one swimming pool , **but** without an admission fee, the pool was poorly maintained.

22a Recognizing comma splices and fused sentences

When you link two sentences (independent or main clauses—see 16c) *by a comma alone,* you create a **comma splice.**

305

COMMA
SPLICE

Eight inches of rain fell in twenty-four hours, all the creeks swelled rapidly.

> READER'S REACTION: **I had to read the sentence twice because at first I couldn't tell where one part ended and the next began.**

EDITED

Eight inches of rain fell in twenty-four hours **, and** all the creeks swelled rapidly.

When you provide *neither a punctuation mark nor a connecting word* to show where one main (independent) clause ends and the next begins, you create a **fused sentence** (often called a **run-on sentence**).

FUSED
SENTENCE

That night the river overflowed its banks and spread over the lowlands thousands of people were left homeless by the time the waters receded.

> READER'S REACTION: **When I first read that the river "spread over the lowlands thousands of people," I imagined a mass of people being pushed over the land.**

EDITED

That night the river overflowed its banks and spread over the lowlands **; as a result,** thousands of people were left homeless by the time the waters receded.

You can edit comma splices and fused sentences in many ways, but first you need to identify them.

1 Identifying comma splices and fused sentences

As you edit, look for sentences containing more than one word group that could stand on its own as a sentence. (Consider marking such word groups in some way, such as drawing a line, in order to focus your attention on them.) Take note of those word groups that are joined by a comma alone (comma splice) or that are joined without any punctuation at all (fused sentence).

22a
cs/fs

COMMA
SPLICE

In a typical Navajo family, the husband serves as trustee/the mother and her children are the real owners of the family's property.

> WRITER'S REACTION: **When I drew a line to separate the two word groups that could stand alone, I noticed I had created a comma splice by joining them with only a comma.**

FUSED

The engineering and social work programs get the most public attention/the medical technology and marketing programs get the largest enrollments.

> WRITER'S REACTION: **Putting a line between the word groups that could be sentences on their own helped me see how the lack of any punctuation between them makes the sentence hard to read.**

Pay attention to writing likely to contain comma splices or fused sentences. When you are drafting quickly, adding idea to idea and clause to clause, you may sometimes use commas to string word groups together, creating comma splices—or you may leave out punctuation entirely. Writing of this sort often occurs when you are working under pressure or rushing to record ideas and details.

Pay attention to long sentences. Fused sentences can occur in sentences of any length, but as you edit, pay special attention to long sentences without internal punctuation. Check to see if they contain freestanding (main) clauses joined without punctuation. (Look at the commas in long sentences, too, in order to identify any that are creating comma splices.)

STRATEGY

As you edit, ask, "How many statements are there in this sentence?" A fused sentence is not a single unit but two (or more) units whose relationship is not clearly signaled to readers. If a sentence appears to contain more than one statement, check for appropriate punctuation and connecting words.

FUSED SENTENCE — The scientists had trouble identifying the fossil skeleton it resembled both that of a bird and that of a lizard.

COMMENT: **The sentence makes two statements: one about the troubles encountered by scientists and one about the nature of the skeleton.**

EDITED — The scientists had trouble identifying the fossil skeleton **because** it resembled both that of a bird and that of a lizard.

DID YOU KNOW?

22a
cs/fs

Preferences in punctuation and sentence style can change over time. Today, when you join two main clauses with a coordination conjunction (*and, but, for, nor, yet,* or *so*), you must also punctuate with a comma. A hundred years, ago, however, in *A New English Grammar for Schools* (1900), Thomas W. Harvey gave this advice: "A clause, introduced by *for, but, and* or an equivalent connective, is often set off by a semicolon" (294). As a correct example, Harvey gave the following sentence that contrasts with our modern taste for short, direct sentences: "The person he chanced to see, was, to appearance, an old, sordid, blind man; but upon his following him from place to place, he at last found, by his own confession, that he was Plutus, the god of riches, and that he was just come out of the house of a miser" (244).

Thomas W. Harvey, *A New English Grammar for Schools* (New York: American Book, 1900).

2 Noticing sentence patterns that may lead to comma splices and fused sentences

By joining sentences, you can emphasize their relationship. Some kinds of related sentences follow patterns that lead to more than their fair share of comma splices and fused sentences, however.

- Sentences with the same subject
- One sentence illustrated by another
- Balanced sentences with contrasting ideas
- Sentences with related ideas

STRATEGY

Use the list of sentence patterns (above) as an editing checklist, and when you identify any comma splices or fused sentences, correct them in ways that emphasize their relationship. (See 22b for ways to correct comma splices and fused sentences.)

- Sentences (main clauses) with the same subject

  COMMA SPLICE The ice cream cake had begun to melt, it was dripping onto Grandmother's lace tablecloth.

  EDITED The ice cream cake had begun to melt, **and** it was dripping onto Grandmother's lace tablecloth.

- One sentence (main clause) illustrated by another

  FUSED SENTENCE Children with Down syndrome feel the same emotions as the rest of us they get sad, puzzled, and silly.

  EDITED Children with Down syndrome feel the same emotions as the rest of us; they get sad, puzzled, and silly.

- Balanced sentences (main clauses) with contrasting ideas

  COMMA SPLICE The engineering and social work programs get the most public attention, the medical technology and marketing programs get the largest enrollments.

  EDITED The engineering and social work programs get the most public attention; **nonetheless,** the medical technology and marketing programs get the largest enrollments.

- Sentences (main clauses) with related ideas

  FUSED SENTENCE Health costs are rising rapidly solutions to the problem are not clear.

  EDITED Health costs are rising rapidly; **moreover,** solutions to the problem are not clear.

22a
cs/fs

When is a comma joining two word groups not a comma splice? When one of the word groups cannot stand on its own as a sentence—when it is one of a variety of modifying or dependent word groups. To identify comma splices (or fused sentences), check that each word group can form a sentence. Don't assume that a long cluster of words is automatically a sentence, even if it does present an idea or make a statement.

Although the elementary school has a good reputation, it is overcrowded and has run-down facilities.

PART 1   Although the elementary school has a good reputation.
(not a sentence)

PART 2   It is overcrowded and has run-down facilities.
(sentence)

(For help in identifying word groups that cannot form sentences, see 21a, 16c, and 16d.)

Exercise 1

A. First, use the strategies discussed in 22a to identify the comma splices in the following passage.

The subarctic region provides little variety in food, therefore, Eskimo diet includes large quantities of meat such as seal and caribou. The cold weather and the available materials determine dressing habits, a loose shirt with a hood, trousers, stockings, and mittens (often made of caribou skin and fur) are a common outfit for men, women, and children alike. Social affairs are important in Eskimo communities, favorite gatherings include carnivals, Christmas parties, and feasts of game brought in by hunters. Children in Eskimo communities begin school at the age of five or six, most quit by the time they are twelve in order to go to work. Boys usually go hunting with their fathers, girls learn to sew and cook.

22a
cs/fs

Next, draw a double vertical line between each of the independent (main) clauses making up the following fused sentences.

EXAMPLE

Casinos used to operate legally in only a few states // they are now springing up all over the country as states make casino gambling legitimate.

1. The gaming industry is one of the fastest-growing industries in some areas it is a major employer.

2. Legalized gambling takes many forms bingo, lotteries, casinos, and video games are run under government supervision in many states.
3. State lotteries are popular they may also encourage people to gamble unwisely.
4. The economic and law enforcement objections to legalized gambling get the most public attention the moral and psychological objections may deserve the most attention.
5. Legalized gambling now goes beyond people in casinos betting on roulette or sports events it includes people playing bingo at a charity event or playing video poker in a family restaurant.

B. Working in a group, decide which, if any, of the sentences in the first passage in Exercise 1A follow sentence patterns likely to lead to comma splices or fused sentences, and identify the patterns.

22b Editing comma splices and fused sentences

Here are six strategies for correcting comma splices and fused sentences. As you revise, choose a strategy that brings your ideas into sharper perspective, creates emphasis, and highlights relationships.

1. Create separate sentences.
2. Join main clauses with a comma plus a coordinating conjunction (*and, but, or, for, nor, so,* or *yet*).
3. Join main clauses with a semicolon.
4. Join main clauses with a semicolon plus a conjunctive adverb or transitional expression (*however, moreover, for example, in contrast,* and similar words or phrases).
5. Subordinate one of the clauses.
6. Join main clauses with a colon.

1 Create separate sentences

When the ideas in main clauses are loosely related, you can generally express them best in separate sentences.

COMMA SPLICE AND FUSED SENTENCE   Costa Rica's political life has been relatively free of damaging conflict, the same cannot be said of its neighbors El Salvador and Nicaragua, in particular, have long histories of civil unrest.

EDITED   Cost Rica's political life has been relatively free of damaging conflict● **The** same cannot be said of its neighbors● **El Salvador** and Nicaragua, in particular, have long histories of civil unrest.

22b
cs/fs

2 Join main clauses with a comma plus a coordinating conjunction

When main clauses convey ideas or information of approximately equal importance, consider linking the clauses with a comma plus a coordinating conjunction (*and, but, or, for, nor, so,* or *yet*) that indicates their relationship.

COMMA
SPLICE

The more experienced teams use complicated strategies for offense and defense, the inexperienced teams concentrate on the basics.

EDITED

The more experienced teams use complicated strategies for offense and defense**, but** the inexperienced teams concentrate on the basics.

FUSED
SENTENCE

Schizophrenia is a mental illness its causes may be physical.

EDITED

Schizophrenia is a mental illness**, yet** its causes may be physical.

Three or more closely related clauses can be punctuated as a series in order to emphasize their relationship. Be sure to include the conjunction before the last item.

We collected the specimens, we cleaned them with a mild detergent**, and** we measured them.

3 Join main clauses with a semicolon

You can use a semicolon to emphasize the similar importance of two main clauses.

COMMA
SPLICE

During flight an airplane tends to drift up or down, left or right because of air turbulence. An autopilot is a device that detects and corrects drift, the system senses changes in the aircraft's motion and reacts accordingly.

EDITED

During flight an airplane tends to drift up or down, left or right because of air turbulence. An autopilot is a device that detects and corrects drift**;** the system senses changes in the aircraft's motion and reacts accordingly.

22b
cs/fs

4 Join main clauses with a semicolon plus a conjunctive adverb or transitional expression

However, nonetheless, therefore, consequently, moreover, thus, and similar words (conjunctive adverbs) specify relationships between word groups.

Transitional expressions such as *for example*, *in contrast*, and *in addition* can be used for similar purposes. Use them with a semicolon.

FUSED SENTENCE   Commercially raised animals such as chickens or beef cattle can reach marketable size within a matter of months or a year the American lobster must grow for an average of six to eight years before it reaches the proper size.

EDITED   Commercially raised animals such as chickens or beef cattle can reach marketable size within a matter of months or a year**;** **in contrast,** the American lobster must grow for an average of six to eight years before it reaches the proper size.

Words like *however*, *nonetheless*, and *thus* (conjunctive adverbs) and expressions like *for example* and *on the other hand* (transitional expressions) can appear *within* a second main clause as well as at the beginning. Wherever they appear, the words must be set off with a comma(s) and the clauses themselves joined by a semicolon.

AT BEGINNING   The Great Lakes once supported a thriving fishing industry; **however,** in recent decades pollution has reduced the catch greatly.

IN MIDDLE   The Great Lakes once supported a thriving fishing industry; in recent decades, **however,** pollution has reduced the catch greatly.

AT END   The Great Lakes once supported a thriving fishing industry; in recent years pollution has reduced the catch greatly, **however.**

5 Subordinate one of the clauses

Subordinators such as *although*, *while*, *when*, *because*, *since*, and *unless* and relative pronouns such as *who*, *which*, or *that* enable you to specify a wide range of relationships (see 28b).

COMMA SPLICE   Margaret Atwood is best known for her novels, her essays and poems are also worth reading.

EDITED   **Although** Margaret Atwood is best known for her novels, her essays and poems are also worth reading.

6 Join the clauses with a colon

When a clause summarizes, illustrates, or restates a preceding clause, you can join the two with a colon (see 34b).

FUSED SENTENCE   Foreign study calls for extensive language preparation vaccinations and a passport are not enough.

EDITED   Foreign study calls for extensive language preparation⁝ vaccinations and a passport are not enough.

Exercise 2

22.2

A. Identify and edit in *two* ways each of the following comma splices and fused sentences. Use the methods of revision indicated in brackets after each sentence.

EXAMPLE

Children often fight among themselves, these conflicts pose many challenges for parents. [comma plus coordinating conjunction; semicolon]

Children often fight among themselves, and these conflicts pose many challenges for parents.

Children often fight among themselves; these conflicts pose many challenges for parents.

1. Some parents refuse to become involved in their children's squabbles, they fear the children will resent the interference. [subordination; semicolon]
2. Siblings have special reasons to fight competing for space and playthings or for attention from a parent can turn playmates into rivals. [colon; semicolon plus transitional phrase]
3. Sibling fights offer an opportunity for children to become sensitive to the feelings of others, the arguments pose dangers as well. [comma plus coordinating conjunction; semicolon plus conjunctive adverb]
4. Bickering is common and normal excessive fighting can be a sign of more serious trouble. [semicolon plus conjunctive adverb; separate sentences]
5. By adolescence, most children have worked out compatible relationships with their siblings, they may still occasionally argue. [subordination; comma plus coordinating conjunction]

22b
cs/fs

B. Working with a group, edit each of the following sentences in two ways, using strategies discussed in 22b. You may need to make changes in wording or punctuation.

1. One group claims that cattle raising is hard on the environment another group argues that raising wheat and other cereal grains causes water pollution and destroys topsoil.

2. In Central Florida, cattle waste has polluted Lake Okeechobee runoff from fertilizer has greatly increased the growth of algae in the lake.

3. The waters of Long Island's south shore are also polluted the main culprit is lawn fertilizer.

4. In my state, pesticides from potato farming have polluted the groundwater pig and chicken farming have caused problems.

5. Our large population makes a massive farming industry necessary we are going to have to deal with the problems caused by large-scale farming and livestock raising.

CHAPTER 23

PRONOUN REFERENCE

Words like *they, it, she, who,* and *which* (pronouns) help you make sentences less repetitive and easier to understand, while also enabling you to build links among ideas.

Freud made **the claim** that slips of the tongue reveal subconscious thoughts and desires, yet **he** offered no real evidence to support **it**.

For this linking process (called **pronoun reference**) to work, readers must recognize the word to which a pronoun refers, known as its **headword** (or **antecedent**).

When the relationship is not clear, readers may be confused.

CONFUSING   Much of my supposedly glamorous life with the circus consisted of leading the elephants from their cages and hosing **them** down.

           READER'S REACTION: **What got hosed down? The elephants? The cages? Both?**

By creating clear pronoun reference, however, you can tie sentences and ideas together and guide your readers.

CLEAR   Much of my supposedly glamorous life with the circus consisted of hosing the **elephants** down after leading **them** from **their** cages.

23a Recognizing and editing unclear pronoun reference

As long as your readers can clearly identify the word or group of words acting as a single antecedent, pronoun reference will help you tie statements together.

23a
pr ref

Calvin Klein, **Liz Claiborne**, and **Donna Karan** started out as clothing designers. **They** now head major corporations bearing their names.

Watch out for pronouns that can easily refer to more than one possible
antecedent or that are widely separated from their antecedents. Both of these
can confuse your readers.

1 Watch for pronouns with several possible antecedents

Look for passages containing a pronoun and two or more words or word
groups to which it might *possibly* refer. If your readers cannot easily identify the
appropriate antecedent, they will have trouble understanding the meaning.

AMBIGUOUS
REFERENCE

Detaching the measuring probe from the glass cylinder is a
delicate job because **it** breaks easily.

READER'S REACTION: **Which is especially fragile, the probe or the cylinder?**

> ### STRATEGY
>
> You can correct passages with **ambiguous reference** in two ways.
>
> 1. Replace the troublesome pronoun with a noun.
>
>   Detaching the measuring probe from the glass cylinder is a del-
>   icate job because **the probe** breaks easily.
>
> 2. Reword the sentence.
>
>   Because the measuring probe breaks easily, detaching it from
>   the glass cylinder is a delicate job.

23a
pr ref

In addition, watch for pronouns that can refer to each of two or more
subjects in earlier sentences.

AMBIGUOUS
REFERENCE

Robespierre and Danton disagreed over the path the French
Revolution should take. **He** was convinced that the Revolution
was endangered by its internal enemies; **his opponent** believed
the Revolution had been won.

EDITED
(ADD NOUNS)

Robespierre and Danton disagreed over the path the French
Revolution should take. **Robespierre** was convinced that the
Revolution was endangered by its internal enemies; **his oppo-
nent** believed the Revolution had been won.

When you use *said* or *told* to report in a general way what someone has
said (**indirect quotation**), you may sometimes create confusion.

AMBIGUOUS   When the project was finally completed, Jennifer's supervisor said **she** needed a few days off because she had been working so hard.

READER'S REACTION: **Who needs the time off, Jennifer or her supervisor?**

Edit this problem by (1) reporting the person's words exactly (**direct quotation**) or (2) rewriting with nouns rather than pronouns.

DIRECT
QUOTATION   When the project was finally completed, Jennifer's supervisor said, "**You** need a few days off because **you** have been working so hard."

REWRITTEN
WITH NOUN   When the project was finally completed, her supervisor said that **Jennifer** needed a few days off because **she** had been working so hard.

2 Pay attention to pronouns widely separated from their antecedents

When you place a pronoun at a distance from its antecedent, your readers may have a hard time recognizing the connection—even though no other possible referent comes between them.

REMOTE REFERENCE
James Van Allen designed an instrument that the first American space satellite used to detect what are now known to be two doughnut-shaped rings of high-energy particles extending from between several hundred to fifty thousand kilometers above the earth. The belts were eventually named for **him**.

To edit for this problem, either bring the pronoun closer to its antecedent or rename the noun or pronoun to which it refers.

EDITED
James Van Allen designed an instrument that the first American space satellite used to detect what are now known to be two doughnut-shaped rings of high-energy particles extending from between several hundred to fifty thousand kilometers above the earth. They were eventually named **the Van Allen belts after the man instrumental in their discovery**.

23a
pr ref

3 Pay attention to the location of *who, which,* and *that*

Keeping pronouns and antecedents close together is especially important for word groups beginning with *who, which,* and *that* (relative pronouns). Avoid confusion by placing the pronoun right after its antecedent.

CONFUSING	As I lay on the carpet in my old bedroom, I noticed two stale pieces of bubble gum under **the dresser that I loved to chew as a boy**.
EDITED	As I lay on the carpet in my old bedroom, I noticed under the dresser two stale pieces of **the bubble gum that I loved to chew as a boy**.

Exercise 1

A. Rewrite each of the following sentences to create clear pronoun reference.

EXAMPLE

Someone needs to pick up the weekend shipment ~~at the airport~~ that
        at the airport
may arrive late Saturday night.
                      ^

1. Both Carlo and Andy agree that he will be responsible for getting the cartons of replacement parts from the air terminal.
2. The accountant has told his client that he will be answerable for any problems with billing.
3. Airfreight offers weekend shipment and is cheaper, which means that work doesn't have to stop on Monday morning while workers wait for delivery of the replacement parts.
4. The van used to pick up shipments is the old one the company's owner purchased right after her divorce which is covered with rust spots.
5. The sales projections used to order supplies are often inaccurate because the sales manager calculates them using a formula on a spreadsheet that is overly optimistic.

B. Working with a group of fellow students, compare the choices each of you made in editing the sentences in Exercise 1A.

4 Create clear reference chains

You can guide readers through a passage using a chain of pronouns to connect sentences. A **reference chain** begins with an antecedent stated in the first sentence of a passage and throughout directs readers' attention to the topic you are addressing.

STRATEGY

- State the antecedent clearly in the opening sentence.
- Make sure other possible antecedents do not interrupt links in the chain.

- Do not interrupt the chain and then try to pick it up after several sentences.
- Call attention to the links by giving the pronouns prominent positions (usually the beginnings of sentences); vary their positions only slightly.

UNCLEAR

Sand paintings were a remarkable form of Pueblo art from the Southwest and Southern California. An artist would sprinkle dried sand of different colors, ground flower petals, corn pollen, and similar materials onto the floor to create **them**. The sun, moon, and stars as well as animals and objects linked to the spirits were represented in the figures **they** contained. **Their** purpose was to encourage the spirits to send good fortune to humans.

Because the pronouns *them* and *they* are buried at the ends of sentence in the middle of the paragraph, readers can easily lose sight of the paragraph's topic, sand paintings.

EDITED TO CREATE A REFERENCE CHAIN

Sand paintings were a remarkable form of Pueblo art from the Southwest and Southern California. To create **them**, an artist would sprinkle dried sand of different colors, ground flower petals, corn pollen, and similar materials onto the floor. **They** contained figures representing the sun, moon, and stars as well as animals and objects linked to the spirits. **Their** purpose was to encourage the spirits to send good fortune to humans.

DID YOU KNOW?

College instructors view problems with pronoun reference as among the most irritating and potentially confusing errors they encounter in student writing. They also think that appropriate and careful use of pronoun reference is a key tool for writers who wish to guide and focus the attention of readers.

Chris M. Anson and Robert A. Schwegler, "A Survey of Attitudes Toward Error Among Instructors at Four Colleges," unpublished ms.

23a
pr ref

Exercise 2

A. Revise the following sentences so that they form a reference chain giving appropriate emphasis to the information provided in the passage. You will need to emphasize some ideas and details more than others.

When it comes to reading material, Americans have some clear favorites. In terms of circulation, the top five newspapers in the country are the *Wall Street Journal*, *USA Today*, the *New York Daily New*, the *Los Angeles Times*, and the *New York Times*. Sales of softbound books far outnumber sales of hardbound books. Our favorite subject areas for books are medicine, history, fiction, sociology and economics, religion, and technology. The top three magazines in terms of revenue are *Time*, *Sports Illustrated*, and *People*. More people subscribe to *Modern Maturity* and the *AARP Bulletin* than to any other magazines, including *Reader's Digest*, which is number three on the subscription list. *1,001 Home Ideas* and *The Elks Magazine* have larger paid circulations than *Vogue*, *Rolling Stone*, and *Mademoiselle*.

B. Working with a group of writers, share your versions of the passage in Exercise 2A. Choose two versions that give the information different emphases. Identify the ways each writer has created a reference chain, and indicate which ideas and details have been highlighted and which have been moved to the background.

23b Recognizing and editing pronoun reference that is not specific

If readers say they "get lost" reading your work or "can't quite figure out what you are saying," part of the problem may be pronoun reference that is not specific enough. **Specific pronoun reference** points out for readers the precise relationships among statements. When pronouns refer to antecedents that are implied rather than stated, however, or when pronouns refer too broadly to a preceding passage, readers become confused.

1 Use *it, which, this,* and *that* with care

It, *which*, *this*, and *that* are useful words but also easy to misuse. You are most likely to misuse these pronouns when you want to refer to the entire idea of a preceding sentence, sentence part, or group of sentences. Used carefully, however, the words can help you refer effectively to an entire idea, as does the writer of the following pair of sentences.

> Every few million years an extremely large asteroid collides with the earth. **This** has not happened in historic times, so we have no experience of the consequences of **that** event.
>
> —ROBERT JASTROW, *Journey to the Stars*

Such **broad pronoun reference** can help you sum up ideas in order to comment on them, as in the preceding example. On the other hand, *overly* broad reference can easily confuse readers by failing to make clear the *specific* antecedent of *it, which, that,* or *this.*

OVERLY BROAD
REFERENCE

Redfish have been heavily harvested for years, but in the last decade they have been subjected to oil pollution and to the destruction of their mangrove swamp habitat by waterfront building. **That** has led to a recent and rapid decline in the redfish population.

READER'S REACTION: **Does *that* refer to the destruction of habitat, to oil pollution, to overfishing, or to some combination?**

STRATEGY

23.2

Look for words like *it, which, this,* and *that,* and then see if you have provided a specific word or group of words to which the pronoun clearly refers. If not, edit using one of these techniques: *specify, replace,* or *reword.*

- **Specify.** Right after *this, that,* or another troublesome word, add a word or phrase that specifies (or explains) the pronoun's referent.

EDITED
(SPECIFIES)

Redfish have been heavily harvested for years, but in the last decade they have been subjected to oil pollution and to the destruction of their mangrove swamp habitat by waterfront building. That **combination** has led to a recent and rapid decline in the redfish population.

EDITED
(EXPLAINS)

Redfish have been heavily harvested for years, but in the last decade they have been subjected to oil pollution and to the destruction of their mangrove swamp habitat by waterfront building. That **increasingly serious set of challenges** has led to a recent and rapid decline in the redfish population.

23b
pr ref

- **Replace.** Drop the pronoun, and use a noun or noun phrase in its place.

VAGUE

One test conducted by the Mars lander discovered some evidence of life on Mars, but the other uncovered no evidence whatsoever. This led many scientists to conclude that there is no life on the planet.

REPLACED

One test conducted by the Mars lander discovered some evidence of life on Mars, but the other uncovered no evidence whatsoever. **The reliability of the second test** led many scientists to conclude that there is no life on the planet.

- **Reword.** Rewrite so that the pronoun is no longer needed.

| RE-WORDED | One test conducted by the Mars lander discovered some evidence of life on Mars, but the second and more reliable test uncovered no evidence whatsoever, leading many scientists to conclude that there is no life on the planet. |

2 Look for *it* used in more than one sense

You can employ *it* in many ways.

REPLACING A NOUN
I threw the blender out after **it** broke for the third time.

WAY OF POSTPONING SUBJECT
It is the lack of sunshine in winter that often causes depression.

IDIOMATIC EXPRESSION
It is raining.

But you may confuse readers if you use *it* in more than one sense in a sentence or short passage.

| CONFUSING | When I was young, I always found **it** surprising that my father would come home from a hard day at his job and go out to the garden to work in **it**, even when **it** was raining. |

| EDITED | When I was young, I was always surprised when my father came home from a hard day at his job and went out to work in the garden, even when **it** was raining. |

23b
pr ref

3 Watch for antecedents that are implied rather than directly stated

Often, writers have an antecedent in mind but fail to communicate it to readers.

| IMPLIED | In the West, **they** often prefer Japanese cars; in the center of the country, **they** drive mostly Detroit-made autos; and in the Northeast and Southeast, **they** often choose European models. |
| | READER'S REACTION: I am guessing that *they* means "people in general." But it could mean rich people, people under forty, or some other group. |

By stating an antecedent directly, you eliminate both guessing and possible misunderstanding.

EDITED   In the West, **people under forty** prefer Japanese cars; in the center of the country, they drive mostly Detroit-made autos; and in the Northeast and Southeast, they often choose European models.

   Of course, if you have an antecedent in mind as you write, but do not actually state it, you may have trouble identifying the problem during editing. As you edit, therefore, check that you have provided readers with a *stated* antecedent for pronouns rather than an *implied* one. Watch out, as well, for the following troublesome words and contexts.

They or it without an antecedent. During conversation, listeners can usually figure out the meaning of *they* or *it*. Writing, especially academic writing, needs to provide precise and clear statements, so make sure your readers can identify an antecedent in the text itself.

IMPLIED   In February, frost damaged most of the citrus groves in the state, but **it** has not been determined.
READER'S REACTION: I can't be sure what *it* is.

EDITED   In February, frost damaged most of the citrus groves in the state, but **the extent of the loss** has not been determined.

You without an antecedent. When you intend to address the reader directly ("you, the reader"), *you* is acceptable in most writing.

ACCEPTABLE   In implementing the recommendations, **you** may find that staff members resist the report's suggestions for patient care. The following statistics should help **you** convince them the new procedures are useful.

   When *you* refers indefinitely to experiences, situations, and people in general, it often leads to misleading and wordy sentences.

MISLEADING   In Brazil, you pay less for an alcohol-powered car than for a gasoline-powered one.
READER'S REACTION: Who is *you*? After all, I'm not likely to be buying a car in Brazil.

EDITED   In Brazil, alcohol-powered cars cost less than gasoline-powered ones.

EDITED   In Brazil, consumers pay less for an alcohol-powered car than for a gasoline-powered one.

23b
pr ref

Possessive as antecedent. Remember to pair possessive nouns with possessive pronouns: *Kristen's . . . hers.*

UNCLEAR   The **company's** success with a well-known jazz fusion artist led **it** to contracts with other musicians.

EDITED   The **company's** success with a well-known jazz fusion artist led to **its** contracts with other musicians.

REWRITTEN   Success with a well-known jazz fusion artist led the company to contracts with other musicians.

When readers encounter the following pattern in academic writing, they will consider it inappropriate because the pronoun refers to the possessive form of a noun. (This pattern is more acceptable in informal writing.)

INAPPROPRIATE   In William Faulkner's *The Sound and the Fury*, he presents the first part of the story from the point of view of a mentally retarded person.

            William Faulkner, not *William Faulkner's* should be the antecedent of *he*.

EDITED   In *The Sound and the Fury*, William Faulkner presents the first part of the story from the point of view of a mentally retarded person.

Modifier mistakenly treated as antecedent. A modifier (like *experimental*) may *suggest* an antecedent (like *experiment*) without directly stating it. If you mistakenly rely on an implied antecedent of this sort, you force readers to guess at your intentions.

CONFUSING   A product's successful marketing may depend on how many demographic studies were conducted. As a result, people trained in it often get good jobs in major corporations.

            READER'S REACTION: What field do the people get training in? *Demographic*? That's not the name of a field.

EDITED   A product's successful marketing may depend on how many demographic studies were conducted. As a result, people trained in **demography** often get good jobs in major corporations.

Antecedent implied by another word. If you make a pronoun refer to a word that is not actually in a sentence but merely implied by some other word, your sentence is likely to be clumsy or hard to understand.

CLUMSY   Growing up in the Southwest, Alice dreamed of studying oceanography, though she had never seen **one**.

EDITED   Growing up in the Southwest, Alice dreamed of studying oceanography, though she had never seen **an ocean**.

UNCLEAR   Rosalind Franklin participated in the discovery of DNA's molecular structure, though she is seldom given credit for **it**.

            READER'S REACTION: **For what should she receive credit: the discovery? the structure? her participation?**

EDITED   Rosalind Franklin participated in the discovery of DNA's molecular structure, though she is seldom given credit for **her participation**.

Exercise 3

A. Revise the following sentences to eliminate vague pronoun reference and provide specific antecedents.

EXAMPLE

     The committee's report

~~In the committee's report~~ it₍ₐ₎ points out that students generally benefit from participating in a music program.

(*or* In its report, the committee points out . . .)

1. Many people study a musical instrument in high school though few students intend to become one.
2. At most secondary schools they offer a variety of music programs.
3. Last February, the town began investigating the quality of its high school band program, but it has not yet been completed.
4. In many regional high schools in the West, the band's large size mirrors the role it plays in the school's social life.
5. In the Northwest you quickly get used to marching and playing in the rain.

B. Compare your revised versions of the sentences in Exercise 3A with those of other writers. As a group, choose the best version of each sentence, and state the reasons for your choice.

23c Matching *who, which,* and *that* to antecedents

Who refers to people and may refer to animals with names. *Which* refers to animals and things (including ideas). *That* refers to animals, to things, and to anonymous people or people viewed collectively.

23.2

WHO   Branford and Wynton Marsalis, **who** are brothers, rank among the top contemporary jazz musicians.

WHICH   Quantum theory, **which** includes the work of Einstein, Planck, and Bohr, was the chief contribution of early twentieth-century physics.

THAT   Rheumatoid arthritis is a disease **that** affects the entire body, and the patients **that** this clinic serves get extended therapy for the disease.

Some readers will expect you to use *which* or *who* with **nonrestrictive clauses** and *that, which,* or *who* with **restrictive clauses** (see 33c for discussion of these two kinds of modifiers). Other readers may pay little attention to the distinction. In formal writing, however, you should generally pay attention to the difference.

RESTRICTIVE (ESSENTIAL, LIMITS MEANING)
Drugs **that** limit tissue rejection are necessary for the survival of transplant recipients.

NONRESTRICTIVE (NONESSENTIAL)
The license, **which** will cost you thirty dollars, permits you to fish anywhere in the state for seven days.

Exercise 4

A. Revise the following sentences to correct inappropriate pronoun references. Indicate which sentences, if any, contain appropriate pronoun reference.

EXAMPLE

Many scholars ~~which~~ *who* are interested in Buddhism have begun to study Tibetan religious practices.

1. The gathering was addressed by the Dalai Lama, a man which is one of the spiritual leaders of Tibetan Buddhism.
2. Tibetan Buddhism is characterized by large monastic organizations who practice yoga and other spiritual and intellectual rituals.
3. It is also true that this form of Buddhism retains features that it inherited from the folk religions of Tibet.
4. Up until the recent Chinese invasion, that occurred in 1959, Tibetan life was dominated by religious practices.
5. Although Lamaism has its greatest influence in Tibet and in countries who are nearby, such as Nepal and Mongolia, it is beginning to spread its influence in the West, including North America.

B. At a library, find a magazine with somewhat complicated, information-filled articles. Choose an article that interests you, and identify several paragraphs in which the author uses a variety of the pronoun reference patterns discussed in this chapter. Make enough copies of these paragraphs to share with a group of fellow students. As a group, identify each of the pronoun reference strategies and try to decide why the author used each one.

23c
pr ref

CHAPTER 24

MISPLACED, DANGLING, AND DISRUPTIVE MODIFIERS

The following sentences leave readers with unanswered questions.

MISPLACED MODIFIER   When I was at the store last week, I only looked at the DVD player.

> READER'S REACTION: *Only* is confusing. Do you mean you just looked and didn't try the DVD player out? You didn't have time to look at other equipment? You were the only person who looked at the DVD player?

DANGLING MODIFIER   Rushing to get to the post office before it closed, my bicycle nearly hit an unwary young woman.

> READER'S REACTION: Who was rushing to the post office—I, the bicycle, or the young woman?

The relationship between a modifier and the word(s) it modifies needs to be clear to readers. If it is unclear, it will result in unanswered questions and confusion.

A **misplaced modifier** is not placed closely enough to the word(s) it is intended to modify and appears to modify something else. A **dangling modifier** appears in a sentence that contains no word or phrase to which the modifier can be reasonably linked.

A modifier can also be disruptive, separating closely connected elements such as a subject and a verb and making a sentence difficult to read and understand.

DISRUPTIVE MODIFIER   The chief accountant, **even though her assistant first uncovered evidence that the company president had been embezzling funds**, assumed the responsibility of reporting the crime to the police.

Careful editing can make clear the relationship between a modifier and the word(s) being modified.

EDITED   When I was at the store last week, I looked only **at the DVD player.**

EDITED   Rushing to get to the post office before it closed, **I** nearly hit an unwary young woman while riding my bicycle.

EDITED   **Even though her assistant first uncovered evidence that the company president had been embezzling funds,** the chief accountant assumed the responsibility of reporting the crime to the police.

24a Recognizing and editing misplaced modifiers

Misplaced modifiers take many forms, yet you can readily develop your ability to recognize them by using these techniques (discussed in detail in the pages that follow).

- Look for a *word that fails to modify the word(s) you intend* and instead appears to modify some other word or group of words.
- Pay attention to a modifier's *location*.
- Pay attention to limiting modifiers such as *only*, *hardly*, and *exactly*.
- Pay attention to squinting modifiers that appear to modify *both* the word *before* and the word *after*.
- Pay attention to groups of words beginning with *who*, *which*, or *that*.

Editing misplaced modifiers involves either moving the modifier or rewriting the sentence.

STRATEGY

Try these two techniques for editing misplaced modifiers.

- *Move* the modifier closer to the word(s) it should modify.

  MISPLACED MODIFIER   After you have installed the fan, follow the directions for the wiring connections on the back of the cover plate.

  READER'S REACTION: **Are the wiring connections on the back of the cover plate?**

  MOVED   After you have installed the fan, follow the directions **on the back of the cover plate** for the wiring connections.

- *Rewrite* or *modify* a sentence so that the connection between modifier and words to be modified is clear.

MISPLACED MODIFIER	People who abuse alcohol frequently have other problems.
	READER'S REACTION: **Does *frequently* refer to the rate of alcohol abuse or the likelihood of problems?**
REWRITTEN	People who abuse alcohol tend to have other problems as well.

1 Pay attention to a modifier's location

You can word a sentence in many different ways to create emphasis and meaning. With so many choices, don't be surprised if you position a modifier inappropriately on the first try. As you edit, therefore, check that modifiers are placed closely enough to the word(s) they are intended to modify that the relationship is clear.

DRAFT	After a divorce, toddlers demand to be fed often instead of feeding themselves.
	READER'S REACTION: **I think this could be read as a statement that *all* toddlers regress, not just that this happens *often*.**
EDITED	After a divorce, toddlers **often** demand to be fed instead of feeding themselves.

Look at the end of sentences. During drafting, you may occasionally add new ideas and details to the end of a sentence, modifying a word you do not actually intend to modify.

MISPLACED MODIFIER	The wife believes she sees a living figure behind the wallpaper in the story by Charlotte Perkins Gilman, which contributes to her sense of entrapment.
	READER'S REACTION: **This sounds as if the story itself causes a feeling of entrapment.**
EDITED (MODIFIER MOVED)	The wife **in the story by Charlotte Perkins Gilman** sees a living figure behind the wallpaper, which contributes to her sense of entrapment.

24a
mm/
dm

Check the order of modifying phrases. You may sometimes draft sentences that present modifying phrases in confusing order. (Pay special attention to prepositional and participial phrases—see 16c-1 and 4.)

CONFUSING	It was not a good idea to serve food to the guests standing around the room on flimsy paper plates.
	READER'S REACTION: **Surely the guests were not standing on their plates!**
EDITED (MODIFIER MOVED)	It was not a good idea to serve food **on flimsy paper plates** to the guests standing around the room.

Exercise 1

Identify and correct the misplaced modifiers (words or phrases) in the following sentences. You may decide either to move the modifier or to rewrite the entire sentence.

EXAMPLE

   in pet store windows
Puppies spend a lot of time staring at people ~~in pet store windows~~.
     ^

1. They decided to buy the beagle puppy confused by the many exotic breeds of dogs.
2. This dog would replace the one killed by a truck running across a busy highway.
3. They forgot to buy a dog bed distracted by the crowd of people in the store.
4. Hurriedly, John sighed and began tearing up newspapers in order to begin house-training the puppy.
5. The parents could hear the children playing outside with the dog yelling and laughing.

2 Pay attention to *only, simply, even,* and other limiting modifiers

You can alter the meaning of a sentence considerably by moving around words like *only, almost, hardly, just, scarcely, merely, simply, exactly,* and *even* (called **limiting modifiers**). As you edit, by moving a modifier or rewriting to achieve the meaning you intend, remember that a limiting modifier generally applies to the word that immediately follows, though not always.

24a
mm/
dm

DID YOU KNOW?

In some languages, such as Latin or German, words change form to indicate their role in a sentence. In English, however, modifiers tend to change location, not form, to show which words they describe; for that reason, that position can make a big difference in meaning. As J. N. Hook points out, magazine editors pay considerable attention to the placement of modifiers.

Should you write "Smith only wanted one" or "Smith wanted only one"? A study by Bryant reported in 1962 that 86 percent of magazines placed *only* as in the second sentence. Logic supports that placement: it was *only one* that Smith wanted. Bryant added that in spoken English, sentences like the first predominated. Her findings, although dated, still appear valid.

J. N. Hook, *The Appropriate Word* (Reading, MA: Addison Wesley, 1990), 180.

During difficult economic times, **only** charities for disabled children maintain their normal levels of support.
They are the sole charities able to maintain normal levels.

During difficult economic times, charities for disabled **only** children maintain their normal levels of support.
The charities are for disabled children from families with one child.

During difficult economic times, charities for disabled children **only** maintain their normal levels of support.
They do not increase the levels of support.

3 Be alert for squinting modifiers

When readers encounter a modifier that appears to modify *both* the word(s) before and the word(s) after, they become understandably confused. To identify such **squinting modifiers**, read your sentences with attention not just to the meaning you intend but also to other possible readings that a reasonable reader might notice. To edit, ask yourself which word or word group you intend to modify, then move the modifier into a position that repairs the ambiguity.

SQUINTING
MODIFIER
People who enjoy listening to Aaron Copland's music **often** claim that he was the finest American composer of the twentieth century.

READER'S REACTION: **Does this mean that they *listen often* to the music or that they *often claim* something about Copland?**

EDITED
People who enjoy **listening often** to Aaron Copland's music also tend to claim that he was the finest American composer of the twentieth century.

EDITED
People who enjoy listening to Aaron Copland's music **will often** claim that he was the finest American composer of the twentieth century.

24a
mm/
dm

Exercise 2

A. Each of the following sentences contains either ambiguity caused by a squinting modifier or a limiting modifier that can be moved to different positions. Indicate the type of problem in each sentence.

EXAMPLE
Adults over age thirty who return to college frequently complete both undergraduate and advanced degree programs. *(squinting modifier)*

1. Adults entering college after working or raising a family officially are classified "non-traditional students" by many colleges.

2. "Non-trads" defer college entry often until after a major life event.
3. Following divorce or job loss, returning to college temporarily provides a boost to self-esteem.
4. Experts report that non-traditional students earn high grade point averages easily exceeding those of traditional students.
5. Nonetheless, failing to take into account the special needs of "non-trads" causes them to drop out frequently.

B. Working with a group of other writers, edit the sentences in Exercise 2A by rewriting each in two different ways.

4 Pay attention to clauses beginning with *who, which,* and *that,* or other subordinators

You should generally place a modifying clause beginning with *who, which,* or *that* right after the word(s) it is intended to modify. (See 16c-5 on relative clauses.)

MISPLACED
MODIFIER

The environmental engineers discovered another tank behind the building that was leaking toxic wastes.

READER'S REACTION: I know a building can leak, but I'll bet the writer meant to identify the tank as the culprit.

EDITED

Behind the building, the environmental engineers discovered another tank that was leaking toxic wastes.

Modifying clauses that begin with other subordinators, such as *when, although, because,* and *while* (see 16a-7), allow more flexibility in placement. Nonetheless, you still need to check that they convey your intended meaning.

MISPLACED
MODIFIER

The company switched from the old health plan to one offered by a competing insurance company because premiums are rising rapidly.

EDITED

Because premiums are rising rapidly, the company switched from the old health plan to one offered by a competing insurance company.

24a
mm/
dm

24.1

Exercise 3

A. Revise the following sentences to eliminate any misplaced modifiers.

EXAMPLE

I $my\ leg$
Sliding into second base, ~~my leg~~ broke.

1. The coach tossed out the practice balls to the players, wet and soft from yesterday's rain.
2. They worked on hitting and catching for fifteen minutes before the first game which was the only practice time they had.
3. The coach who was known as a strict disciplinarian of the championship Little League team invented a rigorous new set of conditioning exercises.
4. A proposal to follow the infield fly rule was defeated by the coach's committee which no one understood.
5. The coach is unable to present the award given in memory of Father Baker because he is sick.

B. Compare your edited versions of the sentences in Exercise 3A with those of other students. As a group, decide which versions you prefer and why you prefer them.

24b Recognizing and editing dangling modifiers

Pay attention to modifying words or phrases at the beginning of sentences. If the modifier does not mention the person, idea, or thing being modified, readers will expect you to name it as the subject of the main clause immediately following. If neither the modifier nor the subject of the main clause mentions clearly what you intend to modify, then the modifier is a **dangling modifier**. Often vague, illogical, or unintentionally humorous, dangling modifiers can needlessly distract readers or leave out important information.

DANGLING MODIFIER	**Leaking in several places**, the scouts abandoned their tents for the dry cabin.
EDITED	**Their tents leaking in several places**, the scouts decided to spend the night in the dry cabin.
EDITED	The scouts decided to spend the night in the dry cabin **because their tents were leaking in several places**.

24b
mm/
dm

Remember, even if you can find the word(s) to which a modifier should refer somewhere else in a sentence (in some position other than as the sentence's subject), the result will still be a dangling modifier.

DANGLING MODIFIER	Jumping into the water to save the drowning swimmer, the crowd cheered the lifeguard.
EDITED	Jumping into the water to save the drowning swimmer, **the lifeguard** was cheered by the crowd.

A modifier in the body of a sentence can dangle, too, when there is no word or phrase to which it can reasonably refer.

DANGLING MODIFIER	The emergency repairs were completed by noon, having become aware of the problem only at ten o'clock. READER'S REACTION: **Who became aware of the problem?**
EDITED	The emergency repairs were completed by noon, **the telephone company** having become aware of the problem only at ten o'clock.

STRATEGY

To correct a dangling modifier, take *one* of the following steps.

1. Add a subject to the modifier.

DANGLING   While shopping for a birthday gift for my brother, the stuffed alligator caught my eye.

EDITED   While **I was** shopping for a birthday gift for my brother, the stuffed alligator caught my eye.

2. Change the subject of the main clause.

DANGLING   Trying to decide where to hold the fundraiser, the new restaurant was attractive.

EDITED   Trying to decide where to hold the fundraiser, **the committee** was attracted to the new restaurant.

3. Rewrite the entire sentence.

DANGLING   After debating new regulations for months without a decision, the present standards were allowed to continue.

EDITED   The commission debated new regulations for months without a decision, then allowed the present standards to continue.

24b
mm/ dm

[www] 24.2

Exercise 4

A. Rewrite each of the following sentences in the *two* ways indicated in brackets, in order to eliminate dangling modifiers.

EXAMPLE   *Marion designed her research poorly.*
Unable to meet with an advisor, ~~Marion's research was poorly designed.~~
[add subject to main clause; rewrite]

Because Marion was unable to meet with an advisor, she designed
her research poorly.

1. Because of a failure to gather enough data, her study was incomplete. [rewrite; add subject to modifier]
2. Lacking the money to pay skilled interviewers, minimally trained volunteers were relied upon. [add subject to main clause; rewrite]
3. Many subjects were not asked appropriate questions because of poor training. [add subject to modifier; add subject to main clause]
4. Anxious and tired, the two-day attempt to write the research report was unsuccessful. [add subject to modifier; add subject to main clause]
5. After spending over twenty hours writing at the computer, the report was still not satisfactory. [rewrite; add subject to modifier]

B. Compare your edited versions of the sentences in Exercise 4A with those of another student, and decide which versions are the most successful and why.

24c Recognizing and editing disruptive modifiers

Readers generally expect sentence elements like subjects and verbs to stand close to each other. The same is true for verbs and the sentence elements that follow them (objects or complements). Modifiers that come between such elements may be disruptive, making a sentence difficult to understand.

DISRUPTIVE
MODIFIER
The researcher, **because he had not worked with chimpanzees before and was therefore unaware of their intelligence**, was surprised when they purposely undermined the experiment he was trying to conduct.

1 Pay attention to separated subjects and verbs

Some modifiers placed between subject and verb are disruptive; others are not. How can you recognize the difference?

- Modifiers providing information related to both the subject and the verb are disruptive.
- Modifiers providing information related to the subject alone are generally not disruptive.

subject   modifier
DISRUPTIVE Work on the building, **due to problems with the construc-**
verb
tion permits, was completed three months late.

24c
mm/
dm

	subject	modifier	verb

NOT
DISRUPTIVE

The electronics mall **that opened last month** has drawn crowds of customers.

To edit a potentially disruptive modifier, move it from between subject and verb.

DISRUPTIVE
MODIFIER

Contractors, **because house building is a boom-or-bust business**, should be ready to do home repairs when housing starts are down.

EDITED

Because house building is a boom-or-bust business, contractors should be ready to do home repairs when housing starts are down.

2 Pay attention to separations between verbs and objects (or complements)

Edit by moving the disruptive modifier.

CLUMSY

Joanne began collecting, **with special attention to survey results**, data for her study of dating preferences.

EDITED

With special attention to survey results, Joanne began collecting data for her study of dating preferences.

3 Be alert for split infinitives or verb phrases

Look for words that come between the parts of an infinitive (*to* plus a verb, as in *to run* or *to enjoy*), making it hard for readers to understand the relationship between the parts. Edit by moving the intervening words.

UNCLEAR

The office designer tried **to** respectively **address** each of the workers' concerns.

EDITED

The office designer tried **to address** each of the workers' concerns **respectively**.

Even when a **split infinitive** is easy to understand, you might consider revising it because some readers find split infinitives irritating. At times, however, a split infinitive is the clearest and most concise way of phrasing a statement.

Our goal is to more than halve our manufacturing errors.

The alternatives are more wordy and complicated—for example, "Our goal is a rate of manufacturing error less than half the present rate."

24c
mm/
dm

You will usually cause no difficulty for readers if you separate the parts of a verb phrase (helping verb plus main verb, as in *had been digging*) by adding one or more adverbs.

CLEAR   The archaeologists had been **carefully** digging at the site for three years.

Longer word groups within a verb phrase may be disruptive, however.

DISRUPTIVE   The archaeologists had been, **because of initial discoveries made during construction of a new house**, digging at the site for three years.

CLEAR   **Because of initial discoveries made during construction of a new house**, archaeologists had been digging at the site for three years.

Exercise 5

A. Rewrite each of the following sentences to eliminate disruptive modifiers and to make the sentence easier to read and understand.

EXAMPLE   ~~The architect,~~ because she was unfamiliar with eighteenth-century interior design and furnishings, *the architect* had to do some research before completing the project.

1. The overall design of a building and its interior decoration ought to thoughtfully and harmoniously work together.
2. Furniture design has at least for the past several centuries been greatly influenced by a handful of designers, including Hepplewhite, Chippendale, Sheraton, and, most recently, Eames.
3. Design in Colonial America, because of economic limitations and social customs, was generally simple and practical.
4. Americans had, by the early 1800s in what is now known as the Federalist period, developed more refined and expensive tastes.
5. Today, magazines like *Architectural Digest* and *House Beautiful* illustrate the tendency for styles in interior design to rapidly change and to add considerably to the cost of a home.

B. Working with a group of fellow writers, compare your revisions of the sentences in Exercise 5A. Decide which versions you prefer and why.

24c
mm/
dm

24d Using absolute phrases effectively

An **absolute phrase** consists of a noun or pronoun, a participle, and modifiers (for example, *the water level having risen* and *her view of market conditions changing almost daily*). It modifies an entire sentence rather than a specific word or group of words. Absolute phrases can add variety and flair to your writing; nonetheless, many people avoid them for fear of creating dangling modifiers. However, an absolute phrase provides its own noun or pronoun subject, so it does not dangle.

> **The water level having risen**, people in the valley feared that the dam was about to burst.
> **The absolute phrase sets the scene for the rest of the sentence.**

> The stockbroker began pelting her clients with urgent and sometimes contradictory advice, **her view of market conditions changing almost daily**.

CHAPTER 25

SHIFTS

In the course of almost any kind of writing, you are likely to ask readers to shift their attention many times—from events in the past to plans for the future, for example, or from what you are saying to what other people have said. As long as such shifts are signaled clearly, your readers should have little trouble following them. In speaking, you may be able to make rather abrupt shifts knowing that the people with whom you are talking will understand. In writing, however, inconsistent and confusing shifts may cause readers to wonder about your meaning.

INCONSISTENT **I** am thinking of taking out a two-year certificate of deposit because **you** can get a high interest rate on it.

> READER'S REACTION: **I don't think the writer means that** *she* **may buy the certificate of deposit because** *someone else* **can get a good interest rate.**

You need to identify and edit misleading shifts so they do not undermine readers' confidence in your writing.

EDITED **I** am thinking of taking out a two-year certificate of deposit because **I** can get a high interest rate on it.

25a
shift

25a Recognizing and editing shifts in person and number

Person refers to the ways you can use words like pronouns and nouns to shape the relationships among you, your readers, and your subject.

FIRST PERSON (*I, WE*)

- Use *I* to refer to yourself as the writer or as the subject of an essay.
- Use *we* when more than one person is author or subject.
- Use *we* for both yourself and your readers when discussing shared experiences or understandings.

- Use *we* in some academic fields such as the study of literature ("In this part of the poem we begin to see . . .") but not in others (for example, chemistry or engineering).

SECOND PERSON (*YOU*)
- Use *you* to refer directly to the reader.
- Do not use *you* in most kinds of academic and professional writing unless called for by the situation, as in a set of instructions.

THIRD PERSON (*HE, SHE, IT, THEY; ONE, SOMEONE, EACH,* AND OTHER INDEFINITE PRONOUNS)
- Use third person for the ideas, things, and people you are writing about.
- *People* and *person* are third person nouns, as are names of groups of things, ideas, and people (for example, *students, teachers, doctors*).

1 Pay attention to shifts in person

Look for shifts in person in your writing. In particular, watch for inconsistencies created by illogical shifts between **I** and **you** or between **you** and **he**, **she**, **it** or a noun in the third person.

INCONSISTENT   If a **person** is looking for an even higher interest rate, **you** might consider a corporate bond.

EDITED   If **you** are looking for an even higher interest rate, **you** might consider a corporate bond.

2 Pay attention to shifts in number

When you edit, look for shifts in number, especially with words that identify groups or members of a group, such as *business executives* or *a student* or with words like *person* or *people*. Remember that *person* is singular and *people* is plural. For logic and consistency, check that pronouns and their antecedents agree in number (see 19c).

25a
shift

SHIFTED   When **a business executive** is looking for a new job, **they** often consult a placement service.

READER'S REACTION: I think this writer had business executives in mind as a group, even though the sentence mentions only one *business executive.*

EDITED   When **business executives** are looking for **new jobs, they** often consult a placement service.

SHIFTED   If **a person** has money to invest, **they** should talk to a financial consultant.

EDITED   If **people have** some money to invest, **they** should talk to a financial consultant.

READER'S REACTION: I know that *a person . . . he or she* would also be correct, but it seems more complicated than necessary.

Exercise 1

A. Rewrite the following sentences to make them consistent in person and number.

EXAMPLE

Each person has ~~their~~ *a* favorite fast-food restaurant.

1. A would-be restaurant owner often fails to carefully consider the competition they will face from other restaurants of all kinds, both fancy and informal.
2. Good franchise chains survey competition, tell potential owners how much money they will need to open the business, and help you with the many problems a restaurant owner faces.
3. Admittedly, running a doughnut shop or a pizza place gives one less prestige than you get from owning a gourmet restaurant.
4. I would still rather run a successful business than one where you lose money.
5. Not all franchise arrangements are good ones, so people should do some research before he or she decides to open a franchised restaurant.

B. Working with a group of fellow students, write a brief paragraph on a topic of general interest. Choose a topic about which the group members have some knowledge—for example, finding a good summer job, developing effective study habits, or buying good clothing cheaply. Then rewrite the paragraph so it contains several nouns and pronouns that do not agree in person and number. Give a copy of the faulty paragraph to another group as a "quiz." Correct the paragraph they have created, in turn, for you.

25b Recognizing and editing shifts in tense and mood

When you change verb **tense** within a sentence or group of sentences, you signal a change in time and the relationship of events in time (see Chapter 18). When you choose a particular verb **mood**, you indicate an aim or attitude (see 18g).

1 Pay attention to shifts in tense

As you edit, watch out for unnecessary, illogical shifts in verb tense that can mislead your readers and that contradict your meaning.

ILLOGICAL   Scientists digging in Montana **discovered** nests and clutches of eggs that **indicate** how some dinosaurs **take care** of their young.

Indicate (present tense) is appropriate because the scientists interpret the evidence in the present. *Take care* (present tense) is inappropriate because the dinosaurs clearly acted in the past.

LOGICAL   Scientists digging in Montana **discovered** nests and clutches of eggs that **indicate** how some dinosaurs **took care** of their young.

Watch especially for any narration of events in the past tense that shifts suddenly to the present tense under the mistaken assumption that doing so will make events seem more vivid.

TENSE SHIFT   We **had been digging** at the site unsuccessfully for several weeks when suddenly Tonia **starts yelling**, "Eggs! I think I've found fossil eggs!"

EDITED   We **had been digging** at the site unsuccessfully for several weeks when suddenly Tonia **started yelling**, "Eggs! I think I've found fossil eggs!"

2 Watch for tense shifts in indirect quotation

In an **indirect quotation** you *report* what someone has said, rather than quoting word for word as in **direct quotation**. Use the past tense for indirect quotations.

DIRECT   A report said that in 2004, "The region will face increased environmental problems over the next ten years."

INDIRECT   A report **says** that in 2004, the region **will** encounter an increase in the damage to the air, water, and land caused by pollution.

INCONSISTENT   A report **said** that in 2004 the region **would** encounter an increase in the damage to the air, water, and land caused by pollution.

In contrast, use the present tense when you summarize or comment on a written work, film, television show, or similar source.

INCONSISTENT   In the novel's opening, Ishmael **arrives** at New Bedford with the intention of shipping out on a whaler, which he soon **did**.

CONSISTENT   In the novel's opening, Ishmael **arrives** at New Bedford with the intention of shipping out on a whaler, which he soon **does**.

25b
shift

DID YOU KNOW?

Watching for inappropriate shifts is one job done by a copy editor who reads and corrects an author's manuscript. Talking to copy editors, Elsie Myers Stainton says that the work of an author, living or dead, may be discussed as

> living, existing in the present. [. . .] The choice of tense usually depends on a nearby verb: "Whitman *was* just a clerk in the Attorney General's office, but he said, 'I celebrate myself.'" If excerpts are quoted from the poet's work as though from the living present, the present tense can be used: "Whitman *says*: 'Sing on, there in the swamp!/O singer bashful and tender!'"

Elsie Myers Stainton, *The Fine Art of Copyediting* (New York: Columbia UP, 1991) 54.

3 Be alert for shifts in mood

Choose the *mood* of a verb according to your purpose: to make a command or request (**imperative mood**), to present a statement or question (**indicative mood**), or to offer a conditional or hypothetical statement (**subjunctive mood**). (See 18g.)

subjunctive   indicative

INCONSISTENT   It is essential that our company **cut** costs and **increases** revenue.

subjunctive   subjunctive

EDITED   It is essential that our company **cut** costs and **increase** revenue.

When you are giving directions, use the imperative consistently so your directions will be less wordy and easier to understand.

INCONSISTENT   To reduce costs, **order** refilled cartridges for printers, and **you should** encourage employees to use email in place of paper memos.

CONSISTENT   To reduce costs, **order** refilled cartridges for printers, and **encourage** employees to use email in place of paper memos.

25b
shift

Exercise 2

A. Rewrite the following sentences to make them consistent in tense and mood.

25.1

EXAMPLE

I went to the video store last week, and after half an hour I still ~~can't~~ *couldn't*
figure out which movies I ~~want~~ *wanted*.

1. The video store manager said that if I bought two DVDs I will get a third one free, and then he tells me about several of his favorite DVDs.
2. In the movie *Sacrifice for Glory*, set in World War II, a British Mosquito bomber crashes in the jungle, and only the copilot managed to survive the long walk through the tropical heat back to civilization.
3. The hot sun beat on the shoulders of the copilot as he wades through the waist-deep, crocodile-infested swamp.
4. In *The Phantom Menace*, Anakin is a child with the power of the Force, but later in the series he turned to the Dark Side as Darth Vader.
5. In *Ghoulish Lunch*, the main character was reaching into the refrigerator around the guacamole dip for the last piece of apple pie when suddenly a cockroach crawls out from under the crust.

B. In a newspaper or magazine, locate a brief review of a movie, performance, book, or recording. Make sure the review contains numerous shifts in tense and mood. Make a copy of the review to share with a group of fellow students. After looking over all the reviews brought in by the group, choose one with particularly complex shifts. As a group, identify each shift and describe its nature. Continue working through as many reviews as you can.

25c Recognizing and editing shifts in voice

To recognize a verb in the **active voice**, see if the *agent* (or *doer*) of the action acts as the sentence's subject. To recognize a verb in the **passive voice**, see if the *goal* of the action acts as the sentence's subject. (See 18e.)

ACTIVE
subject   verb   object
The lava flow **destroyed** twelve houses.
agent   action   goal

PASSIVE
subject   verb
Twelve houses **were destroyed** [by the lava flow].
goal   action   [agent]

Note that you can choose whether or not to mention an agent when a sentence uses the passive voice.

In general, stick to either active or passive voice within a sentence, and be alert as you edit for unwarranted shifts that blur a sentence's focus and confuse readers.

INCONSISTENT
> active
>
> Among the active volcanoes, Kilauea **erupts** most frequently, and over 170 houses **have been destroyed** since 1983.
>
> READER'S REACTION: The first part of the sentence focuses on Kilauea, but the second part doesn't mention it, leading me to wonder if some of the other volcanoes share responsibility for the destruction.

EDITED
> Among the active volcanoes, Kilauea has erupted most frequently in recent years, and **it has destroyed** over 170 houses since 1983.

Occasionally, you may need to shift between active and passive voice to highlight a sentence's subject or emphasize your meaning.

> passive   active
>
> Hawaii **was built** by volcanic activity, and the island still **has** active volcanoes.
>
> **The shift between passive and active keeps Hawaii as the sentence's focus.**

When you write instructions, shifts between active and passive voice can make your directions hard to follow.

CONFUSING
> **You can purchase** hiking clothes from an outdoor equipment store, and picks, specimen bags, and other rock-collecting equipment **may be obtained** from a geological supply Web site.

EDITED
> **You can purchase** hiking clothes from an outdoor equipment store, and **you can obtain** picks, specimen bags, and other rock-collecting equipment from a geological supply Web site.

Exercise 3

25c
shift

A. Rewrite the following sentences to make them consistent in voice.

EXAMPLE
We enjoyed the expedition, ~~and much was~~ *and much* learned about fossils.

1. In the morning we dug in the base of the ravine, and during the afternoon the walls were explored.
2. The team found fossils of trilobites, and other fossils were also found at the site.
3. Team members learned many things about the science of paleontology, and much was learned about the geological history of our area as well.

4. A chart helped in identifying fossilized animals, and we also learned useful identifying strategies from the lecture given by Bill Gonzales, the team leader.

5. After you fill out the application for next month's dig, the form should be given to Bill or sent to his office.

B. Working in a group, use the sentences in Exercise 3A as the basis for a brief narrative telling the story of the "dig." Add sentences to fill in the information needed to make the story believable and interesting. Make your narrative consistent in voice.

25d Avoiding shifts between direct and indirect quotation

In **direct quotation** you present a speaker's or writer's exact words, set off by quotation marks. Through **indirect quotation** you present the substance of what was said, but in your own words and without quotation marks.

Try to avoid mixing direct and indirect quotation within sentences. As you edit, rewrite any mixed sentences to make them less confusing and easier to read.

MIXED   Writing about the Teenage Mutant Ninja Turtles, Phil Patton names cartoonists Peter Laird and Kevin Eastman as their creators and says, "They were born quietly in 1983, in the kitchen of a New England farmhouse."

EDITED   Writing about the Teenage Mutant Ninja Turtles, Phil Patton says, "Cartoonists named Peter Laird and Kevin Eastman dreamed up the characters," who "were born quietly in 1983, in the kitchen of a New England farmhouse."

Be especially alert for sentences mixing indirect and direct quotations without quotation marks to indicate the difference.

**25d
shift**

CONFUSING
Before we set out on the hike, the guide told us to stay in line and you should obey all orders immediately.

EDITED TO INDIRECT QUOTATION
Before we set out on the hike, the guide told us to stay in line and to follow every order right away.

EDITED TO DIRECT QUOTATION
Before we set out on the hike, the guide told us, "You should stay in line and obey all orders immediately."

Exercise 4

25.2

A. Rewrite each of the following sentences twice. First use direct quotation consistently, and then use indirect quotation consistently. (Feel free to invent direct quotations in order to complete the exercise. Be sure to change direct quotations into your own words when you present them as indirect quotations.)

EXAMPLE

The article began by saying, "People often fear bees" and that this fear is a result of ignorance.

The article began by saying, "People often fear bees, and this fear comes from ignorance."

The article began by saying that the widespread fear of bees is caused by ignorance.

1. I once heard a beekeeper claim that unless beekeeping becomes more popular as a hobby, "I believe that agriculture in this country may suffer."
2. At a meeting last night, the county agriculture commissioner argued that increased beekeeping would aid agriculture in our area and "We should be willing to provide beekeepers with financial support for their efforts."
3. Having eaten honey every day for sixty years, my grandfather says, "I may not look as good as I did when I was younger," but that he feels just as good.
4. My grandfather also says that he has stayed mentally alert because "I manage a large beekeeping and honey business."
5. My neighbor told me, if you are too busy to sell your honey at a roadside stand I should see if the supermarket in town would sell it for me.

B. Share your edited sentences from Exercise 4A with a group of your fellow students. Decide which versions of each sentence are best and why.

25d
shift

CHAPTER 26

MIXED AND INCOMPLETE SENTENCES

When someone you are talking with switches topics abruptly, you can ask for an explanation. When you are reading, however, you can't ask the author to explain a confusing shift of topic that comes in the middle of a sentence, as in the following example.

SHIFTED TOPIC   One **skill** I envy is **a person** who can study despite noise and other distractions.

Clearly, a *skill* is not a *person*.

EDITED   One **skill** I envy is **the ability** to study despite noise and other distractions.

Just as confusing are sentences that begin with one grammatical pattern then shift to another.

SHIFTED STRUCTURE   Because the new television show did poorly in the ratings **explains why** programming executives decided to move it to a slot between two hit shows.

EDITED   Because the new television show did poorly in the ratings, **programming executives** decided to move it to a slot between two hit shows.

Sentences with confusing shifts (called **mixed sentences**) confuse readers by undermining patterns they rely on as they read. An **incomplete sentence** that omits wording necessary to make a logical and consistent statement does the same. For example, if you start by writing "*X* is larger," you should be ready to complete the comparison: "*X* is larger *than Y.*"

INCOMPLETE   When they are first introduced, electronic products are likely to cost three times as much.

READER'S REACTION: Are the new products likely to cost more when they are first introduced than they will cost later? Or are they likely to cost more than products being sold now?

26 mixed

348

EDITED   When they are first introduced, electronic products are likely to cost three times as much **as the most expensive products currently available**.

(Fragments are incomplete sentences lacking grammatical completeness. See Chapter 21.)

26a Recognizing and editing mixed sentences

Mixed sentences shift topics or grammatical structures without warning and for no clear reason. They throw readers off the track and make illogical statements. To recognize mixed sentences, you need to keep certain basic sentence patterns in mind, and watch for some troublesome phrases.

1 Recognizing topic shifts

Keep this basic sentence pattern in mind:

The subject *announces a topic.*
The predicate comments on or renames *the same topic.*

　　　　subject　　　　　　　　　　　predicate
The Old PC Network publishes a newsletter about outdated computers.
　　　　topic　　　　　　　　　　　　comment

　　　　subject　　　　predicate
The Apple IIe is an out-of-date but still usable computer.
　　　　topic　　　　topic renamed

You create confusion if you mistakenly make each part of a sentence address a *different* subject. (The resulting problem is sometimes called a **topic shift** or **faulty predication**.)

SHIFTED TOPIC   The **presence** of ozone in smog is the **chemical** that causes eye irritation.
Presence is not a chemical, though that is what the sentence says.

EDITED   The **ozone** in smog is the **chemical** that causes eye irritation.

26a
mixed

STRATEGY

To identify shifted topics, try asking the question "Who does what?" or "What is it?" If the answer is illogical, the sentence needs editing.

SHIFTED	In this factory, **flaws** in the product noticed by any work-er **can stop** the assembly line with the flip of a switch. QUESTION: **Who does what? Certainly flaws can't stop the line or flip a switch.**
EDITED	In this factory, **any worker** who notices flaws in the prod-uct **can stop** the assembly line with the flip of a switch.
SHIFTED	An **actuary** is the **process** of determining insurance risks and premiums. QUESTION: **What is it? An actuary is a person, not a process.**
EDITED	An **actuary** is a **person** who determines insurance risks and premiums.

2 Editing topic shifts

In general, you can eliminate problems with topic shifts by making sure the topic in both parts of a sentence, subject and predicate, is the same. You can also use the following techniques to edit some common patterns of topic shifting: rename the subject, cut *is when* or *is where*, omit *the reason is . . . because*, and edit for intervening words.

Rename the subject. When you build a sentence around the verb *be* (*is, are, was, were*) you may choose to have the predicate rename the subject in order to create a definition. When you do, make sure the topics on each side of the verb are roughly equivalent.

SHIFTED TOPIC	**Irradiation** is **food** that is preserved by the use of radiation. READER'S RESPONSE: **Irradiation is a process of preservation, not the food itself.**
EDITED	**Irradiation** is a **process** that can be used to preserve food.

Cut *is when* or *is where*. The phrases *is when* and *is where* make it impossi-ble to balance the topics in a definition built around the verb *is*. Cut them and rewrite to create balance and eliminate a shift in topic.

NOT BALANCED	**Blocking** is **when** a television network schedules a less pop-ular program between two popular ones.
EDITED	**Blocking** is the **practice** of scheduling a less popular televi-sion program between two popular ones.

Omit *the reason . . . is because*. In conversation, the phrase *the reason . . . is because* causes little confusion. In writing, however, readers will recognize that it creates an illogical statement. Why? A phrase opening with *because* is a modifier that cannot logically rename the topic (subject) of the first part of a sentence.

NOT LOGICAL	One **reason** for research into alternative fuels **is because** of the need to reduce air pollution.
EDITED	One **reason** for research into alternative fuels is **the need** to reduce air pollution.

STRATEGY

Rewriting a sentence to eliminate *the reason . . . is because* is an obvious editing strategy, yet this approach may occasionally prove to be surprisingly difficult. When it does, try either of the following techniques.

- Drop *the reason . . . is.*

INCORRECT	**The reason** he took up figure skating **is because** he wanted something to do during the long winter.
EDITED	He took up figure skating **because** he wanted something to do during the long winter.

- Change *because* to *that.*

EDITED	**The reason** he took up figure skating **is that** he wanted something to do during the long winter.

Edit for intervening words. Watch for words and phrases coming between a subject and a verb. You may sometimes mistakenly treat these intervening words as the sentence's topic.

SHIFTED TOPIC	Programming **decisions** by television executives generally keep in mind the need to gain audience share.
	READER'S REACTION: I know that network executives can keep an audience in mind, but according to this sentence it is programming decisions that are thinking about the viewers.
EDITED	**Television executives** making programming decisions generally **keep** in mind the need to gain audience share.

26a
mixed

Exercise 1

A. Rewrite the following sentences to eliminate topic shifts.

EXAMPLE

Hides ~~that are~~ treated with tanning chemicals turn ~~them~~ into leather.

1. Tanning is when animal hide is made supple and resistant to decay.
2. The first step is when the hides are thoroughly scraped and cleaned.
3. The use of diluted acid is the substance that pickles the hides to prepare them for tanning.
4. The reason leather is supple is because it is lubricated with oil after pickling, then dried and impregnated with resins.
5. The final steps are when the leather is dyed and given a shiny surface through compression.

B. Compare your edited sentences for Exercise 1A with those produced by other writers. Decide which versions you prefer and why you prefer them.

3 Recognizing shifts in grammatical pattern

Occasionally, you may begin a sentence with one grammatical pattern in mind only to shift to another partway through. The resulting sentence confuses readers.

SHIFTED PATTERNS

Because of the rebellious atmosphere generated by protests against the Vietnam war helps explain the often outrageous fashions of the time.

READER'S REACTION: When I encounter a word like *because,* I expect it to be attached to some main statement and to add to (modify) the core statement in a sentence. But that doesn't happen here. The sentence simply says the same thing twice: *because* and *helps explain.*

EDITED (MAIN CLAUSE ADDED)

Because of the rebellious atmosphere generated by protests against the Vietnam war, **fashions of the time became outrageous**.

EDITED (REWRITTEN)

The rebellious **atmosphere** generated by protests against the Vietnam war **helps explain** the often outrageous fashions of the time.

26a
mixed

The following techniques can help you recognize shifted grammatical constructions (which can take so many different forms that they are often difficult to identify).

> ## STRATEGY
>
> These three strategies may help you spot shifts in grammatical patterns.
>
> - Pay attention to the *meaning* of sentences, checking that all the elements, especially subjects and predicates, stand in clear and reasonable relationships to each other. Read aloud sentences that seem potentially confusing.

- Ask "What is the topic of this sentence, and how does the rest of the sentence comment on or rename the topic?"
- Check that the sentence clearly indicates *who does what to whom.*

SHIFTED By wearing bell-bottom pants, love beads, long hair, and tie-dyed T-shirts was how many young people expressed their opposition to mainstream values.

READER'S REACTION: **I can puzzle out the meaning, but this sentence really doesn't make clear who did what to whom.**

EDITED By wearing bell-bottom pants, love beads, long hair, and tie-dyed T-shirts, many young people expressed their opposition to mainstream values.

4 Editing shifts in grammatical pattern

Sentences can mix grammatical patterns in many different ways, so you may have to study a sentence with an inappropriate shift very carefully in order to decide how to edit it. The following four kinds of grammatical shifts are quite common, however.

- Sentences that begin twice
- Whole sentences used as subjects
- Adverb phrases used as subjects
- Subordinating clauses used as subjects

The techniques described below can help you edit these problems.

Sentences that begin twice. When you try to give more emphasis to a topic than the structure of a sentence allows, you may mistakenly start the sentence over again, treating the sentence's object as a second subject.

STRATEGY

26a
mixed

To edit sentences that begin twice, rewrite the sentence, moving most or all of the information in one of the two main clauses to a modifying phrase or clause.

MIXED PATTERNS **The new procedures for testing cosmetics, we** designed them to avoid cruelty to laboratory animals.

READER'S REACTION: **It seems that the writer starts this sentence again with the word *we*.**

EDITED **We** designed **the new procedures for testing cosmetics** to avoid cruelty to laboratory animals.

EDITED **The new procedures for testing cosmetics** were designed to avoid cruelty to laboratory animals.

Whole sentences used as subjects. Another way you may mistakenly give emphasis to a topic is to put it in a complete sentence (main clause), which you then use incorrectly as the subject of another sentence.

STRATEGY

Rewrite so that most (or all) of the information in one of the two main clauses appears instead in a modifying phrase or clause.

MIXED PATTERNS
In 1872, Claude Monet exhibited the painting *Impression, Sunrise* was the source of the term *Impressionism*.

EDITED (PHRASE CREATED)
The source of the term *Impressionism* was the painting *Impression, Sunrise*, **exhibited by Claude Monet in 1872**.

EDITED (CLAUSE CREATED)
In 1872, Claude Monet exhibited the painting *Impression, Sunrise*, **which was the source of the term *Impressionism***.

Adverb phrase used as subject. When readers encounter a phrase like "By designing the questionnaire carefully" at the beginning of a sentence, they expect it to be followed by the sentence's subject. They do not expect it to act as the subject.

STRATEGY

Either add a new subject, or alter the form of the phrase so that it can act as a subject.

		adverb phrase
MIXED PATTERNS		**By designing the questionnaire carefully** made Valerie's psychology study a success.
EDITED		By designing the questionnaire carefully, **Valerie made** her psychology study a success.
EDITED		The **careful design** of the questionnaire **made** Valerie's psychology study a success.

26a
mixed

Adverb clause used as subject. When readers encounter a word like *when, because, if, while, as,* or *despite* (subordinating conjunction) at the head of a clause beginning a sentence (adverb clause), they expect it to be followed by a main clause, not to act itself as the sentence's subject.

STRATEGY

Either add a subject, or rewrite the sentence by dropping the subordinating word and turning the introductory clause into a subject.

MIXED

subordinate clause
Even if an audition gets off to a bad start does not mean giving up hope of getting the part.

EDITED (SUBJECT ADDED)

Even if an audition gets off to a bad start, **you** should not give up hope of getting the part.

EDITED (SUBORDINATING WORD DROPPED)

An audition that gets off to a bad start does not mean you should give up hope of getting the part.

Exercise 2

A. Rewrite the following sentences to eliminate shifts in grammatical pattern.

26.1

EXAMPLE   ~~S~~

~~Many people used to die from infectious diseases was why~~ scientists
                                                                           ^
worked hard to develop vaccinations, *because many people used to die*
                                      from infectious diseases.

1. By observing that farm workers who had cowpox were resistant to smallpox led Jenner to develop an inoculation for smallpox in the 1790s.
2. Paying attention to Jenner's methods was why Pasteur was able to develop vaccines for chicken pox, rabies, and human anthrax.
3. Vaccinations produce antibodies are the sources of immunity.
4. Because they are not effective against all infections means that vaccinations are not a perfect solution for diseases.
5. Making sure your vaccinations are up to date, you need to do this during your regular medical checkup.

B. In a group, compare your edited sentences for Exercise 2A with those produced by other writers. Identify those edited versions you consider correct, consistent, and clear.

26b | **inc**

26b Recognizing and editing incomplete sentences

Sentences that fail to complete an expected logical pattern, such as a comparison, or leave out words necessary to meaning or logic are called **in-**

complete sentences. They make readers do extra, unnecessary work. (Sentences missing a *grammatical* element are fragments; see Chapter 21.)

1 Recognizing and avoiding incomplete or illogical comparisons

When readers encounter a comparison, they expect to learn something about the relationship of the things being compared, for example, that *X* is *greater/lesser* than *Y*. If you leave out one of the elements (*X* is *larger*) or if the things you try to compare are not logically comparable, you will fail to meet your readers' expectations and perhaps even confuse them.

Recognize missing elements and supply them. Check that you have included both of the items being compared. Omitting one creates an **incomplete comparison**. To edit, supply the missing element.

INCOMPLETE   The picture quality of the DVDs is much better.

READER'S REACTION: **The picture quality is better than what? Than the quality on DVDs used to be? Than the quality was on analog (VHS) tapes?**

EDITED   The picture quality of the DVDs is much better than **it was on VHS tapes.**

Look also for places where you have omitted a word or words necessary to complete a comparison or make it clear, and then supply them.

AMBIGUOUS   The most experienced members of the maintenance staff respect the new supervisor more highly than their fellow workers.

READER'S REACTION: **Do the experienced staff members respect the supervisor more than they respect their fellow workers, or do they respect the supervisor more than their fellow workers do?**

CLEAR   The most experienced members of the maintenance staff respect the new supervisor more highly **than do** their fellow workers.

CLEAR   The most experienced members of the maintenance staff respect the new supervisor more highly **than they respect** their fellow workers.

Occasionally, however, you can omit part of the wording of a comparison when the meaning is clear without it, and when the meaning can be easily inferred by readers.

CLEAR   Most customers like dealing with a bank teller better than [dealing with] a machine.

The second *dealing with* can be left out because the sentence has only one possible meaning.

Watch for illogical comparisons (especially within and between groups).

As you review comparisons, ask, "Can these things be reasonably compared?" If a comparison seems to be illogical, try one of the following editing techniques.

STRATEGY

To make seemingly illogical comparisons reasonable, consider using either of these strategies:

- Fill in the missing words.
- Use the possessive.

ILLOGICAL
Even a small hamburger's fat content is higher than a skinless chicken breast.

READER'S REACTION: The writer probably wants to compare the fat content of two foods, but the sentence actually compares one *kind* of food (chicken breast) to the *fat content* of the other.

EDITED (WORDS PROVIDED)
The fat content of even a small hamburger is higher than **that of** a skinless chicken breast.

EDITED (POSSESSIVE USED)
Even a small **hamburger's** fat content is higher than a skinless chicken **breast's**.

Groups pose special problems for comparisons. When you are comparing items belonging to the *same group*, you need to distinguish each item (for example, field hockey) from other members of the class to which it belongs (all *other* team sports). Otherwise, your comparison will be illogical.

The word *other* serves to keep the two things separate by marking off the group as a whole from one of its members.

Field hockey has a higher percentage of women players than does any **other** team sport.

Therefore, if you leave out the word *other* when comparing members of a group or class, your comparison will be illogical.

26b
inc

ILLOGICAL   At times, more cargo was loaded onto ships docked at New Orleans than at **any** city in North America.

READER'S REACTION: **Do you mean that New Orleans is not a city in North America?**

EDITED   At times, more cargo was loaded onto ships docked at New Orleans than at any **other** city in North America.

For *different groups*, however, a comparison using the word *other* is inappropriate and illogical.

ILLOGICAL   Though he wrote in the 1800s, Dickens painted as vivid a picture of oppressive government and society as **any other** author writing today.

READER'S REACTION: **Do you mean that Dickens is still writing even though he is dead?**

EDITED   Though he wrote in the 1800s, Dickens painted as vivid a picture of the ways government and society can oppress people as **any** author writing today.

2 Recognizing appropriate and inappropriate omissions

Leaving out repeated words or phrases can often make sentences easier to read, yet careless omissions have the opposite effect.

Repeated words and phrases. Look for sentences containing repeated words and phrases (common in compound constructions). As long as omitting these repetitions does not undermine meaning or confuse readers, you should consider cutting them to create **elliptical constructions** that make writing concise and effective.

LEFT IN   Some presidents spend much time mastering the facts before making a major decision; others spend little **time mastering the facts before making a major decision**.

OMITTED BUT CLEAR   Some presidents spend much time mastering the facts before making a major decision; **others spend little**.

You can also frequently eliminate the word *that* from sentences where it introduces a noun clause after a verb: "Artists know [that] there is a difference between oil and acrylic paints."

Careless omissions. Beware of careless omissions (of articles, prepositions, pronouns, or parts of verbs) whenever you are writing hurriedly or are focusing on the information and ideas rather than on the details of your writing. Careful editing (including reading passages aloud) is normally the best way to identify such omissions.

26b
inc

INCOMPLETE   A corporation issues common stock a way raising money.

EDITED   A corporation issues common stock **as** a way **of** raising money.

Exercise 3

A. Rewrite the following sentences to eliminate any incomplete or illogical constructions.

EXAMPLE   *other*
Both Shannon and Bill like tennis more than any ˄ game.

1. His tennis serve has more speed and accuracy than Bill.
2. He also has better sense of where an opponent is going hit ball.
3. Bill's commitment to tennis is greater than his family.
4. He has more fun playing tennis.
5. Like many exercise-addicted people, Bill would be exercising than eating, and he would rather be playing tennis than doing anything else.

26.2

B. In a small group, compare the effectiveness of your edited sentences in Exercise 3A with those of your fellow writers. Make sure the members of your group agree on what is incomplete or illogical in the original version of each sentence.

26b
inc

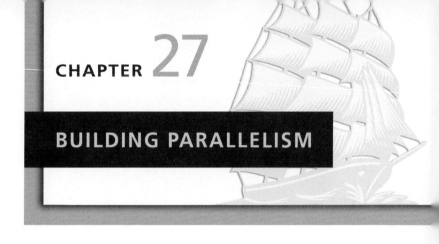

CHAPTER 27

BUILDING PARALLELISM

Parallelism is the expression of similar or related ideas in similar grammatical form, as in the following sentence.

I furnished my first apartment

with **purchases** | **from department stores,**
items | **from the want ads,**
and **gifts** | **from my relatives**.

Parallelism enables you to present ideas concisely while highlighting their relationships.

Parallelism can also offer pleasure and surprise. You can use it to create intriguing sentence rhythms while highlighting unexpected images and contrasts.

According to **how** and **when** you said it, zydeco meant either **the kind of music itself**, or **the kind of two-step touch-dancing that you did at parties to the music**. In theory, this meant that you could **zydeco** to **zydeco** at the **zydeco**.

—Susan Orlean, *Saturday Night*

27a Building parallelism

Readers generally find a sentence with parallel elements easy to read and understand. They also appreciate the touch of style parallelism can bring even to everyday sentences.

In deciding which elements to make parallel and where to place them, you should consider each sentence's message as well as the emphasis you wish to create within an entire passage. In the following selection, for example, the poet Nikki Giovanni uses parallel structures to point out similarities between people who often see themselves as different.

The true joy, perhaps, of being a Black American is that we really have no home. **Europeans bought** us; but the **Africans sold**. If we are to be human we must forgive **both** . . . **or neither**. It has become acceptable, in the last decade or so, for intellectuals to concede Black Americans **did not come here** out of our own volition; yet, I submit that just as **slavery took away our choice, so also did** the overcrowded, disease-ridden cities of Europe; **so also did** religious persecution; **so also did** the abject and all but unspeakable Inquisition of the Spanish; **so also did** starvation in Italy; **so also did** the black, rotten potatoes lying in the fields of Ireland. **No one came** to the New World in a cruise ship. **They all came** because they had to.

—Nikki Giovanni, "Pioneers: A View of Home"

27b Recognizing and editing problems with parallelism

Once you begin a parallel pattern in your writing, you need to complete it. Incomplete or **faulty parallelism** disappoints readers' expectations and may make sentences confusing and hard to read. Moreover, with the following common writing strategies, your readers will expect you to employ parallelism.

- Series
- Paired elements, including those created by words such as *and, or, either . . . or,* and *neither . . . nor,* as well as comparisons and contrasts
- Lists

To create parallelism as you write or edit, whether with words, phrases, or clauses, you need to make sure all the elements employ the same grammatical forms. To recognize lack of parallelism, look for shifts in grammatical forms.

27b
//

FAULTY
PARALLELISM

Consider swimming if you are looking for exercise that **aids** cardiovascular fitness, **overall** muscle strength, and probably **will not cause** injuries.

PARALLEL

Consider swimming if you are looking for exercise that **aids** cardiovascular fitness, **develops** overall muscle strength, and **causes** few injuries.

1 Check for parallelism in a series

When you place items in a series, check that they are parallel in grammatical form. A series without this consistency can seem clumsy and distracting.

To check for parallelism in a series, first identify a series: . . . *x, y, and z* (the series may have more than three elements). Then mentally isolate each element and check that each takes the same grammatical form.

NOT PARALLEL   patient, tactful, and **to display tolerance**

PARALLEL   patient, tactful, and **tolerant**

Remember, the elements in a series can be words, phrases, clauses—even a series of separate sentences.

To edit, put the elements in similar grammatical form. You don't have to create word-for-word parallels. Sentence elements that differ somewhat in length and wording can still be parallel as long as they have the same structure.

WORDS (NOT PARALLEL)   To get along with their parents, teenagers need to be patient, tactful, and **to display tolerance**.

WORDS (PARALLEL)   To get along with their parents, teenagers need to be patient, tactful, and **tolerant**.

PHRASES (NOT PARALLEL)   The singer Jim Morrison is remembered for his innovative style, his flamboyant performances, and for behavior that was self-destructive.

PHRASES (PARALLEL)   The singer Jim Morrison is remembered for his innovative style, his flamboyant performances, and **his self-destructive behavior**.

CLAUSES (NOT PARALLEL)   In assembling the research team, we looked for engineers whose work was innovative, with broad interests, and who had boundless energy.

CLAUSES (PARALLEL)   In assembling the research team, we looked for engineers whose work was innovative, **whose interests were broad**, **and whose energy was boundless**.

27b //

The final position in a series often receives the greatest emphasis from writers and the most attention from readers. You can use this knowledge to create sentences with a strong cumulative effect, directing attention to the final element.

When VG Industries moved, the town was left with abandoned buildings, unused rail lines, and **thousands of unemployed workers**.

2 Decide which words to repeat

In creating parallelism, make sure you repeat all words necessary to the meaning of a sentence, including all the words called for by grammatical structures or idiomatic expressions. You need not repeat a lead-in word, however, if it is the same for all elements in a series.

Mosquitoes can breed in puddles, ~~in~~ ponds, and ~~in~~ swimming pools.

If the lead-in words differ, you must include them.

You need to **chop** the cilantro, **grind** the coconut, and **grate** the nutmeg.

STRATEGY

As you edit, pause when you encounter a series. Read it carefully with the structure of the full sentence in mind so you can decide what words are necessary to the meaning.

INCOMPLETE The main character from the novel *Tarzan of the Apes* has appeared on television, films, and comic books.

> **READER'S REACTION: Do you really mean to say he appeared *on* films and *on* comic books?**

EDITED The main character from the novel *Tarzan of the Apes* has appeared *on* television, *in* films, and *in* comic books.

Exercise 1

A. Underline the parallel structures in each of the following sentences.

27.1

1. We've told you about the bombs, the fires, the smashed houses, and the courage of the people.
   —EDWARD R. MURROW, "From London, September 22, 1940"

2. She looked at a man because she liked the way the hair was tucked behind his ears, or she liked the question-mark line of a long torso curving at the shoulder and straight at the hip.
   —MAXINE HONG KINGSTON, "No Name Woman"

3. But far below, in the warren of passages on the starboard side forward, in the forward holds and boiler rooms, men could see that the *Titanic's* hurt was mortal.
   —HANSON W. BALDWIN, "R.M.S. *Titanic*"

4. In that context three groups of wounded soldiers are identified: those whose survival depends on their receiving immediate treatment; those who need medical attention but will survive even if they do not get it immediately; and those who are hurt so badly they would not survive even with medical attention.
   —RUTH MACKLIN, *Mortal Choices*

27b
//

5. For in each American marriage there is a special code, developed from the individual pasts of the two partners, put together out of the accidents of honeymoon and parents-in-law, finally beaten into a language that each understands imperfectly.

—MARGARET MEAD, *Male and Female*

B. Working in a group, rewrite the following sentences to correct faulty parallelism and create appropriate emphasis. Include all necessary words. If a sentence can be rewritten in several ways, choose the version the group considers most effective.

1. What kind of job would be appropriate for a person who enjoys sailboarding, skiing, and to skydive?
2. The college's career counselor suggested that Rosalie write out her personal goals, read some materials on choosing a profession, or that she might take a career test.
3. Optimism, stamina, and being a good thinker are three traits of a good sales representative.
4. If you wish to choose a career at which you can succeed, you might start by making a list of the things you like to do, anything you are very good at, and also jobs or experiences you always try to avoid.
5. You can locate possible jobs in newspaper ads, friends, and employment agencies.

3 Pay attention to parallelism with paired sentence elements

When you are creating paired sentence elements to emphasize similarities and heighten contrasts, you will call attention to the relationship if you use parallelism—and readers will expect you to present the paired elements in parallel form.

And, but, or, for, nor, so, **and** *yet.* Take notice of sentence elements you have joined with *and, but, or, for, nor, so,* and *yet* (**coordinating conjunctions**). In general, present the words, phrases, or clauses in parallel form, to direct your readers' attention to the relationship of the elements and make the sentence easier to read.

27b
//

WORDS NOT PARALLEL

A well-trained scientist learns to keep a detailed lab notebook and make the entries accurately.

PARALLEL

A well-trained scientist learns to keep a **detailed and accurate** lab notebook.

PHRASES NOT PARALLEL

First-year chemistry courses are supposed to teach students <u>how to take notes on an experiment</u> and <u>the ways of writing a lab report</u>.

PARALLEL

First-year chemistry courses are supposed to teach students **how to take notes on an experiment** and **how to write a lab report**.

CLAUSES NOT PARALLEL

Because she is interested in science and organizing complex information intrigues her, Lynn has decided to become a technical writer.

PARALLEL

Because she is interested in science and intrigued by organizing complex information, Lynn has decided to become a technical writer.

Both . . . and, not only . . . but also, either . . . or, neither . . . nor, and *whether . . . or.* When you wish to call special attention to a relationship or a contrast, you may choose to employ pairs of connectors such as *both . . . and, not only . . . but also, either . . . or, neither . . . nor,* or *whether . . . or* (**correlative conjunctions**). If you use these connectors, check to make sure you also use parallel forms for the elements you are joining.

Our dilemma is clear: **either** we must reduce manufacturing costs **or** we must file for bankruptcy.

The items you link with correlative conjunctions should be clearly related in meaning and similar in grammatical form. If the elements following the first and second connectors do not match, the sentence may be hard to follow or unclear in meaning.

AMBIGUOUS

Leon Blum's election represented a significant change in French politics and society because he was not only the first Socialist premier but also the first Jew.

PRECISE (PARALLELISM ADDED)

Leon Blum's election represented a significant change in French politics and society because he was not only the **first Socialist premier but also the first Jewish premier**.

27b
//

Comparison and contrast. Be alert for places in your writing where you are comparing or contrasting items, and use parallel forms to help call attention to them.

DRAFT	This new ingredient will reduce the calories in our frozen yogurt, and the yogurt will have more taste.
EDITED	This new ingredient in our frozen yogurt **will reduce the calories** and **improve the taste**.

When you use *who(m)*, *which*, or *that* (relative pronouns) to begin two parallel clauses, check that you use the same word to begin both. If you do not, the clauses will lack parallelism because they will not have the same grammatical form.

LACKS PARALLELISM	The sailor embarking on hazardous voyages and who wore one earring of his lover's matched pair believed he would always be reunited with her.
PARALLEL	The sailor **who** embarked on hazardous voyages and **who** wore one earring of his lover's matched pair believed he would always be reunited with her.

Exercise 2

A. Rewrite the following sentences to eliminate faulty parallelism.

EXAMPLE

In choosing a career, you should plan carefully and ~~also~~ some research ~~is needed~~.
(do / ^)

1. Anthony could not decide whether he wanted to be a lawyer or if investment banking was a more promising career.
2. His friends thought Anthony's career plans were not suited to his abilities and his interests didn't fit the plans either.
3. After thinking about his goals, Anthony realized that the two things he wanted most from a career were stability and an income that was reasonable.
4. The counselor suggested that he might consider either working for the federal government or a job with a large, stable corporation.
5. Anthony had been reading about corporations in financial trouble and which had been laying off employees, so he decided to look carefully at government jobs.

27b
//

B. Working with a group of fellow students, gather a number of pamphlets offering advice. Campus offices, libraries, clinics, banks, and similar places usually provide pamphlets on all kinds of subjects, from health care and home safety to job hunting. Choose one of the pamphlets, identify those places where parallelism is used effectively with paired sentence elements, and edit to correct any faulty parallelism.

Enhance the parallelism when appropriate in order to highlight ideas and their relationships.

27c Creating parallelism beyond the sentence

As you write and revise, you can create parallelism beyond the sentence level to organize clusters of sentences and even paragraphs. Parallelism of this sort can clarify complicated information or highlight the overall pattern of an argument or explanation.

27.2

1 Creating parallel sentence clusters

By adding parallelism to groups of sentences, you call attention to **sentence clusters**, groups of sentences that develop related ideas or information. The parallel elements can link related items or guide readers though an explanation or argument.

One way to draw readers' attention to a sentence cluster is through parallel sentence openers, as in the following passage, which also uses parallel elements to reinforce the writer's opening point about conflicting values.

> Each of us probably belongs to several organizations whose values are in conflict. **You may belong to** a religious organization that **endorses restraint** in alcohol use or **in** relationships between the sexes while at the same time **you belong to** a social group whose activities seem to endorse a contrasting set of values. **You may belong to** a sports team **that endorses** conflict and winning and a club **that promotes** understanding among people and conflict resolution. **You may belong to** a political club whose platform contradicts the policies of your professional organization.

2 Creating parallel paragraphs

By creating paragraphs that are parallel in structure and wording, you can reinforce the overall pattern of a report or essay and alert readers to your line of argument or explanation. The parallel element can be as simple and unobtrusive as parallel opening phrases for a series of paragraphs.

> **One reason for acting** on this recommendation is that the flooding gets worse every spring. [. . .]
>
> **A second reason for action** is that the city currently has a budget surplus that could be spent on drainage improvement. [. . .]
>
> **A third, and most important, reason for taking immediate steps** is that the health and safety of city residents is endangered by the floods.

27c
//

DID YOU KNOW?

Many well-known writers make frequent and skillful use of parallelism. Here is an example from Annie Dillard.

Back in New Orleans where he was headed they would play the old stuff, the hot, rough stuff—bastardized for tourists maybe, but still the big and muddy source of it all. Back in New Orleans where he was headed the music would smell like the river itself, maybe, like a thicker, older version of the Allegheny River at Pittsburgh, where he heard the music beat in the roar of his boat's inboard motor; like a thicker, older version of the wide Ohio River at Louisville, Kentucky, where at his family's summer house he'd spend his boyhood summer mucking about in boats.

Annie Dillard, *An American Childhood* (New York: HarperCollins, 1987) 6.

Exercise 3

A. Underline all examples of parallelism in the following passage.

Large computers have some essential attributes of an intelligent brain: they have large memories, and they have gates whose connections can be modified by experience. However, the thinking of these computers tends to be narrow. The richness of human thought depends to a considerable degree on the enormous number of wires, or nerve fibers, coming into each gate in the human brain. A gate in a computer has two, or three, or at most four wires entering on one side, and one wire coming out the other side. In the human brain, a gate may have as many as 100,000 wires entering it. Each wire comes from another gate or nerve cell. This means that every gate in the human brain is connected to as many as 100,000 other gates in other parts of the brain. During the process of thinking innumerable gates open and close throughout the brain. When one of these gates "decides" to open, the decision is the result of a complicated assessment involving inputs from thousands of other gates. This circumstance explains much of the difference between human thinking and computer thinking.

—Robert Jastrow, "Brains and Computers"

B. Working in a group, decide what each example of parallelism in Exercise 3A contributes to the effectiveness of the individual sentence or the entire passage. Note any differences of opinion, and discuss whether these differences reveal alternative ways of viewing the meaning or purpose of the passage.

27c
//

27d Creating parallelism in lists

Lists can summarize key points, instructions, or stages in a process. To avoid confusing readers, make sure the elements in lists are as nearly parallel as possible.

UNEDITED (CONFUSING)

The early 1960s were characterized by the following social phenomena.

1. A growing civil rights movement
2. Kennedy pursued a strongly anticommunist foreign policy.
3. An emphasis on youth in culture and politics
4. Taste in music and the visual arts was changing.
5. Government support for scientific research increased greatly.

EDITED (CLEAR)

The early 1960s were characterized by the following social phenomena.

1. **A growing** civil rights movement
2. **A strongly** anticommunist foreign policy (encouraged by President Kennedy)
3. **A youthful** emphasis in culture and politics
4. **A changing** taste in music and the visual arts
5. **A marked** increase in government support for scientific research

If you present every item in a list in a different grammatical form, readers must shift expectations often and will find it difficult to concentrate on the differences and similarities between the items. Parallelism makes it easy for readers to pay attention to the ideas and information in the list, and it encourages readers to compare the items covered in the list.

Exercise 4

27d
//

A. Arrange the following materials into a list whose elements maintain parallel form.

The awards for arts and entertainment for 1985 offer an interesting picture of American culture in the middle of the decade.

Academy Award: *Out of Africa* (Best Picture); William Hurt, *Kiss of the Spider Woman* (Best Actor); Geraldine Page, *The Trip to Bountiful* (Best Actress); Don Ameche, *Cocoon* (Best Supporting Actor); Anjelica Huston, *Prizzi's Honor* (Best Supporting Actress).

The Emmy Awards went to *The Golden Girls* (Outstanding Comedy Series), *Cagney & Lacey* (Outstanding Drama Series), William Daniels and Sharon Gless (Outstanding Lead Actor/Actress in a Drama Series), and Michael J. Fox and Betty White (Outstanding Lead Actor/Actress in a Comedy Series).

Tony Awards for Broadway Theater. Best Play: *As Is* by William Hoffman. Best Musical: *Big River* by Roger Miller.

MTV Video Music Awards. Best Video: Don Henley, "The Boys of Summer." Best Male Video: Bruce Springsteen, "I'm on Fire." Best Female Video: Tina Turner, "What's Love Got to Do with It." Best Group Video: USA for Africa, "We Are the World."

B. Compare your list for Exercise 4A with the lists of several other students. Note any differences in the ways your lists are organized.

CHAPTER 28

COORDINATION AND SUBORDINATION

Suppose you were asked to revise a report containing the following passage, which is filled with short, choppy sentences that fail to emphasize connections among the ideas.

> California's farmers ship fresh lettuce, avocados, and other produce to supermarkets. They never send fresh olives. Fresh olives contain a substance that makes them bitter. They are very unpleasant tasting. Farmers soak fresh olives in a solution that removes oleuropein, the bitter-tasting substance. They make sure just enough is left behind to produce the tangy "olive" taste.

You might decide to **coordinate** the sentences, linking them in ways that show how the sentences are related while giving equal emphasis to each statement. (Resources for **coordination**: words like *and* and *but*; words like *however*; and punctuation marks like the semicolon.)

COORDINATED

California's farmers ship fresh lettuce, avocados, and other produce to supermarkets, **but** they never send fresh olives. Fresh olives contain a substance that makes them bitter, **so** they are very unpleasant tasting. Farmers soak fresh olives in a solution that removes oleuropein, the bitter-tasting substance; **however**, they make sure just enough is left behind to produce the tangy "olive" taste.

Or you might try specifying the relationships and relative importance of ideas by using **subordination**: making some of the sentences modify others by employing subordinating words (such as *because*, *although*, and *since*) and attaching the subordinated sentences to the others.

SUBORDINATED

California's farmers ship fresh lettuce, avocados, and other produce to supermarkets, **though** they never send fresh olives. **Because** fresh olives contain a substance that makes them bitter, they are very unpleasant tasting. **When** farmers soak fresh olives in a solution that removes oleuropein, the bitter-tasting substance, they make sure just enough is left behind to produce the tangy "olive" taste.

28a Recognizing and creating coordination

When you want to link words or groups of words, the techniques of coordination—some quite common, such as *and* or *but*; others less familiar, such as *however* or a semicolon—enable you to give equal weight to the different elements.

WORDS	trims **and** shapes
CLUSTERS OF WORDS	in the shallow water, near the islands, **or** in the middle of the main channel
MAIN CLAUSES	The winter freeze prevents boats from sailing; **however**, the residents are still able to fish through holes in the ice.

To recognize coordination, look for the words and punctuation marks used to create it (listed below).

CREATING COORDINATION

JOINING WORDS AND CLUSTERS OF WORDS (PHRASES)

1. **Use *and, but, or, nor,* or *yet*** (coordinating conjunctions).

   cut **and** hemmed   smooth **or** textured   intrigued **yet** suspicious

2. **Use pairs like *either . . . or, neither . . . nor,* and *not only . . . but also.***

   either music therapy **or** pet therapy
   not only a nursing care plan **but also** a psychological treatment program

JOINING MAIN (INDEPENDENT) CLAUSES

1. **Use *and, but, or, for, nor, so,* or *yet* (coordinating conjunctions) preceded by a comma.**

   The students observed the responses of shoppers to long lines, **and** they interviewed people waiting in line. Most people in the study were irritated by the checkout lines, yet a considerable minority enjoyed the wait.

2. **Use a semicolon** (see 33a).

The wait provoked physical reactions in some people; they fidgeted, grimaced, and stared at the ceiling.

3. **Use words like** *however, moreover, nonetheless, thus,* **and** *consequently* **(conjunctive adverbs) preceded by a semicolon.**

Store managers can take simple steps to speed up checkout lines; **however**, they seldom pay much attention to the problem.

4. **Use colon** (see 33b).

Tabloids and magazines in racks by the checkout counters serve a useful purpose: they give customers something to read while waiting.

By creating effective coordination you can specify and highlight relationships among ideas.

RELATIONSHIPS NOT SPECIFIED	Cats have no fear of water. They do not like getting their fur wet and matted. Cats like to feel clean and well groomed.
CLEAR RELATIONSHIPS	Cats have not fear of water, **but** they do not like getting their fur wet and matted; they like to feel clean and well groomed.
CHOPPY	Cats are able to swim. A hungry cat will gladly jump into water to catch a fish. House cats are usually well fed. They are not willing to get soaked for an extra bite to eat.
SMOOTHER	Cats are able to swim, **and** a hungry cat will gladly jump into water to catch a fish. House cats are usually well fed; **therefore,** they are not willing to get soaked for an extra bite to eat.

Exercise 1

28a
coord

A. Combine each of the following pairs of sentences into a single sentence using coordination. Make sure you use each of the strategies listed in the preceding table for joining main clauses, and do not use any particular conjunction (such as *and* or *however*) more than once. Rewrite the sentences if necessary to avoid awkwardness or confusion.

EXAMPLE
                                                                , so
Winter weather makes outdoor exercise difficult. Winter has its own
                                                      ^
forms of exercise.

1. Ice skating can be enjoyable. It is also physically demanding.

2. Recreational skaters need to be in good shape physically. They should exercise to increase their fitness.
3. Skaters who are not in good shape get tired quickly. These skaters are also more likely to pull a muscle or fall.
4. To get in shape for skating, try a program of regular exercise for at least several weeks. Pay special attention to exercises focusing on knees and ankles.
5. Other areas to exercise are hip and leg muscles. Exercises aimed at each muscle group are best.

B. Working with a group of fellow writers, prepare a brief paragraph (five to seven sentences) offering advice on some subject: fitness, cooking, appliance repair, gardening, or the like. Make sure all but one or two of the sentences are compound sentences containing at least two main clauses. Connect the clauses using a variety of strategies for coordination, making sure they are appropriate for your subject and purpose.

28b Recognizing and editing problems with coordination

Problems with coordination generally take two forms: excessive use of a strategy, and illogical linking of ideas and sentence elements.

1 Look for excessive coordination

If you use words like *and*, *so*, or *but* merely to string together groups of loosely related sentences, you risk boring readers with excessive coordination.

28b
coord

STRATEGY

These approaches may help you spot excessive coordination in your writing.

- Look for sentences that make several statements (usually three or more) and also contain several connectives like *and* or *so*. When you have identified a sentence like this, read it carefully to see if it contains too much coordination and too many conjunctions so that the result is a "stringy," hard-to-follow sentence.

    STRINGY   The toy was designed in Japan, **but** its parts are made in Brazil, **and** it is assembled in Mexico, **so** what is the country of origin for tax purposes?

EDITED   The toy was designed in Japan, **but** its parts are made in Brazil, **and** it is assembled in Mexico. What is the country of origin for tax purposes?

- Pay attention to *when* and *how* you wrote a passage. Often during drafting when you jot down ideas quickly, the result is excessive coordination. Remember which passages you wrote quickly, look them over, and edit to complete the job of specifying relationships.

DRAFT   Ripe fruit spoils quickly, **and** the fresh grapefruit for sale in supermarkets is picked before it matures to avoid spoilage, **and** it can taste bitter, **but** the grapefruit in cans is picked later, **and** it tastes sweeter.

EDITED   Ripe fruit spoils quickly. The fresh grapefruit for sale in supermarkets is picked before it matures, **so** it can taste bitter. The grapefruit in cans is picked later; **consequently,** it tastes sweeter.

Try arranging three or more coordinated main clauses as a series in order to create emphasis. Place a coordinating conjunction only before the last clause.

The lawyers drew up the contract, the accountants checked it for accuracy, **and** we signed it in good faith.

2 Check for illogical coordination

Check that clauses you have linked (or plan to link) by coordination are related closely enough to deserve equal emphasis within a single sentence. To identify loosely related elements (illogical coordination), take on a reader's perspective and question the relationship, perhaps asking "How are these two elements linked?" To correct illogical coordination, try adding information to a sentence or changing its emphasis.

28b
coord

ILLOGICAL   Antarctica is a remote continent with an unusually harsh climate, and scientists are now studying its unique animal life in detail.
READER'S REACTION: **What do the remoteness and the climate have to do with either the scientists or the animals?**

EDITED   Antarctica's remoteness and harsh climate **have made exploration difficult,** and scientists are **only now beginning detailed study** of its unique animal life.

EDITED   Antarctica is a remote continent with an unusually harsh climate; **therefore,** much of its animal life is unique.

Make sure you link clauses in ways that indicate their relationships precisely and clearly.

VAGUE   Penguins swim in frigid water and stand on ice, **and** their feet never seem to freeze.

EDITED TO SHOW CONTRAST   Penguins swim in frigid water and stand on ice, **yet** their feet never seem to freeze.

Exercise 2

A. Revise the following passage to eliminate excessive or illogical coordination. Use coordination to combine short sentences when appropriate, to clarify relationships and eliminate choppiness.

28.1

> Working for someone else can be unrewarding, and this is also true of working for a large corporation, so many people in their early thirties decide to open businesses of their own, but they often do not have very original ideas, so they open restaurants or small retail stores, for these are the small businesses they are most familiar with, yet they are also the ones that are most likely to fail, and they face the most competition. Franchises are small businesses, and they often provide help to people getting into business on their own for the first time. Fast-food restaurants are often franchises, and they are quite expensive to start up, or they face a lot of competition. What many potential small-business owners fail to investigate are the many less familiar kinds of franchise operation. Enterprising people can own the local office of an armored car service, or they can run a regional unit of a nationwide cleaning service for commercial buildings, and they can open hardware stores with the name of a national chain over the front door. Electronics stores, fabric stores, and real estate offices can be locally owned yet parts of a national chain, so people who want to be their own bosses have many opportunities.

B. Work with a group of fellow writers to produce two versions of the passage in Exercise 2A, each with a different emphasis.

28c Recognizing and creating subordination

When you want to help readers understand links between ideas or information, you can use **subordination,** having one clause modify or comment on another. In using subordination, you create a sentence with unequal elements: one presenting the central idea (main clause), and one or more beginning with a subordinating word like *because, although, who, which,* or *that* and acting as a modifier (subordinate clause).

MAIN CLAUSES   Most first-time home buyers are people in their late twenties or early thirties. They have tired of paying rent.

SUBORDINATED   Most first-time home buyers are people in their late twenties or early thirties **who** have tired of paying rent.

READER'S REACTION: **The information after** *who* **adds to the statement presented at the beginning of the sentence and ties the ideas together.**

SUBORDINATED   Sales of single-family homes are up, **although** sales of the more expensive homes are still depressed.

READER'S REACTION: **The clause following** *although* **not only qualifies the meaning of the opening statement—it also takes the sentence in a new direction.**

SUBORDINATED   I am saving money **so that** I can make a down payment **as soon as** I find an affordable house.

READER'S REACTION: **I like the way the subordinate clauses add more and more focus to the opening statement.**

Recognizing subordination means recognizing subordinating words and the effects they create. The following list should help you identify subordinators and the messages they convey.

CREATING AND RECOGNIZING SUBORDINATION

MEANING	SUBORDINATOR
Time	before, while, until, since, once, whenever, whereupon, after, when
Cause	because, since
Result	in order that, so that, that
Concession or Contrast	although, though, even though, as if, while, as though
Place	where, wherever
Condition	if, whether, provided, unless, rather than
Comparison	as
Identification	that, which, who

28c
sub

Subordination enables you to put some information in the foreground (in a main clause) and other information in the background (in a subordinate clause). Thus, you can help readers distinguish primary statements from secondary statements, new information and ideas from old, and important information from background.

SECONDARY/ PRIMARY	**Although** energy costs are increasing, costs for raw materials have dropped more than thirty percent in the past six months.
OLD/NEW	**Though** most biographies of Charles Dickens have spent much time examining his childhood, his latest biographer pays little attention to this period.
IMPORTANT/ BACKGROUND	Raymond Carver, **who** died in 1990, created a stir with his "minimalist" short stories.

You can also vary the meaning of a sentence considerably, depending on the subordinating conjunction you choose.

As soon as the copier is repaired, we can print the newsletter.

Whenever the copier is repaired, we can print the newsletter.

If the copier is repaired, we can print the newsletter.

Short, choppy sentences can become smooth and graceful through careful subordination.

CHOPPY	For each moon, the Seneca have a name. They draw the name from the season. The sixth moon is called the Strawberry Moon. Strawberries ripen in June.
EDITED	For each moon, the Seneca have a name **that** they draw from the season. **Because** strawberries ripen in June, the sixth moon is called the Strawberry Moon.

28c
sub

LOCATING AND PUNCTUATING SUBORDINATION

SUBORDINATING CONJUNCTIONS

You can use a subordinating conjunction such as *although, because,* or *since* (see list on page 377) to create a subordinate clause at the beginning or end of a sentence (see 15d).

PUNCTUATION WITH SUBORDINATING CONJUNCTIONS

Use a comma *after* an introductory clause that begins with a subordinating conjunction. At the end of a sentence, do not use commas if the clause is *essential* to the meaning of the main clause (restrictive); use commas if the clause is *not essential* (nonrestrictive). (See 22c.)

BEGINNING	**Once she understood the problem,** she had no trouble solving it.
END	Radar tracking of flights began **after several commercial airliners collided in midair.** Essential

END   The present air traffic control system works reasonably well, **although accidents still occur.**
Nonessential

RELATIVE PRONOUNS

You can use a relative pronoun (*who, which, that*) to create a relative clause (also called an adjective clause) at the end or in the middle of a sentence. (See 15d.)

PUNCTUATION WITH RELATIVE PRONOUNS

If the modifying clause contains information that is *not essential* to the meaning of the main clause, the modifying clause is nonrestrictive and you should set it off with commas. If the information is *essential*, the modifying clause is restrictive and you should not set it off with commas. (See 22c.)

RESTRICTIVE   The anthropologists discovered the site of a building **that early settlers used as a meetinghouse.**

NONRESTRICTIVE   At one end of the site they found remains of a smaller building, **which may have been a storage shed.**

RESTRICTIVE   The people **who organized the project** work for the Public Archaeology Lab.

NONRESTRICTIVE   A graduate student, **who was leading a dig nearby,** first discovered signs of the meetinghouse.

Exercise 3

A. Use subordination to combine each of the following pairs of sentences. Choose appropriate subordinating conjunctions, and create emphasis consistent with each sentence's meaning. Rewrite the clauses if necessary to produce effective sentences.

28c
sub

EXAMPLE

Newspapers often contain reports of car accidents. ~~The accidents~~ *that* were preventable.

1. Comedian Sam Kinison died in a car crash. A pickup truck swerved across the road and hit his car.
2. Kinison was not wearing a seat belt. A seat belt might have saved his life.
3. Driving quickly off the road to the right is one thing you can do. This will help you avoid collisions.
4. Drive a large car. Big, heavy cars and passenger vans are much safer in crashes.

5. Buying a car with front and side impact air bags is an excellent way to reduce your chances of getting injured or dying. These cars cost more money.

B. Working with a group of fellow students, conduct research to determine which subordinating words are widely used. Each person should locate a five- to seven-paragraph segment of a magazine article and make a list of all the subordinating words in it, tallying the number of times each word appears. (The list on page 377 and a dictionary can help you decide whether a word is a subordinator.) Pool your lists, and determine how often the various words appear in the articles you sampled.

28d Recognizing and editing problems with subordination

Problems with subordination generally take two forms: illogical or unclear relationships and excessive use of a strategy.

1 Be alert for illogical or unclear relationships

Sometimes the subordinating word you choose may not specify a clear relationship, or it may indicate an illogical relationship.

STRATEGY

- To identify illogical subordination, state a sentence's meaning to yourself with slightly different wording.

  Ask yourself, "Does the original sentence convey my intended meaning?"

  Ask yourself, "Can the subordinating word I have chosen convey several conflicting meanings?"

  If your answer to either question reveals a problem, revise the sentence by choosing a more appropriate subordinator (see page 377 for alternatives).

  UNCLEAR EMPHASIS   Since she taught junior high school, Jean developed keen insight into the behavior of twelve- and thirteen-year-olds.

    READER'S REACTION: I'm not sure whether *since* here means she developed insights *because* she was a teacher or *after* she quit teaching.

**28d
sub**

EDITED   **Because** she taught junior high school, Jean developed keen insight into the behavior of twelve- and thirteen-year-olds.

- To identify unclear subordination, look for sentences that confuse readers by presenting key ideas in a subordinate clause and secondary ideas in a main clause. Correct this problem by making sure the main clause presents the sentence's most important statement.

FAULTY   His training and equipment were inferior, although Jim was still able to set a school record throwing the discus.
READER'S REACTION: **Isn't Jim's achievement the key point?**

EDITED   **Although** his training and equipment were inferior, Jim was still able to set a school record throwing the discus.

2 Be careful with troublesome subordinators: *as/while, and which, but that,* and *who*

When you use the following coordinators, be especially careful, for they can be especially ambiguous, confusing, or irritating to readers: (1) *as* and *while,* and (2) *and which, but that,* and *and who.*

As, while. You can use *as* correctly to create a comparison, or you can use it to indicate simultaneous events.

COMPARISON   Our team spent **as much** time on the accounting problems **as** the other, less successful teams did.

TIME   They began interviewing students **as** the semester was coming to an end.

28d
sub

However, if you use *as* to point out a cause-effect relationship, you will probably confuse some readers. Other readers may consider this use of *as* unacceptable in standard written English.

AMBIGUOUS   **As** the level of achievement in the morning and afternoon classes differed, the researchers looked for possible explanations.
READER'S REACTION: **Does *as* mean "while" or "because"?**

EDITED   **Because** the level of achievement in the morning and afternoon classes differed, the researchers looked for possible explanations.

Do not use *as* in place of *whether* or *that*. This substitution is always incorrect in writing and formal speaking.

INCORRECT   They were not sure **as** the differences in achievement were significant.

EDITED   They were not sure **whether** the differences in achievement were significant.

EDITED   They were not sure **that** the differences in achievement were significant.

While can indicate events occurring at the same time. *While* can also signal a concession.

SIMULTANEOUS   I can get some work done at home **while** the children are at
EVENTS   school.

CONCESSION   **While** she thinks the presentation was a success, I am not so sure.

Nonetheless, *while* may be ambiguous in some sentences, and you may need to replace it with another, clearer subordinator.

UNCLEAR   **While** they interviewed the students, the researchers did not come to any conclusions.
     READER'S REACTION: **Does *while* mean "although" or "when"?**

EDITED   **When** they interviewed the students, the researchers did not come to any conclusions.

EDITED   **Although** they interviewed the students, the researchers did not come to any conclusions.

28d
sub

In addition, *while* is never an acceptable replacement for *but* or *and*.

INCORRECT   One researcher claimed that teachers in the morning classes were more effective than those in the afternoon, **while** the other researcher disagreed.

CORRECT   One researcher claimed that teachers in the morning classes were more effective than those in the afternoon, **but** the other researcher disagreed.

And which, but that, and who. When you place *and* or *but* at the head of a clause along with *which*, *that*, or *who*, you add an unnecessary word and confuse readers by obscuring the relationship signaled by the subordinating word.

CONFUSING The research was funded by the Champlin Foundation, **and which** also published the results.

EDITED The research was funded by the Champlin Foundation, **which** also published the results.

3 Watch out for excessive subordination

When you use too much subordination in a sentence, you create a pattern of relationships so intricate that it overloads readers. To clear up such confusion, separate your ideas into several sentences, and rewrite them so that readers can grasp your meaning more easily.

CONFUSING The election for mayor will be interesting this year because the incumbent has decided to run as an independent while his former challenger for the Democratic nomination has decided to accept the party's endorsement even though the Republican nominee is her former campaign manager who switched parties last week.

EDITED The election for mayor will be interesting this year. The incumbent has decided to run as an independent. His former challenger for the Democratic nomination has decided to accept the party's endorsement even though she will have to run against her former campaign manager. He switched parties last week to become the Republican nominee.

Exercise 4

A. Revise the following sentences to eliminate illogical, incorrect, or excessive subordination. When appropriate, combine short sentences through subordination to clarify relationships and eliminate choppiness.

EXAMPLE

Because
~~Since~~ my doctor said I need more exercise, I have been looking for a sport I might enjoy.

1. As I am not particularly good at athletics, I want a sport that is not too demanding. I would also like a sport that is fun.
2. I enjoy volleyball, although it is a serious, highly competitive sport demanding considerable quickness and coordination. Volleyball is not the answer.
3. Since I have played tennis, I have thought about trying out for the tennis team. I have also thought about talking this idea over with the tennis coach.

28d
sub

28.2

4. Some of my friends think I should give the tennis team a try while others think the idea is laughable.

5. What I really want to find is a brand-new sports program, and which will give me the training I need, because I don't have the experience necessary to succeed in established sports, although I am willing to work as hard as I need to in order to bring my skills up to a competitive level.

B. Working in a group, share your revisions of the sentences in Exercise 4A. Decide which versions of the sentences are the best, and be ready to explain and defend your choices.

ESL ADVICE: GRAMMATICAL STRUCTURES FOR COORDINATION AND SUBORDINATION

Use both coordinators and subordinators, but avoid mixing the two grammatical structures.

MIXED **Although** frogs can live both on land and in water, **but** they need to breathe oxygen.

This sentence has both a subordinator, *although*, and a coordinator, *but*. Use one pattern, but not both.

main clause   main clause

CONSISTENT COORDINATION Frogs can live both on land and in water, **but** they need to breathe oxygen.

subordinate clause   main clause

CONSISTENT SUBORDINATION **Although** frogs can live both on land and in water, they need to breathe oxygen.

ESL

28d
sub

Editing for Word Choice

CHAPTER 29

CHOOSING APPROPRIATE WORDS

When you search for appropriate words, you will want first to ask yourself whether you have used the correct word to express your intended meaning. Consider the following sentence.

Dr. Parsippani [*caused to die*] Mr. Rollet.

In this sentence, several words meaning "cause to die" could fill the slot, including *killed*, *slaughtered*, *assassinated*, and *murdered*. Choosing the best word means first avoiding words that are incorrect or inaccurate. *Assassinate* would be ruled out unless Mr. Rollet were an important political figure; *slaughtered* usually applies to livestock and borders on slang when used for humans; *murdered* indicates foul play. If you meant none of these more specific meanings, *killed* might be the simplest and most precise word to use.

Choosing the right words also means choosing words appropriate to your intended purpose, audience, and context. In a formal paper, writing "This guy's theories, well, I think they're just plain garbage" represents an inappropriate choice of words and phrases, or **diction**. A word like *guy* does, in fact, refer to a person (usually male), so technically it's not *incorrect*. But as slang, it would violate any reader's expectations if it were used in the context of a formal academic paper, and it is therefore *inappropriate*.

29a Thinking about word choice

Whenever you choose specific words while you draft and revise, you base your decisions partly on your writing situation, which includes your purpose, audience, context, and persona (the image of yourself that you project in your writing).

1 Adjust your diction to your readers' needs

The characteristics of your readers should play a major role in your choice of words (see Chapter 6). Whenever you write for teachers or students in college, you should maintain a fairly high level of formality in your diction (the exceptions being deliberately informal notes, responses, journal entries, or quoted speech). Avoid **colloquialisms**.

TOO INFORMAL   The stock market crash didn't seem to **faze** many of the investors with **megabucks stashed** in property assets.

>   READER'S REACTION: **This seems really colloquial; I'm not sure I trust the writer's authority.**

EDITED   The stock market crash did not significantly affect investors with extensive property assets.

A WORD ABOUT SPEAKING

Audiences are especially sensitive to diction because, unlike readers, they have no way to stop and check the meaning of a word or reread a passage. Because much college work assumes academic, sophisticated diction, it's easy to forget that not all audiences are experts who will recognize complex vocabulary. College student Steven Hoecht discovered this as he edited his talking points for an activity he wanted to use in his volunteer work at a nearby elementary school.

TOO TECHNICAL   In order to create effective leaf silhouettes, it is necessary first to procure several preferably truncated and partially dehydrated leaves.

EDITED   To start making your leaf rubbing, first you need to gather a few large, partly dried leaves.

---

2 Adjust your diction to your purpose

Your *purpose* for writing plays an important role in determining your diction (see Chapter 5). In much academic writing, your main purpose will be to inform your readers, providing them with a balanced, detailed assessment of a topic. Using inflammatory, highly emotional, unreasoned, or outrageous language will only subvert your own purposes.

29a
words

BIASED   Most proponents of rock-music censorship grew up listening to pablum and thinking even wimpy bands like the Beach Boys were a bunch of perverts.

>   READER'S REACTION: **I thought this was a paper weighing the sides of the rock-music censorship debate. This seems too biased and emotional.**

EDITED   Proponents of rock-music censorship may unfairly stereotype all of rock-and-roll culture as degenerate or evil.

3 Adjust your diction to your persona

Writing can portray you in many different roles. Through your choice of words, you can sound like a mean-spirited, unyielding demagogue or a reasonable, open-minded arbiter of conflicting opinion. Your **persona** as a writer refers to the public role or character you assume. Thinking carefully about how *you*, as a writer, portray yourself can help you to choose appropriate words.

For example, your persona in a clinical experiment will be objective and detached; using too many personal references may call into question the accuracy of the experiment. But such clinical diction may convey too cold and unfeeling a persona for other occasions.

TOO CLINICAL   [*in a classified ad selling unpedigreed puppies*] Three domestic canines, *Canis familiaris*, type Shetland sheepdog, @29 centimeters, 0.522 kilograms; age: 8 weeks; iris: brown; coloring: burnt umber with variegated blond diameters; behaviorally modified for urination and defecation; inoculated. $25 per canine.
READER'S REACTION: **The writer seems uncaring, treating puppies like laboratory specimens.**

EDITED   Three healthy shelty puppies 8 weeks old, brown with light spots, housebroken, all shots. $25 each.

ROBOTLIKE   The river having been reached, it was decided to portage to the campsite. A camp was set, and dinner was prepared and eaten. The sunset was observed at the lake. Then eight hours of sleep ensued.
READER'S REACTION: **This narrative lacks vitality. The characters seem like robots.**

EDITED   When we reached the river, we decided to portage to the campsite. There, we set camp, cooked dinner, enjoyed the sunset at the lake, and slept for eight hours.

29a
words

4 Use specialized diction appropriately

If you're writing in a specific field or discipline, you need to adjust your diction to your context. For example, in a history course, readers of your papers will expect certain terms and language that might not be appropriate in a physics course.

Many specialized terms eventually find their way into general usage, two examples being *ego* from Freudian psychology and *modem* (modulator-demodulator) from computer science. When you write for general audiences, your readers will find highly specialized language inappropriate. If you use diction too general for readers in a specialized field, however, your writing may seem naive *in that context*. Revise your drafts to include specific terms used in the field (if you actually understand those terms, and if they improve accuracy and economy).

TOO GENERAL   [*in an analysis of a painting for an art history course*] Tiepolo's *Apotheosis of the Pisani Family* (1761) is a lively painting with lots of action going on in it, with nice colors, and typical of the period when it was painted.

READER'S REACTION: **The diction seems too general for a specialized analysis in my field of art history.**

EDITED   Tiepolo's *Apotheosis of the Pisani Family* (1761) shows affinities with typical rococo frescoes of the period, including bright colors with characters in various highlighted actions set against dark border accents.

When you learn new words in one field, you may inadvertently use those words in another field in which they are inappropriate.

TOO COMPLEX   [*in an economics paper on the influence of sexuality in the marketplace*] Ego gratification, originating in the neo-erotic domains of the pleasure principle, remains one of the chief factors influencing the attractiveness of sexuality in marketing.

READER'S REACTION: **I'm an economics major, not a Freudian psychoanalyst. Talk in my language, please.**

EDITED   Freudian theory can help us to explain why sexuality sells in the American marketplace. According to Freud, humans are biologically caught in a kind of sexual rhythm. This rhythm causes us to seek certain kinds of gratification not always explicitly sexual.

Exercise 1

29a
words

A. Assume that the following paragraph is part of a brochure on dental hygiene found in a dentist's office. Examine the passage, and circle words and phrases you find inappropriate. Write a paragraph explaining the problems in diction that you identified in the passage. Consider its intended audience, purpose, context, and persona.

Brushing and flossing of human dentin has been shown to be instrumental in the systematic reduction of invasive caries. When brushing, it is advisable to rotate the cusp of the preventive maintenance tool at alternating angles during upward and downward motion. When flossing, it is advisable to insert and retract the flossing material several times between the dentitial spaces.

B. In a group, compare your responses to Exercise 1A. Which choices of diction did everyone find inappropriate? As a group, try editing the passage.

29b Using precise diction

Because you may write most fluently when you're not weighing every word you put on the page, you'll find it helpful to work with diction during the editing process. Think of this as adjusting your prose to match your intended meaning.

1 Choose specific words

Try whenever possible to edit for more specific, accurate words.

TOO VAGUE   [in a do-it-yourself brochure describing bathroom remodeling] Note: Do not place flooring over uneven floor or with wood rot. Remove damaged area first.

READER'S REACTION: The language is vague and imprecise. What do I do with a "damaged area"?

EDITED   Note: Do not install any new flooring over existing floors that are weak or uneven or show signs of wood rot. Replace any damaged flooring material before installing new flooring.

2 Choose words with appropriate connotations

English is full of **synonyms**, words that are identical or nearly identical in meaning. When you make a choice between two words, you will often consider the words' **connotations**—"shades" of meaning, or associations that words acquire over time. When editing, look for any inappropriate connotations in your choice of words.

IMPRECISE   The senator **retreated** from the gathering.

READER'S REACTION: Did the senator feel attacked, bewildered, or overcome? Or did she just leave?

EDITED   The senator **left** the gathering.

3 Edit for stuffy language

English is filled with Latin words that entered the language centuries ago, creating an abstract, educated way of speaking and writing that may be alluring because it sounds sophisticated. Heavily Latinized language, however, can make your writing seem unnecessarily wordy and complicated (see

29b words

Chapter 31). Notice how direct the following words are compared with their more abstract synonyms.

PLAIN WORD	LATIN-BASED
bathroom	lavatory
bickering	disputatious
die	expire
drunk	intoxicated
graveyard	cemetery
split	bifurcate
stingy	penurious
think	cogitate

In general, use simple, direct diction unless the context of your writing calls for specialized language or unless a more abstract term better reflects your intended meaning than its concrete counterpart.

LATINATE   The reflections upon premarital cohabitation promulgated by the courts eventuated in the orientation of the population in the direction of moral relaxation on this issue.

READER'S REACTION: **The diction seems stuffy. Say it more plainly, please.**

EDITED   Court decisions about living together before marriage led to greater public acceptance of this practice.

4 Edit for archaic words and neologisms

The English language constantly changes. Some words are doomed to become obsolete. New words enter the vocabulary by the hundreds. Still others shift their meanings, as in the case of *gay*, which used to mean "carefree" but now almost exclusively means "homosexual."

Most **archaic words**—words that are rarely used any more but are still found in older literature—will be labeled as such in the dictionary. In general, you should avoid archaic words unless you're using them for a special reason. **Neologisms**—words coined very recently—may not be in the dictionary at all. You may have a harder time recognizing neologisms because they tend to be used in casual speech. Whenever you suspect that a term is too new to be acceptable in writing, identify it as a neologism and define it, or else avoid it altogether.

29b
words

ARCHAIC/   Good reviews of our previous play had been scarce (**save** in
NEOLOGIC   *Fanfare*), and this time around we had to **forfend** the **trashing** of the critics again.

READER'S REACTION: *Save* and *forfend* seem old-fashioned, and what's *trashing*?

EDITED   Good reviews of our previous play had been scarce (**except** in *Fanfare*), and this time around we had to **defend ourselves against** the critics' **attacks** again.

5 Edit for idiomatic and trite expressions

Idioms are words and phrases whose meanings have changed, usually to something quite different from their literal definitions. These terms often have "forgotten histories." Here are some common idioms.

29.1

IDIOM	MEANING
bust a gut	work extremely hard
get in the fast lane	be ambitious, rise up; lead a fast-paced, self-destructive lifestyle
get some z's	sleep, take a nap
lose your marbles	go insane
meet your maker	die
pack it in	quit, resign
stack the deck	cheat
take a spin	go for a ride
toss cookies	vomit
wipe the slate clean	start over

DID YOU KNOW?

Some idiomatic expressions have interesting histories. For example, the phrase *kick the bucket* (meaning "to die") is thought to come from a crude method of suicide in which the victim stood on a bucket, put a noose around his or her neck, and then kicked away the bucket. However, the term may have come from medieval slaughterhouses. Immediately after being slaughtered and hung on the "buckets" (or beams), the livestock would inevitably "kick the buckets" as they died. The phrase *rule of thumb* also has a disputed history, possibly coming from brewers' practice of gauging the temperature of a brew by dipping a thumb into the vat. However, others believe the word comes from centuries-old English common law and refers to the maximum size (the diameter of a human thumb) of the instrument with which women were permitted to be beaten. Some people now avoid the term because of its possibly sexist history.

Ebenezer Cobham Brewer, *Brewer's Dictionary of Phrase and Fable*, rev. ed. (New York: HarperCollins, 1963), and William Morris and Mary Morris, *Morris' Dictionary of Word and Phrase Origins* (New York: HarperCollins, 1962).

29b
words

In most academic writing, idioms are too informal or have become trite from overuse. Replace them with precise words.

IDIOMATIC   The winning team was **placed high upon a pedestal**, while the losers, **wallowing in a slough of despond**, reminded themselves of what a **dog-eat-dog** world it is in sports.

EDITED   The winning team was idolized and cheered by the fans, while the losers, despondent and humorless, consoled themselves over their defeat.

Exercise 2

A. Read the following paragraph and identify as many cases as you can of inappropriate diction. Look for imprecise, misused, stuffy, or trite words, checking in a dictionary if you need to. Then edit the passage by replacing the misused words or expressions with more appropriate ones.

> The inaugural time I witnessed someone parachuting from a plane was when I was in college. The parachuting establishment was located in the desert of Arizona. First we apprised ourselves on the diminutive single-prop plane and shackled ourselves into the seats. Three employees of a local business were the jumpers. We circled around until we reached the pinnacle for jumping, about 6,000 feet up. The first customer was about to detort but became lugubrious with fear and couldn't jump. The second man faced us with his back to the open side of the plane and a verecund expression on his face, then fell back deliberately and dejected himself from the craft, spinning downward toward the verdurous desert.

B. In a small group, compare your edited versions of the passage in Exercise 2A. Discuss all your choices, and then try to reach consensus on the best substitutions.

29c
words

29c Using strategies for editing diction

Having a wide-ranging vocabulary—not just *knowing* lots of words, but knowing how to use them thoughtfully—is clearly helpful for editing your diction. But even the most experienced writers will tell you that when it comes to choosing words, they always search for just the right flavor. Use the following strategies when you think common sense isn't enough.

ESL ADVICE: USING DICTIONARIES

Sometimes you want to express an idea or concept in writing, but you do not know what word or words would express it in English. Bilingual dictionaries are usually a good starting point to find a possible translation. However, for every word, they list several options. It is important that you consult an English dictionary to ensure that you choose the most appropriate word. These dictionaries contain definitions and examples that can help you decide which word best matches your intended meaning and your diction.

1 Use the dictionary

As Chapter 30 suggests, the dictionary will be your most important tool when you work on diction. Dictionaries give you precise definitions as well as usage notes.

STRATEGY

When editing your work, circle any words that you have learned fairly recently or have not used often; then look them up to be sure you've used them correctly.

IMPRECISE   Employees should know that their contracts may be terminated if they deliberately **abrogate** their usual work hours.

READER'S REACTION: **The term** *abrogate* **means to abolish or nullify, usually by some formal means. Do you really mean this?**

EDITED   Employees should know that their contracts may be terminated if they **miss work**.

---

2 Use a thesaurus

A thesaurus provides lists of synonyms that are useful when you're editing diction and want to replace an existing word that you question for some reason. But be careful. Be sure you're familiar with a synonym and its connotations before simply substituting it, or you could fall prey to "thesaurusese," a disease that leads to the proclivity for excessively prolix and convoluted linguistic verbiage that can stray several standard deviations from definitional accuracy. In plainer English, this condition may lead you to reject good, common words, choosing instead to pepper your prose with sophisticated-sounding synonyms, often without knowing whether you're using them correctly.

When using a thesaurus, ask yourself whether your new word choice captures your meaning more accurately, gives more flavor, or avoids redundancy more effectively than your original choice. When in doubt, stick with words you know.

ORIGINAL   She was **angered** to the point of frustration and could no longer hold her dissatisfaction inside.

> WRITER'S REACTION: **I'm not satisfied with** *anger.* **My thesaurus suggests the alternatives** *vexed, irritated, exasperated, infuriated, inflamed, miffed,* **and** *enraged.*

IMPRECISE   She was **enraged** to the point of frustration.

> WRITER'S REACTION: **This word is too strong and does not convey the woman's true feelings.**

EDITED   She was **irritated** to the point of frustration.

3 Use the slash/option technique

Sometimes you already have several alternatives in mind for a particular word while you're writing. Stopping to weigh the alternatives may break your train of thought.

STRATEGY

Write down the alternative words and separate them with slashes. Later, as you revise and edit, you can choose which word most accurately fits your intended meaning.

DRAFT   Steve and Esme stopped their chess matches only long enough to enjoy John's delicious **culinations/cuisine/cooking/delectables/repasts/meals**.

EDITED   Steve and Esme stopped their chess matches only long enough to enjoy John's delicious **meals**.

29c
words

4 Fight insecurity with simplicity

29.2

Vagueness, words with wrong connotations, overused expressions—you can slice all these from your prose if you develop a keen eye for style and clarity in your writing. But the problem of overblown, deliberately complex diction—diction intended to puff up your writing with "sophisticated" language—often has its roots in insecurity. When writers worry about their intellectual status, they often toss away good, direct vocabulary in favor of gobbledygook. Professionals in advanced fields have earned the right to use words with *specialized* meanings. They sound sophisticated because, in their fields, they *are*. But using overly complex prose out of a fear of sounding naive only makes you sound *more* naive.

Whenever you have the slightest urge to puff up your prose with jargon or needlessly complicated diction, *stop*. Ask yourself what kind of salesperson in an audio store you would be more likely to trust—one who talks to you in simple, honest language about the pros and cons of various DVD players, or one who uses dozens of alien-sounding words for acoustic features and for complex mechanisms inside the machines. Then return to your draft. Be direct; choose concrete, lively words when you can.

Exercise 3

A. Locate a short passage in a newspaper or magazine article. Rewrite the passage, substituting words that are inappropriate or inaccurate.

B. Make several copies of your original passage and the changed version in Exercise 3A. In a group, work on each other's passages to "repair" the damage. When you finish, compare your edited versions with the original passages. How close did you come to the originals? What differences can you see between your "repaired" versions and the originals?

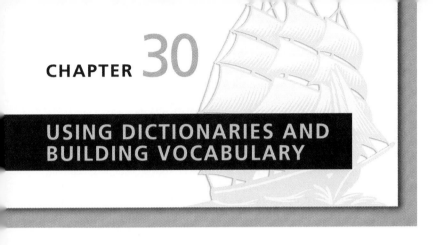

CHAPTER 30

USING DICTIONARIES AND BUILDING VOCABULARY

In cultures that have no writing, all the words in the language must be passed orally from generation to generation. The entire "dictionary" exists in the memories of the speakers. In societies with advanced literacy, such as ours, no one could hope to know all the words in the language. Most educated Americans use a working vocabulary of about 25,000 words. That's less than 3 percent of the total vocabulary of the English language, which exceeds 1 million words. Under these circumstances, it's easy to see why the dictionary is such an important tool for any writer or reader. But there are many kinds of dictionaries, for many purposes. What are your special needs as a writer?

30a Choosing dictionaries to serve your needs

As you work with your writing, you will need different kinds of dictionaries for different purposes, even beyond the typical need to check on the correct spelling, pronunciation, and definition of a word. Here are some common questions writers ask about dictionaries and their use.

- *What's the best kind of all-purpose dictionary I can get?*
  Desk dictionaries are suitable for most routine academic and professional tasks. Although they don't pretend to give an exhaustive list of English vocabulary, they are still quite substantial reference works. Desk dictionaries are often called *college dictionaries* because they represent the standard of vocabulary used by educated people. Less bulky and less expensive than full-length dictionaries, they're widely used in most homes and workplaces.
- *What if I don't want to lug around a huge book when I'm working on my writing away from home?*
  Most people use a **pocket dictionary** for quick checks on spelling or syllable division. Pocket dictionaries are **abridged dictionaries**,

meaning that they contain far fewer words and much less information than standard dictionaries. They are inexpensive and convenient, but you'll still want to use a more substantial dictionary for checking definitions and etymologies (the origins of words).

- *What's a good place to get really full information on a word? What's the most authoritative source?*

If your desk dictionary doesn't answer your questions or contain the word you're looking up, you can consult much more comprehensive **unabridged dictionaries**, which are found in most libraries and schools. These dictionaries contain many more words than desk and pocket dictionaries. They usually provide detailed information about words in common use, and they include specialized words from various fields, archaic words, words "borrowed" into English from other languages, and so on. Unabridged dictionaries often provide notes on usage as well as complete etymological information.

The *Oxford English Dictionary* (OED for short) is the most comprehensive dictionary ever compiled in English. It takes up many volumes, but a compact version is available in two massive books of 4,116 pages accompanied by a magnifying glass for reading the very small print. There is also a new "shortened" edition of two (legible) volumes. For every word listed, the OED quotes the earliest known use of the word in a written document and explains or illustrates many uses that followed. Because they provide such complete etymological and other information, dictionaries like the OED are considered research tools.

- *Sometimes I feel that I use the same words over and over. Is there a book that can help me to find alternatives?*

A **thesaurus** is a dictionary of **synonyms** and **antonyms**—words related or opposite in meaning to each other. A thesaurus is useful when you want to find an alternative to a word you've already considered, or perhaps to remember a word that has temporarily slipped your mind. Under the word *funny*, for example, *Webster's Collegiate Thesaurus* lists the synonyms *laughable, comic, comical, droll, farcical, gelastic, ludicrous, ridiculous*, and *risible*. Obviously, not every synonym listed means exactly what the word *funny* does; your choice of word will depend on your context. The thesaurus lists the related words *antic, bizarre, fantastic*, and *grotesque*. It gives as an idiom *too funny for words*, and it provides the contrasting words *doleful, dolorous, lugubrious, melancholy*, and *plaintive*, along with the single antonym *unfunny*.

- *What if I just want to check on correct spelling?*

Spelling dictionaries are dictionaries without definitions. They provide spellings and information on word division (**syllabification**). Spelling dictionaries range from lists of the one hundred most commonly misspelled words (these brief lists are often preferred by secretaries because they're so easy to use) to much more substantial works with thousands of words. If you own a good desk dictionary, you probably won't need a spelling dictionary unless you're a frequent misspeller or do a good deal of your writing away from your desk.

- *Occasionally when I'm writing poetry I need to find rhymes for words. Is there a reference that can help me?*

    If you want to rhyme a word, you can consult a **rhyming dictionary**. Most rhyming dictionaries are organized into clusters of rhymed words accessible through an index.

- *I've often needed to know the complete history of a specific word. What reference should I use?*

    Most good dictionaries include etymological information, and research dictionaries, especially the OED, will give you very complete accounts. **Etymological dictionaries**, however, specialize in the history of words (**etymology**) and will often give fuller histories of some words. A few, such as John Ciardi's *A Browser's Dictionary*, make enjoyable reading.

- *I've noticed that some words just aren't in the standard dictionary. How can I find their proper spellings and meanings?*

    Most formal dictionaries don't include every word that might be heard in casual conversation, much less the sort of jargon found among computer enthusiasts, avid sports fans, surfers, and the like. Dictionaries of colloquialisms, slang, idioms, and informal usage fill the gaps. They're revised often to keep up with new expressions, such as *za*, *undertoad*, or *mommy track*.

- *In some of my classes, I hear words that I can't find in the dictionary, probably because they're specialized. Where can I look them up to make sure I understand them and can use them correctly?*

    Many disciplines use and require complex vocabularies that sound like a foreign language to the average person. To ensure the precise use of specialized terms, these disciplines have their own academic and professional dictionaries. It's a good idea to ask a librarian or teacher to help you locate such dictionaries for your field of study. As you gain expertise in your chosen field, you may want to add such resources to your personal reference library.

30a
dctnry

Exercise 1

A. Conduct a brief "anatomy exam" of your own dictionary by answering the following questions.

1. What kinds of information does your dictionary give for each word?
2. How complete are the entries?
3. How have the definitions been determined?
4. How many separate entries does the dictionary include? (A good reference dictionary should contain at least 150,000 words.)

5. Are variant uses, definitions, and spellings given?
6. Does the dictionary contain acronyms (such as SIDS, ARC, NATO, FDA)?
7. Does it contain abbreviations?
8. Does it include often-used foreign words such as *tête-à-tête*, *pied-à-terre*, *calzone*, *karate*, and *kibosh*?
9. Does the dictionary show when to *italicize* words such as *cogito ergo sum* or *mea culpa*?
10. What is contained in the introduction or preface? Is there an appendix? Are there any special features?

B. Compare your notes from Exercise 1A (and your dictionaries) with those of other students.

DID YOU KNOW?

Most people think of dictionaries as timeless authorities on matters of spelling, word division, and definition. But dictionaries constantly change. As you're reading this, experts called *lexicographers* are working to keep abreast of important changes in the word stock of American English. One of their jobs is to decide whether certain new words should be put into the dictionary. Special reference works like the *Barnhart Dictionary of New English* compile new words not yet found in conventional dictionaries.

30b Using a dictionary

In one sense, you already know how to use a dictionary. You've done it hundreds of times: flipped the book open, found the word, checked the spelling or the definition, and slapped the book shut again. But have you really *used* the dictionary to its fullest potential? If anything in an entry has seemed like so much needless fine print to you, you may have skipped over some useful information.

The annotated illustration of the word *college* (Figure 30.1) appears in *Webster's Third New International Dictionary of the English Language* (Unabridged). As you read the annotations, note what sorts of important information are provided.

This brief example shows that deciphering the more technical and abbreviated language of dictionary entries is not difficult if you use the explanations and keys found in the front of the book. And once you start looking *carefully* at dictionary entries, you'll find yourself thinking more critically and deeply about the word stock of your language, especially as you choose appropriate words for your papers.

Grammatical
Word   function
division   Pronunciation (part of speech) Etymology

col•lege \ 'kälij, -ēj\ *n* -s *often, attrib* [ME, fr. MF, fr. L *colle-gium* society, fr. *collega* colleague—more at COLLEAGUE] **1:** a body of clergy living in common on a foundation **2:** a building or a number of buildings used in connection with some specific educational or religious purpose: as **a:** the precinct of an English cathedral **b:** a dormitory for students **3** [ME, fr. ML *collegium*, fr. L, society] **a:** a self-governing constituent body of a university offering living quarters and instruction, sometimes limited, but not granting degrees <Balliol and Magdalen *Colleges* at Oxford> **b:** UNIVERSITY <Edinburgh *College*> **c:** preparatory or high school <Eton *College*> <Girard *College*> **d:** an independent institution of higher learning offering a course of general studies and usu. preprofessional training leading to a bachelor's degree **e:** a part of a university offering a specialized group of courses <this university has a ~ of dentistry> <the ~ of engineering at the university> **f:** an institution offering instruction usu. in a professional, vocational, or technical field <teachers ~> <business ~> <army war ~> <barber ~> <~ of embalming> **4 a:** COMPANY, ASSEMBLAGE, COTERIE, CLUB <a ~ of courtesans> <some dusty ~ of pedants> **b:** a meeting or reunion of companions or associates <a ~ of Collegiants> **5:** an organized body, guild, society, or group of persons engaged in a common pursuit, having common interests or a common duty or role and sometimes a charter or special rights and privileges <a ~ of cardinals serving as papal councillors and electors> <a ~ of craftsmen> <a ~ of witches was entrusted with the duty of annually choosing a beautiful girl to be the bride of the water-god—J.G. Frazer>; *specif:* COLLEGE OF ARMS **6 a:** a collection of persons treated in law in one or more respects as a unit **b:** a body of electors—see ELECTORAL COLLEGE **7** *slang:* PRISON, REFORMATORY **8:** a course of study or of lectures <taking three ~*s* a year> **9:** a charitable foundation in England providing residence and care: ASYLUM, HOSPITAL **10:** the faculty, students, or administrative body of a college <the ~ stood behind any move to improve education> <the ~ was at the football game in force>

Meaning

Examples

Examples in context

Example in quotation

Slang or idiomatic form

FIGURE 30.1 Detail from *Webster's Third New International Dictionary of the English Language* (Unabridged). Springfield, MA: G. & C. Merriam, 1993.

30b
dctnry

Exercise 2

A. Using a good college-level dictionary, look up one or more of the following words:

     caduceus   hoist   surprise   denizen   picnic

Using the annotation of college in Figure 30.1 as a guide, list the types of information your dictionary provides for each word—part of speech, etymology, definitions, hyphenation for word division, and so on. Be sure to look at every piece of information given for each word. What did you learn about each word that you looked up for this exercise?

B. In a small group, compare your answers to Exercise 2A. Look for differences in what your dictionaries say about these words and how easily you can access that information.

30c Using dictionaries in the age of technology

Dictionaries and dictionary-like programs are readily available for computers and can also be accessed online. Those used most often are actually simple spelling checkers that scan your document for any words that don't fit the spellings in the computer's memory. Most spelling checkers are little more than matching programs; they don't contain definitions or guides to usage. A few programs, however, do. Software and CD-ROM versions of major dictionaries contain definitions, notes on correct usage, hyphenation information, and spelling correctors. Some have accompanying thesauruses capable of producing a million responses for as many as 40,000 entries. These programs can provide acronyms, synonyms, antonyms, contrasted words, compared words, and related words. A few programs boast average access times of less than one second and can insert a replacement word directly into a document.

Computerized dictionaries have several advantages over typical printed dictionaries. For one thing, they are far less bulky. They can be upgraded more easily and more quickly than a book can be edited, updated, and republished. You can also personalize many computer dictionaries, adding your own special words to the dictionary's memory (good mainly for spelling checks). Computerized dictionaries have other advantages for the user, including prompts that allow you to find a word that you're not sure how to spell.

Computerized dictionaries also have their limitations. It's more difficult to browse through them. They may cost three or four times more than a good college dictionary. If you like to write in different locations, you won't

30c
dctnry

30.1

be able to use your dictionary without a computer (and power to drive it). Computerized dictionaries, unlike a good sturdy book, can easily be damaged or become corrupted. (This is not true, of course, for online dictionaries.) Still, many avid computer users find them a valuable resource in lieu of or in addition to standard desk dictionaries.

30d Building vocabulary

A rich, varied vocabulary is the mark of an educated person—and is essential to effective writing and easier reading. Consider this passage.

> It was increasingly surreal, this internecine feud that had pitted Reverend Willis against his own congregation. Willis had long ago inveighed against their recidivism, but only to his inner circle. Now they were getting the full force of his resentment as he turned his sermons from missals into invectives, from evangelizing into blame.

Did you stumble over any words in this passage? Clearly, the better your vocabulary, the more easily you'll recognize words as a reader and listener, and the more able you'll be to choose effective words as a writer and speaker.

1 Vocabulary and the writing process

If you don't give yourself many options for word choice, you essentially put a stranglehold on your prose, limiting its variety, its accuracy, and its metaphoric potential. Consider the six versions of one line written by Johanna Vaughan in her paper about food-shelf programs.

Without the help of local and state government, the food-shelf program in Seattle will become **ineffective**.

Without the help of local and state government, the food-shelf program in Seattle will become **obsolete**.

Without the **beneficence** of local and state government, the food-shelf program in Seattle will **die**.

Without the beneficence of local government, the food-shelf program in Seattle will die **of starvation**.

Without the **financial nurturing** of local government, Seattle's food-shelf program will die of **nutritional neglect**.

Without the financial **sustenance** of local government, Seattle's food-shelf program will **slowly** die of starvation.

30d
vocab

Many of Vaughan's changes depend on more than the substitution of individual words, but it's hard to overlook the role her vocabulary plays in her writing process. She can revise more effectively *because she has more options*—she can experiment with words like *sustenance, beneficence,* and *obsolete.*

Although it can become tedious to keep moving between your emerging sentences and that 1,500-page dictionary on your desk, there is something to be said for some modest vocabulary development during the process of completing each of your writing assignments. Especially while revising, take time to consider alternatives to some of your words, perhaps circling those that seem repetitive or bland, then listing alternatives or using a dictionary or thesaurus (as long as you're confident that you know the exact meaning of the replacement words).

2 Vocabulary and the reading process

Every time you pick up a book or newspaper, you're exposed to new words. If you're like most people, you probably pass over them, as long as you're not hopelessly confused without knowing their meaning. In many cases, the mere exposure to these words, in their contexts, helps you to acquire them as part of your vocabulary. But a few deliberate techniques can help.

STRATEGY

- Each day, select one word from something you've read, look up its definition, and check its etymology. Then, without sounding too unnatural, try incorporating the word into your speech at least three times during the day. If that's not possible, just make up sentences on your own, and say them silently to yourself. You'll find that the word stays with you, and you'll begin using it more regularly.
- Keep an ongoing list of unfamiliar words, look them up, and review them periodically, crossing them out when they've become part of your vocabulary. Your journal is an excellent place to do this (see Chapter 2). This method works much more effectively than the one recommended by some self-improvement books, which advise you to cram dozens of words into your brain each day in the hope that you'll actually remember them later and be able to use them accurately. The words on your list should come directly from material you're reading and studying, from the daily newspaper to the most complex textbook chapters.
- Every time you look up a word for its meaning, check its etymology. Most English words have Anglo-Saxon, Latin, Greek, or French origins. When you look up a word's roots, you will further develop your vocabulary. Over time, you'll become able to make educated guesses at the meanings of new words on the basis of their parts.

Learning about a word's origins is a particularly interesting and useful way to expand your vocabulary. The word *elevate*, for example, comes to us from Latin *elevatus*, "lightened" or "lifted up." The parts of the word include a prefix, *e-*; the form *lev(is)*, which means "light" (as in "not heavy"); and the suffix *-ate*. The root word *lev(is)* is found in several related words (*levitate, elevator, elated*) If you didn't know the meaning of the word *levitate,* your knowledge of the etymology of *elevate* might help you, and the context of the word might do the rest to define it for you.

Many word origins will also surprise you and reveal the linguistic diversity of English, which has absorbed words from dozens of other languages. The word *cookie*, for example, comes from the Dutch spoken by early settlers of Manhattan. The word *alcohol* is from Arabic. The word *typhoon* hails originally from the Chinese *tai fung*, "great wind." *Chicago* was an Algonquian word meaning "place of the wild onion" or "foul-smelling place." The *tomatoes* you eat have their name origins in Nahuatl, an indigenous language spoken in Mexico and Central America. *Hibachi* is Japanese. *Goober* is African. *Cockroach* is Spanish. *Sauna* is Finnish.

Exercise 3

A. To practice studying the etymologies of words, look up the following interesting examples in a good, full-length (unabridged) dictionary. (The best source will be the OED in your college library.) Look for anything unusual or interesting about the history of these words.

EXAMPLE: KANGAROO

The OED says that the word probably comes from an indigenous aboriginal language of Australia and meant "I don't know" or "I don't understand," the response given to visitors who asked the aborigines the name of the animal.

barbecue	guillotine	mesmerize	sadist
blimp	juke (box)	muscle	sandwich
blurb	ketchup	OK or okay	serendipity
dollar	laser	robot	voodoo

B. In a group, compare your etymologies for the words in Exercise 3A. What surprised you about the origins of these words?

30.2

30d
vocab

CHAPTER 31

WORDINESS

As a writer, you can state similar thoughts in different ways to achieve different effects on your readers. For example, you can create a short, direct sentence.

Incentive pay improves work quality.

You can then add words to anticipate readers' reactions and guide the effect of the sentence.

Incentive pay **often encourages** work **of higher** quality.

Or you can bury the message with unnecessary language that clogs the meaning and frustrates or bewilders your reader.

There is evidence that the use of pay **as an** incentive **can be a contributing or causative factor** in the improvement **of the** quality **of** work.

Wordy writing includes words not necessary to the meaning or desired effect of a passage. Of course, even the best writing often starts out wordy. While drafting, you may pay more attention to exploring ideas and conveying information than to writing concisely. Most rough drafts contain sentences that need pruning.

Avoiding **wordiness** does not always mean using the fewest words possible. It means including all the words appropriate for your meaning, purpose, and audience, but no more. Defining every medical term in an article on a rare skin disorder might seem wordy to specialists in the field but appropriate for general readers. Other aspects of wordiness are more universal, such as redundancy or overblown vocabulary. To make sure your final drafts are concise, you need to learn how to edit for wordiness, a process that involves cutting unnecessary words and phrases, substituting better words, and rewriting entire sentences.

31a Editing for common types of wordiness

Redundancy can creep into your writing when you use everyday phrases and patterns of expression. Their familiarity disguises their wordiness.

1 Eliminate empty words and phrases

Cut empty phrases. Empty phrases like *at this point in time, totally overcome, due to the fact that,* or *each and every* add length but little meaning to your writing. Cut them.

WORDY   **At this particular juncture**, the fire damage **makes it incumbent** upon us to decide whether **or not** to rebuild the old plant.
READER'S REACTION: **What exactly is a "particular juncture"? What does "incumbent upon" mean? Doesn't deciding "whether" imply "or not"?**

CUT   The fire damage **now** forces us to decide whether to rebuild the old plant.

Reduce redundant pairs. English is rich in pairs (or larger groups) of synonyms and near-synonyms. Because they say the same thing twice, **redundant pairs** are always candidates for editing.

above and beyond	free and clear	questions and problems
aid and abet	full and complete	ready and willing
any and all	kith and kin	various and sundry
around and about	one and only	way, shape, or form
each and every	part and parcel	will and testament

WORDY   To encourage innovation, the manager spoke with **each and every individual** team assigned to the project. Team One made a complex task manageable by dividing it into **bits and pieces**.

CUT   To encourage innovation, the manager spoke with **each** team assigned to the project. Team One made a complex task manageable by dividing it into **pieces**.

REPHRASED   To encourage innovation, the manager spoke with **each** team assigned to the project. Team One made a complex task manageable by **splitting it up**.

Shorten wordy phrases. You can shrink many familiar phrases to just one or two words. The shorter versions are easier to read, and they convey your message more effectively.

31a
wordy

WORDY	Carbon 14 can be used to date a site only **in the event that** organic material has survived. **In a situation in which** rocks need dating, potassium-argon testing is appropriate.
CUT	Carbon 14 can be used to date a site only **if** organic material has survived. **When** rocks need dating, potassium-argon testing is appropriate.

Wordy phrases are so familiar that they may be hard to recognize. Use the following list as a guide until you develop the habit of turning wordy phrases into one or two words.

COMMON WORDY PHRASES

PHRASE	REPLACEMENT
as a result of	because, since
being that	
due to the fact that	
for the reason that	
on account of	
on the grounds that	
has the capability of	can
is able to	
possesses the ability to	
at the present moment	now
at this juncture	
at this point in time	
within the current time frame	
a considerable proportion of	many, most
a large number of	
the greater number of	
the substantial majority of	
a case in point is	for example
an example of this would be	
in regard to	
in the case of	
with attention to	
it is evident that	clearly, obviously
it should be obvious that	
concerning the matter of	about

31a
wordy

PHRASE	REPLACEMENT
circumstances dictate that it is imperative that	should, must
it is incumbent upon it is of great importance that there is a need for	
at a time which during an occasion when in a situation in which on the occasion of	when
despite the conditions that even taking into consideration the fact that even though regardless of the fact that	although
at all times	always

Cut intensifying phrases. Intensifying phrases meant to add force (*for all intents and purposes*, *in my opinion*, and *all things considered*, for example) carry little meaning. Your reader will find your sentences more effective and forceful without them.

WORDY   **As a matter of fact**, most archaeological discoveries can be dated accurately.

CUT   Most archaeological discoveries can be dated accurately.

Shorten or rewrite redundant phrases. Redundant phrases say the same thing twice, adding unnecessary words to your writing. Sometimes an adjective simply repeats the meaning of the noun it modifies; *true facts*, *free gifts*, or *final outcomes* are redundant because by definition facts are true, gifts are free, and outcomes are final.

31a
wordy

added bonus	baby puppies	each individual
end result	fresh news	future plan
necessary requirements	past history	terrible tragedy
unintentional mistake	cheap bargain	unexpected surprise

Similar repetition occurs in redundant verb phrases (*completely finished*, *totally overcome*, and *revert back*).

Some redundancies occur when you use a specific word that implies a more general term you've used with it. *Blue*, for example, clearly implies the category *color*, so it is redundant to state both (*blue in color*).

aggressive ~~by nature~~   circle ~~around~~
consensus ~~of opinion~~   curved ~~in form~~
expensive ~~in cost~~   first ~~in order~~
handsome ~~in appearance~~   ~~in a~~ clumsy ~~manner~~
~~in a~~ grumpy ~~mood~~   old ~~in age~~
plans ~~for the future~~   small ~~in size~~

WORDY   Because it was sophisticated **in nature** and tolerant **in style**, Kublai Khan's administration aided the development of China in the late 1200s.

CUT   Because it was **sophisticated and tolerant**, Kublai Khan's administration aided the development of China in the late 1200s.

REWRITTEN   Kublai Khan's **adept and tolerant administration** aided the development of China in the late 1200s.

Edit or rewrite to cut all-purpose words. They sound serious and important, yet **all-purpose words** like *factor, aspect, situation, type, field, range, thing, kind, nature, character,* and *angle* are often fillers. By eliminating the fillers and rewriting, you can make sentences easier to understand.

WORDY   Viewed **from a** sociological **perspective**, the president's popularity **factor** might be **a type of** result of the changing **nature of** our attitude toward authority.

EDITED   Viewed sociologically, the president's popularity might be a result of our changing attitude toward authority.

All-purpose modifiers include *very, totally, major, central, secondary, unlikely, peripheral, great, really, surprisingly, definitely, absolutely, marginal, quite, superlative,* and similar terms. They are appropriate when used precisely and sparingly but can easily become clutter.

WORDY   In the short story, Young Goodman Brown is so **totally** overwhelmed by **his own** guilt that he becomes **extremely** suspicious of the people around him and **absolutely** destroys his relationships. [*30 words*]

EDITED   In the short story, Young Goodman Brown is so overwhelmed by guilt that he becomes suspicious of the people around him and destroys his relationships. [*25 words*]

REWRITTEN   In the short story, Young Goodman Brown's **overwhelming** guilt makes him suspicious **of everyone** and destroys his relationships. [*18 words*]

Exercise 1

A. Edit the following sentences to make them more concise. Use one of the three editing options for wordiness: cut unnecessary words, substitute better words, or rewrite the sentence entirely. Keep track of your changes.

31.1

EXAMPLE

~~In spite of the fact that~~ *Although* ^ most ~~ordinary~~ middle-aged people ~~say they generally~~ feel ~~physically~~ healthy, ~~and in good shape, severe physical~~ catastrophes such as ~~debilitating~~ strokes ~~and/~~or heart attacks can strike ~~suddenly~~ at any time.

1. As a matter of fact, my uncle had just come back from playing nine holes of golf when he suffered the terrible tragedy of his heart attack.
2. We all thought my aunt was absolutely in the very best of health, but she also died extremely suddenly.
3. For me, the end result of these experiences has been regular visits to the doctor to check on my health.
4. On account of my last visit to the doctor, I have started exercising on a regular basis.
5. A regular exercise program helps me to a better kind of feeling about myself.

B. In a small group, compare your revised versions of the sentences in Exercise 1A. Create a "best" version of each sentence by pooling the changes in your group. Try to base your decisions on which version gets the writer's point across most concisely.

DID YOU KNOW?

Legal writing is full of redundancies, perhaps because the law is written to exclude as much uncertainty as possible. Because many legal expressions have a long history, they tend to change slowly. However, recent trends in the law have begun to eliminate such wordy expressions as *cease and desist*, *null and void*, and *give and bequeath*.

31a
wordy

2 Edit wordy and repetitive sentences

Some sentence patterns encourage wordiness, which will annoy your readers. You should always treat them as likely candidates for cutting and rewriting.

Rewrite sentences with expletive constructions. Beginning a sentence with a construction like *there is*, *there are*, or *it is* allows you to hold off announcing the subject—a strategy sometimes useful for creating emphasis or surprise. You should use this technique sparingly, however (see 10b). Using strong verbs in the place of expletive constructions can yield shorter, more forceful sentences.

OVERUSED **It was** between 1346 and 1350 **that** the bubonic plague struck swiftly and horribly. **There were** over 20 million deaths from the plague—one-fourth of Europe's population. **It is** not surprising that records from the period are confusing and incomplete.

REWRITTEN Between 1346 and 1350, one-fourth of Europe's population— about 20 million people—died swiftly and horribly from the bubonic plague. Not surprisingly, records from the period are confusing and incomplete.

Substitute active for passive constructions. Sentences in the active voice often strike readers as livelier and more direct than their passive counterparts. (See 18e.) This impression may come from the presence of a strong verb closer to the beginning of the sentence, tied to the subject or doer of the action. Favor the active voice in your writing unless you have good reason to use the passive.

PASSIVE Even more unanswered questions **are posed** by Mercury, the smallest planet. Pictures of Mercury **were taken** from within 300 kilometers.

ACTIVE Mercury, the smallest planet, **poses** even more unanswered questions. *Mariner X* **took** pictures of Mercury from within 300 kilometers.

31a wordy

Substitute verbs for nominalizations. A **nominalization** is a verb transformed into a noun or an adjective.

VERB	NOMINALIZATION
analyze	analysis
combine	combination
fail	failure
move	movement
propose	proposition
recognize	recognition
vary	variable

Some professions and disciplines heavily nominalize their prose. However, you can resist this tendency and create shorter, livelier sentences if you turn nominalizations into verbs.

NOMINALIZED   The committee held **a discussion of** the new regulations for airplane safety. **A limitation on** flammable seat materials now is necessary.

EDITED   The committee **discussed** the new regulations for airplane safety. Airlines now **must limit** flammable seat materials.

Turn clauses into phrases and phrases into words. You can often shorten clauses and phrases or reduce them to single words. Look for clauses beginning with *which, who,* or *that* and phrases beginning with *of.*

CLAUSES   The Comstock Lode, **which was a vein of high-quality silver ore**, was named after Henry T. P. Comstock, **who staked one of the first claims**.

CUT TO PHRASES   The Comstock Lode, **a vein of high-quality silver ore**, was named after Henry T. P. Comstock, **one of the first claimants**.

CLAUSES   A driver **who has been drinking too much** can turn a car into a weapon **that is potentially lethal**.

CUT TO WORDS   An **intoxicated** driver can turn a car into a **potentially lethal** weapon.

PHRASES   Bridge joints **covered with paint** cannot flex to relieve pressure or to avoid **fatiguing of the metal**.

CUT TO WORDS   **Painted** bridge joints cannot flex to relieve pressure and avoid **metal fatigue**.

Eliminate unnecessary repetition. When you are writing quickly, you may become repetitive. Such careless repetition, which will tire and annoy your readers, can occur even when you are actually varying your wording of ideas. As you revise and edit, look for ideas *already stated or implied* elsewhere in your sentence or paragraph.

31a
wordy

WORDY   GPS is a **navigation** system that helps sailors and pilots **navigate**. By getting information **about their position** from **orbiting** satellites, travelers can pinpoint their **global** position **on a chart**.

EDITED   GPS is a system that helps sailors and pilots navigate. By getting information from satellites, travelers can pinpoint their position.

Good writing may repeat information in order to help readers keep track of an explanation or argument. On the other hand, excessive repetition makes a passage dull and difficult to read.

REPETITIVE   **Our proposal** outlines a **three-step** program for **converting the building** into a **research center** for the study of literature, film, and culture. Each of the **three steps** discussed in **our proposal** should be complete in six months. We expect that **the building** will be **converted** to its new use as a **research center** eighteen months from the time work is begun.

CUT   Our proposal outlines a **three-step** program for **converting the building** into a center for the study of literature, film, and culture. Each **step** should be completed in six months. We expect that **the building** will be **converted** to its new use eighteen months from the time work is begun.

REWRITTEN   We propose **three steps** for **converting the building** into a center for the study of literature, film, and culture. At six months per **step**, the project should be completed in eighteen months.

Exercise 2

Rewrite the following sentences to make them less wordy.

EXAMPLE

My

It was an interest in ancient cultures that first sparked my interest in an anthropology course taught by (Professor Donaldson's.) *attracted me to*

1. There is much information and detail in this informative course about the civilizations of the pre-Columbian Americas.
2. Anthropologists have spent a great deal of time studying and investigating Machu Picchu, which was the center point of an advanced culture high in the Andes Mountains.
3. There are many excavations in the area that have received support from American universities.
4. It seems to be true that the ruins are a breathtaking sight.
5. Proposals for further exploration are now being made to funding organizations by several groups of anthropologists.

**31b
wordy**

31b Editing for clichés, generalizations, and overblown language

Many writers in college choose language that is either overused (clichéd) or too stuffy or complicated (see 29b). They may do this because they're unfamiliar with a specialized topic or think they must sound "smart" to their reader, a teacher with considerable knowledge. But most teachers are more irritated than impressed by such language.

1 Omit clichés and vague generalizations

Much wordiness stems from a lack of the tough, careful attention to language characteristic of the best writing. **Clichés** and **vague generalizations** are like the sayings in fortune cookies, empty of meaning until the reader plugs in some concrete association. But it's a serious mistake to assume that your reader will do your work for you.

CLICHÉD	In **today's modern world**, college graduates **stumble across a startling discovery** before they **strike out on their own**. The best jobs are not necessarily the ones that give you a **shot at big money** but the ones that **turn you on** personally.
EDITED	Almost before they have received their diplomas, today's college graduates begin to rethink the idea of employment. The glamour of high-salary positions soon wears thin, replaced by hopes of happiness, job security, and friendly colleagues.

www
31.2

A passage with vague generalizations may be short but still wordy because it offers relatively little information. To revise, *add specific details* or *combine sentences* to eliminate repetition and highlight relationships.

WORDY	Glaciers were of central importance in the shaping of the North American landscape. They were responsible for many familiar geological features. Among the many remnants of glacial activity are deeply carved valleys and immense piles of sand and rock.
COMBINED	Glaciers carved deep valleys and left behind immense piles of sand and rock, shaping much of the North American landscape in the process.
DETAILS ADDED	Glaciers carved deep valleys and left behind immense piles of sand and rock, shaping much of the North American landscape in the process. Cape Cod and Long Island are piles of gravel deposited by glaciers. The Mississippi River and the Great Lakes were left behind when the ice melted.

31b
wordy

2 Edit overblown language

Overblown language consists of words too formal or technical for the writer's purpose and audience. Students often use formal language and technical terms in an attempt to impress their instructors and sound authoritative. Rein in your formal diction and technical words, using them only when you are sure of their meaning and when they contribute directly to your point.

OVERBLOWN	Under the **present conditions of** our society, marriage **practices** generally **demonstrate a high degree of** homogeneity.
APPROPRIATE	In our culture, people tend to marry others who are like themselves.

3 Eliminate excessive writer's commentary

In certain contexts, talking directly to readers can be an acceptable strategy. If you use such **writer's commentary**, do so cautiously. You can use phrases like *as previously stated* or *I intend to demonstrate* to remind your readers of a point you made earlier or to set the stage for what's to come, but such phrases can become superfluous if you use them too often.

IRRITATING	**As I have already shown**, considerable research suggests that placebos (pills with no physical effect) can sometimes lead to improvements or a cure. However, **my paper documents the tendency of** experts in medical ethics to question the ethics of placebo use, calling it a form of lying. **I intend to show** that the effects of placebos (**mentioned above**) overcome any moral concerns **such as the one I have just described**.
EDITED	Considerable research has shown that placebos (pills with no physical effect) can sometimes lead to improvements or a cure. Experts in medical ethics, however, question the ethics of placebo use, calling it a form of lying. **This paper** will argue that the effects of placebos overcome any such moral concerns.
TOO OVERT	**The thesis of my paper is that** American culture associates the pursuit of knowledge with social ineptitude and the denial of emotion. **I have chosen to focus on** Mr. Spock from the *Star Trek* series as an exemplar of this unfortunate public attitude toward education.
EDITED	American culture associates the pursuit of knowledge with social ineptitude and the denial of emotion. This unfortunate public attitude toward education is well represented in the character of Spock, the brilliant but only half-human Vulcan in the *Star Trek* series.

**31b
wordy**

Exercise 3

A. Rewrite the following passage to eliminate overblown language, unnecessary commentary, vague generalizations, and clichés. As you revise, make the passage more concise.

The social psychologist and student of human behavior Peter Marsh several years ago published a tome entitled *Tribes* in which he set forth the challenging, and for many readers, downright revolutionary, conception that the denizens of our modern world perpetuate the primitive form of social organization known as a tribe. According to Marsh in his book, as a reaction against the tendency of our modern society to break up the social networks characteristic of the more rural lifestyles of earlier decades and centuries, many people form formal and informal groups based on their preferences in food, clothing, recreation, and work. Some of these groupings are of remarkably short duration, consisting of what we might call fads. Let me point out that, in my opinion, Marsh is trying to be critical of many of these groups, particularly those that seek to raise the social status of members by excluding nonmembers from certain privileges. Yet I think that a careful reading of Marsh's book would also indicate that he is favorably predisposed toward the tendency of modern people to form tribes.

B. In a small group, compare your revisions of the passage in Exercise 3A. What specific changes did you and your peers make that were especially effective?

31b
wordy

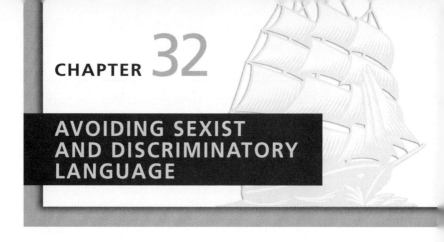

CHAPTER 32

AVOIDING SEXIST AND DISCRIMINATORY LANGUAGE

Prodded by the women's movement, writers and editors strive to eliminate sexist language from published work. But what is **sexist language**? People disagree about some common terms. For example, *seminal* is widely used to mean "highly original and influencing future events or developments"—but the literal meaning of the word is "pertaining to, containing, or consisting of semen." As such, it represents a potentially sexist usage: why should originality and creativity be associated with maleness? Some people think the term should be dropped in favor of words like *important* or *influential;* others argue that it's perfectly acceptable to use the common English word *seminal* to describe an important and influential work.

No matter how you feel about the issue of gender, as a writer you *must* be concerned with the reactions of your readers to the way you represent men and women and members of minority groups. You don't want to alienate your readers, to prejudice people against your ideas, or to perpetuate unhealthy attitudes.

32a Recognizing and editing sexist language

As you edit your writing, try to read what you've written from the perspective of a person of the opposite gender or another culture. If you're a man, for example, ask yourself whether women might object to anything you've said. If you're white, think about your paper from the perspective of an African American or a member of another minority group. Be especially sensitive when you're characterizing such groups, discussing occupational roles, or referring to all human beings.

1 Avoid demeaning characterizations of women

Your readers are likely to object to language that demeans women or plays into negative stereotypes of women's behaviors, roles, and attributes.

DEMEANING	Pasquale's defense attorney called on **three blonde babes** to testify that they had seen him in a bar on the night Smith was shot.
EDITED	Pasquale's defense attorney called on **three women** to testify that they had seen him in a bar on the night Smith was shot.

DEMEANING	Two undergraduates and **a co-ed** were jointly awarded the prize for the most unusual recipe. READER'S REACTION: **I'm angered by the implication that women aren't real students.**
EDITED	**Three undergraduates** were jointly awarded the prize for the most unusual recipe.

DEMEANING	Driving **like a typical woman**, Susan backed her car into the shopping cart. READER'S REACTION: **This unfairly stereotypes women as incompetent.**
EDITED	Susan **inadvertently** backed her car into the shopping cart.

2 Avoid gender-stereotyping roles and occupations

Our use of language has not entirely kept pace with social changes in men's and women's roles, especially in the area of occupation. Be on the look-out for unfair or inaccurate stereotyping.

STEREOTYPED	The most important thing **a mother can do** to facilitate language growth in **her** child is to read aloud to **him** as much as possible. READER'S REACTION: **I'm the father of a little girl. I object to the implication that only mothers can care for their children or that all these children are boys.**
EDITED	The most important thing **parents can do** to facilitate language growth in **their children** is to read aloud to **them** as much as possible.

STEREOTYPED	Setting industry standards, the OnCall Pager is **smaller than most doctors' wallets and easier to answer than a phone call from their wives**. READER'S REACTION: **I'm a woman and a doctor. I'm insulted by the assumption that all doctors are male and the negative reference to "wives."**
EDITED	Setting industry standards, the OnCall Pager **will appeal to doctors because of its small size and ease of operation**.

32a
discrm

3 Beware of male terms used generically

The most common form of sexist language uses *mankind* or *men* for humankind; *he*, *his*, or *him* for all people; and a host of words that imply male roles for occupations (*fireman*, *policeman*, and the like). Most cases are easily edited: *police officer* for *policeman*, *garbage collector* for *garbageman*. Editing out the generic *he*, however, may prove more difficult. When possible, try first to make the construction plural. For example, you can substitute *their* for *his* or for the clumsy *his or her*.

32.1

SEXIST	Every child should bring **his** lunch money to school with **him** each day.
AWKWARD	Every child should bring **his or her** lunch money to school with **him or her** each day.
BETTER	All children should bring **their** lunch money to school with **them** each day.

| SEXIST | The Alejandro Restaurant serves **man-sized** portions of paella. |
| EDITED | The Alejandro Restaurant serves **heaping** portions of paella. |

Some nonsexist style manuals suggest avoiding the use of generic *he* by making a pronoun plural even if it does not agree in number with the subject (see 19c). Some readers, however, object more strenuously to the error in agreement than to the sexist language. The solution is to avoid both problems whenever possible.

ORIGINAL	**Everyone** has at one time or another squandered **his** money at a casino.
PROBLEMATIC	**Everyone** has at one time or another squandered **their** money at a casino.
BETTER	**Most people have** at one time or another squandered **their** money at a casino.
	Everyone has at one time or another squandered money at a casino.

32a
discrm

Exercise 1

A. The following list of words and proposed replacements ranges from the obviously sexist (and therefore inflexible and in need of revision) to the highly debatable and even absurd. For each word, decide whether you would accept the alternative term, and explain why. (Tip: Consult a dictionary when in doubt.)

1. *Persondible* for *mandible*
2. *People-eating tiger* for *man-eating tiger*
3. *Personic depressive* for *manic depressive*
4. *Face-to-face talk* for *man-to-man talk*
5. *Sanitation employee* for *garbageman*
6. *Actor* for both *actor* and *actress*
7. *"Our parent, who art in heaven . . ."* for *"Our Father, who art in heaven . . ."*
8. *Chair* or *chairperson* for *chairman*
9. *Waitperson* or *waitron* for *waiter* and *waitress*
10. *Flight attendant* for *steward* and *stewardess*

B. Compare your responses to Exercise 1A with those of your fellow writers. (And, while you're at it, add *fellow* to your list in Exercise 1A.)

DID YOU KNOW?

In 1990, staff administrators for the city of Sacramento decided to eliminate the term *manhole cover* from city documents, suggesting *maintenance access cover* as a suitable substitute. The access holes are used by both male and female maintenance workers, and it is misleading and inappropriate to characterize them in male terms. Such a change is not all that different from the now widespread use of *flight attendant* for *stewardess*, *police officer* for *policeman*, or *letter carrier* or *postal worker* for *mailman*.

Anne Rudin (former Sacramento mayor), telephone interview, 17 September 1993.

4 Avoid implying sexist views

Whenever you revise your prose, pay special attention to the ways you characterize men and women and their roles and relationships. Avoid making any offhand remarks that could be interpreted as sexist.

32a
discrm

SEXIST   **Being a girl**, Sondra was chosen to be at the top of the cheerleading pyramid.
READER'S REACTION: **I'm not comfortable with what's being implied about girls' abilities here.**

EDITED   **Being the lightest person on the team**, Sondra was chosen to be at the top of the cheerleading pyramid.

SEXIST   **Naturally**, Mike wrestled with the flat tire while Natasha **tried to seduce someone into pulling over and helping**.
READER'S REACTION: **This stereotypes men as inherently strong and capable and women as sex objects.**

EDITED   Mike **struggled to change the tire** while Natasha **tried to flag down a car for help**.

5 Avoid making unwarranted claims

Much sexism finds its energy in misunderstandings about the biological and intellectual nature of men and women. Men are assumed to be stronger, more agile, and more aggressive. Women are assumed to be weaker, worse at math and science but better at language (especially stereotypically "effeminate" forms such as poetry), and less able to manage and negotiate. Many of these assumptions either are unsubstantiated or have come about as self-fulfilling prophecies. In your writing, avoid reinforcing such unfair and incorrect notions.

STEREOTYPED   The anti-abortion protest became more heated when several people appealed to the **instinctive nurturing emotion of the women** in the crowd.
READER'S REACTION: **Aren't men nurturers too?**

EDITED   The anti-abortion protest became more heated when several people appealed to the **feelings of nurture among the parents** in the crowd.

STEREOTYPED   **Behaving like a wimp**, Roger chose to stay home and read instead of playing football with his friends.
READER'S REACTION: **This attaches negative stereotypes to men who engage in intellectual activities.**

REVISED   Roger chose to stay home and read instead of playing football with his friends.

Exercise 2

A. Examine the following paragraph. Then revise its sexist language. Add to the original if you wish.

32a
discrm

Preschool programs for children in poor families have always been under-funded and at best only a stopgap measure for more permanent educational reform. This was the message delivered by the man-and-wife team, Dr. and Mrs. Herbert Kline, Ph.D.s, at the Eleventh Regional Conference on Preschool Education. About seven hundred elementary school teachers came to the conference to hear the Klines debunk some old wives' tales about education. The Klines also focused on what the future holds for those interested in becoming public school teachers, including the need to balance work with attending to one's husband and family. Every teacher of young children, Mrs. Herbert Kline pointed out, must not only practice her craft well but also keep abreast of new theory and research which she can then integrate into her classroom in a way rewarding to her and to her students.

B. In a small group, compare your responses to Exercise 2A. What strategies did you use to revise the sexist language?

32b Avoiding discriminatory language

Members of minority groups often suffer from discriminatory practices, especially those that are manifested in language. Most readers won't tolerate racism, and as soon as they encounter **discriminatory language**, they'll stop reading or throw the material away.

1 Avoid derogatory terms

You may be used to hearing certain derogatory terms and epithets in others' speech. Make sure that they don't appear in your writing or you may anger and alienate your readers.

RACIST
: The economic problems in the border states are compounded by an increase in the number of **wetbacks** from Mexico, some of whom are illegally trying to rip off jobs from good, taxpaying citizens.

  READER'S REACTION: **I object to characterizing a group of people this way. This derogatory name is offensive.**

EDITED
: The economic problems in the border states are compounded by an increased number of illegal immigrants from Mexico, some of whom are able to get jobs in this country.

HOMOPHOBIC
: The talk show included a panel of **fags** who spoke about what it's like to be a **homo**.

  READER'S REACTION: **Using emotionally loaded names for people doesn't encourage reasonable discussion. You'll have to be more objective than this if you want me to pay attention to your ideas.**

EDITED
: The talk show included a panel of gay guests who shared their thoughts about homosexuality.

DEROGATORY
: In a typically **white-male** fashion, the principal argued against the schoolteachers' referendum.

  READER'S REACTION: **The fact that white men are in the majority doesn't give you permission to stereotype all white males negatively.**

EDITED
: The principal argued against the schoolteachers' referendum.

32b
discrm

DISCRIMINATORY   The Johnsons **welshed on** their response.

READER'S REACTION: **What made you think that you could say this without offending people of Welsh descent? Casual stereotyping is just as offensive as deliberate insults.**

EDITED   The Johnsons were not true to their word.

2 Revise unfair stereotypes

Some racial and cultural stereotypes are so ingrained in our society that you may not notice them at first. Try to maintain a critical consciousness about these stereotypes, and then edit sentences or words that run the risk of unfairly stereotyping various groups. Don't rely on your intentions here; think first about how your reader *might* construe your words.

RACIST/ELITIST   The streets in St. Paul are so confusing that they must have been planned by a bunch of **drunken Irishmen**.

READER'S REACTION: **I object to the off-hand acceptance of this stereotype and the condescending attitude toward a group of people.**

EDITED   The streets in St. Paul are so confusing that no one appears to have done any planning.

DEMEANING   My paper focuses on the **weird** courtship rituals of a **barbaric** Aboriginal tribe living in southwestern Australia.

READER'S REACTION: **Your paper already sounds biased. How can you fairly inform me about this topic if you don't speak respectfully about this tribe yourself?**

EDITED   My paper focuses on the unusual courtship rituals of an Aboriginal tribe living in southwestern Australia.

In attempts to create an ideally just world, some social critics have proposed new names and terms for various groups, such as the homeless, the physically and mentally disabled, and even the short or the fat. The terms *vagabond*, *bum*, and *tramp*, for example, are no longer acceptable; *homeless* is now generally preferred. More questionable, however, are the terms *differently abled* for *disabled*, *vertically challenged* for *short*, and *pre-woman* for *girl*. Debates about such proposed substitutions don't seem likely to subside in the near future. The best advice on this matter is to test your choices on your readers and keep up with changes in the language.

32b
discrm

32.2

3 Choose appropriate group names and terms

Just as the issue of sexism in language continues to evolve, the representation of various groups, especially minorities, cannot be seen as "finally" corrected. Making informed decisions about how to identify different groups may require some thought or consultation. The term *American Indian* is still widely accepted, but a preferred form, *Native American*, has entered the vocabulary. Some Native American groups prefer their tribal names (*Hopi, Navajo, Havasupai*). In the 1960s, the word *Negro* gradually gave way to *black*, but not without considerable overlap in usage and much debate in both the black and white communities, including whether the terms should be capitalized. The term *colored* has been out of use for some time, but *people of color* is now preferred for members of any "nonwhite" minority group. (Many people also object to the term *nonwhite*.) *African American* itself has been gaining popularity in place of *black*, though even African Americans do not agree on which is preferred. Terms for people of Hispanic descent can also be confusing, from *Chicano* (and its feminine form, *Chicana*) for Mexicans to *Latino* and *Latina* for people from South and Central America more generally.

How, then, should you decide what terms to use to describe members of various groups?

1. Whenever possible, use the term preferred *by the group itself*.
2. When there is disagreement within the group itself about the preferred name or term, choose the *most widely accepted term* or the one favored by a majority of the group's members.

Exercise 3

A. The chief editor of a large city newspaper received several complaint letters from readers about a sportswriter's use of the word *niggardly* to characterize the owner of a major football team who was reluctant to pay the salary asked by a new superstar player. In a column, the chief editor explained that the word *niggardly* means "stingy" or "cheap" (from Old Norse) and has absolutely no etymological connection with any racial terms. Yet some readers were offended. And, he argued, as long as they were simply *reminded* of a more offensive word, he had a duty to avoid it. He subsequently asked all reporters and editors to use alternative words. In your judgment, did the chief editor do the right thing? What issues are at stake here? Write a position statement.

B. Share your position statement from Exercise 3A with your classmates.

32b
discrm

Editing for Punctuation

CHAPTER 33

COMMAS

Of all the punctuation marks in English, the comma is probably the one you find easiest to misuse. At some places in a sentence, commas are mandatory; at others, they are optional. Moreover, unneeded or inappropriate commas can confuse your readers or disrupt a sentence's meaning. Consider the following sentence.

> During interviews avoid dominating the discussion because doing so especially with reticent subjects can affect whatever they say cut off the free flow of their ideas and contaminate your data.

Clearly, it's difficult to read this sentence with the commas missing. But where should you use them? In the following version, the correctly used commas make the sentence easier to read and understand.

> During interviews, avoid dominating the discussion because doing so, especially with reticent subjects, can affect whatever they say, cut off the free flow of their ideas, and contaminate your data.

33a Using commas to help join sentences

Whenever you wish to use *and, but, or, for, nor, so,* or *yet* (coordinating conjunctions) to link two word groups that can stand alone as sentences (main clauses—see 16c), you need to use a comma before the conjunction.

The air was cold **, and** he could see his breath.

He heard the dog barking on the other side of the field **, so** he decided to investigate.

The ground was rough **, yet** the dog still ran quickly through the grass.

Remember that a comma alone isn't enough; join main clauses with a comma *plus* a coordinating conjunction. If you join the clauses with only a comma, you create a comma splice, a serious sentence error that can distract or irritate readers (see 22a).

LINKING SENTENCES WITH A COMMA
PLUS A COORDINATING CONJUNCTION

main clause + **,** + (and, but, or, for, nor, so, yet) + main clause

We wanted to take a hike **,** **but** the weather was too bad.

If the main clauses you plan to join are quite short, you can sometimes omit the comma.

The temperature dropped **and** the snow began falling.

A comma is appropriate even with short clauses, however.

When you use a comma plus a coordinating conjunction to join main clauses, make sure you do not distract readers by adding commas at the following inappropriate places.

- After *and, but, or, nor, so, yet,* or *for* linking main clauses rather than before.

  INCORRECT   I coated the table with varnish and **,** I sanded it again.

  EDITED   I coated the table with varnish **,** and I sanded it again.

- Between sentence elements other than main clauses—words, phrases, or clauses—that are linked by a coordinating conjunction.

  INCORRECT   We sanded **,** and stained the old oak table.
  The comma splits parts of a compound verb that belong together.

  EDITED   We sanded and stained the old oak table.

  INCORRECT   I bought a wood stain that was inexpensive **,** and that cleaned up easily.
  The comma comes between subordinate clauses, not main clauses.

  EDITED   I bought a wood stain that was inexpensive and that cleaned up easily.

33a
∧
,

33.1

Exercise 1

A. Combine each of the following sentence pairs into a single sentence, using commas and coordinating conjunctions.

EXAMPLE

Shopping by mail can be convenient. It sometimes helps save money. ˌ *and it*

1. Jim wanted to buy paper for his copier. He went to all the office supply stores in town.
2. The stores had plenty of paper. It cost more than Jim was willing to pay.
3. Jim then heard about a mail-order office supply company. He called the company for a catalog.
4. The catalog contained more than fifty different kinds of reasonably priced copier paper. The paper was available in packs of one thousand sheets. For an even greater discount, the paper came in bulk orders of five thousand sheets.
5. He ordered five thousand sheets of medium-quality paper. It lasted for the next three months.

B. Compare your versions of the sentences in Exercise 1A with those produced by a group of classmates. Decide which versions are the most effective and why.

33b Using commas to set off introductory phrases

A comma can help your readers sort sentence parts that might otherwise run together and create confusion. The simplest sentences need no comma.

noun phrase   verb phrase
Jessica mowed the lawn.

When you add another layer to this basic sentence—a word or a word group—you may need to signal the addition with a comma.

Tirelessly , Jessica mowed the lawn.

On Saturday , Jessica mowed the lawn.

After running five miles , Jessica mowed the lawn.

In spite of the throbbing pain in her ankle , Jessica mowed the lawn.

STRATEGY

Place a comma after an introductory sentence element when the comma makes the sentence easier to read and understand.

The following sentence needs a comma to avoid confusing readers.

CONFUSING   Forgetting to remove the hose Jessica mowed the lawn.

EDITED   Forgetting to remove the hose **,** Jessica mowed the lawn.
The comma lets readers know where the introductory word group ends and the main sentence begins.

In contrast, the following sentences are easy to understand without a comma.

CLEAR   By noon Jessica will be finished mowing the lawn.

CLEAR   Suddenly it started raining and Jessica quit mowing.

In general, you need to put a comma at the end of a long introductory element to let readers know where the main sentence begins.

CONFUSING   When Ruane came home and saw the chopped pieces of hose she was furious at Jessica.

CLEAR   When Ruane came home and saw the chopped pieces of hose **,** **she** was furious at Jessica.

You should also use a comma with a short introductory element that might otherwise briefly confuse readers.

CONFUSING   By six boats began showing up.

EDITED   By six **,** boats began showing up.

CONFUSING   Adamant that man kept shouting at the bank teller.

EDITED   Adamant **,** that man kept shouting at the bank teller.

You can insert a comma to tell readers which of two possible meanings you intend.

Curious **,** George went deeper into the cave.

Curious George went deeper into the cave.
***Curious George* is a character in a series of children's books.**

Well **,** over there was where I saw him, officer.

Well over there was where I saw him, officer.
***Well over there* is a location.**

33b
∧
,

1 Use a comma after an introductory clause beginning with *because, although, if,* and similar words

When you open a sentence with a clause (see 28b-1 on subordinate clauses) that begins with a word such as *since, although, because,* or *when* (subordinating conjunctions—see 28b-2 for a detailed list), place a comma after the clause to mark the beginning of the main sentence.

> **Although I am healthy,** I see a physician for a regular checkup.

> **When I need to see my doctor because I feel ill,** I can usually schedule an appointment within a day.

2 Use a comma after an introductory phrase

Phrases lack one or more elements necessary to form a complete sentence, such as a subject, a predicate, or both (see 16b). When you start a sentence with a phrase, you generally add a comma to signal the boundary between the phrase and the main sentence.

> **During the past decade,** Dr. Bandola has worked for an HMO.

> **Growing tired of the HMO's management,** she decided last year to open her own medical practice.

> **Worried about the costs of a new office,** she consulted a real estate broker specializing in medical and dental offices.

> **To furnish her waiting room,** she went to a discount office furniture company.

> **Her office now furnished,** she is ready to begin seeing patients.

DID YOU KNOW?

Writers sometimes claim that commas (and other punctuation) ought to appear where someone reading a text aloud would be likely to take a breath. They often use this argument to excuse their highly personal or inconsistent punctuation. As William Bridgwater points out, however, if you try to follow the punctuation marks when you read aloud, you may find yourself "panting like a dog on a hot day." Bridgwater admits that "in English punctuation there are fashions, just as there are in dress and in popular use of phrases," yet he observes that many punctuation practices are "fairly stable" while others, such as the use of commas with nonrestrictive modifiers, "are almost universally accepted by English-speaking readers." His job as a copy editor is to recognize the conventions and "promote punctuation that will aid the reader today."

William Bridgwater, "Copyediting," in *Editors on Editing*, ed. Gerald Gross (New York: HarperCollins 1985) 79–81.

33b
∧
,

3 Use a comma after introductory words like *however* or transitional phrases like *for example*

Words like *however, nonetheless,* and *moreover* are **conjunctive adverbs** (see 16a-6). *For example, in addition, in contrast,* and similar word groups are **transitional expressions.** Set off both of these elements with a comma when they begin a sentence.

> **Nonetheless,** I do not think we should ban all use of chemical pesticides in the region.

> **In contrast,** a group of organic farmers has been urging us to rely on natural methods of pest control.

You may occasionally wish to open a sentence with an interjection, such as *yes, no, well,* or *oh.* When you do, follow it with a comma unless an exclamation mark is more appropriate as a way to express strong emotion.

> **Yes,** I cleaned the beakers and the test tubes.

> **No!** I do not want to attend any more meetings on the problem.

Exercise 2

A. Edit the following sentences by placing commas after introductory elements where necessary.

EXAMPLE

In the past mailboxes usually had simple designs.

1. In contrast mailboxes today come in many surprising designs.
2. Occasionally people in the suburbs choose an unusual mailbox, but residents of small towns generally display the most imagination.
3. On a recent trip through rural Iowa I noticed mailboxes in the shape of log cabins, igloos, Eiffel Towers, cows, cats, and even parrots.
4. One morning I drove down a block on which each mailbox took the shape of a different kind of fish, including bass, trout, bluegill, shark, pike, and salmon.
5. Whenever you start thinking that people in big cities or suburbs are more creative than people in small towns remember the mailboxes.

B. Working in a group, combine each of the following pairs of sentences by making one an introductory element for the other. Insert commas when appropriate.

33b
^
,

EXAMPLE

Because

~~The~~ morning was gray and foggy⁄ ~~M~~any people woke up late.

1. People felt sleepy. They still had to go to their offices and plants for a full day's work.
2. People were trying to get to work on time. They jammed the highways and commuter trains.
3. Avi felt rested and alert. The gloomy weather did not bother him.
4. Avi worked hard throughout the afternoon. The other people in Avi's office were exhausted by two o'clock in the afternoon.
5. Avi still felt awake at seven o'clock in the evening. He went to see a movie.

33c Using commas to set off nonrestrictive modifiers

Restrictive and nonrestrictive modifiers are common midsentence elements. You use a **restrictive modifier** to present information that is essential to the meaning of a passage. You use a **nonrestrictive modifier** to add information that is interesting or useful but that is not essential to the meaning (see 23c).

STRATEGY

When the information in a modifier is essential to the meaning of a passage, present it without commas so that readers will regard it as a necessary, integral part of the sentence (that is, restrictive clauses need no commas).

RESTRICTIVE   The charts **drawn by hand** were hard to read.

> READER'S REACTION: This sentence implies that the other charts, presumably those that were computer-generated, were easier to read than the hand-drawn ones.

When the information in a modifier adds to a passage but is not essential to its meaning, set it off with commas so that readers will regard it as providing helpful but not necessary detail (that is, nonrestrictive modifiers require commas).

NONRESTRICTIVE The charts**,** **drawn by hand,** were hard to read.

> READER'S REACTION: This sentence says that all the charts were hard to read. It adds the detail that the charts were hand-drawn but doesn't indicate that this was necessarily related to the problem with legibility.

Because of the difference between restrictive and nonrestrictive modifiers, you can change the meaning of a sentence considerably by deciding whether to set off a modifier with commas.

1 Recognize nonrestrictive modifiers

As you edit, you need to recognize nonrestrictive modifiers and set them off with commas. You also need to be able to recognize restrictive modifiers, which require no commas to set them off.

STRATEGY

To identify a nonrestrictive modifier, try eliminating the modifier from a sentence. If you can do so without altering the sentence's essential meaning, then the modifier is nonrestrictive and you should use commas with it. Remember, eliminating a nonrestrictive modifier may make a sentence less informative but will not change its basic meaning.

UNEDITED SENTENCE	Their band **which performs primarily in small venues like clubs** has gotten many fine reviews for its music.
WITHOUT MODIFIER	Their band has gotten many fine reviews for its music.
	The meaning is retained, though the sentence does not offer as much interesting information. The modifier is nonrestrictive.
EDITED	Their band **,** **which performs primarily in small venues like clubs ,** has gotten many fine reviews for its music.

If eliminating a modifier changes a sentence's meaning, the modifier is restrictive. Do not set it off with commas.

UNEDITED SENTENCE	Executives **,** **who do not know how to cope with stress ,** are prone to stress-related illness.
WITHOUT MODIFIER	Executives are prone to stress-related illness.
	The intended meaning of the original sentence is that _some_ executives are susceptible to stress-related problems; in contrast, the shortened sentence says they _all_ are. The modifier is restrictive.
EDITED	Executives **who do not know how to cope with stress** are prone to stress-related illness.

33c
∧
,

2 Use commas with nonrestrictive modifiers

If a nonrestrictive modifier appears in the middle of a sentence, enclose it with commas. Place a comma after one coming at the beginning of a sentence and before one coming at the end.

> **main clause begins ,** **nonrestrictive modifier ,** **main clause ends**
> The public hearing **,** scheduled for 7 p.m. **,** will gather responses to cable TV rates.

> **nonrestrictive modifier ,** **main clause**
> Unable to meet their rising costs **,** the cable companies have requested a rate hike.

> **main clause ,** **nonrestrictive modifier**
> Many residents oppose the hike **,** which is larger than last year's.

3 Pay special attention to modifying clauses, phrases, and appositives

In recognizing nonrestrictive (and restrictive) modifiers as you edit, keep in mind that they can be clauses, phrases, or words (see 23c).

Look for modifying clauses beginning with *who* and *which*. Pay special attention to clauses beginning with *who, which, that, whom, whose, when,* or *where* (see 16c-5 and 23c), and decide whether or not they should be set off with commas. These common modifying elements can appear in the middle or at the end of a sentence.

NONRESTRICTIVE   Preventive dentistry **, which is receiving greater emphasis ,** may actually reduce the number of times each of us has to visit a dentist's office.

NONRESTRICTIVE   At the heart of preventive dentistry are toothbrushing, flossing, and rinsing **, which are all easily done**.

RESTRICTIVE   Dentists **who make a special effort to encourage good oral hygiene** often provide helpful pamphlets and samples of toothbrushes and floss.

Watch for modifying phrases. Be alert as well for phrases (word groups lacking a subject, a predicate, or both) that are nonrestrictive and should be marked with commas. These modifying elements can appear at the beginning, middle, or end of sentences.

NONRESTRICTIVE   **Occupying the daily headline of the local newspaper for the last two weeks ,** our city's budget crisis now threatens to spread to the state budget.

33c
^
,

NONRESTRICTIVE | The governor has called for a conference of the people most directly involved in trying to solve the budget problem **, including the mayor, state legislators, and the city's budget director**.

RESTRICTIVE | City services **popular with voters** are seldom cut from the budget.

Look for appositives. An **appositive** is a noun or pronoun that renames or stands for a preceding noun. Since most appositives are nonrestrictive, you generally need to set off appositives with a comma. Be on the lookout for an occasional restrictive appositive, however, and do not use commas with it.

NONRESTRICTIVE | Amy Nguyen **, a poet from Vietnam ,** recently published her second collection of verse.

NONRESTRICTIVE | The athletic performance drink **, a concoction of electrolytes, vitamins, minerals, and fructose ,** contributed to Jose's endurance in the marathon.

NONRESTRICTIVE | Stump grinding **, a method for removing old tree roots with a special machine ,** is much easier than digging the roots out with a shovel.

RESTRICTIVE | The well-known executive **Louis Gerstner** went from heading RJR Nabisco to the top job at IBM.

RESTRICTIVE | The terms *cognitive* **and** *neural pathways* are familiar to anyone involved in brain research.

Exercise 3

A. Edit the following sentences to set off all nonrestrictive modifiers with commas and to eliminate any commas that unnecessarily set off restrictive modifiers.

EXAMPLE
My mother who is ninety lives in the retirement residence called South Bay Manor.

1. Fifty years ago, a residence that served retired people, was called an old folks' home.
2. These homes which provided few services for residents were apartment buildings with dining rooms.
3. A retirement residence today offers many things to do including recreational activities, fitness programs, trips, classes, and social events.

33c
∧
,

4. The image of infirm people, sitting in rocking chairs, has been replaced by one of senior citizens, who are vigorous and involved.
5. Retirement residences often known as retirement communities are
small towns, where people go to lead active lives.

B. Have each member of a small group bring in a paragraph from a
magazine article, both in original form and rewritten to eliminate the
commas setting off all nonrestrictive modifiers. As a group, first attempt to restore the commas to the rewritten versions; then check the
originals to see if you agree with their punctuation.

33d Using commas to set off parenthetical expressions

Remember that the basic structure of a sentence can be interrupted
with all sorts of words and word groups that add information or modify the
sentence's various elements, including conjunctive adverbs (like *however* or
nonetheless), transitional terms (like *in contrast*), and parenthetical remarks.

Use commas to set off conjunctive adverbs like *however* and *moreover*
(see 16a-6, 22b). Do the same with transitional expressions like *on the other
hand* or *for example* and with parenthetical remarks like *in fact* or *more importantly* (sometimes called **interrupters**).

TRANSITIONAL EXPRESSION	The hailstorm last week, **on the other hand**, caused severe damage.
INTERRUPTER	**In fact,** the hailstorm was so powerful that it broke a dozen priceless stained glass windows on the west side of the church.
CONJUNCTIVE ADVERB	We should not be surprised, **therefore,** if someone takes up a collection for the windows' repair.

You should also use commas to set off tag questions, statements of contrast, and words indicating direct address.

TAG QUESTIONS	We should be ready to contribute to the cause even if we don't attend the church, **shouldn't we?**
STATEMENT OF CONTRAST	The windows' beauty touched all of us in the community, **not just the church members**.
DIRECT ADDRESS	Please remember, **friends of beauty,** that your contribution will help restore the windows to their former magnificence.

33d
∧
,

Exercise 4

Edit the following sentences to add or delete commas as appropriate.

EXAMPLE

Scheduling may be ˄in fact˄the toughest job any manager faces.

1. Project schedules need to be arranged so that the job gets done on time of course.
2. Moreover meetings need to be set up so they do not interrupt people's work, unnecessarily.
3. Most staff members are cooperative however, and may even offer suggestions for scheduling.
4. Management training programs should, I think offer instruction in scheduling techniques.
5. Remember your staff's time is too valuable to be wasted.

33e Using commas in a series

Whenever you list items in a series and give each roughly equal status, you should separate the items with commas. In one sense, commas take the place of a repeated *and*, which appears only before the last item in the series.

HARD TO READ   Harvey's favorite novels are *Moby Dick* **and** *The Awakening* **and** *Jane Eyre* **and** *Things Fall Apart.*

EDITED   Harvey's favorite novels are *Moby Dick*, *The Awakening*, *Jane Eyre*, **and** *Things Fall Apart.*

33.2

Note how difficult the following sentence is to read when the series lacks commas.

HARD TO READ   Tiffany's favorite novels, however, are *War and Peace Of Time and the River Heart of Darkness* and *The Color Purple.*

EDITED   Tiffany's favorite novels, however, are *War and Peace*, *Of Time and the River*, *Heart of Darkness*, and *The Color Purple.*

33e
˄
,

Placing a comma before the *and* that introduces the last item in a series helps avoid confusion. Many readers prefer this practice, especially in academic and professional writing. Editors of newspapers and some magazines, however, do not use this comma.

CONFUSING The ingredients for the casserole are peas, potatoes, ham, caramelized sugar and bread crumbs.

READER'S REACTION: **Does *caramelized sugar* and *bread crumbs* refer to some special mixture, or are they two separate ingredients?**

EDITED The ingredients for the casserole are peas, potatoes, ham, caramelized sugar, and bread crumbs.

A numbered or lettered list that is part of a sentence should be punctuated as a series.

To make sure your analysis is complete, you should (1) check the bottom of the container for residue, (2) measure the salinity of the water, (3) weigh any organic waste in the filter, and (4) determine the amount of dissolved oxygen in the water.

If the items in a list are long and complex or if they contain commas, separate the items with semicolons rather than commas (see 34a).

CONFUSING The company is marketing a line of jigsaw puzzles of cities, like San Antonio, Texas, states, like Michigan and Montana, and countries, like Mexico, Japan, and France.

EDITED The company is marketing a line of jigsaw puzzles of cities, like San Antonio, Texas; states, like Michigan and Montana; and countries, like Mexico, Japan, and France.

33f Separating coordinate adjectives with a comma

In a pair of **coordinate adjectives**, each adjective modifies a noun on its own. Therefore, separate coordinate adjectives with commas to indicate that they apply to the noun (or pronoun) in an equal manner.

COORDINATE (EQUAL) These drawings describe a **quick, simple** solution to the drainage problem.

With **noncoordinate adjectives**, the first adjective modifies the entire noun phrase formed by the next adjectives plus the noun. Usually noncoordinate adjectives are of different categories. For example, one adjective may describe a quality and another a nationality, as in the phrase *friendly Dutch student* (see 20a). Do not separate noncoordinate adjectives with a comma. In the following example, the adjective *flexible* modifies *plastic pipe*.

NONCOORDINATE (UNEQUAL) We can use **flexible plastic** pipe to carry water away from the building.

In place of a comma, you can connect coordinate adjectives with *and* or *but.*

COORDINATE   These drawings describe a **quick and simple** solution to the drainage problem.

STRATEGY

To identify coordinate adjectives, ask one of the following questions. If the answer is *yes,* the adjectives are coordinate and should be separated with a comma.

- Can you place *and* or *but* between the adjectives?

COORDINATE   Through irrigation, the region's farmers have turned dry infertile [*dry and infertile?—yes*] land into orchards.

EDITED   Through irrigation, the region's farmers have turned dry **,** infertile land into orchards.

NOT COORDINATE   Five percent of the budget goes to new telecommunications [*new and telecommunications?—no*] equipment.

- Can you easily invert the adjectives without creating an awkward sentence?

COORDINATE   We wanted to move from our small cramped [*cramped small?—acceptable*] apartment.

EDITED   We wanted to move from our small **,** cramped apartment.

NOT COORDINATE   We decided to move to a small Manhattan [*Manhattan small?—awkward*] apartment.

33f
∧
,

Exercise 5

A. Edit the following sentences so that any series and any coordinate adjectives are correctly punctuated. Let any correct sentence stand.

EXAMPLE
McDonald's Burger King and Wendy's are worldwide symbols of American culture.

1. McDonald's and the others offer quick appetizing meals and clean pleasant surroundings.

2. In the late 1940s, the McDonald brothers opened a restaurant serving a limited inexpensive menu, including fifteen-cent hamburgers french fries and shakes.
3. The brothers did not want to expand their modestly successful restaurant into a chain.
4. Ray Kroc, a manufacturer of milkshake machines, recognized the potential of the brothers' innovations joined their business to help it expand and, frustrated by their lack of ambition, eventually bought them out.
5. Kroc continued to develop innovative imaginative ways to serve customers, and these fast efficient practices have come to characterize today's fast-food restaurants.

B. Working with a partner, exchange your current papers. Edit your partner's draft so that all series and coordinate adjectives are correctly punctuated.

33g Using commas with dates, numbers, addresses, place names, people's titles, and letters

You should separate the elements in dates, place names, long numbers, and addresses according to conventional practice. Separate the elements whether or not they appear in sentences.

1 Dates

Put a comma between the date and the year and between the day of the week and the date.

> The first computer in this office arrived on August 17, 1985.

> The workshop will begin on Wednesday, September 11.

In the middle of a sentence, follow the year with a comma when you are giving the full date.

> On February 4, 1961, the woman destined to be my mother was born in the middle of a snowstorm.

Do not use commas when the date contains only a month and year or a month and a day.

> A test version of the software will be available in January 2003. The regular version will be shipped to stores on June 1.

33g
∧
,

Likewise, do not use commas with dates stating a season and a year.

The fall 2002 issue of the magazine arrived late.

You do not need to use commas when you present the elements of a date in inverted order: 5 July 1993.

2 Numbers

In order to help your readers understand long numbers, use commas to create groups of three, beginning from the right. In numbers with four digits, you may choose whether or not to use the comma, but keep your practice consistent within an essay or report.

During the livestock census on the ranch, we counted **1,746** sheep, **835** beef cattle, and **3,589** chickens.

The combined income for people in our rural town is $8,543,234.

The best high-speed server costs $3,525 at Electronics World.

Omit commas in addresses or page numbers of four numbers or more.

18520 South Kedzie Drive   page 2054

ESL ADVICE: NUMBERS

In writing long numbers, make sure you use commas to create groups of three. Periods are used only to indicate decimals.

1.000 = one   1,000 = one thousand

ESL

33g
∧
,

3 Addresses and place names

Separate names of cities and states with commas.

Kansas City, Missouri, is a larger town than Kansas City, Kansas.

For addresses appearing within a sentence, place a comma between all elements *except* the state and zip code.

You can order the zucchini and carrot seeds from Fredelle and Family, Seed Brokers, Box 389, Holland, Michigan 30127.

Do not place a comma after the zip code unless the punctuation of some other sentence element requires one.

NO COMMA Send the bill to Mr. Robert Mfume at 82 Nassau Avenue, Kenmore, New York 11327-8501 for a full refund.

COMMA NEEDED The pamphlet can be obtained from Bradley Hospital, Veterans Memorial Parkway, East Providence, Rhode Island 02915, a children's psychiatric center.

4 People's names and titles

Place a comma before a title or initials that come after a person's name.

The report on possible lung damage among plant employees was prepared by **Luis Aguayo, M.D.**

If the name and title come at the beginning of a sentence or in the middle, use a comma after the title as well.

We hired **Crystal Bronkowski, A.I.A.,** to design the new building.

When you give a person's surname (last name) first, separate it from the first name with a comma: **Shamoon, Linda K.**

5 Salutations and closings of letters

Use a comma after the salutation of personal or informal letters.

Dear Tiffany,   Dear Volleyball Players,

Use a colon after the salutation in business and formal letters.

Dear Specialty Metals Customers: Dear Sir or Madam:

Use a comma after a letter's closing, just before the signature.

Sincerely,   Best wishes,   With affection,   Regards,

33g
∧
,

Exercise 6

A. Edit the following sentences by adding or eliminating commas as appropriate.

EXAMPLE
My mother remembers assembling her first jigsaw puzzle in autumn⸝
1985, several months before my birth on January 22 1986.

1. Puzzles have fascinated me for the last thirty years, and last year I spent exactly $2479.83 on them.
2. For my birthday this year, one cousin gave me a map of Chicago Illinois in the form of a jigsaw puzzle, and another cousin gave me a puzzle of a seventeenth-century print from the Beinecke Library at Yale University New Haven Connecticut.
3. I have ordered a puzzle map of Atlanta Georgia from Buffalo Games, Inc. P.O. Box 85 601 Amherst Street Buffalo New York 14207 and a puzzle of Edward Hopper's painting, *Nighthawks* from Galison Books 36 West 44th Street New York New York 10036.
4. From January through June 1994, I assembled one puzzle a week, with the puzzles ranging from 500 to 1250 pieces each for a total of somewhere between 10500 pieces and 26250 pieces.
5. I am planning to have a business card made up with both my official and unofficial titles, Jessica Montoya Ph.D. Puzzle Assembler.

B. Working in a group, share copies of magazine or newspaper articles that contain numbers, addresses, people's names and titles, or openings and closings of letters. Check the articles to see whether they follow the same conventions for comma use as those described in 33g. If not, or if the author uses commas inconsistently, edit each article so that it agrees with the recommendations for comma use covered in 33g.

33h Using commas with quotations

When you introduce or conclude a quotation by indicating its source or explaining the context, you should remind readers of the difference between your explanation and the quotation itself by using commas to separate them.

At the grand opening, he said **,** "This facility is dedicated to the physical and mental health of the citizens of Oakdale."

"Some books are meant to be chewed **,**" said Francis Bacon **,** "and others to be digested."
Because the explanatory words interrupt the quotation, the first part ends with a comma.

"The fire doors need to be replaced before the school can be reopened **,**" the commissioner wrote.

When a quotation ends with a question mark or an exclamation point, you should keep this punctuation even if you provide an explanation after the quotation.

33h
^
,

"We can't afford the $30,000 to replace the doors right away**!**" the schoolboard president responded angrily.

"Why can't you understand the paramount importance of fire safety**?**" the commissioner retorted.

If your explanation ends with *that* just before the quotation, do not include a comma.

Lorene Cary begins her story by saying that "they had just come home from Woolworth's, where they both worked at the cheap-and-greasy fountain on Friday nights and Saturdays in a town they and their friends called 'Tacky' Darby."

When you quote a person's words indirectly (rather than word for word in quotation marks), do not use a comma after *that*.

FAULTY   He testified that**,** he did not damage the machinery as a pro-
                  test during the strike.

EDITED   He testified that he did not damage the machinery as a protest
                  during the strike.

Exercise 7

A. Edit the following passages by adding, deleting, or moving commas so that quotations are appropriately punctuated.

"Ice cream is virtually the only food we eat frozen, which means that its flavor, which we define as a composite of taste and smell, is only fully released upon melting" explains Arun Kilara, a 43-year-old professor of food science at Penn State and one of the world's ac-knowledged authorities on ice cream.

Not surprisingly, few true ice cream connoisseurs are fond of the industry's use of fat substitutes, such as the complex protein found in NutraSweet's Simplesse. "The search for the perfect fat sub-stitute" Kilara says "is like a contemporary version of alchemy—lots of useful discoveries, but they'll never turn lead into gold." While some protein-based fat substitutes approximate fat's texture, or "mouth feel" he explains, they cannot dissolve flavor compounds in the same way.

"The smaller the ice crystals, the smoother the ice cream" says Kilara. "You get the smallest crystals when the drop in temperature is the most rapid and when agitation is most vigorous."

"There's one basic truth about ice cream—its quality begins deteriorating from the moment it is made" Kilara concludes. "Over the product's lifetime, ice cream's air escapes, its fat clumps, its ice melts, and its water freezes."

—LAWRENCE E. JOSEPH, "The Scoop on Ice Cream"

B. Working in a group, write a paragraph that presents information drawn from a newspaper or magazine article. Include several quotations from the article in your paragraph. Indicate the source or context for the quotations, and use commas appropriately to introduce or conclude the quoted material.

33i Using commas to make your meaning clear

Even if no rule specifies a comma, you may still include one in a sentence if it is necessary to make your meaning clear to readers, to remind them of deleted words, or to add emphasis.

CONFUSING	When food is scarce, animals that can expand their grazing territory at the expense of other species.
EDITED	When food is scarce, animals that can, expand their grazing territory at the expense of other species.
HARD TO READ	Anyone who can afford to buy this high-speed file management program should.
EDITED	Anyone who can afford to buy this high-speed file management program, should.
	The comma reminds readers that should means "should do so."
UNEMPHATIC	Stocks go up and down.
EMPHATIC	Stocks go up, and down.
	The comma emphasizes the contrast.

33j
no ∧
,

33j Avoiding commas that do not belong

When they are not sure precisely where to put commas, some writers insert them at every possible point. The result is confusing and irritating to readers. Try to avoid scattering commas throughout your writing with no clear purpose in mind. If you are not sure whether to add a comma, leave it out until you have checked to make sure one is required. In addition, avoid using commas in the situations discussed in this section.

1 Do not insert a comma after words like *although* and *because* that introduce a clause

Certain conjunctions and other words may mislead you into thinking you need a comma. Among the most common words of this type are subordinating conjunctions like *although*, *when*, and *since* (see 28b-2 for a detailed list). They introduce an entire subordinate clause and should not be set off with commas. One reason writers set off subordinating conjunctions with commas is that they mistake the words for conjunctive adverbs (like *however*) and transitional expressions (such as *for example*), which should be set off with commas (see 22b).

INCORRECT   **Although,** Jim had just started to learn how to ski, we took him to the most expert slope on his first trip up the mountain.

EDITED   **Although** Jim had just started to learn how to ski, we took him to the most expert slope on his first trip up the mountain.

2 Do not insert a comma between a subject and a predicate

Unless subjects and predicates are separated by a modifying clause, don't insert a comma between them.

INCORRECT   Cézanne's painting *Rocks at L'Estaque*, hangs in the Museu de Arte in São Paulo, Brazil.

EDITED   Cézanne's painting *Rocks at L'Estaque* hangs in the Museu de Arte in São Paulo, Brazil.

3 Do not overuse commas

Today readers generally prefer a style in which commas are not used heavily. Too many commas, even when they are correctly used, can lead to a style that is choppy and hard to read. Whenever possible, avoid sentence structures that call for a large number of commas. If necessary, edit and rewrite to eliminate excessive comma use.

33j
no ˄ ,

TOO MANY COMMAS   Samantha, always one, like her mother, to speak her mind, loudly protested the use of force, as she called it, by two store detectives, who had been observing her while she, looking for bargains, absentmindedly slipped a pair of gloves into her jacket pocket.

EDITED   Always one to speak her mind, like her mother, Samantha loudly protested what she considered the use of force by two store detectives who saw her absentmindedly slip a pair of gloves into her jacket pocket while she was looking for bargains.

In the first passage, none of the commas are incorrect, but the comma is clearly overused. In the second passage, careful editing turns a nine-comma sentence into one with two commas.

Exercise 8

A. Edit each of the following sentences in two ways: (1) by removing any unnecessary commas and (2) by rewriting to create sentence structures that contain fewer commas, all of which are necesssary.

EXAMPLE

When ⌐they realized they had no job prospects, the five friends⌐

formed ⌐a company, which they called Home Restorers, Inc.

When they realized they had no job prospects, the five friends formed Home Restorers, Inc.

1. Because, she likes the outdoors, Sandy, a devoted gardener, takes care of landscaping, grass cutting, and outdoor cleanup.
2. Strong, tireless Jun, does roofing, paving, and similar work.
3. Interior design was, Padmaja's major, so she, everyone agrees, is the person best qualified to do interior decorating.
4. Having painted, her parents' house one summer, Rachael was, chosen, by her partners, as the company's painting supervisor.
5. Desperate, for a place in the company, Joel decided that, marketing, because it would draw on his undergraduate work in sociology, was the best thing for him to do.

B. Exchange draft papers with another writer, and edit each other's work to eliminate unnecessary commas. When you encounter a sentence that might be rewritten to reduce the number of commas, underline it. When your partner returns your paper, check over the editorial changes and consider rewriting any underlined sentences.

33j
no ⌃,

CHAPTER 34

SEMICOLONS AND COLONS

Semicolons and colons help you connect words, word groups, or sentences in useful and varied ways. Compare the following brief passages.

On April 12, 1861, at 4:30 a.m., one of Beauregard's batteries fired upon Fort **Sumter. The** Civil War had begun.

On April 12, 1861, at 4:30 a.m., one of Beauregard's batteries fired upon Fort **Sumter; the** Civil War had begun.

On April 12, 1861, at 4:30 a.m., one of Beauregard's batteries fired upon Fort **Sumter: the** Civil War had begun.

All three examples are correct, yet each encourages readers to take a different perspective. In the first version there is no *necessary* connection between the two sentences. Readers may choose whether to view the sentences as a simple statement of facts or as the presentation of a dramatic moment. In the second version, however, the *semicolon* connects the two statements and encourages readers to link the firing of a gun battery to the beginning of the Civil War. In the third sentence, the *colon* provides even more direction to readers. It encourages them to view the guns' firing as a dramatic and significant moment: the beginning of the Civil War.

34a
;

34a Using semicolons

A semicolon joins two main clauses that could act as complete sentences on their own. The semicolon indicates that the clauses are linked logically; at the same time, it creates a brief reading pause between them.

1 Try joining main clauses with a semicolon

You can use a semicolon to join two complete sentences (main clauses— see 16c-2) into a single unit. Think of a semicolon as an alternative to using a period and starting a new sentence.

TWO SENTENCES	The demand for paper products is at an all-time high. Business and industry alone consume millions of tons of paper each year.
ONE SENTENCE	The demand for paper products is at an all-time high; business and industry alone consume millions of tons of paper each year.

You signal the relationship between main clauses by joining them with a semicolon, though you do not specify the logical link as you might by joining clauses with a conjunction such as *and*, *but*, or *yet* (see 28a). A semicolon can highlight the close relationship of ideas or dramatically emphasize a contrast between clauses.

The city council wants more parks, an expanded recreation program, and a civic center; the mayor wants to cut expenses and limit services.

When you join main clauses with a semicolon, make sure readers will be able to recognize the logical relationship without having to puzzle over the sentence.

STRATEGY

Check for correct use of a semicolon by seeing if the clauses on either side of the semicolon can stand on their own as complete sentences. If they can't, the semicolon has probably been misused.

INCORRECT	The demand for recycled paper has also increased greatly; with manufacturers rushing to develop reliable supplies of scrap paper.
TEST	The demand for recycled paper has also increased greatly. **The first clause is a complete sentence.**
	With manufacturers rushing to develop reliable supplies of scrap paper. **The second part is a sentence fragment.**
CORRECT	The demand for recycled paper has also increased greatly; manufacturers are rushing to develop reliable supplies of scrap paper.

34a
;

2 Use a semicolon with transition words such as *however, on the other hand*

When you use a semicolon by itself to link main clauses, you ask readers to recognize the logical link; in contrast, when you use a transition word like *however* or a transitional expression like *on the other hand*, you specify the relationship for readers. The effect on readers is something like the following.

assertion → semicolon → transition → assertion
(*pause*)   (*consider relationship*)

I like apples **;**   **however,** I hate pears.
assertion pause   **contrast**   **assertion**

To specify the transition between clauses, you can choose a **conjunctive adverb** such as *however, moreover, thus,* or *therefore* (see 28b-2 for a detailed list) or a **transitional expression** like *for example, in contrast,* or *on the other hand*. The linking word or phrase can appear between clauses (just after the semicolon), within one of the clauses, or at the end of a clause. If such a transition comes between clauses, right after a semicolon, it must be followed by a comma; if it comes within a clause, it must be preceded and followed by commas; if it comes at the end of a clause, it must be preceded by a comma.

BETWEEN CLAUSES	Joe returned from the Arctic **;** **however,** Alan was never found.
WITHIN A CLAUSE	Joe returned from the Arctic **;** Alan**,** **however,** was never found.
AT END OF CLAUSE	Joe returned from the Arctic **;** Alan was never found**,** **however**.

Consider joining a series of short to medium-length sentences with semicolons when (1) the sentences are logically linked; (2) as a group, the unlinked sentences seem choppy or disconnected; and (3) commas do not separate the elements enough to encourage readers to consider each one fully.

CHOPPY	The shelty took first prize. The German shepherd took second. The poodle walked away in third place.
BETTER	The shelty took first prize, the German shepherd took second, **and** the poodle walked away in third place.
MOST EFFECTIVE	The shelty took first prize **;** the German shepherd took second **;** and the poodle walked away in third place.

3 Use a semicolon with deleted structures

There are exceptions to the rule that semicolons must join main clauses (clauses that can stand on their own as sentences). In some cases, elements within a second clause can be deleted if they "match" elements in the first clause. The two clauses can be joined with a semicolon even though the second could not stand on its own as a sentence.

ELEMENTS INCLUDED
In winter, **the hotel guests enjoy** the log fire in the dining room **;** in summer, **the hotel guests enjoy** the patio overlooking the river.

ELEMENTS DELETED
In winter, **the hotel guests enjoy** the log fire in the dining room **;** in summer, the patio overlooking the river.

4 Use a semicolon with a complex series

Most of the time, you can use commas to highlight and separate elements in a series, with no risk of confusion (see 33e). When some of the items themselves contain commas, however, readers may have a hard time deciding which commas mark the parts of the series and which belong within the items, as in the following example.

CONFUSING
For the project, I interviewed Debbie Rios, my roommate, Liza Marron, my former employer, and my calculus instructor.

READER'S REACTION: **How many people were interviewed? Three, four, or five?**

To avoid confusion, put semicolons between elements in a series when one or more of the elements contain commas or some other internal punctuation, such as a dash, parentheses, or a colon.

EDITED
For the project, I interviewed Debbie Rios, my roommate **;** Liza Marron, my former employer **;** and my calculus instructor.

Exercise 1

A. The following passage contains some semicolons used correctly and some used incorrectly. It also contains some sentences that might be more effective if joined with semicolons and others that would be better as separate sentences. Rewrite the passage, adding or eliminating semicolons and making any other changes necessary to create a more effective piece of writing.

The Grateful Dead came back into my life recently; largely because of my children's interest. My daughter has been *associated* with the group; I find it difficult to apply the common description of a fan as a Deadhead; since she was fifteen. Her school band; the Cosmic Country Sound, was patterned after the Grateful Dead; she was its lead singer and tambourine player.

34a
;

34.1

I had no idea that my son, four years younger; had any interest in the group. His room is decorated with posters of Boris Becker and Albert Einstein. But then a year ago he let his hair grow into a mane; started wearing beaded necklaces and rope wristlets, and, sure enough; turned up one day at my study door to announce, "Dad; there's this concert I'd like to go to . . . ."

Both of my children have urged me to go to a Grateful Dead concert. I hadn't taken them up on the offer until this summer; when by chance I met someone way up in the band's hierarchy who gave me not only some tickets to a concert at the Meadowlands in New Jersey; but also a backstage pass. I told my son. His eyes widened at the news. He invited three of his friends. His sister; with a job on the West Coast, was devastated that she couldn't be on hand.

—Adapted from GEORGE PLIMPTON, "Bonding with the Grateful Dead"

B. The passage in Exercise 1A can be rewritten in many ways, depending on the focus and stylistic effect a writer wishes to create. Share your version of the passage with a group of fellow students. Each group member should be ready to explain the reasons for his or her choices when they differ from those of other writers in the group. As a group, rewrite the passage, and share that version with the class.

34b Using colons

You can use a colon to introduce or set up an example, illustration, list, or quotation. By calling attention to what follows, a colon seems to say "Here is . . ." or "Pay attention to this." In most cases, the words coming *before* a colon form a complete sentence while those coming after take the form of a dependent clause, a phrase, or even a single word.

WORDS   Bring these things with you: paintbrushes, a drop cloth, and gloves.

WORDS, PHRASES, AND CLAUSES   Each year the river claims something that optimistic humans have built on its banks: part of a yard, a toolshed, a driveway edged with bushes, or a house that people admired for its dramatic view from the bluff.

Sometimes, however, you may wish to use a colon to join two sentences, the first providing a relatively broad statement and the second offering a sharper focus, a summary, or a change in direction.

After searching through the house most of the day, she finally admitted the obvious: her grandmother's ring was lost.

1 Use a colon to introduce examples, statements, and lists

You can use colons to introduce examples and concluding generalizations. Commonly, a colon comes after the first part of a sentence, which offers a statement or generalization that the remainder of the sentence (following the colon) illustrates, explains, or makes concrete and particular.

> Mulholland believed that the growing city at the edge of the desert would have to tap another source of water **:** the Owens Valley, several hundred miles away.

> Remember this important selling guideline **:** Know your customer!

By asking readers to pause partway through a sentence, a colon calls special attention to the second half of the statement and avoids the run-together effect that a comma may create.

RUN TOGETHER   After saving for eleven years, the Cranes finally had enough money to get what they wanted **,** a ranch in Wyoming where they could live out their own version of self-reliance.

EDITED   After saving for eleven years, the Cranes finally had enough money to get what they wanted **:** a ranch in Wyoming where they could live out their own version of self-reliance.

A colon can also introduce a more formal series or list.

> Though baseball doesn't reign in England, the British enjoy a wide variety of sports **:** soccer, golf, rugby, cricket, tennis, croquet, polo, and billiards, to name just a few.

> The prosecutor introduced into evidence the following exhibits **:** a nine-inch knife, a piece of clothing belonging to the victim, and a bloodstained rag from the suspect's car.

When a complete sentence follows a colon, you can choose to begin it with either a capital or a lowercase letter. Stick to one style or the other throughout an essay.

34b
:

CORRECT   The airline lost the bag containing my insulated jacket, pants, and boots **: our** long-awaited winter hike in the Rockies was ruined.

ALSO CORRECT   The airline lost the bag containing my insulated jacket, pants, and boots **: Our** long-awaited winter hike in the Rockies was ruined.

When the word group following a colon is not a sentence, begin it with a lowercase letter.

LOWERCASE   The symptoms are as follows **:** **sore** throat, joint pain, fever, and headache.

2 Use a colon to introduce quotations

You can also use a colon as a convenient way to introduce quotations, either short ones that you integrate into your own words or longer ones that you set off from the body of your text (see Chapter 36). The word group before the colon must be a complete sentence; if it is not, use a comma instead.

Ms. Johnson responded to criticism of the sales campaign **:** "For a program launched in the middle of a recession, sales were actually quite strong."

3 Use a colon to separate titles and subtitles

Colons separate the main titles of books, movies, and the like from their subtitles.

Ballroom Dancing for the Absolute Novice **:** *An Introduction*

Freddie's Dead **:** *The Final Nightmare*

Alcohol Policy **:** A Major Problem on Today's Campuses
The title of your own paper should not be italicized.

Colons are also used in separating hours from minutes (10:32); in certain chapter and verse notations, such as those in the Bible (John 8:21–23); and in some reference styles, such as that of the Modern Language Association (MLA) (see Chapter 51).

4 Use a colon to join sentences

A colon is one of the strategies you can use to join complete sentences (main clauses). (See 22b.) It works most effectively when the second sentence sharply focuses, sums up, or illustrates the first.

Hearing a sound like both rushing water and cloth being ripped, she knew it was too late to abandon her house in the canyon **:** The mud slide had begun.

In the middle of a week filled with heavy rain and mud slides, Joel thought of the bushes and grasses now sprouting **:** Next summer the hillside might be on fire.

5 Avoid overuse and misuse of colons

Because colons add emphasis to examples and assertions, you may be tempted to use them often. Don't. Vary your style. Remember that anything is weakened by overuse.

34b

COLON OVERUSED   Suzanne had an obsession for books **:** there were bookshelves in her kitchen, her bathrooms, and even her closets. She read voraciously **:** in the morning, at lunch, after dinner, and late at night. Her house soon turned into a lending library **:** friends and relatives borrowed books by the dozen. And she liked everything **:** classics, mysteries, pulp romances, autobiographies.

34.2

EDITED   Suzanne had an obsession for books. There were bookshelves in her kitchen, her bathrooms, and even her closets. She read voraciously **whenever she could, from morning to** late at night. Her house soon turned into a lending library, friends and relatives borrow**ing** books by the dozen. And she liked everything **:** classics, mysteries, pulp romances, autobiographies.

You can use a colon to introduce a list at the end of a complete sentence. When you introduce a list with a word group other than a complete sentence, however, do not use a colon.

INCORRECT   Her three favorite activities were **:** jogging, volunteering at the local homeless shelter, and cooking.

EDITED   Her three favorite activities **were jogging**, volunteering at the local homeless shelter, and cooking.

EDITED   **She had three favorite activities :** jogging, volunteering at the local homeless shelter, and cooking.

INCORRECT   The room had **:** a fireplace, oak floors, and an oak buffet.

EDITED   The room **had a** fireplace, oak floors, and an oak buffet.

The colon and the words introduced by it should appear only at the end of a sentence, not in the middle.

INCORRECT   Keep in mind these elements **:** introduction, body, and conclusion, while preparing your presentation.

EDITED   Keep in mind these **elements—**introduction, body, and conclusion**—while** preparing your presentation.

34b

Exercise 2

A. Edit the following sentences by deleting misused or overused colons, adding colons where needed, and retaining any colons that are appropriate. You may need to rewrite some sentences to correct overuse or misuse of colons.

EXAMPLE

For the Hirsches͠ retirement meant a trip to France.

1. They prepared for the trip by: first looking for inexpensive hotels in Paris.
2. The Residence Rivoli seemed like a good value clean, centrally located: private bath.
3. Mr. Hirsch, however, wanted to splurge: He argued that an upper-bracket hotel would be so much more enjoyable: a shining marble bath, plush dining room, and elegant meals. There would be parking as well: essential for anyone with a car.
4. But Mrs. Hirsch wasn't impressed: the expensive hotels would be comfortable, but she wanted atmosphere: and small, charming hotels would have that in abundance.
5. Finally, they reached a compromise; they would: stay in a chateau near the Loire, which would be cheaper than a fancy Paris hotel but afford plenty of atmosphere. Then they could: drive into Paris; enjoy the sights; and have a peaceful night: all without driving more than an hour or so each way.

B. Share your edited versions of the sentences in Exercise 2A with a group of classmates. For each sentence, choose one version the group considers both correct and effective. Then share your chosen sentences with other groups in order to see how often you have made similar and different choices.

34b

CHAPTER 35

APOSTROPHES

Like the dot above the *i*, the apostrophe may seem trivial. But without the help of apostrophes, your readers would stumble over your sentences and might have to reread them to figure out what you're saying. Misplaced apostrophes are also distracting.

MISUSED OR LEFT OUT   James horse cant canter, but two months rest and his leg's will heal, and then well see him in race's at Blueberry Down's again.

No doubt you had difficulty reading this sentence. You weren't sure which words were possessives, which were contractions, and which were plurals; the omitted and misplaced apostrophes misled you into putting some words into the wrong categories. Try reading it again.

CORRECTED   **James's** horse **can't** canter, but two **months'** rest and his **legs** will heal, and then **we'll** see him in **races** at Blueberry **Downs** again.

Apostrophe use seems complicated, but the correct use of apostrophes eventually becomes second nature.

35a
'
∨

35a Using apostrophes to mark possession

A noun that expresses ownership is said to be a **possessive noun**. In writing, you must mark possessive nouns to distinguish them from plurals. In the phrase *the cats meow*, for example, a reader will assume that *cats* is plural and *meow* is a verb, and will expect certain kinds of structures to follow (such as *all night* or *in the house*), to complete the sentence.

APOSTROPHE MISSING	The **cat s** meow is becoming fainter.
CORRECTED	The **cat's** meow is becoming fainter.

Without a way of distinguishing between the plural and the possessive in writing, readers would be misled and frustrated by many such constructions.

1 Add an apostrophe plus -*s* to mark possession in singular nouns

In general, when you write a singular possessive noun, you will follow it with an apostrophe plus -*s*.

Bill's coat

the dog's collar

New Mexico's taxes

When a noun ends with -*s*, though, showing possession may be tricky. Writers follow two different conventions in such circumstances (and editors will usually adopt one of these and stick to it).

1. Add an apostrophe and another -*s*, just as you would do with any other noun. This is the more common and preferred method.

   Chris's car   Elliott Ness's next move

2. Alternatively, simply add an apostrophe to the final -*s*.

   Chris' car   Elliott Ness' next move

For nouns ending in -*s*, choose one of these conventions and stick to it throughout an essay.

INCONSISTENT	After driving closer to the **lioness'** cub, we discovered that **Hess's** camera had no film.
EDITED	After driving closer to the **lioness's** cub, we discovered that **Hess's** camera had no film.

To avoid the awkward sound of possessives for nouns ending in -*s* ("the bass's solo part," "the pass's success"), try revising the construction ("the part of the solo bass," "the success of the pass").

When creating possessives from proper names ending with -*s*, which can sound awkward when pronounced ("Hodges-es"), you can indicate the typical pronunciation (with only one -*s* sound) by using only the apostrophe (Hodges').

35a
⌄

Be careful with personal pronouns. You may be tempted to add an apostrophe plus -s to these, but they're already possessive.

INCORRECT   If the car was **your's**, why did you tell Jose that it was Lida's and then take **her's** and dent **it's** fender?

EDITED   If the car was **yours**, why did you tell Jose that it was Lida's and then take **hers** and dent **its** fender?

Be especially wary of confusing *it's* and *its*. Practice expanding the contraction *it's* (*it* + *is*) whenever you use it in writing, and you'll locate such slips more easily.

DRAFT   **Its** not the muffler shop employees who were responsible for the fraud, but **its** managers.

EXPANDED   **It is** not the muffler shop employees who were responsible for the fraud, but **it is** managers.

EDITED   **It's** not the muffler shop employees who were responsible for the fraud, but **its** managers.

2 Add an apostrophe to mark possession in plural nouns

Most English nouns end in -s or -es in the plural. When you want to make a plural noun possessive, simply add an apostrophe after the -s.

PLURAL POSSESSIVE   The **Solomons'** house had its lead paint removed.

PLURAL POSSESSIVE   The **roses'** petals had begun to wither.

35.1

Some irregular nouns form their plurals differently (*mice, children, fish*). In these cases, the word will be plural without ending in -s or -es. Mark possession by adding an apostrophe plus -s, even if the word does not change in the plural (*deer/deer, fish/fish*).

IRREGULAR PLURAL   The livestock show included several **oxen**.

PLURAL POSSESSIVE   The livestock show featured the **oxen's** plowing abilities.

Even though third person singular verbs end in -s, remember that these are not possessive nouns, so they don't require an apostrophe.

INCORRECT   The *Enterprise* **speed's** out of the galaxy with the Klingons in hot pursuit.

EDITED   The *Enterprise* **speeds** out of the galaxy with the Klingons in hot pursuit.

35a

3 Add an apostrophe plus -*s* or an apostrophe to only the last word in a noun phrase

Hyphenated and **multiple-word nouns** are becoming increasingly common in English. As a general rule, treat the entire noun phrase as a single unit, marking possession on the last word.

HYPHENATED
NOUN

My **father-in-law'** s library is extensive.

MULTIPLE-WORD
NOUN

The **union leaders'** negotiations fell through at the last minute.

When you use a compound noun phrase (two or more nouns connected by *and* or *or*) as a possessive, you'll need to decide whether these nouns function as separate items or as a single unit.

SEPARATE ITEMS

Billy' s and **Harold'** s lawyers were ruthless.

READER'S REACTION: Billy must have one lawyer and Harold another, since the possessive is marked on both.

SINGLE UNIT

Billy and Harold' s lawyers were ruthless.

READER'S REACTION: Billy and Harold must have shared the same team of lawyers, since the entire noun phrase is marked as possessive.

Exercise 1

A. Edit the possessive forms in the following sentences so that each uses possessive apostrophes correctly. You may also have to add or move apostrophes, but do not change any correct forms.

EXAMPLE

France longest river, the Loire, has its source in Vivarais and winds its way some six hundred miles to the Atlantic.

1. The rivers name is especially associated with the many chateaux that line its bank's.
2. Serious sightseers visits to the Loire Valley should include tours of several of this regions beautiful castles.
3. The Loires reputation is also founded on its renowned cuisine and its sophisticated wines.
4. Barton and Jone's wine import businesses have flourished in the United States ever since Jones came up with the companys award-winning advertising campaign.
5. Several other companies have found an eager market for Frances excellent wine's.

B. In a small group, compare your corrections to Exercise 1A, and discuss any especially difficult cases.

35b Using apostrophes to mark contractions and omissions

You can use the apostrophe to indicate omission of one or more letters when two words are brought together to form a **contraction**. Contractions suggest an informal style to which some academic, work, or professional readers may object. When in doubt, err on the side of formality.

For those times when you do want to use contractions, follow a simple rule: learn exactly where the apostrophe goes. Most contractions are so common that you've already memorized them. But you still may inadvertently omit apostrophes from even simple words. For example, perhaps you've written *your* (a possessive pronoun) when you really meant *you're* (*you are*).

1 Use an apostrophe to contract a verb form

You can contract pronouns and verbs into a single unit by "splicing" them, eliminating the first part of the verb and substituting an apostrophe. Use the following chart to check your work.

it's	=	it	+	is
who's	=	who	+	is
they're	=	they	+	are
can't	=	can	+	not
you'll	=	you	+	will
you're	=	you	+	are

You can also splice nouns followed by *is.* Avoid such forms in most formal writing.

INFORMAL   **Shoshana's** going to the ballet, but her **seat's** in the very last row of the theater, and **she's** concerned that **she'll** miss the action.

MORE FORMAL   **Shoshana is** going to the ballet, but her **seat is** in the very last row of the theater, and **she is** concerned that **she will** miss the action.

Edit your papers *very* carefully for contractions before turning them in. Take note of these often-confused forms.

they're	=	they + are
there	=	an adverb
their	=	a pronoun
you're	=	you + are
your	=	a possessive pronoun
who's	=	who + is
whose	=	a possessive pronoun
it's	=	it + is
its	=	a possessive pronoun

2 Use an apostrophe to mark plural letters

When you want to make individual letters plural, add an apostrophe plus -*s*.

Mind your **p's and q's**.

The **x's** mark the spots.

You can omit the apostrophe in the plurals of numbers.

I'll take two size **5s** and two size **7s**.

They walked out in **twos** and **threes**.

The apostrophe is often omitted from the plural form of abbreviations, especially if it runs the risk of making the word look like a possessive. "I took all my freshman courses from **TAs**" might be just as acceptable as "**TA's**" because the abbreviation is capitalized.

3 Use an apostrophe to abbreviate a year

You can abbreviate years by omitting the first two numbers of the century as long as the century is understood by your reader. Such contractions represent informal usage.

INFORMAL   Sam has an ⁹85 Johnson class M sixteen-foot sailboat for sale.

UNCLEAR   Victorian details on houses in our neighborhood remained popular throughout the ⁹90s.

READER'S REACTION: **Does this mean the 1890s (in the Victorian period)? I'm confused.**

EDITED   Victorian details on houses in our neighborhood remained popular throughout the **1990s**.

4 Use an apostrophe to show colloquial pronunciation

When quoting people, you can use apostrophes to indicate certain omissions and other features of colloquial speech and dialects.

DIALECT   I'm **a-goin**⁹ to the post office first **an**⁹ then home.

Exercise 2

A. The following paragraph contains sentences with some contracted words that require apostrophes and some "lookalikes" that do not. All these words appear in italics. Insert apostrophes where they belong.

35.2

Many medical scholars believe that the age of molecular biology *didnt* really begin until April 1953 when Watson and Crick's article on the double helix appeared in a scientific journal. These researchers *werent* sure at that time how influential their ideas would become. *Its* generally thought, for example, that if several important researchers *hadnt* immediately seen the underlying brilliance of the double helix, the whole idea *wouldnt* have gained such a quick following. "*Your* basic educator," Professor Ewell Samuels asserts, "*couldnt* have seen beyond what was already a given in biology. *Its* when *youre* presented with many scholars *whose* ideas agree that things really begin to happen. *Whos* going to argue with a whole field jumping on the bandwagon of a new theory?"

35b

B. In a small group, compare your corrections to the passage in Exercise 2A. After reaching agreement on which cases are actual errors, try to decide as a group which contractions in the passage, if any, are too informal. Would you use no contractions in this passage? Some?

CHAPTER 36

QUOTATION MARKS

You learn about some of the many uses for quotation marks almost as soon as you begin to read.

> The three soldiers went on to the house of Albert and Louise.
>
> **"**Could you spare a bit of food? And have you some corner where we could sleep for the night?**"**
>
> **"**Oh no,**"** said Albert. **"**We gave all we could spare to soldiers who came before you.**"**
>
> **"**Our beds are full,**"** said Louise.
>
> —Marcia Brown, *Stone Soup*

And when you start reading about pets, you encounter some other uses.

> Whereas no reptile alive today can be considered aerial, we do come close with the Asian genus of **"**flying dragons,**"** *Draco.*
>
> —Robert G. Sprackland, Jr., *All About Lizards*

36a
" "

You use quotation marks in still other ways when you incorporate other people's words and ideas in your writing.

> As Ruth Macklin points out in *Mortal Choices,* however, **"**many state laws now permit involuntary hospitalization of mental patients only if they are judged dangerous to themselves or others.**"**

Quotation marks have many important roles, so keeping track of the various conventions for their use is both difficult and necessary.

36a Marking quotations

Use quotation marks whenever you quote someone else's words. Quotation marks tell readers which words are someone else's (and which words

466

are yours). Quoted material can make your writing lively and interesting while providing explanation and support for your ideas.

To use quotation marks effectively and correctly, you need to know whether you are quoting words directly or indirectly, on their own or within another quotation.

1 Direct quotations

Whenever you quote someone directly, use double quotation marks (" ") both before and after the quotation—unless the quotation is long or needs special emphasis (see 36b). Make sure that the words within the quotation marks are the exact spoken or written words of your source.

DIRECT QUOTATION (SPOKEN)
"The loon can stay beneath the water for several minutes," the park ranger told us as we walked along the shore.

DIRECT QUOTATION (WRITTEN)
Samuel Gross has written that "every generation looks with scorn upon its offspring's own developing culture."

As you edit, check that you have placed quotation marks around all directly quoted material.

QUOTATION NOT FULLY MARKED
"Had it not been for the flight navigator," the pilot said, we wouldn't have been able to make the emergency landing.

READER'S REACTION: **The second part of the sentence doesn't have any quotation marks, so at first I didn't notice that it was also something the pilot said.**

EDITED
"Had it not been for the flight navigator," the pilot said, "we wouldn't have been able to make the emergency landing."

Make sure you use quotation marks within a sentence to separate quoted material from the words you use to introduce or comment on it. This is an especially important practice when your words interrupt a quotation.

QUOTATION MARKS MISSING
"I'm grateful, too, commented one passenger dryly, though I would have gladly missed the whole experience."

READER'S REACTION: **"Commented one passenger dryly" seems like part of the quotation.**

EDITED
"I'm grateful, too," commented one passenger dryly, "though I would have gladly missed the whole experience."

36a
" "

2 Indirect quotations

Whenever you **paraphrase** or **summarize** someone else's speaking or writing, do not use quotation marks. Reserve the marks for cases when you quote someone's words exactly.

INDIRECT QUOTE (PARAPHRASE)
The pilot told us that if it hadn't been for the flight navigator, the plane would not have made a safe landing.

INDIRECT QUOTE (SUMMARY)
Samuel Preston believes that after just one generation, the social consequences of a major war have almost completely vanished.

3 Quotations inside quotations

Whenever a direct quotation contains another quotation, use single quotation marks (' ') for the inside quotation and double quotation marks (" ") for the one enclosing it.

> Goddio became interested in searching for the sunken ship *San Diego* after reading an account by De Morga who "wrote of a struggle 'obstinately and bitterly waged on both sides so that it lasted more than six hours,' until the pounding of the battle caused his ship to 'bust asunder at the bows.'"

Note how the comma is placed inside the single quotation marks and the period is inside both the single and double quotation marks. (See 33h.)

36b Using block quotations

When you quote more than four typed lines of prose, you should use a **block quotation** rather than quotation marks. To create a block quotation, begin on a new line after the sentence preceding the quotation, indent ten spaces (or one inch on a word processor), and present the quotation double-spaced without quotation marks. Do not indent the opening line of the quotation if you are quoting only one paragraph or part of a paragraph.

> According to Postman, we can no longer ignore the profound effects of technology on all aspects of American life:
>
> > To be unaware that a technology comes equipped with a program for social change, to maintain that technology is neutral, to make the assumption that technology is always a friend to culture is, at this late hour, stupidity plain and simple.

36b
" "

In a longer quotation, indent three spaces (or one-fourth inch) for the first line of each full paragraph. In addition, include any quotation marks that appear within the original, but do not add any at the beginning or end of the block quotation.

> Clifford Geertz's discussion of cockfights on the island of Bali illustrates the personal, almost informal tone of much contemporary anthropology:
>
> > My wife and I were still very much in the gust-of-wind stage, a most frustrating, and even, as you soon begin to doubt whether you are really real after all, unnerving one, when, ten days or so after our arrival, a large cockfight was held in the public square to raise money for a new school.
> >
> > Now, a few special occasions aside, cockfights are illegal in Bali under the Republic (as, for not altogether unrelated reasons, they were under the Dutch), largely as a result of the pretensions to puritanism radical nationalism tends to bring with it. The elite, which is not itself so very puritan, worries about the poor, ignorant peasant gambling all his money away, about what foreigners will think, about the waste of time better devoted to building up the country. It sees cockfighting as "primitive," "backward," "unprogressive," and generally unbecoming an ambitious nation. And, as with those other embarrassments--opium smoking, begging, or uncovered breasts--it seeks, rather unsystematically, to put a stop to it.
> >
> > —Clifford Geertz, "Deep Play: Notes on the Balinese Cockfight."

36b
" "

(See 49b for a discussion of parenthetical documentation with block quotations; see 34b-3 for the use of colons to introduce block quotations.)

When you are quoting more than three lines of verse, present them in a block quotation, beginning on the next line after an introductory sentence and indented ten spaces from the left margin. If the verse contains any quotation marks, include them, but do not add any of your own at the beginning and end of the quotation.

> Donald Hall also uses lines of uneven length and varying rhythm in his poem "The Black-Faced Sheep."
>
> > If one of you found a gap in a stone wall,
> > the rest of you--rams, ewes, bucks, wethers, lambs;

mothers and daughters, old grandfather-father,
cousins and aunts, small bleating sons--
followed onward, stupid
as sheep, wherever
your leader's sheep-brain wandered to.
My grandfather spent all day searching the valley
and edges of Ragged Mountain,
calling **"**Ke-<u>day</u>!**"** as if he brought you salt,
"Ke-<u>day</u>! Ke-<u>day</u>!**"**

36c Writing dialogue

When writing dialogue, use the conventions for direct quotations (see 36a). Whenever a new person speaks, indent as if you're beginning a new paragraph, and begin with new quotation marks.

36.1

Finally the old man woke.

"Don't sit up,**"** the boy said. **"**Drink this.**"** He poured some coffee in a glass.

The old man took it and drank it.

"They beat me, Manolin,**"** he said. **"**They truly beat me.**"**

"*He* didn't beat you. Not the fish.**"**

"No. Truly. It was afterwards.**"**

—Ernest Hemingway, *The Old Man and the Sea*

36c
" "

DID YOU KNOW?

The most common way to quote someone's words directly is by enclosing the words with quotation marks. Writers in the past and some contemporary writers striving for special effects have used other devices to mark the start of quoted speech. For example, the King James version of the Bible uses no quotation marks, even though dozens of people are quoted throughout its pages. Instead, each quotation is introduced with a comma and starts with a capital letter:

Then cried a wise woman out of the city, Hear, hear; say, I pray you, unto Jo'ab, Come near hither, that I may speak with thee.

—2 Samuel 20:16

Other devices, including colons and semicolons, can be used for introducing quoted speech. These devices are rare, but you may encounter them in your reading.

When a character in a written dialogue speaks for more than one paragraph with no interruption, begin each new paragraph with quotation marks, but don't end with them. End only the *last* paragraph with quotation marks.

CORRECT

❝And then that imbecile crowd down on the deck started their little fun, and I could see nothing more for smoke.

❝The brown current ran swiftly out of the heart of darkness, bearing us down towards the sea with twice the speed of our upward progress. [. . .]❞

—JOSEPH CONRAD, *Heart of Darkness*

36d Labeling titles of short works

You should use quotation marks to enclose titles of short works, such as articles, essays, stories, songs, and short poems; parts of a larger work or series, such as chapters in a book, episodes in a television series, or sections of a musical work; and unpublished works, such as doctoral dissertations or speeches.

QUOTATION MARKS WITH TITLES

ARTICLES AND STORIES

"TV Gets Blame for Poor Reading"	newspaper article
"A Political Identity Crisis"	magazine article
"The Idea of the Family in the Middle East"	chapter in book
"Baba Yaga and the Brave Youth"	story
"The Rise of Germism"	essay

POEMS AND SONGS

"A Woman Cutting Celery"	short poem
"Evening" (from *Pippa Passes*)	section of a long poem
"On the Road Again"	song

EPISODES AND PARTS OF LONGER WORKS

"All Day Long"	episode of a TV series
"All We Like Sheep" (from Handel's *Messiah*)	section of a long musical work

UNPUBLISHED WORKS

"Renaissance Men—and Women"	unpublished lecture
"Sources of the Ballads in Bishop Percy's Folio Manuscript"	unpublished dissertation

36d
❝ ❞

Never put the title of your own paper in quotation marks. This is a common mistake that irritates many teachers. If your title contains quoted material, place that material, not the entire title, in quotation marks.

INCORRECT   "The Theme of the Life Voyage in Crane's 'Open Boat' "

EDITED   The Theme of the Life Voyage in Crane's "Open Boat"

36e Indicating special meanings of words and phrases

You can use quotation marks to set off words and phrases you are using in a special sense or to indicate terms that are part of a technical vocabulary or that are unusual in some way. In using quotation marks to call attention to words and phrases, remember an important principle: Go lightly to avoid distracting readers with too many highlighted words.

36.2

Most disciplines use a host of specialized words that readers *within* the discipline readily recognize. If you are writing for a general audience, however, consider calling attention to specialized terms and phrases by setting them off with quotation marks. Quotation marks can also help you highlight a term you are defining. (Italics can be used for this purpose as well; see 40a-4.)

> The phenomenon that draws each person into the crowd's irrational and often destructive and confrontational behavior is known among social psychologists as "crowd contagion."
>
> The term "FSBO" (sometimes actually pronounced as "fizbo") is generally used in the real estate industry to refer to a home that is "for sale by owner."

When deciding whether to use quotation marks to set off specialized terms, ask yourself whether the term is likely to be known to your intended readers. Ask also whether the term is unusual enough to require highlighting or will seem clear to readers. In the following sentence, for example, a well-known writer includes quotation marks that most readers will probably consider unnecessary.

UNNECESSARY
The number of these folds varies from individual to individual and each adult has a characteristic "frown pattern" of one, two, three or four lines.

—DESMOND MORRIS, *Body Watching*

READER'S REACTION: I have no trouble figuring out what a frown pattern is, so for me the quotation marks make the sentence appear cluttered.

Clichés and idioms, perhaps because they seem informal or slang-like, often fool writers into placing them in quotation marks. Doing so, however, only calls more attention to their presence, further weakening the prose. Instead of placing such expressions in quotation marks, simply replace them with stronger words and phrases.

Exercise 1

A. Add quotation marks to the following passage as appropriate.

The shame of illiteracy—or so Robert Cullany puts it—affects millions of adults in the United States alone, but the problem is not nearly as prevalent as innumeracy, Cullany's term that means being unable to use numbers. Cullany writes, illiteracy and innumeracy are a national blight on our intellectual landscape, and cannot be tolerated. He also points out that they cripple our productivity, lead to familial dysfunction (poor family structures), and deny people the ability to become what Cullany calls self-learners. The ALVC, or Adult Literacy Volunteer Corps, is made up of dedicated people who believe they can help this so-called mind plague.

B. Working in a small group, share your edited versions of the passage in Exercise 1A. Which quotation marks did you all agree on? Which ones did members of your group miss or disagree on?

36f Indicating irony, sarcasm, and authorial distance

You can—*sparingly*—use quotation marks to indicate irony or sarcasm, or to show a reader that you don't "lay claim" to a specific term or expression.

36f
" "

To the people who oppose animal rights, the suffering of helpless animals is somehow justified by the "great medical advances" that are encouraged by what they view as "legitimate research" on animals.

This strategy is easy to misuse or overuse, and careful word choice is generally a more effective way of conveying disapproval (see 29a-1 and 2).

Exercise 2

A. Edit the following passage by adding or deleting quotation marks as appropriate. Leave in place any quotation marks that are correctly used.

On April 12, 1633, Galileo was interrogated by the Inquisitor for the Holy Roman and Universal Inquisition. The focus was Galileo's book, the "*Dialogue on the Great World Systems*," in which he posited the theory of a "spinning" earth that "circulated" around the sun. The theory itself was "bad" enough given the Pope's "beliefs," but one of the "characters" in the book's "dialogue" was cast as a "simpleton," and the Pope thought that perhaps it referred to him because he didn't go along with Galileo's "theory." At one point, the Inquisitor asked Galileo, "Did you obtain permission to write the book? To which Galileo replied, I did not seek permission to write this book because I consider that I did not disobey the instruction I had been given. "Did you disclose the Sacred Congregation's demands when you printed the book?" asked the Inquisitor. "I said nothing, Galileo replied, when I sought permission to publish, not having in the book either held or defended opinion. In the end, "Galileo" had to retract his "book," and was also shown instruments of torture "as if" they were going to be used—a "scare tactic," to be sure.

—Adapted from Jacob Bronowski, *The Ascent of Man*

B. Working in a small group, share your edited versions of the passage in Exercise 2A. Discuss each of the changes, and note any that gave you trouble. Indicate whether all group members agreed about each change.

36f
66 99

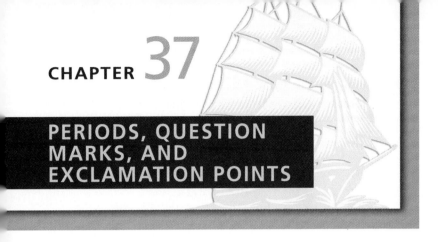

CHAPTER 37

PERIODS, QUESTION MARKS, AND EXCLAMATION POINTS

When you speak, you mark boundaries between sentences with changes in pitch or with pauses of various lengths. When you write, however, you must mark these divisions with visual symbols because your reader can't "hear" a rising pitch in a word or a pause between sentences. When you want to mark the end of a sentence, you will use one of three symbols: a period, a question mark, or an exclamation point.

37a Using periods

Use a period when you want to mark the end of a sentence. A sentence is like a train, sometimes moving directly from one location to another, sometimes taking a few structural diversions before completing its journey. For each sentence, a period marks the end of the line. The period can also be used in abbreviations.

1 End a sentence with a period

No matter how long or complicated, all sentences that are *statements* must end with periods. However, sometimes a sentence will contain embedded clauses that appear to be something other than statements. Use a period to end a sentence when the main, or "outer," sentence is a statement.

INCORRECT   Ten-year-old Naomi affectionately kissed her little brother on the forehead but wondered whether he really knew that she was sorry for startling him**?**

> READER'S REACTION: **The sentence as a whole is a statement; the question in the second half is being reported in the sentence, but the sentence doesn't ask the question.**

EDITED   Ten-year-old Naomi affectionately kissed her little brother on the forehead but wondered whether he really knew that she was sorry for startling him•

2 Use periods in abbreviations

Periods are also used to punctuate abbreviations and to mark decimal points in numbers. Most abbreviations require periods to let the reader know that something has been eliminated from the word or term.

Dr.	Mrs.	Ms.	Ph.D.
pp.	in.	abbr. (for *abbreviation*)	
a.m. (or A.M.)		B.C. (or B.C.E.)	

Many common abbreviations, including *a.m.* and *p.m.*, come from Latin, and, for brevity, have been "permanently" shortened (it would seem odd to spell out *a.m.* and *p.m.* as *ante meridiem* and *post meridiem*).

Some abbreviations, especially acronyms (see 43a), may not require periods at all. When the entire term is capitalized, periods are generally not used (NASA, EU, SALT). Use of periods in abbreviations varies considerably. When in doubt, use the preferred choice in a dictionary. Remember too that some academic disciplines have their own styles for abbreviations. (See Chapters 51–54.)

When an abbreviation that requires a period occurs at the *end* of a sentence, that period will also end the sentence.

CORRECT   Before he became a freelance writer, Richard Rodriguez earned a Ph.D.

If the abbreviated word occurs in the *middle* of a sentence, the period may be followed by another punctuation mark, such as a comma, dash, colon, or semicolon.

INCORRECT   Officials from the paper industry testified until **10 p.m,** well before the meeting adjourned.

EDITED   Officials from the paper industry testified until **10 p.m.,** well before the meeting adjourned.

37a

Exercise 1

37.1

Edit the following sentences so that periods are used correctly, adding or omitting punctuation as appropriate.

EXAMPLE
Every two years the French department at St. Joseph's College organizes a group trip to a foreign country.

1. On our trip to France, we visited the medieval city of Carcassonne

2. As we approached the inner city, which was surrounded by high walls and a real moat, we wondered whether we were still in the twentieth century?
3. "Have we fallen into a time warp or something" Trish said?
4. As we climbed up to the ramparts at 10 p.m, we decided that the experience was almost as good as watching a N.A.S.A. space shuttle launch.
5. Mr Siefert, the hotel manager, told us that the Bastille Day fireworks would begin at 9:30 p.m.

DID YOU KNOW?

The use of periods in pronounceable acronyms often follows a pattern of change. The common word *laser* was originally an acronym meaning "*l*ight *a*mplification by *s*timulated *e*mission of *r*adiation." The abbreviation process began with periods separating the capital letters designating each word: *L.A.S.E.R.* Soon the periods disappeared, yielding *LASER*. Then the capital letters disappeared, though in some contexts the first letter may still have been capitalized. Finally, the term became a common, lowercase, pronounceable word, which has even been clipped into the verb *to lase*. Similar processes appear to have happened for other pronounceable acronyms, including *scuba* (*s*elf-contained *u*nderwater *b*reathing *a*pparatus), *TV*, and *telex*.

37b Using question marks

A question mark indicates that something has been asked, either directly or hypothetically.

37b
?

1 End a direct question with a question mark

Always end a direct question with a question mark.

DIRECT   When is the train leaving?

DIRECT   Considering all the attention given in the media to the issue of homestead tax breaks, why aren't more homeowners filing for the exclusion?

When a sentence (like the preceding example) has more than one clause, the main clause will usually determine the proper punctuation. Occasionally you may embed a direct question within an outer statement, generally using parentheses to set off the embedded question.

EMBEDDED   The telephone repair technician arrived only after the electricians had removed the power lines (did they pose a danger?) and disconnected the service box.

End **indirect questions** with a period. These are sentences whose main clause is a statement and whose embedded clause asks a question.

INDIRECT   Phil wondered whether to support the department's proposal to create a new program.

INDIRECT   Carlos asked if he could help out on the bid for the highway project.

When you present the exact words, your quotation is *direct* rather than *indirect*, and you need to include the question mark.

QUOTED   It was Laitan who asked, "Why is the temperature in the solution rising so quickly?"

2 Watch for other uses of question marks

Question marks may appear in writing for more specialized reasons. In various kinds of informational writing, for example, a question mark may signal a date or other fact that is uncertain or that has been questioned.

David Robert Styles, 1632?–1676

Meadville, pop. 2,330?

Occasionally writers will call attention to or mock other people's statements by including a parenthetical question mark. Sometimes this may come from a genuine doubt or lack of information; more often it's a device for sarcasm.

PARENTHETICAL   The veterinarian informed us that our Siamese cat had contracted a rare (?) ailment.

SARCASTIC   We dispute R & D's finding that the lubricant burns off (?) under high heat.

Such a use of question marks is usually colloquial or informal; in general, try to find other ways to convey the same message in academic writing.

37b
?

Unless you're writing very informally (in a note to a friend, for example), avoid using more than one question mark for emphasis or combining question marks and exclamation points.

INAPPROPRIATE   Can you believe they arrested him for parking in front of the building**?!** How can they do that**?????**

EDITED   Can you believe they arrested him for parking in front of the building**?** How can they do that**?**

Exercise 2

A. Edit the following passage by removing any inappropriate question marks or adding any that are required.

> Are you bat-phobic. Although bats have been hated and feared for centuries, most species are harmless to humans and beneficial to the environment. In his article "Are We Batty Over Bats," Harlan Sneed wonders whether our destruction of bats is really justified? Should we be smoke-bombing caves that are breeding places for thousands of bats, just because we are afraid of them. Sneed also gives examples of cultures that are contributing to the extinction of bats not through fear but through excessive trapping—for food; they are a delicacy (!?) in some parts of the world. Sneed ends his article with a reminder: "Environmental protection is as much a matter of the way we think as the way we act. Maybe you have never *acted* against your environment but are you entirely inculpable in your thoughts and attitudes."

B. In a small group, compare your edited versions of the passage in Exercise 2A. Create one collaboratively edited version.

37c Using exclamation points

When you use an exclamation point, you make your statement emphatic, alerting your reader to its importance. You can also use exclamation points to indicate commands or, in quotations, words that are shouted.

1 End an emphatic statement with an exclamation point

Exclamation points are often used to end emphatic statements such as commands or warnings.

EMPHATIC   Keep all the camp children away from the precipice**!**

Avoid overusing exclamation points to do the work that should be assigned to strong, carefully chosen words. Treat the exclamation point like a rare and powerful spice: If you don't saturate your text with exclamation points, they will carry much more flavor when you do decide to use them. When you want to make your prose more dramatic, try some revision and add vivid details.

OVERUSED   I couldn't believe it! Andrea and I were face to face with a small black bear! We were terrified! I screamed! Andrea jumped back into the tent and buried herself under her sleeping bag! That left me holding an entire bag of delicious corn chips right under the hungry creature's nose!

REVISED   Suddenly, I began to realize we were not alone. Out of the shadows, just three feet from the front of our tent, appeared the black nose and sharp, glinting teeth of a small black bear.

Also avoid using more than one exclamation point at the end of any sentence. A single exclamation point is worth exactly as much as a hundred.

INCORRECT   The bear was grunting right outside our tent!!!!!

EDITED   The bear was grunting right outside our tent!

2 Watch for other uses of exc]lamation points

37.2

37c
!

Like question marks, exclamation points can be used parenthetically or marginally in casual writing to express dismay, outrage, shock, or strong interest. In more formal contexts, look for other ways to emphasize the word or idea in question.

INAPPROPRIATE   Emergency rescue workers spent several hours (!) trying to reach the stranded toddler.

EDITED   Emergency rescue workers spent several **agonizing** hours trying to reach the stranded toddler.

When you quote people's words directly, you can use exclamation points to indicate emphatic statements or commands.

QUOTED   Halfway to the airport, Sybil suddenly shouted, "Oh, no! We forgot the plane tickets!"

Use exclamation points sparingly and realistically in quotations and dialogue. Few people continue to speak emphatically for very long.

Remember that when you use an exclamation point, you are punctuating the end of your sentence. Don't add another mark, such as a comma, when you write an emphatic sentence within an outer sentence.

INCORRECT   "Stop**!** **,**" yelled Steve.

EDITED   "Stop**!**" yelled Steve.

Exercise 3

A. Edit the following passage by removing or adding exclamation points to make them correct and stylistically acceptable.

> Seventy-five miles (!) from anywhere, Frank's old Buick decided to sputter and stall out on the edge of Route 61. Meanwhile, the temperature had fallen to 16 below!!!! To make matters worse, the wind had whipped up to 30 miles per hour! That's an incredible wind chill of around 75 below zero!!!!! "Hey," yelled Bill, "don't anyone leave this car. If we stay put, maybe the highway patrol will spot us." "Who are you kidding!!??," shouted Frank. "It's 3 a.m.!"

B. In a small group, compare your edited versions of the passage in Exercise 3A. Discuss any differences, and create one collaboratively edited version.

37c
!

CHAPTER 38

SPECIAL PUNCTUATION MARKS

Punctuation symbols—dashes, commas, semicolons, colons, slashes, ellipses, quotation marks, and the like—make up a kind of toolbox for writing. You can use the tools in various ways to change the style and sense of your prose and its effects on your readers. Five "special" punctuation marks—parentheses, brackets, dashes, ellipses, and slashes—can be useful strategies for guiding readers through complex sentences, and for providing emphasis appropriate to your purpose for writing.

38a Using parentheses

Parentheses *enclose* a word, sentence, or clause: you can't use just one. Whatever you write between two parentheses takes on the quality of an aside—something in a "softer" voice than that of the rest of a sentence. Or it becomes information and ideas presented in the background rather than the foreground.

1 Use parentheses to set off words or sentences

With parentheses, you can set off a word, a group of words, an entire sentence, or groups of sentences from the rest of your text. By using parentheses to place some information in the background, you can direct your readers' attention to the main assertions and details in a passage without having to omit worthwhile (though potentially distracting) secondary material.

> **INFORMATION SET OFF WITHIN A SENTENCE**
> Although most of the team always eats a hearty and varied breakfast (if also a little high in fats and cholesterol), Jim feels he performs much better with less food in his stomach. Invariably, this means only one thing: a bowl of Cheerios (without milk).

INFORMATION SET OFF IN A SEPARATE SENTENCE

Consuelo had tried for two years to get a hearing about her immigration status. (Her employer, during this time, had been unsympathetic to her pleas.) Then, in June, she finally received a letter.

Use parentheses sparingly and carefully. Too many parenthetical statements can clutter your sentences, distracting readers and obscuring your main assertions.

DISTRACTING Handico, Inc., decided (early in 1993) to use its waste milling chips (which had been warehoused in Detroit) to manufacture pencils (described as "environmentally friendly") to donate to public schools (which gave the company a tax credit).

CLEAR Early in 1993, Handico, Inc., decided to use its waste milling chips (warehoused in Detroit) to manufacture "environmentally friendly" pencils. These they donated to public schools, resulting in a tax credit for the company.

2 Watch for special uses of parentheses

You can use parentheses to present information that is not part of the structure of a sentence. You can also use parentheses in numbered lists.

NUMBERS AND LISTS Harry's Bookstore has a fax number (349-0934) for (1) ordering books, (2) inquiring about the availability of specific items, or (3) requesting publication information.

3 Punctuate parenthetical statements correctly

Don't use a comma *before* a parenthetical statement placed in the middle of a sentence. *After* the closing parenthesis, use whatever punctuation would normally occur at this point in the sentence if the parenthetical statement were not there.

38a ( )

WITHOUT PARENTHESES If you sign up for Telepick by August 15, you are eligible for one hour of free long-distance calls.

WITH PARENTHESES If you sign up for Telepick by August 15 (and list up to four commonly called numbers), you are eligible for one hour of free long-distance calls.

When a parenthetical statement *inside a sentence* comes at the end of the sentence, always place the sentence's end punctuation *after* the closing parenthesis.

INCORRECT   People on your Telepick list can also call you at the same dis-
            counted rate (as long as they, too, use Coombs Communication
            as their long-distance carrier.)

CORRECT   People on your Telepick list can also call you at the same dis-
            counted rate (as long as they, too, use Coombs Communication
            as their long-distance carrier).

When parentheses enclose an entire freestanding sentence, however, place
the end punctuation *inside* the closing parenthesis.

38.1

CORRECT   You can sign up for Telepick's "Free Hour" program until
            August 10. (This offer does not include international calls.)

38b Using brackets

Use brackets to indicate that you have added words of your own to a
quotation, or to act as parentheses within parentheses.

1 Use brackets for interpolations

Sometimes you need to introduce your own words into a quotation to
help clarify a word or a statement for readers, or to provide important background information. To indicate that the words are your own, and not those
of the writer or speaker being quoted, enclose the **interpolation** in brackets.

INTERPOLATION   My friends Paula and Kent decided to have their wedding on
                a sailboat off Key West. When I asked them if the ceremony
                would take place at a specific place offshore, Kent said, "It's
                a surprise even to us. Captain Sims [the boat's owner] has
                chosen a special place within two hours of Key West."

38b
[ ]

2 Use brackets within parentheses

When you need to include a parenthetical statement *within* a parenthetical statement, use parentheses first, and then use brackets for the inner
statement. Try to limit your use of brackets because they can make your writing seem unnecessarily complex.

You can contact Rick Daggett (Municipal Lumber Council [Violations
Division], Stinson County Municipal Center) to report violations of
the rules governing logging of old-growth trees.

38c Using dashes

You can use dashes, like parentheses, to set off material within a sentence. Dashes call more attention to a word or group of words than parentheses do; use them to create emphasis or indicate a change in tone. Dashes differ in function from hyphens, which are used to connect words or to separate words into parts (see Chapter 40). On typewriters and computers, dashes appear as two unspaced hyphens, with no space before, between, or after them: --. In professional typesetting, the dash is represented by a single line: —.

1 Use dashes for emphasis

Use dashes in pairs to highlight a word or group of words in the middle of a sentence.

MATERIAL SET OFF IN THE MIDDLE
After picking out two pet mice—**one brown with white spots and one white with a brown forehead**—the little boy realized he had only enough money to buy one of them.

When the word or words you want to emphasize appear at the *end* of a sentence, however, use one dash to introduce the material. Conclude with the appropriate end punctuation for the sentence.

MATERIAL SET OFF AT THE END
Heartbroken at the thought that someone might buy the mouse, the boy offered his six quarters as a deposit—**along with his Mickey Mouse watch and his school notebook**.

You can use dashes to create contrasts in tone or structure within a sentence. When you use dashes, you don't need to make the material within them part of the grammatical structure of the sentence or make it consistent in tone with the rest of the sentence. Inside the following sentence, for example, the dashes enclose another complete sentence.

FULL SENTENCE SET OFF
The mice—**by this time they were fully domesticated**—frolicked in the cedar chips.

Remember that dashes call attention to the material within them. In contrast, enclosing material in commas provides no real emphasis, and using parentheses de-emphasizes the enclosed material.

38c
—

STRONG EMPHASIS
When the boy—**clutching three weeks' allowance**—returned to the store, it had already closed.

NO SPECIAL EMPHASIS
When the boy, **clutching three weeks' allowance,** returned to the store, it had already closed.

LOSS OF EMPHASIS
When the boy **(clutching three weeks' allowance)** returned to the store, it had already closed.

2 Use dashes to set off introductory and concluding ideas

You can use dashes to set off an idea or a series of items. This is a dramatic way of opening a sentence or calling attention to the assertion it makes.

ITEMS SET OFF IN OPENING
Extended TV hours, better meals, and more physical exercise— these were the inmates' three major demands for prison reform.

You can also use dashes instead of a (nonemphatic) colon to list a series of items at the *end* of an assertion.

ITEMS SET OFF AT THE END
Charles had learned several ways to forestall the effects of long flights—**drinking lots of water, avoiding alcohol, and moving around the cabin as much as possible during the flight**.

3 Avoid overuse of dashes

The use of dashes can become addictive, resulting in sentences and paragraphs that seem to be clusters of fragmented statements.

OVERUSED   There had been some interest—chiefly by Stockton—in an automated navigation system—a way to track cars by telecommunication and let drivers know if they are going in the right direction—or give them directions.

   READER'S REACTION: **This sentence highlights so many points with dashes that it is hard to tell what the writer considers the most important point.**

MORE EFFECTIVE   There had been some interest, chiefly by Stockton, in an automated navigation system—a way to track cars by telecommunication and let drivers know if they are going in the right direction or give them directions.

38c
—

If you find yourself using too many dashes in your writing, look over a draft and circle the dashes that seem really important—those that help emphasize the key point in an entire section of an essay, for example. Then either replace the other dashes with commas, colons, or parentheses, or create emphasis through word choice and sentence structure. (See Chapter 10 for advice on creating emphasis within sentences.)

Exercise 1

A. Some dashes and parentheses have been added to the following paragraph. Edit the paragraph to make it more effective, deciding which of these punctuation marks should stay and which should be replaced. Change sentence structure and strategy if necessary.

> The next morning—their donkeys carried them—to the site of the excavation. Carter and his assistant—A. R. Callender—had already begun clearing the stairway (again). As more of the doorway was exposed, the seals (of Tutankhamun) could be seen—in addition to those of the royal necropolis. When all sixteen steps had been cleared (and the entire doorway could be seen), Carter got a jolt— holes had been cut into the (upper) part of the door. The damage had been repaired—and bore the seals of the necropolis, but the question remained—had this tomb, too, been pillaged?
> —Metropolitan Museum of Art, *The Treasures of Tutankhamun*

B. Compare your edited version of the passage in Exercise 1A with those created by some of your fellow students. Remember that there will be no single—or "most correct"—answer. Compare the relative strengths and weaknesses of each version.

38d Using ellipses

The **ellipsis** (from Greek *elleipsis*, "an omission") is a series of three *spaced* periods telling your reader that something has been left out. You will use ellipses chiefly for two purposes: to omit parts of a quotation and to suggest gaps in a sentence, either in dialogue or in quoted speech.

1 Place and space ellipses correctly

Correct placement and spacing of ellipses can be tricky. The following guidelines should cover most cases.

- Use three spaced periods • • • for ellipses within a single sentence. If you are preparing a paper using Modern Language Association Style

(MLA), place brackets around the ellipsis marks $\big[\, \bullet \; \bullet \; \bullet \,\big]$ as discussed in Chapter 51.

- Use a period before an ellipsis that falls at the end of a sentence $\bullet$ $\bullet$ $\bullet$
- Leave a space before the first period $\bullet$ $\bullet$ $\bullet$ and after the last period of all ellipses.
- When another punctuation mark occurs before omitted words, you can eliminate it if it is not necessary to the grammar of the sentence, but you must retain it if it is necessary to the grammar.

EXAMPLE   The newspapers reported that "Officer Hatt testified solemnly , $\bullet$ $\bullet$ $\bullet$ often staring at his hands and slowly shaking his head."

2 Use ellipses in quotations with omitted words

Ellipses are especially useful when you want to quote some (but not all) words in a passage. You may wish to omit the material because it doesn't offer relevant ideas or information, because it makes the quotation too long for your purposes, or because you want to "skip" from one part of a long quotation to the next without including everything between. The following examples from a student's paper on sailing show his original draft, from which he wanted to cut the boldfaced sentence in the block quotation, and his edited draft, in which he has used ellipses to do so.

ORIGINAL   Drummond, in his *Complete Guide to Sailing*, blames the instability of the sandbagger on its sail-to-hull ratio:

Extremely fast, sandbaggers were very wide and shallow. They carried an enormous amount of sail area on an expanded rig. **As a result, when they were raced, they carried twenty-five or more bags of sand in the cockpit as ballast. When a boat came about, a crew of husky men quickly shifted the bags of sand to the windward side.** The boats ran from eighteen to twenty-eight feet in length, and carried a bowsprit almost as long as the hull and a main boom that extended ten feet or more beyond the stern.

38d
$\bullet\bullet\bullet$

EDITED   Drummond, in his *Complete Guide to Sailing*, blames the instability of the sandbagger on its sail-to-hull ratio:

Extremely fast, sandbaggers were very wide and shallow. They carried an enormous amount of sail area on an expanded rig $\bullet$ $\bullet$ $\bullet$ The boats ran from eighteen to twenty-eight feet in length, and carried a bowsprit almost as long as the hull and a main boom that extended ten feet or more beyond the stern.

You can also eliminate *parts* of a sentence. When you do so, maintain normal sentence structure and grammatical form; don't just rip out words at random. The following example from a student's interview paper shows the original quotation from his notes; the way he incorporated this into his rough draft (with ellipses); and his corrected, edited version.

ORIGINAL QUOTATION	"We've always played well against Duke. Year before last, we creamed them. Last year their defense fouled us up, but we still won. This year we've got a deep bench. I bet we'll take them to the cleaners, for sure."
INCORRECT DRAFT	When I pressed him to predict the team's performance, Coach Harms paused for a minute, then said with determination, "We've always played well against Duke. Year before last, we creamed them. Last year • • • but we still won • • • we'll take them to the cleaners • • • •
EDITED	When I pressed him to predict his team's performance, Coach Harms paused for a minute, then said with determination, "We've always played well against Duke. Year before last, we creamed them. Last year • • • we still won. This year • • • we'll take them to the cleaners • • • •"

If you omit a line or two of poetry within a block quotation in a paper following MLA style (see Chapter 51), put brackets around a series of spaced periods to show the omission.

3 Use ellipses for other gaps

Occasionally you may want to indicate a pause or a gap in your own writing, not just in quoted material. In fiction and personal narrative, for example, ellipses are often used to show suspense, hesitation, or uncertainty, or to suggest continuing action.

FOR SUSPENSE	When we returned to our campsite, we were stunned. The tent was in a shambles. Our food was strewn everywhere. Our water jug was fifty yards away. Muddy claw marks were everywhere • • • •

38e Using slashes

You will use slashes mainly to indicate alternative forms of words. You can also use slashes in a more specialized way to quote lines of poetry when those lines are not already set off from your text.

1 Use slashes with alternative words

When used to indicate alternative words, the slash translates as "or" or "and." It is a shorthand often used in technical documents and manuals.

Be certain that the **on/off** switch is in the vertical position.

There is no exemption from the Composition **101/102** sequence.

Combinations such as *he/she* and *him/her* are not entirely acceptable in formal writing. Many good alternatives for these combinations are available. (See 32a.) The term *and/or* appears primarily in legal writing, but it can be used in moderation elsewhere. Different fields or professions may have particular functions for the slash or may use the slash in specific terms.

2 Use slashes when quoting lines of poetry

When you quote lines of poetry *within* your text rather than setting off the material in a block quotation, separate the lines of verse with a slash. Type a space before and after the slash.

38.2

The speaker in Sir Philip Sidney's sonnet addresses the moon by saying, "With how sad steps, O Moon, thou climb'st the skies, **/** How silently, and with how wan a face."

Exercise 2

A. Find or create a short paragraph that uses as many of the punctuation marks described in this chapter as possible: parentheses, brackets, dashes, ellipses, and slashes. Choose one example of each case, and explain what purpose it serves in the paragraph.

38e
/

B. Write or type out another version of the paragraph in Exercise 2A, stripped of its special punctuation. Make two copies to exchange with classmates. Ask the members of your group to edit the two copies, which lack parentheses, brackets, dashes, ellipses, and slashes. They should insert these punctuation marks wherever they think the marks are appropriate. Then compare your original and the versions punctuated by your classmates. Decide which marks of punctuation you consider effective and ineffective, and give reasons for your judgments.

Proofreading for Mechanics and Spelling

CHAPTER 39

CAPITALIZATION

Capital letters call attention to themselves and to words containing them. Your readers expect capitalization to signal the start of sentences or to identify specific people, places, and things. Capitalization that follows convention not only makes reading easier but also reflects a general sense that certain people and things deserve the kind of recognition that capital letters can provide. In the passage that follows, notice how hard it is to pay attention to specific details when some capitals have been removed.

> Then, as i cross the state line, i remember a florence, alabama, composer named william christopher handy. After moving to memphis and writing songs about boss crump, beale street, st. james infirmary, and st. louis, he became known as "the father of the blues." Maybe i should turn north. —Hugh Merrill, *The Blues Route*

The general rules for capitalization are easy to remember.

- Use a capital letter at the beginning of a sentence.
- Capitalize proper nouns, proper adjectives, and most words in titles of works.

Specific conventions are often harder to keep in mind, and sometimes you may need to consult this chapter for answers to your questions: Should I capitalize a sentence after a colon? What about the beginning of a sentence within parentheses? When should I use *president* and *President*? How can I recognize when a noun is "proper" and requires capitalization?

39a Using a capital at the beginning of a sentence

Sentences begin with capital letters. This convention applies to regular sentences and sentence fragments used appropriately as partial sentences. (See 21c on partial sentences.)

Two national parks, Yellowstone and Grand Teton, are in Wyoming.
Are camping spots in the parks hard to get in the summer?
Make your reservations early!
No camping without a reservation.

1 Capitalize the opening word in a quoted sentence

When you quote someone else's words or sentences, you will ask, "When should I capitalize within the quotation?" The answer generally depends on the relationship between the main (outer) sentence and the material you are quoting within it.

Capitalize the first word in the quotation when it is a complete sentence or when it begins your own sentence.

COMPLETE
SENTENCE
QUOTED
> Speaking of *Blind Man with a Pistol*, James Lundquist says, "**T**he novel begins with an opening chapter that, without exaggeration, is one of the strangest in American literature."

If you interrupt a quotation with your own words, do not capitalize after the interruption.

QUOTATION
INTERRUPTED
> "**T**he novel," claims James Lundquist, "**b**egins with an opening chapter that, without exaggeration, is one of the strangest in American literature."

Also drop the capitalization if you integrate the quotation into the structure of your own sentence.

INTEGRATED
QUOTATION
> On the other hand, James Lundquist claims that "**t**he novel begins with an opening chapter that, without exaggeration, is one of the strangest in American literature."

If you are quoting only part of someone else's sentence, capitalize the quoted material when you use it to open your sentence but not when you place it in the middle or at the end. (Indicate any changes in capitalization in brackets.)

39a
cap

OPENING
QUOTATION
> "[O]ne of the strangest in American literature" is how Lundquist describes the first chapter.
>
> **The first word is not capitalized in the source, so the writer indicates the change in brackets.**

CONCLUDING
QUOTATION
> James Lundquist overstates his case when he argues that the first chapter remains "**o**ne of the strangest in American literature."

2 Capitalize a freestanding sentence in parentheses

Capitalize the first word of any sentence that stands on its own within parentheses.

FREESTANDING   By this time, the Union forces were split up into nineteen sec-
SENTENCE   tions. (**G**rant was determined to unite them.)

However, when you place a sentence within parentheses (or dashes) inside another sentence, do not begin the enclosed sentence with a capital.

ONE SENTENCE   Saskatchewan's economy depends heavily on farming (**o**ver
INSIDE ANOTHER   half of Canada's wheat crop comes from the province), though oil production and mining have also become important in recent decades.

3 Capitalize the first word of a line of poetry

Lines of poetry generally begin with a capital letter, regardless of where the initial word appears in the "sentence."

> **L**ong since, we pulled brown oak-leaves to the ground
> **I**n a winter of dry trees; we heard the cock
> **S**hout its unplaceable cry, the axe's sound
> **D**elay a moment after the axe's stroke.
>
> —LOUISE BOGAN, "Old Countryside"

For special effect, however, poets sometimes ignore this and other conventions of capitalization.

> **n**ew **h**ampshire explodes into radio primary,
> **n**ewspaper headlines & beer—
> **w**ell-weathered tag-lines from lips of schoolchildren.
> **w**e triumph by not being clear.
>
> —T. R. MAYERS, "(snap)shots"

When you are quoting poetry, follow the author's practice.

39a
cap

39.1

4 Decide whether to capitalize following a colon

If a complete sentence follows a colon, you can choose to capitalize it or put it in lowercase (see 34b on colon use). Since either choice is correct, you might make your decision on the basis of style or emphasis. But be consistent.

CORRECT	The province of New Brunswick is bilingual both by law and in practice: **O**ne-third of the population is French-speaking and the remainder English-speaking.
ALSO CORRECT	The province of New Brunswick is bilingual both by law and in practice: **o**ne-third of the population is French-speaking and the remainder English-speaking.

In general, if the word group following the colon is not a sentence, you do not need a capital letter.

> Foremost among the educational issues in New Brunswick is another problem related to language: **b**ilingualism in the schools.

There are some special cases in which the word group after a colon takes a capital letter even if it is not a complete sentence. If the word group after a colon states a principle or aphorism, for example, use a capital letter.

> Remember this rule as you go through life: **A**lways look on the bright side.

5 Decide whether to capitalize elements in a series or list

You can treat questions in a series or elements in a list in a variety of ways.

Questions in a series. You can choose whether to use capital letters to highlight the opening of each question in a series.

CORRECT	Should we spend our limited campaign funds on television ads? **O**n billboards? **O**n smaller signs and posters? **O**n flyers?
ALSO CORRECT	Should we spend our limited campaign funds on television ads? **o**n billboards? **o**n smaller signs and posters? **o**n flyers?

Stick to one style throughout an essay.

39a
cap

Run-in lists. If the items in a **run-in list** (a list whose items aren't placed on separate lines) are simple, you may use commas to separate them and a lowercase letter for the first word in each item. If the items themselves in a run-in list contain commas or are very complex and lengthy, you may decide to separate them with semicolons.

> In estimating the project's costs, remember that you need to pay for the following: (1) **l**ab facilities, (2) **u**tilities, and (3) **m**easuring equipment.

In estimating the project's costs, remember the following: (1) **l**ab facilities must be rented; (2) **l**ight, heat, and other utilities need to be charged to the project's account; (3) **m**easuring equipment should be leased.

If the list following the colon consists of complete sentences, capitalize the first word of each item.

In estimating the project's costs, remember the following: **F**irst, lab facilities must be rented. **S**econd, light, heat, and other utilities need to be charged to the project's account. **F**inally, measuring equipment should be leased.

Vertical lists. You may choose whether to capitalize the elements in a **vertical list** when they are either words or partial sentences. You must use capitalization with complete sentences, unless they appear in an outline without periods (see 4b on outlining).

CORRECT   When you estimate the project's costs, remember the following:

1. **L**ab facilities
2. **U**tilities
3. **M**easuring equipment

ALSO
CORRECT   When you estimate the project's costs, remember the following:

1. **l**ab facilities
2. **u**tilities
3. **m**easuring equipment

Use the same pattern of capitalization in all the lists in a paper, and make sure the items in each list are parallel in form (see 27d).

39b
cap

DID YOU KNOW?

In other languages, capitalization conventions can be quite different from those for English. In German, for example, nouns and pronouns are capitalized: *Ich werde Sie ihrer Blumen zurückgeben* (I will give you your flowers back). In Spanish, pronouns and the names of days and months are not capitalized: *Almuerzo con ella los lunes* (I lunch with her on Mondays).

39b Using capitals for proper nouns and adjectives

To capitalize a word is to highlight its importance. Readers pay special attention to words naming specific people, places, and things (proper nouns) and to adjectives created from these nouns (proper adjectives). When readers come across the title of a work, they are also aided if you identify this title with capitals.

1 Capitalize proper nouns and adjectives

You should capitalize the names of specific people, places, and things (**proper nouns**) as well as adjectives derived from them (**proper adjectives**).

PROPER NOUNS	PROPER ADJECTIVES
Brazil	Brazilian music
Dickens	Dickensian portrait
Venice	Venetian architecture

An article (*a*, *an*, or *the*) preceding a proper noun or adjective should not be capitalized unless it begins a title or starts a sentence.

All other nouns and adjectives are **common nouns** and **common adjectives**. Do not capitalize them except in special contexts, such as at the beginning of a sentence, in titles of works, or as parts of proper nouns.

COMMON NOUN (LOWERCASE)	PART OF PROPER NOUN (CAPITALIZED)
lake	Lake Jackson
river	Danube River
park	Prospect Park
computer company	Mesa Computer Company

Some company and institutional names include both a proper and a common noun. Both parts are capitalized because together they form a proper name.

proper common	proper common
Sandberg **U**niversity	**R**obinson **C**orporation

People writing documents under the auspices of an institution (for example, a memo to university staff or a corporate annual report) may decide to capitalize the common noun when it is used as a shortened name for the institution.

Sandberg **U**niversity is pleased to announce plans for renovating Smith Hall.

The **U**niversity has contracted with Jacksonville Construction for the project.

If the subject of your paper has a common noun as part of its name, you may wish to follow the same procedure, after first giving the subject's full

39b
cap

name, in order to help your readers readily distinguish references to the subject from more generic uses of the word.

> The Democratic **P**arty has always been the dominant **p**arty in this county. However, recently other political groups have begun to encroach upon the **P**arty's territory.

Sometimes a time period such as a week or season refers to a specific event. In such cases the time period is capitalized because it is part of the name of the event.

PART OF THE EVENT'S NAME
At Bardstown College, **F**all **O**rientation runs from September 3 to 5.

NOT PART OF THE NAME
The **f**all **o**rientation at Bardstown College runs from September 3 to 5.

The following categories should help you recognize words that need to be capitalized.

CAPITALIZATION OF NOUNS AND ADJECTIVES

CAPITALIZED	LOWERCASE
INDIVIDUALS	
President Clinton	the president
Michael Jordan	her boyfriend
Georgia O'Keefe	my teacher's father
RELATIVES	
Aunt Rosa; Uncle Jack	an uncle; my cousin
Mother; Dad	your mother; her dad
GROUPS OF PEOPLE AND LANGUAGES	
Caucasian	black (preferred in general usage)
Japanese	
Hopi	
Negro	
African American	
Russian	
Native American	
TIME PERIODS, HOLIDAYS, AND SEASONS	
Thursday; October	spring; summer; fall; winter
Easter; Ramadan; Yom Kippur; Labor Day	holiday

CAPITALIZED	LOWERCASE
RELIGIONS AND RELATED SUBJECTS	
Judaism, Jews	
Christianity, Christians	
Islam, Muslims	
Catholic	catholic (meaning "universal")
Protestant	
Hinduism	
Buddhist practices	
Talmud; Bible	talmudic; biblical
God; Jesus Christ	a god, goddess; godly
ORGANIZATIONS, INSTITUTIONS, AND MEMBERS	
Chicago Bulls, the Bulls	the team
Democratic Party, Democrat	democratic (referring to democracy)
Heritage Foundation; Conservative Party; Tory	conservative (referring to a political philosophy)
Girl Scout; Boy Scouts of America	the scout
Metropolitan Opera; Cincinnati Symphony	the opera; the string quartet
Rolling Stones	a band
Florida State Police	the police, the state police
Coast Guard; Virginia Board of Ethics	the sailors; the board
House of Commons; U.S. Senate, the Senate	a member of parliament; a senator
Air Line Pilots Association	the union, union member
PLACES, THEIR RESIDENTS, AND GEOGRAPHIC REGIONS	
Malaysia, Malaysian	the country; the citizen
Cape Verde Islands, Cape Verdean	the state; the resident
Tibet, Sino-Tibetan	
Berlin, Berliner	the city; the resident
Erie County; Nassau Avenue	the county; the street
South China Sea; Volga River	the sea; the river
Amazon Basin; Mars	the region; the planet
the Southwest, the East; East Coast	southwest, east southwestern, eastern (directions)
BUILDINGS AND MONUMENTS	
Taj Mahal; Peace Bridge	Jim's garden; our backyard
Tower of London; Busch Stadium	the tower; a stadium
Space Needle; Getty Museum	a landmark; a museum
Piazza Navona; Grant's Tomb	the piazza; her tomb
HISTORICAL PERIODS, EVENTS, AND MOVEMENTS	
Thirty Years' War; Dorr's Rebellion	the war; the rebellion
Algerian Revolution	the revolution

39b
cap

(*continued*)

CAPITALIZATION OF NOUNS AND ADJECTIVES *(Continued)*

CAPITALIZED	LOWERCASE
Ming Dynasty	a dynasty
Romantic period; Impressionism	the period or style
First Great Awakening; Postmodernism	the movement; a trend
Jazz Age; Renaissance	a cultural epoch

ACADEMIC INSTITUTIONS AND COURSES

Auburn University; Utica College	a university
English Department	an English department
Department of Chemistry	chemistry department
Sociology 203; English 101	sociology or English course

VEHICLES

Airbus A300; Pontiac Grand Prix	a passenger plane; my car
J Boat	a sailboat

COMPANY NAMES AND TRADE NAMES

Samsung; Monsanto Chemical	the company; the chemical company
Intel; Fuji Heavy Industries; Xerox	a manufacturer; an employer
Luvs; New Balance; Kleenex; Toblerone; Patagonia	diapers; shoes; tissues; chocolate bar; outdoor equipment

SCIENTIFIC, TECHNICAL, AND MEDICAL TERMS

Big Dipper; Earth (planet)	earth (ground)
Marxism	marxian theory
Heisenberg's uncertainty principle	
Alzheimer's disease; Down syndrome	tuberculosis
organ of Corti	pancreas
Pistacia vera; *Gazella dorcas*	pistachio tree; gazelle

2 Use capitals in titles of works

In titles, you should capitalize the first word, the last word, and all words in between *except* articles (*a*, *an*, and *the*), prepositions under five letters (such as *in*, *of*, and *to*), and conjunctions under five letters (such as *and* or *but*). These rules apply to titles of long works, short works, and parts of works as well as titles for your own papers. If a colon divides the title, capitalize the first word after the colon.

> *The Mill on the Floss*
> "Factory of the Future: A Survey"
> *Reservoir Dogs*
> *Briefing for a Descent into Hell*
> "Politics and the English Language"

Fragile Glory: A Portrait of France and the French
"Just like Romeo and Juliet"
"The Civil Rights Movement: What Good Was It?"
"Sumer Is Icumen In"
Developing a Growth Plan for a Small Retail Business [your own title]

(For the rules governing the use of italics and quotation marks in titles, see 40a and 36d.)

3 Capitalize the pronoun *I* and the interjection *O*

Whenever **I** try to argue with my parents, they make me feel as if **I'm** still a child.

Trust in him, **O** people, and pour out your heart.

Although *oh* would seem to be capitalized by analogy with *O*, convention requires that *oh* remain in lowercase unless it begins a sentence or is capitalized in material you are quoting.

"**O**h dear, no," said the housekeeper.
—WILKIE COLLINS, *The Woman in White*

Exercise

A. Add capitalization wherever necessary in the following sentences. Replace any unnecessary capitals with lowercase letters. Circle the cases that seem the toughest to figure out.

39.2

EXAMPLE
Over the next ten years, ̷india will become an increasingly important
trading partner for ̷north ̷america.

39b
cap

1. Located on a subcontinent in the southern part of asia, the republic of india has a territory of about 1.2 million Square Miles.
2. India's population of almost 800 Million falls into two main groups, dravidians and indo-aryans, which in turn are made up of many other cultural groups.
3. Dravidians live mainly in the south, an area that is dominated geographically by the deccan plateau.
4. The religion of the Majority is hinduism, though other religious groups such as sikhs and muslims are important.
5. Recently, religious conflicts have broken out in the provinces of kashmir and uttar pradesh.

6. Indian History is long and complicated, but in Modern Times it has been dominated by the british rule over the Country and by attempts to escape that rule and found a democratic State.
7. British Rule over most of the country began after the sepoy rebellion of 1857–58.
8. It ended after world war II with the independence movement led by mahatma gandhi.
9. The move toward industrialization has been the main goal of indian leaders since Independence, though this movement has at times been complicated by the problem of overpopulation and by conflicts stemming from the hindu social (or caste) system.
10. The dominant political Party since Independence has been the congress Party, with leaders such as jawaharlal nehru, indira gandhi, and rajiv gandhi.

B. In a small group, compare your list of difficult cases from Exercise A. What did you do to figure out your answer to each difficult case? Compare your answers.

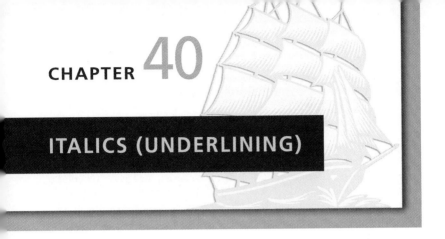

CHAPTER 40

ITALICS (UNDERLINING)

Type that slants to the right—***italic type***—gives special emphasis to words and ideas. In handwritten or typed texts, <u>underlining</u> is the equivalent of italic type: <u>The Color Purple</u> = *The Color Purple*.

Convention requires you to use underlining (or italics) to give distinctive treatment to titles of full-length works such as books and films, foreign words, names of vehicles, and words named as words. (Titles of shorter works, such as stories and articles, or parts of works, such as chapters, require quotation marks rather than italics; see 36d and 39b-2.)

If you write your papers out in longhand, you will underline all such words and phrases. (A typewriter will also provide underlining.) A computer word-processing program may give you the option of *italics*, though some readers may prefer you to underline.

TYPEWRITTEN   Alice Walker's novel <u>The Color Purple</u> has been both praised and criticized since it appeared in 1982.

COMPUTER PRINTOUT   Alice Walker's novel *The Color Purple* has been both praised and criticized since it appeared in 1982.

You can also occasionally use underlining or italics to add emphasis to your writing and clarify your meaning.

> Not only was he one of the captains of the Permian team, not only was he number one in his class, but now he was thinking of applying to Harvard.
> *Harvard?*
> Never in a thousand years could Tony Chavez have imagined it turning out this way. Never in a million.
>
> —H. G. Bissinger, *Friday Night Lights*

40
it/und

40a Following conventions for underlining (using italics)

Knowing when to use underlining (italics) can sometimes be difficult. As you proofread, therefore, you may need to consult the lists and discussions that follow in order to answer your questions. For example, should Stephen Crane's novel be written as *Maggie: A Girl of the Streets* or as "Maggie: A Girl of the Streets" (in quotation marks)? Should the borrowed French word "quiche," meaning a dinner pie with a filling, be written *quiche* (italicized or underlined) or quiche (in plain type)? Should the name of the famous Star Trek vessel be written as *The Enterprise*, the *Enterprise*, "The Enterprise," or The Enterprise?

1 Underline titles of long or major works

Underline (italicize) titles of most long works, such as books, magazines, and films, and of major works such as paintings and sculptures. For parts of works, however, and for short works such as stories, reports, magazine or newspaper articles, and episodes in a television series, use quotation marks rather than underlining. Some titles, such as those of sacred books (like the New Testament, Pentateuch, or Koran), require neither underlining nor quotation marks. (See the following list.)

TREATMENT OF TITLES

UNDERLINE OR ITALICIZE	USE QUOTATION MARKS
BOOKS AND PAMPHLETS	
Generations: The History of America's Future, 1584 to 2069 (nonfiction book)	"Boomers" (book chapter)
Maggie: A Girl of the Streets (novel)	"Preface" (chapter in a novel)
Beetroot (collection of stories)	"The Purloined Letter" (story)
The White Album (collection of essays)	"Once More to the Lake" (essay)
Tracing Your Family's History (pamphlet)	"List Your Relatives" (section of a pamphlet)
POEMS	
Paradise Lost (long poem)	"Richard Cory" (short poem)
The One Day (long poem)	"Whoso list to hunt" (first line of a poem, used as a title)
PLAYS	
King Lear	
Angels in America	
Fences	

MOVIES AND TELEVISION PROGRAMS

Queer as Folk (TV show)

Saving Private Ryan (film)

20/20 (TV news show)

"The Long Suit" (episode in a TV series)

"Daycare Dilemmas" (report from a news program)

PAINTINGS AND SCULPTURE

Nude Descending a Staircase (painting)

Winged Victory (sculpture)

MUSICAL WORKS

Nixon in China (opera)

Nutcracker Suite (work for orchestra)

Some Kind of Blue (album)

Camille Saint-Saëns's *Organ Symphony*

"Luck Be a Lady" (song in a musical)

"Waltz of the Flowers" (section of a longer work)

"Big Money" (song on an album)

Saint-Saëns, Symphony no. 3 in C Minor, op. 78

MAGAZINES AND NEWSPAPERS

Discover (magazine)

Review of Contemporary Fiction (scholarly journal)

the *New York Times*

"What Can Baby Learn?" (article in magazine)

"From Krazy Kat to Hoodoo: Aesthetic Discourse in the Fiction of Ishmael Reed" (scholarly article)

"Asbestos Found in Schools" (newspaper article)

NO UNDERLINING, ITALICS, OR QUOTATION MARKS

SACRED BOOKS

Bible, Koran, Talmud, Bhagavad Gita

PUBLIC, LEGAL, OR WELL-KNOWN DOCUMENTS

United States Constitution

Last Will and Testament

TITLE OF YOUR OWN PAPER

The Attitudes of College Students Toward Intramural Sports (paper for a sociology class)

The Role of Verbal Abuse in *The Color Purple* (title of a work being discussed is italicized)

Exception: If your paper has been published and you are citing it, enclose the title in quotation marks.

40a
it/und

A reader needs to know whether certain end punctuation (such as a question mark) is part of a title or part of your own sentence in which the title appears. Underline any punctuation *only* when it's part of the title.

INCORRECT	What did he think of <u>Jumanji?</u>
CORRECT	What did he think of <u>Jumanji</u>?
CORRECT	The book <u>What's Up, Doc?</u> provides an intriguing history of cartoons.

> **The comma and question mark are part of the title, so they need to be underlined.**

2 Underline names of specific vehicles

Underline (italicize) the names of specific ships, airplanes, trains, and spacecraft, but not the names of *types* of vehicles. Note that USS and SS are not underlined. (See also 39b-1.)

SPECIFIC VEHICLES	TYPES OF VEHICLES
Voyager VI	Boeing 767
Orient Express	Sea-Doo
USS *Corpus Christi*	Arctic Cat snowmobile
SS *Norway*	Chevrolet Impala
Memphis Belle	Ducati 750
Mir	Boston Whaler

3 Underline foreign words and phrases

Foreign words and phrases pass through stages of familiarity as they are first adopted and then become more and more common. When a word or phrase has not moved into common use and still seems very foreign, highlight it with underlining or italics. Extremely common words and phrases—for example, "quiche," "junta," "taco," and "kvetch"—have lost their foreignness. You need not underline such words. When you can't decide whether to treat a word or phrase as part of the language, look it up in a dictionary.

FOREIGN	The code of <u>omertà</u> supported a kind of order in the criminal world.
FOREIGN	Many lawyers contribute to their communities by doing <u>pro bono</u> work.
COMMON	I served the vegetables grilled on skewers like shish kebab.

Scientific names for the genus and species of plants and animals also require underlining; the common names do not.

SCIENTIFIC NAME   The seaweed <u>Chrodus crispus</u> turns up in processed form in ice cream, in nondairy creamer, and even in hamburgers.

SCIENTIFIC NAME   Anthropologists speculate about the social arrangements practiced by early human species such as <u>Homo habilis.</u>

COMMON NAME   Tests found algae growing in the Swansons' pool.

4 Underline words, letters, and numbers named as words

When you focus attention on a word, letter, or number by discussing it as itself, you should underline it.

40.1

DISCUSSED   In several Boston accents, r is pronounced ah, so that the words car and park become <u>cah</u> and <u>pahk</u>.

Also underline a word or phrase you are defining.

DEFINED   Electricity can also be generated from a <u>piezoelectric crystal,</u> a piece of quartz or similar material that responds to pressure by producing electric current.

DID YOU KNOW?

Most of this book is printed in the familiar vertical letters known as roman type. The slanted letters discussed in this chapter, however, are in *italic* type. Italic type was developed around 1500 from a kind of swift handwriting that scholars and scribes of the period used to write out manuscripts. Italic type first appeared in 1501 in an edition of the work of the Latin poet Virgil published in Venice by the famous Italian printer and print designer Aldus Manutius.

40a
it/und

Exercise 1

The following sentences contain words that need to be highlighted by underlining (italics) or by quotation marks. Edit each by supplying any necessary underlining or quotation marks. Star the items that are the most challenging to edit.

40.2

EXAMPLE
The well-known "<u>Old Farmer's Almanac</u>" contains information about the weather and articles on various topics.

1. I first learned about this famous American almanac from a newspaper article, You Can Look It Up There, that appeared in my local paper, the Record-Advertiser.
2. GQ and Cosmopolitan probably would not print an article like Salt: It's Still Worth Its Salt, which appeared in a recent edition of the almanac.
3. According to this article, the word salary comes from the Latin term for wages paid to some soldiers, salarium argentum, that is, salt money.
4. In an essay on the historic effects of weather, the author points out that freezing temperatures on January 28, 1986, led to the space shuttle Challenger disaster.
5. If you are interested in learning about the ocean, you can find out that high tides occur twice a month at syzygy, the times when the sun and moon are lined up on the same side of the earth or on opposite sides.

40b Underlining for emphasis

By underlining (italicizing) a word or phrase, you give it special emphasis. You should make use of this strategy on a *very* limited basis, however, since readers become annoyed when you rely too often on underlining to do the work your words should be doing on their own.

EMPHASIZES CONTRAST

A letter of recommendation mixing strong praise with a few reservations seems direct and realistic; a letter filled with <u>faint</u> praise makes the endorsement seem lukewarm.

ADDS FORCE

In releasing themselves from the single ideal of the dependent woman, women have more or less incidentally released a lot of men from the single ideal of the dominant male. The one mistake the feminists have made, I think, is in supposing that all men need this release, or that the world would be a better place if all men achieved it. It would just be duller.   —NOEL PERRIN, "The Androgynous Man"

HIGHLIGHTS IMPORTANT INFORMATION

Whenever you start the generator, <u>make sure there is sufficient oil in the crankcase.</u>

Many kinds of informal writing, such as notes, journal entries, and personal letters, rely on underlining to add a certain "oral" emphasis to the prose. Be careful not to rely on underlining for this purpose when writing formal papers and other documents.

INFORMAL   Next time, <u>hand</u> the receipts to me instead of <u>dropping</u> them on my desk.

MORE FORMAL   In the future, give the receipts to me personally instead of placing them on my desk.

Exercise 2

A. For each of the following sentences, add any underlining required by convention or needed for appropriate emphasis. Circle any words that are underlined but should not be. Star any items that are challenging to edit.

EXAMPLE

In 1957, Chevrolet produced the <u>Bel Air</u>, a model now considered a classic.

1. As David Halberstam points out in his book The Fifties, automobiles from the period were so hot they were cool.
2. Cars from that period, with <u>enormous</u> tailfins and <u>lots</u> of chrome, are still <u>eye-catchers</u> today.
3. The musical Grease is set in the same era.
4. Television shows from the period included the Ed Sullivan Show and Lassie.
5. Readers could choose from such now-defunct publications as the Herald Tribune newspaper and Look magazine.

B. In a group, compare your corrections to Exercise 2A. Which were the hardest to make, and why?

40b
it/und

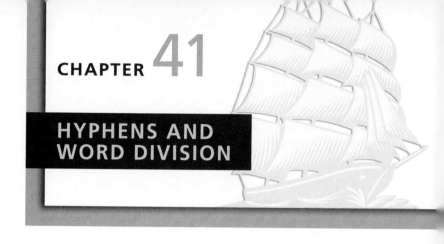

CHAPTER 41

HYPHENS AND WORD DIVISION

Hyphens divide words and tie them together as well. At the end of a line, you may need to split a word, completing it on the next line. A hyphen (-) tells readers to treat the divided word as one word, not two.

Hyphens also help to divide words that are hard to read without a break (for example, *anti-intellectual,* not *antiintellectual*), and they link familiar compound words (*three-quarters, commander-in-chief*).

41a Using hyphens to divide words

To make your readers' job easier, use a hyphen to split a word at the end of a line. Also hyphenate words that may be misleading or hard to read without a visual break. As you proofread, moreover, check that you have divided words whenever necessary and that the hyphens come at appropriate points in words.

1 Divide words at the end of a line

When you don't have enough room at the end of a line to complete a word of *two or more syllables,* type it on the next line unless doing so will create a right margin that is very jagged and distracting. To create a reasonably even margin, split the word *between syllables,* and mark the break with a hyphen at the end of the line.

DISTRACTING   The rate of change in home appliance manufacturing has accelerated rapidly over the past decade. Increasingly sophisticated consumers, international competition, and the need for an ozone-safe refrigerant to replace CFCs (chlorofluorocarbons) have provided the impetus.

HYPHENATED The rate of change in home appliance manufacturing has accelerated rapidly over the past decade. Increas‐ ingly sophisticated consumers, international compe‐ tition, and the need for an ozone-safe refrigerant to replace CFCs (chlorofluorocarbons) have provided the impetus.

If there is no space for a word at the end of a line, a word-processing program will automatically move the word to the next line. This process is called *word wrapping*. In proofreading a word-processed document, you need to be alert for jagged margins created by this process, and hyphenate to make margins more regular.

A hyphen is a short line used to divide words at syllables or to join parts of compound words and word clusters. Type a hyphen as a *single* line (-) with no space on either side. A dash, in contrast, interrupts sentences (see 38c). Type a dash as *two* lines (--) with no space on either side or in between.

INCORRECT one — fourth of the workforce
HYPHEN

CORRECT HYPHEN one‐fourth of the workforce

INCORRECT DASH surprising ingredients — peanut butter, raisins, and whipped cream

CORRECT DASH surprising ingredients——peanut butter, raisins, and whipped cream

Although it may seem simple, dividing words at the ends of lines can be tricky. The following tips may help you to follow convention.

Divide words only between syllables. Readers will have a hard time recognizing words that are split at a place other than a syllable break. For example, the word *adjustable* can be correctly divided in only two places: *ad-just-able*.

CONFUSING Experts disagree about the wisdom of **adju‐ stable** rates for mortgages.

CLEAR Experts disagree about the wisdom of **adjust‐ able** rates for mortgages.

Consult a dictionary to determine where to divide a word. If you rely entirely on your own pronunciation, you may divide some words incorrectly, especially those you encounter in reading but seldom use in conversation. For example, *irrevocable* is divided as *ir-re-vo-ca-ble*, not *ir-rev-oc-able*; *milieu* is *mi-lieu*, not *mil-ieu*. Your pronunciation of a familiar word may also differ from the standard one given in the dictionary and expected by readers. (For

41a
-

example, you may pronounce the word *nuclear* in two syllables, *nuc-lear*, rather than with the three syllables listed in the dictionary, *nu-cle-ar*.)

Some word-processing programs will hyphenate words at the ends of lines for you. This feature can be timesaving and helpful, yet the programs often split words incorrectly, especially less common terms. Consequently, the programs allow you to accept or reject proposed word divisions, and effective proofreading includes checking on the accuracy of the hyphenations you are offered.

Leave more than one letter at the end of a line and more than two at the beginning.

INCORRECT   Two designers announced they are considering an **a-greement** to produce a line of affordable clothes for professional women.

EDITED   Two designers announced they are considering an **agreement** to produce a line of affordable clothes for professional women.

INCORRECT   The concert ended because a stagehand **disconnect-ed** the power supply for the main amplifiers.

EDITED   The concert ended because a stagehand **discon-nected** the power supply for the main amplifiers.

Divide compound words at natural breaks. Generally, divide a compound word at the break between the words making it up. If a compound already includes a hyphen, divide it at that point.

DISTRACTING   If the sports car is the classic European car, the **Volkswa-gen** is the classic California car.

EDITED   If the sports car is the classic European car, the **Volks-wagen** is the classic California car.

DISTRACTING   In his new movie, the actor plays a bumbling, **acci-dent-prone** police detective.

EDITED   In his new movie, the actor plays a bumbling, **accident-prone** police detective.

Don't divide one-syllable words. Even relatively long words such as *touched*, *drought*, *kicked*, and *through* have no stopping points in pronunciation and should be left intact. If the undivided word doesn't fit on a line, move it to the next line.

41a
–

Avoid confusing divisions. When some words are correctly divided, they form other words with meanings that may be distracting.

DISTRACTING   The school board is proposing a solution for **sin—gle** parents unable to afford child care.

CLEAR   The school board is proposing a solution for **single** parents unable to afford child care.

Don't split abbreviations, numerals, or contractions. Abbreviations and acronyms (NATO, DVD, NCAA), numerals (528; 100,000), and contractions (didn't, should've) can be sounded out with syllables, but splitting them will distract your readers.

DISTRACTING   Foreign policy experts disagree about funding the NA—TO alliance at present levels.

CLEAR   Foreign policy experts disagree about funding the **NATO** alliance at present levels.

Exercise 1

A. Look at each hyphen in the following sentences, and decide whether to retain it, to change the division within the word, or to eliminate it in favor of placing the entire word on the next line. Use your dictionary if you need to, and keep track of the toughest cases.

EXAMPLE
Although receiving a present can be very pleasant, gift-~~giv~~-
  giving
~~-ing~~ can be equally rewarding.

1. Looking for a job that would be challenging, Jen thou-ght long and hard about taking the position at Hammond's Gift Shop.
2. By the next Saturday, however, she was unpacking a truck-load of the exquisite vases and figurines that the gift shop sells.
3. Hank wanted only one thing for his birthday: an ornamental Chinese vase that was way beyond Rachel's budget.
4. When he came home one afternoon and saw the vase on the man-tle, Hank went right out to get flowers as a way of saying "thank you."
5. The bouquet was lovely, redolent of roses, tulips, and baby's-breath.

B. In a small group, compare your edited sentences from Exercise 1A. Which were the most difficult, and why?

41a
-

2 Divide words to prevent misreading

You can use a hyphen to help readers distinguish between words that are spelled the same but have very different meanings.

In the spirit of **reform** politics, the party sought to **re‑form** a defunct citizens' action committee.

For **recreation**, the Prichards staged a hilarious **re‑creation** of the argument between Joe and Arnold.

You should also hyphenate words that are difficult to read because of repeated letters or odd combinations of letters.

anti‑imperialism (*not* antiimperialism)

post‑traumatic (*not* posttraumatic)

co‑owner (*not* coowner)

41b Using hyphens to join words

Instead of *dividing* whole words, hyphens are often used to *tie together* the elements of compound words and phrases. The conventions for linking compounds, however, tend to be quite mixed; should the mechanical heart regulator be written as *pacemaker*, *pace maker*, or *pace-maker*?

1 Check hyphens in compound words

A compound word is made from two or more words. Some compounds are hyphenated (*double-decker*, *time-lapse*), some are treated as one word (*backfire*, *timekeeper*), and some are treated as separate words (*mail carrier*, *time bomb*). A dictionary will tell you how to treat a particular compound. Make sure the dictionary is up to date, however, because usage changes. Today's *baby-sitter* can quickly become tomorrow's *babysitter*.

2 Hyphenate familiar compounds correctly

Some familiar compounds generally require hyphens.

Numbers. You should hyphenate all numbers between twenty-one and ninety-nine when they are spelled out.

forty‑one   eighty‑six   twenty‑five

This rule holds even if the number is part of a larger number.

fifty‑eight thousand   twenty‑three million

41b
‑

Use a hyphen to show inclusive numbers.

pages 163–78   volumes 9–14

Fractions. Hyphenate fractions when you spell them out.

five–eighths of the liquid in the container

two–thirds the size of last year's convention

Prefixes and suffixes. Hyphenate a prefix attached to a capitalized word or a number.

Cro–Magnon   non–Euclidean   post–Victorian   pre–1989
mid–October   pre–Clinton   trans–Canadian   post–1066

Hyphenate a capital letter and a word that together form a compound.

A–frame   I–beam   T–shirt
B–movie   O–ring   X–factor

Some specialized terms, such as those used in music, do not require a hyphen.

A minor   G sharp   C clef

The prefixes *ex-*, *self-*, and *all-* and the suffixes *-elect* and *-odd* should generally be hyphenated in compounds.

all–encompassing   self–centered   president–elect
ex–partner   self–denial   twenty–odd

3 Hyphenate compound modifiers correctly

When you ask two or more words to work as a single modifier and you place them *before* a noun, hyphenate them.

BEFORE NOUN   The **second–largest** supplier of crude oil to the United States is Nigeria.

BEFORE NOUN   Ayn Rand's works are among the most popular **twentieth–century** novels.

When the modifiers come *after* a noun, you generally do not need to hyphenate them.

AFTER NOUN   Many of the drugs used to treat cancer are **nausea inducing**.

41b
–

41.1

Remember that modifying compounds can mean something quite different from the sum of their independent meanings. Hyphens help readers to know which meaning to assign the compound.

The director needed three **extra wild** monkeys for the scene.

The director needed three **extra-wild** monkeys for the scene.

The **bird eating** spiders flew away.

The **bird-eating** spiders have enormous fangs.

Do not hyphenate compound modifiers containing *-ly* adverbs or comparative and superlative forms.

The new products were developed by the company's **highly regarded** research team.

Nigeria is the **most populous** country in Africa.

(Compound modifiers differ from coordinate adjectives, which are joined with a comma. See 33f.)

4 Use hyphens to create new compounds

To add vividness and emphasis to your writing, you can occasionally create (or "coin") a new compound word or phrase. Join the elements in such a compound with hyphens to indicate its original, temporary nature.

She entered the program with a **prove-it-to-me** attitude.

DID YOU KNOW?

41b
-

Short compound words are common in English, with and without commas, but in other languages, long compounds occur quite frequently. As Bill Bryson points out:

German is full of jaw-crunching words like *Wirtschaftstreuhandgesellschaft* (business trust company), *Bundesbahnangestelltenwitwe* (a widow of a federal railway employee), and *Kriegsgefangenanentschädigungsgesetz* (a law pertaining to war reparations), while in Holland companies commonly have names of forty letters or more, such as Douwe Egberts Koninlijke Tabaksfabriek-Koffiebranderijen-Theehandal Naamloze Vennootschap (literally Douwe Egberts Royal Tobacco Factory–Coffee Roasters–Tea Traders Incorporated; they must use fold-out business cards).

Bill Bryson, *The Mother Tongue* (New York: Morrow, 1990) 19.

Exercise 2

A. Insert hyphens in the following sentences wherever appropriate. Consult a dictionary if necessary.

41.2

EXAMPLE

The company hired a well‿regarded accounting firm as part of its financial reorganization.

1. Alejo enjoys painstakingly exact work, such as building scale model ships.
2. While working, he likes to listen to Francis Poulenc's jazz influenced classical music.
3. One fourth of all his model ships are sold at auction.
4. Tony, his assistant, keeps track of the profits in a pre and post auction sale log.
5. Although his creations are awesome, Alejo harbors many insecurities that are mostly selfinflicted.

B. In a small group, compare your edited versions of the sentences in Exercise 2A. Which were the most difficult decisions, and why? Did your dictionaries give all members of the group the same advice?

41b

CHAPTER 42

NUMBERS

You can convey numbers in several ways in your writing—as numerals (37; 18.6), as words (eighty-one; two million), or as a combination of numerals and words (7th, 2nd). Understanding the appropriate ways to present numbers is important because unconventional or inconsistent usage can mislead your readers. This chapter shows you how to present numbers appropriately in general academic writing. For advice about the use of numbers in business, technical, and professional writing, see the reference guides listed in Chapters 51–54.

42a Spelling out numbers or using numerals

Whenever you use numbers in your writing, you need to decide whether to spell them out (twenty-five) or use numerals (25). The rules that follow tell you how to use numbers in general writing, including much academic writing. Conventions for the use of numbers may vary according to academic discipline and profession, however, so check with your instructor or with one of the style sheets describing conventions for specific fields (see Chapter 48).

1 Spell out numbers of one or two words

Spell out a number if you can write it in one or two words.

CORRECT   We are ordering **twenty-seven** personal computers.

CORRECT   Folktales have been popular in children's storybooks for the past **two hundred** years.

Treat hyphenated numbers (see 41b-2) as a single word.

CORRECT   Last year, our farm produced more than **seventy-eight thousand** eggs.

2 Spell out numbers that begin a sentence

Readers expect every sentence to begin with a capital letter. To avoid unsettling your readers, spell out any number that opens a sentence, even if the number contains more than two words. If the number is long enough to be distracting, rewrite so that it appears elsewhere in the sentence.

INAPPROPRIATE   **428** of the houses in Talcottville are built on leased land.

DISTRACTING   **Four hundred twenty-eight** of the houses in Talcottville are built on leased land.

EASY TO READ   **In Talcottville, 428** houses are built on leased land.

3 Express related numbers in a consistent form

When the numbers in a sentence or passage refer to the same category, treat them consistently by sticking to either words or numerals. If one of the numbers would require numerical form on its own, expressing the rest in numerals will help you keep sentences direct and concise.

INCONSISTENT   Café Luna opened with a menu of **twenty-six** items, which soon expanded to **eighty-five** and then **104** items as word spread about the good food.

42.1

CONSISTENT   Café Luna opened with a menu of **26** items, which soon expanded to **85** and then **104** items as word spread about the good food.

DID YOU KNOW?

Although numbers might seem unimportant, they may have led to the very birth of writing as a communicative medium. The most ancient written texts (inscribed on stone tablets several thousand years ago) recorded sales, exchanges, cattle, and other possessions—subjects that required a way to represent numbers. Without a way of writing numbers, ancient people would have been unable to record and convey much of the information they considered important.

42b
num

42b Following special conventions

In using numbers as part of dates, measurements, addresses, and the like, you need to follow some special conventions.

1 Use numerals when appropriate

ADDRESSES AND ROUTES
1005 Avenue of the Americas   Interstate 6   Route 102
2450 Ridge Road, Apartment B3, Alhambra, CA 91801

DATES
September 7, 1989   2002   1880–1910
class of '01 (informal)   the '80s (informal)   1930s
486 B.C. (or B.C.E.)   A.D. 980 (or 980 C.E.)
from 1955 to 1957   between 1872 and 1876

PARTS OF A WRITTEN WORK
Chapter 12   page 278
Macbeth 2.4.25–28 (or act II, scene iv, lines 25–28)
Genesis 1:1–6 (reference to the Bible)

MEASUREMENTS USING SYMBOLS OR ABBREVIATIONS
128 MB   65 mph   80 kph
6'4"   47 psi   21 ml

PERCENTAGES, DECIMALS, AND FRACTIONS
7 5/8   27.3   67 percent (or 67%)

TIME OF DAY
10:52   2 p.m.   6:17 a.m.
12 p.m. (noon)   12 a.m. (midnight)

EXCEPTION   seven o'clock, not 7 o'clock

MONEY (SPECIFIC AMOUNTS)
$7,883 (or $7883) $4.29 $7.2 million (or $7,200,000)

SURVEYS, RATIOS, STATISTICS, AND SCORES
7 out of 10   3 to 1   a mean of 23
a standard deviation of 2.5
the Bills defeated the Packers 21 to 17

CLUSTERED NUMBERS
paragraphs 2, 4, 9, and 13–15 (or 13 through 15)
units 23, 145, and 210

2 Spell out numbers when appropriate

DATES AND TIMES
the sixties   October seventh   the nineteenth century

four o'clock (or four in the morning)
times rounded to the quarter hour: half past eight, a quarter after one

ROUNDED NUMBERS OR ROUNDED AMOUNTS OF MONEY
about three hundred thousand citizens
close to eleven thousand dollars
sixty cents (and other small dollar or cent amounts)

RANGES OF NUMBERS

LESS THAN 100	Supply the full second number.
	9–13 27–34 58–79 94–95
OVER 100	Simply supply the last two figures of the second number unless more are needed to prevent confusion. Do not use a comma in four-digit page numbers.
	134–45 95–102 (not 95–02) 370–420
	1534–620 (not 1534–20) 1007–09
YEARS	Supply both years in a range except when they belong to the same century.
	1890–1920 1770–86 476–823 42–38 B.C.
LARGE NUMBERS	For especially large numbers, combine numerals and words.
	75 million years 2.3 million new automobiles

42c Avoiding too many numbers

Using too many numbers in a sentence or passage can confuse readers. If numbers come next to each other, first check for any needed hyphens (see 41b).

CONFUSING	For the company picnic we can buy either **forty six packs** of soda pop or **twenty two liter** bottles.
HYPHENS ADDED	For the company picnic we can buy either **forty six-packs** of soda pop or **twenty two-liter** bottles.

When a passage contains so many numbers that readers might have trouble keeping track of the relationships, consider organizing the numbers in a table or chart.

DETAILED DESCRIPTION
The origins of Canada's population include the British Isles (40%), France (27%), other European regions (20%), and Indian (indigenous) or Eskimo (1.5%).

42c
num

Canadian Population

ORIGIN	PERCENTAGE
British Isles	40.0
France	27.0
Other European	20.0
Indian (indigenous) or Eskimo	1.5

This alternative is appropriate only when the numbers identify comparable categories. In other instances, you can avoid confusing readers by rewriting in order to simplify or to separate numbers so they are easier to understand.

Exercise

A. In the following sentences, correct any errors in the use of numbers. Circle any especially difficult items. You may need to rewrite some sentences.

42.2

EXAMPLE

When the list of cities for the Rock and Roll Hall of Fame was narrowed down to *1̸* *one*, the choice was Cleveland.

1. Of the groups and individuals elected to the Rock and Roll Hall of Fame from 1986 to 1990, 5 were female and 68 were male.
2. The Hall of Fame is increasing its membership goals from nineteen thousand to twenty-one thousand five hundred.
3. 411 of the 2000 questionnaires about favorite rockers were returned by the deadline.
4. This year the Hall of Fame purchased twenty-six articles of clothing, 127 signed memorabilia, and 232 unused concert tickets for the museum.
5. Although subscribers were told the museum would open by 10:30 in the morning on the twelfth, the personnel weren't ready for the large crowd until about 2 o'clock.

42c
num

B. In a small group, compare your edited versions of the sentences in Exercise 1A. Which cases gave you the most trouble? How did you resolve them?

CHAPTER 43

ABBREVIATIONS

When they are understood and agreed upon by both writer and reader, abbreviations act as a kind of shorthand, making a sentence quicker to write and easier to read.

SPELLED OUT   In her course Reporting Economic Issues, new faculty member **Doctor** Marian Hwang will be drawing heavily on her prior employment at both the **Internal Revenue Service** and **the National Broadcasting Company**.

ABBREVIATED   In her course Reporting Economic Issues, new faculty member **Dr.** Marian Hwang will be drawing heavily on her prior employment at both the **IRS** and **NBC**.

Improper or badly placed abbreviations, however, can make a sentence *harder* to read and understand.

CONFUSING   The legal theory known as Law **&** Economics has a strong advocate in **Jg. Rich.** Posner. He is a former **U of C** law **prof.** who now sits on the Seventh **U.S. Cir. Ct. of App.** in Chicago.
READER'S REACTION: **Am I supposed to know all these abbreviations? What is "Cir. Ct. of App."? Is "U of C" the University of California? Cincinnati? Chicago?**

CLEAR   The legal theory known as Law **and** Economics has a strong advocate in **Judge** Richard Posner. He is a former **University of Chicago** law **professor** who now sits on the Seventh U.S. **Circuit Court of Appeals** in Chicago.

Abbreviations should aid your readers, not distract them. This chapter provides some basic rules for abbreviating words and phrases in your writing.

43
abbrev

43a Using familiar abbreviations

Many abbreviations are so widely used that readers have no trouble recognizing them. These abbreviations are acceptable in all kinds of writing as long as you present them in standard form.

1 Abbreviate titles with proper names

When people's titles come right before or after their names, you should use standard abbreviations such as *Dr.*, *Rev.*, *Ms.*, and *Prof.*

BEFORE NAME	**Dr.** Antoinette Plocek; **Mr.** William Choi; **Ms.** Rutkowski; **Mrs.** Stephanie Chenier; **Rev.** Richard Valantasis; **Hon.** Patricia Hacaj; **St.** Rose of Lima.
AFTER NAME	Christine Carruthers, **M.D.**; Cathy Harrington, **D.V.M.**; Angelo Iacono, **Jr.**; James Guptil, **Sr.**; Ralph Romero, **S.J.**; Jane Berger, **M.A.**; Rosemary Anzaldua, **C.P.A.**

If the person's title is preceded by *the*, the title should be spelled out.

The **Reverend** Robert Marsh

The **Honorable** Judith Loesser

When you give a person's entire name, you may abbreviate his or her title, but if you use the title *as part of your reference to the person*, spell out the entire title.

INCORRECT	The list included **Prof.** Levesque, **Brig. Gen.** Washington, and **Rep.** Schroeder.
ACCEPTABLE	The list included **Professor** Levesque, **Brigadier General** Washington, and **Representative** Schroeder.
ALTERNATIVE	The list included **Prof. Roland** Levesque, **Brig. Gen. William** Washington, and **Rep. Patricia** Schroeder.
EXCEPTIONS	**Rev.** Mills and **Dr.** Smith were not invited.

Spell out a title when it does not come next to a proper name.

INCORRECT	You should consult the **Dr.** about that knee.
EDITED	You should consult the **doctor** about that knee.
EDITED	You should consult **Dr. Boyajian** about that knee.

43a
abbrev

Use only one form of a person's title at a time.

INCORRECT	**Dr.** Vonetta McGee, **D.D.S.**
CORRECT	**Dr.** Vonetta McGee
CORRECT	Vonetta McGee, **D.D.S.**

Academic titles such as *M.A.*, *Ph.D.*, *B.S.*, *Ed.D.*, and *M.D.* can be used on their own in abbreviated form.

| ACCEPTABLE | The university offers an **Ed.D.** specifically designed for school-teachers who want to become administrators. |

2 Abbreviate references to people and organizations

Your readers may be more familiar with some abbreviations (3M, IBM, NAFTA) than with the names for which they stand (Minnesota Mining and Manufacturing, International Business Machines, North American Free Trade Agreement). Such abbreviations are almost always acceptable, as are those that simplify complicated names (AFL-CIO for American Federation of Labor and Congress of Industrial Organizations).

In some abbreviations the letters are pronounced singly (YMCA, USDA). In others, called **acronyms**, the letters form a pronounceable word (AIDS, SALT). Abbreviations and acronyms in which each letter stands for a word are usually written in capitals without periods.

ORGANIZATIONS	NAACP, AMA, NBA, FDA, NCAA, UNESCO, IBEW
CORPORATIONS	USX, PBS, GM, CNN, AT&T, PBS, BBC
COUNTRIES	USA (*or* U.S.A.), UK (*or* U.K.)
PEOPLE	JFK, LBJ, FDR, MLK
THINGS OR EVENTS	FM, AM, TB, MRI, AWOL, DWI, TGIF

43a
abbrev

43.1

If your reader won't recognize an unfamiliar abbreviation, you can still use it in your document as long as you give the full word or phrase once and show the abbreviation in parentheses. From then on, you can use the abbreviation without confusion.

| EXPLAINED | The **American Library Association (ALA)** has taken stands on access to information. The **ALA** opposes book censorship and favors privacy for records of the books borrowed by an individual. |

This technique is especially useful in academic or technical writing because it enables you to shorten complicated and often-repeated terms.

3 Abbreviate dates and numbers correctly

Abbreviations of dates and numbers may be used only when they *specify* a number or amount; they are not a substitute for the general term.

ABBREVIATION	MEANING
A.D. or AD	*anno Domini*, meaning "in the year of Our Lord"
B.C. or BC	*before Christ*
B.C.E. or BCE	*before common era*, used by some writers in place of *B.C.*
C.E. or CE	*Common Era*, used by some writers in place of *A.D.*
a.m.	*ante meridiem*, meaning "morning"; some writers use *A.M.*
p.m.	*post meridiem*, meaning "after noon"; some writers use *P.M.*
no.	number
$	dollars

INCORRECT   Because of the lack of capable leadership, the bill providing **$** for inspection of meat-processing plants was not passed until late in the **p.m.**, just before the legislature adjourned.

EDITED   Because of the lack of capable leadership, the bill providing **money** for inspection of meat-processing plants was not passed until late in the **evening**, just before the legislature adjourned.

You may use either *a.m.* and *p.m.* or *A.M.* and *P.M.* in handwritten or typewritten papers. Book and magazine printers generally set these abbreviations in small capitals (A.M., P.M.). Your word processor may allow you to do this.

43a
abbrev

DID YOU KNOW?

Each day we use some common abbreviations without knowing that they were originally longer words or expressions (a famous example being *OK*, which has many proposed origins but most likely comes from an African word pronounced *ah-keh* or *wah-keh*). The term *good-bye*, for example, was abbreviated from the phrase *God be with you*, a kind of blessing and simple statement of departure. The substitution of *good* for *God* may have come about by association with similar phrases like *good day* or *good night*. Today we have gone a step further with the shortened form *bye* or the curious repetition *bye-bye*.

In a hurried, informal note, you can use abbreviations to avoid spelling out words as long as your reader understands your shortcuts. In formal writing, however, use only familiar, acceptable abbreviations.

INFORMAL   If I'm not in the office during the **a.m.**, leave your **ID no.** and have the **$** delivered to **Dr. B.** at the Oak **Blvd.** office.

FORMAL   If I'm not in the office during the **morning**, leave your **identification number** and have the **money** delivered to **Dr. Baruti** at the Oak **Boulevard** office.

43b Using abbreviations sparingly

You can shorten many words and turn most names into initials, but the resulting sentences are likely to be hard to read and irritating. Their only real use is in shorthand notes to yourself or as a quick drafting technique (see 7b).

UNREADABLE   The descr. in the opening ch. is ~ to that in B. House except for the hum. tone and the emph. on a single char.'s pt. of view.

In most formal writing, your readers will expect words in full form except for certain familiar abbreviations (discussed in 43a). In special situations, such as research papers and scientific or technical writing, you can draw on a wider range of appropriate abbreviations to save space, particularly in documenting sources. (See Chapter 48 on abbreviations to use in documentation and in specialized writing.)

1 Avoid inappropriate abbreviations

The following lists should help alert you to inappropriate abbreviations.

DAYS, MONTHS, AND HOLIDAYS

AVOID	Thurs., Thur., Th.	Oct.	Xmas
USE	Thursday	October	Christmas

PLACES

AVOID	Wasatch Mts.	Lk. Erie	Phil.	Ont.	Ave.
USE	Wasatch Mountains	Lake Erie	Philadelphia	Ontario	Avenue

EXCEPTION   988 Dunkerhook Road, Paramus, **NJ** 07652
Use accepted postal abbreviations in all addresses with zip codes.

43b
abbrev

If an abbreviation is officially part of a company name, you may use it (for example, Sugarn *& Son Mfg.* for Sugarn *and Son Manufacturing*). Otherwise, spell out the entire name.

COMPANY NAMES

QUESTIONABLE   The switches were installed by **LaForce Bros. Electrical Conts.**

EDITED   The switches were installed by **LaForce Brothers Electrical Contractors**.

Some contexts require you to use abbreviations in a particular way. The Modern Language Association (MLA) reference style, for example, requires abbreviations of publishing companies; thus, Holt, Rinehart and Winston, Incorporated, becomes just Holt (see 51a). Otherwise, spell out the entire name.

PEOPLE'S NAMES

AVOID   Wm. and Kath. Newholtz will attend.

EDITED   William and Katherine Newholtz will attend.

DISCIPLINES AND PROFESSIONS

INCORRECT	econ.	bio.	poli. sci.	phys. ed.	OT
EDITED	economics	biology	political science	physical education	occupational therapy

Abbreviations may be acceptable in particular contexts; for example, reports in medicine or education routinely refer to PT (physical therapy) and OT (occupational therapy).

PARTS OF WRITTEN WORKS

IN DOCUMENTA-TION	ch.	p.	pp.	fig.
IN WRITTEN TEXT	chapter	page	pages	figure

Check style guide for academic field or profession (see Chapter 47).

43b
abbrev

Use symbols such as @, #, =, ~, and + only in tables or graphs, not in the text of a paper. In general, spell out units of measurement such as *quart* and *mile* when you use them in sentences. You may, however, abbreviate phrases such as *rpm* and *mph*, with or without periods. You may also use @ when including an email address in text.

Write to her at jmjones@adcorp.com.

SYMBOLS AND UNITS OF MEASUREMENT

AVOID	pt.	qt.	in.	mi.	kg.
USE	pint	quart	inch	mile	kilogram

CORRECT	Above 5600 **rpm**, viscosity breaks down.
CORRECT	Above 5600 **r.p.m.**, viscosity breaks down.

2 Limit Latin abbreviations

Limit your use of Latin abbreviations such as *et al.* and *e.g.* to documenting sources and making parenthetical comments.

c.f.	compare (*confer*)	i.e.	that is (*id est*)
e.g.	for example (*exempli gratia*)	N.B.	note well (*nota bene*)
et al.	and others (*et alii*)	viz.	namely (*videlicet*)
etc.	and so forth (*et cetera*)		

INCORRECT	Many products, **e.g.**, laptops, have flat-screen displays.
APPROPRIATE IN PARENTHESES	Many products (**e.g.**, laptops) have flat-screen displays.
PREFERABLE	Many products, **such as** laptop computers, have flat-screen displays.

The abbreviation *et al.* is very often used incorrectly. Meaning "and others," *et al.* comes from the longer Latin phrase *et alii*. No period appears at the end of the word *et*, but a period *always* appears at the end of *al.* because it is an abbreviation. Making the phrase possessive can be awkward; avoid such constructions as "Johnson et al.'s new book." Instead, use "a new book by Johnson et al."

Exercise

A. Revise the following sentences, adding or correcting abbreviations when appropriate and spelling out or rewriting any inappropriate abbreviations. Assume that these sentences are all written in a fairly formal academic context.

43b
abbrev

EXAMPLE   *New York, Los Angeles*
People think of ˄NY, LA, and Montreal as international cities, but many small- to-medium-sized towns are just as cosmopolitan.

1. At a drugstore in a small Montana town, I talked with a clerk who told me about the Wine Appreciation Guild, Ltd. (155 Conn. St., San Francisco, CA 94107), which publishes nonfiction books on food, wine, etc., e.g., *Wine Technology and Operations* by Yair Margalit, PhD.

2. According to a study by Ernest D. Abrams Consulting, smaller towns like Sioux City, IA, and Vero Bch., Fla., are even more likely to be the homes of inventors and innovators.

3. In one town in upstate NY, an engineer, Chas. D'Angelis, has created a device that measures rpms by counting the # of times a gear with a single tooth interrupts a laser beam.

4. While I was driving through the rural Midwest, I visited Rich. Forer, D.O., who examined my sore back, prescribed an innovative exercise rout. he had developed, and gave me an Rx for a mild painkiller.

5. In a city of twenty thou. people in eastern Tenn. I came across a health coop. that is pioneering a new phys. therapy program.

B. Meet in a small group and compare your editing of the sentences in Exercise A. Which ones seemed the hardest? Why?

CHAPTER 44

STRATEGIES FOR SPELLING

Consider the fact that the sounds in the word *see* (an *s* and an *e*) can be spelled in at least a dozen different ways, as illustrated in the words *see*, *senile*, *sea*, *scenic*, *ceiling*, *cedar*, *juicy*, *glossy*, *sexy*, *cease*, *seize*, and *situ*. Or consider the six different pronunciations of the letters *ough* in the words *cough*, *tough*, *bough*, *through*, *though*, and *thoroughfare*. English spelling is often difficult, and unless you have been gifted with a marvelous visual memory for the way words are spelled, the best you can do is to develop some practical strategies for identifying spelling problems and choosing correct spellings.

44a Spelling as you write

Spelling errors are most likely to occur as you draft. You can deal with them immediately, during drafting, or later, as you edit and proofread. If correct spelling is hard for you, try to keep this difficulty from turning into a fear of misspelling that distracts you from what you are trying to write. Worrying about spelling can draw your attention away from the most important parts of drafting and revising—exploring ideas and expressing them in effective ways. Stopping to check every word you *might* have misspelled is a sure way to disrupt your train of thought.

Giving special attention to spelling is therefore something often best reserved for proofreading. Nonetheless, you can take some positive steps to deal with spelling errors as you write.

1 Recognize possible errors

To recognize possible spelling errors as you draft, consider the following sources of incorrect spelling.

Inattention. You know the correct spelling of a word, but you don't use it. You might make a typing mistake. You might focus so hard on what you want to say or how to say it that you let a misspelling creep in. Usually, you can recognize errors of this sort quickly when you glance back over what you have written.

Guessing. You don't know the correct spelling of a word, so you guess on the basis of reason or of similar-sounding words. You know, for example, that the words *irreconcilable, reasonable, honorable, justifiable,* and *probable* all end with *-able,* so you reason that the word you don't know, *irresistible,* must do the same—and you get it wrong.

"Sounding out." You don't know the correct spelling of a word, so you "sound it out." Although this strategy works occasionally, it can often lead you astray because of the sound/spelling discrepancies in English. And if you mispronounce a word, your spelling will probably be wrong. Many a motel billboard has mistakenly offered "congradulations" to a graduating class. Perhaps the most common spelling error in the United States is the infamous *alot,* incorrectly spelled as one word because, when spoken, the *a* and the *lot* blend together. Sounding out a word can be helpful during the drafting process, when you need to get the word down on the page and can't, for the moment, look it up. Nonetheless, you can recognize right away that the spelling *might* be wrong.

2 Note possible misspellings as you draft

Instead of interrupting your thoughts to check every possible spelling error while you draft, try the following strategy.

> **STRATEGY**
>
> Circle possible misspellings as you write. As you draft, you regularly glance back over a sentence or two in order to review what you have said. When you do this, circle any obvious spelling errors that have slipped into your work as well as any words you think *might* be spelled wrong. You may want to correct some errors right away, but don't allow correcting to distract you from the more important practice of drafting and developing your ideas. Come back to the circled words later, after you have completed drafting, and check them for misspellings.

44b Recognizing and correcting spelling errors

As you edit and proofread, you can use one or more of the following methods to recognize and correct misspellings.

1 Pause to think

While you are editing and proofreading, remind yourself to pay attention to spelling. If you suspect for whatever reason that a word might be misspelled, pause to check the spelling. Think about the sequence of letters, concentrating especially on sequences that are likely to be misspelled. Correct any words whose spelling you know; look up any unfamiliar spellings (see 44b-2). Develop some way to remember the correct spelling for future use. For example, if you often misspell the plural of *quiz,* try to remember that *quizzes* has two *z*'s—perhaps by associating quizzes with boredom (*zzzzzzz*).

2 Look it up

A dictionary will give you the correct spelling of a word, and it may even offer spelling advice. *Merriam-Webster's Collegiate Dictionary* (10th ed.), the *New World Dictionary of the American Language,* the *American Heritage Dictionary of the English Language,* or any other standard dictionary is a good place to start. If you have a general idea of how a word is spelled, especially how it begins, you can usually locate it in a dictionary with a little looking around. If you know how a word sounds but are not sure about the spelling, you can use the lists of correspondences between sound and spelling that some dictionaries offer. If you still can't find your word, you may wish to use a specialized dictionary or handheld electronic speller designed for people who have considerable trouble with spelling. These dictionaries list words both

in·fer \in-'fər\ *vb* **in·ferred; in·fer·ring** [MF or L; MF *inferer,* fr. L *inferre,* lit., to carry or bring into, fr. *in-* + *ferre* to carry — more at BEAR] *vt* (1528) **1 :** to derive as a conclusion from facts or premises ⟨we see smoke and ∼ fire —L. A. White⟩ — compare IMPLY **2 :** GUESS, SURMISE ⟨your letter . . . allows me to ∼ that you are as well as ever — O. W. Holmes †1935⟩ **3   a :** to involve as a normal outcome of thought   **b :** to point out : INDICATE ⟨this doth ∼ the zeal I had to see him —Shak.⟩ **4 :** SUGGEST, HINT ⟨another survey . . . ∼s that two-thirds of all present computer installations are not paying for themselves —H. R. Chellman⟩ ∼ *vi* : to draw inferences ⟨men . . . have observed, *inferred,* and reasoned . . . to all kinds of results —John Dewey⟩ — **in·fer·able** *also* **in·fer·ri·ble** \in-'fər-ə-bəl\ *adj* — **in·fer·rer** \-'fər-ər\ *n*
in·fer·ence \'in-f(ə-)rən(t)s, -fərn(t)s\ *n* (1594) **1 :** the act or process of inferring: as   **a :** the act of passing from one proposition, statement, or judgment considered as true to another whose truth is believed to follow from that of the former   **b :** the act of passing from statistical sample data to generalizations (as of the value of population parameters) usu. with calculated degrees of certainty **2 :** something that is inferred; *esp* : a proposition arrived at by inference **3 :** the premises and conclusion of a process of inferring
in·fer·en·tial \ˌin-fə-'ren(t)-shəl\ *adj* [ML *inferentia,* fr. L *inferent-, inferens,* prp. of *inferre*] (1657) **1 :** relating to, involving, or resembling inference **2 :** deduced or deducible by inference
in·fer·en·tial·ly \-'ren(t)-sh(ə-)lē\ *adv* (1691) : by way of inference : through inference

FIGURE 44.1 Detail from *Merriam-Webster's Collegiate Dictionary,* 10th ed. Springfield, MA: Merriam-Webster, 1993.

under the correct spelling (*phantom*, for example) and under likely mis-spellings (*fantom*). Electronic spellers work like computer spelling checkers.

As shown in the samples from *Merriam-Webster's Collegiate Dictionary* (10th ed.), a dictionary entry will tell you a word's correct spelling and also the spelling of its various forms (see Figure 44.1 on p. 533). The entry will indicate preferred spellings and alternative forms, and it will contain listings for related words. It will also provide information about the word's roots and history, and this information may help you remember the spelling.

Exercise 1

A. Assume that you've circled the following words in italics in one of your papers. You're done with your draft, and now you want to double-check your spellings. Look up each word, make any necessary corrections, and then write out one way to remember each correct spelling. Do this whether or not you already know how to spell the word.

EXAMPLE *pal*
school *principle*

> *The school principal is not always every kid's "pal."*

coal *minor*   *precede* to the gate   *stationery* car
vacume the rug   she was *lieing*   *likelyhood*

B. In a group, share your devices for remembering the spellings in Exercise 1A. Write out those the group thinks are best, and share them with the rest of the class.

---

3 Be alert for common patterns of misspelling

Many words contain groups of letters that can trip up even the best spellers. Other words have plural or compound forms that may be confusing, and others add suffixes and prefixes that need special attention.

Plurals. For most words, you can form a plural simply by adding *-s* (*novel, novels; experiment, experiments; contract, contracts*). Watch out for words that end in *-o* preceded by a consonant; they often add *-es* for the plural.

ADD *-ES*   potato, potatoes   tomato, tomatoes
              hero, heroes   zero, zeroes

ADD *-S*   cello, cellos   memo, memos

When a vowel comes before the *-o*, add *-s*.

ADD *-S*   stereo, stereos   video, videos

44b
spell

44.1

For words ending in a consonant plus -*y*, change *y* to *i* and add -*es*.

etiology, etiologies   gallery, galleries   notary, notaries

Exception: Add -*s* for proper nouns (*Kennedy, Kennedys; Tanury, Tanurys*).

For words ending in a vowel plus *y*, however, keep the *y* and add -*s*.

day, days   journey, journeys   pulley, pulleys

For words ending in -*f* or -*fe*, you often change *f* to *v* and add -*s* or -*es*.

hoof, hooves   knife, knives   life, lives   self, selves

Remember, however, that some words simply add -*s*.

belief, beliefs   roof, roofs   turf, turfs

Words ending with a hiss (-*ch*, -*s*, -*ss*, -*sh*, -*x*, or -*z*) generally add -*es*.

bench, benches   bus, buses   bush, bushes
buzz, buzzes   fox, foxes   kiss, kisses

A number of one-syllable words ending in -*s* or -*z* double the final consonant: *quiz, quizzes*.

Though most plurals follow these simple rules, some do not, and you need to be alert for their irregular forms. Words with foreign roots often follow the patterns of the original language, as is the case with the following words drawn from Latin and Greek.

alumna, alumnae (female)   criterion, criteria
alumnus, alumni (male)   datum, data
bacterium, bacteria   vertebra, vertebrae

44b
spell

Some familiar words form irregular plurals: *foot, feet; woman, women; mouse, mice; man, men.* (If you suspect that a word has an irregular plural, be sure to check a dictionary for its form.)

For compound words, use the plural form of the last word except in those few cases where the first word is clearly the most important.

basketball, basketballs   pegboard, pegboards
meadowland, meadowlands   snowflake, snowflakes

Exception: sister-in-law, sisters-in-law.

Word beginnings and endings. **Prefixes** do not change the spelling of the root word that follows.

>   precut   dissatisfied   misspell   unendurable

The prefixes *in-* and *im-* have the same meaning, but you should use *im-* before the letters *b*, *m*, and *p*.

USE *IN-*	incorrect	inadequate	incumbent
USE *IM-*	immobile	impatient	imbalance

   Suffixes may change the spelling of the root word that comes before, and they may pose spelling problems in themselves.
   Retain the silent *-e* at the end of a word when you add a suffix beginning with a consonant.

KEEP *-E*	fate, fateful	gentle, gentleness

Exceptions: words like *judgment*, *argument*, *truly*, and *ninth*.

Drop the silent *-e* when you add a suffix beginning with a vowel.

DROP *-E*	imagine, imaginary	generate, generation
	decrease, decreasing	define, definable

Exceptions: words like *noticeable* and *changeable*.

   Four familiar words end in *-ery*: *stationery* (paper), *cemetery*, *monastery*, *millinery*. Most others end in *-ary*: *stationary* (fixed in place), *secretary*, *primary*, *military*, and *culinary*.
   Most words with a final "seed" sound end in *-cede*: *precede*, *recede*, and *intercede*, for example. Only three are spelled *-ceed*: *proceed*, *succeed*, and *exceed*. One is spelled *-sede*: *supersede*.
   The endings *-able* and *-ible* are easy to confuse because they sound alike. Add *-able* to words that can stand on their own and *-ible* to word roots that cannot stand on their own.

USE *-ABLE*	charitable, habitable, advisable, mendable
	Drop the e for word roots ending in one e *(comparable, detestable)*, but keep it for words ending in double e *(agreeable)*.
USE *-IBLE*	credible, irreducible, frangible

Words containing *ie* and *ei*. Here is an old rhyme that tells you when to use *ie* and *ei*.

I before *e*
Except after *c*,
Or when sounding like *a*
As in neighbor and weigh.

Most words follow the rule.

USE *IE* believe, thief, grief, friend, chief, field, niece

USE *EI* receive, deceit, perceive, ceiling, conceited

Exceptions: weird, seize, foreign, ancient, height, either, neither, their, leisure, forfeit.

4 Watch for commonly misspelled words

Words that sound like each other but are spelled differently (*accept/except, assent/ascent*) are known as **homophones**. Writers often confuse them, creating errors in both spelling and meaning.

INCORRECT The city will not **except** any late bids for the project.

EDITED The city will not **accept** any late bids for the project.

The list on pages 538–540 of homophones and other often-confused words is designed to help you recognize errors in spelling or meaning as you proofread.

5 Try alternatives to the dictionary

Sometimes when you want to use a particular word, you can't find the correct spelling in a dictionary, no matter how hard you look. Try the alternatives listed in the following strategy.

44b
spell

STRATEGY

- List as many possible spellings as you can, even if they seem odd. Try looking them all up. Often you will find the right area in the dictionary and will be able to locate the word with a little more searching.
- Try a thesaurus (see 29c) if you know a suitable synonym; the word may be listed there in its correct spelling.
- Ask friends or classmates if they know the spelling, especially for technical terms; then look up the word in the dictionary to be sure you got good information.

- Check the indexes of books that deal with the topic the word relates to.
- Check your textbook, class notes, or handouts to see whether the word appears there.

6 Get help

All writers make some spelling errors that they simply can't fix because they don't know the word is misspelled. If at all possible, ask members of a revision group to identify any spelling errors you haven't caught. But first clean up all the errors you already know, even if you simply circle the words to identify them as misspelled. If someone else finds any more misspellings in your paper, you have the chance not just to fix them before sending the paper on to its reader but also to learn the correct spellings along the way.

COMMONLY MISSPELLED OR CONFUSED WORD PAIRS

WORD	MEANING	WORD	MEANING
accept	receive	brake	stop
except	other than	break	shatter, destroy; a gap; a pause
affect	to influence; an emotional response	capital	seat of government; monetary resources
effect	result	capitol	building that houses government
all ready	prepared		
already	by this time	cite	quote an authority
allusion	indirect reference	sight	ability to see; a view
illusion	faulty belief or perception	site	a place
ascent	upward movement	complement	to complete or supplement
assent	agreement	compliment	to praise
assure	state positively	desert	abandon; sandy wasteland
ensure	make certain		
insure	indemnify	dessert	sweet course at conclusion of meal
bare	naked		
bear	carry; an animal	discreet	tactful, reserved
board	get on; flat piece of wood	discrete	separate or distinct
		elicit	draw out, evoke
bored	not interested	illicit	illegal

WORD	MEANING	WORD	MEANING
eminent	well known, respected	patience	calm endurance
immanent	inherent	patients	people getting medical treatment
imminent	about to happen	peace	calm or absence of war
fair	lovely; light-colored; just	piece	part of something
fare	fee for transportation	plain	clear, unadorned
foreword	prefatory comment in book	plane	woodworking tool; airplane
forward	advance, ahead	persecute	harass
forth	forward	prosecute	take legal action against
fourth	after *third*	personal	relating to oneself
gorilla	an ape	personnel	employees
guerrilla	kind of soldier or warfare	precede	come before
hear	perceive sound	proceed	go ahead, continue
here	in this place	principal	most important; head of a school; invested money
heard	past tense of *hear*	principle	basic truth, rule of behavior
herd	group of animals		
hole	opening	rain	precipitation
whole	complete	reign	to rule; period of ruling
its	possessive form of *it*	rein	strap for guiding an animal
it's	contraction for *it is*	raise	lift up or build up
later	following in time	raze	tear down
latter	last in a series	right	correct
lessen	make less	rite	ritual
lesson	something learned	write	compose; put words into a text
meat	flesh	road	street
meet	encounter	rode	past tense of *ride*
loose	not tight	scene	section of a play: setting of an action
lose	misplace	seen	visible
no	negative	stationary	fixed in place or still
know	understand or be aware of	stationery	paper for writing
passed	past tense of pass		
past	after; events occurring at a prior time		

(continued)

44b spell

COMMONLY MISSPELLED OR CONFUSED WORD PAIRS (continued)

WORD	MEANING	WORD	MEANING
straight	unbending	waist	middle of body
strait	water passageway	waste	leftover or discarded material
than	compared with		
then	at that time; next	which	one of a group
their	possessive form of *they*	witch	person with magical powers
there	in that place	who's	contraction for *who is*
they're	contracton for *they are*	whose	possessive of *who*
		your	possessive of *you*
to	toward	you're	contraction for *you are*
too	in addition, also		
two	number after *one*		

44C Using long-term strategies to improve your spelling

Improving your spelling in general is like improving anything that develops slowly: you need to practice. Here are three useful ways to become a more effective speller.

1 Use memory devices and pronunciation aids

The use of **mnemonics** (memory aids) can greatly improve your spelling by reminding you of odd spelling conventions that don't correspond with pronunciation. In *Beyond the "SP" Label*, Patricia McAlexander, Ann Dobie, and Noel Gregg offer a number of memory aids, including the following.

All right is spelled like *all wrong*.

A lot is like *a little*.

Emigrant, immigrant: An emigrant leaves; an immigrant comes in.

Separate: sep_arate rates two *a*'s; there's a rat in *separate*.

Use these as models to create memory aids of your own.

Some words get misspelled because they are often pronounced partially or incorrectly. You need to develop an ear for "careful" pronunciations equivalent to spelling. Instead of hearing *new-cue-lar*, a common pronunciation of *nuclear*, hear the word in its carefully pronounced (spelling) form: *new-clee-ar*.

DID YOU KNOW?

Experts frequently argue over just how difficult the English spelling system is. In his book *The English Language*, David Crystal tries to show that the system isn't really as bad as we think. He claims that only four hundred words have "irregular" or idiosyncratic spellings and cites a study showing that 84 percent follow some sort of general (learnable) pattern, such as *purse, nurse, curse* and *hatch, catch, latch*.

David Crystal, *The English Language* (New York: Viking, 1988) 69.

---

2 Read more and attend to spellings

Nothing boosts literacy (spelling included) so powerfully as reading. The more you read, the more likely you are to see words spelled correctly. When reading, keep a list of words you might use (and might otherwise misspell) someday. Focus consciously on words with difficult spellings (if you've been doing that in this chapter, you may already have learned the spellings of *mnemonic* and *nuclear*).

3 Build your own speller

The most useful spelling aid should look like someone's personal telephone book: filled with names and numbers generally meaningless to other people. If you keep track of words you commonly misspell, perhaps in a little notebook or file, you'll find yourself looking up possible candidates for misspellings much more quickly. As you begin learning and remembering the correct spellings, you can cross some words off your list as you're adding new ones.

Exercise 2

44c
spell

A. Without using a dictionary, circle the words that are misspelled in this list.

supercede	conceed	procede
idiosyncracy	concensus	accomodate
dexterous	impressario	irresistable
rhythym	opthalmologist	diptheria
anamoly	afficianado	caesarian
grafitti	judgement	liason

B. Working with a partner or in a small group, compare your answers to Exercise 2A, and *then* resolve any debates with a dictionary.

44d Spelling and the computer

You're no doubt aware of the virtues of the spelling checker, a program that searches your document for misspellings and asks you whether they're correct. But spelling checkers need to be used with care.

1 Understand how spelling checkers work

Most spelling checkers on personal computers work in conjunction with a dictionary that must be present in the computer's memory. Often these computer dictionaries hold several thousand basic words. When you ask the computer to screen your document for any spelling errors, it compares each word in your text with the words in the dictionary. If the word matches a word in the dictionary, the computer assumes the word is correctly spelled, and it moves on to the next word.

When the computer encounters a word that does *not* match any word in its dictionary, it asks you whether the word is misspelled. If it is, you can select an alternative spelling or type in the correction, and the computer then moves on until it finds the next possible error. A typical program also allows you to add words to its often limited dictionary. In this way, you can personalize the dictionary so that an unusual word or technical term won't be flagged every time the computer finds it in your paper.

44.2

2 Use a spelling checker cautiously

Using a spelling checker, especially on longer documents, is likely to reveal at least one or two errors. But whatever you do, don't rely *entirely* on a spelling checker to fix your writing.

A spelling checker can't reveal words that are properly spelled but used incorrectly. If it runs across the sentence "The Lakewood High quarterback lead his team to victory in the semifinals," a spelling checker will ignore *lead* because this is a correctly spelled word in the dictionary. But here, *lead* should be *led*.

The computer may flag a word as misspelled and then, on command, offer you other correct spelling options. If you're not careful, you can mistakenly choose the wrong word to be inserted in place of the misspelled one.

44d
spell

PART 5

Using Research Strategies: Reading and Writing Within a Research Community

CHAPTER 45

PARTICIPATING IN RESEARCH COMMUNITIES: ACADEMIC, WORK, AND PUBLIC

As a customer, you've probably walked past the perfume areas of department stores many times. What would happen if on every such occasion, you found yourself overcome with a fit of sneezing? You might share the experience with other people and get their reactions, or you might try some informal experiments, perhaps seeing how close to the perfume area you could get without sneezing. Eventually, though, your curiosity would get the best of you, and you would begin searching for an explanation: what's the relationship between perfume and sneezing?

At that moment, you would be embarking on a research journey—a systematic investigation of a question, phenomenon, or topic. Your personal interest might well turn into a full-scale research paper for a course, perhaps starting with an Internet search for a site that reports the results of studies on the relationship between perfume and allergies (such as the Health and Environmental Resource Center—<http://www.herc.org>).

You may be the only person you know who sneezes in the perfume section of a department store. But hundreds of other people, in businesses, universities, and communities, are conducting and reporting on research relating to this topic, for many different reasons. Responding to letters from consumers about perfumed advertisements, for example, the director of a department store's mail advertising division recognizes her responsibility to investigate and report on potential customer-related problems. She looks up articles on legal liability for allergic reactions to perfumed ads and billing statement inserts, and incorporates this research into her management report outlining the problem and suggesting ways to avoid it. A parent's concern about his child's allergic reaction to perfumed junk mail leads him to join a community group that is collecting information on healthy school environments. Similarly, an academic such as a sociologist might study changes in people's attitudes toward allergy-triggering junk mail, and then publish her research in a sociology journal. Motivations like these are what lead people to become part of research communities and contribute to the advance and dissemination of knowledge.

45a Recognizing research communities

Over the years, the ubiquitous college research paper has developed a poor image: a boring, tedious exercise in which you show a teacher that you can collect a bunch of information and dump it into a paper that has lots of correctly formatted references. But consider this: almost every aspect of your life—the LCD watch that beeped you awake, the chemical in your toothpaste that helped remove plaque from your teeth, the UVA-filtering lenses in the sunglasses you put on as you went out, the internal combustion engine that got you to school (and what it did to the environment along the way), the

45.1

GENERAL COMMUNITY GOALS FOR PRINT, ELECTRONIC, AND FIELD RESEARCH			
	ACADEMIC	**WORK**	**PUBLIC**
GOALS	Explain or prove, offer well-supported interpretations or conclusions, advance knowledge, analyze or synthesize information for use in other settings	Document problems, propose a project or course of action, compare information, improve performance	Support arguments for a policy or course of action, inform or advise for the public good
AUDIENCE EXPECTATIONS	Detailed evidence from varied sources including quotations, paraphrases, and summaries; documented sources that acknowledge scholarship	Clear, direct, and precise information; appropriate detail; less formal documentation	Accessible, fair, and persuasive information with evidence; informal documentation
TYPICAL QUESTIONS	What does it mean? What happened? How does it occur? How might it be modified?	What is the problem? How can we solve it? What course of action will help us achieve our goals?	How can this policy be made better? What do people need or want to know?
TYPICAL FORMS	Interpretive (thesis) paper, informative paper, research report, grant report	Proposal, report, feasibility study, memorandum	Position paper, editorial, proposal, informative article, pamphlet, guidelines
SAMPLE RESEARCH TOPIC (COSMETICS)	Gender roles in cosmetics advertising (refer to *Social Sciences Index*)	International marketing strategies for cosmetics (refer to *BIZZ—Business Index*)	Animal testing of cosmetics (refer to *Reader's Guide to Periodical Literature*)
SAMPLE RESEARCH QUESTION	What roles (and values) for women and men are reinforced by advertising?	How should trade-marked packaging be modified for regional markets?	Is animal testing necessary? How good are the alternatives?

trigger mechanisms in the stoplights on the street, even the process that resulted in 70 percent of your newspaper being composed of recycled products—all this and much more is the direct or cumulative result of **research**. Even phenomena that are not the products of research, such as the good feeling you got when you alerted someone that they had dropped a ten dollar bill on the street, or the way your body's immune system fought off the virus you unknowingly ingested at the cafeteria, are the subjects of intense, sustained investigation by communities of researchers and scholars.

Although we like to think that some specific person "invented" microwave technology or "discovered" that Pluto may not be a planet but a moon or "found" the principle of ego gratification, research questions almost always exist and are pursued by a **research community**, a web of people and texts preserving and adding to the understanding of a subject. Without such communities, knowledge couldn't possibly build on itself, and we would all be living in a state of intellectual darkness.

Although anyone engaged by a general subject like "the relationship between cell phone use and car accidents" has a common interest, a researcher's domain or subject of investigation defines the community of readers, writers, and speakers who are investigating certain aspects of that question. They share a perspective on the scope of a focused matter of interest— a **research topic**. They agree on what's worth asking about the topic, **research questions** that set goals for gathering and examining information. They also use common terms, key words that form a research thread linking topics, questions, and resources.

45b Developing a research question

As a researcher and writer, how can you arrive at a focus for your work that lets you pull together current knowledge about a subject and ask (and sometimes answer) new questions that go beyond that knowledge? Begin by avoiding broad subjects. Aim for limited topics: specific elements of a subject or particular issues and unanswered questions arising from it. For example, while it might not be too difficult for you to gather and report information and ideas about subjects like "the effects of exercise" or "gender and advertising," it would be a very challenging task indeed to conduct the kind of detailed inquiry necessary to arrive at fresh insights of your own on such broad subjects.

While some people can develop intriguing research topics of their own, most worthwhile research writing grows from *issues* or *questions* developed within a research community. Typically, the members of such a community focus their reading, writing, and oral communication on the most puzzling, controversial, or intriguing aspects of a subject. For example, recent academic discussions of the effects of exercise have asked whether regular exercise helps relieve depression, what effects exercise has on self-image, and whether exercise habits influence dating and marriage. In short, by paying attention to what others are thinking, saying, and asking about a subject, you can discover ways to focus your research and arrive at a limited topic worth exploring.

For your research to be productive, the research topic should be well focused and manageable, and address aspects of the subject (issues, questions) that your readers will consider worth your attention and theirs. Try one or more of the following approaches to focus your topic.

1 Consider the assignment

Usually, your research papers in college will be prompted by specific assignments. Even when that assignment specifies a subject for research, you'll probably need strategies to help identify a focused research topic.

STRATEGY

- If the assignment comes in written form, read it carefully, looking for key words and phrases that specify a topic or question and that either limit or open up your choices. If the assignment takes oral form, ask questions to identify key words and phrases or concerns you will need to address. If the project begins with an occasion or problem, write down words and phrases you or your readers are likely to associate with it.
- If a word or phrase immediately suggests a topic, write it down, followed by a list of synonyms or alternative terms. Draw on this list as you develop guiding questions for your research (see 45a-4), follow a research thread (see 45a-5), and write your paper or report.
- If you can't identify a topic right away, take key words and phrases, write them down, and brainstorm (see 2c-2) related words and phrases along with the topics they suggest.
- Consider asking the person or people who made the assignment what they think of a potential topic—and for further topic suggestions. Consider asking potential readers for their reactions.

In an intermediate composition course, Summer Arrigo-Nelson and Jennifer Figliozzi were asked to "investigate the psychological or social dimensions of a local or campus problem" by drawing on print or electronic sources and field research of their own, and to present their conclusions in the form of an academic research report. They underlined the words *psychological or social dimensions* and *campus problem* in the assignment, and made a list of campus problems.

45b
resrch

low class attendance	new majors	date rape
inadequate library	role of sports	student alcohol use
living conditions	canceled classes	student fees
parking	drugs	crime

They chose "student alcohol use" as a focus. The topic interested them. They also thought they could easily find some research sources and that doing field research of their own wouldn't be too difficult. Some initial reading and brainstorming led them to wonder about the role of parents in determining the drinking habits of college students, and they decided to address this question in their research.

2 Consider your audience

As you join the "conversations" that various research communities may be having about your topic, remember that readers in each community expect different things from the documents they read, so your own collection of sources won't all look alike. Academic readers look for detailed evidence from a variety of sources and expect carefully documented sources and quotations. Readers in work settings expect a clear and direct presentation, accurate information, and detail appropriate to the subject and the audience's expertise, along with less formal documentation. And readers in public communities expect information and supporting evidence that is accurate, clear, accessible, and persuasive, without quite as much attention to documentation. While college research papers typically address academic audiences, they don't have to; your own paper may take one of many forms and be addressed to one of many different communities of readers.

45.2

STRATEGY

An **audience inventory**—a checklist or set of questions adapted to a specific audience—tailors your research to the specific concerns of your audience. An inventory works best when you know your audience well, as is common in work settings, or when your audience is a local one (such as the residents of a town, a campus community, or the members of an organization). Try answering the following questions.

What problems or issues has the audience been facing?
What new discoveries or information might interest or be useful to the audience?
What policies or programs are causing your readers difficulty or might be helpful to them?

45b
resrch

Summer Arrigo-Nelson and Jennifer Figliozzi prepared an audience inventory to help plan their paper on the effects of alcohol consumption among college students. Below is a sample of their inventory, which focused on the audience of their own campus community.

AUDIENCE INVENTORY QUESTION	*What new discoveries or information about student alcohol use might benefit the campus community?*
SUMMER AND JENNIFER'S RESPONSE	*Our conclusion about the relationship between student drinking behavior in college and parental permissiveness for drinking in the home could be important for a campus program aiming to reduce student alcohol use.*

A WORD ABOUT SPEAKING

Creating an audience inventory and linking it to your research question is especially important for oral presentations in which you summarize, synthesize, or report on the results of others' research. What has your audience come to hear about? How can you most effectively stimulate their interest in your research question? What will they already know, and what will they want to learn? Is the community engaged in research on your topic substantially different from your audience, and if so, how should you translate or present the information from that community for this different audience?

3 Explore and browse

Good research questions often begin in a general area of interest, something that you'd like to know more about. For example, you might be curious about why some people believe that the United States fooled the world by "staging" the Apollo moon voyages in the 1960s and '70s to win the space race against the Russians. This general interest is a good place to begin browsing sources, always keeping in mind that you will need to *narrow* and *refine* your focus to a specific question for investigation. In the process of searching broadly for information on a topic, you'll begin to find more specific areas of interest that can help you narrow your focus.

STRATEGY

Try using some Internet **search engines**, Web sites where users can look for information or browse through collections of **links** to other sites. Be aware that such search engines use differing principles for organizing their results—by the "most consulted," for example, or by the best match with your key words, or even by how much a site is willing to pay to be included in the top ten results. Also be very

45b
resrch

careful to do some preliminary analysis of a Web site's credibility and authority, rejecting bogus sites before you spend time consulting them fully.

Popular search engines include:

Google at <http://www.google.com>
AltaVista at <http://www.altavista.com>
HotBot at <http://www.hotbot.lycos.com>
Lycos at <http://dir.lycos.com/>
Ask Jeeves at <http://www.ask.com>

In browsing through the results of his *Google* search for information on the "moon walk conspiracy," Sam Roles found several sites that related to the psychology of conspiracy theories. Because he hadn't known that psychologists and sociologists were actively researching this phenomenon, he found his focus shifting and becoming more defined—an *angle* on the moon walk conspiracy. As he explored this angle, he found many other case studies of conspiracy theory in recent and historical events, including the death of Princess Diana, the "purported" death of the Beatles' Paul McCartney cryptically "explained" in hidden messages on their albums, and government cover-ups of encounters with aliens.

4 Locate and track your topic in a domain

As you explore a general topic area, you'll inevitably find your focus both expanding outward to a broader domain and contracting inward to some specific aspect of the topic. This expansion outward allows you to choose new, more specific focuses. As your focus sharpens, it may once again expand as you learn more about the topic. Being completely open to possibilities within the constraints of your assignment can lead you to make many interesting discoveries and lead you into an area you're really motivated to explore. Along the way, you're also learning where your final focus is "positioned" within a broader area of research.

STRATEGY

Try mapping out the process of your topic exploration according to the levels of specificity within an area. Begin with your first topic choice; as you explore, place any exploration that **broadens** your focus on the left of your topic choice, and any exploration that **narrows** your focus on the right of your topic choice. If a new focus emerges from your exploration, connect it to the area it derived from and continue the diagram from there.

Sam Roles had begun with "moon walk conspiracy" as his first choice of a topic area. He soon found that this topic was located within a broader topic, conspiracy theory. Exploring this more general topic led him to more cases of conspiracy theory roughly parallel in specificity to the moon walk case (see Figure 45.1). One of these was the theory that the government is hiding information about (and actual physical evidence of) encounters with aliens. This, in turn, led to an even more specific case, the "Roswell" encounters.

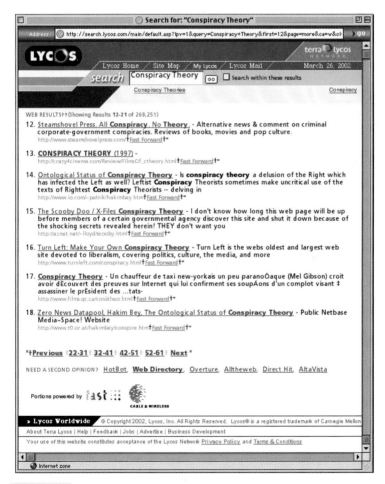

FIGURE 45.1   Results page from a *Lycos* search using the term "Conspiracy Theory"

You can also explore a general topic and locate the level of your question(s) within that topic by tracing discussions of a topic online. **Usenet newsgroups** can offer you a wide range of opinions and perspectives, and if you trace a research thread through them, you're likely to encounter fresh information, interesting or controversial ideas, and new developments. **Discussion lists** can help you identify the most current knowledge of a subject or the most recent state of a discussion. For more information on discussion lists and newsgroups, see Chapter 13.

5 Identify and apply keywords to your search

As you've no doubt discovered with Internet search engines, successfully locating relevant information depends on the terms you use in your search. Sometimes these terms are predictable in advance; sometimes you'll need to figure out which terms work best as you search for information. For example, searching under "conspiracy" for purported cases (like Princess Diana's death) will yield millions of sites on every conceivable aspect of conspiracy—a very ineffective way to get the information you need. Searching under "conspiracy theory" narrows the possibilities a little, but still offers a hodgepodge of material. "Cases of conspiracy theory" provides a crisper, more refined set of links, including one to material that emerged from a recent academic conference on the John F. Kennedy assassination and the conspiracy theories surrounding it. One link provides a definition of conspiracy theory, other examples of it, and a bibliography of twenty-four books and articles—clearly a productive find within a mass of potentially useless information.

STRATEGY

Brainstorm a list of keywords on your topic to get started. As you try these out in your preliminary searches, keep track of which new terms or variants emerge, so you know what to continue searching under. These terms will help you later on as you refine your focus and develop a thesis for your paper.

Remember that the Internet isn't likely to provide everything you need for your research paper. Depending on your topic, it might provide very little. But it's a good place to begin. For example, by going to some of the most academic-sounding links in your preliminary search for information on conspiracy theories, you might see a reference to a published collection of essays on the subject, perhaps Nancy Lusignan Shultz's *Fear Itself: Enemies Real and Imagined in American Culture* (1999), which includes scholarly essays on various aspects of conspiracy theory in the United States. Finding this book in your library will inevitably yield many other sources in the essays' bibliographies. Using the Internet to **get started** is an excellent strategy; relying on it for all your information may result in a paper that lacks coherence and appears to be a random assortment of ideas.

6 Develop guiding research questions

All research is an attempt to answer questions. When you've chosen an interesting topic to investigate, you need to ask questions about that topic in order to move forward. **Guiding questions** are questions that help you set goals for gathering and examining information, and help you focus on the most important ideas as you comb through print and electronic sources, or analyze data gathered from field research.

> **STRATEGY**
>
> Work toward two or three questions early on in your research process. As you do so, relate your questions to your general and specific goals. What you're trying to answer is based on what you're trying to provide to your audience. Design your questions to enlighten you and your readers.

Summer Arrigo-Nelson and Jennifer Figliozzi developed the following questions for their academic research project on the relationship of parental behaviors to college student drinking.

> *Will students with permission to drink at home show different drinking behaviors at college than those without permission to drink at home?*
>
> *Do the students feel that a correlation exists between drinking behaviors at home and at college?*

Exercise 1

A. Choose one of the following general topic areas as if you were going to write a research paper on it. Using the strategies in this section, consider possible audiences for the research, explore the topic (and note your movement within and beyond the topic area), list two or three keywords and/or phrases that usually yield relevant information, and create several guiding questions for your research.

Whole language versus phonics in reading instruction
Road rage
Cures for Lyme disease
"Slow growth" methods for containing suburban sprawl
Rising acceptability of body piercing and tattoos
Threat of biological warfare

45b
resrch

Hormone replacement therapy and breast cancer
Irradiation of perishable foods

B. Exchange work from Exercise 1A with at least two other students. How do your questions differ? Which questions identify points that need to be clarified? What possible audiences could be addressed, and in what form of writing?

45c Mapping research communities

When you learn about a topic, you begin by collecting and exploring a lot of information—the more the better. At first everything may seem relevant, especially if you haven't yet decided on your focus and research question(s) and are still exploring the topic. The result is a mass of information, and you must begin making sense of it and deciding what material is really relevant to your project.

This can be challenging, because people focusing on your topic may be working in different research communities, some of them with academic goals, some with work-related goals, and some with public or civic goals. Each community may be asking specific questions about the topic from particular perspectives. They may recognize that other communities are working in the same area but that those communities are not asking the same questions for the same reasons. An anti-handgun coalition, for example, may be collecting reliable statistics on accidental handgun deaths among children to argue that gun control is a good and necessary thing to reduce these needless deaths. The National Rifle Association, meanwhile, may be collecting related data to argue that education and protective measures among gun owners, not government control, is a better solution to the problem. These communities are not the same—in fact, they're opposed to each other—but both are conducting similar kinds of research on the same subject and offering different interpretations and recommendations for specific purposes.

As you collect and sift through information on your topic (the "what") you need to begin figuring out the source this information is coming from (the "who" or "where"), the ways in which they work with and around the topic (the "how"), and what purposes or goals the community is trying to accomplish (the "why"). Such analysis requires that you stand back from the information itself and figure out its context.

1 Analyzing the "who" of research communities

As you collect information about your topic, look for clues about the people providing that information and about their affiliations. As Sam Roles explored conspiracy theory, for example, he began to see some hints about the communities of researchers exploring this topic. Some of the sites he explored had links to organizations, papers, and conferences associated with the terms "psychology" and "social psychology." Others seemed connected to two related fields: "American studies" and "cultural studies" (both of which also happened to have departments at Roles's own university). Still others clustered around "political science" or "government," while a few were associated with "history," especially those focusing on the JFK assassination and "holocaust conspiracy theory." Each cluster of sources appeared to be loosely affiliated, to share a common ground.

STRATEGY

For each article, book, or online document you find on your topic, look for clues about the community from which it emerged— the "who" or the "where." Be aware that Web sites may contain multiple sources of information or links to other sources, creating crisscrossing communities. Analyze *each* document and link separately.

- What can you find out about the author? What is the author's affiliation?
- Is the source and/or author linked in any way to an organization, department, sponsor, business, or other entity?
- Are there any references in your source? If so, are they, in turn, linked to a specific group or community on the basis of their titles and publication outlets?

As Summer Arrigo-Nelson and Jennifer Figliozzi explored their general topic of college drinking, several research communities began to emerge from their analysis. Most of their sources seemed to cluster around two research communities: the academic discipline of psychology, and the field of college administration, especially student services (dorm life, campus environment, etc.). Their tips came mostly from the journal titles their searches yielded: in psychology, *Psychological Bulletin, Psychological Addictions*, and *Psychological Review*; in college administration, *Journal of College and University Student Housing, Journal of American College Health*, and *Higher Education Handbook*. Some publications, such as *Journal of Educational Psychology*, seemed to bridge communities, and cited works in common. Another cluster of sources came from state and federal government agencies, as well as various nonprofit groups. But a few sources also had commercial sponsors, including the Anheuser-Busch corporation.

2 Analyzing the "how" of research communities

Every research community is tied together by common assumptions about the object of its research, by common language and terminology, and

45c
resrch

by common methods of analysis and interpretation. Communities don't always harmoniously agree on these assumptions, of course; in some fields, for example, scholars debate whether their research questions are best answered through **quantitative** research (such as statistical measures) or **qualitative** research (such as careful description and analysis). Sometimes, these arguments can lead a research community to divide itself into more specific communities on the basis of methodology. Still, the communities are closely aligned and their scholars are often located in the same places, such as specific academic departments or government agencies.

As Sam Roles began recognizing the communities of his sources, for example, he also found that their terminology, questions, and research methods differed. While the historians were sifting through facts and evidence, or analyzing the way in which conspiracy theorists were presenting facts and evidence, the cultural studies scholars were commenting in more open-ended ways on the collective mindset of Americans. Although the latter frequently showcased and analyzed texts from conspiracy theorists, they did so in a looser framework of interpretation than did the historians.

STRATEGY

After beginning to identify the communities from which clusters of your sources have emerged, look for patterns in the way they approach your topic.

- Do they use any common terminology or language? How specialized is it? Does it assume a general or specialized audience?
- How are they coming to their conclusions—through observation? speculation? anecdote? data collection? Do they use the same methods for getting and interpreting information?
- How do they present information—clinically? anecdotally? Are their texts organized in similar ways, such as "Introduction, Methods, Results/Discussion, Implications?"

In recognizing one community of researchers (psychologists) interested in college drinking, Summer Arrigo-Nelson and Jennifer Figliozzi soon began to see patterns in the way members of this community conducted and reported on their research. The terminology appeared clinical and abstract, and included phrases like "cultural stimuli," "social-psychological properties," "male-dominated social norms," and "recreational use of psychoactive substances." The articles tended to report on controlled experiments in which "subjects" were "tested" by being exposed to certain "conditions." Many of the results were presented numerically, using complicated statistical analyses, but also had readable conclusions. In contrast, the community these students characterized as "college administrators," while they still worked with statis-

45c
resrch

tics and sometimes reported on studies of data, tended to use phrases like "student growth and development," "organizational properties of a campus," "peer pressure," and "awareness programs." The introductions to their articles were longer, devoting less space to defining terms and more to outlining a general problem. While the psychological articles always included extensive literature reviews in separate sections, most of those in educational administration wove references to other literature into their introductions and throughout their essays.

3 Analyzing the "why" of research communities

The communities that sponsor, engage in, and report on research are driven by various *goals and objectives*. Sometimes these are very specific: solve a particular social problem, develop a new product, work a bug out of a process. Usually these specific objectives are part of a broader set of goals: understand the nature of human behavior, completely eliminate a cause of death, create the most profitable organization manufacturing a product line. To understand the research community of each of your sources—to be able to *interpret* that source—you need to figure out the "why" of the community: its goals and objectives.

In browsing material about conspiracy theories, Sam Roles located the Web site of an organization called The Committee for the Scientific Investigation of Claims of the Paranormal (csicop.org). After deciding on the authority of this organization (which was founded by noted scientists and authors such as Carl Sagan and Isaac Asimov), Roles began analyzing the "why" of the organization. He soon found its mission statement: it encourages "the critical investigation of paranormal and fringe-science claims from a responsible, scientific point of view and disseminates factual information about the results of such inquiries to the scientific community and the public. It also promotes science and scientific inquiry, critical thinking, science education, and the use of reason in examining important issues." With this "why" information, Roles could begin to read with a fuller critical understanding the extensive publications the organization has issued on the subject of the 1947 "alien spaceship crash" in Roswell, New Mexico, and the "conspiracy theory" that the U.S. military has covered up its knowledge (and evidence) of the incident for over fifty years.

STRATEGY

After gaining an understanding of the community from which a source has emerged, analyze the community's motivation or goals for producing or disseminating information about your topic.

- If the source is connected to an organization, can you find its mission statement or statement of purpose?

45c
resrch

- If the source is connected broadly to an academic or scholarly discipline, what can you learn about the discipline from the mission statements of its central organizations? (Consider looking at several departmental descriptions at major research-oriented universities.)
- In the absence of any direct information about the general or specific goals of the community from which a source comes, can you speculate about those goals on the basis of the document itself? Is there a thesis or conclusion that might suggest those goals?

Summer Arrigo-Nelson and Jennifer Figliozzi found some information about college drinking at a Web site sponsored by the Anheuser-Busch corporation. This site described the company's "consumer awareness and educational programs," including a "college issues" initiative aimed at responsible drinking and the curbing of illegal and underage consumption of alcohol. The site itself didn't contain lots of factual information, instead describing campus programs sponsored by Anheuser-Busch. Arrigo-Nelson and Figliozzi interpreted the information in the context of the company's overriding goal (to be a profitable marketer of beer); therefore, its noble attempts at public service could not conflict with that overriding goal (for example, by advocating universal sobriety instead of "responsible, legal-age drinking").

Exercise 2

A. Locate two sources of information about the topic you chose for Exercise 1. Using the strategies described in 45c, write informal analyses of the "who/where, how, what, and why" of each source.

B. Share your analyses in a small group, explaining what clues provided the information that led to your analysis.

45d Planning your research

By their very nature, college research projects require a sustained effort, usually over several weeks or months. By planning your project carefully and making the most efficient use of your time, you can avoid the increasing stress of a looming deadline and the fear that you'll be turning in an incomplete or substandard paper. Planning involves dividing up your work

45d
resrch

and sticking to a schedule. By being methodical in the process of your research, you'll make the most efficient use of your time.

1 Plan your research

Managing all the decisions and activities involved in research is like juggling: you need to plan your moves. To manage time and effort effectively, pay attention to three decision points.

1. **How much time do you have?** When should your report or document be in final form? Do you have to produce any intermediate assignments, such as a progress report, drafts, or notes?
2. **What kind of report or document will you be creating, and for whom?** What form will your work take? What resources will you have to gather or develop in order to produce such work? What audience or community of readers will you be addressing? What will you need to learn about them and their expectations? Will you need to share or discuss the project with them while you're researching and writing?
3. **What kind of research must you do?** Will you be doing research in printed or library sources (books, articles, documents, microfilms, databases)? In electronic sources (Internet, World Wide Web, email, CD-ROM databases)? In field settings through interviews, surveys, observations, experiments, or ethnographic study?

STRATEGY

Create a research and writing plan by working backwards from the due date for a project. Even if you don't follow the plan exactly, a calendar, list of dates, or chart of activities can help you get started on a project and give you a sense of direction. It can also help you avoid the problem of leaving too many activities for the last moment. Your plan should take the shape dictated by your topic, audience, purpose, and resources.

45.3

Here is brief plan that reflects some activities you might include in your own research plan.

ACTIVITY	COMPLETE BY
Analyze task and audience; focus topic.	
Figure out guiding questions.	October 22
Do preliminary research; look for research thread.	

45d
resrch

ACTIVITY	COMPLETE BY
Do journal writing, freewriting, outlining, or sketching out of ideas to identify goals and necessary resources for the project.	October 29
Go to library and identify print resources. Make appointments for interviews. Go online and identify electronic resources. Prepare working bibliography.	November 6
Do research in print resources and take notes. Conduct interviews; transcribe them or take notes. Do electronic research, take notes, and download information. Summarize ideas and information in notes, outlines, or preliminary drafts of parts of the report.	November 20
Create a tentative plan and thesis. Draft the report or document.	November 27
Share the draft with colleagues. Begin a list of works cited.	December 4
Revise the paper. Check citations and list of works cited. Proofread and submit final paper.	December 12

2 Build a working bibliography

If you work haphazardly and too quickly, especially when locating sources for your project, you may find yourself later having to spend valuable time backtracking—getting lost references, relocating passages in a text, or trying to retrieve an Internet site that you didn't bother to bookmark.

STRATEGY

Build a **working bibliography**. Include any and every source that has potential to be included in your paper. Don't include sources that you're not reasonably sure you'll be able to obtain. As you select sources, be sure to make complete and accurate entries. Entries in a working bibliography should contain the following:

45d
resrch

BOOKS	ARTICLES	ELECTRONIC SOURCES
Call number	Author(s)	Name of source
Author(s), editor(s), translator(s)	Title and subtitle	Address/URL/access route/vendor
Title and subtitle	Periodical name	receipt of
City of publication, name of publisher, and date of publication	Volume and issue, and number (if used)	information
	Date	Name of person responsible for
	Page number(s)	writing or posting information or name of sender
		Original publication information (online or in print, if available)

Also choose a format to record your bibliographic entries: note cards, a research notebook, or electronic notes. Use a backup system (photocopies for paper and separate disks or drives for electronic material); you don't want the horrible experience of losing all your hard work and having to start over.

3 Take clear, careful notes

There are two kinds of useful notes you can take when reading and considering your source material: **analytical notes** and **critical notes**. Analytical notes are informational; they record facts and details from your source (including quotations), and they focus on material that is relevant to your research question. Critical notes are your own interpretations of and comments on the source. If analytical notes are the "what's there" of your source, then critical notes are the "what does it mean" or "how might we assess this" of your source.

Summer Arrigo-Nelson and Jennifer Figliozzi located an online government publication on the relationship between environment and college drinking. In their analytical notes, they included the following description of the online document.

Provides an overview of the research on this relationship between environment and drinking behavior on college campuses, focusing mainly on the physical, organizational, and social-psychological properties of campuses relative to drinking behaviors and problems caused by alcohol use. Offers six main conclusions from the literature review, most importantly that the college environment has very powerful influences

45d
resrch

on students, especially those who seek peer acceptance, and also that anti-drinking campaigns have been ineffective. Each conclusion yields a series of recommendations about campus environment and student drinking behavior.

In their critical notes, they evaluated the source highly for its excellent summary of the research on this aspect of their topic, but also noted that it did not account very fully for the prior environmental influences that students brought with them to college.

A WORD ABOUT SPEAKING

In any presentation that reports on or summarizes the research or scholarship of others, your audience will probably not want to get mired in details; they will want an overview or summary, something that gives them a useful perspective on a topic. Your analytical and critical notes should be geared toward this audience need as well as to the need for substantiating information that you might not present. For example, an audience member might question a conclusion you present from the research, and you should be ready to explain how that conclusion was reached, even though you might not provide all those details during your presentation.

CHAPTER 46

USING PRINT AND ELECTRONIC RESOURCES

When you start your research, the number of resources you find immediately will depend in part on how narrowly or broadly you've defined your topic or research question. An Internet search under a term such as "genetics" will yield an astonishing number of sources—so many that it's impossible to begin your work in earnest. Conversely, a search for information on "the exploitation of dwarfism in the history of the Ringling Bros. circus" will yield little. Clearly, your search will be most effective if you've developed an appropriate focus. In the first case above, you would need to focus on a much more specific aspect of genetics to get started; in the second case, you would have to pan back from a single circus or a single abnormality to something broader, such as the history of exploitation in circus freak shows.

As you adjust your focus, you'll almost never be justified in reporting to your instructor that "there's nothing out there on my topic." Library and electronic resources are filled with easily accessible information and also offer many strategies for locating harder-to-access sources. With a careful and thorough search strategy, and a willingness to refocus your topic as you explore, you'll probably uncover plenty of sources, more than you can possibly use. This wealth of information will let you write with authority and sophistication about your research area.

46a Developing search strategies

A **search strategy** begins with your topic and research questions. It helps you select, examine, and evaluate resources most appropriate for your task, from the general through the specific. A search strategy is not a detailed plan. You can't know the specific twists and turns your research will take until you encounter them as you trace a thread of information and ideas. As your research goes forward, you can make more specific plans, reflecting your growing understanding of your subject and the shape your report or document will take.

46a
source

1 Pay attention to *where* research takes place

- **Library research** focuses primarily on print or electronic resources: books, articles, pamphlets, microfilms, databases, recordings, films, artworks, and reproductions. Your skill with indexing and reference systems will help you work with materials in library settings.
- **Electronic (online) research** focuses on information and documents on disk or available through networks: texts, data, graphics, pictures, audio, film, and email. Your skill with computer software and search engines will give you access to materials in electronic settings.
- **Field research** focuses mainly on events and oral texts gathered through observation, interviews, surveys, note taking, and recording. It requires skills in interviewing, administering surveys, observing, and interpreting.

2 Pay attention to the differences between primary and secondary sources

Primary sources consist of information and ideas in their original (or close-to-original) form: historical documents, works of literature, email resources, letters, tapes of interviews, survey data, videotapes, raw statistics, and other kinds of basic information that contain little or no interpretation by the observer or gatherer. **Secondary sources** consist of works that analyze, summarize, sort, interpret, or explain the information in primary sources. Secondary sources tell you what others have said about your area of research. For example, in his research on the purported 1947 "alien spaceship crash" in Roswell, New Mexico, Sam Roles could examine primary documents such as transcripts of oral testimonials from eyewitnesses or secondary documents such as analyses of the nature or veracity of those testimonials.

46.1

3 Move from preliminary sources, to general sources, to specialized sources

As you begin your research, you'll usually skim the most general and broadly informative sources such as encyclopedias, magazine articles, ready references, general information books, or Web pages (see 46b). These **preliminary sources** are helpful in focusing on a topic, arriving at research questions, and identifying keywords to use in searching indexes and databases or with search engines on the Web and Internet (see 46c).

General sources provide background information on a topic and help identify issues, problems, and ideas you might examine more closely. They include books, articles in general-interest magazines and academic journals, online news sites, Web pages devoted to specific topics, introductions to databases, and postings to listservs or electronic bulletin boards.

46a
source

Specialized sources provide information and ideas that add substance to the explanations, interpretations, and arguments you advance in a paper. They include research or project reports, technical documents, surveys, entries in a specialized database, field notes, theoretical books, specialized newsletters, electronic discussion groups and newsgroups, reports from industry or public interest groups, scholarly articles, and scientific reference works.

STRATEGY

- **Write.** Begin by jotting down your ideas about the directions your research might take, including notes about the resources you might consult first and those you might consult later on. Ask yourself whether you're likely to do library, electronic, or field research, or some combination. Consider whether you're likely to consult primary sources, secondary sources, or both.
- **List.** Next, create a list of the steps you plan to take in your research process (consult preliminary sources, focus on topic, decide on research questions, consult general sources to identify issues, prepare and administer survey, etc.), including specific resources to consult.
- **Be prepared.** Review your research questions and search strategy whenever you do library or online research. Keep a list of key terms handy so you focus on the same research thread each time you work.
- **Stay aware of the direction of your work.** Work from broad, general sources to narrower, specific ones. Look for a variety of sources and fair, representative information. Balance online resources such as Web sites, discussion groups, and databases with traditional library resources. (In academic settings, instructors may require you to use more than one kind of resource.)
- **Revise.** Review and revise your research questions, keywords, and search strategy in the course of your research (and writing).

In his research on the Roswell incident, Sam Roles mapped out several areas he thought would yield some useful information.

Earliest newspaper accounts of the incident, especially local ones around the Roswell area of New Mexico. These are useful descriptions of what eyewitnesses say they saw or thought they saw.

National newspaper and magazine articles after the incident. These provide preliminary commentary on the general American reception of the reports.

46a
source

Information on alien encounters: Too much! Narrow to commentaries on Roswell after the fact.

Information on conspiracy theory: Narrow to anything about the origins and history of the theory that the U.S. military covered up an alien encounter in Roswell and is still hiding the evidence.

To decide on the kinds of research appropriate for your project, ask the following questions.

1. Has your topic been frequently discussed in books, articles, Web sites, electronic discussion groups, or newspapers? (Do library and electronic research so your writing can build on what others have said.)
2. Is your subject a text (book, poem, Web page, document), an object (painting, sculpture), or an event (play, musical performance, video, film) that you need to locate in a library, museum, or theater; on disk; or through the Internet? (Obtain the material from a library or in electronic form along with the record of what others have said about it. Or do field research by witnessing a performance and observing the behavior of the audience.)
3. Is your subject a historical event that you can study only through written documents, films, or pictures? (Do research in library and electronic resources.)
4. Is your subject an event, a situation, a set of attitudes, or a pattern of behavior that has not been widely studied and that you can investigate directly? (Do field research, using observation, interviews, questionnaires, or surveys to gather data.)
5. Is your subject one of current interest to researchers and others who use electronic means of exchanging ideas, including email? (Consult electronic sources like newsgroups.)

An important caveat: It may seem easier to sit at a computer than to make a trip to the library, but this doesn't mean online research is the best method for your project. Some materials are available *only* in book or other print form in the library. Some libraries have "local" computer resources and systems that are much easier to access on their own terminals than from a remote computer via the Web. As you begin your research, don't let the possible inconvenience of a trip to the library prevent you from using the material that you can obtain only there.

4 Keep refining your keywords

46a
source

Many people begin searching for sources using general terms to identify their topic, only to discover that these are not the terms used in an index.

Indexes, databases, library catalogs (see 46b-3), and many other reference sources are arranged (or searched) by **keywords**. If you can identify the keyword (for a printed index) or a series of keywords (for an electronic index), you can usually locate all the resources you need. If you don't, you may waste precious time going down the wrong paths and locating useless sources.

Of course, you may not know which terms and phrases are most preferred until you begin your search (see 45b-4), and there may be some necessary trial and error in your work. Sometimes it helps to have two or three alternative keywords or phrases, so that if a particular database or other resource yields little under one, you can try the others before moving to another resource.

Exercise 1

A. Consider Sam Roles's preliminary brainstorming plan for his research on the Roswell incident. In addition to the sources of information he has considered, what else comes to mind as potentially productive avenues for his research? How might his purpose, audience, and kind of writing help him decide which information is the most valuable? (Think up some specific purposes, audiences, and genres of writing.)

B. In a group, compare your responses to Exercise 1A. How expansive were your additions to what Roles had started? How much did the constraints of purpose, audience, and text rein them in?

46b Identifying print and electronic resources

Your topic, guiding questions, or search strategy will probably lead you to a rich variety of resources: books, articles, microfilms, indexes, CD-ROM databases, Web pages, Internet files, or electronic messaging. You need to be familiar with the categories in which these resources are commonly arranged and the ways you can best consult them.

You also need to be familiar with resources that have been assembled for your use. Many universities provide access to databases and references via their library Web pages. Businesses and organizations frequently subscribe to databases; professional organizations (legal, medical, scientific, or scholarly) often maintain collections of articles and reference materials in electronic form. Government organizations provide electronic access to documents and records for public use. University, corporate, public, and government libraries make an astonishing range of printed and visual resources readily available.

46b
source

1 General references

You can use general references to gain a broad overview of a topic, including background information and a sense of relationships to other subjects. General references can also provide names, keywords, and phrases useful for tracing a topic, as well as bibliographies of potential resources. Commercial Internet services like America Online and Compuserve offer access to online reference works (such as *Grolier Multimedia Encyclopedia*), databases (such as *The Digital Tradition Folk Song Database*), reference services (such as *Medline*), and collections of resources (such as Electric Library).

- **General encyclopedias, ready references, maps, and dictionaries** (such as *The New Encyclopedia Brittanica (CD-ROM)*, *National Atlas of the United States*, or *The American Heritage Dictionary of the English Language*) provide very basic information on a wide range of topics. These are good places to start to conduct research for an overview of your topic, but they don't usually provide in-depth information.
- **Specialized encyclopedias and dictionaries** (such as the *Encyclopedia of Pop, Rock, and Soul* or the *McGraw-Hill Encyclopedia of Science and Technology*) provide more in-depth coverage of a specific topic or area. Such works can be easily located in a library's catalog (see 46b-3) or by searching online. The range of resources is wide.
- **Bibliographies** (such as the *International Bibliography of the Social Sciences*) provide organized lists of citations (sometimes annotated) to works on a specific topic.

2 Specialized indexes for periodicals, books, documents, and electronic collections

Periodicals are publications containing articles by different authors. **General-interest magazines** appear once a month or weekly, with each issue paginated separately. **Scholarly journals** generally appear less frequently than magazines, perhaps four times a year, with the page numbering running continuously throughout the separate issues making up an annual volume. Newspapers generally appear daily or weekly and frequently consist of separately numbered sections. **Online (electronic) periodicals** are available through the Internet, with past issues or selected articles sometimes available in electronic archives. **Web sites** may act like periodicals, offering a selection of articles and materials with links to other, related sites. Print periodicals generally appear at regular intervals. Electronic sites may add materials at irregular intervals, whenever new material is available or the person responsible for the site updates it.

You can locate articles in print and electronic sources like these by consulting some of the many readily available print and electronic **indexes**, and by consulting Internet services or search engines. Many of these aids are quite specialized in coverage, provide lists or electronic links to related resources, and offer brief summaries (or abstracts) of the contents of articles and books.

- **General and newspaper indexes** (such as *InfoTrac* [online], *Reader's Guide to Periodical Literature,* and the *New York Times Index*) give you a way to search for topics in the news and in magazines and periodicals intended for the general public.
- **Specialized indexes** (such as *Anthropological Literature* [online] or *Education Index*) provide a way to search for publications in more specialized and academic sources.
- **Abstracts** (such as *Abstracts of English Studies* or *Language and Language Behavior Abstracts*) provide brief summaries of articles.
- **Electronic databases** are files of information available in electronic form on disks or through the Internet. To find electronic databases covering your topic, you might consult a catalog such as the *Gale Directory of Databases,* the *Federal Database Finder* (a directory of free and fee-based databases and files available from the federal government), or one of the many other guides available in bookstores and libraries.

STRATEGY

Get to know the organization of your campus library's Web site, or that of a nearby research library or other preferred site for research. Most libraries provide both electronic databases and lists of print materials, such as indexes, for research. Sometimes these are organized so that you can begin with a list of general resources, such as a virtual reference collection and catalogs, then continue to narrow your search to more and more specific indexes and abstracts within particular fields. Without knowing how your library's resources are organized, you can't begin a search strategy for your project. Your reference librarians can also help you to find the resources most relevant to your topic.

In searching for material on the Roswell incident, Sam Roles started at the reference section of his library's Web site. This section was organized hierarchically, from the most general lists of indexes and databases to the most specific. After starting with "Electronic Resources by Subject," Roles was led to a dozen broad categories, such as "Medicine and Health" and "Engineering and Technology." He chose "Humanities and Social Sciences," which opened a page of eighteen more specific subjects, such as "Philosophy" and "History." One of these, "Communication and Media," led him to a page that contained almost fifty separate databases in this area. A database called "Academic Search" (with some full-text articles) seemed like a good bet for getting infor-

46.2

46b
source

mation on the Roswell incident. After accessing this database with his university User ID, he was led to a search page, where he tried the words "Roswell incident and aliens." This yielded eight articles, half of which were relevant to his paper and one of which, published in the *Journal of the American Medical Association*, commented on the psychological aspects of Americans' belief in aliens. In about two minutes, Sam had already found some potentially useful material for his paper. (And there were dozens of databases yet to search.)

3 Library catalogs

Once you have a list of resources on your topic and a start for your working bibliography (see 47a), your next job is to locate the resources. Your library's catalog is mostly likely to be an **online catalog**, though **card catalogs** are sometimes still used. You can search under the *author's name*; the *title of a work* or a periodical or series containing the work; or the *subject area*.

Here is what Sam Roles found in a subject search of his topic by using a Web-based electronic catalog at his school (see Figure 46.1) This entry indicates that the book *The UFO Invasion: The Roswell Incident, Alien Abductions, and Government Coverups* is available at the library's main branch. Highlighted options on Sam's screen let him get help, do a more specific search, move forward or backward in the string of entries yielded by his search (under "alien encounters"), or return to the catalog search screen. The page includes information on where the book is located in the library, and whether it's checked out. It also includes a list (not shown) of the book's contents and other information.

If your library doesn't have a particular title, you may be able to get it through a lending service called **interlibrary loan**—ask a reference or circulation librarian. Some libraries now give you the option of electronically requesting interlibrary loan materials.

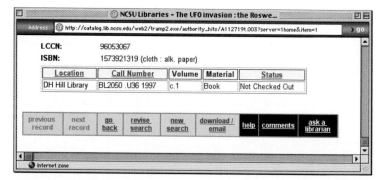

FIGURE 46.1   Online catalog page showing the main listing for the book, *The UFO Invasion*

4 Government documents and other resources

Libraries, the Internet, and electronic sites have a variety of resources other than books and articles. **Government documents** include reports, pamphlets, and regulations issued by Congress, federal agencies, and state or local governments. These rich sources of information, both general and technical, are sometimes housed in separate collections in a library. The *Monthly Catalog of U.S. Government Publications* can also aid your search.

Library **special collections** include rare books, manuscripts, and documents, including those of local historical interest. **Audiovisual collections** contain videotapes, films, and audio recordings. A **microform collection** contains microfilms and microfiches of books, periodicals, newspapers, and unpublished documents.

Almost all libraries can arrange for interlibrary loans within a few days. Many have overnight arrangements with local libraries and college or university reference libraries within a region. Some library online catalogs even list the holdings of regional libraries.

46c Search strategies for electronic environments

The **Internet** links computers of all kinds through email, discussion groups, resource sites, and the World Wide Web. **Web sites** provide text and graphics with numerous links to related sites so that you can move quickly ("surf") from site to site following a research thread. Though the Internet and Web provide almost unlimited access for anyone with a computer and the knowledge to use it, they are nonetheless populated by distinct communities. Try to keep in mind the differences among academic, work, and public communities as you search the Internet and the World Wide Web for sources to use in a research project. Some examples follow.

COMMUNITY	TOPICS OF INTEREST	SITE
ACADEMICS	Music (from Tanzania; Russian panpipes; hip-hop performance)	*EOL: Peer-Reviewed Multimedia Web Journal* (<http://www.research.umbc.edu/eol/2/index/html>)
SPECIALIZED TECHNOLOGY BUSINESSES	Manufacturing techniques, new technologies, especially for production	*Michigan Manufacturing Center* (<http://www.iti.org/mmtc/>)
PEOPLE ACROSS THE UNITED STATES	Drunk driving policies and related topics	*NCADD* (National Commission Against Drunk Driving) (<http://www.ncadd.com>)

46c source

1 Conducting a Web search

The Web consists of documents ("pages" or "sites," which are collections of pages) that you can access using an address known as a **URL** (uniform resource locator) or by selecting a **link** embedded in a Web document (usually a logo or a highlighted portion of text). To contact a Web site, you need a **browser**, such as *Netscape Navigator* or *Internet Explorer*.

To locate sites relevant to your research, use a **search engine**, an electronic search tool that matches keywords to millions of sites on the Internet. You can access these through the search button on your browser or by using their URLs. (Some sites, such as <http://searchenginewatch.com> and <http://cui.unige.ch/meta-index.html>, provide useful lists of dozens of search engines like the following. See 45b-3 for an additional list of major search engines.)

Excite	<http://www.excite.com>
WebCrawler	<http://www.webcrawler.com>
News Resource	<http://www.newo.com/news>
DogPile	<http://www.dogpile.com>
Metacrawler	<http://www.go2net.com>
Yahoo!	<http://www.yahoo.com>
Northern Light	<http://www.northernlight.com>
Direct Hit	<http://www.directhit.com>
Fast Search	<http://www.alltheweb.com/>

Remember that search engines are not all organized the same way. Some provide links in the order of "most often accessed," while others create a statistical probability of the match between your keywords and the site's content. Some even allow site owners to pay to have their Web pages listed before others'.

Typing keywords into a general search engine like the ones above will usually yield a huge variety of results. The most common search error among students using the Web to write research papers happens when they give all these links the same scholarly "weight" or relevance to their topic. *Don't do this.* Using general search engines to get information for an academic paper is like being at a huge flea market. You have to search through stall after stall of useless junk to find something really worthwhile.

At the same time, don't skim past every site that doesn't give you the definitive word on your topic. In searching for information on alcohol use in college, for example, Summer Arrigo-Nelson and Jennifer Figliozzi found two sites they thought worthless at first glance. One was a site promoting (and selling) a beer-drinking board game invented by some college students. The other was the personal Web page of a college graduate who wrote extensively about his battle with alcohol while in school and its effects on his performance. Although neither site seemed useful in their review of the scholarly research literature on alcohol use in college, these students recognized that this material had potential value for their introduction or their discussion and conclusions.

STRATEGY

To expand or limit your electronic search, try using **Boolean logic**, linking terms with the operators OR, AND, and NOT. Check any instructions on the main page of the search engine to see if this strategy will help. *Google*, for example, does not require Boolean operators because they are built into the system.

OR (expands): X OR Y — Search for either term (documents referring to either X or Y)

AND (restricts): X AND Y — Search for both terms (documents referring to both X and Y, but not to either alone)

NOT (excludes): X NOT Y — Search for X unless X includes the term Y (documents referring to X except for those documents that also refer to Y)

Figure 46.2 on page 574 shows the results of a query sent to the *Google* Internet search engine using two keywords, "alcohol" and "college." *Google* does not require the "AND" operator; however, it makes use of other search strategies mentioned at its information page.

Before using any search engine extensively, it helps to learn something about its features and operating procedures.

46.3

STRATEGY

At the main page of your search engine, find the link to the page that explains the system ("search tips," "about this site," etc.). Find answers to at least the following questions, if possible.

- How is the system organized? How does it search for sites?
- What are the basic search procedures?
- Does the engine recognize Boolean operators? Which ones?
- Does the engine exclude "stop words," such as *where* and *how*, which slow down a search? If so, what command executes that exclusion?
- What are the advanced search features? What procedures can you use to conduct a search *within* preliminary results?
- Can you personalize the engine to save yourself time whenever you use it?
- How are results displayed? Can you vary the parameters of that display, such as increasing the number on each page while decreasing the length of the annotations, or vice versa?

46c
source

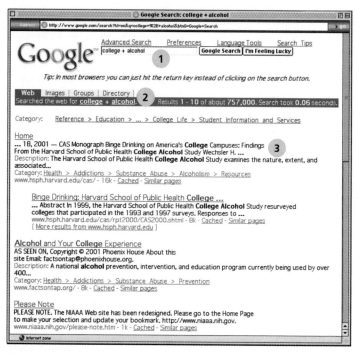

1 Keywords used in search
2 Results of search
3 One source with annotation

FIGURE 46.2 Results of a *Google* search query using the keywords "alcohol" and "college"

Exercise 2

A. In addition to the general search engines like those listed above, there are also smaller, more scholarly sites with prescreened and categorized information, such as the following.

AlphaSearch	<http://www.calvin.edu/library/as/>
BUBL Information Service	<http://bubl.ac.uk/>
Infomine	<http://www.infomine/urc/edu/Main/html/>
Librarian's Index to the Internet	<http://www.sunshine.berkeley.edu>
Scout	<http://www.ilrt.bris.ac.uk/mirrors/ scout/toolkit/bookmarks/index.html>
The WWW Virtual Library	<http://www.vlib.org/Home.html>

46c
source

Access one of these sites or one of the larger search engines discussed earlier. Then answer all the questions in the Strategy box that precedes this exercise.

B. Compare your notes with other students in a small group. What differences and similarities do you see between the ways in which each site is organized and how best to use it?

2 Evaluating Web search results

While the Internet provides a wealth of information on almost every imaginable topic, remember how it got there. Anyone can put information on a Web site, and that site may appear in your search. How do you know that the information has any validity whatsoever? No one is "policing" the truth or accuracy of information on the Web—that's entirely up to you to figure out. If you're too hasty about pulling information from the Internet and dropping it into your paper, you may fall prey to the "snake oil syndrome"—trying to pass off fakery and untruth as academic material with scholarly integrity. This is rarely a problem in more traditional library research, because most print materials have already undergone a rigorous process of academic scrutiny and judgment. Published books and articles in the library are usually "presanctioned." Many Web sites are not.

This is not to say that you can't trust anything on the Web. Thousands of sites are created collaboratively by experts and authorities on specific subjects. Information about the history of bicycles at the Smithsonian Institution's Web site can be trusted, while an unreferenced historical sketch found at the personal Web page of a bike enthusiast may be suspect.

When you find a Web site that could be useful for your project, check first to see whether it actually addresses your topic. Some search engines list sites in order of probable relevance based on the occurrence of keywords, but you really need to do the work yourself by looking at the summaries provided by the search engine and then scanning the sites themselves. If a site addresses your topic, check to see whether it contains the kind of information and ideas you need and whether it's appropriate to the research community you're addressing. (An extremely academic site may contain material that is not appropriate for general public consumption, for example, unless you "translate" it.)

Then spend some time figuring out the source of the information. Who created it? What authority do they have? How can you trust the information?

STRATEGY

Use the following questions to evaluate Web sites you locate in your search.

1. Who is responsible for the site? Does the responsible person or organization have a reputation for accuracy or expertise that will make the source acceptable to your audience? Papers for an

46c
source

economics course that cite statistics from the Federal Reserve Bank's Web site at (<http://www.bog.frb.fed.us/releases/>) will usually be on more solid ground than those citing online opinions from stockbrokers (for example, at (<http://www.thestreet.com)>), though the brokers' opinions may be perfectly appropriate for a business report, especially if they come from the Web site of a source like the *Wall Street Journal* at (<http://info.wsj.com/>).

2. How much detail does the site provide? Are sources cited? Is the writing effective? A site providing detailed information and supporting evidence is likely to be more reliable than one lacking in detail, especially if it gives references whose accuracy you can check. Though good writing and high-quality graphics don't guarantee honesty or accuracy, they are evidence of the care taken in producing a site.

3. Are other opinions taken into account? If other people's perspectives are acknowledged and presented fairly, it's more likely that the conclusions offered in a site rest on careful thought and attention to evidence.

3 Coping with complexity

As you search electronic and other resources for your research, especially for larger writing projects, you may begin to feel overwhelmed with information. Chapter 47 provides some strategies to help you read, analyze, and sort such information. It helps to do at least some preliminary organization, however, during even the early stages of research for your project. Keeping track of sources, classifying and filing information, and saving electronic materials in labeled folders or on separate disks can make the job of retrieval much easier later on, when you'll also have important issues in your drafting and revising to worry about.

STRATEGY

To keep track of your research materials and begin pulling them together as you work, try the following tips.

- Gather your notes, photocopies, electronic printouts, and other relevant materials.
- Sort your resources. Make a note of missing material, and track it down.
- Using your research questions as a guide, identify major points and subtopics. Use keywords, color coding, stacks of material, or some other method to sort your resources by category.

46c
source

- If one category contains little information, decide whether to drop it or do further research.
- If a category contains a great deal of information, decide whether to break it into subtopics.
- If you feel you have not found enough appropriate material, ask for help from a reference librarian, an instructor, a colleague, or a specialist in the field you are researching.
- Reexamine and regroup your resources until you are ready to plan and draft your paper.

Exercise 3

A. To familiarize yourself with the resources of your library, take tours or library introduction sessions offered by the staff, or locate the following resources on your own (using any maps the library provides): general and specialized encyclopedias, bibliographies, print indexes, electronic indexes and databases, government documents, and the periodical collection. Learn how to access the catalog electronically and search for books and other information, and find out whether there are any electronic resources at the library that are not accessible from computers located outside the library.

B. Each person in a work group should look up entries for a particular topic in one or more of the kinds of resources listed in Exercise 3A, then report back to the group. You may all research a topic someone in the group is working on, or each of you may look up the topic you are researching for a paper of your own.

46c
source

READING CRITICALLY AND EVALUATING SOURCES

You can't identify, gather, and use research sources without reading them. But if you read your sources in superficial ways, your research project and your writing will suffer. Careful reading—analytical and critical—adds depth and insight to your work. Approaching your sources as a critical reader also means working with them in a writerly way, reshaping and synthesizing information and ideas, experiencing insights, and accomplishing your own purposes and those of your readers. The process of critical reading begins with careful, insightful note taking.

47a Reading print and electronic sources analytically

A research project calls for two types of reading, analytical and critical. Both are challenging, and they're often intertwined. When you read *analytically*, you try to understand the ideas and information presented in a source. When you read *critically*, you interact with the source, assessing its strengths, limitations, and biases; analyzing its relationships to other texts produced by a research community; and identifying questions or issues it leaves unaddressed.

Both kinds of reading contribute in significant ways to the outcome of a research project. Analytical reading leads to the summaries, paraphrases, syntheses, quotations, and details you develop into much of the content of a research report or paper. Critical reading leads to many of the insights you contribute to an understanding of the topic. It helps you determine what use to make of information and concepts from your source, as shown below.

ANALYTICAL READING	CRITICAL READING
What does it say? (literal)	What does it mean or imply?
—summary	(interpretive)
—paraphrase	—interpretation
—synthesis	—position of author

ANALYTICAL READING	CRITICAL READING
—quotations	—nature of publication
—details	—use in one's own ideas
	—reception of audience

Of course, analytical reading and note taking require critical thought. Selecting quotations that accurately represent a source's main points, paraphrasing and summarizing, understanding ideas and information—all these call for critical comprehension. Critical reading goes even further; it assesses and decides on the value of information and ideas, generally with an eye toward developing insights and perspectives you can develop in your own writing.

In a **summary**, you present the essential information in a text without interpreting it. A summary is shorter than the original, *compressing* the information and presenting only the key ideas and support. In a **paraphrase**, you restate an author's ideas in your own words, retaining the content and sense of the original but providing your own expression. A **synthesis** brings together summaries of several sources and points out the relationships among the ideas and information.

1 Summarizing

A summary helps you understand the key ideas and content in an article, part of a book, a Web site, or a cluster of paragraphs. You can also create summaries as a concise way of presenting ideas and information from a source in your own writing. In an **objective summary**, you focus on presenting the content of the source in compressed form and avoid speculating on the source's line of reasoning. In an **evaluative summary**, you add your opinions, evaluating or commenting on the original passage.

STRATEGY

To prepare a summary of information relating to your topic, follow this process.

- **Read** the selection, looking for the most important ideas, evidence, and information. Underline, highlight, or make note of key points and information that you think should be mentioned in your summary.
- **Scan** (reread quickly) the selection to decide which of the ideas and bits of information you noted during your first reading are the *most* important. Try also to decide on the writer's main purpose in the selection and to identify the major sections of the discussion.

47a
source

- **Summarize** *each section* of the source (each step in the argument, each stage in the explanation) in a *single sentence* that mentions the key ideas and information.
- **Encapsulate** the *entire passage* in a *single sentence* that captures its main point or conclusion.
- **Combine** your summaries in (1) with your summary in (2) (above) to produce a draft summary of the main point, other important points, and the most important information.
- **Revise** to make sure your summary is logical and easy to read. Check against the source for accuracy.
- **Document** clearly the source of your summary using a standard style of documentation (see Chapters 51–54).

In a summary, you can present the key ideas from a source without including unnecessary detail that might distract readers. Summer Arrigo-Nelson and Jennifer Figliozzi used two one-sentence summaries of research to help introduce one of the questions for their academic research paper.

> First, research has shown that adolescents who have open and close relationships with their parents use alcohol less often than do those with conflictual relationships (Sieving 1996). For example, a survey given to students in seventh through twelfth grades reported that approximately 35 percent of adolescent drinkers were under parental supervision while drinking (Dept. of Education 1993). Based on this research, we are interested in determining if students who were given permission to drink while living with their parents would possess different drinking patterns, upon reaching college, than those who did not previously have permission to drink.

2 Paraphrasing

A good paraphrase doesn't add to or detract from the original but often helps you understand a difficult work. When you want to incorporate the detailed ideas and information from a passage into your own writing but don't want to quote your source because the wording is too dense or confusing, then a paraphrase can be the answer.

STRATEGY

47a
source

To paraphrase part of a source, put the information in your own words, retaining the content and ideas of the original as well as the sequence of presentation. (Many paraphrases contain sentences that correspond with the original except for changes in wording and sentence structure.)

- **Read** the selection carefully so that you understand the wording as well as the content.
- **Write** a draft of your paraphrase, using your own words and phrases in place of the original. Rely on synonyms and equivalent expressions. You can retain names, proper nouns, and the like from the original, of course.
- **Revise** for smooth reading and clarity. Change sentence structures and phrasing to make sure your version is easier to understand than your source.
- **Document** clearly the source of your paraphrase using a standard style of documentation (see Chapters 51–54).

As part of her research for an editorial supporting a new alcohol abuse program on her campus, Jennifer Figliozzi encountered the following passage in a report on current programs at various schools.

> The university also now notifies parents when their sons or daughters violate the alcohol policy or any other aspect of the student code of conduct. "We were hoping that the support of parents would help change students' behavior, and we believe it has," says Timothy F. Brooks, an assistant vice-president and the dean of students at the University of Delaware.

Because she wanted to avoid long quotations and instead integrate the information smoothly into her discussion, Jennifer paraphrased part of the passage.

> Officials at the University of Delaware thought that letting parents know when students violate regulations on alcohol use would change students' drinking habits, and one administrator now says, "We believe it has" (Reisberg 42).

Exercise 1

A. Choose an article that interests you in a magazine such as *Natural History* or *Scientific American*. Paraphrase the first paragraph or two or any passage of a few lines or more. Do as Jennifer has done above, and try to integrate the passage into an imaginary research report, putting much or most of the passage into your own words.

B. In a group, paraphrase the same passage and then compare paraphrases. Discuss which paraphrases are the most accurate and thorough, yet the most concise.

47a
source

3 Synthesizing

By bringing together summaries of several sources and pointing out their relationships in a synthesis, you can use your sources in some special ways: to provide background information, to explore causes and effects, to look at contrasting explanations or arguments, or to bring together ideas and information in support of a thesis.

STRATEGY

To create a synthesis of your source materials use the following strategy:

- **Identify** the role a synthesis will play in your explanation or argument as well as the kind of information and ideas you wish to share with readers.
- **Gather** the sources you plan to synthesize.
- **Read** your sources, and prepare to summarize them.
- **Focus** on the purpose of your synthesis, and draft a sentence summing up your conclusion about the relationships of the sources.
- **Arrange** the order in which you will present your sources in the synthesis.
- **Write** a draft of your synthesis, presenting summaries of your sources and offering your conclusion about the relationship(s).
- **Revise** so that your synthesis is easy to read. Make sure readers can easily identify the sources of the ideas and information.
- **Document** clearly the sources for your synthesis using a standard style of documentation.

Many academic papers begin with a summary of prior research designed to identify a need for further research and to provide justification for the research questions. The opening section of Summer Arrigo-Nelson and Jennifer Figliozzi's academic research paper uses synthesis for this purpose.

> Research dealing with student alcohol use most often focuses on children's perceptions of their parents' actions and on the relationship between child and parent. Studies conducted with high school students have supported the hypothesis that positive family relationships are more likely to be associated with less frequent alcohol use among adolescents than are negative relationships. Adolescents model the limited substance use of their parents where there is a good or moderate

47a
source

```
parent/adolescent relationship (Andrews, Hops, and Dunkin
1997). Other factors the studies found to be associated with
positive family relationships, along with substance use, were
academic achievement, family structure, place of residence,
self-esteem, and emotional tone (Weschler, Dowdall, Davenport,
and Castillo 1995; Martch and Miller 1997).
```

Work and public writing often use synthesis in a similar fashion to identify a problem that needs to be addressed or a policy that needs to be examined or reconsidered.

4 Analyzing electronic and visual sources

Print sources consist mostly of text, so that when you're summarizing, paraphrasing, or synthesizing, you're putting someone else's words into your own words. In contrast, electronic sources, especially Web pages, may include pictures, drawings, charts, and even video or sound, which convey both information and ideas. (Print documents make use of graphics, too, of course.) Public writing may use pictures to convey or reinforce values and may use graphs to present detailed information in accessible form. Workplace writing and academic writing sometimes use charts and drawings to present complex data and explain causes, consequences, or relationships.

STRATEGY

You can "quote" pictures and graphic representations by reproducing them within your own text (with appropriate documentation). Paraphrasing and summarizing are more difficult, though not impossible. To paraphrase pictures, drawings, or graphic presentations, you need to "extract" information and concepts from them and "translate" the material into your own words. Instead of paraphrasing a paragraph reporting the results of a study on car theft in major U.S. cities, for example, you would describe the bar graph that reports the statistics.

47b Reading print and electronic sources critically

To read critically, you must be able to do four things: (1) *identify* in your sources any unanswered questions (academic), unsolved problems (work), or unresolved issues (public) that you can make the focus of your research and writing; (2) *synthesize* different perspectives among sources; (3) *interpret* your sources; (4) *evaluate* your sources.

47b
source

1 Identifying questions

A final research report or essay often begins by identifying an unanswered question, an unsolved problem, or an unresolved issue in a way that highlights its importance for readers, going on to address this concern in detail. As you read and reflect on your topic, use note cards or your research journal (or even the margins of photocopies) to record and explore unanswered questions, unsolved problems, and unresolved issues. Try stating them as concisely as you can in a *question paragraph* (or a *problem* or *issue paragraph*). Such a paragraph can suggest ways for you to develop your paper or report, and you may even include all or part of it in the finished product. Here is a critical note card Lily Germaine made for a paper about bodybuilding.

Tucker, Larry A. "Effect of Weight Training on Self-Concept: A Profile of Those Influenced Most." Research Quarterly for Exercise and Sport, Introduction, pp. 389-91.

Tucker uses the word "although" at least four times when summarizing other studies, and he tends to use phrases such as "only a few studies have shown . . . ". He's being nice on the surface but is setting his readers up to find fault with the other studies. That basic fault is their lack of objective methodology, which he seems to plan on rectifying by using mathematical measurements and rigid definitions of terms. A glance through the rest of the article reveals lots of

equations and two tables of statistics. He seems to think he can be completely objective in determining such a slippery thing as "self-concept." I really have to question this assumption.

Lily's question paragraph begins with insights and wording from her notes.

> Does bodybuilding affect self-concept? Before we
> can answer this question, we need to ask if we can
> accurately measure such a slippery thing as "self-concept."
> Some researchers, like Tucker, believe that self-concept can
> be accurately gauged using mathematical measurements
> and rigid definitions of terms. For several reasons, however,
> this assumption is questionable. . . .

2 Synthesizing perspectives

To offer your readers an in-depth understanding of a subject, use a **critical synthesis** to bring together perspectives, opinions, interpretations, and evidence from a variety of sources and explore their potential connections. Like an **analytical synthesis**, a critical synthesis provides readers with a unified discussion reflecting your understanding of the various perspectives, but it also pays special attention to highlighting and summarizing differences and to presenting your conclusions about the sources.

Be alert to agreements and disagreements as you read and take notes on your sources, identifying and exploring the various perspectives in critical notes or a research journal. When you are drafting your paper, consider preparing a critical synthesis that may become an important element of the finished project, such as a review of prior research (academic), a consideration of alternative responses to a problem (work), or an overview of differing stands on an issue (public).

Look over your sources and notes, and then synthesize (sum up) the main ideas, positions, or facts of your sources, building on the techniques you use to prepare an analytical synthesis. To do this, imagine that you're an expert on the topic and that you're trying to give someone a quick state-of-the-art overview based on your sources. Here are some guidelines.

1. Be true to the ideas and information in your sources.
2. Suggest relationships (among conclusions, opinions, ideas, and facts) that go beyond those relationships discussed in your sources.

47b
source

3. In a thesis statement (5c) or a statement of the central idea of the synthesis, summarize the relationships you observe.
4. Be selective. Focus on material that relates directly to your central idea.
5. Be balanced. Acknowledge facts, opinions, and alternative perspectives that contradict the central idea of your synthesis.
6. Base your synthesis on your own thinking as well as material from your sources.

Here is a critical synthesis Kimlee Cunningham used to introduce the thesis of her academic paper on three Disney animated feature films.

> It is probably an exaggeration to say that a character like Belle in Beauty and the Beast is a lot like a contemporary feminist, as one critic suggests: "She wants adventure and he wants commitment; he holds a mirror and she hugs a book" (Showalter). However, we should not simply ignore an interpretation like this by claiming "that it takes a classic fairy tale, and turns it around and analyzes it from a modern feminist view" (Hoffman). Even if many people view a film like Beauty and the Beast (or Aladdin) as "just a love story" (Hoffman), the films nonetheless grow out of the complicated values and roles that shape relationships today. Disney's contemporary portrayal of women characters shows a willingness to change with the times but also a reluctance to abandon traditional values and stereotypes.

3 Interpreting sources

Most research papers or reports should present a point of view about their topic: a conclusion about its meaning or causes, a commitment to a particular course of action, or a stand on an issue. At the same time, you need to share with your readers the differing outlooks embodied in your sources, and to indicate why readers should accept your interpretation as an alternative. Here are some basic questions concerning the outlook (or bias) of your sources.

1. Does the source display a balanced perspective in offering its conclusions?
2. Does the source advocate strongly, though fairly, for a particular point of view?
3. Does the source display one-sided bias, including misrepresentation of facts and distortions of others' positions?

47b
source

In an **interpretation**, you build on synthesis (see 47b-2) by explicitly including your opinions and giving priority to your own ideas and points of view. Interpreting involves **generalizing** (coming to broad conclusions about what your research has to say about your topic) and **extending** (going beyond this to connect your source's ideas to your own).

> ### STRATEGY
>
> Begin an interpretation by stating the point of view of your source(s) as accurately as possible. Add your own ideas and conclusions. Take into account any strong advocacy (or questionable bias) in the source(s).
>
> 1. Present material from your sources accurately. Select material most relevant to the point you want to make, but do not suppress contradictory, biased, or partisan material that contradicts other ideas.
> 2. Present your point of view, and provide supporting evidence, perhaps comparing the perspective of one source to that of another and to your own.
> 3. Add interpretations and conclusions of your own not present in the sources, or present in a different form.

4 Evaluating print sources

To be published, print material usually goes through an editorial process that gives the source some degree of credibility and authority. An article in an academic journal, for example, was first submitted by a scholar to the journal's editor, who then sent it out to one or more other experts for anonymous review. Using a set of evaluation questions, these experts told the editor whether the essay was suitable for publication and, if it was, what further revisions were required. The editor then worked with the author to produce the most authoritative article possible, one that would make the best contribution to the work of the field. The article also underwent one or more cycles of editing, often with the help of a professional editor. With published books, the process is just as rigorous and may have taken years instead of months. Unlike Internet sources (see 47b-5), *academic* publications are, on the whole, relatively trustworthy because academic disciplines thrive on intellectual integrity in their search for truth.

Not every source you encounter, however, is equally valuable, accurate, or persuasive. One important part of your work as a researcher is to evaluate sources, even academic sources, in order to decide what material to treat as authoritative and what to reject or refute. Furthermore, almost no area of inquiry is without some degree of bias. Deciding to use a source means seeing that source in the context of its author's or organization's motivations and dispositions. If you use a particular source, it's equally important to share the results of your evaluation with your readers. (See also 46c-2.)

47b
source

STRATEGY

1. Consider the reputation of the publisher or organization responsible for the source. Does the publisher or journal have a reputation for balance and accuracy? Is the writer or organization an advocate whose views require caution?
2. Consider the reputation of the author. Is the author's reputation clear from the outset? What do other sources think of the author's trustworthiness, fairness, and importance?
3. Ask how accurate your source is, especially if it presents facts as truth. Can you spot obvious errors? Which points are detailed and well documented?
4. Find and test generalizations in the source. How does the writer support them? Do they go beyond the facts in the text? Are they consistent with your knowledge of the topic?
5. Compare the source with others. Are the ideas generally consistent with those in your other sources? If different, do they seem original and insightful or misleading and eccentric?
6. Use questionable sources with caution. Does a print source have current, exciting ideas but also contentious or half-developed notions? Does material apply only to a specific setting? Is the source's information outdated or biased? Do experts cited have particular political or financial interests?
7. Consider the expectations of your audience or research community. Academic audiences look for detailed explanations, evidence, and acknowledgment of scholarship on the subject. Work audiences look for precise, clear, and accurate presentation of facts. Public audiences look for fairness in presenting opinions and alternatives.
8. Look for documentation. Does the source either appropriately document information, quotations, and ideas, or clearly indicate that the author is responsible for them?

When you draw information from a source, use it to support your conclusions, or disagree with its perspective, you may need to share your evaluation of it with readers.

1. Support your judgments with examples from the texts or data you are evaluating.
2. Explain your judgments of one text or body of data by comparing it to other texts or data.
3. Base your evaluation on your own ideas, but feel free to draw on evaluations you have found in other sources.

47b
source

Exercise 2

A. Read an entire print article, preferably one that is relevant to a writing project you're working on. First write an objective summary of the article that tries to capture its main points as clearly as possible. Next, using one or more of the strategies in 47b, write a critical commentary on the piece, identifying gaps or unanswered questions, authorial biases, or problems with the credibility or stance of the source.

B. In a small group, share your critical commentaries and objective summaries. Discuss what you see in the relationship between the two types of writing, focusing especially on how the objective summary can help you to support (with clear, careful reasoning) some of the evaluative assertions you made in your critical commentary.

5 Evaluating Internet and Web sources

47.1

Internet and World Wide Web sources pose special problems for evaluation (see 47b-5). Many Web sites or Internet documents are produced without the editorial checks and balances that make books from reputable publishers or articles in scholarly journals and well-known magazines relatively trustworthy sources. You can begin evaluating Internet and Web sources using questions developed by Paula Mathieu at the University of Illinois, Chicago, as part of the *Critical Resources in Teaching with Technology* (CRITT) project featured at <http://www.engl.uic.edu/~stp>.

Evaluation questions

1. **Who benefits? What difference does that make?** The Web pages accessible at <http://www.whymilk.com/milku/diet_nutri_101.htm>, for example, seem dedicated entirely to the reader's health, as illustrated in Figure 47.1 on page 590. Perhaps the three cups will indeed benefit most readers. With a little bit of critical thinking, however, these readers can easily recognize that milk producers and distributors will also benefit from sales of those three cups a day.

2. **Who's talking? What difference does that make?** The "speaker" responsible for all the positive facts about milk is not clearly identified in the pages except as "we" at the bottom of some pages in the invitation to call for more information. "We" is the Milk Council, an organization of milk producers and distributors. Can readers trust the "facts" presented by this group that goes unnamed in the pages? Perhaps. But it seems unlikely that all the "facts" will appear on the pages, especially those that might call into question an unqualified endorsement of milk's goodness.

   In contrast, consider the Web page at <http://liberator.enviroweb.org/fall94/milk.html> (see Figure 47.2 on p. 591). This site provides a

① Commercial site

② Includes features designed to appeal to readers

③ Offers personal analysis of diet and exercise

④ Advocates drinking milk

⑤ Uses graphics to convey information

⑥ Offers more information

READER'S REACTION: **Why are you sharing all this? How do you benefit? How do I know this is accurate, complete information?**

FIGURE 47.1   Web page sponsored by "Why Milk"

contrary voice, linking milk drinking to disease. The article was first published in *Animal Life*, founded by an advocacy group, Cornell Students for the Ethical Treatment of Animals (CSETA). The author tells us nothing about himself, leaving readers to judge what he says based on the quality of his evidence and reasoning. He does seem to provide scientific support, but some readers may find the reasoning strained and the tone a bit extreme.

47b
source

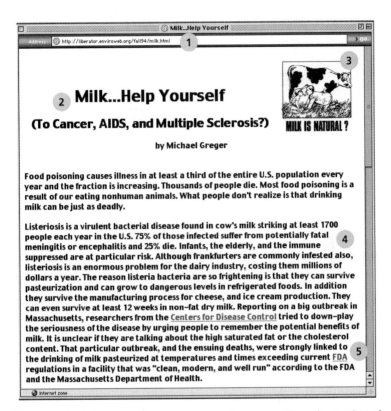

<table>
<tr><td>

1 Organizational site

2 Uses title to introduce position

3 Uses graphics to highlight point of view

4 Uses statistics

5 Cites authority
</td><td>

READER'S REACTION: Given the number of milk drinkers, how serious is this risk? Isn't this view a bit extreme?
</td></tr>
</table>

FIGURE 47.2   Web page sponsored by the EnviroLink Network

A third Web site, <http://www.niddk.nih.gov/health/digest/pubs/lactose/lactose.htm>, offers an additional perspective on milk and dairy products, pointing out that between 30 and 50 million Americans are lactose intolerant, including 75% of African Americans and Native Americans and 90% of Asian Americans (see Figure 47.3 on p. 592). This site, sponsored by the National Digestive Diseases Information Clearinghouse (an organization that is part of the federal government's National Institute of Health), certainly can be trusted for its authority

47b
source

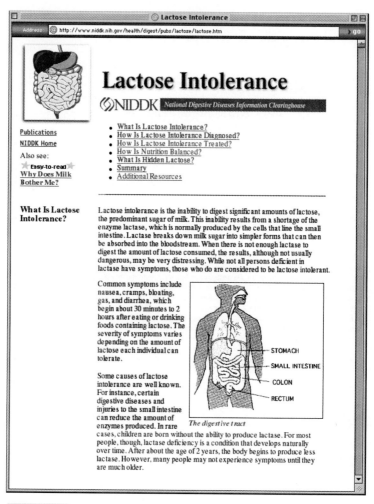

Lactose Intolerance

⑤NIDDK *National Digestive Diseases Information Clearinghouse*

Publications

NIDDK Home

Also see:

☆ Easy-to-read ☆
Why Does Milk
Bother Me?

- What Is Lactose Intolerance?
- How Is Lactose Intolerance Diagnosed?
- How Is Lactose Intolerance Treated?
- How Is Nutrition Balanced?
- What Is Hidden Lactose?
- Summary
- Additional Resources

**What Is Lactose
Intolerance?**

Lactose intolerance is the inability to digest significant amounts of lactose, the predominant sugar of milk. This inability results from a shortage of the enzyme lactase, which is normally produced by the cells that line the small intestine. Lactase breaks down milk sugar into simpler forms that can then be absorbed into the bloodstream. When there is not enough lactase to digest the amount of lactose consumed, the results, although not usually dangerous, may be very distressing. While not all persons deficient in lactase have symptoms, those who do are considered to be lactose intolerant.

Common symptoms include nausea, cramps, bloating, gas, and diarrhea, which begin about 30 minutes to 2 hours after eating or drinking foods containing lactose. The severity of symptoms varies depending on the amount of lactose each individual can tolerate.

Some causes of lactose intolerance are well known. For instance, certain digestive diseases and injuries to the small intestine can reduce the amount of enzymes produced. In rare

STOMACH

SMALL INTESTINE

COLON

RECTUM

The digestive tract

cases, children are born without the ability to produce lactase. For most people, though, lactase deficiency is a condition that develops naturally over time. After about the age of 2 years, the body begins to produce less lactase. However, many people may not experience symptoms until they are much older.

FIGURE 47.3   Web page sponsored by the National Digestive Diseases Information Clearinghouse

and integrity. Notice that the authors, who "are" the NDDIC, don't make any judgments about the value of dairy products; their role is to present information impartially and truthfully.

To critically analyze and interpret these sites, the motivations of each "author" clearly must be taken into account. One has a commercial interest: sell as much milk, and as many dairy products, as possible, regardless of the consequences. Another has an organizational interest: stop the consumption of dairy products in order to stop the exploitation and destruction of animals. A third has an informational interest: give the public up-to-date, factual information and recommendations from the most authoritative research and sources possible, regardless of what consequences that information may have to different organizations and businesses.

47.2

STRATEGY

Some Web pages may provide you with no information about the source or author. How, then, can you begin to figure out where it came from? Start by looking carefully at the URL. Web searches often take you to a page deep in the hierarchy of a Web site. You may need to "back up" to a higher level. Remember that main Web sites end in several major suffixes (*org*, *edu*, *gov*, and *com*, meaning "organization," "educational institution," "government site," and "commercial site"). To get back up to higher pages, erase a section of the subsidiary suffix and enter that address into your browser. To get to the main or "home" page, erase everything after the *org*, *edu*, *gov*, or *com*. The "Milk . . . Help Yourself" article, for example, has the URL <http://liberator.enviroweb.org/fall94/milk.html>. Erasing the suffix after "org" yields an online publication, the *Liberator*. A link at the bottom of the page takes us to the organization that publishes the *Liberator*, "AnimalConcerns.org," an "online community concerned about the welfare of animals." Another link at the bottom of the *Liberator* page takes us to an organization called EnviroLink Network, the "Online Environmental Community." A note at the top of this page explains that a superordinate organization, Network for Change, is creating the site in partnership with the EnviroLink Network and Animal Concerns Community. A Webmaster is also listed at the bottom of the page.

3. **What's missing? What difference does that make?** In the first Web site, under the heading "All Kinds of Milk" appears the following: "Fat free skim, 1% lowfat, 2%, whole—there are lots of different kinds of milk to fit your fancy." Why does this list ignore soy milk, rice milk, goat's milk, sheep's milk, coconut milk? The selective nature of the presentation, its commercial purpose, and its strategies become even clearer when a reader asks what is left out and why. In the second site, nothing is said about the possible health consequences of eliminating milk and other dairy products from one's diet, including the loss of calcium, which is crucial in the development and sustenance of bones. Furthermore, if the author's real purpose is to stop the killing of cows (which implies that he is also opposed to eating beef or using any other cattle products), why doesn't he argue that we should stop breeding cattle, since they have no other use to us on a large scale?

47b
source

CHAPTER 48

TURNING RESEARCH INTO WRITING

How do you know when to begin *writing* your research paper or report? Actually, there's no set time. When you've gathered enough material to begin seriously creating a draft of your research paper, you can piece together some of your preliminary and less formally written material from notes or a journal, then add significant new material to make a more complete and coherent text. Instead of trying to draft your paper by launching right into the first word of the first line, start by thinking strategically about the nature and shape of your task.

48a Moving from research questions to a plan and a thesis

The research questions that focus and guide your research (see 45b and 46a) should have evolved as you worked, reflecting your developing knowledge of your subject. Consider using the latest versions of your research questions to create a plan for drafting your report or document.

1 Review your research questions

Arrange your research questions in a logical *order*: in what sequence do you want to address them in your essay or report? Add any further questions you now think you ought to address. Use your list as a tentative guide for your drafting. As you answer the questions, think about the way the blocks of information connect with each other. Don't be too concerned about getting the sequence just right at this point, but keep your structure in the back of your mind as you work.

2 Envision your readers

As you begin drafting, asking questions about your audience can help you provide clear explanations, arguments, and sufficient supporting evidence.

Begin by writing informally about your imagined readers. What are the interests and values of your readers? What questions do they want answered? What are their likely reactions to what you have to say? How do issues of gender, age, position, or background affect the way readers may respond to the material in your research?

3 Examine your purpose

Think about your general goals (to inform, to persuade) as well as your specific ones (to get a committee to adopt a policy; to show that your interpretation is the most plausible one). Ask yourself what you want your paper to *do*. Then ask what form it might take, given this purpose. What do you want your audience to learn, to do, or to feel? Does your research suggest an argument or position paper? Does it suggest a history, a case study, an action proposal, or a research report?

> ### STRATEGY
>
> A **purpose structure** is a series of statements that briefly describe what you intend to do in each section of a paper and that help you begin to visualize the finished product. (See Chapter 5.) Try to create a purpose structure as you review your notes and questions.

Jim Nowak created the following purpose structure for his paper on intellectual property rights.

Beginning	Explain the importance of copyrights, patents, and intellectual property rights, especially for computer software.
Middle	Discuss questions of intellectual property rights as they evolved in three legal controversies: Sun Microsystem's Java language versus Microsoft's version of Java; Lotus 1-2-3 versus similar spreadsheets; and Apple's Macintosh user interface versus Microsoft's Windows.
Ending	Describe recently proposed solutions to the problem of establishing ownership of software designs.

4 Develop a thesis

Develop a thesis statement in a sentence or two as a way of giving your planning a focus and maintaining this focus as you draft and revise. Begin with a **tentative** (or **draft**) **thesis statement** (see Chapter 5), perhaps based on your research question(s). Modify it as you draft and in your final version,

48a
plan

perhaps breaking it into several sentences to make it easier to read. You might develop your thesis from the research questions you created earlier in the process (see 45b). Consider using your thesis statement as an organizing strategy for your final draft, repeating parts of it in modified form at key points in the paper.

A WORD ABOUT SPEAKING

In an oral presentation, your audience will need to know not only your overarching goal or purpose but how your presentation will unfold, and they'll expect this information early on. It helps to answer two questions relating to your thesis and your purpose structure: First, what are you going to say (or show or argue or demonstrate)? Second, how will you do this in your presentation, in terms of its overall structure or use of time?

In her presentation on fetal alcohol syndrome, Brittany Sherson included in her talking points the following statement of purpose and presentation outline.

> In this presentation, I will show
>
> —that even a single alcoholic beverage during pregnancy can harm the developing fetus, and
> —that the vast majority of Americans are unaware of the effects of alcohol on their unborn children.
>
> My presentation will
> first: provide an overview of the research on the effects of alcohol on the fetus;
> second: argue that Americans are ill-informed by providing statistics about fetal alcohol syndrome;
> third: offer some recommendations for how to remedy this national crisis.

48.1

48b
draft

48b Planning and drafting your paper

The moment you begin your research, you're planning your project. But when you've collected most of the information you need, you'll need to focus more sharply on the organization and content of your paper.

Outlining. A traditional outline is often too detailed for a long research essay because writers become frustrated trying to fit into the outline all the bits of information they have gathered—information that doesn't always prove useful as they develop their reasoning in a draft. Consider making a **working outline** that shows the general sequence of information along with the relationships (transitions) between segments of information.

> ## STRATEGY
>
> In an informal outline, quickly block out the main parts of your paper. Write detailed transitions between the parts. Focus on the largest units of your paper first, and then work on smaller organizational chunks such as sections and paragraphs. This will give you a clear sense of how the parts fit together and how the paper will progress.

Grouping information. Grouping your information (3b) is useful if you have many bits of information but not a particularly clear idea of how they relate.

> ## STRATEGY
>
> Write down or describe separate pieces of information (such as major points from your sources, informal paraphrases or summaries, or thoughts and ideas you want to include) on pieces of paper. If you took notes on cards, you may be able to use these. Now arrange the pages or cards in relation to one another. As you begin to see patterns emerge, you may think of additional information that fits into one grouping or another.

Cutting and pasting. If you've been using a research journal to record and reflect on research, you may already have the segments of your draft. Instead of spending a lot of time writing, try moving around the pieces you've already sketched.

> ## STRATEGY
>
> If you've written on both sides of your journal pages or don't want to cut up the original, photocopy the relevant pages. Now cut out the separate entries. Arrange the entries to reflect a cohesive relationship, and think of or draft transitions. Depending on how extensive your journal entries are, you may end up with a rough draft by the time you finish cutting and pasting.

48b
draft

Cutting and pasting can be done easily using a word-processing program. Choose relevant passages from your journal or research notes, and then paste them into a new file wherever they seem to fit. Print out the results from time to time so you can see the overall pattern emerging.

Focusing on the introduction and conclusion. Sometimes you might want to write the introduction and the conclusion first. You'll have to consider your readers' level of interest and familiarity with your topic, and you'll have to predict your paper's design and goals. You may find your research question(s) helpful in developing your introduction or conclusion.

STRATEGY

In writing the introduction, ask yourself, "How can I engage readers from the start and make them want to read on?" Think of interesting ways to begin—even formal academic papers don't have to have dull openings. Write two or more different openings, experimenting with style and content.

In writing the conclusion, ask, "How can I make my readers want to keep thinking about the topic?" Don't hide behind a quotation. Avoid sentimental or patriotic clichés, and don't merely summarize. Try several versions.

In thinking of a way to begin his research paper on the Roswell incident as a case study in the cultural implications of American conspiracy theories, Sam Roles knew that he already had an intriguing topic. Not too many readers would turn away from an account of a mysterious alien spaceship crash in New Mexico and the notion that the military hid the evidence from a paranoid, reactionary public for over fifty years. He decided to begin his paper *as if* the incident were true, thus seducing his readers into the same mindset as those who believe the crash really happened.

> One night early in the month of July, 1947, witnesses near the town of Roswell, New Mexico, saw a brilliant disk-like object streak down and crash in the desert. Later, however, when one witness tried to locate the debris, he was stopped and turned away by military personnel. The first press releases on the incident claimed that Army forces had discovered a "flying disk" (*Roswell Daily News*), but when invesigators went to the

```
office of Major Jesse Marcel, who had been sent to look into
the incident and had in his possession pieces of the wreckage,
the "wreckage" had mysteriously become the remnants of a
weather balloon (Berlitz). Aliens had crashed on United States
soil, but believers were told it was nothing more than a few
routine Air Force tests.
```

Exercise 1

In a group, choose one of the planning methods in 48a and collaboratively apply it to one person's project. If the group chooses to write an introduction and conclusion, everyone should prepare a separate one-paragraph introduction and a brief (one- or two-sentence) conclusion. Compare all the versions.

48c Integrating print and electronic sources into your writing

48.2

Although your research paper is an original contribution to a subject area—something *you* create through your thorough sleuthing for information and your particular way of pulling all that information together and presenting it for others to learn from—it's also about *other people's* work. It's your way of representing what a community of scholars and researchers and commentators has said about a topic or how this community has tried to answer a question. *All* secondary research is about what others have said or written; *most* primary research begins with an acknowledgment or synthesis of the current state of knowledge on a topic before the researcher provides his or her own report of an original experiment, investigation, or analysis. For these reasons, learning how to acknowledge the work of others and incorporate it into your research paper is among the most important skills you can develop, and is crucial to the success of your final product.

Written sources can be integrated into your paper in several ways: as quotations, paraphrases, or summaries. Furthermore, not all sources will appear in words; for example, you might want to include charts of facts, details, and statistics, or other visuals such as pictures, graphs, and screen shots.

1 Integrating words and phrases into sentences and paragraphs

When you quote, paraphrase, or even summarize a source, you retain something of the original: the exact wording, the sequence of ideas and details, or the general point.

48c
source

Quotations.   Quoting someone's words means putting them into your paper or oral presentation in the *exact* way that they appeared in the original text. (This is why it's so important for you to be accurate when taking notes during the research stage of your project.) Avoid stringing quotations together or using many long quotations set off in blocks (which may look like padding). Instead, use quotations for these reasons:

- To support your conclusions by showing that a recognized authority or someone who writes with style and insight agrees with your conclusions
- To show that you're accurately representing ideas that you want to challenge, modify, or extend
- To preserve an especially stylish, persuasive, or concise way of saying something
- To show vividly and dramatically what other people think
- To provide a jumping-off point for your thoughts, or a change of pace

You can quote entire sentences from a source and let them stand on their own, with proper attribution.

> Yet alcohol awareness campaigns have seen only moderate success. "Although heavy drinking and monthly and daily alcohol use among high school seniors have declined since the 1980s, the decline is less among college-bound seniors, and binge drinking is a widespread problem on college campuses" (Bradley and Miller 1).

Or you can use an embedded quotation if it is less than a line or two.

EFFECTIVE   Yet a 1994 government investigation of the Roswell incident "located no records at existing Air Force offices that indicated any 'cover-up' by the USAF or any indication of such a recovery" of alien debris (Weaver 1).

A **block quotation** is a longer passage from a source, set off from your own prose because of length. Remember that readers expect you to *do* something with block quotations, not just insert them.

> Research has also shown that conspiracy theories can be more prevalent among historically oppressed or persecuted populations, as demonstrated in a recent study of African American attitudes and beliefs.

48c
source

> Our survey of 1,104 African Americans in Louisiana
> shows that there is a strong belief in many different
> conspiracy theories. A large percentage of African
> Americans do suspect some type of conspiratorial plot
> by the government aimed specifically at their race.
> More alarming, over half of the respondents believed
> that the government was involved in some type of
> genocidal plot against African Americans, and this
> was before the recent reports surfaced of possible
> CIA involvement in crack cocaine distribution in
> Los Angeles. (Parsons, Simmons, Shinhoster, and
> Kilburn 217)

Paraphrases and summaries. To make your writing smoother and more sophisticated, be selective in using quotations. Usually, you can summarize, even combining several sources, or paraphrase rather than quoting sources directly.

> Yet at first, government officials denied they had any tests
> underway in New Mexico. Many officials were as baffled as the
> general public, including Captain Tom Brown, AAF information
> officer, who told reporters that he and his colleagues were as
> mystified as everyone else about the phenomena. (Albuquerque
> Journal)

2 Integrating facts, details, and statistics

You can build entire paragraphs around facts, details, and statistics drawn from your sources as long as you indicate clearly the sources of your information. You may retain some of the emphasis of your source in using these materials; more likely, you'll end up integrating these details into prose that reflects your own purposes.

3 Visuals

Visuals (drawings, photos, graphs, and the like) can sometimes present or emphasize data better than words. If you copy a visual from print or download it from an electronic resource, you'll need to cite the source, and you may need permission to use it. Whether you create a visual yourself or draw it from your research, make sure it adds to the written text and doesn't simply substitute for it. Visuals that add to a written explanation or extend it imaginatively can increase the credibility and effectiveness of your writing. (See Chapter 14.)

**48c
source**

STRATEGY

- Put the visual as near to the relevant written text as you can without disrupting the flow of the text or distorting the visual.
- Don't interrupt the writing in ways that make it hard to read.
- Make sure your visuals are of good quality and of appropriate size for the page.
- Ask one or more readers whether your visuals are easy to understand and whether they add to the text's ideas and effect.
- Label each visual (*Figure 1, Figure 2* . . . ; *Table 1, Table 2* . . .).

CHAPTER 49

UNDERSTANDING DOCUMENTATION AND AVOIDING PLAGIARISM

Unlike assignments such as personal narratives and persuasive essays, research papers will be a quilt of other people's ideas, opinions, and scholarly work. What's "original" about most research papers is the integration of these other people's work into your own synthesis. The biggest challenge in writing up research is to bring this outside work into your thinking—and your own text. To do so effectively, you need to think carefully about what information or words you should document (that is, give credit for). *When* should you cite a source? What exactly is considered plagiarism, even when a source is cited?

49a Recognizing when to document sources

In general, you need to document the words, ideas, and information you draw from another person's work. Bear in mind the three most important reasons for documenting sources: (1) to add support to your conclusions and credibility to your explanations by showing that they're based on careful research; (2) to acknowledge another person's hard work; and (3) to show your readers where they can obtain the materials you cite (and from there, perhaps others). Decisions on what needs documenting may vary from audience to audience. If you're writing to a general audience, readers may expect you to cite sources for your discussion of subatomic particles. If you're writing for a physics professor or an audience of physicists, you can probably assume that such matters are common knowledge.

YOU MUST DOCUMENT
- Word-for-word (direct) quotations taken from someone else's work
- Paraphrases or summaries of someone else's work, whether published or presented more informally in an interview or email message
- Ideas, opinions, and interpretations that others have developed and presented, even if they are based on common knowledge

49a
source

- Facts or data that someone else has gathered or identified if the information is not widely known enough to be considered common knowledge
- Information that is not widely accepted or that is disputed
- Illustrations, charts, graphs, photographs, recordings, original software, performances, interviews, and the like

BUT DO NOT DOCUMENT
- Ideas, opinions, and interpretations that are your own
- Widely known ideas and information—the sort you can locate in common reference works or that people writing or speaking on a topic usually present as common knowledge
- Commonly used quotations ("To be, or not to be")

After Sam Roles had finished all his research on the Roswell incident as a case study in American conspiracy theory, he knew that most of his first paragraph, which introduced the subject of conspiracy theory in general, didn't have to include any references. As he transitioned into more academic definitions of conspiracy theory, however, he cited two articles in sociology journals whose authors provided precise definitions of conspiracy theory. The "general" introduction needed no references because it came from Sam's knowledge and was rendered entirely in his own words. He referenced the definitions, however, to acknowledge the work of experts and the fact that he was quoting their ideas and their words.

49.1

49b Understanding plagiarism

As the student conduct codes of almost every college and university in this country will tell you, plagiarism is a serious ethical breach and a possible violation of the law. Committing plagiarism can lead to a failing grade on your paper, a failure in your course, academic probation, or expulsion from your institution. In work settings, plagiarism can result in major lawsuits involving large damages. In public settings, they can lead to legal action and even jail time. Yet not all forms of plagiarism are equal. They arise from several circumstances:

- **Wholesale, conscious plagiarism**: A writer knowingly takes someone else's words and/or ideas and passes them off as his or her own. In school, turning in a paper obtained from the Web or a fraternity file, or having someone else write your paper and then putting your name on it, constitutes this form of plagiarism. So does taking published material and putting it into your paper as if it had come from your own mind.

- **Conscious lapses in citation**: A writer knowingly leaves out a reference to the author of a work or provides an inaccurate reference, perhaps because of an inability to retrieve the original source.
- **Inadvertent or unconscious plagiarism**: A writer doesn't understand when and how to cite sources, and fails to acknowledge his or her sources out of ignorance. Or, in summarizing or paraphrasing a source, the writer doesn't pay enough attention to the relationship between his or her own words and the words of the source material.

The material in this section shows how not to fall prey to the second and third kinds of plagiarism. We have little advice about the first kind except to say, as loudly as we can, *don't do it*. Internet resources, including plagiarism detection sites, are now so powerful that teachers can and will find cases of malicious plagiarism very quickly. More to the point, research paper assignments are designed to help you learn about a topic and develop crucial writing and research skills for college and beyond. Passing off others' work as your own damages *you* more than anyone else.

A WORD ABOUT SPEAKING

When giving an oral presentation on research, you'll also want to think carefully about summarizing, paraphrasing, and synthesizing information. But because you're doing so in a different context—for a live audience in "real time" instead of a reader—you need to think carefully about your reasons for each choice. Synthesis can be especially useful when you want to move through a lot of information quickly without boring or overwhelming your audience.

49c Avoiding plagiarism

When you include quotations, paraphrases, and summaries in your writing, you *must* acknowledge their sources. If you don't, you're treating someone else's work as your own.

- Be sure you enclose someone else's exact words in quotation marks.
- Make sure that paraphrases and summaries are in your own words.
- Be sure to cite the source of any ideas or information that you quote, paraphrase, or summarize.

The following paraphrase is too close to the original to be presented without quotation marks and would be considered plagiarized.

49c
plag

ORIGINAL PASSAGE

   Malnutrition was a widespread and increasingly severe problem throughout the least developed parts of the world in the 1970s, and would continue to be serious, occasionally reaching famine conditions, as the millennium approached. Among the cells of the human body most dependent upon a steady source of nutrients are those of the immune system, most of which live, even under ideal conditions, for only days at a time. (From Laurie Garrett, *The Coming Plague*, New York: Penguin, 1994, p. 199)

PLAGIARIZED VERSION

   Garrett points out that malnutrition can give microbes an advantage as they spread through the population. Malnutrition continues to be a severe problem throughout the least developed parts of the world. The human immune system contains cells that are dependent upon a steady source of nutrients. These cells may live, even under ideal conditions, for only days at a time.

As the highlighted words show, the writer of the plagiarized version made only minor changes in some phrases and "lifted" others verbatim.

APPROPRIATE PARAPHRASE

   Garrett points out that malnutrition can give microbes an advantage as they spread through the population. The human body contains immune cells that help to fight off various diseases. When the body is deprived of nutrients, these immune cells will weaken (Garrett 199).

Because this writer's paper focused on the general threat of global disease, he also could have simply summarized the passage.

APPROPRIATE SUMMARY

   It has been suggested that malnutrition can weaken the immune system and make people more susceptible to diseases they would otherwise fight off (Garrett 199).

STRATEGY

   Inadvertent plagiarism—really a kind of sloppiness in your writing process—often happens when you are working between your source material and your developing paper. You *think* you're using your own words but the words of your source are so fresh in your mind that they creep in and "become" yours. Whenever you paraphrase or summarize a source, be sure to look back at the source and

49c
plag

compare your words with those in the source. If any phrases or sentences are too close to the original, either quote the material directly and exactly (using quotation marks), or revise your summary or paraphrase so that you're not using the author's words as your own.

1 Be aware of different conventions in the use of sources

Academic research usually acknowledges and draws on the work of previous scholars and researchers. The writer indicates where he or she fits into the tradition of research on a topic and explains any agreements and disagreements with previous work. In this community, much value is placed on a thorough presentation of data and evidence, along with precise, formal documentation in the style appropriate to the subject matter or academic field (MLA, APA, CMS, CBE, or COS—see Chapters 51–54). The following excerpt from Summer Arrigo-Nelson and Jennifer Figliozzi's research report shows their careful integration (and critique) of a research study.

49.2

> First, although both questions 1 and 4 looked to determine student alcohol use within the home, a discrepancy appeared between the percentage of people who replied that they were offered alcohol at home and those who said that their parents believed alcohol was only for those over twenty-one years of age. This discrepancy could have arisen if the students in the sample were not thorough in their evaluation of their parents' views, in which case, correlations drawn from this data should not be relied upon (Aas, Jakobsen, and Anderssen 1996).

When you read academic research, you'll find that many of the conventions for citation and for the quoting of material will be relevant to your own papers, which will most often assume a similar academic orientation. Material from other settings, however, may follow somewhat different conventions. Work audiences will expect concise treatment of things they already know and extended summaries, tables, graphs, and illustrations—all carefully documented with a recognizable citation system (see Chapters 50–54). Material designed for general public consumption may cite sources in a somewhat informal fashion; texts with many footnotes or academic-sounding references can confuse or put off some public audiences.

The following paragraphs are excerpted from a publication of the "Exxon Valdez Oil Spill Trustee Council" <http://www.oilspill.state.ak.us> that contains documents of public interest, with special focus on the Exxon Valdez cleanup effort and that spill's impact on the Alaskan shoreline environment. Notice how several important and scientifically complex studies are condensed into a research synthesis that is readily understandable by a reasonably educated public audience, but does not overwhelm the reader with complex references, preferring to provide alternative ways, at the Web site, to access the actual research studies.

> Cormorants are large fish-eating birds that spend much of their time on the water or perched on rocks near the water. Three species typically are found within the oil-spill area. Carcasses of 838 cormorants were recovered following the oil spill, including 418 pelagic, 161 red-faced, 38 double-crested, and 221 unidentified cormorants. Many more cormorants probably died as a result of the spill, but their carcasses were not found.
>
> No regional population estimates are available for any of the cormorant species found in the oil-spill area. In 1996, the U.S. Fish and Wildlife Service Alaska Seabird Colony Catalog, however, listed counts of 7,161 pelagic cormorants, 8,967 red-faced cormorants, and 1,558 double-crested cormorants in the oil-spill area. These are direct counts at colonies, not overall population estimates, but they suggest that population sizes are small. In this context, it appears that injury to all three cormorant species was significant. Counts on the outer Kenai Peninsula coast suggested that the direct mortality of cormorants due to oil resulted in fewer birds in this area in 1989 compared to 1986. In addition, there were statistically significant declines in the estimated numbers of cormorants (all three species combined) in the oiled portion of Prince William Sound based on pre- and postspill boat surveys in July 1972–73 compared to 1989–91. More recent surveys (through 1998) have not shown an increasing population trend since the oil spill, and for that reason these species are considered to be not recovered.

If you cite such work in your own papers or projects, you may wish to "unpack" the general references into specific citations. In more informal and less research-oriented public writing, be sure that you check any quotations or material that appears to be from some other source than the public document itself. If you encounter an unreferenced quotation, try contacting the organization or author of the document to get the full citation of his or her source.

In contrast, consider an excerpt from a document at the same oil spill Web site that is clearly intended for other researchers and scholars with technical backgrounds, such as academics in marine biology departments at research universities, or members of the Environmental Protection Agency who monitor coastal pollution. Notice especially how careful the authors are to cite the sources of their information. Notice, too, how much more specialized is their language and terminology.

49c
plag

> The composition, distribution, abundance, and productivity of plant and animal plankton communities in the GOA have been reviewed by

Sambrotto and Lorenzen (1986); Cooney (1986); Miller (1993); and Mackas and Frost (1993). In general, dramatic differences are observed between pelagic communities over the deep ocean, and those found in shelf, coastal, and protected inside waters (sounds, fjords, and estuaries). Specifically, the euphotic zone seaward of the shelf edge is dominated year round by very small phytoplankters—tiny diatoms, naked flagellates, and cyanobacteria (Booth 1988). Most are smaller than 10 microns in size, and their combined standing stocks (measured as chlorophyll concentration) occur at very low and seasonally stable levels. It was originally hypothesized that a small group of large oceanic copepods (Neocalanus spp. and Eucalanus bungii) limited plant numbers and open ocean production by efficiently controlling the plant stocks through grazing (Heinrich 1962). More recent evidence, however, indicates the predominant grazers on the oceanic flora are not the large calanoids (Dagg 1993), but instead abundant populations of ciliate protozoans and heterotrophic microflagellates (Miller et al. 1991a, 1991b, Frost 1993).

A WORD ABOUT SPEAKING

Famous cases of plagiarism in speeches and public addresses abound. This usually happens when a speaker uses someone else's words without any acknowledgment of their source, making it appear that the words (and ideas) are the speaker's own. Numerous parenthetical references during a presentation, however, can also bore or frustrate your audience. It's a good idea to hand out a list of all the references you use in your talk, so that your audience has them in one place. Then, instead of citing full references the way you would in a paper, weave them artfully into your presentation: "As Warnock has pointed out in her research on [. . .]," "Several studies, notably the Jones, Argyle, and Pollock references on your sheet, have shown that [. . .]," or "In my summary of the research, I'll be drawing on the references listed in the handout."

Exercise 2

A. Choose a passage from one of your secondary sources, and write a summary and paraphrase of it. Then embed a quotation from the source into a sentence of your own.

B. With a group or partner, discuss your writing for Exercise 2A. Does any of it seem plagiarized? If so, help each other to rewrite. Talk about how to improve the passages. How can you make them read more smoothly? How can you make them more concise?

49c
plag

CHAPTER 50

DOING FIELDWORK

Although much of the academic research you've done in school has focused on print sources (books and articles), large numbers of researchers engage in **field research**. Field researchers gather information and ideas firsthand—directly from **informants**, people they interview or survey, or from observation of events, places, and phenomena. Consider, for example, the range and variety of field research being conducted in various settings.

- **Academic settings**. Field research in disciplines like sociology, psychology, business, education, or urban planning generally means studying people's behaviors or outlooks in order to identify patterns or causes and effects. Anthropologists, for example, often study cultures or groups of people by immersing themselves as much as possible in the culture, making observations, taking copious notes, and engaging in cultural and social analysis. When field research takes the form of scientific inquiry in fields like chemistry, engineering, or pharmacy, it inquires into how substances, organisms, objects, or machines work or can be constructed.
- **Work settings**. Field research in businesses or other organizations often looks at the way customers (or staff) act and interact, focusing especially on problems, programs, or future actions and choices. Researchers may study a particular manufacturing plant to see if they can find inefficiencies in production; market researchers may conduct extensive polls and surveys to gauge the public's interest in a certain product (in some cases recruiting people to take taste tests or engage in "focus groups" to provide information for improving a product or refining a marketing strategy).
- **Public settings**. Field research in public settings often aims to gather (and measure) people's opinions, attitudes, and values, especially in relationship to policies, public programs, and institutions, as well as to issues affecting all or part of a society. In addition, government-sponsored

research in the public interest provides important information that can have profound effects on laws and regulations. Researchers working for the Environmental Protection Agency, for example, collect samples of soil, water, and air from specific or general areas of the country in order to test the levels of certain pollutants or contaminants in those samples.

In these and thousands of other cases, research involves the direct collection and analysis of data, often "on location," hence in the "field."

Field work doesn't exclude information from print resources. In most cases, field researchers supplement their work with data gathered by other researchers and writers, or refer to prior research in order to extend or refine it. Still, your field work will yield original results, meaning that the material in your research paper or report is the product of your own work, not borrowed from somebody else's research, and that the information and ideas you present are more likely to be fresh and original.

Good field research also involves interpretation. Be prepared to give the data you collect the same kind of critical "reading" and analysis you give to print and electronic resources (see 47b). These same secondary sources may also suggest kinds of conclusions you can draw from your data, or uses you can make of it. Of course, the goals of your field work and the method you employ should depend on both your writing tasks and the research community you're addressing.

If you launch into original field research too quickly, you might overlook important perspectives or miss the chance to think about your data-gathering process more carefully. It helps to do some background research before beginning field research. What have other people said or found out about your topic? What problems or unanswered questions arise from their work? Be sure to plan your field work carefully (see Chapter 46), so that you won't feel you've missed something important after the field experience is over.

50a Preparing surveys, polls, and questionnaires

A common type of field research for college papers involves collecting attitudinal or factual data from students, faculty, or people in the vicinity of a campus. Research in public and work settings often relies on these techniques, but they're common in academic research as well.

Polls, surveys, and questionnaires are most often done on paper; increasingly, however, the World Wide Web is allowing researchers to collect information more widely using electronic surveying techniques. Regardless of whether you'll use paper-and-pencil surveys, live questionnaires (in person or over the phone), or electronic surveys, you'll need to think through

50.1

50a
field

your questions very carefully and test your instrument before you administer it for real.

1 Surveys and polls

Surveys and **polls** collect short answers, often in *yes/no* form. They provide statistics you can present in charts and tables, measure against research findings, or use to support your opinions.

> ### STRATEGY
>
> - Begin your survey or questionnaire with a clear sense of what you want to find out and why. Creating and refining a research question (see 45b) will help you to focus on relevant questions or data.
> - Consider the people you'll survey or poll. Do you want to poll on the basis of gender, age, or occupation? For example, if you were comparing the opinions of college students and parents about alcohol use, you would want a large enough sample from each group to enable you to generalize about any differences.
> - Anticipate responses and design questions accordingly. If you ask a *yes/no* question, will either a yes or no answer give you sufficient information about the question? If you ask an open-ended question (requiring a freeform written or oral response), how will you organize and make sense of the responses?
> - Consider the task relative to your survey respondents and their motivations. If your questionnaire is very long or complicated, will they tire and toss the survey away? Consider providing a reward of some sort for lengthy surveys and questionnaires.
> - Consider the nature of the information you're requesting. Will your respondents be uncomfortable? Are they able to provide the information without becoming frustrated or finding that it all "depends"?
> - Always draft, test, and revise your questions to make them as effective as possible.
> - Think carefully about where you'll conduct your survey or poll, because the location you choose may determine the particular groups of people who answer your questions. Polling people in a bar about their attitudes toward alcohol use will yield quite different information than the same poll conducted in the parking lot of a health food co-op.

50a
field

Here are a few of the questions Shane Hand asked people about recycling. As they answered, he put a mark on a tally sheet.

Do you . . .

Use coffee mugs instead of polystyrene cups?	(Yes)	No
Reuse plastic wrap, foil, and plastic bags?	Yes	(No)
Recycle newspapers and/or magazines?	(Yes)	No

Are you willing to . . .

Take your own bags to the store?	(Yes)	No
Shop at a store that's harder to get to, but carries biodegradable products?	Yes	(No)

2 Questionnaires

Questionnaires allow you to gather in-depth information, sometimes from a large number of people. Because they're usually mailed, most questionnaires don't require the "live" contact time of interviews, but they need to be prepared carefully so they don't confuse respondents and ruin a project.

> **STRATEGY**
>
> 1. Consider the form of your questionnaire. Will you ask respondents to write out explanations, check boxes, or circle answer choices? Will you use a multiple-choice format or a rating scale?
> 2. Draft a list of questions that will yield the information you want. Scrutinize your wording carefully, and test your draft on at least two or three people. Ask them to describe points at which they were confused or needed more information.
> 3. Revise the questionnaire and prepare it for distribution. Try to fit your questions on one page (front and back) if possible, but leave enough room for longhand comments if you have time to analyze them.

In a project for the student activities board on his campus, Eric Poritsky designed a questionnaire to find out how much time students spent using computer terminals on campus (outside of dorm rooms). The board used the results in a proposal to persuade the Coffee Bean, a national chain coffee house with a franchise in the union, to install a dozen computer terminals in their facility so that students and faculty could access the Internet while having coffee. Among Eric's questions were a cluster that asked respondents to estimate their time using terminals at different locations on campus, thus mixing a poll-like question with some more open-ended questions about computer use, including an estimate of how often the respondents might use computer terminals inside the Coffee Bean.

50a
field

50b Conducting interviews

You can use interviews to supplement your research in print and electronic resources, either by talking with experts, or by contacting people whose experiences may help you test the validity of conclusions offered in your other sources. You might also decide to make interviews your main method of research. Such a strategy would be especially appropriate for research on an organization or a program (such as a juvenile justice system or an emergency medical response program) currently facing a number of problems.

STRATEGY

1. List possible interviewees. Begin by writing down the questions you'd like to have answered; then list people who might be able to answer them. Consider whether you'll need to do a thorough, lengthy interview or just collect short answers to a few questions.
2. Write out questions you want to ask your interviewees. Arrange your questions logically; avoid those that can be answered by yes or no, unless you plan follow-up interviews. If possible, rehearse with friends to discover those questions that are likely to be ineffective.
3. Be courteous when you contact your interviewees. Explain your project and ask their permission for the interview.
4. Use your list of questions, but don't be shackled by it. Follow the train of new information and ideas as long as it serves your purpose.
5. Consider tape-recording your interview instead of writing everything down. This will let you focus on the content of the interview. Always ask permission to use a recorder, and bring along extra tapes or disks and batteries.
6. After the interview, send a thank-you note to each interviewee, both for politeness and because you may need a follow-up interview.

Exercise 1

A. Imagine you're writing an interview paper describing someone's occupation. Choose an occupation. Then draft a list of questions you might ask a person in that occupation during an interview.

B. In a small group, compare and discuss your list of questions. Consider especially the forms of the questions and the sorts of information they might elicit. Consider role-playing parts of your interviews to tease out some of the potential problems in the phrasing of the questions, and explore the ways in which the interviewer might follow up on them during the interview.

A WORD ABOUT SPEAKING

If you're giving an oral presentation on the results of your field work, you will want to spend considerable time preparing materials that summarize and display what you've found. For questionnaires, polls, and surveys, consider creating simple, well-organized charts or graphs that clearly display the results of your research. Several popular kinds of software can help to convert numbers into visual displays. If your research material has come from more open-ended field research techniques, such as questionnaires and observations, look for ways to group or cluster the information so that you can display your interpretations more convincingly.

50c Ethnographies

50.2

You can use **ethnographic research** to interpret the practices, behaviors, language, and attitudes of particular groups that are tied together by their interests or ways of understanding and acting in the world. Such cultural analyses are at the heart of much important research on human belief and ritual. Ethnography means, literally, the writing (*-graphy*) of culture (*ethno-*). The written report of ethnographic research (an **ethnography**) aims to provide an in-depth understanding of its subject. For this reason, you may need to use several methods to gather detailed information about your subject, including **observation** of people, events, and settings; **interviews** with **informants** (people who provide you with information about the group to which they belong); and the collection of **artifacts** (material objects characteristic of a group or culture). Most full-scale ethnographies require months or even years of participation in a community; you can use the principles of ethnographic research, however, for more modest "quasi-ethnographies" or "qualitative" sorts of investigations.

To understand your subject in depth, focus your fieldwork on a specific setting, activity, person, or group of people to which you can devote enough time and energy to arrive at worthwhile conclusions. Conduct **structured observations** in which you carefully and objectively look at a situation, behavior, or relationship in order to understand its elements and processes. For instance, in researching the ways preschoolers use language during play, you could arrange and plan in detail a series of structured observations at a daycare center.

50c
field

STRATEGY

1. Choose the site, and, if necessary, get permission to conduct your observations.
2. Decide how to situate yourself. Will you move around or remain inconspicuous? How will you explain your presence to the people you are observing?
3. Decide what information you want to gather and why. Consider how you will use it in your report.
4. Consider your means for recording information: tape recorder, camera, notepad, or video camera.
5. Make a list of problems that might arise, and develop strategies for dealing with them.

Most universities have a group, board, or committee in charge of "human subjects consent." (Many also have such groups to ensure the ethical and humane treatment of animals in experiments.) Human subjects consent boards review proposals in which people will be the objects of research or experiments, usually to be sure that those people are not exploited or potentially harmed. Check with your instructor to see whether you need to submit your proposal for field research to such a board or committee and, if necessary, get approval from them before starting your research.

PART 6

Using Citation Styles

CHAPTER 51

DOCUMENTING SOURCES: MLA

The MLA (Modern Language Association) documentation style offers you a convenient system for acknowledging your sources for ideas, information, and quotations and for directing readers to these sources. It consists of an in-text citation (generally in parentheses) and a list of works cited (presented at the end of the text). (For advice on what to document and what not to document, see 49a.)

51.1

USE MLA DOCUMENTATION STYLE IN . . .

ACADEMIC SETTINGS

When writing in humanities fields such as English and foreign languages

When writing for publications or groups requiring use of MLA style

When writing papers for an instructor who asks for a simple form of parenthetical documentation such as MLA style

CONSIDER USING MLA DOCUMENTATION STYLE
(PERHAPS A MODIFIED FORM) IN . . .

WORK AND PUBLIC SETTINGS

When readers are not expecting a specific form of documentation

When you feel your subject and audience are best served by a simple, direct documentation style that seldom uses footnotes or endnotes

When other writers in the setting use either MLA style or a similar, though informal, system

If the MLA documentation style does not meet your needs, consider using these other documentation styles: APA (Chapter 52), CSE (Chapter 53), or CMS (Chapter 54).

For detailed treatments of the MLA documentation system, see the *MLA Handbook for Writers of Research Papers* (5th ed., New York: MLA, 1999) or the *MLA Style Manual and Guide to Scholarly Publishing* (2nd ed., New York: MLA, 1998); and recent changes online at <http://mla.org/>.

51a Using in-text citations

The **MLA documentation style** uses a citation in the text (generally an author's name) to identify a source for readers. The citation helps readers locate the source in the list of works cited appearing at the end of the paper. Many in-text citations provide a page number to indicate exactly where in the source readers can find the particular information.

> **IN-TEXT CITATION**
> Although the average Haitian peasant calls himself a Catholic and views himself as such, he generally continues to call on his African ancestors' gods, or loa, for spiritual and emotional support. As one peasant put it, "One must be Catholic to serve the loa" (Metraux 59).
>
> —Fredza Léger, College Student

> **ENTRY IN THE LIST OF WORKS CITED**
> Metraux, Alfred. Haiti: Black Peasants and Their Religion. London: Harrap, 1960.

Citations may appear within parentheses or as part of the discussion itself. They may refer to a work in general or to specific parts of a source (by including a page number).

Author's name inside parentheses. You can choose to provide the author's name in parentheses. For a quotation or for specific information, include the page number to indicate where the material appears in the source, as in (*Jenkins 134*). *Do not* place a comma between an author's name and a page number; *do not* use *p.* or *pp.* to indicate page(s).

> Comparing the writing styles of individual authors in classic Chinese literature is difficult because ancient China had "no concept of single authorship" (Liu 30).

Author's name as part of discussion. You can make the author's name (or other information as well) part of the discussion.

> James Liu reminds us that it is difficult to compare the writing styles of individual authors in classic Chinese

literature because ancient China had "no concept of single authorship" (30).

General reference. A **general reference** enables you to refer to the main ideas in a source or to information presented throughout the work, not in a single place. It may also refer to a book, an article, or some other source as a whole. You need not provide page numbers for a general reference.

PARENTHETICAL Many species of animals have developed complex systems of communication (Bright).

The statement summarizes one of the work's main points, so the reference cites the work as a whole, not a specific page or pages.

AUTHOR NAMED According to Michael Bright, many species of animals
IN DISCUSSION have developed complex systems of communication.

Specific reference. A **specific reference** enables you to document words, ideas, or facts appearing in a particular place in a source.

People have trouble recognizing sound patterns dolphins use to communicate. Dolphins can perceive clicking sounds "made up of 700 units of sound per second," yet "in the human ear the sounds would fuse together in our minds at 20-30 clicks per second" (Bright 52).
The page number gives the specific location of the quotation.

According to Michael Bright, dolphins recognize patterns consisting of seven hundred clicks each second, yet such patterns begin to blur for people at around twenty or thirty clicks each second (52).
The page number cites the specific source.

Punctuation and abbreviations are kept to a minimum when you use in-text parenthetical citations following the MLA documentation style. You do not place a comma between an author's name and a page number in a parenthetical reference, for example, nor do you use *p.* or *pp.* to indicate page(s). (For advice on punctuating sentences containing parenthetical references, see "Placement and Punctuation of Parenthetical Citations," on page 621.)

STRATEGY

Use the following questions to help decide whether to make in-text citations general or specific and whether to make them parenthetical or part of the discussion.

- Am I trying to weave broad concepts into my own explanation or argument (general), or am I looking for precise ideas and details to support my conclusions (specific)?
- Will this part of my paper be clearer and more effective if I draw on the author's own words (specific) or if I merely point out that the author's text as a whole presents the concepts I am discussing (general)?
- Do I wish to highlight the source by naming the author (part of discussion), or to emphasize the information itself (parenthetical)?
- Will this passage be more concise, emphatic, or effective if I put the author's name in parentheses or if I work it into the discussion?
- Do I wish to refer to more than one source without distracting readers (parenthetical), or do the several sources I am citing need individual attention (part of discussion)?

PLACEMENT AND PUNCTUATION OF PARENTHETICAL CITATIONS

In general, put parenthetical citations close to the quotation, information, paraphrase, or summary you are documenting. Place the parenthetical citation either at the end of a sentence (before the final punctuation) or at a natural pause in the sentence.

> Wayland Hand reports on a folk belief that going to sleep on a rug made of bearskin can relieve backache (183).

If the citation applies to only part of the sentence, put it after the borrowed material at the point least likely to disrupt the sentence.

> The folk belief that "sleeping on a bear rug will cure backache" (Hand 183) is yet another example of a kind of magic in which external objects produce results inside the body.

When you place an in-text parenthetical citation at the end of a long quotation set off as a block (see 36b), leave a space after the ending punctuation and then add the citation.

> Many athletes are superstitious, especially baseball players, but perhaps the most superstitious of all are pitchers.
>> On the days they are scheduled to appear, many pitchers avoid activities that they believe sap their strength and therefore detract from their

```
            effectiveness, or that they otherwise generally
            link with poor performance. Many pitchers avoid
            eating certain foods on their pitching days. Some
            pitchers refuse to walk anywhere on the day of the
            game in the belief that every little exertion
            subtracts from their playing strength. One pitcher
            would never put on his cap until the game started
            and would not wear it at all on the days he did not
            pitch. (Gmelch 280)
```

If the material you are quoting contains quotation marks, use double quotation marks to enclose the quotation as a whole and single quotation marks to enclose the interior quotation.

```
    According to Dubisch, "Being a 'health food person' involves
    more than simply changing one's diet or utilizing an
    alternative medical system" (61).
```

51b Creating MLA in-text citations

In-text citations following MLA documentation style may take slightly differing forms depending on the number of authors, the number of volumes in a work, and the number of works being cited. (For advice on placing in-text citations within a passage and providing appropriate punctuation, see the box, "Placement and Punctuation of Parenthetical Citations," on page 621.)

GUIDE TO MLA FORMATS FOR IN-TEXT CITATIONS

1. One Author
2. Two or Three Authors
3. Four or More Authors
4. Corporate or Group Author
5. No Author Given
6. More than One Work by the Same Author
7. Authors with the Same Last Name
8. Indirect Source
9. Multivolume Work
10. Literary Work
11. Bible
12. Two or More Sources in a Single Citation
13. Selection in an Anthology
14. Electronic or Other Nonprint Sources

51b
MLA

1. One author

Provide the author's last name in parentheses, or make either the full name or last name alone part of the discussion.

PARENTHETICAL   During World War II, government posters often portrayed

homemakers "as vital defenders of the nation's homes"

(Honey 135).

AUTHOR NAMED   According to Maureen Honey, government posters during
IN DISCUSSION

World War II often portrayed homemakers "as vital

defenders of the nation's homes" (135).

2. Two or three authors

Give the names of all the authors in parentheses or in the discussion.

PARENTHETICAL   By the time Elizabeth I died, Francis Bacon had amassed

considerable debt (Jardine and Stewart 275).
If the book had three authors, the citation would read (Jardine, Stewart, and Ringler 275).

AUTHOR NAMED   Jardine and Stewart provide a partial list of Francis
IN TEXT

Bacon's debts from the year Elizabeth I died (275).

3. Four or more authors

Supply the first author's name and the phrase *et al.* (meaning "and others") within parentheses. To introduce the citation as part of the discussion, use a phrase like "Chen and his colleagues point out . . . ."

More funding would encourage creative research of complementary

medicine (Chen et al. 82).

If you give all the authors' names rather than *et al.* in the works cited list, then give all the names in the in-text citation.

4. Corporate or group author

If an organization or government agency is named as the author, use its name (shortened, if cumbersome) in the citation.

Concerns over the quality of local news programs led to a

proposed system of standards ("benchmarking") for raising the

quality of journalism (Project for Excellence 189-91).
"Project for Excellence" is the shortened name of Project for Excellence in Journalism.

5. No author given

When no author's name is given, use the title instead (in a shortened version if it is long). Begin the abbreviated title with the word used to alphabetize the work in the list of works cited.

> On January 1, 1993, the former state of Czechoslovakia split
>
> into two new states, the Czech Republic and the Slovak Republic
>
> (Baedeker's 67).

The shortened title refers to *Baedeker's Czech/Slovak Republics,* **a book for which no author is given.**

6. More than one work by the same author

When the list of works cited includes more than one work by the same author, add the title in shortened form to your citation.

> The members of some Protestant groups in the Appalachian region
>
> view the "handling of serpents" during worship "as a supreme
>
> act of faith" (Daugherty, "Serpent-Handling" 232).

"Serpent-Handling" is a shortened version of "Serpent-Handling as Sacrament." In a parenthetical citation, add a comma between the author's name and the title.

7. Authors with the same last name

When the authors of different sources have the same last name, identify the specific author by giving the first initial (or the full first name, if necessary).

> Medical errors remain a major problem (D. Adams 1); however,
>
> new electronic information systems may help reduce them (J.
>
> Adams 309).

8. Indirect source

When your source provides you with a quotation (or paraphrase) taken from yet another source, you need to include the phrase *qtd. in* (for "quoted in") to indicate the original source.

> For Vitz, "art, especially great art, must engage all or almost
>
> all of the major capacities of the nervous system" (qtd. in
>
> Feuch 65).

Feuch is the source of the quotation from Vitz.

When referring to an indirect source, you should generally include in your discussion the name of the person from whom the quotation is taken. If the same information were presented in a parenthetical citation—(*Vitz, qtd. in Feuch 65*)—some readers might mistakenly look for Vitz rather than Feuch in the list of works cited.

9. Multivolume work

Give the volume number followed by a colon and a space, then the page number: (*Franklin 6: 434*). When referring to the volume as a whole, use a comma after the author's name and add *vol.* before the volume number: (*Franklin, vol. 6*).

> In 1888, Lewis Carroll let two students call their school paper
>
> Jabberwock, a made-up word from Alice's Adventures in
>
> Wonderland (Cohen 2: 695).

The author is Cohen, the volume number is 2, and the page number is 695.

10. Literary work

When you refer to a literary work, consider including information that will help readers find the passage you are citing in any of the different editions of the work. Begin by giving the page number of the particular edition followed by a semicolon; then add the appropriate chapter, part, or section numbers.

> In Huckleberry Finn, Mark Twain ridicules the exaggerated
>
> histrionics of provincial actors through his portrayal of the
>
> King and the Duke as they rehearse Hamlet's famous soliloquy:
>
> "So [the duke] went to marching up and down, thinking, and
>
> frowning horrible every now and then; then he would hoist up
>
> his eyebrows; next he would squeeze his hand on his forehead
>
> and stagger back and kind of moan; next he would sigh, and next
>
> he'd let on to drop a tear" (178; ch. 21).

Note that there is a semicolon after the page number, followed by *ch.* (for "chapter"). If you also include a part number, use *pt.* followed by a comma and the chapter number, as in (*386; pt. 3, ch. 2*). For a play, note the act, scene, and line numbers, if needed, as in this reference to *Hamlet*: (*Ham. 1.2.76*). For poems, give line numbers (*lines 55–57*) or, if there are part divisions, both part and line numbers (*4.220–23*).

11. Bible

MLA style uses a period between the chapter and verse numbers (*Mark 2.3–4*). For parenthetical citations, use abbreviations for names of five or more letters, as in the case of Deuteronomy: (*Deut. 16.21–22*).

12. Two or more sources in a single citation

When you use a parenthetical citation to refer to more than one source, separate the sources with a semicolon.

> Differences in the ways people speak, especially differences in
> the ways men and women use language, can often be traced to who
> has power and who does not (Tannen 83-86; Tavris 297-301).

13. Selection in an anthology

If your source is a reprint of an essay, poem, short story, or other work appearing in an anthology, cite the work's author (not the editor of the anthology), but refer to the page number(s) in the anthology.

> John Corry argues that pornographic material is not really
> available "with just the click of a button" (114).

The selection appears on page 114 of the anthology *Pornography: Opposing Viewpoints.*

14. Electronic or other nonprint sources

Provide the name of the author, the title, or any other information readers need to find the appropriate entry in your list of works cited. You need not include a page number for electronic sources of a single page or without page numbering. For numbered paragraphs, give the number and use the abbreviation *par(s)*.

> In contrast, the heroine's mother in the film Clueless died in
> an ironic and contemporary fashion: the victim of an accident
> during liposuction.

51C Informative footnotes and endnotes

At times you may wish to comment on the usefulness or reliability of a source, provide some additional background details, or discuss a specific point at length. You recognize, however, that doing so would disrupt the flow of the discussion and would be useful for only a few readers. Informative footnotes (or endnotes) offer a solution. Place a number (raised slightly above the line of the text) at a suitable point in your discussion. Then provide the note itself, labeled with a corresponding number at the bottom of a page (for a footnote) or at the end of the paper before the list of works cited on a page titled "Notes" (for an endnote).

[1]Anyone still inclined to question the intricacy of video games and the conceptual challenges they pose might consider investigating the numerous publications devoted to strategies for games like Riven, Myst, and even the various versions of Doom.

51d Creating an MLA list of works cited

In an alphabetized list titled "Works Cited," placed on a new page that follows the last page of your paper or report, provide readers with detailed information about the sources you have cited in the text. To indicate all the works you consulted, even if you did not cite them all, you may provide a list titled "Works Consulted."

In your list of works cited, alphabetize the entries by the author's last name or by last and first names for authors with the same last name. If a source does not identify an author, alphabetize by the first word in the title (other than *A*, *An*, or *The*).

GUIDE TO MLA FORMATS FOR A LIST OF WORKS CITED

1. BOOKS AND WORKS TREATED AS BOOKS

1. One Author
2. Two or Three Authors
3. Four or More Authors
4. Corporate or Group Author
5. No Author Given
6. More Than One Book by the Same Author
7. One or More Editors
8. Author and an Editor
9. Translator
10. Edition Other Than the First
11. Reprinted Book
12. One or More Volumes of a Multivolume Work
13. Book in a Series
14. Book Published Before 1900
15. Book with a Publisher's Imprint

51d
MLA

53. Online Book
54. Selection from Online Book
55. Online Journal Article
56. Online Magazine Article
57. Online Newspaper Article
58. Online Government Document
59. Online Editorial
60. Online Letter to the Editor
61. Online Interview
62. Online Review
63. Online Database, Information Service, or Scholarly Project
64. Online Source from Computer Service
65. Online Abstract
66. Online Videotape or Film
67. Online Television or Radio Program
68. Online Recording
69. Online Artwork
70. Online Map or Chart
71. Online Cartoon
72. Online Advertisement
73. Other Online Sources
74. FTP, Telnet, or Gopher Site
75. Email
76. Online Posting
77. Synchronous Communication
78. CD-ROM, Diskette, or Magnetic Tape
79. CD-ROM Abstract

1 Books and works treated as books

MODEL FORMAT FOR BOOKS AND WORKS TREATED AS BOOKS

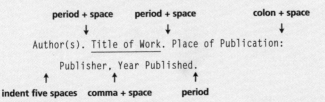

- **Author(s).** Give the author's last name first, followed by the first name (spelled out unless the author uses initials), any middle name or initial, and a period. Do not include titles like *M.D.* or *SJ*, but include other parts of a name, like *III* or *Jr.*, placing them at the end of the name preceded by a comma: *Valantasio, Louis, Jr.* (See Entries 2 and 3 for sources with more than one author.)

- **Title of work.** Give the title of the work, including any subtitle. (Use a colon to introduce a subtitle unless the primary title ends with a question mark, dash, or exclamation point.) Capitalize the main words, and end with a period unless the title ends with some other mark of punctuation. Underline the title, but not the period.

- **Publication information.** After the title, provide the city where the work was published, followed by a colon and a single space. If not obvious, add the country (abbreviated, as in *Dover, Eng.*). If more than one place of publication appears in the work, use the first one in your citation. Then give the publisher's name (followed by a comma) and the date of publication (followed by a period). You may omit unnecessary words such as *Publisher, Inc.*, and *Co.* (For example, use just *McGraw*, not *McGraw-Hill, Inc.*) Substitute the letters *U* and *P* for the words *University* and *Press* where they appear in the publisher's name (for example, *U of Chicago P*). If any of the basic publication information is missing, use *n.p.* ("no place" or "no publisher") or *n.d.* ("no date").

- **Spacing.** Double-space all entries, and indent five spaces for the second and any additional lines in each entry. Leave spaces between each of the major elements in an entry (author's name, title of work, and publication information).

1. One author

Twitchell, James B. ADCULTusa: The Triumph of Advertising in

American Culture. New York: Columbia UP, 1996.

2. Two or three authors

Give the first author's name, starting with the last name, followed by the other names in regular order. Use commas to separate the names, and introduce the second of two names or the third name with *and*.

Kress, Gunther, and Theo van Leeuwen. Reading Images: The

Grammar of Graphic Design. London: Routledge, 1996.

3. Four or more authors

Use the first author's name and then the phrase *et al.* (meaning "and others"). You may choose to give all the names, but if you do, you must list them in any parenthetical citations (see p. 623).

Bellah, Robert N., et al. <u>Habits of the Heart: Individualism</u>

<u>and Commitment in American Life</u>. Berkeley: U of California

P, 1985.

All authors listed: Bellah, Robert N., Richard Madsen, William M. Sullivan, Ann Swidler, and Steven M. Tipton

4. Corporate or group author

Treat the corporation, organization, or government agency as the author, alphabetizing by the first main word of the organization's name. If the organization is also the publisher, repeat its name again, abbreviated if appropriate.

United Nations Educational, Scientific, and Cultural

Organization. <u>A Short Internet Guide</u>. New York: UNESCO,

2001.

5. No author given

List the work alphabetically according to the first main word of its title.

<u>Guide for Authors</u>. Oxford: Blackwell, 1985.

6. More than one book by the same author

List multiple works by an author alphabetically by the first main word of the title. For the first entry, include the full name(s) of the author(s). For additional entries, use three hyphens in place of the name, followed by a period and a space, but only if the author or authors are *exactly* the same for each work. If the authorship differs in any way, include the name(s) in full.

Tannen, Deborah. <u>The Argument Culture: Moving from Debate to</u>

<u>Dialogue</u>. New York: Random, 1998.

---. <u>That's Not What I Meant! How Conversational Style Makes or</u>

<u>Breaks Your Relations with Others</u>. New York: Morrow, 1986.

7. One or more editors

Begin with the editor's name followed by a comma and the abbreviation *ed.* or *eds.*

Achebe, Chinua, and C. L. Innes, eds. <u>African Short Stories</u>.

London: Heinemann, 1985.

8. Author and an editor

Begin with either the author's or the editor's name depending on whether you are using the text itself or the editor's contributions.

> Weber, Max. <u>The Theory of Social and Economic Organization</u>. Ed.
>
>   Talcott Parsons. Trans. A. M. Henderson and Talcott
>
>   Parsons. New York: Free, 1964.

9. Translator

Refer to the book by its author, not its translator, even though the English words are the translator's. Abbreviate the translator's title as *Trans.*

> Baudrillard, Jean. <u>Cool Memories II: 1978-1990</u>. Trans. Chris
>
>   Turner. Durham: Duke UP, 1996.

10. Edition other than the first

Give the edition number (*3rd ed.*) or description (*Rev. ed.* or *1998 ed.*, for example) after the title.

> Coe, Michael D. <u>The Maya</u>. 6th ed. New York: Thames, 1999.

11. Reprinted book

Supply the original publication date after the title. If pertinent, include the original publisher or place of publication. Then follow with the publication information from the work you are using.

> Ondaatje, Michael. <u>The Collected Works of Billy the Kid</u>. 1970.
>
>   Harmondsworth, Eng.: Penguin, 1984.

12. One or more volumes of a multivolume work

Indicate the total number of volumes after the title (or after the editor's or translator's name).

> Tsao, Hsueh-chin. <u>The Story of the Stone</u>. Trans. David Hawkes.
>
>   5 vols. Harmondsworth, Eng.: Penguin, 1983-86.

If you are citing a particular volume instead of the whole work or several volumes from the whole work, supply only the particular volume number and publication information. Indicate the total number of volumes at the end of the entry.

> Tsao, Hsueh-chin. <u>The Story of the Stone</u>. Trans. David Hawkes.
>
>   Vol. 1. Harmondsworth, Eng.: Penguin, 1983. 5 vols.

13. Book in a series

Give the series name and any item number after the title of the work. Use abbreviations for familiar words in the name of the series (such as *ser.* for *series*).

> Hess, Gary R. <u>Vietnam and the United States: Origins and Legacy</u>
>
> <u>of War</u>. Int. Hist. Ser. 7. Boston: Twayne, 1990.

14. Book published before 1900

For books published before 1900, include the publisher's name only if it is relevant to your research. Use a comma rather than a colon after place of publication.

> Darwin, Charles. <u>Descent of Man and Selection in Relation to</u>
>
> <u>Sex</u>. New York, 1896.

15. Book with a publisher's imprint

For a book issued with a special imprint name, give the imprint name first, followed by a hyphen and the main publisher's name.

> Sikes, Gini. <u>8 Ball Chicks: A Year in the Violent World of Girl</u>
>
> <u>Gangs</u>. New York: Anchor-Doubleday, 1997.

16. Anthology or collection of articles

To refer to an anthology or a collection of scholarly articles as a whole, supply the editor's name first, followed by *ed.*, and then the title of the collection.

> Sharma, Arvind, ed. <u>Our Religions</u>. New York: HarperCollins,
>
> 1993.

To cite a selection within an anthology or collection, see Entries 33 and 34 on pages 638–639.

17. Government document

Begin with the government or agency name(s) or the author, if any. Start with *United States* for a congressional document or a report from a federal agency; otherwise, begin with the name of the government and agency or the name of the independent agency. For congressional documents, write *Cong.* (for *Congress*), identify the branch (*Senate* or *House*), and give the number and session (for example, *101st Cong., 1st sess.*). Include the title of the specific document and the title of the book in which it is printed. Use *GPO* for *Government Printing Office*.

```
United States. Office of Juvenile Justice and Delinquency
     Prevention. Promising Strategies to Reduce Gun Violence.
     By David I. Sheppard and Shay Bilchik. Washington: GPO,
     1999.
United States. Cong. Senate. Committee on Commerce, Science,
     and Transportation. Internet Filtering Systems. 105th
     Cong., 2d sess. Washington: GPO, 1998.
```

18. Title within a title

When a book title contains another work's title, do not underline the title of the second work. If the second title would normally be enclosed in quotation marks, add them and underline the entire title.

```
MacPherson, Pat. Reflecting on Jane Eyre. London: Routledge,
     1989.
Golden, Catherine, ed. The Captive Imagination: A Casebook on
     "The Yellow Wallpaper." New York: Feminist, 1992.
```

19. Pamphlet

Use the same form for a pamphlet as for a book.

```
Vareika, William. John La Farge: An American Master
     (1835-1910). Newport: Gallery of American Art, 1989.
```

20. Published dissertation

Treat a published doctoral dissertation as a book. Include the abbreviation *Diss.*, the school for which the dissertation was written, and the year the degree was awarded.

```
Said, Edward W. Joseph Conrad and the Fiction of Autobiography.
     Diss. Harvard U, 1964. Cambridge: Harvard UP, 1966.
```

21. Unpublished dissertation

Use quotation marks for the title; include the abbreviation *Diss.*, the school for which the dissertation was written, and the date of the degree.

```
Anku, William Oscar. "Procedures in African Drumming: A Study
     of Akan/Ewe Traditions and African Drumming in
     Pittsburgh." Diss. U of Pittsburgh, 1988.
```

22. Conference proceedings

Begin with the title unless an editor is named. Follow with details about the conference, including name and date.

> Childhood Obesity: Causes and Prevention. Symposium Proc., 27
>
> Oct. 1998. Washington: Center for Nutrition Policy and
>
> Promotion, 1999.

2 Articles and selections from books

MODEL FORMAT FOR ARTICLES AND SELECTIONS

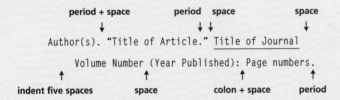

- **Author(s).** Give the author's last name first, followed by the first name, any initial, and a period. If the piece has more than one author, give subsequent names in regular order separated by commas with *and* preceding the final name.
- **Title of article.** Give the article's full title in quotation marks, concluding with a period unless the title ends with a question mark or an exclamation point.
- **Title of journal, periodical, or book.** Give the publication's title, underlined, but not including an opening *The*, *A*, or *An*. Do not end the title with a period.
- **Publication information.** Supply the volume number (and sometimes the issue number), the year of publication (in parentheses), and the page numbers for the full article or selection. The volume number is always found on the publication's cover or title page; even if it is in Roman numerals, use Arabic numerals for your entry. For a scholarly journal, you don't need to include the month or season (e.g., Winter). Introduce the page numbers with a colon.
- **Spacing.** Double-space all entries, and indent five spaces for the second and any additional lines in each entry. Leave a space between each of the major elements in an entry (author's name, article or selection title, and journal title along with publication information). Leave a space between the colon and the page number and also after the journal title and the volume number.

23. Article in journal paginated by volume

Each volume consists of several issues, paginated continuously; that is, each issue begins where the preceding left off—at page 354, for example. Give the volume number after the journal's title.

> Rockwood, Bruce L. "Law, Literature, and Science Fiction: New
>
>   Possibilities." Legal Studies Forum 23 (1999): 281-89.

24. Article in journal paginated by issue

The issues making up a volume are paginated separately. Give the volume number first, followed by a period and the issue number.

> Adams, Jessica. "Local Color: The Southern Plantation in
>
>   Popular Culture." Cultural Critique 42.1 (1999): 171-87.

25. Article in weekly magazine

Put the day first, then the month (abbreviated except for May, June, and July), and then the year followed by a colon. Give inclusive page numbers. If the pages are not consecutive, give the first page with a plus sign (for example, *23+*). (Treat biweekly magazines in a similar fashion.)

> Wright, Robert. "The Power of Their Peers." Time 24 Aug. 1998:
>
>   67.

26. Article in monthly magazine

Treat a monthly or bimonthly magazine as a weekly magazine (Entry 25), but without listing the day.

> Jacobson, Doranne. "Doing Lunch." Natural History Mar. 2000:
>
>   171-87.

27. Unsigned article in magazine

Begin with the title (ignoring *A*, *An*, and *The* when alphabetizing).

> "Horseplay." New Yorker 5 Apr. 1993: 36-38.

28. Article in newspaper

Treat a newspaper as a weekly magazine, including citation of pages (see Entry 25), but include the section number or letter with the page number. Omit *A*, *An*, or *The* at the beginning of a newspaper's name. For a local newspaper, give the city's name in brackets after the title unless the city is named in the title.

Willis, Ellen. "Steal This Myth: Why We Still Try to Recreate

the Rush of the 60s." New York Times 20 Aug. 2000: AR1+.

29. Editorial or letter to the editor

Supply the title first for an unsigned editorial and the author's name first for a signed editorial. Identify with the word *editorial*.

"A False Choice." Editorial. Charlotte Observer 16 Aug. 1998:

2C.

Use the word *letter* to identify a letter to the editor.

Varley, Colin. Letter. Archaeology May-June 1993: 10.

30. Interview—published

Treat the person interviewed, not the interviewer, as the author. For untitled interviews, include the word *Interview* (without underlining or quotation marks) in place of a title.

Stewart, Martha. "I Do Have a Brain." Interview with Kevin

Kelly. Wired Aug. 1998: 114.

31. Review

Give the title after the name of the reviewer. Cite an unsigned review by its title.

Munoz, Jose Esteban. "Citizens and Superheroes." Rev. of The

Queen of America Goes to Washington City, by Lauren

Berlant. American Quarterly 52 (2000): 397-404.

For a review with no title, give the name of the reviewer followed by *Rev. of* ("Review of"), the work's title, a comma, the word *by*, and the author of the work.

Asante, Molefi Kete. Rev. of Race and the Writing of History:

Riddling the Sphinx, by Maghan Keita. Journal of Black

Studies 31 (2001): 699-701.

32. Article from encyclopedia or reference volume

Begin with the author's name or with the article's title if no author is named. You need not include the publisher or place of publication for a common reference work or series; instead, note the edition and the date. If entries are arranged alphabetically, you need not note the volume or page(s).

Oliver, Paul, and Barry Kernfeld. "Blues." The New Grove
    Dictionary of Jazz. Ed Barry Kernfeld. New York: St.
    Martin's, 1994.

"The History of Western Theatre." The New Encyclopaedia
    Britannica: Macropedia. 15th ed. 1987. Vol. 28.

33. Selection in anthology or chapter in edited book

List the author of the selection or chapter and give the title in quotation marks (but underline titles of novels, plays, and other works first published on their own). Next, provide the underlined title of the book containing the selection or chapter. If the collection has an editor, follow with the abbreviation *Ed.* and the name(s) of the editor(s) in regular order. Conclude with publication information and the selection's inclusive page numbers.

Atwood, Margaret. "Bluebeard's Egg." "Bluebeard's Egg" and
    Other Stories. New York: Fawcett-Random, 1987. 131-64.

If you are citing the original source for a selection reprinted in a collection, use the phrase *Rpt. in* ("Reprinted in") followed by information about the original source.

Atwood, Margaret. "Bluebeard's Egg." "Bluebeard's Egg" and
    Other Stories. New York: Fawcett-Random, 1987. 131-64.
    Rpt. in Don't Bet on the Prince: Contemporary Feminist
    Fairy Tales in North America and England. Ed. Jack Zipes.
    New York: Methuen, 1986. 160-82.

34. More than one selection from anthology or collection (cross-reference)

When you cite two or more works from an anthology or collection, include an entry for the collection and provide cross-references for individual selections.

Howard, Jean E., and Marion F. O'Connor, eds. Shakespeare
    Reproduced: The Text in History and Ideology. New York:
    Methuen, 1987.
Entry for collection.

Erickson, Peter. "The Order of the Garter, the Cult of
    Elizabeth, and Class-Gender Tension in The Merry Wives of
    Windsor." Howard and O'Connor 116-42.
Individual selection.

```
Goldberg, Jonathan. "Speculation: Macbeth and Source." Howard
    and O'Connor 242-64.
```
Individual selection.

35. Preface, foreword, introduction, or afterword

Indicate whether the selection is a preface, foreword, introduction, or afterword. Give the title of the work and the name of its author, preceded by the word *By*.

```
Tomlin, Janice. Foreword. The Complete Guide to Foreign
    Adoption. By Barbara Brooke Bascom and Carole A. McKelvey.
    New York: Pocket, 1997.
```

36. Letter—published

Treat the letter writer as the author. Indicate the date or the collection number of the letter if the information is available.

```
Garland, Hamlin. "To Fred Lewis Pattee." 30 Dec. 1914. Letter
    206 of Selected Letters of Hamlin Garland. Ed. Keith
    Newlin and Joseph B. McCullough. Lincoln: U of Nebraska P,
    1998.
```

37. Dissertation abstract

For an abstract of a dissertation published in *Dissertation Abstracts International* (*DAI*) or *Dissertation Abstracts* (*DA*), follow the author's name and the title with the abbreviation *Diss.* (for "Dissertation"), the institution's name, and the date of the degree. Conclude with publication information for the particular volume of abstracts.

```
Hawkins, Joanne Berning. "Horror Cinema and the Avant-Garde."
    Diss. U of California, Berkeley, 1993. DAI 55 (1995):
    1712A.
```

3 Field resources and other printed resources

Use the following formats for sources other than books or articles.

38. Interview—unpublished

Give the name of the person interviewed. Then indicate the type of interview: *Personal interview* (you did the interview in person), *Telephone interview* (you talked to the person over the telephone), or *Interview* (someone else conducted the interview, perhaps on a radio or television program). If a recorded or broadcast interview has a title, give it in place of the word *Interview*. Give the date of the interview or appropriate citation information for a broadcast or address (URL) for electronic source.

```
Coppola, Francis Ford. Interview with James Lipton. Inside the

    Actors Studio. Bravo. 10 July 2001.

Schutt, Robin. Personal interview. 7 Oct. 2002.
```

39. Survey or questionnaire

MLA does not specify a form for these field resources. When citing your own field research, you may wish to use the following format.

```
Arrigo-Nelson, Summer, and Jennifer Emily Figliozzi.

    Questionnaire on Student Alcohol Use and Parental

    Values. University of Rhode Island, Kingston. 15-20

    Apr. 1998.
```

40. Observations

MLA does not specify a form for this type of field research. You may wish to use the following form to cite your notes on field observations.

```
Williams, Keyshawn. Observations of ATM Patrons. Aurora, CO. 11

    Mar. 1998.
```

41. Letter or memo—unpublished

Give the author's name, a brief description (for example, *Letter to Jane Cote*), and the date of the document. For letters addressed to you, use the phrase *Letter to the author*; for letters between other people, give the name and location of any library holding the letter in its collection.

```
Hall, Donald. Letter to the author. 24 Jan. 1990.
```

42. Performance

Following the title of the play, opera, dance, or other performance, supply the name of the composer, director, writer, theater or place of presentation, and city where the performance took place as well as the date (include actors when relevant).

```
The Producers. By Mel Brooks and Thomas Meehan. Dir. Susan

    Stroman. St. James Theatre, New York. 8 July 2001.
```

43. Oral presentation

Identify speaker, title or type of presentation, and details of the meeting, sponsoring group, location, date; include electronic address, if any.

```
Dunkelman, Martha. "Images of Salome in Italian Renaissance
    Art." The Renaissance Woman, II. Sixteenth Century Studies
    Conf., Adams Mark Hotel, St. Louis. 11 Dec. 1993.
```

44. Map or chart

If the source is electronic, conclude with its address (URL).

```
Arkansas. Map. Comfort: Gousha, 1996.
```

45. Cartoon

Provide the cartoonist's name and the title, if any. Include the word *Cartoon* and publication information (or electronic address).

```
Guisewite, Cathy. "Cathy." Cartoon. Providence Sunday Journal
    23 July 1995: F3.
```

46. Advertisement

Begin with the name of the subject of the advertisement (product, company, or organization). Include the electronic address (URL), if any.

```
Toyota. Advertisement. GQ July 2001: 8.
```

4 Media resources

47. Film or videotape

Alphabetize according to the title of the work. The director's name is almost always necessary; names of actors, producers, writers, musicians, or others are needed only if they are important to identification or to your discussion. Include the distributor, the date, and other relevant information including the URL for electronic sources.

```
Rosencrantz and Guildenstern Are Dead. Dir. Tom Stoppard. Perf.
    Gary Oldman, Tim Roth, and Richard Dreyfuss. Cinecom
    Entertainment, 1990.
```

For a videotape, filmstrip, or similar resource, indicate the medium—*videocassette, videodisc,* and so forth. If the date of the original version is important, add this just before the description of the medium.

<u>Rosencrantz and Guildenstern Are Dead</u>. Dir. Tom Stoppard. Perf.

    Gary Oldman, Tim Roth, and Richard Dreyfuss.

    Videocassette. Buena Vista Home Video, 1990.

48. Television or radio program

Begin with the episode title, and use it to alphabetize the entry. Give the program's name and, if they are pertinent to the discussion, include names for writer, director, actors, or others. Use abbreviations for their roles, for example, *Writ.*, *Dir.*, *Prod.*, *Perf.*, *Cond.*, *Introd.*, or *Narr.* Conclude with the URL for an electronic source, if appropriate.

"Love Comes to the Butcher." <u>All in the Family</u>. Dir. Paul

    Bogart. CBS. 15 Jan. 1978.

49. Recording

Begin the entry with the title of the recording or with the name of the person whose role in the recording you wish to emphasize, for example, the performer, the composer, the conductor, or the speaker. Underline the title of the compact disc, tape, or record. Put the name of a specific work in quotation marks unless the piece is identified by key, form, or number, such as *Symphony in A minor, no. 41*. Continue with performers or others involved, the manufacturer, and the year when the recording was issued. Indicate the medium if it is anything other than a compact disc (for example, *audio-cassette*, or *LP* for a record).

The Goo-Goo Dolls. <u>Dizzy Up the Girl</u>. Warner, 1998.

Mozart, Wolfgang Amadeus. Symphony no. 40 in G minor. Vienna

    Philharmonic. Cond. Leonard Bernstein. Audiocassette.

    Deutsche Grammophon, 1984.

50. Artwork

Give the name of the artist, the title of the work, and the location of the work. Because many museum and gallery names are similar, indicate the city.

Uccello, Paolo. <u>Saint George and the Dragon</u>. National Gallery,

    London.

5 Internet, Web, and electronic resources

The following models demonstrate the guidelines for citing electronic sources according to the 1999 *MLA Handbook for Writers of Research Papers*. The MLA recommends the following general conventions.

- **Publication dates.** For sources taken from the Internet, include the date the source was posted or last updated or revised; give also the date the source was accessed.
- **Uniform resource locator.** Include a full and accurate **URL** for any source taken from the Internet (with access-mode identifier—*http*, *ftp*, *gopher*, or *telnet*). Enclose the URL in angle brackets < >. When a URL continues from one line to the next, break it only after a slash. Do not add a hyphen.
- **Page numbering.** Include page or paragraph numbers when given by the source.

51. Professional Web site

History of the American West, 1860-1920. 25 July 2000. Denver

    Public Library. 16 Oct. 2001 <http://memory.loc.gov/

    ammem/award97/codhtml>.

52. Individual Web site

Give the name of the person who created the site, a title or description such as *home page,* and any sponsor.

Baron, Dennis. Home page. 20 Apr. 1999. Dept. of English,

    U of Illinois, Urbana-Champaign. 13 June 1999

    <http://www.english.uiuc.edu/baron/index.htm>.

53. Online book

Include the author's name and the title; the name(s) of any editor, compiler, or translator (if relevant); electronic publication information (sponsoring organization and date of publication if the online text has not been published before); information about print publication (if any); date of access; the scholarly project containing the work (if any) and date posted (see following example); and URL.

London, Jack. The Iron Heel. New York: Macmillan, 1908.

    The Jack London Collection. 10 Dec. 1999.

    Berkeley Digital Library SunSITE. 15 July 2001

    <http://sunsite.berkeley.edu/London/Writing/IronHeel/>.

54. Selection from online book

Muir, John. "The City of the Saints." Steep Trails. 1918. 17

    July 2001 <http://encyclopediaindex.com/b/sttrl10.htm>.

55. Online journal article

Give the author; the title of the article (if any); the name of the periodical; details about the volume, issue, and item number; and date of publication (in parentheses). If the number of pages or paragraphs is available, place a colon after the parentheses containing the date and give the number. Finally, give your access date and add the electronic address in angle brackets.

```
Dugdale, Timothy. "The FAN and (Auto)Biography: Writing the

    Self in the Stars." Journal of Mundane Behavior 1.2

    (2000). 19 Sept. 2000 <http://www.mundanebehavior.org/

    issues/v1n2dugdale.htm>.
```

56. Online magazine article

Supply the same information required for an online journal article.

```
Anderson, Christopher. "In Search of the Perfect Market."

    The Economist 14 Sept. 1997. 5 Jan. 1998

    <http://www.economist.com/editorial/freeforall/

    14-9-97/ec1.html>.
```

57. Online newspaper article

When citing an editorial, a review, or a letter to the editor, indicate it as you would a similar print source. See Entries 29 and 31 for examples. Otherwise supply the author's name, the title of the article, the name of the online version of the newspaper followed by the date of publication, and the date of access and electronic address.

```
Colker, David. "Seven Days of Spam." Los Angeles Times 3

    May 2001. 15 July 2001 <http://www.latimes.com/tech.../

    la0000371/17/1Jun30.story?coll=la%2Dfeaturees%2Dtechnolog>.
```

58. Online government document

```
United States. Dept. of Commerce. Bureau of the Census. Census

    Brief: Disabilities Affect One-Fifth of All Americans.

    Dec. 1997. 18 July 2001 <http://www.census.gov/prod/

    3/97pubs/cenbr975.pdf>.
```

59. Online editorial

Ely, Jane. "For the Young, Get Houston the Games."

    Editorial. Houston Chronicle 17 July 2001. 17 July 2001

    <http://www.chron.com/cs/CDA/story.hts/editorial/970112>.

60. Online letter to the editor

Hadjiargyrou, Michael. "Stem Cells and Delicate Questions."

    Letter. New York Times 17 July 2001. 18 July 2001

    <http://www.nytimes.com/2001/07/18/opinion/

    L18STEM.html>.

61. Online interview

Payan, Victor. Interview with David Riker. San Diego

    Latino Film Festival. 1999. 17 July 2001

    <http://www.sdlatinofilm.com/video.html#Anchor=David=64709>.

62. Online review

Harvey, De. Rev. of Bossa Nova, dir. Bruno Barretto. Film

    Monthly 1.10 (2000). 28 Aug. 2000 <http://

    freehosting2.at.webjump.com/84f640...Playing/

    Articles/BossaNova/BossaNova.htm>.

63. Online database, information service, or scholarly project

Begin with the title of the project or database and the name of its editor. (When citing specific material from the project, begin with the author and the title in quotation marks.) Follow with the name of the project or database. Include information such as version number, date of electronic publication or update, and name of any sponsoring institution. Conclude with date of access and electronic address.

"Imaging Radar." Ed. Robert Mah. Fact Sheets. Aug 1996.

    NASA Jet Propulsion Laboratory. 3 Jan. 1999

    <http://www.jpl.nasa.gov/facts/>.

64. Online source from computer service

If you use a source from a service (such as Dialog, Nexis, or Lexis) and the source has been published in print as well as online, cite the source according to the appropriate model (that is, journal, newspaper, or abstract). Add information on the online version, including the name of the database (underlined), the word *Online*, the name of the computer service, and the date of access. Give the electronic address (URL) or the keyword or topic labels (path) you use to reach it. If you used a service to which a library subscribes (such as EBSCOhost), give the name of the database (underlined), the name of the service, the library, and the date you accessed the source. If you know the electronic address (URL), give it at the end.

> Margolis, Robin. "Happy, Healthy, and Interfaith." Beliefnet.
>
> Online. America Online. 16 July 2001. Keyword:
>
> Spirituality.

65. Online abstract

> Prelow, Hazel, and Charles A. Guarnaccia. "Ethnic and Racial
>
> Differences in Life Stress Among High School Adolescents."
>
> Journal of Counseling & Development 75.6 (1977). Abstract.
>
> 6 Apr. 1998 <http://www.counseling.org/journals/
>
> jcdjul197.htm#Prelow>.

66. Online videotape or film

> Coppola, Francis Ford, dir. Apocalypse Now. 1979.
>
> Film.com. 17 July 2001 <http://ramhurl.filmcom/
>
> smildemohurl.ram?file=screen/2001/clips/
>
> apoca.smi>.

67. Online television or radio program

> Edwards, Bob. "Adoption: Redefining Family." Morning Edition.
>
> Natl. Public Radio. 28-29 June 2001, 17 July 2001
>
> <http://www.npr.org/programs/morning/features/2001/
>
> jun/010628.cfoa.html>.

68. Online recording

> Malcolm X. "The Definition of Black Power." 8 Mar. 1964.
>
>> Great Speeches. 2000. 18 July 2001 <http://
>>
>> www.chicago-law.net/speeches/speech.html#lm>.

69. Online artwork

> Elamite Goddess. 2100 B.C. (?). Louvre, Paris. 16 July 2001
>
>> <http://www.louvre.fr/louvrea.htm>.

70. Online map or chart

> Beirut [Beyrout] 1912. Map. Perry-Castaneda Library Map
>
>> Collection. 16 July 2000. <http://www.lib.utexas.edu/
>>
>> maps/historical/beirut2_1912.jpg>.

71. Online cartoon

> Auth, Tony. "Spending Goals." Cartoon. Slate 7 Sept. 2001. 16
>
>> Oct. 2001 <http://cagle.slate.msn.com/politicalcartoons/
>>
>> pccartoons/archives/auth.asp>.

72. Online advertisement

> Mazda Miata. Advertisement. 16 July 2001 <http://
>
>> www.mazdausa.com/miata/>.

73. Other online sources

When citing electronic sources other than those explained above (such as a photo, work of art, film, or interview), adapt MLA models for their nonelectronic equivalents. Include the date of access and electronic address.

> NASA/JPL. "Martian Meteorite." Photo. Views of the Solar
>
>> System: Meteoroids and Meteorites. Ed. Calvin J. Hamilton.
>>
>> <http://spaceart.com/solar/eng/meteor.htm#views>.

74. FTP, Telnet, or Gopher site

For sources obtained through FTP (file transfer protocol), telnet, or go-pher, supply information as you would for a similar source obtained via the World Wide Web, with the appropriate electronic address in angle brackets at the end.

```
Clinton, William Jefferson. "Radio Address of the

    President to the Nation." 10 May 1997. 29 June 1999

    <ftp://OMA.EOP.GOV.US/1997/5/10/1.TEXT.1>.
```

75. Email

Begin with the writer's name and the title of the communication (in quotation marks), a description of the message including recipient, and the date.

```
Smithee, Alan. "The Director Confesses." E-mail to the author.

    17 Sept. 1995.
```
Note that *e-mail* is spelled with a hyphen in MLA citations.

76. Online posting

Give the name of the author, the title of the posting as in the subject line, and follow it with the label *Online posting.* Next give the date of posting and name of forum. Conclude with date of access and electronic address. For a forwarded posting, give the writer, title, and date of the document, then the phrase *Fwd. by* and the name of the person forwarding it, followed by the phrase *Online posting*, the date of the posting, name of the forum, and electronic address.

```
Palmer, Megan. "Global Warming." Online Posting. 15 May 2001.

    Environmental Science Bulletin Board. 18 July 2001.

    <http://www.escribe.com/science/es/bb/index.html?bID=29>.
```

Many discussion groups maintain archives. For your readers' convenience, cite archived versions whenever possible.

```
Sawyer, Nede. "Electric Cars." Online Posting. 1 Mar. 1999.

    ENVIRON. 18 July 2001. <http://gimli.worc.mass.edu/

    scripts/wa.exe?A2=ind9903&L=environ&F=&S=&P=507>.
```

When citing a Usenet newsgroup, give the information on the author, title, the phrase *Online posting*, and date of posting. Give the date of access. Next, in angle brackets, give the name of the newsgroup, with the prefix *news*.

```
Jarvilehto, Timo. "How Far Can Unity of the Organism-
    Environment System Be Maintained?" Online posting. 18 Dec.
    1998. 19 Dec. 1998 <news:sci.journals.psycoloquy>.
```

Again, citing an archived posting from a newsgroup is preferable. In that case, give the name of the group after the date of posting and follow the access date with the electronic address.

```
Jarvilehto, Timo. "How Far Can Unity of the Organism-
    Environment System Be Maintained?" Online posting. 18 Dec.
    1998. PSYCOLOQUY. 18 Dec. 1998 <http://x2.dejanews.com/
    =liszt/getdoc.xp?AN=424430517.1&CONTEXT=915464904.
    1241448542&hitnum=0>.
```

77. Synchronous communication

When citing material from a MUD, MOO, or other form of synchronous communication, begin with the speaker's name if you are citing only one. Give a description of the event, its date, its forum (e.g., *CollegeTownMOO*), and the date of access. End with the prefix *telnet://* and the electronic address in angle brackets.

```
Finch, Jeremy. Online debate "Can Proust Save Your Life?"
    3 Apr. 1998. CollegeTownMOO. 3 Apr. 1998 <telnet://
    next.cs.bvc.edu.7777>.
```

For your readers' convenience, cite an archived version of material from a synchronous communication forum when possible. Provide the same information as above, but substitute the electronic address of the archived version for the electronic address of the forum at the end.

78. CD-ROM, diskette, or magnetic tape

Databases containing information or texts come in portable forms (such as CD-ROM) or online. Begin entries with author and title, provide publication information about the printed source (if any); give the title of the database or service (underlined), the medium (e.g., *CD-ROM, Online*), the name of the vendor or computer service, and the publication date (for CD-ROM) or date of access (for online sources).

```
Shakespeare, William. All's Well That Ends Well. William
    Shakespeare: The Complete Works on CD-ROM. CD-ROM.
    Abingdon, Eng.: Andromeda Interactive, 1994.
```

79. CD-ROM abstract

For abstracts, include information about an article being summarized, the electronic version, and any printed version of the abstract.

> Straus, Stephen. "Separating Remedies from Snake Oil." New York
>
>   Times 3 Apr. 2001: D5+. Abstract. Infotrac. CD-ROM. 19
>
>   July 2000.

51.2

Exercise

A. Rewrite the following sentences to add MLA-style in-text citations.

1. After the fact, however, Johanson and Edey admitted, "Neither of us was prepared for the explosion of interest that followed the formal disclosure of *afarensis* in print."

    The quotation is from page 294 of Donald Johanson and Maitland Edey's book *Lucy: The Beginnings of Humankind* (New York: Simon & Schuster, 1990).

2. In Samoa during the 1930s, girls separated socially from their siblings at about age seven and began to form close and lasting relationships with other girls their age.

    The reference is to Margaret Mead's discussion in *Coming of Age in Samoa*, originally issued in 1928 and reprinted in 1961 by Morrow Publishers in their Morrow Quill paperback series. It cites the general discussion in Chapter 5, "The Girl and Her Age Group," on pages 59 through 73 of the 1961 edition.

B. Create a list of works cited using MLA style, and include the following items.

1. An article reviewing books on Latin American families. The author is Elizabeth Anne Kuzenesof. Her review is titled "The History of the Family in Latin America." It appeared in the Spring 1989 issue of *Latin American Research Review* on pages 168–189 (paginated by issue). This issue of the journal was number 2 in volume 24.

2. An interview of Donald Davis published in the October 1992 edition (volume 67) of the *Wilson Library Bulletin*. The interviewer was Judith O'Malley, and the interview appeared on pages 52 and 53. The periodical appears monthly.

3. A book of 280 pages by Vera Rosenbluth titled *Keeping Family Stories Alive*. The subtitle is *A Creative Guide to Taping Your Family Life and Lore*. It was published in 1990 by Hartley and Marks, a publisher in Point Roberts, Washington.

4. A collection of the stories of Shalom Aleichem titled *Around the Table: Family Stories of Shalom Aleichem*. The collection was edited

by Aliza Shevron and translated by her. The book was illustrated by Toby Gowing. Scribner Publishers in New York issued the book in 1991. It contains 364 pages.

5. A scholarly article by Beverly Whitaker Long and Charles H. Grant III in volume 41 of the journal *Communication Education*. Volume 41 is dated 1992, and the article runs from page 89 to page 108. The title of the article is "The 'Surprising Range of the Possible': Families Communicating in Fiction."

51e
MLA

51e Sample MLA paper

The following paper was written by a student using the MLA documentation style. The *MLA Handbook* recommends beginning a research paper with the first page of the text, using the format shown on Shane Hand's first page. Because his teacher required a title page and an outline as well, he prepared both of these, too. In the margins of the paper is a running commentary on the elements of the paper, from considerations of audience and purpose to organizational strategy, style, and format.

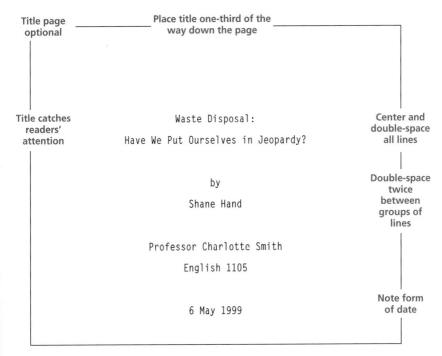

Title page optional ———————— **Place title one-third of the way down the page**

Title catches readers' attention

Waste Disposal:

Have We Put Ourselves in Jeopardy?

Center and double-space all lines

by

Shane Hand

Double-space twice between groups of lines

Professor Charlotte Smith

English 1105

6 May 1999

Note form of date

51e
MLA

Center
heading
|

Outline

Double-space
below heading
|

Thesis statement: Using landfills as a way to dispose

of solid and hazardous wastes is no longer a valid

Keep thesis
statement
short—one
or two
sentences

option because we now know of the potential long-term

dangers to our soil and groundwater that landfills

represent. We must both find new technologies that

safely dispose of waste and reduce our own consumption.

Outline
optional:
check with
instructor

I. Mainly two types of waste pollute our

environment: solid and hazardous (toxic).

A. Most solid waste consists of packaging

residues: aluminum cans, glass and plastic

bottles, paperboard cartons, and wooden

crates.

B. Most hazardous waste consists of chemical

toxins, by-products of manufacturing

processes, or ingredients in a wide range

of products.

Outline uses
sentences
(rather than
topics or
phrases); ask
instructor's
preference

II. Americans are finally becoming aware of the

problems with dumping wastes in landfills.

A. Space is the most obvious problem--people

do not want a landfill in their local area.

B. Pollution of soil and groundwater is a more

threatening problem.

III. The key to solving the waste disposal problem

is public commitment.

A. People should take political action.

Hand ii

1. They should urge politicians to pass recycling regulations.

2. They should force businesses to become environmentally responsible.

3. They should work to develop local and national recycling programs.

B. People should change their own consumer habits.

IV. A poll shows that most people already have changed their consumer habits.

V. Along with public commitment, new waste disposal technologies must also be developed.

A. Currently, landfills with clay and plastic linings reduce leakage into groundwater.

B. Currently, incineration reduces the amounts and toxicity of hazardous wastes.

C. New technology should not give anyone the excuse not to change consumption habits. Recycling is still the best approach to solving this problem.

Align all entries of same level

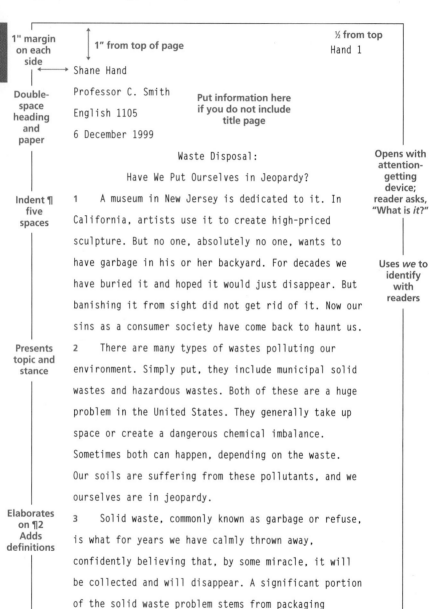

51e
MLA

1" margin on each side

1" from top of page

½ from top
Hand 1

Shane Hand

Double-space heading and paper

Professor C. Smith

English 1105

6 December 1999

Put information here if you do not include title page

Waste Disposal:

Have We Put Ourselves in Jeopardy?

Indent ¶ five spaces

1   A museum in New Jersey is dedicated to it. In California, artists use it to create high-priced sculpture. But no one, absolutely no one, wants to have garbage in his or her backyard. For decades we have buried it and hoped it would just disappear. But banishing it from sight did not get rid of it. Now our sins as a consumer society have come back to haunt us.

Presents topic and stance

2   There are many types of wastes polluting our environment. Simply put, they include municipal solid wastes and hazardous wastes. Both of these are a huge problem in the United States. They generally take up space or create a dangerous chemical imbalance. Sometimes both can happen, depending on the waste. Our soils are suffering from these pollutants, and we ourselves are in jeopardy.

Elaborates on ¶2 Adds definitions

3   Solid waste, commonly known as garbage or refuse, is what for years we have calmly thrown away, confidently believing that, by some miracle, it will be collected and will disappear. A significant portion of the solid waste problem stems from packaging residues, specifically containers. Aluminum cans, glass and plastic bottles, paperboard cartons, and

Opens with attention-getting device; reader asks, "What is *it*?"

Uses *we* to identify with readers

1" bottom margin

Hand 2

wooden crates are thrown away in massive numbers,
never to be used again. An average landfill today
consists of six main types of trash. Paper takes up
about 50 percent by volume; plastic covers are close
to 10 percent; metals take up 6 percent; glass holds
1 percent; organic materials cover about 13 percent;
and about 20 percent is miscellaneous substances
(Rathje 116). These numbers may seem meaningless, but
when we think about the nation's daily output of these
materials (500,000 tons), it becomes clear that the
landfills are filling very quickly, so fast that our
soils cannot degrade the waste fast enough to balance
the space with the input. In fact, some pollutants
never degrade.

Adds facts and statistics

Cites author and page

4   The average person assumes that hazardous
wastes account for a small percentage of today's
environmental problems. However, hazardous wastes
are generated by almost all sectors of the economy.
These wastes are a general consequence of the
industrialized society in which we live. They reflect
our need for packaging, appliances, cleaning supplies,
beauty aids, pharmaceuticals, and other manufactured
products. As with solid wastes, for many years toxic
wastes were considered safely gone as soon as they
were carted out of sight; as one report reminds us,
however, "As with other environmental concerns,
it is only within the past twenty to thirty years
that the possible adverse environmental quality and

Defines solid waste in larger context

51e
MLA

health problems have been recognized and addressed"

Uses title in citation; author unknown

(Hazardous Waste 3). In the past, hazardous waste

disposal was accomplished in the quickest and least

costly manner, frequently by open dumping and

uncontrolled burning. These practices have been found

to present a hazard to human health and the

environment. The magnitude of this problem can be best

presented by totaling the amount of hazardous wastes

Cites source second time; page number only

produced each year, which the Office of Technology

Assessment puts at about 250 million metric tons (5).

As our industrial society grows, finding ways to

eliminate these wastes while allowing the same or an

improved standard of living should be an overall goal.

Uses generalization to shift from definitions to argument

5   When the land was young, it was wide-open and

unspoiled. Yet as the population grew, the spoilage

grew. But the problem has now reached such magnitude

that Americans are finally becoming concerned about

what happens to their refuse. To some extent this

concern is due to some misconceptions about the

viability of continued landfilling of municipal solid

wastes. One misconception is that the United States is

running out of landfill space. This does not appear to

be the case, as argued by a recent study done on

landfills. According to the study, "at the current rate

Uses expert source to make key point

Uses brackets to set off added explanation

of landfilling, all the MSW [municipal solid waste]

generated by the country over the next thousand years

could easily be contained within a 30-by-30 mile area

Long quotation might have been paraphrased

using current landfill technology" (Wiseman 9).

However, this does not resolve the problem since this idea is impractical. The space problem is distinctly regional, and no one region will consent to be the site for such a landfill. And where landfill siting is most a problem--along the northeastern seaboard, for instance--it is more often due to political opposition than to a lack of available space. This opposition goes back to the "not in my backyard" syndrome.

6   Space is not the only problem these landfills have. There is a grave threat to the environment through the creation of leachate. Leachate is created when surface water contributes to the large amount of water already existing in solid waste. The water percolates through landfills, releasing toxic constituents and heavy metals into soil and groundwater. Leachate is not only dangerous but also expensive since it must be collected, conveyed, stored, treated, and disposed (Organic). It also has the potential to generate gases, including methane, that could have long-term environmentally destructive effects. A more immediate threat is that the gases could cause spontaneous explosions and fires. Even ordinary household items, once they are in landfills, can become hazardous wastes. A seemingly innocent bottle of nail polish puts more than six toxic chemicals into a landfill. All of these toxic constituents take hundreds and even thousands of years to disappear.

Moves from topic of space to topic of environmental damage

Makes information "real" to readers

51e
MLA

Presents one part of two-pronged proposal

7   The key to solving the waste problem once and for all is public commitment. The public should urge the politicians to pass recycling regulations and force businesses to become environmentally responsible.

Specifies public commitments

Public action must be taken to develop and institute recycling programs on the local and national level. Some may argue that recycling programs are expensive and thus not practical, but isn't our environment more important than a price tag? In other countries, such as Germany, recycling efforts have increased as much as 40 percent (Rathje 120). Funding for these programs comes from the government with the approval of the taxpayers (121). The public can also make a commitment even on a small scale. As seen in the above breakdown of a landfill's contents, at least 50 percent of a landfill's space is occupied by items that can be recycled. Reusing products and refusing to buy products that are not recyclable or do not contain recycled materials are two ways we as consumers can bring about change. All of these ideas will help control the space problem and relieve our soils. These kinds of efforts could be encouraged by local, state, and federal governments by increased tax incentives akin to tax reduction programs in place that spur the cleanup and redevelopment of brownfields (Pennsylvania).

8   With these ideas in mind, I turned to the public to find out whether any of these ideas were practiced or acceptable. I used a survey (Hand, see appendix)

Hand 6

which consisted of a series of questions to find out
people's habits and attitudes. My results are based
on a collection of roughly three hundred responses.
The participants in this survey were either from the
Virginia Tech area or from a subdivision in Upper
Marlboro, Maryland (my hometown). Their ages ranged
from about seventeen to fifty years old, which
provided a wide range for the average consumer. Upon
tabulating the responses, I obtained the following
results.

Places
complete
survey form
in appendix
so it does
not disrupt
argument

Already Do

Use coffee mugs instead of polystyrene cups	55%
Reuse plastic wrap, foil, and plastic bags	64%
Recycle newspapers and magazines	46%
Recycle glass	57%
Recycle plastic containers	38%
Recycle aluminum cans	65%

Results
could also
be in a table
or graph

Willing to Do

Take own bags to the store	66%
Shop at a store that's harder to get to but carries biodegradable products	59%
Recycle plastic containers	59%
Pay more for products in low-waste packaging	55%
Pay more for recycled paper	54%

9   It is important to remember that this survey
represents only a small region of the United States.
These results could be different in other parts of the
country. It is also possible that my respondents wanted

51e
MLA

to make themselves out to be more environmentally

Caution about results helps make presentation seem balanced

responsible citizens than they really are. Still, I was favorably surprised by my results. It seems that many people do take some steps to preserve the environment and are willing to take other steps once they are made aware of them. This demonstrates how important it is to educate the public about the environment.

Presents second part of proposal

10   Of course, along with public commitment, there must be technological improvement of waste disposal.

Space and toxicity problems in landfills can be

Specifies technology that could be developed further

overcome or minimized by state-of-the-art landfill technology. Landfills lined with clay interposed between multiple layers of plastic sheeting greatly reduce the risk of contaminating the groundwater, especially if they are equipped with a system that collects and treats the substances that filter to the bottom of the landfill. Such a system does not need continuous removal of the substance since "landfills have an inherent capacity to lessen the toxicity of the substances introduced or generated in them" (Wiseman 9). This reduction in toxicity can also be accelerated by maintaining landfills as "biochemical" systems. As for the gases created, they can be collected and even marketed as fuel.

Reconnects to first proposal

11   The preferred method for management of hazardous wastes is waste elimination. If wastes are not generated as the result of residential, commercial, and industrial actions, disposal is not necessary. If

**51e
MLA**

waste is not eliminated, then steps should be taken to reduce the amount generated. Due to extensive research efforts in the past few years, more is known about incineration technology than any of the other waste management alternatives. For one, incineration provides a high level of toxic control. The by-product--ash--takes up little space in a landfill. On the other hand, when the ash by-product of incineration is placed in a landfill, it returns some heavy metals and other harmful organic compounds to the soil (Montague). In addition to the possible threat to the soil, many suspect that incineration emissions may contribute to health problems such as Down syndrome, asthma, and other respiratory problems in humans as well as premature deaths and deformities in farm animals (Farley). Without a doubt, incineration should play an increasing role in hazardous waste management.

12   Still, though new advances in waste management technology are moving toward resolving this environmental problem, they do not give anybody the excuse not to recycle since recycling is far more beneficial to the environment than any technology. We, as individuals, neighborhoods, and communities, need to urge, by example and by political action, the federal government to act now. Together, we can clean up our garbage mess so our country can once again be healthy and beautiful. We owe it to ourselves as well as to future generations.

Specifies another technology

Repeats need to change habits in conclusion

Uses *we* and *our* to strengthen appeal to readers

51e
MLA

↕ 1″ from top of page

½″ from top   Hand 9

Page numbers continue

Center heading

Works Cited

First line of entry not indented

———

Additional lines indented five spaces

List sources mentioned in paper

———

Double-space

Farley, Rose. "Bottom of the Ninth: Permit Hearings
    Begin in TXI's Quest to Become the Nation's
    Largest Toxic Waste Incinerator." 12-18 Feb. 1998.
    Dallas News Observer. 19 Jan. 1999 <http://
    www.dallasobserver.com/archives/1998/021298/
    news2.html?cat=nfc&query=TXI>.

Hand, Shane. Questionnaire on Consumer Habits and
    Attitudes Toward Recycling. Blacksburg, VA, and
    Upper Marlboro, MD. 21-25 Feb. 1999.

Hazardous Waste Incineration. New York: American
    Society of Mechanical Engineers, 1988.

Montague, Peter. "New Study Shows Incinerator Ash More
    Dangerous Than We Realized." 29 Aug. 1988.
    Rachel's Hazardous Waste News 92. 19 Jan. 1999
    <http://www.enviroweb.org/pubs/rachel/rhwn092.htm>.

Organic Waste Technologies Inc. "Leachate Evaporation."
    19 Jan. 1999 <http://www.owtinc.com/
    leachate_1.htm>.

Pennsylvania Department of Environmental Protection.
    "Brownfields Tax Incentive." 19 Jan. 1999
    <http://www.dep.state.pa.us/dep/deputate/airwaste/
    wm/landrecy/Tax/tas.htm>.

Rathje, William L. "Once and Future Landfills."
    National Geographic May 1991: 116-34.

Wiseman, Clark A. "Impediments to Economically
    Efficient Solid Waste Management." Resources 105
    (1991): 9-11.

Hand 10

Works Consulted

Includes all works consulted even if not cited in the paper

Brown, Kirk W. Hazardous Waste and Treatment. Woburn:

  Butterworth, 1983.

Bugher, Robert D. Municipal Refuse Disposal. Danville:

  Interstate, 1970.

Farley, Rose. "Bottom of the Ninth: Permit Hearings

  Begin in TXI's Quest to Become the Nation's

  Largest Toxic Waste Incinerator." 12-18 Feb. 1998.

  Dallas News Observer 19 Jan. 1999 <http://

  www.dallasobserver.com/archives/1998/021298/

  news2.html?cat=nfc&query=TXI>.

Flack, J. E. Man and the Quality of His Environment.

  Boulder: U of Colorado P, 1967.

Hand, Shane. Questionnaire on Consumer Habits and

  Attitudes Toward Recycling. Blacksburg, VA and

  Upper Marlboro, MD. 21-25 Feb. 1999.

Hazardous Waste Incineration. New York: American

  Society of Mechanical Engineers, 1988.

Montague, Peter. "New Study Shows Incinerator Ash More

  Dangerous Than We Realized." 29 Aug. 1988.

  Rachel's Hazardous Waste News 92. 19 Jan. 1999

  <http://www.enviroweb.org/pubs/rachel/

  rhwn092.htm>.

Organic Waste Technologies Inc. "Leachate Evaporation."

  19 Jan. 1999 <http://www.owtinc.com/

  leachate_1.htm>.

Pennsylvania Department of Environmental Protection.

  "Brownfields Tax Incentive." 19 Jan. 1999

Hand 11

<http://www.dep.state.pa.us/dep/deputate/airwaste/
wm/landrecy/Tax/tas.htm>.

Rathje, William L. "Once and Future Landfills."

National Geographic May 1991: 116-34.

Van Tassel, Alfred J. Environmental Side Effects of

Rising Industrial Output. Lexington: Heath, 1970.

Wiseman, Clark A. "Impediments to Economically

Efficient Solid Waste Management." Resources 105

(1991): 9-11.

Appendix

Intro:

My name is Shane and I am taking a survey in order to study the habits of the average consumer. I am interested in seeing how your habits affect the environment. Please take a few moments to answer some questions.

Survey:

Do you . . .

Use coffee mugs instead of

    polystyrene cups?   Yes   No

Reuse plastic wrap, foil, and

    plastic bags?   Yes   No

Recycle newspapers and/or magazines?   Yes   No

Recycle glass?   Yes   No

Recycle plastic containers?   Yes   No

Recycle aluminum cans?   Yes   No

Are you willing to . . .

Take your own bags to the store?   Yes   No

Shop at a store that's harder to get to

    but carries biodegradable products?   Yes   No

Recycle plastic containers?   Yes   No

Pay more for products in low-waste

    packaging?   Yes   No

Pay more for recycled paper?   Yes   No

Includes clean copy of any survey, questionnaire, or other primary research document

CHAPTER 52

DOCUMENTING SOURCES: APA

The documentation style developed by the APA (American Psychological Association) identifies the source of information, ideas, or quotations by providing the author's name and the date of publication for the source within the parentheses. For this reason, APA style is often called a name-and-date style. The information in the parenthetical citation enables readers to locate more detailed information about the source in a **reference list** at the end of a paper or report.

Many writing situations call for either the APA style or a name-and-date style loosely based on the APA style but adapted to the needs of specific audiences. APA style can be easily modified and lends itself to informal uses; as a result, it is an important resource for writers looking for a direct, simple documentation system that does not disrupt the reading of a text with detailed information or require readers to turn to a footnote or endnote.

52.1

USE APA STYLE IN . . .

ACADEMIC SETTINGS

When writing in social science fields such as psychology, sociology, business, economics, education, and political science.

For publications or professional groups requiring use of APA style.

When writing papers for an instructor who requests documentation in a name-and-date style.

WORK AND PUBLIC SETTINGS

For readers whose professions are linked to academic fields in the social sciences (personnel managers, social workers, or school administrators, for example).

When you are drawing heavily on research in the social sciences to support your paper.

When writers or publications addressing audiences similar to yours regularly use APA style or a modified form of the style.

CONSIDER USING APA STYLE (PERHAPS IN A MODIFIED FORM) IN . . .

WORK SETTINGS

In business, because many business audiences prefer a name-and-date system, in part because it indicates how current the writer's sources are. (Professional audiences often have similar expectations.)

PUBLIC SETTINGS

When you need a simple, direct system to identify your source and its date.

APA documentation style makes the year of publication part of an in-text citation, as in (*Tannen, 1998*), and gives the date right after the author's name in a reference list to which the in-text citation refers.

> Tannen, D. (1998). *The argument culture: Moving from debate to dialogue.* New York: Random House.

For more detailed discussion of this documentation style, consult the *Publication Manual of the American Psychological Association* (5th ed., 2001) or check for updates online at <http://www.apastyle.org>.

52a Using in-text citations

The APA system provides parenthetical citations for quotations, paraphrases, summaries, and other information in the text of a paper. For advice on what to document and what not to document, see 49a. For an APA in-text citation, you include the author's name and the year of publication, separating these items with a comma. You may choose to name the author (and give the date) either within the parenthetical citation or within your text.

Author's name inside parentheses. Include the author's name and the year of publication inside parentheses, separating these items with a comma. When you are documenting the source of a quotation, follow the date with a comma, *p.* or *pp.*, and the page number or numbers on which the quoted material appears in the source.

> One recent study points out that while "women radio news directors have exceeded the men in yearly salary, that may not be the case in other radio news positions" (Cramer, 1993, p. 161).

To indicate the specific location of information or the source of paraphrased or summarized material, give the page number of the source.

> In the mid-1960s, Tom Wolfe began writing unconventional
> and insight-filled essays about American popular culture.
> Despite his Ph.D. in American Studies from Yale, Wolfe and his
> work were at first ignored by most intellectuals, both inside
> and outside universities, who viewed serious or high-brow
> culture as far more important than popular culture (Aronowitz,
> 1993, p. 198).

Author's name as part of discussion. When you make an author's name part of the discussion, give the date of the source in parentheses after the name. For quoted or paraphrased material, provide the page number in the source within parentheses following the quotation or paraphrase.

> As Cramer (1993) points out, "Although women radio
> news directors have exceeded the men in yearly salary, that
> may not be the case in other radio news positions" (p. 161).

When you supply the author's name and the date in your text or in an in-text citation, your readers will be able to identify a source in the list of references you provide at the end of your paper.

52b Using content footnotes

Occasionally you may wish to expand information presented in the text or discuss a point further without making the main text of your paper more complicated or harder to follow. A content footnote allows you to do this, but you should use such footnotes sparingly because too many footnotes or long footnotes can distract your readers.

To prepare a content footnote, place a number slightly above the line of your text that relates to the footnote information. Make sure that you number the footnotes in your paper consecutively.

TEXT OF PAPER   I tape-recorded all the interviews and later
transcribed the relevant portions.[1]

On a separate page at the end of your paper, below the centered heading "Footnotes," present the notes in the order in which they appear in your text. Begin each note with its number, placed slightly above the line. Indent five to seven spaces, the same as a paragraph, for the first line only of each footnote, and double-space all notes.

FOOTNOTE ¹Sections of the recordings were hard to hear and understand because of problems with the tape recorder or background noises. These gaps did not substantially affect information needed for the study.

Your instructor may prefer that you type any footnote at the bottom of the page with the text reference.

GUIDE TO APA FORMATS FOR IN-TEXT CITATIONS

1. One Author
2. Two Authors
3. Three to Five Authors
4. Six or More Authors
5. Corporate or Group Author
6. No Author Given
7. Specific Page or Section
8. Work Cited More Than Once
9. Authors with the Same Last Name
10. Two or More Sources in a Citation
11. Personal Communications, Including Interviews and Email

52c Creating APA in-text citations

1. One author

Supply the author's last name and the date of the publication in parentheses, separated by a comma and a space. If the author's name appears in the text, give only the date in parentheses. If both the name and the date are included in the text, no other information need be cited.

> Mallory's 1995 study of magnet schools confirmed several of the trends proposed earlier (Jacobson, 1989) and also updated the classification by Bailey (1991) based on district demographics.

2. Two authors

Include both names in citations. In a parenthetical reference, separate the names by an ampersand (&); in the text, use the word *and*.

> Given evidence that married men earn more than unmarried men (Chun & Lee, 2001), Nakosteen and Zimmer (2001) investigate how earnings affect spousal selection.

3. Three to five authors

Include all the authors' names, separated by commas, for the first citation. For parenthetical citations use an ampersand (&) rather than *and*.

> Biber, Conrad, and Reppen (1998) point out that "the language you use to write a term paper is different from the language you use when talking to your roommate" (p. 135).

In the second and other following citations, give only the first author's name followed by *et al.* and the date (for example, "Biber et al. (1998) present evidence that . . .").

An exception to this would occur when two or more citations, after being shortened, become identical. In that case, cite more than one author, separated with commas, to differentiate the references, providing the minimum number of authors necessary to prevent ambiguity, followed by *et al.* and the date.

4. Six or more authors

Give the name of the first author followed by *et al.* and the date in all citations: (*Lichtenberg et al., 1998*). An exception to this would occur when two or more citations, after being shortened, become identical. In that case, cite more than one author, separated with commas, to differentiate the references, providing the minimum number of authors necessary to prevent ambiguity, followed by *et al.* and the date.

Supply the names of the first six authors in the reference list at the end of your report. For more than six authors, list the first six and shorten any remaining authors to *et al.*

5. Corporate or group author

Spell out the name of an association, corporation, or government agency for the first citation, following with an abbreviation of a cumbersome name within brackets. You may use the abbreviation for later citations.

FIRST CITATION
> Besides instilling fear, hate crimes limit where women live and work (National Organization of Women [NOW], 2001).

LATER CITATION
> Pending legislation would strengthen the statutes on bias-motivated crimes (NOW, 2001).

6. No author given

Give the title or the first few words of a long title (*The Great Utopia: The Russian and Soviet Avant-Garde, 1915–1932* might appear in a citation as *Great Utopia*) and the year.

```
Art and design in 1920s Russia mixed aesthetically startling
images with political themes and an endorsement of social
change (Great Utopia, 1992).
```

When the word *Anonymous* designates the author, use it in the citation: (Anonymous, 2002).

7. Specific page or section

Indicate the part of the work you are citing: *p.* (for "page"); *chap.* ("chapter"), *fig.* ("figure"), for example. Spell out any words that may be confusing.

```
Teenagers who survive suicide attempts experience stages of
recovery, and these stages have distinct symptoms (Mauk &
Weber, 1991, Table 1).
```

8. Work cited more than once

When you cite the same source more than once in a paragraph, repeat the source as necessary to clarify a specific page reference or show which information comes from one of several sources. If a second reference is clear, do not repeat the date.

```
Personal debt has become a significant problem in the past
decade. Much of the increase can be linked to the lack of
restraint in spending people feel when using credit cards
(Schor, 1998, p. 73). The problem is so widespread that "about
one-third of the nation's population describe themselves as
either heavily or moderately in financial debt" (Schor, p. 72).
```

9. Authors with the same last name

When your reference list contains works by two different authors with the same last name, provide each author's initials for each in-text citation, both for works by a single author and for works by several authors.

```
Scholars have looked in depth at the development of African
American culture during slavery and reconstruction (E. Foner,
1988). The role of Frederick Douglass in this process has also
been examined (P. Foner, 1950).
```

10. Two or more sources in a citation

If you are summarizing information found in more than one source, include all the sources—names and years—within the citation. Separate the authors and years with commas; separate the sources with semicolons. List sources alphabetically by author (as in your list of references; see p. 700), then oldest to most recent for several sources by the same author.

> Several researchers have found that work performance is affected by personality (Furnham, 1992; Gilmer, 1961, 1977).

11. Personal communications, including interviews and email

In your text, cite letters, memos, interviews, email, telephone conversations, and similar personal communications by giving the initials and last name of the person, the phrase *personal communication*, and the date. Readers probably will have no access to such sources, so you need not include them in your reference list.

AUTHOR NAMED IN TEXT

> According to J. M. Hostos, the state has begun cutting funding for social services duplicated by county agencies (personal communication, October 7, 2002).

PARENTHETICAL REFERENCE

> The state has begun cutting funding for social services duplicated by county agencies (J. M. Hostos, personal communication, October 7, 2002).

52d Creating an APA reference list

Immediately after the last page of your paper, you need to provide a list of references to enable readers to identify and consult the sources you have cited in your report.

- **Page format.** One inch from the top margin of a separate page at the end of your report's text (before notes or appendixes), center the heading "References" without underlining or quotation marks.
- **Alphabetizing.** List works cited in the report alphabetically by author or by the first main word of the title if there is no author. Arrange two or more works by the same author from the oldest to the most recent according to year of publication.
- **Spacing.** Double-space all entries and between entries.
- **Indentation.** Do not indent the first line, but indent five to seven spaces for the second and additional lines.

GUIDE TO APA FORMATS FOR REFERENCES

1. BOOKS AND WORKS TREATED AS BOOKS

1. One Author
2. Two or More Authors

52d
APA

52d
APA

1 Books and works treated as books

MODEL FORMAT FOR BOOKS AND WORKS TREATED AS BOOKS

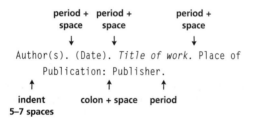

- **Author(s).** Give the author's last name followed by a comma and the initials of the first and middle names. For a book with more than one author, use the same inverted order for each author. Separate the names with commas, using an ampersand before the final name.
- **Date.** Provide the year of publication (in parentheses) followed by a period.
- **Title of work.** Give the title in italics followed by a period. Use a capital only for the first word of the main title, the first word of any subtitle, and any proper nouns.
- **Publication information.** For U.S. publishers, give the city and state followed by a colon and a space; then supply the publisher's name, leaving out unnecessary words such as *Inc.* or *Publishers.* Abbreviate the name of the state using the standard postal abbreviation. You do not need to name the state for the following familiar publishing locations: Baltimore, Boston, Chicago, Los Angeles, New York, Philadelphia, and

San Francisco. For publishers outside the United States, give the city and the abbreviated name of the country. No country is needed for these familiar locations: Amsterdam, Jerusalem, London, Milan, Moscow, Paris, Rome, Stockholm, Tokyo, and Vienna.

- **Spacing.** Double-space all entries, and indent five to seven spaces, the same indentation that you choose for paragraphing, for the second and any additional lines.

1. One author

Wilson, W. J. (1996). *When work disappears: The world of the new urban poor.* New York: Knopf.

2. Two or more authors

List each author's last name first, followed by first and middle initials.

Biber, D., Conrad, S., & Reppen, R. (1998). *Corpus linguistics: Investigating language structure and use.* Cambridge, Eng.: Cambridge University Press.

For a book with more than six authors, name the first six, followed by a comma, then add *et al.* to indicate the rest.

3. Corporate or group author

Treat the organization or agency responsible for the work as an individual author, and alphabetize by the first main word. When author and publisher are the same, give the word *Author* following the place of publication instead of repeating the name.

Amnesty International (2001). *Annual Report 2001.* [Brochure]. London: Author.

4. No author given

Give the title first, then the date. Use the first significant word of the title to alphabetize the entry. If the word *Anonymous* is used for the author, designate the author with it and alphabetize under *anonymous.*

Boas anniversary volume: Anthropological papers written in honor of Franz Boas. (1906). New York: Stechert.

5. More than one work by the same author

List works in chronological order. Include the author's name in each entry.

```
Aronowitz, S. (1993). Roll over Beethoven: The return of
     cultural strife. Hanover, NH: Wesleyan University Press.
Aronowitz, S. (2000). From the ashes of the old: American labor
     and America's future. New York: Basic Books.
```

If the same lead author has works with different co-authors, alphabetize these entries based on the last names of the second authors.

6. More than one work by the same author in the same year

List in alphabetical order works appearing in the same year by the same author. Add lowercase letters after dates (e.g., *1992a, 1992b*). Alphabetize by the first main word in the title. For in-text citations, provide both the date and the letter (*Gould, 1987b*).

```
Gould, S. J. (1987a). Time's arrow, time's cycle: Myth and
     metaphor in the discovery of geological time. Cambridge,
     MA: Harvard University Press.
Gould, S. J. (1987b). An urchin in the storm: Essays about
     books and ideas. New York: Norton.
```
Alphabetized under *urchin*, not *An*.

7. One or more editors

Include (*Ed.*) or (*Eds.*) after the name(s) of the editors.

```
Bowe, J., Bowe, M., & Streeter, S. C. (Eds.). (2001). Gig:
     Americans talk about their jobs. New York: Three Rivers
     Press.
```

8. Translator

Include the translator's name, in normal order, after the title, followed by *Trans.*

```
Bourdieu, P. (1990). In other words: Essays towards a reflexive
     sociology (M. Adamson, Trans.). Stanford, CA: Stanford
     University Press.
```

9. Edition other than the first

Include information about the specific edition in parentheses after the title (for example, *Rev. ed.* for "revised edition" or *3d ed.* for "third edition").

Groth-Marnat, G. (1996). *Handbook of psychological assessment*

(3rd ed.). New York: Wiley.

10. Reprint

Butler, J. (1999). *Gender Trouble.* New York: Routledge.

(Original work published 1990)

11. Multivolume work

Include the names of the editors or authors, making sure you indicate if they are editors. Then provide the inclusive years of publication. If the work is a revised edition or has a translator, give this information after the title. Then identify in parentheses the volumes you are using for your paper.

Strachey, J., Freud, A., Strachey, A., & Tyson, A. (Eds.).

(1966-1974). *The standard edition of the complete*

psychological works of Sigmund Freud (J. Strachey et al.,

Trans.) (Vols. 3-5). London: Hogarth Press and the

Institute of Psycho-Analysis.

12. Anthology or collection of articles

Give the name of the editor(s) first, followed by the abbreviation *Ed.* or *Eds.* in parentheses.

Cobley, P. (Ed.). (1996). *The communication theory reader.*

London: Routledge.

Ghosh, A., & Ingene, C. A. (Eds.). (1991). *Spatial analysis in*

marketing: Theory, methods and applications. Greenwich,

CT: JAI.

13. *Diagnostic and Statistical Manual of Mental Disorders*

The manual known in short form as the *DSM-IV* is widely cited in fields such as psychology, social work, and psychiatry because its definitions and guidelines often have legal force and determine patterns of treatment. Because of the volume's importance, the APA *Publication Manual* recommends the following specific form for the entry.

American Psychiatric Association. (1994). *Diagnostic and*

statistical manual of mental disorders (4th ed.).

Washington, DC: Author.

In your text, following an initial full citation, you may use the standard abbreviations for this work: *DSM-III* (1980), *DSM-III-R* (1987), *DSM-IV* (1994), or *DSM-IV-TR* (2000).

14. Encyclopedia or reference work

> Winn, P. (Ed.). (2001). *Dictionary of biological psychology.*
>
> London: Routledge.

15. Unpublished dissertation

> Conrad, S. (1996). *Academic discourse in two disciplines:*
>
> *Professional writing and student development in biology*
>
> *and history.* Unpublished doctoral dissertation, Northern
>
> Arizona University, Flagstaff.

16. Government document

> Select Committee on Aging, Subcommittee on Human Services,
>
> House of Representatives. (1991). *Grandparents' rights:*
>
> *Preserving generational bonds* (Com. Rep. No. 102-833).
>
> Washington, DC: U.S. Government Printing Office.

17. Report

Begin with the name of the author, whether an individual or a group or government agency. If the agency also publishes the report, use the word *Author* in the publication information instead of repeating the group's name.

> Advisory commission to study the Consumer Price Index. (1996).
>
> *Toward a more accurate measure of the cost of living.*
>
> Washington, DC: Senate Finance Committee.

If the report has a number, give it in parentheses after the title with no punctuation between the title and parentheses. When several numbers are listed in the report, choose the one most likely to help readers obtain the document.

> Dossey, J.A. (1988). *Mathematics: Are we measuring up?* (Report
>
> No. 17-M-02). Princeton, NJ: Educational Testing Service.
>
> (ERIC Document Reproduction Service No. ED3000207)

2 Articles and selections from books

MODEL FORMAT FOR ARTICLES AND SELECTIONS

```
period +   period +        period +
 space      space            space
   ↓          ↓                ↓
Author(s). (Date). Title of article. Title of

    Periodical, Volume Number, Page numbers.
 ↑                    ↑          ↑
indent             number      comma
5–7 spaces       italicized   italicized
```

- **Author(s).** Give the author's last name and initials followed by a period and a space.
- **Date.** Supply the date in parentheses followed by a period and a space.
- **Title of article.** Give the article title, capitalizing only the first word (and the first word of any subtitle along with any proper names). Do not use quotation marks with the title. End with a period and a space.
- **Title of journal, periodical, or book.** Give the journal title in italics with all main words capitalized, the volume number (also in italics), and the page numbers. Use commas to separate these.
- **Spacing.** Double-space all entries, and indent five to seven spaces, the same indentation that you choose for paragraphing, for the second and any additional lines.

18. Article in journal paginated by volume

You do not have to include the particular issue number because page numbers run continuously throughout the different issues making up a volume.

Iran-Nejad, A., McKeachie, W. J., & Berliner, D. C. (1990). The multisource nature of learning: An introduction. *Review of Educational Research, 60*, 509–515.

Macklin, M. C. (1996). Preschoolers' learning of brand names from visual cues. *Journal of Consumer Research, 23*, 251–261.

For references with up to six authors, supply the names of all the authors in the reference list entry. For more than six authors, list the first six and shorten the remaining authors to *et al.*

All in-text citations for references having two authors should include both authors. For three to five authors, list all authors at the first citation; thereafter, give only the name of the first author followed by *et al.*, as in (*Albertini et al., 1986*). For six or more authors, cite the first author's surname followed by *et al.* and the date for all citations, including the first.

19. Article in journal paginated by issue

When each issue of a journal begins with page 1, include the issue number in parentheses immediately (with no space) after the volume number. Do not italicize the issue number.

> Wurzbacher, K. V., Evans, E. D., & Moore, E. J. (1991). Effects
>
> of alternative street school on youth involved in
>
> prostitution. *Journal of Adolescent Health, 12*(7),
>
> 549-554.

20. Special issue of journal

Begin with the special issue's editor (if other than the regular editor); otherwise, place the title at the beginning, then the date. Indicate in brackets that it is a special issue. You need not include page numbers.

> Balk, D. E. (Ed.). (1991). Death and adolescent bereavement
>
> [Special issue]. *Journal of Adolescent Research, 6*(1).

21. Article in popular magazine (weekly or biweekly)

Supply the same information as you would for an article in a monthly magazine (see Entry 22), but add the specific date.

> Adler, J. (1995, July 31). The rise of the overclass. *Newsweek,*
>
> *126,* 33-34, 39-40, 43, 45-46.

When an article is continued, list all the different pages, separated by commas.

22. Article in popular magazine (monthly)

Include the month and year of the magazine. Spell out months. Add the volume number and pages. If there is no author, put the title first, before the date.

> Dold, C. (1998, September). Needles and nerves. *Discover, 19,*
>
> 59-62.

23. Article with no author given

Begin the entry with the article's title, and alphabetize using the first main word in the title.

> True tales of false memories. (1993, July/August). *Psychology*
>
> *Today, 26,* 11-12.

24. Article in newspaper

Use *p.* or *pp.* to introduce the section and page numbers for newspaper articles. If no author is given, put the title first.

Murtaugh, P. (1998, August 10). Finding a brand's real essence.

Advertising Age, p. 12.

25. Letter to the editor or editorial

Treat a letter to the editor like another newspaper article, but label it in brackets.

Ellis, S. (2001, September 7). Adults are problem with youth

sports [Letter to the editor]. USA Today, p. 14A.

26. Interview—published

Although APA does not specify a form for published interviews, you may wish to employ the following form, which is similar to other APA references.

Dess, N. K. The new body-mind connection (John T. Cacioppo)

[Interview]. Psychology Today, 34(4), 30-31.

27. Review with a title

Following the title of the review, indicate in brackets the kind of work (*book, film, video program, television program,* and so on) and the title (italicized) of the work being reviewed.

McMahon, R. J. (2000). The Pentagon's war, the media's war

[Review of the book Reporting Vietnam: Media and military

at war]. Reviews in American History, 28, 303-308.

28. Review without a title

Begin with the name of the reviewer. If the review article does not have a title, substitute a description in brackets consisting of the phrase *Review* followed by the type of material and the title of the book, motion picture, television show, or other topic of the review.

Van Meter, E. J. (1994). [Review of the book Preparing

tomorrow's school leaders: Alternative designs].

Educational Administration Quarterly, 30, 112-117.

29. Article from encyclopedia or reference work

If no author is identified, begin with the title of the article. Use *In* before the work's title, and follow it with the volume and page numbers.

> Chernoff, H. (1978). Decision theory. In *International*
>
> *encyclopedia of statistics* (Vol. 1, pp. 131-135). New
>
> York: Free Press.

30. Chapter in edited book or selection in anthology

For a selection from an anthology, begin with the author's name, the year the book was published, and the title of the selection. Following the word *In*, cite the editors, the title of the collection, and the page numbers.

> Chisholm, J. S. (1999). Steps to an evolutionary ecology of
>
> mind. In A. L. Hinton (Ed.). *Biocultural approaches to the*
>
> *emotions* (pp. 117-150). Cambridge, England: Cambridge
>
> University Press.

31. Dissertation abstract

> Yamada, H. (1989). American and Japanese topic management
>
> strategies in business conversations. *Dissertation*
>
> *Abstracts International, 50*(09), 2982B.

If you consult the dissertation on microfilm, give the University Microfilms number at the end of the entry in parentheses: (*UMI No. AAC–9004751*).

3 Field resources

32. Interview—unpublished

To refer to an interview you have conducted yourself, provide the information only as part of an in-text citation: (*R. Gelles, personal communication, September 14, 1993*). (See Entry 33, below.)

33. Personal communication (including email)

Letters, email, telephone conversations, and similiar communications cannot be consulted by your readers, so do not include them in your reference list. Instead, cite them in text. (See p. 672 and Entry 32 for examples.)

34. Paper presented at a meeting

52d
APA

For an unpublished paper presented at a conference or symposium, include the month as well as the year, and list both the name and location of the meeting.

Nelson, J. S. (1993, August). *Political argument in political*

  science: A meditation on the disappointment of

  political theory. Paper presented at the annual

  meeting of the American Political Science Association,

  Chicago.

35. Unpublished raw data

When you use data from field observations, a survey, or similar kinds of research, briefly describe the contents of the data within brackets following the date. Conclude the entry with the phrase *Unpublished raw data.*

Williams, S. (1999). [Survey of student attitudes toward

  increased library fees]. Unpublished raw data.

4 Media resources

36. Motion picture

Begin with the name or names of the people primarily responsible for the work, and indicate each person's role (for example, *Director* or *Producer*) in parentheses following the name. Italicize the title, and then indicate the medium (for example, *Motion picture or Slides*) in brackets. At the end of the entry, within parentheses, indicate the location and name of the distributor (for example, *WGBH, Boston*). If the distributor is not well known, supply the address. For motion pictures, give the country of origin and the name of the studio.

Simon, T. (Producer), & LeBrun, N. (Writer). (1986). *Atocha:*

  Quest for treasure [Motion picture]. (Available from

  Columbia Tristar Home Video, 3400 Riverside Drive,

  Burbank, CA 91505-4627)

Coen, E. (Producer), & Coen, J. (Director). (2000). *O Brother,*

  Where Art Thou? [Motion picture]. United States: Universal

  Pictures.

37. Television or radio program

Begin the entry for a series of programs with the name of the script writer, the producer, the director, or any other person whose role you wish to indicate. Give the title of the program or series (italicized) followed by *Television series* in brackets. Conclude with the location and name of the network or channel responsible for the broadcast.

> Moyers, B. (Executive Editor). (1993). *Bill Moyers' journal*
>
>   [Television series]. New York: WNET.

A specific episode in a series is treated much like an anthology. List the script's writer as you would an author, then the name of the director, with each of these followed by his or her function in parentheses. Follow the episode title with *Television series episode* in brackets, then indicate the producer in the editor position, before the italicized title of the series.

> Moyers, B. A. (Writer), & Grubin, D. (Director). (1993). A life
>
>   together [Television series episode]. In D. Grubin
>
>   (Producer), *Bill Moyers' journal*. New York: WNET.

38. Recording

Begin by giving the name of the writer and the date of copyright (in parentheses). Following the song title, supply the name of the recording artist in brackets, if this is someone other than the writer. Indicate the medium in brackets after the album title; include a number for the recording within the brackets if one is necessary for identifying the recording and obtaining a copy.

Give the location, followed by a colon and the name of the recording label. Include the recording date, if different from the copyright date, in parentheses, with no period after the final parenthesis.

> Freeman, R. (1994). Porscha [Recorded by R. Freeman & The
>
>   Rippingtons]. On *Sahara* [CD]. New York: GRP Records.
>
>   (Recording date, if different from copyright date)

5 Internet, Web, and electronic resources

39. Web site

Include the information specified in Entry 42.

> Ringertz, N. (1998, December 2). Alfred Nobel's health and his
>
>   interest in medicine. [Essay posted on Web site *The*

Electronic Nobel Museum Project]. Retrieved December 31,

1998, from http://www.nobel.se/alfred/ringertz/index.html

40. Online book or document

For texts lacking a publication date, use *n.d.* ("no date").

Frary, R. B. (n.d.) *A brief guide to questionnaire development.*

Retrieved August 8, 1998 from http://ericae.net/ft/

tamu/upiques3.htm

41. Selection from online book or document

Lasswell, H. D. (1971). Professional training. In *A pre-view of*

policy sciences (chap. 8). Retrieved May 4, 2002, from

http://www.policysciences.org/spsresources.htm

42. Online journal article

Begin with the author(s) and the date of posting. Add the title, list the source with the volume and issue numbers, and list the page numbers if given. If you have viewed the article online only, add the words *Electronic version* in brackets after the article. Retrieval date and electronic address should be included when there is a possibility that the material has been changed from its printed form, as shown here:

Sheridan, J., & McAuley, J. D. (1998). Rhythm as a cognitive

skill: Temporal processing deficits in autism [Electronic

version]. *Noetica, 3,* 8. Retrieved December 31, 1998,

from http://www.cs.indiana.edu/Noetica/OpenForumIssue8/

McAuley.html

43. Online article identical to print version

If online and print articles are identical, you may use the print format but identify the online version you used.

Epstein, R. (2001). Physiologist Laura [Electronic version].

Psychology Today, 34(4), 5.

44. Online newletter article

Cashel, J. (2001, July 16). Top ten trends for online

communities. *Online Community Report.* Retrieved

October 18, 2001, from http://www.onlinecommunityreport.com/
features/10/

45. Online newspaper or news service article

Begin with as much information as possible that would be provided for
a printed source. Give the date of retrieval, a colon, and the electronic address.

Sonner, S. (1998, December 31). Psychologist ponders horse
killer. *Washington Post Online.* Retrieved December 31,
1998, from http://search.washingtonpost.com/
wp-rv/WAPO/19981231/V000412-123198-idx.html

46. Online organization or agency document

Arizona Public Health Association (n.d.). *Indigenous health
section.* Retrieved September 6, 2001, from
http://www.geocities.com/native_health_/AzPHA.htm

47. Online government document

U.S. Department of Labor, Women's Bureau. (2001). *Women's jobs
1964-1999: More than 30 years of progress.* Retrieved
September 7, 2001, from http://www.dol.gov/dol/wb/public/
jobs6497.htm

48. Online document from academic site

Cultural Studies Program. (n.d.) Retrieved September 9, 2001,
from Drake University, Cultural Studies Web site:
http://www.multimedia.drake.edu/cs/

49. Online report

Amnesty International. (1998). *The death penalty in Texas:
Lethal injustice.* Retrieved September 7, 2001, from
http://www.web.amnesty.org/ai.nsf/index/AMR510101998

50. Online report from academic site

Vandell, D. L., & Wolfe, B. (2000). *Child care quality:
Does it matter and does it need to be improved?*
(Special Report No. 78). Available from University of
Wisconsin, Institute for Research on Poverty Web site:
http://www.ssc.wisc.edum/irp/sr/sr78.pdf

51. Online abstract

For an abstract, give the source of the original work and the location of
the abstract.

Globus, G. (1995, August). Quantum consciousness is cybernetic.
PSYCHE, 2(12). Abstract retrieved January 8, 1998, from
http://psyche.cs.monash.edu.au/v2/psyche-2-12-curran.html

52. CD-ROM abstract

Schroeder, E. (1988). Therapy for the chemically dependent
family [CD-ROM]. *Journal of Chemical Dependency, 2,*
95-129. Abstract retrieved from: SilverPlatter File:
PsycLIT Item: 76-37924.

53. Journal article from online database

Piko, B. (2001). Gender differences and similarities in
adolescents' ways of coping. *Psychological Record, 51(2),*
223-236. Retrieved August 31, 2001, from InfoTrac Expanded
Academic database.

54. Newspaper article from online database

Sappenfield, M. (2002). New laws curb teen sports drugs. *The
Christian Science Monitor,* June 24, 2002. Retrieved June
26, 2002, from America Online: News Publications database.

55. Presentation from virtual conference

52d
APA

```
Brown, D. J., Steward, D. S., & Wilson, J. R. (1995). Ethical
    pathways to virtual learning. Paper presented at the
    Center on Disabilities 1995 virtual conference. Retrieved
    September 7, 2001, from http://www.csun.edu/cod/95virt/
    0010.html
```

56. Online posting or archived discussion list

Give the name of the author and in parentheses the date the message was posted, followed by a period. Next write the title of the message from the subject line and in brackets any identifier for the message. Finally, write the words *Message posted to* and the Uniform Resource Locator (URL), or electronic address.

When listing URLs, do not allow your word processor to hyphenate at the right margin. Instead, break lines either before a period or after a slash. (This can be accomplished with most word processors by inserting an extra space where you want the line to break.) Do not use a period after URLs.

```
Morrison, A. (1998, September 11). Chlorambucil [Msg 1].
    Message posted to http://www.acor.org/lists/cancer/
    ws/98/09/0078.html
```

57. Computer program

You need not reference standard, off-the-shelf software. However, if the software is in limited distribution, identify the source as computer software or computer programming language after the title. If the program's author owns specific rights to it, begin the entry with the author's name. Otherwise, begin with the name of the material. Give the location and name of the organization producing the program. Add any version number or retrieval information at the end in parentheses unless it is part of the title.

```
Checkmate [Computer software]. (1993). Memphis, TN: Psych
    Development Software. (Windows version)
```

Exercise

52.2

A. Turn to Exercise A in Chapter 51. Rewrite the sentences supplied there to add in-text citations in APA style.

B. Turn to Exercise B in Chapter 51. Rewrite the items supplied there to create a list of references in APA style.

C. Working with a partner or a small group, compare your answers to Exercise A and B above. Correct any errors in your answers, using your handbook or your instructor's advice to resolve any differences of opinion.

52e
APA

52e Sample APA paper

Supply abbreviated title (50 characters maximum) for heading

Cyclists   1

Number title page and all others using short title

Running head: CYCLISTS

Center title and all other lines

Competitive Cyclists: Who Are They?

Steven King

University of Rhode Island

Supply name and institution

Double-space twice between groups of lines

Professor Hasan Danesh

Sociology 150

Section 10

November 24, 1998

Ask your instructor if instructor's name, course name, and date are necessary

52e
APA

Center
heading

Supply
one ¶
and do
not
indent

Summarize
paper in
no more
than about
120 words

Use short
title and
page
number

Double-
space
abstract
and rest
of
paper

Abstract

Cyclists at a race were asked to fill out a
questionnaire about attitudes toward cycling,
demographics, and self-perception of social status.
Responses to the questionnaire provided general
support for an initial hypothesis regarding the low
level of women's participation in competitive cycling
but not for a hypothesis regarding enjoyment of
extreme physical exertion and pain as a reason for
undertaking competitive cycling. In addition, the
responses suggested further hypotheses concerning the
relative lack of participation by cyclists under 25
years old and the likelihood that people of different
ages, marital status, and levels of education
undertake competitive cycling for different reasons.

**Besides the abstract, typical
sections in an APA paper are
Introduction, Method, Results,
and Discussion**

First part is
introduction
but no
heading is
used

Indent ¶
five to
seven
spaces

Use
introduction
to present
problem or
subject,
background
information,
and
hypothesis
or guiding
question

1" margin
each side

Follows
general
APA
practice,
discussing
subjects,
materials,
and
procedure
for the
study

1" top margin →   Cyclists   3

**52e
APA**

Repeat and
center title

Be
consistent
for ¶s and
references

Citation
uses title;
no author

Competitive Cyclists: Who Are They?

1   Bicycle riding is the third most popular

participant sport in the United States, with an

estimated 55.3 million people riding a bike at least

once a year (*Interbike*, 1992) for varying reasons and

with widely differing perspectives (Meyer, 1997;

Worthington, 1998; Zimberoff, 1996). Another report,

from the Bicycle Institute of America (1990), estimates

that 25 million American adults ride a bicycle an

average of once a week. That same survey indicates that

220,000 adults took part in bicycle races during the

year, or less than 1% of those who ride frequently.

2   In this paper I report on a group of people who

entered a particular bicycle race. I collected data

through a survey taken at the race. The survey asked

for demographic data as well as information about level

of commitment and motivation. I then summarized and

analyzed the data. Although the purpose of my study was

primarily descriptive, I also was able to estimate the

kind of support available for two hypotheses I

developed before beginning the study. In addition, the

study suggested several more hypotheses useful for

further research.

[The introduction goes on to provide background
information on competitive cycling as a sport.]

Method

3   I gathered the data for this paper at a bicycle

race held in Westerly, Rhode Island, on Sunday,

Explains
how the
study was
carried out

Center
section
heading

↓ 1" bottom margin

Cyclists   4

September 27, 1998. Called "The First Annual
Charlestown 40 Kilometer Time Trial," the event
consisted of each entrant's riding the course
individually "against the clock." The course was on
smoothly paved roads and was relatively flat. There
were 37 entrants, 34 male and 3 female.

Supplies cross-reference to survey in Appendix

4   The respondents filled out a survey (see Appendix)
after they had completed the event and were waiting for
the results. I circulated through the parking area and
asked the entrants to go to the registration table and
complete the survey. My original plan was to have the
entrants complete the survey prior to the race at
registration. My goal was a 100% response. As it worked
out, I achieved an 88% response rate (32 of 36 possible
respondents; I was the 37th entrant).

5   The questionnaire requested basic demographic
information including a question regarding self-
perception of social status. It also asked respondents
to rate their cycling ability and indicate how many
years they had been active in cycling competition. A
question about the distance traveled to get to the race
was intended to provide some indication of the level of
commitment to cycling competition. Traveling a
substantial distance to the race involves a considerable
time commitment and willingness to pay for transportation
and meals in addition to race entry fees. A final open-
ended question asked for three to five reasons why the
respondent entered competitive cycling events.

52e
APA

Literature Review

6   The factors motivating competitive cyclists do not appear to be a major issue in sociology or psychology at the present time. No journal articles that deal directly with the topic were found. Nonetheless, articles on body image, weight loss, and health risk-taking provide useful background for the present study.

7   In an article relating body image and exercise, David and Cowles (1991) make interesting comparisons between men and women and between younger and older men. Older men (over 25) and women of all ages are likely to desire to lose weight when asked to consider their own bodies. Women are far more dependent on dieting to lose weight than men, who seem more likely to exercise. Drewnowski and Yee (1987) also emphasize the tendency of women to turn to dieting and of men to turn to exercise in order to control weight. Schneider and Greenberg (1992) found that participants in individual sports such as swimming, jogging, tennis, and cycling tend to take fewer behavioral health risks in other aspects of their lives than do participants in team sports.

8   A physiological study of the determinants of endurance in well-trained cyclists found that cyclists with 5 or more years of cycling experience had superior endurance compared to similarly trained cyclists with 2 to 3 years of experience (Coyle, Coggan, Hopper, & Walters, 1988). This study suggests a link between

Provides theoretical background for study and context for methods and conclusions; Literature Review section often follows Introduction

Cite up to five authors in first reference to a work

Cyclists   6

performance and years of cycling experience. Because
responses to the survey were anonymous, this study was
unable to test the hypothesis by linking experience to
performance in the race.

Hypotheses

Section added to discuss hypotheses in detail

9   This study was intended to be descriptive and to
produce hypotheses for further research rather than to
test them. Nonetheless, I began the study with two
tentative hypotheses designed to help interpret the
data. On the basis of my experience with cycling, I
predicted that the percentage of women entrants in the
race would be approximately 10% and would not exceed
20%. In addition, on the basis of my experience and my
reading about cycling (Matheny, 1986), I predicted that
a common response to the survey question on motivation
would be a half-humorous suggestion of "love of pain"
or "love of suffering." Pain and suffering in fact
can be powerful if complex motivators in sport.
Members of one bicycling group who race to remind
the public about the effects of asbestos and toxic
chemicals explain:

> We tell the public that the temporary pain
> we experience racing bicycles is nothing like
> the pain a mesothelioma or cancer patient
> faces every hour of every day. As bike
> racers, we choose to suffer swollen legs
> and burning legs when climbing mountains or
> sprinting for the win. We know that a

terminal asbestos patient does not have this
choice--his pain and anguish was [sic] forced
upon him and his family. We do not take our
health for granted! (Worthington, 1998, p. 1)
This study aims to discover whether
motivations of this sort are widespread.

Results

10   The gender split among respondents was 93.8% male
and 6.3% female. This closely matches the overall
registration proportion of 92.3% male and 7.7% female.
The mean age of respondents was 36.6 years, ranging
from a low of 16 to a high of 62. Only 1 entrant was
under 25 while 5 were over 50. Just under half (46.9%)
the respondents indicated they were married. No
respondents indicated a household size of 6 or more.
Mean educational level was 14 years.

11   The question rating level of cycling ability
brought about a respondent-created category. Three
respondents felt so torn between the intermediate and
advanced categories that they drew a large circle
around both. If only one person had done this, I would
have made an assignment based on other criteria, but
with 3 out of 32 choosing this option, I decided to
label it an additional category. There was also one
crossed-out and recircled response to this question,
indicating that at least one more person had
difficulty with the distinction between the two
categories.

Provides detailed summary of questionnaire responses

Cyclists   8

Detailed information could be presented in table or chart

12   The mean number of seasons involved with competitive cycling was 4.2 years, ranging from 1 (5 cases) to 10 years (5 cases). Many of the athletes probably had experience in other aerobic sports prior to or overlapping with cycling. A high proportion (71.9%) of the respondents traveled over 50 miles one way to enter a race within the past year. Over two-thirds (69.2%) of those who traveled this distance did so with some frequency, four or more times during 1992.

Includes results that do not support hypothesis

13   The open-ended question regarding reasons for entering bicycle races produced 22 different responses. The most popular cluster was enjoyment of competition at 75%, followed by enjoyment of training at 59%, friendship with other cyclists at 40%, and health benefits of cycling at 31.3%.

Discussion

Analyzes results and their implications

14   In terms of the number of seasons of cycling experience, those respondents older than the mean of 36.6 years averaged exactly twice as many years' experience as those younger than the mean (5.8 years to 2.9 years). Only one cyclist (7%) over age 36 was in the first year of competition, while four (22.2%) age

Might be organized more clearly to correspond with questionnaire items or previous discussion

36 or under were in the first year. More of the young riders traveled 50 miles to a race (77% to 64%), but the older riders who did travel did so more frequently than their younger counterparts. Only 2 (11.2%) of the younger group traveled 7 or more times, compared to 6 (42.8%) of the older group. It seems that perhaps the

older group is more committed one way or the other--to travel and compete regularly or to stay home.

15   Due to the low number of female entrants/respondents, it is not appropriate to make statistical comparisons between male and female respondents. I will say, though, that the responses of the 2 women who completed the survey show little to distinguish them from the male respondents. It may be that this particular survey did not bring out gender-based differences, or it may be that the cycling experience transcends gender. The data are too slim to support even a preliminary conclusion.

16   Drawing on the results, I compared married respondents to all others. I found that married racers tend to live in larger households, with 53.3% living in households of 3 or more versus 17.6% of the nonmarried group. Of interest is that there are no beginning-level cyclists among the married respondents but 25% among the nonmarried group. It is tempting to hypothesize that married people are less likely to take up a new competitive sport such as bicycle racing, but I'm restrained by personal knowledge of many cyclists who have started competing after being married. Married people also mentioned health benefits as a reason for competing more frequently than nonmarrieds (53.3% to 12.5%). Health benefits were also more important to older cyclists (42%) than younger cyclists (22%).

Explores relationships among answers, suggesting tentative conclusions and research issues

Cyclists   10

17   There was no apparent relationship between age and marital status. The mean age of the entire sample (36.635) and the mean age of the married cyclists (36.60) is within .035 years. When I controlled for marital status (married) and household size (3 or more), I discovered a drop in the percentage that travel from 66.7% to 50%. Both respondents who mentioned cycling as a stress release are married and in a larger household. By the same token, there was almost perfect agreement between these age and marital status subgroups and the entire sample on the two most popular reasons for competing, enjoyment of competition and enjoyment of the training process.

18   Splitting the group on the basis of level of education showed that 90% of those with no college degree traveled 50 miles to a race at least once. But only 1 (10%) mentioned racing for fun and only 1 (10%) mentioned racing for health benefits while 40% mentioned competing to achieve personal goals. Health (40%) and fun (31%) were both more important among those with a college degree while achievement of personal goals was relatively less important (13.6%).

[The discussion continues with a critique of the survey and its administration. The writer raises questions about the representativeness of the sample and the timing of the questionnaire's administration. He also discusses some problems with the phrasing of individual questions.]

Continues discussion of relationships discovered through analysis of results

Cyclists   11

Conclusions

19   This study had three goals: to describe the group being studied, to test the viability of two hypotheses, and to formulate additional hypotheses. The survey responses provide a rough but interesting description of competitive cyclists and suggest that the group deserves further study.

20   Of the two proposed hypotheses, the one regarding the level of women's participation seems likely to be supported by further research. This research also needs to look at the reasons for the relatively low level of women's participation, perhaps beginning with the literature suggesting that women in general tend to depend on diet rather than exercise to control weight. Questions of body image and the difficulty of cycling while overweight may also be worth considering. Other factors having nothing to do with weight may be significant. For instance, women may be drawn to mountain biking more than bicycle racing because of more equitable distribution of sponsorships, media coverage, and prize money (Meyer, 1997). Also, women may perceive road training for bicycle racing as more hazardous than other sporting activities (Zimberoff, 1996).

21   The second hypothesis regarding "love of pain" as a reason for cycling received little support from the data. This response was not even among the top 10 on the questionnaire.

52e
APA

Discusses whether the research supports hypotheses or answers guiding questions

|

Sums up goals of research and contributions to discussion of the subject

Might consider whether family responsibilities limit women's participation

52e
APA

Cyclists   12

Suggests
directions
for further
research

22   Several new hypotheses emerged during the study.
One deals with the low number of male competitors
under 25 years of age. It may be the case that the
health and weight concerns of men under 25 and the
benefits of competitive cycling are contradictory.
Some hypotheses regarding reasons for competing seem
worth considering. It may be that people of different
ages, marital status, and education levels have
considerably different reasons for undertaking the
same activity, in this case, racing a bicycle. These
questions are certainly worth further study.

List sources
alphabetically
by last name
of author

Center heading   Cyclists   13

References

Page
numbers
continue

Coyle, E. F., Coggan, A. R., Hopper, M. K., & Walters,

Additional
lines
indented five
spaces, like
paragraphs

T. J. (1988). Determinants of endurance in well-
trained cyclists. *Journal of Applied Physiology,*
64, 2622-2630.

Double-
space all
entries

David, C., & Cowles, M. (1991). Body image and
exercise. *Sex Roles, 25,* 33-34.

First line
of entry
not
indented

Drewnowski, A., & Yee, D. K. (1987). Men and body
image: Are males satisfied with their body weight?
Psychosomatic Medicine, 49, 626-634.

Interbike 1992 directory. (1992). Costa Mesa, CA:
Primedia.

List
source
with no
author by
title

Matheny, F. (1986, February 5). Solo cycling. *Volo News*, 157.

Meyer, J. (1997). Alison Sydor, cyclist, on equity in cycling. Reprinted from *ACTION*, Winter 1994. Canadian Association for the Advancement of Women and Sport and Physical Activity. Retrieved November 9, 1998 from http://www.makeithappen.com/wis/readings/insydor.htm

Schneider, D., & Greenberg, M. (1992). Choice of exercise: A predictor of behavioral risks. *Research Quarterly for Exercise and Sport, 9*, 231-245.

Worthington, R. G. (1998). Labor power racing: Lung busters, leg breakers. [Announcement posted on the World Wide Web]. Washington, DC. Author. Retrieved November 9, 1998 from http://www.mesothel.com/pages/labpower.htm

Zimberoff, B. F. (1996). Ocean to ocean on two wheels: Harassment on the road. *Armchair World NetEscapes*. Retrieved November 9, 1998 from http://www.armchair.com/escape/bike7.html

52e
APA

52e
APA

Add A, B, and so on to heading if more than one appendix

Center heading and name of figure or material

Cyclists   15

Page numbers continue

Appendix

Survey

Please take a minute or two to answer the following questions for a University of Rhode Island study of demographics and motivation of competitive athletes.

1. Sex (circle one) Male Female

2. Date of birth (month/day/year) __/__/__

3. Marital status (circle one)

   Married   Single   Divorced   Widowed   Other

4. Number of people in your household (circle one)

   1   2   3   4   5   6 or more

5. Education level (circle one)

   Haven't finished high school

   High school or equivalency degree

Use clear material, retyped or redrawn if necessary

   Associate degree

   Bachelor's degree

   Master's degree

   Doctoral degree

6. In regard to family income, attitudes, and values, how do you view your social status? (circle one)

   Lower class   Lower middle class

   Middle middle class Upper middle class

   Upper class

7. How do you rate yourself as a competitive cyclist? (circle one)

   Beginner   Intermediate   Advanced   Expert

52e
APA

8. How many years have you been involved in
   competitive cycling? _____

9. Have you traveled more than 50 miles one way to
   enter a bike race, triathlon, or biathlon during
   1992? (circle one) Yes   No
   If you answered yes to the above question,
   approximately how many times did you travel that
   far to enter an event? _____

10. Please list a few (3 to 5) reasons why you enter
    competitive cycling events (including biathlons
    and triathlons).

    I. _____

   II. _____

  III. _____

   IV. _____

    V. _____

    Thank you very much for completing this survey.
                    RIDE FAST!

CHAPTER 53

DOCUMENTING SOURCES: SCIENCE (CSE) AND ENGINEERING

You are preparing a paper in a course in engineering, the sciences, or a technical field. You ask the instructor, "What documentation style should I use for references?" The answer is likely to be either "Use a scientific style" or "Look at the professional journals you've been consulting and follow the style they recommend."

This doesn't sound like much guidance, but it is if you can do three things.

1. Recognize situations calling for scientific or engineering documentation (see below).
2. Recognize the general elements of scientific and engineering style (see 53a).
3. Analyze and understand the documentation style used in a particular scientific, engineering, or technical publication (see 53b).

Students are not the only people who need these skills. Scientists, engineers, technicians, and technical writers also need to be able to choose a documentation style appropriate for a writing situation. Fortunately, some resources are available, though their influence is not as widespread nor as uniform as that of the manuals outlining MLA and APA styles (see Chapters 51 and 52).

The manual endorsed by the Council of Science Editors (formerly the Council of Biology Editors) outlines a general scientific style known as CSE (CBE) style: *Scientific Style and Format: The CBE Manual for Authors, Editors, and Publishers* (6th ed., 1994). The style endorsed by the American Chemical Society is used or adapted widely in engineering, technical, and scientific publications: *The ACS Style Guide: A Manual for Authors and Editors*, ed. Janet S. Dodd (2nd ed., 1997). Some widely used engineering style guides include the following.

ASCE [American Society of Civil Engineers] *Author's Guide to Journals, Books, and Reference Publications*

"Information for IEEE Transactions and Journal Authors,"
http://www.iee.org/organizations/pubs/authors.html

USE A SCIENTIFIC OR ENGINEERING STYLE (IN SOME VARIATION) IN . . .

ACADEMIC SETTINGS

When writing in scientific fields such as biology, chemistry, physics, and related sciences

When writing in engineering fields, including civil, chemical, computer, electrical, biomedical, industrial, or mechanical engineering

When writing in technical and medical fields such as animal science, environmental management, food science, horticulture, medical technology, or nursing

WORK AND PUBLIC SETTINGS

When addressing scientific, engineering, or technical issues for an audience that is reasonably expert in the field and expects you to provide current scientific knowledge

When writing for professional groups or company divisions that expect use of scientific or engineering documentation or require CSE, ACS, or a similar documentation style

---

53a Recognizing elements of scientific and engineering styles

As is the case with other documentation styles, including MLA (Ch. 51) and APA (Ch. 52), scientific and engineering styles contain those kinds of information important for locating a source and presenting them in ways appropriate to a particular discipline or kind of publication.

1 In-text citations

In-text references in scientific and engineering writing take two forms. With the **number method**, numbers, either within parentheses (7) or as superscript figures raised above the line,[7] refer to numbered items in a reference list at the end of the text. The number method saves space (always at a premium in scientific and engineering publications, which are often expensive to publish). It does not disrupt reading, unless the reader decides to turn to the reference list to identify the source. It allows a writer to cite multiple sources (a common practice) in a brief space, for example, (1–3, 5, 7). Yet the number system does not enable readers to identify the author or recency (date) of a source without interrupting their reading.

With the name-and-date method, the name of the author or authors appears in the text along with the date of publication (both generally in parentheses, but not always, see 53b). Without stopping to consult the reference list, therefore, readers can identify how recent the source is and may recognize the particular source from the author's name if they are familiar with work in the field. Name-and-date citations take more space, however, and they can disrupt reading, especially when a citation refers to two or more sources.

2 Reference list

Coming at the end of a text, a reference list provides information necessary to identify a source. This information generally includes the following.

- Author(s) name(s)
- Title of work or article
- Title of publication containing an article
- Publication information (for books—city, publisher, and date of publication; for articles—date, volume and issue number, and page numbers)
- Number of pages (total) (for books) or specific pages used as source
- Electronic address and date of access (for electronic sources)

Entries in a reference list are arranged either alphabetically (to correspond with name-and-date citations) or according to the order of citation in the text (to correspond with number citations).

The form and order of the elements in a reference list may vary slightly according to documentation style.

CSE/CBE

BOOK   Simpson HN. Invisible armies; the impact of disease on American history. Indianapolis: Bobbs-Merrill; 1980. 239 p.

ARTICLE   Yousef YA, Yu LL. Potential contamination of groundwater from Cu, PB, and Zn in wet detention ponds receiving highway runoff. J Environ Sci Hlth 1992;27:1033-44.

ACS

BOOK   Dresselhaus, M.S.; Dresselhaus, G.; Eklund, P.C. *Science of Fullerenes and Carbon Nanotubes;* Academic: New York, 1996; pp 126-141.

ARTICLE   Hill, M.; Fott, P. Kinetics of gasification of Czech brown coals. *Fuel* 1993, *72,* 525-529.

53b Analyzing the documentation style of a publication

Many research publications in science and engineering include guidelines for authors preparing manuscripts for submission, generally with titles like "Information for Authors" or "Editorial Policy and Manuscript Preparation Guidelines." These sections usually contain detailed advice about presenting citations and references, including examples, which you can also supplement by looking for examples in the publication itself.

Here is particularly detailed and helpful advice published in the *Journal of the Air & Waste Management Association.*

> References must be formatted according to the first reference style listed in the *ACS Style Guide* on p. 173; that is, in consecutive order as they are cited within the text, using Arabic numeral superscripts (do not use the author-date format). Do not use an automatic footnoting or referencing function in word processing. Do not use "et al." in references unless there are more than 10 authors; rather, list all authors for each reference. At a minimum, all references should include author, title, publisher, place, year, volume and issue number, and page numbers. Examples of reference styles include the following:
>
> 1. Carson, M.A.; Atkinson, K.D.; Waechter, C.J. An Analysis of Leachate in Groundwater; *J. Biol. Chem.* 1982, *257,* 8115-8121.
> 2. Bockris, J.O.; Reddy, A.K.N. *Modern Electrochemistry;* Plenum: New York, 1970; Vol. 2, p 132.
> 3. Geactinov, N.E. In *Polycyclic Hydrocarbons and Carcinogenesis;* Harvey, R.G., Ed.; ACS Symposium Series 283; American Chemical Society: Washington, DC, 1985; pp 12-45.
> 4. Kanter, H. Ph.D. Dissertation, University of Arizona, December 1984.
> 5. U.S. Environmental Protection Agency. *Quality Control for Pesticides and Related Compounds;* EPA-600/1-79/008; U.S. Government Printing Office: Washington, DC, 1979.
> 6. Roe, A.B. *J. Pharm. Sci.,* in press. [this means that the article has been accepted for publication]
> 7. Roe, A. B. *J. Pharm. Sci.,* submitted for publication.
> 8. Urdal, K.; Fallon, J.D. Structure and Reactivity of Surfaces. In *Proceedings of the 80th Annual Meeting of the A&WMA,* Denver, CO, June 5-8, 1994; pp 173-204.
>
> Authors should look to previous issues of the *Journal,* as well as *The ACS Style Guide,* for reference styles not listed above.

For books, technical reports, and documents not providing guidelines, or for articles photocopied from a journal, consult the text itself for examples of citation and reference style. The following examples are from an article in

IEEE Transactions on Knowledge and Data Engineering titled "Main Memory Database Systems: An Overview" by Hector Garcia-Molina and Kenneth Salem.

IMS, one of the earliest database systems, recognized these access differences, and has provided two systems in one for many years: Fast Path [9] for memory resident data, and conventional IMS for the rest. A recent paper by Stonebraker [25] also discusses some of the issues involved in multilevel database systems and data migration.

References

[9]   D. Gawlick and D. Kinkade, "Varieties of concurrency control in IMS/VS Fast Path," *Data Eng. Bull.,* vol. 8, no. 2, pp. 3-10, June 1985.

[25] M. Stonebraker, "Managing persistent objects in a multi-level store," in *Proc. ACM SIGMOD Conf.,* Denver, CO, May 1991, pp. 2-11.

53c Creating scientific in-text citations (CSE/CBE)

This section and the next, covering a scientific reference list, provide examples in CSE/CBE style. For examples in ACS style, see 53b.

1 Using the name-and-date method

With this method, you include the name of the author or authors along with the publication date of the text. If you do not mention the author's name in the paper itself, include both the name and the year in parentheses; if you do mention the name, include only the year.

PARENTHETICAL REFERENCE

Decreases in the use of lead, cadmium, and zinc in industrial products have resulted in a "very large decrease in the large-scale pollution of the troposphere" (Boutron and others 1991, p 64).

AUTHOR NAMED IN TEXT

Boutron and others (1991) found that decreases in the use of lead, cadmium, and zinc in industrial products have resulted in a "very large decrease in the large-scale pollution of the troposphere" (p 64).

If you cite several works by the same author, all of which appeared in a single year, use letters (*a, b,* and so forth) after the date to distinguish them.

ONE OF SEVERAL APPEARING IN THE SAME YEAR

Decreases in the use of lead, cadmium, and zinc in industrial products have resulted in a "very large decrease in the large-scale pollution of the troposphere" (Boutron and others 1991a, p 64).

2 Using the number method

With this method, you use numbers instead of names of authors. The numbers can be placed in parentheses in the text or raised above the line as superscript figures. The numbers correspond to numbered works in your reference list. There are two ways to use the number method. In one style, you number your in-text citations consecutively as they appear in your paper and arrange them accordingly on the reference page.

Decreases in the use of lead, cadmium, and zinc in industrial products have reduced pollution in the troposphere (1).

In the second style, you alphabetize your references first, number them, and then refer to the corresponding number in your paper. Since only the number appears in your text, make sure you mention the author's name if it is important.

53d Creating a scientific reference list (CSE/CBE)

You may use "Cited References" or just "References" as the heading for your reference list. If your instructor asks you to supply references for all your sources, not just the ones cited in your text, prepare a second list called "Additional References," "Additional Reading," or "Bibliography."

The order of the entries in your reference list should correspond to the method you use to cite them within your paper. If you use the name-and-date method, for example, alphabetize the references according to the last name of the main author or by date of publication for works by the same author(s).

If you use the consecutive number method, the reference list will not be alphabetical but will be arranged according to which work comes first in your paper, which second, and so forth. If you use the alphabetized number method, arrange your list alphabetically, and then number the entries.

Following are some examples of the most commonly used formats for entries. Refer to *Scientific Style and Format: The CBE Manual* for further examples of documentation.

GUIDE TO CBE FORMATS FOR REFERENCES

1. BOOKS AND WORKS TREATED AS BOOKS

1. One Author
2. Two or More Authors
3. Corporate or Group Author
4. Editor
5. Translator
6. Conference Proceedings
7. Technical Report

2. ARTICLES AND SELECTIONS FROM BOOKS

8. Article in Journal Paginated by Volume
9. Article in Journal Paginated by Issue
10. Article with Corporate or Group Author
11. Entire Issue of Journal
12. Figure from Article
13. Selection in Anthology or Collection

3. ELECTRONIC RESOURCES

14. Patent from Database or Information Service
15. Online Article
16. Online Book
17. Online Abstract
18. CD-ROM Abstract

---

1 Books and works treated as books

Formats for entries for the name-and-date method and the number method are the same except for the location of the year. The sample entries for a reference list follow the style for the number method, but model formats are shown for both methods.

MODEL FORMAT FOR BOOKS AND WORKS TREATED AS BOOKS

NAME-AND-DATE METHOD

```
           period +   period +
             space      space        period + space
               ↓          ↓                  ↓
Author(s). Date. Title of work. Place of
Publication: Publisher. Total pages.
                  ↑            ↑
           colon + space  period + space
```

NUMBER METHOD

period +   period +   period +
  space   space   space
   ↓   ↓   ↓

```
1.  Author(s). Title of work. Place of
    Publication: Publisher; Date. Total pages.
```

↑   ↑   ↑
colon   semicolon period +
+ space   + space   space

- **Author(s).** Give the author's name in inverted order, beginning with the last name and followed by *the initials only* (without periods or spaces) of the first and middle names, concluding with a period and a space. For more than one author, follow the same pattern for each author, and separate the names with a comma followed by a space. (Some scientific publications use full names for authors; check if this style is required for your paper.) If no author is given, begin with the word *Anonymous* in brackets.
- **Title of work.** Give the title followed by a period and a space. Do not underline the title, and capitalize only the first word and proper nouns or adjectives. Do not capitalize the subtitle following a colon.
- **Publication information.** Indicate the city, publisher, and date of publication. Put a colon after the city and a semicolon after the publisher. Conclude with a period. To avoid confusion between two cities with the same name or to identify cities likely to be unfamiliar, place a comma and a space after the city and include the abbreviated name of the state or the country.
- **Total pages.** Supply the total number of pages in the work, including the index, but do not add in any preliminary pages with Roman numerals.
- **Spacing.** Double-space your entries. For the name-and-date method, do not indent any lines. For the number method, begin the second and any later lines underneath the beginning of the opening word in the first line. If your instructor gives you other spacing directions, follow these carefully.

1. One author

```
1.  Bishop RH. Modern control system analysis and design using
    MATLAB. Reading: Addison-Wesley; 1993. 239 p.
```

2. Two or more authors

List each author's last name first, and use commas to separate the authors.

```
2.  Freeman JM, Kelly MT, Freeman JB. The epilepsy diet
    treatment: an introduction to the ketogenic diet. New
    York: Demo; 1994. 180 p.
```

3. Corporate or group author

Treat an organization or government agency responsible for a work as you would an individual author. If the author is also the publisher, include the name in both places. You can use an organization's acronym in place of the author's name if the acronym is well known.

> 3. Intergovernmental Panel on Climate Change. Climate change 1995: the science of climate change. Cambridge: Cambridge University Press; 1996. 179 p.

4. Editor

Identify the editor(s) by including the word *editor(s)* (spelled out) after the name.

> 4. Bandy AR, editor. The chemistry of the atmosphere: oxidants and oxidation in the earth's atmosphere. Cambridge: Royal Society of Chemistry; 1995. 437 p.

5. Translator

Give the translator's name after the title, followed by a comma and the word *translator.* If the work has an editor as well, place a semicolon after the word *translato*r and then name the editor and conclude with the word *editor.* Give the original title at the end of the entry after the words *Translation of* and a colon.

> 5. Jacob F. The logic of life: a history of heredity. Spillmann BE, translator. New York: Pantheon Books; 1982. 348 p. Translation of: Logique du vivant.

6. Conference proceedings

Begin with the name of the editor(s) and the title of the publication. Indicate the name, year, and location of the conference, using semicolons to separate the information. Include the total number of pages at the end. You need not name the conference if the title does so.

> 6. Witt I, editor. Protein C: biochemical and medical aspects. Proceedings of the International Workshop; 1984 Jul 9-11; Titisee, Germany. Berlin: De Gruyter; 1985. 195 p.

7. Technical report

Treat a report as you would a book with an individual or corporate author, but include the total number of pages after the publication year. If the report is available through a particular agency—and it usually is—include the information a reader would need to order it. The report listed here can be

obtained from the EPA department mentioned using the report number
EPA/625/7-91/013. Enclose a widely accepted acronym for an agency in
brackets following its name.

> 7. Environmental Protection Agency (US) [EPA]. Guides to
> pollution prevention: the automotive repair industry.
> Washington: US EPA; 1991; 46 p. Available from: EPA Office
> of Research and Development; EPA/625/7-91/013.

2 Articles and selections from books

MODEL FORMAT FOR ARTICLES AND SELECTIONS

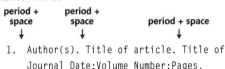

NAME-AND-DATE METHOD

period +   period +
  space   space   period + space
   ↓   ↓   ↓
Author(s). Year. Title of article. Title of
    Journal Volume Number:Pages.

         ↑   ↑
       space   colon + no space

NUMBER METHOD

period +   period +
  space   space   period + space
   ↓   ↓   ↓
1. Author(s). Title of article. Title of
    Journal Date;Volume Number:Pages.

        ↑   ↑   ↑
     space semicolon   colon +
            + no space   no space

- **Author(s).** Give the author's name in inverted order, beginning with
  the last name and followed by the initials only (without periods or
  spaces) of the first and middle names, concluding with a period and a
  single space. For more than one author, follow the same pattern for
  each author, and separate the names with a comma followed by a space.
  If no author is given, begin with *Anonymous*, placed in brackets.
- **Title of article and publication information.** Give the article name,
  journal name, date, volume number and issue number (in parentheses), and page numbers. Do not enclose the article title in quotation
  marks or underline the journal title. Capitalize only the first word and
  any proper nouns in an article's title; do not capitalize the first word in
  a subtitle. For journal titles, follow regular capitalization rules, but use
  abbreviations standard in the field. Conclude the title of the article
  with a period and a space. Place a space but no punctuation between
  the title of the journal and the date. Do not include a space before or
  after the colon separating the volume number from the page numbers
  or between volume and issue numbers.

53d
CSE

- **Pages.** Include the specific pages of the article or chapter.
- **Journal title (abbreviated).** Always abbreviate a journal title unless it is a one-word title. To find out how to abbreviate titles, notice the abbreviations used in your sources and ask your instructor which book lists abbreviations for your field.
- **Spacing.** Double-space all entries. Do not indent the first line or any subsequent lines (name and year); align second and later lines under the beginning of the initial word of the first line.

8. Article in journal paginated by volume

```
8.  Yousef YA, Yu LL. Potential contamination of groundwater
    from Cu, Pb, and Zn in wet detention ponds receiving
    highway runoff. J Environ Sci Hlth 1992;27:1033-44.
```

9. Article in journal paginated by issue

Give the issue number within parentheses immediately (with no space) after the volume number.

```
9.  Boutron CF. Decrease in anthropogenic lead, cadmium and
    zinc in Greenland snows since the late 1960s. Nature
    1991;353(6340):153-5, 160.
```

10. Article with corporate or group author

Treat the corporate or group author as you would any author. If a person's name is part of the corporation, as in this example, do not transpose the first and last names. Alphabetize by the first main word in the corporation name, even if it is a first name.

```
10.  Derek Sims Associates. Why and how of acoustic testing.
     Environ Eng 1991;4(1):10-12.
```

11. Entire issue of journal

Include the title of the main editor or compiler of the specific issue, because this person will often be a guest editor.

```
11.  Savage A, editor. Proceedings of the workshop on the zoo-
     university connection: collaborative efforts in the
     conservation of endangered primates. Zoo Biol 1989;1(Suppl).
```

12. Figure from article

Include the title of the figure (or table, chart, or diagram) and its number, as well as the page on which it appears. Use *p* in this context.

12. Kanaori Y, Kawakami SI, Yairi K. Space-time distribution patterns of destructive earthquakes in the inner belt of central Japan. Engng Geol 1991;31(3-4):209-30 (p 216, table 1).

53d
CSE

13. Selection in anthology or collection

The first name and title refer to the article; the second name and title refer to the book from which the article is taken. Include the page numbers of the article at the end of the citation.

13. Moro M. Supply and conservation efforts for nonhuman primates. In Gengozian N, Deinhardt F, editors. Marmosets in experimental medicine. Basel: S. Karger AG; 1978. p 37-40.

3 Electronic resources

14. Patent from database or information service

The sample below, from the inventors' names through the date, illustrates how to cite a patent. In this instance, information about electronic access is added at the end.

14. Collins FS, Drumm ML, Dawson DC, Wilkinson DJ, inventors. Method of testing potential cystic fibrosis treating compounds using cells in culture. US patent 5,434,086. 1995 Jul 18. Available from: Lexis/Nexis/Lexpat library/ALL file.

15. Online article

15. Grolmusz V. On the weak mod m representation of Boolean functions. Chi J Theor Comp Sci Internet 1995 [cited 1996 May 3] 1995;100-5. Available from: http://www.csuchicago.edu/publication/cjtcs/articles/1995/2/contents.html

16. Online book

16. Darwin C. 1859. On the origin of species by means of natural selection, or the preservation of favoured races in the struggle for life [book online]. London: Down, Bromley, Kent. Available from: ftp://sailor.gutenberg.org/pub/gutenberg/etext98/otoos10.txt via the World Wide Web. Accessed 1999 Feb 12.

53d
CSE

17. Online abstract

Use a form similar to that for journal articles, but give the word *abstract* in brackets following the title.

> 17. Smithies O, Maeda N. Gene targeting approaches to complex
>   genetic diseases: atherosclerosis and essential
>   hypertension [abstract]. Proc Natl Acad Sci USA
>   [Internet]. 1995 [cited 1996 Jan 21]; 92(12):5266-72. 1
>   screen. Available from: Lexis/Medline/ABST.

18. CD-ROM abstract

Indicate the medium (*CD-ROM*) in brackets following the title. Close the entry with the phrase *Available from*, followed by information about the source and retrieval number.

> 18. MacDonald R, Fleming MF, Barry KL. Risk factors associated
>   with alcohol abuse in college students. Am J Drug and Alc
>   Abuse [CD-ROM];17:439-49. Available from: SilverPlatter
>   File: PsycLIT Item: 79-13172.

53.2

Exercise

A. Turn to Exercise A in Chapter 51. Rewrite the sentences supplied there to add either form of in-text citations in CSE or ACS style. Prepare a corresponding list of references.

B. Turn to Exercise B in Chapter 51. Rewrite the items supplied there to create a list of references following either form used in CBE or ACS style.

C. Working with a partner or a small group, compare your answers to Exercises A and B above. Correct any errors in your answers, using your handbook or your instructor's advice to resolve any differences of opinion.

CHAPTER 54

DOCUMENTING SOURCES: CMS

The documentation style outlined in *The Chicago Manual of Style* (the CMS style) provides references in the form of endnotes or footnotes. Endnotes or footnotes are signaled by a superscript numeral in the text (for example,[1]) and a correspondingly numbered reference note at the end of the paper (an endnote) or, less often, at the bottom of the page (a footnote). A bibliography at the end of the paper provides a list of all the sources in alphabetical order. Endnotes and footnotes are less compact than parenthetical references, yet they offer you a chance to cite a source in more specific detail and to include brief explanatory material. Readers especially interested in your sources will find themselves repeatedly turning away from the text itself to consult the notes, however.

USE CMS STYLE IN . . .

ACADEMIC SETTINGS

When writing papers in history and some other fields in the arts and sciences (check with your instructor)

When writing for publications and professional groups requiring use of CMS style or a footnote/endnote style

When writing papers for an instructor who requests documentation using "Turabian" or "Chicago Manual" style or who asks for footnotes or endnotes

WORK AND PUBLIC SETTINGS

When the audience you are addressing expects you to use footnotes/endnotes or when other writers addressing the audience generally use footnotes or endnotes

54.1

CONSIDER USING CMS STYLE (PERHAPS IN A MODIFIED FORM) IN . . .

WORK AND PUBLIC SETTINGS

When you do not wish to distract readers by including authors' names, page numbers, or dates of your sources throughout the text and when you recognize that your readers will not find it necessary to consult every note as they read

54a Using endnotes and footnotes

To indicate a reference in the body of your text, insert a number slightly above the line[2], making sure you number the references consecutively. Insert a number to indicate a reference to the source of a quotation, to alert readers to specific information and ideas borrowed from a source, or to specify the source of paraphrased or summarized material (see Chapter 49). At the end of the paper (in an endnote) or at the bottom of the page (in a footnote), provide detailed information about the source.

TEXT OF PAPER   To emphasize how isolated and impoverished his childhood neighborhood was, Wideman describes it as being not simply on "the wrong side of the tracks" but actually "under the tracks, if the truth be told--in a deep hollow between Penn and the abrupt rise of Bruston Hill."[1]

NOTE   1. John Edgar Wideman, *Brothers and Keepers* (New York: Penguin Books, 1984), 39.

1 Select endnotes or footnotes

Positioning footnotes between the body of the text and the bottom margin can be quite difficult and time-consuming. For this reason, even though it may be a bit easier for readers to look at the bottom of the page for a note than to turn to the end of the paper, you should generally employ endnotes. Most readers mark the page containing the endnotes so they can refer to notes with a minimum of disruption. Because readers may sometimes skip consulting a note unless they are particularly interested in your sources, you should make sure that you place all information necessary for understanding your argument or explanation in the body of your paper and not in the notes.

2 Consider content and explanatory notes

At times you may wish to supplement your text with material that may interest only a few readers. Notes are an appropriate place to do this, but don't make notes so detailed that they distract readers from the main text of the paper. You can also combine explanation with a source reference, though you need to make sure that a long and detailed discussion does not obscure the reference.

TEXT OF PAPER   Another potential source of conflict, or at least misunderstanding, in the contemporary workplace comes from differences in the ways men commonly give orders (directly) and the ways women give orders (indirectly, often in the form of requests or questions).[2]

NOTE   2. Deborah Tannen, "How to Give Orders Like a Man," *New York Times Magazine*, 18 August 1994, 46. It is sometimes easy to oversimplify the differences between the ways men and women use language. Tannen provides a detailed and balanced discussion in *Talking from 9 to 5* (New York: William Morrow, 1994).

54b Creating CMS notes

After you have placed a number slightly above the line of text[3] to indicate the presence of an endnote or footnote and have made sure that your numbering system maintains consecutive order, you need to prepare the note. A typical note provides the author's name in regular order, the title of the work being cited, publication information, and the page number(s).

Place endnotes at the end of a paper, after appendixes but before a bibliography. Supply notes on a separate page with the centered heading "Notes." Indent the first line six spaces. Start the note with the number, followed by a period and a space. Do not indent the second line or any others that follow. Double-space for ease of reading.

GUIDE TO CMS FORMATS FOR NOTES

1. BOOKS AND WORKS TREATED AS BOOKS

1. One Author
2. Two or Three Authors
3. Four or More Authors
4. No Author Given
5. Editor
6. Edition Other Than the First
7. Multivolume Work

2. ARTICLES AND SELECTIONS FROM BOOKS

8. Article in Journal Paginated by Volume
9. Article in Journal Paginated by Issue

1 Books and works treated as books

MODEL FORMAT FOR BOOKS AND WORKS TREATED AS BOOKS

```
         note                  comma
        number               + space    space
          ↓                      ↓         ↓
          1. Author(s), Title (Place of Publication:
    Publisher, Year), Page number(s).
                         ↑
                  comma + space
```

- **Author(s).** Give the name of the author(s) in regular order followed by a comma and a space.
- **Title.** Give the title of the work being cited. Italicize the title of a book and follow the title with a space. (See 39b-2 on capitalization of titles.)
- **Publication information.** Give all publication information within parentheses. Start with the city of publication, followed by a comma and an abbreviation for the state or country if this information is necessary to avoid confusion between two cities with the same name or to identify little-known places. Add a colon and a space then give the publisher's name followed by a comma, a space, and the date of publication. Place a comma followed by a space after the closing parenthesis mark.
- **Page number(s).** Conclude with the specific page numbers containing the information being cited or the passage being quoted, paraphrased, or summarized.

1. One author

1. Ruth Macklin, *Mortal Choices: Ethical Dilemmas in Modern Medicine* (Boston: Houghton Mifflin, 1987), 154.

2. Two or three authors

Separate the names of two authors with *and.* Separate those of three authors with commas as well as *and* before the name of the third author.

2. Mary Knapp and Herbert Knapp, *One Potato, Two Potato . . .: The Secret Education of American Children* (New York: W. W. Norton, 1978), 144.

2. Michael Wood, Bruce Cole, and Adelheid Gealt, *Art of the Western World* (New York: Summit Books, 1989), 206-10.

3. Four or more authors

For works with more than three authors, give the name of the first author followed by *and others.* (Generally, all the names are supplied in the responding bibliography entry.)

3. Anthony Slide and others. *The American Film Industry: A Historical Dictionary* (New York: Greenwood Press, 1986), 124.

4. No author given

If the author is not known, begin the entry with the title.

4. *The Great Utopia: The Russian and Soviet Avant-Garde, 1915-1932* (New York: Guggenheim Museum, 1992), 661.

5. Editor

When a work has an editor, translator, or compiler (or some combination of these), give the name or names after the title preceded by a comma and the appropriate abbreviation, for example, *ed.*, *trans.*, or *comp.*

5. Charles Dickens, *Bleak House,* ed. Norman Page (Harmondsworth, England: Penguin Books, 1971), 49.

Dickens is the author, and Page has prepared the particular edition of the work.

If you wish to emphasize the role of the editor, translator, or compiler, give his or her name at the beginning of the entry.

5. Donald M. Scott and Bernard Wishy, eds., *America's Families: A Documentary History* (New York: Harper & Row, 1982), 177.

The editors are responsible for assembling materials from a variety of sources.

> 5. Robert H. Ferrell, ed., *Dear Bess: The Letters from Harry to Bess Truman 1910-1959* (New York: W. W. Norton, 1983), 71-2.

> **The word *by* with the author's name (*Harry S. Truman*) would be appropriate following the title, but it is not necessary because the author's name appears in the title.**

6. Edition other than the first

Use an abbreviation following the title to indicate the particular edition, for example, *4th ed.* ("fourth edition") or *rev. and enl. ed.* ("revised and enlarged edition").

> 6. John D. La Plante, *Asian Art,* 3d ed. (Dubuque, Iowa: Wm. C. Brown, 1992), 7.

For a work that has been reprinted or appears in a special paperback edition, give information about both the original publication and the reprint.

> 6. Henri Frankfort and others, *The Intellectual Adventure of Ancient Man* (Chicago: University of Chicago Press, 1946; reprint, Chicago: University of Chicago Press, 1977), 202-4 (page citations are to the reprint edition).

7. Multivolume work

A multivolume work can consist of volumes all by a single author (sometimes with different titles for each) or of works by a variety of authors with an overall title. If you are referring to the whole multivolume work, include the number of volumes after the title. To indicate volume and page number for a specific volume, use volume and page numbers separated by a colon and no space. Give the volume number and name for separately titled volumes after the main title and omit the volume number in the page reference.

> 7. Sigmund Freud, *The Standard Edition of the Complete Psychological Works of Sigmund Freud,* trans. James Strachey (London: Hogarth Press, 1953), 11:180.

2 Articles and selections from books

MODEL FORMAT FOR ARTICLES AND SELECTIONS

> 1. Author(s), "Title of Article," *Title of Publication* Volume Number (Date): Page numbers.

- **Author(s).** Give the author's name in regular order.
- **Title.** Put the title of the article or selection in quotation marks. Put a comma inside the closing quotation mark, and leave a space after the quotation mark.
- **Publication information.** Next give the title of the journal or book, italicized, and leave a space after it with no punctuation. Supply the volume number and then the date of publication in parentheses, varying the information and style for different types of publications (see below). Place a colon after the final parenthesis, and leave a space.
- **Page number(s).** Supply the page numbers for the pertinent part of the article or selection.

8. Article in journal paginated by volume

When the page numbers run continuously through the individual issues that make up a volume, give the volume number but do not include the month, season, or number of the individual issue containing the article. Give specific page numbers for the part of the article you are citing. If you wish to refer to the article as a whole, give inclusive page numbers for the entire article, for example, *98–114*.

> 8. C. Anita Tarr, "'A Man Can Stand Up': Johnny Tremain and the Rebel Pose," *The Lion and the Unicorn: A Critical Journal of Children's Literature* 18 (1994): 181.

9. Article in journal paginated by issue

If each issue of a journal begins with page 1, give the volume number followed by a comma, the abbreviation *no.* (for "number"), and the issue number. If the issue is instead identified by month or season, include information just before the year and within the same set of parentheses, for example (*Winter 1994*) or (*February 1996*). Give page numbers for the specific part of the article you are citing or inclusive page numbers for the entire article if you are referring to it as a whole.

> 9. Peter Smagorinsky and Pamela K. Fly, "A New Perspective on Why Small Groups Do and Don't Work," *English Journal* 83, no. 5 (1994): 54–55.

10. Article in popular magazine

Follow the name of the magazine with a comma and the date. Use this order for the date if it includes the day: *25 November 1995*. Place a comma at the end of the date before the page number, and give a page number for the specific part of the article you are citing or inclusive page numbers for the entire article if you are referring to it as a whole.

10. Deborah Tannen, "But What Do You Mean?" *Redbook,*
October 1994, 57-58.

11. Article in daily newspaper

Identify newspaper articles by date (rather than volume number) following the title of the article and the name of the newspaper. Present the date in this order: *4 February 1996.* When the sections of a newspaper are separately paginated, provide the section number or letter and the page number—for example, *sec. B, p. 3*—using *p.* or *pp.* to introduce the page number(s).

11. Debra West, "Stalking Weeds of Spring for Traditional Meals," *New York Times,* 18 May 1995, sec. B, pp. 1, 7.

When an American newspaper's title does not include the city's name, give it at the start of the title (underlined). For less known newspapers, for those outside North America with the city not mentioned in the title, and for those from places easily confused with well-known cities, give the name of the state or country after the title or after the name of the city in the title: *Westerly (R.I.) Sun*; *Times* (London).

12. Chapter in book or selection from anthology

For a selection from an anthology or for a book chapter, give the name of the selection or chapter in quotation marks followed by *in* and the name of book. If the book has an editor, follow the book's title with *ed.* and the editor's name.

12. Fred Pfeil, "'Makin' Flippy-Floppy': Postmodernism and the Baby-Boom PMC," in *Another Tale to Tell: Politics and Narrative in Postmodern Culture* (London: Verso, 1990), 107.
Chapter in a book.

12. W. E. B. Du Bois, "The Call of Kansas," in *W. E. B. Du Bois: A Reader,* ed. David Levering Lewis (New York: Henry Holt, 1995), 173.
Selection from an edited collection of one writer's works.

12. Julie D'Acci, "Defining Women: The Case of Cagney and Lacey," in *Private Screenings: Television and the Female Consumer,* ed. Lynn Spigel and Denise Mann (Minneapolis: University of Minnesota Press, 1992), 169.
Chapter in an edited collection of essays.

3 Field resources
13. Unpublished interview

For unpublished interviews done by someone else, begin with the name of the person interviewed followed by a comma; then give the phrase *interview by*, the name of the interviewer, the date (in this order: *2 May 2001*), any file number, the medium (*tape recording* or *transcript*, for example), and the place where the interview is stored (such as *Erie County Historical Society, Buffalo, New York*). For interviews you conduct, provide the name of the person interviewed, the phrase *interview by author*, a description of the kind of interview, the medium, and the place and date of the interview.

54b
CMS

> 13. Shawon Kelley, interview by author, tape recording, Los Angeles, Calif., 2 May 2000.

> 13. Morton Kosko, telephone interview by author, transcript, Scottsdale, Ariz., 22 January 2002.

4 Media and electronic resources

14. Audio or video recording

Start with the work's title unless the recording features a particular performer, composer, director, or writer. Give names and roles (if appropriate) of performers or others whose participation needs to be noted. Indicate the length of the recording (video), the company responsible, the recording number (audio), the date, and the medium (for example, *audiocassette* or *videocassette*).

> 14. *James Baldwin*, prod. and dir. Karen Thorsen, 87 min., Resolution Inc./California Newsreel, 1990, videocassette.

15. Electronic information service

For information and text you gather through an electronic information service, use whatever format would be appropriate for similar material available in printed form, but at the end of the entry provide the name of the service (such as *Dialog* or *ERIC*), the name of the vendor, and the accession or identifying numbers used by the service.

> 15. Mark Miller, "Two Beaked Whales Wash Up on Beach," *Daytona Beach News-Journal*, 20 January 1994, in Newsbank [database online] [cited 5 March 1995], ENV 3, G6.

16. CD-ROM

Supply information as you would for the print equivalent if it existed. After the title, indicate in brackets the type of medium: *[CD-ROM]*.

> 16. William Shakespeare, *All's Well That Ends Well*. *William Shakespeare: The Complete Works on CD-ROM* [CD-ROM] (Abingdon, England: Andromeda Interactive, 1994).

17. Online book

For a book that has been previously published in print, include all information as required by Entries 1–7. Indicate the medium of the source in brackets following the title: *[book online]*. With the original publication date, give the date you accessed the source. Finally, indicate the URL at which the book is available and the network in brackets: *[Internet]*.

> 17. Charles Darwin, *On the Origin of Species by Means of Natural Selection, or the Preservation of Favoured Races in the Struggle for Life* [book online] (London: Down, Bromley, Kent, 1859 [cited 12 February 1999]); available from ftp://sailor.gutenberg.org/pub/gutenberg/etext98/otoos10.txt; INTERNET.

18. Online article

Include all information required in Entries 8 and 9. Following the publication information, indicate the medium of the source in brackets: *[journal online]*. Indicate the URL at which the book is available and the network in brackets: *[Internet]*. Include the date you accessed the source.

> 18. Aaron Lynch, "Units, Events and Dynamics in Memetic Evolution," *Journal of Memetics--Evolutionary Models of Information Transmission* 2, no. 1 (June 1998) [journal online] [cited 12 February 1999]; available from http://www.cpm.mmu.ac.uk/jom-emit/1998/vol12/lynch_a.html; INTERNET.

5 Multiple sources and sources cited in prior notes

19. Multiple sources

When you wish to cite more than one source in a note, separate the references with semicolons and give the entries in the order in which they were cited in the text.

> 19. See Greil Marcus, *Mystery Train: Images of America in Rock 'n Roll Music* (New York: E. P. Dutton, 1975), 119; Susan Orlean, "All Mixed Up," *New Yorker*, 22 June 1992, 90; and Cornel West, "Learning to Talk of Race," *New York Times Magazine*, 2 August 1992, 24.

20. Book or article cited more than once

The first time you provide a reference to a work, you need to list full information about the source in the note. In later notes you need to provide only the last name of the author(s), a shortened title, and the page(s). Separate these elements with commas.

```
21. Macklin, Mortal, 161.
21. Wood, Cole, and Gealt, Art, 207.
```

If a note refers to the same source as the note before, you can use a traditional scholarly abbreviation, *ibid.* (from the Latin for "in the same place"), for the second note. *Ibid.* means that the entire reference is identical, but if you add a new page reference, the addition shows that the specific page is different.

```
22. Tarr, "'A Man,'" 183.
23. Ibid.
24. Ibid., 186.
```

54c Creating a CMS bibliography

At the end of your paper you need to provide readers with an alphabetical list of the sources cited in your notes. CMS style calls for this list to be titled "Selected Bibliography" or "Sources Consulted" if it includes all the works you consulted. If you want to limit the list to the works appearing in your notes, you might call it "Works Cited," "References," or a similar title.

Place your bibliography on a separate page at the end of your paper, and center the title two inches below the upper edge. Continue the page numbering used for the text. Double-space entries for ease of reading. Do not indent the first line, but indent the second line and any subsequent lines five spaces. Alphabetize the entries according to the authors' last names or the first word of the title, excluding *A, An,* and *The,* if the author is unknown.

GUIDE TO CMS FORMATS FOR BIBLIOGRAPHY ENTRIES

1. BOOKS AND WORKS TREATED AS BOOKS
1. One Author
2. Two or Three Authors
3. Four or More Authors
4. No Author Given
5. Editor
6. Edition Other Than the First
7. Multivolume Work

2. ARTICLES AND SELECTIONS FROM BOOKS
8. Article in Journal Paginated by Volume
9. Article in Journal Paginated by Issue
10. Article in Popular Magazine

1 Books and works treated as books

MODEL FORMAT FOR BOOKS AND WORKS TREATED AS BOOKS

period +   period +   colon +
space   space   space
↓   ↓   ↓
Author(s). *Title*. Place of Publication:
      Publisher, Date.

↑   ↑
indent   comma + space
5 spaces

- **Author(s).** Give the author's last name followed by a comma, then the first and any middle names or initials followed by a period and a space.
- **Title.** Give the title of the work, italicized, ending with a period and space. Capitalize the main words of the title and any subtitle. Do not capitalize *a, an, the,* coordinating conjunctions (such as *and, or,* and *but*), and prepositions. Always capitalize the first and last words of any title or subtitle.
- **Place of publication.** Give the city where the work was published, followed by a comma and an abbreviation for the state or country if necessary to avoid confusion between cities with the same name or to identify little-known places. End with a colon and a space.
- **Publisher.** Give the publisher's name followed by a comma and a single space.
- **Date.** Give the date of publication followed by a period.

1. One author

Macklin, Ruth. *Mortal Choices: Ethical Dilemmas in Modern Medicine.* Boston: Houghton Mifflin, 1987.

54c
CMS

2. Two or three authors

Knapp, Mary, and Herbert Knapp. *One Potato, Two Potato . . . :
The Secret Education of American Children.* New York: W. W.
Norton, 1978.

Wood, Michael, Bruce Cole, and Adelheid Gealt. *Art of the
Western World.* New York: Summit Books, 1989.

3. Four or more authors

Slide, Anthony, Val Almen Darez, Robert Gitt, and Susan Perez
Prichard. *The American Film Industry: A Historical
Dictionary.* New York: Greenwood Press, 1986.

4. No author given

*The Great Utopia: The Russian and Soviet Avant-Garde,
1915-1932.* New York: Guggenheim Museum, 1992.

5. Editor

Dickens, Charles. *Bleak House.* Edited by Norman Page.
Harmondsworth, England: Penguin Books, 1971.

Ferrell, Robert H., ed. *Dear Bess: The Letters from Harry to
Bess Truman 1910-1959.* New York: W. W. Norton, 1983.

Scott, Donald M., and Bernard Wishy, eds. *America's Families: A
Documentary History.* New York: Harper & Row, 1982.

6. Edition other than the first

Frankfort, Henri, H. A. Frankfort, John A. Wilson, Thorkild
Jacobsen, and William A. Irving. *The Intellectual
Adventure of Ancient Man.* Chicago: University of Chicago
Press, 1946. Reprint, Chicago: University of Chicago
Press, 1977.

La Plante, John D. *Asian Art.* 3d ed. Dubuque, Iowa: Wm. C.
Brown, 1992.

7. Multivolume work

Freud, Sigmund. *The Standard Edition of the Complete
Psychological Works of Sigmund Freud.* Translated by James
Strachey. Vol. 11. London: Hogarth Press, 1953.

2 Articles and selections from books

MODEL FORMAT FOR ARTICLES AND SELECTIONS FROM BOOKS

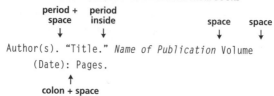

- **Author(s).** Give the author's last name followed by a comma, then the first and any middle names or initials followed by a period and a space.
- **Title.** Give the title of the article within quotation marks, and capitalize the main words of the title and of any subtitle. Do not capitalize *a*, *an*, *the*, coordinating conjunctions (such as *and* and *or*), and prepositions. Always capitalize the first and last words of any title or subtitle. If the article's title contains the title of a work that needs to be italicized or underlined, use underlining; if it contains a title that requires quotation marks, use single quotation marks to enclose the interior title.
- **Name of publication.** Give the title of the journal or magazine containing the article, and italicize it.
- **Volume.** Give the volume number of the periodical; separate it from the name of the publication by a space without a comma or any other punctuation. Include the issue number only for certain kinds of publications.
- **Date.** Provide the year in which the article was published (within parentheses), but indicate the month or season only for certain kinds of publications.
- **Pages.** Follow the parentheses containing the date with a colon and a space; then give the inclusive pages on which the article appears.

8. Article in journal paginated by volume

Tarr, Anita C. "'A Man Can Stand Up': Johnny Tremain and the Rebel Pose." *The Lion and the Unicorn: A Critical Journal of Children's Literature* 18 (1994): 178-89.

9. Article in journal paginated by issue

Smagorinsky, Peter, and Pamela K. Fly. "A New Perspective on Why Small Groups Do and Don't Work." *English Journal* 83, no. 5 (1994): 54-58.

10. Article in popular magazine

Tannen, Deborah. "But What Do You Mean?" *Redbook*, October 1994, 57-58.

11. Article in daily newspaper

West, Debra. "Stalking Weeds of Spring for Traditional Meals."
New York Times, 18 May 1995, sec. B, pp. 1, 7.

12. Chapter in book or selection from anthology

D'Acci, Julie. "Defining Women: The Case of Cagney and Lacey."
In *Private Screenings: Television and the Female Consumer,*
edited by Lynn Spigel and Denise Mann, 169-201.
Minneapolis: University of Minnesota Press, 1992.

Du Bois, W. E. B. "The Call of Kansas." In *W. E. B. Du Bois: A
Reader,* edited by David Levering Lewis, 101-121. New York:
Henry Holt, 1995.

Pfeil, Fred. "'Makin' Flippy-Floppy': Postmodernism and the
Baby-Boom PMC." In *Another Tale to Tell: Politics and
Narrative in Postmodern Culture.* London: Verso, 1990.

3 Other printed and field resources

13. Unpublished interview

Kelley, Shawon. Interview by author. Tape recording. Los
Angeles, Calif., 2 May 2000.

Kosko, Morton. Telephone interview by author. Transcript.
Scottsdale, Ariz., 22 January 2002.

4 Media and electronic resources

14. Audio or video recording

James Baldwin. Produced and directed by Karen Thorsen. 87 min.
Resolution Inc./California Newsreel, 1990. Videocassette.

15. Electronic information service

Miller, Mark. "Two Beaked Whales Wash Up on Beach." *Daytona
Beach News-Journal,* 20 January 1994. Database online.
Available from Newsbank, ENV 3, G6.

16. CD-ROM

Shakespeare, William. *All's Well That Ends Well. William
Shakespeare: The Complete Works on CD-ROM* [CD-ROM].
Abingdon, England: Andromeda Interactive, 1994.

17. Online book

> Darwin, Charles. *On the Origin of Species by Means of Natural Selection, or the Preservation of Favoured Races in the Struggle for Life* [book online] (London: Down, Bromley, Kent, 1859) [cited 12 February 1999]. Available from ftp://sailor.gutenberg.org/pub/gutenberg/etext98/otoos10.txt; INTERNET.

18. Online article

> Lynch, Aaron. "Units, Events and Dynamics in Memetic Evolution." *Journal of Memetics--Evolutionary Models of Information Transmission* 2, no. 1 (1998) [journal online] [cited 12 February 1999]. Available from http://www.cpm.mmu.ac.uk/jom-emit/1998/vol2/lynch_a.html; INTERNET.

5 Multiple sources

19. Multiple sources

When a note lists more than one source, list each one separately in your bibliography, presenting them in alphabetical order among your other sources.

54.2

Exercise

A. Turn to Exercise A in Chapter 51. Rewrite the sentences supplied there to add note numbers in CMS style. Then prepare the corresponding notes for these items.

B. Turn to Exercise B in Chapter 51. Rewrite the items supplied there to create a list of works cited in CMS style.

C. Working with a partner or a small group, compare your answers to Exercises A and B above. Correct any errors in your answers, using your handbook or your instructor's advice to resolve any differences of opinion.

PART 7

Writing Strategies

CHAPTER **55**

WRITING ARGUMENTATIVE PAPERS

If you could prove absolutely, to everyone's satisfaction, that your approach to limiting undergraduate alcohol use (or to waste disposal or the design of a new employee safety program) is the best one, you wouldn't need to argue for your position. You could simply present your conclusion and explain the strong logic and evidence supporting it.

But matters like alcohol use, environmental policy, and business strategy seldom lend themselves to such certainty. Readers (and listeners) will be aware of competing opinions and policies as well as contradictory evidence. They will know that despite their importance, many issues do not allow for absolute answers. This is especially true for value judgments, policy questions, and proposed courses of action. On such questions, members of your audience will probably begin by regarding your opinion as one possibility of many; they will expect you to argue for it with good reasons, logic, evidence, and attention to alternate opinions before they decide to agree with you.

Not all writing is argumentative, of course; much writing aims instead to inform, explain, or share experiences and feelings. Argumentative writing, however, has some specific qualities that set it apart.

- **Argument deals with issues and opinions, not certainties.** It addresses situations in which more than one opinion, interpretation, or course of action is possible.
- **Argument is evaluative.** It takes a stand, presenting and endorsing an outlook, judgment, or opinion.
- **Argument aims at persuasion.** It focuses on reasons, evidence, and values most likely to encourage readers (or listeners) to share an opinion or undertake a proposed action.
- **Argument interacts.** It engages an audience's attitudes and values as well as alternate points of view (pro or con).

55a Recognizing occasions for argument

If you think for a moment of the kinds of writing (and speaking) you may have occasion to do in academic, public, or work settings, you will recognize that much of it is **point driven**, designed to convey and support whatever interpretation, thesis, proposal, or judgment you are offering your audience, and also **argumentative**, designed to persuade readers to share your opinion or perspective rather than a differing point of view.

At the heart of most occasions calling for **argument** is an issue, a topic about which people may hold sharply differing points of view. How you go about building an argument to address an issue may vary from context to context, however. In academic contexts, for example, argumentative writing generally employs forms of expression, reasoning, and evidence appropriate for specific fields of study, such as chemistry, sociology, or literature. (See Chapter 56, "Writing Point-Driven Papers Across the Curriculum," and Chapter 57, "Reading and Writing About Literature," for advice on these kinds of writing.)

In public and work settings, however, as well as in academic texts addressing broad issues, argument takes some relatively general forms, so that developing your ability to recognize public issues can also help you recognize issues (problems) that are worth arguing about for work or academic audiences.

1 Recognizing existing issues

Many arguments you construct will address existing issues. Some, such as gun control or global warming, will have broad relevance; others will be of concern to a specific audience, for example, proposals for a new campus drinking policy or limitations on business or residential development. An existing issue is a matter of ongoing disagreement or of a continuing struggle to find a satisfactory solution or interpretation. Issues of this sort come to you partially formed: other people have already identified the dimensions of disagreement, gathered supporting ideas and information, and taken stances, pro and con.

The presence of so much activity surrounding an issue is generally a sign that it is truly a matter for argument—not a question that can be easily or quickly resolved. The activity also bears witness to the ongoing importance or significance of the questions involved—as long as it is recent activity. Twenty years ago, for example, the policy of requiring deposits on soft drink and beer bottles was widely debated; while the issue is certainly not "resolved" on a national basis, it is no longer a matter of widespread concern or discussion.

List current issues. Keeping in mind the signs of an existing, viable issue—continued disagreement as well as new arguments and counterarguments—you can probably make a list of current issues in varied communities.

	PUBLIC	WORK	ACADEMIC
GENERAL	Genetically altered foods Violence and sex on television	Child care at work Ethnically targeted marketing	Standardized testing Affirmative action in college admissions
LOCAL	A local crusade against a television series	Discipline policies at Abtech's Child-Care Center	Housing regulations at Nontanko River State University

Listing is a good discovery strategy if you are responding to an assignment to prepare a written (or oral) argument about an issue, but it has other uses as well. Listing can help you spot the disagreements or problems that define (or divide) communities; it can help you begin to develop your own responses to the issues.

STRATEGY

Involve yourself in the flow of opinions and ideas surrounding issues.

- **"Talk" to yourself.** In a journal, on a piece of paper, or on a screen, "talk" to yourself about problems, controversies, trends, or ideas that concern you or influence the ways we live. Try making a list, adding to each item a short (one- or two-sentence) summary of at least two different opinions on the subject. To identify and explore different opinions, try adopting different voices in your writing by imagining yourself as a person who has a very different outlook from your usual one.

- **Interview friends, family, or co-workers.** Ask them about questions and problems that concern them and inspire strong opinions. Keep a record of their responses, and add your own ideas. Identify subjects about which there are at least two reasonable and differing opinions. (Issues of limited or local concern—such as oil- versus gas-fired electric generation or possible dredging of a polluted river—may provide a clearer focus and draw more interest than overly broad issues, even ones of global concern.)

- **Read and listen.** Leaf through news and opinion magazines such as *The Nation* and *National Review* or listen to issue-oriented

discussion shows on television and radio. Look at editorials in local and national newspapers (available in your library). Consult
online discussion groups or issue-oriented electronic publications such as *Salon*. List issues interesting to you, and write down
any opposing opinions and important information or ideas.

Exercise 1

A. Using the strategies (described above) for involving yourself in the
flow of opinions and ideas, prepare a list of issues or controversies that
interest you. Choose one, summarize the issue or controversy in a sentence or two, and then summarize the main conflicting opinions (pro
and con), each in a sentence.

B. Working in a group, share your lists of issues. Choose an issue on
someone else's list (other than the issue they have expanded) and expand it in the same manner that you did in Exercise 1A by summarizing the issue and the main conflicting opinions.

2 Recognizing a potential issue

When you focus on a problem others have not identified, offer an
opinion or evaluation likely to be controversial, or propose a change in a
long-agreed-upon policy, you address a potential issue. Though a potential
issue is not yet a focus of argument, you can probably anticipate some members of your audience responding with opposing opinions and contrary proposals that will turn the potential issue into an actual issue.

The strategies you can use to help recognize potential issues are also
techniques of discovery that can deepen your and your audience's understanding of a subject or situation.

STRATEGY

Use these strategies to help recognize potential issues and also as
techniques of discovery that can deepen your and your audience's
understanding of a subject or situation.

- **Review the consequences.** A policy, program, or organization
  often starts out with specific goals. Question and evaluate the consequences of policies or actions as a way of uncovering issues
  worth discussing.

  Have there been unintended consequences? Good or bad?

Has the situation changed? The facts of the matter? Are new responses or conclusions called for?

What problems have appeared? Are there different ways to solve them?

What do participants say about disagreements or problems that emerged? What do outsiders say?

Has the policy or program been successful enough to act as a model for dealing with similar solutions?

- **Question the "taken-for-granted."** The opinions or activity that many people take for granted may mask important disagreements and issues.

Question assumptions. Make a list of some things you think most people take for granted, for example, economic prosperity is good; diesel engines are dirty and polluting. Or make a list of things you think a particular group of people assumes, for example, environmentalists: prosperity increases pollution; regulations lead to cleaner air and water. Then look for contradictions within and among your lists: economic prosperity is good/prosperity increases pollution. Or raise questions about an assumption: Do diesels always pollute? When have regulations made water dirtier?

Question definitions and categories. Use questions to probe taken-for-granted definitions and classifications. People frequently talk and write about "chick flicks," that is, films that appeal to women (*not* men) by focusing on relationships and emotions rather than action. Do men really dislike such films? Do women actually prefer such films to action films or comedies? Are there enough films of other types incorporating the characteristics of "chick flicks" to call into question the existence of the category on its own?

Question evaluations. An evaluation or judgment is an opinion—subject to challenge, of course—and therefore always a potential issue. Raising questions about an evaluation or judgment can help you probe the reasoning behind conclusions and decisions and turn potential issues into real ones:

Opinion: Early decision programs benefit college applicants.
Response: That's what a lot of people say, but really? What about people who need to choose among financial packages? Aren't regular applicants disadvantaged when a large percentage of the spaces in an incoming class are already filled by the time they apply?

Question silence by developing contrasts. An absence of open disagreement does not mean an absence of potential issues. Quite often, people address an issue like the clash between

wildlife and housing developments or discriminatory practices within an institution only when a crisis arises. Try focusing on an organization, community, or policy. Identify a
loosely similar one (two communities with youth sports programs, for example). Use contrasts to identify potential issues.
A seemingly issue-free college athletic administration can
appear as a source of potential controversy when viewed in
contrast with a differently structured, perhaps more successful, program.

- **Offer an evaluation.** When you state a judgment about the
quality of a film, a book, a performance, a policy, a program, or
anything else that can be legitimately evaluated, you create an issue, at least to the extent that you intend for others to share your
opinion and are not simply expressing your personal taste—
which is, of course, a personal statement rather than a subject for
debate.

55a
arg

Exercise 2

A. Use two of the strategies (described above) for identifying potential
issues. Identify at least five potential issues making sure you employ
both of the techniques at least twice. Then summarize each issue in a
sentence or two, and summarize any potentially conflicting opinions
about it in a sentence each.

B. Choose one of the potential issues from your list in Exercise 2A.
Working in a group, present your summary of the issue and then explain briefly why you think an audience should be concerned about it.

3 Recognizing a potential for argument

Your feelings about some things may be so strong that you want to argue with anyone who disagrees with your position. But what if no one really
disagrees? What if no one thinks the subject is worth arguing about?

To have an argument in a formal sense, you must begin with an arguable **issue**, a subject about which your audience can recognize two (or
more) clearly differing, worthwhile opinions. No one, for example, is willing
to say that driving while intoxicated is a good thing; anyone who tried to advance this opinion would be considered foolish, at best. Drunk driving is not
an issue. However, reasonable people disagree about which policies are most
likely to discourage people from driving while intoxicated—strict laws, harsh
punishments, roadblocks, advertising campaigns, door-to-door public infor-

mation programs, programs for high school students, and so on. For most people, this question is certainly an arguable issue, and they would probably be glad to listen to differing opinions in hopes of discovering the best way to deal with the problem.

Use the following questions to help determine whether you have chosen an issue worth arguing about.

55a
arg

1. *Is the issue clearly debatable?* A fact is something about which there can be no debate ("Mice are rodents," "President John F. Kennedy was assassinated on November 22, 1963"). The only facts that can be debated are those that might be reasonably challenged *as* facts. For example, it was widely held as "fact" that peptic ulcers were caused by excess acidity in the diet, and for years treatment involved changes in eating habits, antacids, or acid-inhibiting drugs. New evidence, however, now supports a theory that ulcers are caused by a bacterium able to be treated with antibiotics. The question "Are peptic ulcers caused by diet?" is, in light of this information, a much more debatable issue than the question "Does the earth have a moon?"

2. *Can you explore the issue with something more than pure speculation?* Claims that can't be verified often make for interesting philosophical discussion, but they don't lend themselves fully to argument. The question "Where do we go when we die?" is impossible to answer conclusively and therefore hard to develop into an arguable issue. Statements for which there is only tentative supporting evidence ("There may be life on other planets") also make difficult choices for argument.

3. *Is the issue more than a matter of pure taste or preference?* An author's own values and beliefs need to be supported in argument with sound reasoning or evidence. Statements such as "I hate anything with tomatoes in it" can't be supported with anything more than circular reasoning ("because I hate tomatoes"). However, evaluative statements based on comparisons or analyses, such as those found in reviews (see 56b), can become reasonable supporting evidence for a broader assertion ("The food at Alfredo's Restaurant is highly overrated").

4. *Does the issue avoid assumptions that are so deeply or universally held that they cannot be argued?* Although some of the most important social and political issues of our time seem like good topics for argumentative writing, they may seriously frustrate your composing process. Arguments about topics such as the right to die and capital punishment may invoke systems of belief, including religious belief, that can't be logically debated. Debates between nonreligious students and their fundamentalist peers rarely end in resolution or change—interesting or confrontational though the discussions may be. When you choose a topic, ask yourself whether and how it can be explored through the use of sound reasoning and evidence.

Exercise 3

A. Examine the following five issue statements. Decide which of the issues could be developed into argumentative papers and which would not lend themselves to such development. Explain why.

1. Banning campus visits by environmentally insensitive firms
2. The taste of fresh orange juice
3. The sale of pharmaceuticals (aspirin, sunscreen, condoms, tampons) in campus vending machines
4. Belief in the sacredness of cows
5. The reinstitution of chain gangs (prisoners shackled together at the legs) to do highway work

B. In a small group, compare your analysis of the items in Exercise 3A. Collectively choose two issue statements that would make good argumentative papers.

55b
arg

55b Develop your stance

You construct an argument to help persuade people to accept your opinion. To argue effectively, therefore, you first need a clear idea of your own opinion and of the reasons why you hold it. Even at this early stage, however, thinking about how readers (or listeners) will respond to your reasoning is important. Argument is interactive: to persuade others to accept your perspective, you need to engage their opinions, values, and likely objections.

It is often easy to voice opinions in a lively discussion among friends—if another person disagrees, you can immediately defend or clarify what you have said or you can challenge the person with another point. In written argument (or formal speaking), however, you don't have this luxury. Since readers aren't responding to you "live" (or the audience for a speech isn't interrupting your presentation), you need to anticipate their reactions and counterarguments.

To develop your argumentative stance, you need to do two things.

1. Articulate your opinion along with supporting reasons and information to yourself.
2. Clarify your ideas and supporting evidence through interchange with competing perspectives.

What is crucial is that you do these things through *writing*, especially if your final argument will be written, but also because the act of writing pushes your thinking and reasoning.

STRATEGY

Begin articulating your stance to yourself.

- **Write informally** (perhaps in your journal) about your intuitive reactions to your chosen issue. Does the issue make you feel scornful, pitying, fearful, or outraged? If the issue angers you, exactly what about it makes you angry?
- **List the specific elements of the issue** to which you have responded emotionally, and briefly summarize your responses. Add to this list other points that you may not react to emotionally but that, on an intellectual level, support your first reaction.
- **Identify facts, examples, and ideas** that support your opinions. Also begin thinking about objections to your point of view. If you need to go outside your experience to provide support or to deal with opposing opinions, make a preliminary research plan identifying the kinds of information and ideas you may need to gather.

STRATEGY

Clarify your ideas through interaction with competing perspectives.

- **Read** about the subject, focusing on ways others have defined the issue, on their opinions, on the kinds of support they cite, and on potentially useful information they present.
- **Talk** with people about the issue, gathering their opinions and feelings into an understanding of how perspectives on the subject differ.
- **Listen** to debates in person, on television, or on the radio, and record the differing opinions, supporting ideas or evidence, and counterarguments.
- **Visit** an online discussion group to observe and take note of the varying points of view on an issue as well as the ways participants respond to and counter each others' arguments.

55c Focus on a purpose and create a thesis

As you begin identifying and defining your point of view, try to limit the scope of your argument. If your issue is too broad, you will have a hard time covering it in reasonable space and time and an equally difficult time persuading audiences to agree with you.

Identify your claim. One good way to focus your effort is to ask yourself what kind of **argumentative claim** you plan to make (a **claim** is the opinion you plan to argue for). Do you want to argue that an activity, belief, arrangement, or performance is good or bad (effective or ineffective, healthful or harmful, desirable or undesirable)? If so, you are asking readers (or listeners) to agree with a **value judgment**. Do you want to persuade your audience that a particular course of action ought to be undertaken or avoided? If so, you are asking for agreement on a particular **policy**. Do you want people to agree that a particular explanation is correct or incorrect? If so, you are asking them to endorse or reject an **interpretation**.

55c
arg

Work within your claim. To construct an effective argument, you need to make sure the ideas, supporting information, and organization you choose all help to further your claim. What's more, your claim needs to be relatively specific; after all, when you ask people to agree with you, they will be unlikely to do so unless you can indicate your opinion and purpose clearly and specifically.

STRATEGY

- **Make sure you agree with yourself on the purpose and goals of your argument.** Write a memo to yourself explaining your goals. Use the memo as an opportunity to think out loud and clarify your purpose as you write.

  To: Self
  From: Me
  I find using roadblocks as a way of catching drunk drivers really disturbing. I know it is important to keep drunk drivers off the road, of course. I think this remedy is extreme. I guess what I really want to do is to get my audience to agree that the roadblocks are a violation of civil liberties and should be banned.

- **Revise your claim.** As you construct your argument, bringing together your ideas and evidence to support them, you may decide to modify your argumentative **claim**, that is, the opinion, judgment, or course of action you wish your audience to adopt. A memo to yourself taking into account fresh evidence, new ideas, or counterarguments you have encountered can be a good place to revise and redirect your opinion and the direction of your argument.

To: Self
From: Me
Subject: Roadblocks are effective
Roadblocks violate civil liberties, but the three studies I found
online through NorthernLight.com say that the roadblocks take a
lot of drunk drivers off the road and may reduce accidents. Self,
you've got to deal with this evidence and the arguments for
roadblocks it suggests. Perhaps you can propose an effective
alternative that does not violate civil liberties.

- **Create a clear thesis statement.** An explicit **thesis statement** makes your argumentative claim (opinion or proposal) clear and helps your audience follow your reasoning and evidence.

    Develop a tentative thesis statement as you plan and draft your argument, and revise it as you refine your ideas and evidence. Make sure your thesis statement is not just a general statement of your point of view but an **argumentative thesis** specifying your opinion on an issue. An effective thesis does these things.

1. Identifies a specific issue and your opinion
2. Provides a clear and logical statement of your argumentative claim
3. Suggests a general direction for your argument
4. Indicates any related claims or opinions

Arguments are often complex and involve several closely related claims. Pay special attention to making such relationships clear. For example, imagine that you are working on a thesis statement for your essay arguing that stopping all cars on a highway to search for drunk drivers is a violation of civil liberties, so roadblocks should be replaced with another technique for keeping intoxicated people from driving. You need to recognize that this claim commits you to arguing both a value judgment (roadblocks violate civil liberties) and a policy (another technique for enforcing laws against drunk driving); if you do, you can make sure your thesis (and your essay as a whole) does not blur these points and the evidence you use to support them.

STRATEGY

Create and revise a tentative thesis statement. In a sentence (or at most two sentences) state your argumentative claim (your opinion or proposal) and indicate the general kind of reasoning you will offer to support it.

Suggestion: Try using sentence patterns like "*X* should be altered/ banned/etc. because . . ."; "I propose the following plan/policy/ actions/etc. because . . ."; or "*Y* is inappropriate/ineffective/harmful/ etc. because . . . ."

Next, check specifically whether your tentative thesis blurs your specific purposes for arguing or is illogical.

BLURRED AND ILLOGICAL	Police should stop conducting unconstitutional road-blocks and substitute more frequent visual checks of errat-ic driving to identify people who are driving while intox-icated. **The value judgment and policy proposal are blurred in this thesis statement. In addition, the thesis is potentially illogical because the writer seems to assume that the roadblocks are unconstitutional and does not acknowledge that this value judgment needs to be argued (see "Begging the Question," 55f-5).**

55c arg

Make sure that your thesis either focuses on a single claim or iden-tifies two related claims you will argue in an appropriate order.

SINGLE PROPOSITIONS	Roadblocks used to identify drunk drivers are uncon-stitutional. Police should make more frequent visual checks of errat-ic driving to identify people who are driving while intox-icated.
RELATED PROPOSITIONS	The current practice of using roadblocks to identify drunk drivers is unconstitutional; therefore, police should use an alternative procedure such as instituting more fre-quent visual checks of erratic driving behavior.

A WORD ABOUT SPEAKING

In oral presentations in which you support a position or make an argu-ment, it's important for your audience to know where you stand early on in your remarks. Otherwise they'll have to "figure you out" as you talk, and that can make your presentation either confusing or distracting. It's accept-able for you to state your thesis quite directly if you wish. After a short intro-duction to your topic, for example, you might say, "I hope to show in this presentation why the current practice of using roadblocks to identify drunk drivers is unconstitutional, and what alternatives the police might consider to carry out the important duties of keeping drunk drivers off of our streets."

Exercise 4

A. Examine the following propositions as possible thesis statements for argumentative essays. Decide whether each example provides an adequate thesis, and explain your judgments.

1. The United States should deregulate all mail service in order to increase competition and improve the quality of service.
2. Rap music, which is violent, vulgar, and sexist, should be banned from public consumption, and fines should be imposed on anyone listening to it in public places.
3. The demands for "computer literacy" (knowledge of how to use computers on the job, at home, and in all aspects of public life) will keep increasing with each generation; therefore, public schools should be required to have courses in computer literacy for all students.
4. All Americans select and wear their attire on the basis of a discriminatory class system which, in the schools, distracts students from their education; therefore, we should pass a federal law requiring all students in public schools to wear identical uniforms.
5. Arson is not a crime; it is a mental disease and should be treated as such.
6. If children read when they are growing up, they will become literate.
7. Orange juice tastes better than cranberry juice.
8. Recirculating the hot air from your clothes dryer into your basement during the cold winter months can significantly reduce your heating costs.
9. Humanity's woes began when Eve tasted the forbidden fruit in the Garden of Eden.
10. The telephone resulted in a society less prone to writing, but email will likely lead us right back into the written word as a primary form of communication.

B. In a small group, compare your responses to Exercise 4A. For any propositions that you all agree are inadequate, collaboratively draft a revised proposition that would make an acceptable thesis statement for a short argumentative paper.

55d Develop your reasons and supporting evidence

To encourage readers to agree with your argumentative claim—your opinion, interpretation, or proposal—you need to give them reasons in the form of ideas and evidence that support your proposition.

1 Develop the reasons that support your claim

If you consider your argument from your audience's point of view, the reasoning you use to support your claim is as important as the claim itself. Viewed from this perspective, an argument is a series of reasons that help audience members convince themselves to agree with your point of view and prefer it to competing ones.

STRATEGY

55d
arg

Envision your argument as a claim linked to a series of reasons. One good way to create a link between your claim (opinion) and the reasons supporting it is to envision a working thesis sentence centered on the word *because* (or *since, therefore, consequently,* and the like) followed by the supporting reasons.

CLAIM (IN THE FORM OF A WORKING OR PRELIMINARY THESIS STATEMENT)

Coursework for teacher certification should continue after people have started working as classroom teachers because this approach will be more effective and efficient, because it will help increase the number of new teachers, and because it will help others decide more quickly if teaching is the right career for them.

REASON 1

We learn about a professional skill or activity best while we are also doing it.

[Evidence: compare to examples of medical interships and residencies; examples and charts drawn from research on innovative teacher training programs]

REASON 2

Practicing teachers are often more motivated learners than are pre-service teachers.

[Evidence: information from scholarly article comparing responses of participants in pre-service and in-service courses]

REASON 3

College instructors can design more efficient post- or in-service courses by eliminating the background information pre-service teachers require, leaving time to focus on important issues and the latest research and curriculum resources.

[Evidence: quotations from editorial in magazine dedicated to issues in teaching]

REASON 4

Reducing the amount of time people have to spend before they begin teaching will help increase the number of new teachers available in a time of teacher shortages.

[Evidence: interviews with fellow students; statistics and examples from news reports and online discussion group]

REASON 5

People who decide after teaching for a short time that they have made the wrong career choice will not have spent as much time in coursework and will be able to re-direct their education more easily.

[Evidence: statistics and quotations from online version of report of a state commission on teacher preparation]

REASON 6 (COUNTERARGUMENT)

New teachers will still be capable of doing good work in their first teaching jobs, especially if they are adequately supervised and supported by the schools that hire them.

[Evidence: newspaper reports, interviews with two school superintendents]

55d
arg

2 Think of your argument as reasons *plus* evidence

Reasons alone are seldom enough to convince an audience. They need to be developed with evidence (see the example above) that does a number of things.

- Provides logical justification for the writer's (speaker's) opinions and reasoning
- Encourages audience members to trust the writer's conclusions and proposals
- Enables an audience to understand the reasoning in depth and perhaps draw links between it and their own experiences
- Points out similarities among the values and attitudes underlying the writer's claims or proposals and the values and beliefs of the audience
- Helps readers (listeners) envision a proposed course of action or new policy and regard it as plausible or desirable

3 Draw on varied kinds of evidence

As you explore an issue, examining what others have said about it, pay attention to the ideas and information they use to support their arguments. Think of ways you might acknowledge and incorporate their ideas and details in your own work. Then as you work on your own reasoning, consider the possible sources of support discussed below. Choose those that are most relevant to the reasons supporting your claim and that address most directly your audience's concerns as well as any opposing arguments.

Pay attention to variety and balance in evidence, too. If, for example, all your evidence comes from your own experience, some in your audience might argue that because other people don't share those experiences, your argument is not entirely valid. Try to achieve a balance of facts and statistics, quotations from experts, examples, and personal knowledge.

Examples. Examples drawn from your own experience or from the experiences of others can be among the most persuasive kinds of evidence you can use for support. Events, people, ideas, objects, feelings, stories, images, and texts—all these and similar "instances" can be turned into examples to support a claim and encourage readers to share your point of view.

Relying on examples is something we and our readers do every day. When we are trying to make a decision or form an opinion, we often call to mind our own experiences or those we have read or heard about. Almost without thinking, we then try to decide whether the experiences are representative or unique and whether they apply to the issue or situation we are considering.

In choosing to provide examples in support of an argument, therefore, you need to keep in mind both the readiness of readers to be persuaded by examples and the likelihood that they will approach examples critically. Remember, too, that the power of examples to persuade often rests in the concrete detail a writer provides. Detail serves to illustrate and explain the point being made as well as to support the writer's conclusions.

A fully developed example uses explanation to provide readers with the information they need if they are to come to agree with an opinion or judgment. It uses specific details to help persuade readers of the ethical or emotional importance of a proposition and of its relevance to the reader and to other people. The following extended example does these things by drawing on the writer's experiences.

> I am afraid to grow old—we're all afraid. In fact, the fear of growing old is so great that every aged person is an insult and a threat to the society. They remind us of our own death, that our body won't always remain smooth and responsive, but will someday betray us by aging, wrinkling, faltering, failing. The ideal way to age would be to grow slowly invisible, gradually disappearing, without causing worry or discomfort to the young. In some ways that does happen. Sitting in a small park across from a nursing home one day, I noticed that the young mothers and their children gathered on one side, and the old people from the home on the other. Whenever a youngster would run over to the "wrong" side, chasing a ball or just trying to cover all the available space, the old people would lean forward and smile. But before any communication could be established, the mother would take her child back to the "young" side.
>
> —Sharon Curtin, *Nobody Ever Died of Old Age*

Brief examples often serve more to explain than support, but by providing several related examples, you can often create a cluster of instances with considerable persuasive force, as in the following passage.

> The era of the modern family system had come to an end, and few could feel sanguine about the postmodern family condition that had succeeded it. Unaccustomed to a state of normative instability and definitional crisis, the populace split its behavior from its beliefs.

Many who contributed actively to such postmodern family statistics as divorce, remarriage, blended families, single parenthood, joint custody, abortion, domestic partnership, two-career households, and the like still yearned nostalgically for the *Father Knows Best* world they had lost.

—JUDITH STACEY, "The Family Values Fable"

Quotations and ideas from authorities. By turning to the words or ideas of a recognized authority on a subject or issue, you can add to the reasons for readers to agree with your point of view. After all, we identify people as experts or authorities because we believe that they know more about a subject than we do, and the idea of expertise includes a general willingness to agree with the expert's opinion.

55d
arg

Most readers are nonetheless likely to maintain an intelligently critical attitude toward your use of ideas and quotations from experts. They will expect you to cite generally recognized authorities or to indicate why the person you are citing should be viewed as an authority. They may also reject the perspective of someone whose biases suggest a lack of fairness or balance, particularly if these biases differ from their own. As a result, you may need to present the words or ideas you are citing in ways that make clear that your source is both fair and authoritative, just as the writer of the following passage does.

Another role of the [African-American] family is to pass along different kinds of successful coping strategies against racism. One strategy, the heightened sensitivity to the potential for exploitation by white persons, has been referred to by Grier and Cobbs in *Black Rage* as cultural paranoia. While this heightened sensitivity often has been pathologized by the dominant culture, it is a realistic and adaptive way of approaching situations that have frequently been antagonistic. Hopson and Hopson in *Different and Wonderful* suggest that another important coping strategy and a major source of psychological resilience is reflected in the sharing of African cultural derivatives with children while encouraging them to take pride in their ancestry. In *Long Memory*, Mary Berry and John Blassingame note that each generation of African Americans prepares the next for survival in a society that devalues them by passing along "searing vignettes" about what has preceded them. They view this process as a long collective memory that is in and of itself an instrument of survival.

—BEVERLY GREENE, "African American Families"

Do not expect an authority to do all the work for you. After all, you cite an authority simply to add weight to your own thesis and perspective. You encourage readers to agree with you by pointing out that someone whose opinion carries considerable weight already agrees with you. For this process to be effective, you need to make sure that your words appear along with those of your source. This is important even when you include a quotation because you feel that your source makes a particular point more effectively and persuasively than you can. In the following paragraph, for example, the writer uses the final sentence to make sure readers see how the information he is citing fits his argument.

> Accompanying this modern view of the nuclear family were the sentiments that enlivened it. The first of these was the sentiment, as described by Edward Shorter in *The Making of the Modern Family*, of *romantic love*. Beginning with nineteenth-century individualism, the belief arose that for each of us there is one other individual who was created as our perfect mate. Once we encountered that person, we would know it instantly and proceed to spend the rest of our lives forever "happily-ever-aftering." An essential condition of this romantic ideal was that a young woman would "save" herself for her fated partner. In this romantic context, [her] virginity was a valuable commodity that could be exchanged for a lifelong commitment to the relationship. Romantic love worked to keep couples together even when they were unhappy. **While this ideal was unfortunate for parents in unrewarding relationships, it often benefited children because parents stayed together and usually did not blame the children for the failure of the marriage**.
>
> —David Elkind, "The Family in the Postmodern World"

As you search for examples to support your points, remember the importance of your own writing. No matter how well written your source, readers will ultimately be persuaded by what your own words say rather than by selected statements from someone else.

Detailed information. The range of detailed information available to you on most issues is wide, including statistics, technical information, the results of surveys and interviews, background information, and historical detail. Which of these sources you choose and the role each plays in your writing will depend on the particular issue you are addressing, your point of view, and the views or knowledge of your intended readers. Be alert to these kinds of information as you think about an issue and undertake research, and consider the many different ways you can use the information to support your argument. Here are some examples of different kinds of detailed information used to support an author's thesis.

> Meanwhile, young people find it harder and harder to form or sustain families. According to an Associated Press report of April 25, 1995, the median income of men aged twenty-five to thirty-four fell by 26 percent between 1972 and 1994, while the proportion of such men with earnings below the poverty level for a family of four more than doubled to 32 percent. The figures are even worse for African American and Latino men. Poor individuals are twice as likely to divorce as more affluent ones, three to four times less likely to marry in

55d
arg

the first place, and five to seven times more likely to have a child out of wedlock.

—STEPHANIE COONTZ, "The Way We Weren't"

Visual evidence. Visual evidence is of two kinds: (1) details, facts, and statistics presented in the form of graphs, tables, or other figures, and (2) photographs or drawings that are evidence in themselves. Facts and statistics presented as columns of figures (tables) or in graphs and charts can simplify the presentation of complex evidence. They can also highlight key points. They make evidence easier to understand and more persuasive. For example, comparative data about the relative pace of life in different countries is efficiently summarized in the following table.

55d
arg

55.2

THE PACE OF LIFE IN 31 COUNTRIES			
Country	**Overall Pace of Life**	**Walking Speeds**	**Postal Times**	**Clock Accuracy**
Switzerland	1	3	2	1
Ireland	2	1	3	11
Germany	3	5	1	8
Japan	4	7	4	6
Italy	5	10	12	2
England	6	4	9	13
Sweden	7	13	5	7
Austria	8	23	8	3
Netherlands	9	2	14	25
Hong Kong	10	14	6	14
France	11	8	18	10
Poland	12	12	15	8
Costa Rica	13	16	10	15
Taiwan	14	18	7	21
Singapore	15	25	11	4
USA	16	6	23	20
Canada	17	11	21	22
S. Korea	18	20	20	16
Hungary	19	19	19	18
Czech Republic	20	21	17	23
Greece	21	14	13	29
Kenya	22	9	30	24
China	23	24	25	12
Bulgaria	24	27	22	17
Romania	25	30	29	5
Jordan	26	28	27	19
Syria	27	29	28	27
El Salvador	28	22	16	31
Brazil	29	31	24	28
Indonesia	30	26	26	30
Mexico	31	17	31	26

Visual presentations can also appeal to values and emotions, as does the following map, in which the color red indicates states with what the author considers fewer or inadequate gun control laws.

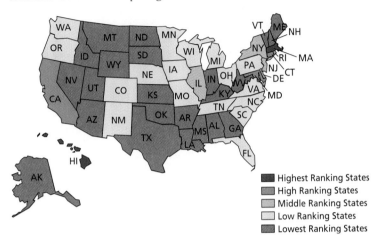

(Note: Using such strategies to add emphasis to weak or questionable evidence is, of course, unethical.)

Photographs and artwork (including line drawings) can highlight evidence's appeal to values and emotions and create vivid representatives of a larger group of examples.

Visuals can also help explain complicated reasoning, as in the following graph highlighting the consequences of failing to decrease birth rates in lesser developed countries.

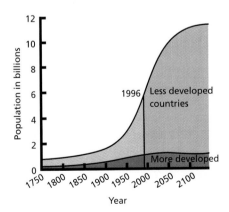

Comparisons. One important way to arrive at a judgment is to compare a particular issue, problem, policy, or situation about which you are uncertain to one about which you are more certain. In trying to decide whether to expand a local recycling program, for example, you might reasonably look at the success of current efforts. In arguing for restrictions on television programs or for wider access to technical information gathered by governments or corporations, you might look at the success or failure of such practices in other countries.

Comparisons can be particularly useful when you are arguing for a particular policy. Your readers will be concerned about the consequences of a policy and its likelihood for success or failure. No one can predict the future, of course, but comparisons can help you persuade because they point to the probability of certain outcomes.

At the same time, you should expect readers to approach comparisons critically, being skeptical of those that are far-fetched or unreasonable and judging whether the comparison speaks directly to the issue at hand. Instead of asking a comparison to stand on its own, therefore, spend some time pointing out its applicability and answering possible objections to it. The author of the following passage, for example, uses comparison to argue for two-parent, child-centered families even though he acknowledges that one-parent families can raise children successfully.

55d
arg

> Infants and children need, at minimum, one adult to care for them. Yet, given the complexities of the task, childrearing in all societies until recent years has been shared by many adults. The institutional bond of marriage between biological parents, with the essential function of tying the father to the mother and child, is found in virtually every society. Marriage is the most universal social institution known; in no society has nonmarital childbirth, or the single parent, been the cultural norm. In all societies the biological father is identified where possible, and in almost all societies he plays an important role in his children's upbringing, even though his primary task is often that of protector and breadwinner.
>
> —DAVID POPENOE, "The American Family Crisis"

STRATEGY

Develop a list of questions that can guide your search for facts, ideas, and experiences that support your proposition. Here are some possible questions.

- What are some good or bad consequences of this policy?
- What do experts say about solutions to the problem?
- What religious or moral values support my position on this issue?
- Are there any comparisons that might help readers understand my perspective?

Trying to answer these questions can help you decide whether you can use your own knowledge to support an assertion or whether you need additional facts, opinions, and information.

A WORD ABOUT SPEAKING

When giving oral presentations, you can use various strategies for presenting evidence for an argument or opinion. One effective method is to create a series of bullet points on an overhead transparency, on the board, or on a handout, which guide you and your audience through the main supporting points in your argument. If you use *PowerPoint* or a similar presentation program, each slide can state one supporting point, perhaps with some elaboration, and you can move through a series of slides to make an effective case for a position or recommendation.

55d
arg

4 Recognize and respond to counterarguments

Traditional argumentation is like debate: you imagine an adversary, someone who doesn't go along with your ideas, and try to undermine that adversary's points or **counterarguments**. Most contemporary approaches to argument aren't quite as battle-like. Your point should be not so much to "win" as to acknowledge other people's perspectives yet still try to convince them of the validity of your views. With either kind of argument, however, you need to anticipate your readers' reactions.

STRATEGY

Use lists and columns to help develop counterarguments. Divide a sheet of paper into three columns. On the left, list the main points supporting your opinion. Write opposing points in the middle column. Put yourself wholly into the other position's point of view when you are listing opposing points. Pretend you are a person diametrically opposed to your original stance. Try to find weaknesses in the points in the left-hand column. Be as critical as possible. In the rightmost column, list the possible defenses to the counterarguments you listed in the middle column. List any known or potential outside sources that would support your argument.

Sometimes it may be difficult to imagine any point of view other than your own. The process of inventing counterarguments may need to move beyond your own frame of reference and beliefs. This is where taking your thesis or position into a more public forum can help. Use various audiences as a "test" for your assertions. Put the idea forward tentatively, so that you will be seen as searching openly for differences of opinion. You might, for example, ask some friends or acquaintances, "What do you think about this issue?" or "Do you think that we ought to do X to solve Y?" Then listen carefully, and take note of the responses. You might gently extend your friends' reasoning by raising a subsidiary issue or counterargument: "But what about the fact that . . . ?" Again, listen.

Exercise 5

A. Using the strategy described in 55c, develop a workable thesis statement. List at least three pieces of supporting evidence or arguments for your assertion.

B. In a small group, use the strategy in 55d-4 to create a list of counterarguments against each member's main supporting arguments. In a discussion of each thesis statement, try collectively to respond to those counterarguments in ways that weaken the objections to the original arguments.

55e Developing a point: Argument in progress

Knowing that he had to begin writing a short argumentative paper, Zachary Carter began jotting ideas in his journal. As he walked through the student union on his way to a class, he noticed a group of students crowding around a table where several members of the Coalition on Animal Rights sat. Large posters on the wall showed cruelties allegedly inflicted on monkeys, dogs, and other animals as a result of medical experiments. The students and the Coalition members were carrying on a lively debate about the animal experiments. As Zachary listened, he knew that he had stumbled on an idea for his paper. He grabbed some leaflets and hurried to class.

1 Identify an issue

At lunch, Zachary glanced through the leaflets he had taken. He couldn't help feeling that they turned an enormous, undefined topic ("animal rights") into something very specific by focusing on only one issue (the morality of performing medical experiments on animals). He started writing about his own feelings on this subject in his journal.

> One day when I was little, I came across some neighborhood kids taunting a frog they'd found. They were kicking it, tossing it to each other, rolling it down the sidewalk. I was horrified, but the kids were a lot bigger than I was, so I just stood a few yards away, ready to run to my house if they turned on me. I found the frog's bashed-up body in the grass the next day.
>
> Animal rights. Maybe this violation was outrageous because there was no purpose but a sick pleasure for the kids. Experiments inflict pain, too, but we're supposed to think it's all for the good of human beings. I don't know. A frog, some experiments. These seem so small. The problem is so much bigger than this. It's humans as a species, multiplying, taking over the planet and pushing out other creatures.

On his way to class, Zachary continued to puzzle over the question of animal rights. The experimentation problem seemed like a complex argument, since people can claim that animal experiments have led to cures for dozens of diseases and thus made our lives better. At the same time, it seemed manageably narrow, since experiments can be studied, monitored, and controlled. But what about other aspects of animal rights? What about the destruction of rain forests, the wiping out of entire species by human development, or pollution killing off organisms by the thousands?

2 Investigate an issue

The day after his encounter with the animal rights group, Zachary was checking his email messages on his computer when he decided to try out his thoughts on an electronic mailing list for students in his writing class.

55e
arg

> Hi, people. I've been thinking about animal rights. (I'm sure you saw the table in the student union.) I guess I'm more worried now than before about what happens to animals in experiments. But I keep thinking that the lab issue is missing the point. It seems so small compared to the huge injustices we keep doing to animals on the whole planet. If we stopped all the experiments in the world, animals still would have no rights because of what we are doing to their environment. What do you think?

Within a day, about a dozen students had posted responses. Several students offered sensible replies and even suggested where Zachary could get more information.

> In response to Zachary Carter's message: Take a situation like human hunger. Big problem, right? So some people create a food-shelf program in one city, and it helps a few dozen families. It doesn't get rid of the problem, but it's a start. Same with taking care of our environment.
>
> Zach Carter: Check out Richard Wagner's book Environment and Man, and while you're at it, Al Gore's Earth in the Balance.

3 Articulate a stance

After thinking about the mailing list responses, Zachary knew that he had to work to articulate his stance. Was he concerned primarily about animal experiments? Or was his point more solution based—that we should do something more fundamental about animal rights? But what was that something? Returning to his journal, he wrote a page exploring his ideas.

A day later, Zachary had narrowed his opinion into something approaching a claim or thesis. In his brainstorming, he realized that he wanted to take a broader view of animal rights, and he settled on a tentative proposition for his paper.

> *In considering the rights of animals, we must begin shifting our focus from small controversies such as animal experiments or the survival of a single species to the true injustice, the large-scale destruction of animals' habitat by humans.*

Zachary felt generally satisfied with his focus but also knew that he really didn't have an argument, just a way of thinking about a problem. What exactly was he proposing—just that we should think more broadly, or that we should take some sort of action?

4 Find supporting evidence

Taking the advice of one of the mailing list respondents, Zachary went to the library in search of the books by Wagner and Gore. He found that they dealt broadly with the issue of the environment. As he read, he was drawn again and again to passages dealing with the issue of human overpopulation. Was there a way to link animal rights to human overpopulation? Searching the electronic databases in his library, he located a series of books by Edward Abbey dealing with the environment. The anthology in his composition course also included a useful article titled "The End of Nature." There was plenty here, he thought, to help him support his ideas. He started jotting down some useful quotations.

> *"Global warming, ozone depletion, the loss of living species, deforestation—they all have a common cause: the relationship between human civilization and the earth's natural balance." (Gore 31)*

Especially powerful for his paper were various proposals for reducing the human population, or at least keeping it from growing out of control. This one main argument, Zachary thought, could lay the foundation for an approach to animal rights in which the earth would be balanced between humans and animals in a harmonious ecosystem.

5 Recognize counterarguments

Because Zachary had already received some email objections to his original thoughts about animal rights, he decided to do most of his work on counterarguments by himself, trying to put himself in the shoes of people (including some of his friends) who would object to the idea. Using a listing strategy (see 55d-4), he divided a piece of paper into three columns, wrote down key supporting points, then imagined what people would say against his supporting points. After trying to come up with valid counterarguments, he looked for ways to defend his original supporting points. The result was a chart of ideas that he could develop in his paper.

Tentative thesis: In considering the rights of animals, we must begin shifting our focus from small controversies such as animal experiments or the survival of a single species to the true injustice, the large-scale destruction of animals' habitat by the overpopulation of humans.

Supporting Points	Opposing Points	Defenses
Humans are pushing the balance of nature askew with their ever-increasing population.	We haven't yet mined the earth for all its resources, so we could support many more people in the future.	Mining all the earth's resources will inevitably destroy the existing ecosystem.
Large-scale tips in the balance of nature will cause a domino effect as inter-dependent species die off.	Entire species have gone extinct without major effects on ecology.	In the past, extinction has happened slowly and naturally because of changing conditions.
More humans need more water, leading to more dams, in turn leading to the destruction of submerged habitat.	Dams create lakes, which create new opportunities for plant and animal life.	Dams like the Glen Canyon Dam upset fragile ecosystems miles downstream.
Male sterilization can effectively curb over-population, as shown in Barbados, etc.	Sterilized men may change their minds about fathering children and then be unable to do so.	Semen can be collected prior to sterilization for later use in artificial insemination.

After creating this list, Zachary felt he was ready to begin more formal work on the structure of his paper in preparation for a preliminary draft. Note how he develops a complex argument that includes a definition of his key terms, adequate quotations from his sources to support his points, and a clear, crisp, readable style to engage his readers.

Animal Rights: The Big Picture

by Zachary Carter

1   The issue of animal rights is a multifaceted one, and, upon examination, it tends to make one follow a circle of logic which leads from one conclusion to the next, without the benefit of a final outcome or decision. But there is a way out of this circle, and that is to shift the focus of the issue away from small controversies such as animal experiments or the survival of a single species of tiny fish to the true injustice, the large-scale destruction of animals' habitat by the overpopulation of humans. Upon exploration, this particular avenue yields astonishing and interesting--even horrifying--results. Clearly an intense effort must be made to preserve the rights of animals (as defined later in this essay) for the benefit of every species involved, including the human race.

2   In order to examine this issue thoroughly, we must find a definition of both "animal" and "rights" and stick to them. So, for the purpose of this essay, "animal" will be defined as any creature that belongs to the kingdom Animalia, which includes reptiles, birds, insects, amphibians, and mammals (even humans). As for a concept of "rights," one must first look at what is most important for the whole of nature. The earth is a vast, spinning ecosystem, teeming with countless forms of life, all in diverse conflict and chaos. Yet amid all the confusion there is an order, a balance, an underlying simplicity. The food chain, photosynthesis, the Krebs cycle, the water cycle, migratory patterns--all these things indicate the presence of an underlying balance, a large-scale cooperation of organisms, the purpose of which is to promote life.

3   Al Gore tells of this in his book Earth in Balance: "All its parts exist in a delicate balance of interdependency" (50). This balance is important to the continuation of life as we know it on earth because "any interruption of this natural process can have a

magnified impact" (51). A large-scale tip in this balance can result in devastating effects on the lives of all creatures, Homo sapiens and other species alike. It is apparent that the preservation of this balance must be the paramount concern of any society because all members in any society are integral parts of nature. If the situation is viewed in this light, then it becomes not only humanity's right and every other species' right, but our duty as well, for the very preservation of life and nature as we know it, to live peacefully within the balance of nature. Consequently, we arrive at the most fundamental definition of "rights": the right to exist within the balance of nature.

55e
arg

4   And now we come to the problem. Humans, driven by natural instinct, are slowly pushing the balance askew and, in the process, trampling on the rights of other species to exist inside the balance. Because of the population boom, humans have spread across every continent, developing, settling, industrializing, mining, setting up agriculture, and so forth. Gore speaks of human intrusion into the balance: "Global warming, ozone depletion, the loss of living species, deforestation--they all have a common cause: the new relationship between human civilization and the earth's natural balance" (31).

5   The human race has destroyed vast areas of native habitat and cut down billions of trees which--at that volume--are virtually irreplaceable. As Gore notes, "when we scrape the forests away, we destroy these crucial habitats along with the living species that depend on them" (116). Predatory species such as the wolf, coyote, and mountain lion, which are an important part of the ecosystem (because they dwell at the apex of the food chain), have been virtually wiped out in many areas. Deer and elk feel this loss through their subsequent boom in population, which in turn causes a demand for food which cannot be met. As a result, there are millions

of starving deer and elk, all because of the destruction of a few
predators.

6   These examples of habitat destruction and the killing of species
are clearly a violation of animals' rights to exist within the
balance. Another type of disruption is the damming of rivers, which
not only submerges vast areas of habitat, but also upsets the fragile
river ecology for hundreds of miles downstream. A prime example of
this is the former Glen Canyon in Utah, now under Lake Powell, a
result of the construction of the Glen Canyon Dam. In South America,
huge amounts of the Amazon rain forest are being burned, leaving
billions, perhaps trillions, of animals homeless if not killed.
Extinctions are on the rise: "Living species of animals and plants
are now vanishing in the world at a rate one thousand times faster
than at any time in the past 65 million years" (Gore 25). The
destruction of an entire species is an example of another clear
violation of the rights of animals to exist within the balance. And
there are more subtle and terrifying problems than these: global
warming, the greenhouse effect, the rising of the oceans. These, in
the words of Bill McKibben, can lead us "if not straight to hell,
then straight to a place with a comparable 'temperature'" (274). But
the underlying cause of all this injustice, the mother of all
problems, is overpopulation.

7   We face a future in which there is no longer physical space on
the earth for the human race, much less the billions of other species
that inhabit the planet. In the words of Edward Abbey:

> The sea will be farmed, all deserts irrigated, whole
> mountains pulverized, the last forests turned to pulpwood
> plantations, in order to satisfy the ever-growing needs
> (no doubt as desperate as in the past) of a human
> population much larger than at present. (Down the River
> 117)

Richard Wagner, author of <u>Environment and Man</u>, states that "adding
four billion more [people] staggers the imagination, for the earth is
barely able to support its present population" (553). He also says
that "overpopulation is one problem the entire world must share"
(538). Clearly the population explosion must be stopped. This is the
only way to make room for all species to have their rightful place
within the balance, for the benefit of human beings and the whole of
the natural world.

8   First, a move must be made to prevent future development of
similar problems, and the only way to do this is to curb the
population explosion. Several things can be used to this end.
Abortion, while morally objectionable to many people, is a natural
form of population reduction. Rabbits in the wild, for example, will
abort their unborn fetuses if the local environment is insufficient
for survival. If moral imperatives preclude the use of this method,
then there are other equally effective chemical and mechanical
methods, "but the most reliable method is sterilization" (Wagner
547). A simple operation performed on a man renders him unable to
conceive offspring, and this does not affect sexual impulses. The
irreversibility of this method can be combated by taking samples of
semen before the operation. Then, at any time, the partner can be
artificially inseminated (Wagner 547). A reduction in population <u>can</u>
be achieved. This is demonstrated by the efforts of "Barbados,
Taiwan, Mauritius, Hong Kong, Tunisia, Singapore, Costa Rica, Egypt,
Chile, and South Korea," which have achieved a reduction (Wagner
554). This proposed reduction in population will help to prevent
further encroachment upon the natural habitat of animal species by
human expansion and exploitation.

9   As for the present, efforts should be made to develop new and
streamline old technology in order to make more efficient use of
resources. Gore says, "It is now an axiom in many fields of science

55e
arg

that more new and important discoveries have taken place in the last ten years than in the entire previous history of science" (31). This trend is expected to continue, and, if so, efficiency of production and use of natural resources should be steered in that direction. Subsequently, waste disposal, energy production, and manufacturing should be improved significantly. Gore also says that "the transformation of the way we relate to the earth will of course involve new technologies, but the key changes will involve new ways of thinking about the relationship [between people and nature] itself" (35).

55e
arg

10   The first and most important imperative is that all individuals make a conscious effort to improve this relationship to the balance of nature, for the sake of animal rights, themselves, and their children. Without this effort to preserve the balance, all members of the human race are on a collision course with destruction, taking millions of innocent species along with them:

> [. . .] developers were bulldozing the last hundred acres of untouched forest in the entire area. As the woods fell away to make way for more concrete, more buildings, parking lots, and streets, the wild things that lived there were forced to flee. Most of the deer were hit by cars; other creatures--like the pheasant that darted into my neighbor's backyard--made it a little further. (Gore 25)

11   An effort to curb these injustices is in order immediately, for the sake of the balance. For "the earth, like the sun, like the air, belongs to everyone--and to no one" (Abbey, Journey 88). And if no effort is made . . . very well then . . . let the world rot.

Works Cited

Abbey, Edward. "The Damnation of a Canyon." Beyond the Wall. New
    York: Holt, 1984.

---. Down the River. New York: Plume, 1991.

---. The Journey Home. New York: Plume, 1991.

Gore, Albert. Earth in the Balance: Ecology and the Human Spirit. New

York: Houghton, 1992.

McKibben, Bill. "The End of Nature." The Informed Argument. Ed.

Robert K. Miller. New York: Harcourt, 1992. 264-74.

Wagner, Richard H. Environment and Man. New York: Norton, 1978.

55f Using critical thinking to strengthen your argument

When you plan and draft a position paper, try to assemble your opinions and supporting evidence in an order that reflects a chain of reasoning supporting your claim (thesis statement). Some of the most effective ways to do this are using different strategies of argument (logical, emotional, imaginative, and ethical) and using data-warrant-claim (Toulmin) reasoning.

1 Build logical strategies

When you employ **logical strategies** for argument, you arrange your ideas and evidence in ways that correspond with patterns of thought that most people accept as reasonable and convincing. You do not have to provide absolute proof for your opinion; if you could, there would be no real need to argue. After all, arguments help to resolve disagreements precisely because an absolutely correct position cannot always be identified. In such a case, an argument helps readers choose among opinions that are reasonable alternatives.

Here are four of the most commonly used logical strategies.

- **Reasoning from consequences.** You argue for or against an action, outlook, or interpretation, basing your argument on real or likely consequences (good or bad).
- **Reasoning from comparisons.** You argue for or against a policy or point of view, basing your argument on similar situations, problems, or actions.
- **Reasoning from authority and testimony.** You draw ideas and evidence to support your outlook from recognized experts or from people whose experience makes them trustworthy witnesses.
- **Reasoning from examples and statistics.** You draw on events, situations, and problems presented as illustrations (examples) or in summarized, numerical form (statistics) to support your point of view.

Induction and deduction are other commonly used logical strategies. A **deductive argument** begins with an explicitly stated **premise** (or assertion or claim) and then goes on to support that premise. It uses **syllogistic reasoning** as the basic logical format. A **syllogism** includes a **major premise**, a **minor premise**, and a **conclusion**. Here is a simple truthful syllogism.

MAJOR PREMISE   All landowners in Clarksville must pay taxes.

MINOR PREMISE   Fred Hammil owns land in Clarksville.

CONCLUSION   Therefore, Fred Hammil must pay taxes.

Faulty syllogistic reasoning is easily illustrated in a flawed syllogism.

55f
arg

MAJOR PREMISE   All Ferraris are fast.

MINOR PREMISE   That car is fast.

CONCLUSION   Therefore, that car is a Ferrari.

In a complex argument, of course, these truthful and faulty kinds of reasoning are much more elaborate. You might begin an argumentative paper, for example, by saying something that your readers would generally hold to be true, go on to show that specific examples of that assertion must also be true, and end with your argumentative assertion. This basic sequence can be used to shape each paragraph as well as to frame the paper as a whole.

In contrast, an **inductive argument** does not explicitly state the premise; rather, it leads readers through an accumulation of evidence until they conclude what the writer wants them to. Such arguments usually begin with a **hypothesis**, which differs from an assertion in being tentative, an idea that the writer wants to consider but as yet has not reached any hard-and-fast conclusion about. Of course, in a finished written argument, this hypothesis is somewhat disingenuous since the writer *does* have a conclusion but withholds it until the readers are convinced by reading through all the supporting points.

This form of argument is effective when you are taking a controversial stand on an issue. If you asserted your stand explicitly at the beginning of the paper, you might put many of your readers on the defensive, ready to criticize your argument right from the start. However, if you hold off your assertion, your readers may also hold off their judgment.

Exercise 6

A. Compose a simple proposition or thesis, and then try to support it with each of the four logical strategies described in 55f-1 (reasoning from consequences, reasoning from comparisons, reasoning from authority or testimony, and reasoning from examples and statistics). Invent authoritative statements or statistics if you wish.

EXAMPLE

> *Simple proposition:* The student senate's proposal to allow alcoholic beverages to be served in the student union should not be passed.
>
> *Reasoning from consequences:* The consumption of alcohol will increase crime on campus, especially personal assaults, drunk driving, and rape.
>
> *Reasoning from comparisons:* Easy availability of alcohol deters students from their academic work; when a bar opened briefly three years ago near fraternity row, every fraternity experienced a drop in average grades.
>
> *Reasoning from authority and testimony:* Having alcohol so easily available on campus may subvert our college's mission by contributing not to students' growth but to their deterioration. According to research conducted by Legman and Witherall, a large percentage of alcoholics over the age of thirty reported that their college binge drinking set a strong pattern for their later addiction.
>
> *Reasoning from examples and statistics:* Bars on campus draw students away from more beneficial activities. Two years after Carmon College opened a wine and beer hall on campus, participation in lectures and special events had dropped by 26 percent; attendance at the film series declined by 18 percent; and weekend library usage between 5 P.M. and midnight dropped by 43 percent.

B. In a small group, compare your theses and logical strategies. Discuss the strength of each strategy as it is used to support the thesis.

2 Draw on emotional strategies

In drawing on **emotional strategies**, you focus on the values, attitudes, belief systems, and emotions that guide people's lives and that are central to any decision-making process.

Values and beliefs. You may present examples, ideas, or statements that confirm or contradict your readers' probable values.

Emotions and values. You may present examples or use language that draws emotional responses (positive or negative) from your readers ("The consequence of this policy will be an increase in the already horrifying flood of bruised, battered, undernourished two- and three-year-olds brought into emergency rooms by parents who deny even the most obvious evidence of abuse").

55f
arg

Be aware that readers often see emotional strategies as weaker support for a point than reason or logic. In an argument against the use of animals for research, for example, an emotional appeal about cruelty to animals could be countered by an emotional appeal about the need for research to cure terrible diseases. A general emotional appeal about animal suffering is not as strong as specific, verifiable accounts of animals being subjected to unbearable pain in the name of research. Often the most powerful emotional appeals will be those directly linked to other forms of logical support.

DID YOU KNOW?

Some people think that the purpose of argument is to win a battle or to discredit the views of people with whom they disagree. A society that relied on such a view of argument to deal with problems and differing points of view would be a rather hostile place to live, however. Belgian scholar Chaim Perelman offers a different view of the aim of argument: to encourage or convince your audience to adhere to your point of view. In other words, argument creates agreement by encouraging people to come together in their beliefs and actions.

Chaim Perelman and L. Olbrechts-Tyteca, *The New Rhetoric* (South Bend: U of Notre Dame P, 1979).

55.3

3 Use data-warrant-claim (Toulmin) reasoning

In *The Uses of Argument* (1964), Stephen Toulmin proposes **data-warrant-claim reasoning**, which draws on several kinds of statements reasonable people usually make when they argue (statements of data, claims, and warrants), highlighting a way of relating these statements in order to convince readers.

Data corresponds to your evidence and *claim* to your conclusion. *Warrant*, however, is a more complex term; it refers to the mental process by which a reader connects the data to the claim. It answers the question "How?" Another way to understand this is to think of data as the indisputable facts and the warrant as the probable facts and assertions. As in an inductive argument, you present the data that lead to your claim, but you also present the warrants, the probable facts and assertions that will encourage readers to accept the validity of your claim.

For instance, as data you might have the results of a detailed study establishing the likelihood of injury in each of the many different models of cars currently on the market. You could make a number of interpretive statements about the data (warrants) and point out patterns you see (probable facts—warrants) in order to provide reasoning that links the data to your claim: for the average consumer, buying a large car is a good way to reduce the likelihood of being injured in an accident.

To argue effectively, you need to show your readers *how* the data and the claim are connected. To warrant such a claim, you could say that there are small, medium, and large cars in the ratings and extend this warrant by pointing out that the large cars have a higher safety rating. To back up this warrant, you point out that although some of the smaller cars on each list are quite safe, in general, the large cars are the safest. You could extend the argument by citing further statistics (data) about safety along with arguments and reasoning from other sources (warrants).

DATA

Ratings of each car model according to likelihood of injury to driver and passenger (scale: 1 = low to 10 = high)

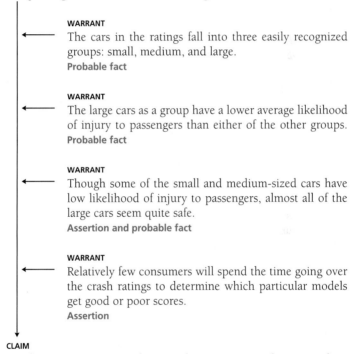

WARRANT
The cars in the ratings fall into three easily recognized groups: small, medium, and large.
Probable fact

WARRANT
The large cars as a group have a lower average likelihood of injury to passengers than either of the other groups.
Probable fact

WARRANT
Though some of the small and medium-sized cars have low likelihood of injury to passengers, almost all of the large cars seem quite safe.
Assertion and probable fact

WARRANT
Relatively few consumers will spend the time going over the crash ratings to determine which particular models get good or poor scores.
Assertion

CLAIM

For the average consumer, buying a large car is a good way to reduce the likelihood of being injured in an accident.

The data-warrant-claim approach to constructing an argument does not assume that an argument can provide absolute proof of a proposition. It aims instead at showing readers that an opinion or proposed action is plausible, grounded on good evidence and reasons, and worth their endorsement. Arguments that employ this kind of reasoning may sometimes seem more like purposeful dialogues than debates. If you employ this approach, you

55f
arg

should take the attitude that your argument is open to other viewpoints, to compromise, and to negotiation.

4 Consider your audience and purpose

Remember that you won't write an effective argument if all you do is stridently voice your opinion on an issue. An argument is effective only if it's part of a relationship between you and your audience. Defining who your audience members are, how you want them to perceive you, and what you want to convince them of is the essential first step to constructing an argument (see Chapter 5).

Your audience is partly determined by your topic and by your own stance. If you are writing about the abortion issue, for example, you need to be clear in your own mind whom you are addressing. Argument papers on this topic are often not well written because the audience is usually a vague "the other side." Remember, it is a fallacy to divide an issue into only two sides (see the discussion of the either/or fallacy in 55f-5). Likewise, it is ineffective to think of your readers as belonging to one of only two camps.

Rogerian argument, based on the theories of psychologist and group therapist Carl Rogers, provides a useful perspective for considering the responses of your audience. Rogers argued that people can more easily be changed when their opponent seems like an ally instead of an enemy. A highly combative or adversarial approach immediately puts a reader on the defensive, thus setting up a barrier to your ideas. The reader's psychological reaction is "Oh yeah? Well, let me tell you something, buster!" rather than "Hmmm, that's an interesting point worth considering."

Identifying alternative views. To practice Rogerian strategies, imagine for a moment that you share the views of someone who is opposed to your actual position or solution. What is your opponent's frame of reference? What assumptions might have led him or her to these views? Giving, for the moment, a charitable response that acknowledges someone else's right to hold an opinion you disagree with, what validity can you see in anything your opponent might say?

Rogers also found that a good way to understand someone's view is to try restating it rather than immediately countering it. When participants in a discussion negotiate their positions, sentences often begin not with statements of judgment or reaction ("Well, I think . . ." or "That point doesn't hold water"), but with statements of reflection and repetition: "What I hear you saying is . . ." or "It sounds to me like you're trying to . . . ." This allows not only for mutual understanding of each person's points but for mutual respect for differences of opinion once those points are clearly articulated.

Making a concession. When you understand your opponent's ideas, you may be prepared to work a **concession** into your argument. You make a concession when you acknowledge or consider a view opposed to one you are arguing. A concession does not have to be so strong that it undermines your entire argument. But placed strategically, it can help your reader to see that you have, in fact, tried to be fair-minded. A reader who recognizes that attitude will be more likely to trust your judgment and listen to you.

Concessions may appear briefly, embedded in the structure of a sentence, or they may be elaborate, sometimes taking one or more paragraphs to describe. Concessions embedded in single sentences often involve words like *although, while, while it may be true that, of course,* or *but.*

In a letter to the editor bemoaning the extinction of local, family-run hardware stores in the shadow of huge, warehouse-sized lumber centers, Angie Krastaat made an extended concession that consumers may be attracted by the lower prices and large selection at the lumber centers, but then countered it with an anecdote that led to a generalization.

55f
arg

Of course, the lumber centers do have their draws: paint in every color, discounted power tools, and items too large to fit into most small stores. But what they gain in selection and pricing they sorely lack in their robot-like relationship with their customers. Where else can you get a single nut, bolt or nail—just one—than a local hardware store? What large lumber center will replace that torn screen or broken window while you wait? Where can you find someone at Mega-Hardware who will work with you in the store to repair something, using ingenuity and bins full of single items?

STRATEGY

To make your argument on "hot" issues more effective, try limiting your audience. Focus on a particular group of people concerned about the issue—on abortion, for example, focus on reaching sexually active teens, unmarried mothers, or the people who protest at abortion clinics. Also consider your image as an arguer. How do you want your readers to perceive you? Do you want to be perceived as erudite, rational, and coolly objective; as passionate and moving; as outraged; as reflective and forgiving?

---

5 Recognize misleading and illogical reasoning

A **fallacy** is a flaw in the reasoning of any persuasive work, whether it's an argumentative essay, an interpretation of a literary work, a report of the results of a study, or a review. Fallacies often show up in advertisements, stated directly in the copy and implied in the visual images. An ad for beer that shows attractive, bikini-clad women and muscular, handsome men romping on a California beach implies (illogically) that drinking the beer will get you that lifestyle. This example of faulty cause-effect reasoning implies that *because* you drink the beer, you'll be like the people in the ad. The same fallacy can be a problem in academic and professional writing as well but may not be as blatant. For instance, if you read an article that says legalizing marijuana will result in a dangerous increase in cocaine use, you ought to question how the writer demonstrates that cause-effect relationship and supplies evidence linking marijuana use to cocaine use.

55f
arg

Faulty cause-effect relationship.   This problem is also called *post hoc, ergo propter hoc* (Latin for "after this, therefore because of this") or just a **post hoc fallacy**. This flawed reasoning attempts to persuade you that just because one event happens after the other, the first event causes the second.

FAULTY
CAUSE-EFFECT

The increase in explicit violence on television is making the crime rate soar.

READER'S REACTION: This *may* be true, but no evidence is presented here linking the two situations.

False analogy.   **Analogies** are comparisons between two things, often on the basis of shared characteristics. In a false analogy, the things may at first glance seem to be comparable but really are not. (See the discussion of the red herring and *ad populum* fallacies in this section.)

FALSE ANALOGY

Raising the national speed limit is like offering free cocktails at a meeting of recovering alcoholics.

READER'S REACTION: I don't see the connection. Most drivers aren't recovering from an addiction to high-speed driving, and a legal limit is not the same thing as self-restraint.

Misleading language/misleading evidence.   This fallacy is also called **equivocation** and **slanted statistics**. A writer can use misleading language by beginning with one definition of a term (usually one everyone agrees with), then shifting to another sense of the word, one that supports the writer's argument but that not all readers may agree with.

MISLEADING
LANGUAGE

Everyone has the right of free speech, so censoring films by rating them Triple X is against one's constitutional rights.

READER'S REACTION: This tries to pass off the *rating* of films as censorship (which it is not) and assumes that *free speech* and *censorship* are directly opposite terms (which they are not necessarily).

Misleading evidence includes statistics, survey results, and expert opinions stacked up in favor of only one side of the argument. For instance, someone who used an opinion poll to argue for the preservation of the spotted owl but polled only people at an environmental rally would have overwhelmingly favorable but misleading evidence.

Red herring. Similar to misleading evidence is the red herring fallacy. A *red herring* is something that distracts readers from the real argument.

RED HERRING   Gun control laws need to be passed as soon as possible to decrease the rate of domestic violence and home firearms accidents. The people who think guns should not be controlled are probably criminals themselves.

READER'S REACTION: **The second sentence doesn't logically follow from the first; it just attacks the people who would oppose the writer's argument instead of supporting the initial assertion.**

Ad populum. *Ad populum* means "to the people" and refers to an argument that appeals to the audience's biases instead of using rational support.

AD POPULUM   All doctors should be tested for AIDS and should not be allowed to practice if they test HIV positive, so they don't spread the disease to their patients. Do you want to be one of those patients?

READER'S REACTION: **This writer is obviously trying to invoke my fear of getting AIDS. The claim that HIV-positive doctors will pass on the disease to patients is not founded on valid research.**

Ad hominem. Another faulty argument based on audience biases is the *ad hominem fallacy*, which means "to the man." This is a personal attack on the opponent rather than a debate on the issue.

AD HOMINEM   Of course Walt Smith would support a bill to provide financial assistance to farmers—he owns several large farms in the Midwest. Besides, how can he be a good senator after cheating on his wife?

READER'S REACTION: **I'd like to hear reactions to Walt Smith's ideas, please. I don't really care whether he had an affair fifteen years ago.**

Bandwagon. This fallacy is also called *consensus gentium*, "consensus of the people." A **bandwagon argument** is one that tries to convince you everyone else agrees with the idea already, so you ought to join in.

BANDWAGON   Each year an increasing number of people are quitting smoking, so you ought to quit, too.

READER'S REACTION: **This writer is trying to convince me to quit by saying that other people are doing it. Even though the assertion may be valid, the support is not.**

Begging the question. This fallacy also is called **overgeneralization** or **hasty generalization**. An argument is begging the question when it presents assumptions as if they were facts, sometimes using words and phrases like *obviously*, *certainly*, *clearly*, *people always/never*, and even the seemingly innocuous *some people say*.

BEGGING
THE QUESTION

Most people these days are trying to be more physically fit; obviously, they are afraid of getting old.

READER'S REACTION: **No evidence is presented for either the claim that most people are trying to be more fit or the claim that they are afraid of getting old. On what basis are these stated as facts?**

**55f
arg**

Either/or. An **either/or strategy** oversimplifies an issue, making it seem as if it has only two sides.

EITHER/OR

On the matter of abortion, there are two positions: either we support a human's right to life, or we allow women to have complete control over their bodies.

READER'S REACTION: **Why can't someone endorse protecting life while also supporting the right to choose what happens to one's body?**

Circular reasoning. *Circular reasoning*, also called **tautology**, is an attempt to support an assertion with the assertion itself.

CIRCULAR
REASONING

The university should increase funding of intramural sports because it has a responsibility to back its sports programs financially.

READER'S REACTION: **All this really says is that the university should fund sports because it should fund sports.**

Exercise 7

A. Choose a controversial topic you know something about—gun control, abortion, the death penalty, the right to die. Now choose any three of the fallacies described in 55f-5, and write one example of each fallacy to make claims about your topic. (Don't identify the names of the fallacies in your response.)

B. In a small group, exchange copies of the fallacious arguments you wrote for Exercise 7A. Discuss each set of fallacies, trying to identify the logical problems and to suggest revisions or identify specific kinds of support needed.

55g
arg

55g The documented argument or position paper

A **position paper** or **documented argument** is a sharply focused form of argumentative writing that draws heavily on research to take a stand on a question of action or policy, generally an issue of considerable concern in public, work or academic communities. A position paper defines its issue, considers its audience, and draws on evidence and logical strategies to make its point.

1 Sample position paper

In the following paper, note how the writer frames her argument with an opening reference to the daily struggle of many people throughout the world to protect their limited food supply against spoilage and contamination. As you read, consider who the writer's audience is, what the main argument is, and how she constructs the support for the argument. What are the counterarguments, and how does she address them? What kind of support, if any, is missing? What fallacies, if any, do you detect?

Food Irradiation: An Idea Whose Time Has Come

by Stephanie Lewis

1   In almost every part of the world people struggle daily to protect their vital food supplies from spoilage. For most Americans, the threats of heat, damp, insect infestation, bacterial contamination, and rot may seem distant. Yet while there is no precise information on just how much of the world's food supply is

Opens with background examples

lost to spoilage, it is clear that the losses are enormous,
especially in less developed countries that can least afford the
waste. In addition, many of these countries have warm climates that
encourage the growth of organisms causing spoilage and that speed up
the normal deterioration process (Thorne). Because the world's
population is growing at a rapid pace, we need to find viable
solutions to the problem of waste and decay.

55g
arg

2   The loss of edible food is only one part of the problem,
however. Food-borne diseases are also some of the most   Uses
                                                                        example
common threats to human health. In particular, a fairly high   plus
                                                                        authority
percentage of raw animal meat is contaminated by bacteria,
resulting in high levels of food-borne illness in most countries
(Thorne).

Supplies
specific
examples

3   Efforts to reduce the price the public pays for food wastage and
food-borne disease began many years ago. The first methods for the
preservation of food were sun drying, salting, smoking, canning, and
cooking. (For people in developed countries, these are now often
techniques of gourmet cooking.) Recently, however, scientists have

Supplies
detailed
information
plus
authority

developed a new method for food preservation, irradiation. In this
method, food is exposed to measured amounts of ionizing radiation.
Scientists have discovered that this form of food preservation can
slow spoilage, reduce insect infestation, and prevent contamination
by other harmful organisms that cause food-borne diseases (Food
Safety). Food irradiation is a particularly promising way to help
reduce the worldwide problems of waste and disease.

4   Nonetheless, the public in this country has not fully accepted
the concept of food irradiation (Lamb). Because of a decades-long
fear of thermonuclear war and well-publicized accidents involving

Supplies
examples

nuclear power (Three Mile Island and Chernobyl), many people fear
anything associated with radiation. This fear persists even if the
radiation is used for a nonthreatening purpose such as the

preservation of food. Often this feeling of apprehensiveness is due to a lack of knowledge and information on the subject of food irradiation. This is also due to some confusion between the phenomenon of radioactive contamination and the process of irradiation used in food preservation.

5   One main reason why food irradiation is not used widely is that governments are still unsure about consumer acceptance of irradiated products. Without such acceptance, food irradiation will be neglected in developing countries as well as in the developed world. Even though about thirty-four countries have given approval for the radiation process of some thirty products, the use of radiation has been slow to materialize. Nonetheless, there is clear evidence that food irradiation is safe and that it effectively controls spoilage. In addition, there is strong proof of its cost-effectiveness in controlling the organisms and bacteria that contribute to waste and reduced shelf life or storage time for food (Lamb).

**55g
arg**

**Presents
statistics
and
detailed
information**

**Cites
authority**

6   Even though radiation has been an aid to health in diagnosing and treating diseases and in sterilizing medical equipment and pharmaceutical products, many people are sincerely scared of anything that appears to raise the risk of radiation exposure. Perhaps the best way to deal with these fears is to address them directly.

7   Is irradiated food safe? The answer to this question is a clear yes. Irradiated food is not harmful because the treatment does not alter the food in any way that would be detrimental to people's health. Are irradiated foods still nutritious? Yes. Even though, as with all methods of food processing, the level of nutrients is lowered by irradiation, the food is still nutritious. It is important to remember that even storing food at room temperature after harvesting can reduce its nutritional value. Moreover, the loss of nutrients is generally unmeasurable or insignificant at low doses of radiation. So not only has it been demonstrated that food irradiation

**Supplies
detailed
information**

is a safe form of food preservation, it is also a method of
preserving the nutrition in food (Blumenthal).   Cites
authority

8   Food irradiation could reduce the amount of waste due to
spoilage of the world's food supply. With the world's population
expected to double during the next century, this form of food
preservation could aid in feeding this growing number of people in a
safe and healthful way at low cost. This technology could improve the
world we live in and change for the better the lives of millions of
people.

55g
arg

[The paper ends with a list of works cited.]

2 Commentary on Stephanie Lewis's position paper

Lewis's focus is clear through most of the paper, even though she waits
until the end of paragraph 3 to offer a thesis statement clearly presenting her
proposition. She acknowledges sympathetically the fears many people have
about food irradiation and offers some scientific evidence of its safety, but she
might have offered even more. In her conclusion she speaks of the low cost
of food irradiation, but she touches on this matter only indirectly earlier in
the paper. Her paper would benefit from revision in these areas; nonetheless,
it argues effectively in many ways.

CHAPTER 56

WRITING POINT-DRIVEN PAPERS ACROSS THE CURRICULUM

Several kinds of point-drivien writing are widely practiced in academic settings. Among these are the critique, the review, and the point-driven essay exam. Each blends argument with the presentation and discussion of information and has as its primary goal convincing readers of the writer's main point (thesis, interpretation, claim).

56a The critique

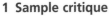

56.1

A formal critique consists of two parts—a summary of the work being discussed and a critical reaction to the work. The summary should objectively condense the whole work, including all of its main ideas. The critical response is a subjective reaction to the work, but this does not necessarily mean a negative reaction. Many students think a critique should tear a work apart, pointing out all its faults, but this is not true. A good critique attempts to explain *how* and *why* a work is written, although questioning both is often an important part of the critique. In writing a critique, you first understand a body of knowledge and opinion, then make a point about it that helps your reader to interpret it and see it from new perspectives.

1 Sample critique

The following selection from a sample critique illustrates how the writer begins with an objective summary of Ortiz's speech and then adds his subjective reaction to Ortiz's ideas. Note the shift in tone as the student moves from summary to critique. Look for sentences that explain how and why Ortiz wrote the speech and for sentences that question Ortiz's ideas.

A Summary and Critique of Alfonso Ortiz's "Some Concerns
Central to the Writing of Indian History"

by Reid Nelson

1   In the speech "Some Concerns Central to the Writing of Indian
History," Alfonso Ortiz addresses the inadequacies created when
non-Native American historians write Native American histories. Ortiz
feels there is a need for historians to develop "greater sensitivity
toward, and respect for, tribal traditions, and of learning Indian
languages" (20).

**56a
arg**

2   Ortiz says Indians place the significance of past traditions in
the place where they originally occurred. Indians therefore think of
the past as occurrences relating to a space and not as events that
took place at a certain time as historians do. This makes specific
dates in the past unimportant to Indians. Ortiz feels that this way
of thinking is illustrated by the Pueblo peoples' saying "When it
has been four times," which unites a sense of time and space
simultaneously by noting when a "distance of four days travel has
passed" or "when a time span of four days has passed" (19).

3   Ortiz's dissatisfaction with historians is deepened by their
tendency to change occurrences that happened in a particular space
into events that took place at a certain time, a practice which does
quite the opposite of that which Indians do. Furthermore, some
historians feel that Indian attempts to represent history in terms
of space and to use metaphors to describe this history are only a
process of mythologization. Ortiz feels that this is an unfortunate
and inaccurate judgment because it precludes the possibility to
better understand Native American cultures.

[The writer continues with three more paragraphs summarizing Ortiz's points.]

7   In this speech Ortiz is both informing and persuading. Ortiz
informs historians about the problems with the way they record
Native American history and attempts to persuade them that their

approach is detrimental to a better understanding of Native Americans.

8   Ortiz has presented his captive audience of historians with a very straightforward and simple argument. His speech utilizes neither complex theorizing nor bewildering vocabulary. Ortiz tells the audience the negative consequences that do occur when the situation goes unchanged, which are the continued misunderstanding of Native Americans and poor relations between the two groups, and strengthens this point by repeating it several times. The reception these ideas receive will depend on two things. It depends first on whether historians agree that there is a problem in the way they write history and second on whether they agree that Ortiz's proposals will benefit non-Native Americans' understanding of Indian history.

56b
arg

[The writer concludes with a summary paragraph and a full reference to the printed source for the speech.]

2 Elements of a critique

An effective critique includes the following elements.

- It does not confuse objective summary with subjective opinion.
- It summarizes all the text's main ideas and important subpoints.
- It expresses a critical opinion of the text fairly, stressing how and why the text works and balancing positive and negative points.
- It gives the reader a clear picture of the text's content, its writer's stance, and the strengths and weaknesses of its argument.

3 Commentary on Reid Nelson's critique

Nelson encountered a common problem with writing critiques—making the summary concise yet understandable. He tries to include everything in Ortiz's speech, which results in his giving equal priority to every point. He could explain the main argument of the speech in more detail in the first paragraph; this explanation would orient the reader more clearly. Nelson could be more concise by cutting out some of the lead-in phrases such as *Ortiz says* and *Ortiz feels* and by using active instead of passive voice. In the critique section, Nelson could more explicitly state the problems with Ortiz's ideas.

56b The review

A common academic writing assignment is the review. A **review** is a critical appraisal of an event, object, or phenomenon, such as an art show,

56.2

a concert, a restaurant, or a book. People read reviews either to help them make a decision about attending or experiencing whatever is being reviewed or to test their own judgments of it against those of another person (usually an expert). When you write a review, you describe, analyze, and evaluate your subject from an informed but clearly opinionated perspective.

Reviews come in many forms and are written from many points of view, from fairly objective and descriptive to very judgmental. The most common reviews are those that describe and evaluate an artistic work or performance: a book, a movie, a concert, a ballet, an opera, an album or CD, an art exhibit, or a play. Reviews can also describe and evaluate objects, such as a new car, a computer program, or a stereo system; events, such as the gala opening of a store or a fashion show; or experiences, such as dining at a restaurant or touring an amusement park. You can review almost anything that can be experienced by others, although your choice of what to review may depend on the interests of your intended audience.

Reviews typically both describe and evaluate, but there is no formula for how to include these two perspectives. Some reviews use a simple two-part structure, with a description followed by an evaluation. Many reviews, however, begin with an evaluative point in a kind of thesis statement: such-and-such was or is a success or failure, good in these areas but poor in these, worth experiencing or a waste of time and money.

Despite the different formats for reviews, however, some important principles tie reviews together as one kind of point-driven writing. First, good reviews are *considered*. They don't just state an opinion but support it with specific information and details. Second, good reviews are *authoritative*; most professional reviewers have experienced whatever they review hundreds of times. In writing your own reviews, for example, try to choose something you have experienced before, such as a movie, book, or CD.

1 Sample review

This book review assignment asked the students to develop a thesis based on the book's contents; the thesis could agree or disagree with the book's author if the book took a position on an issue. As you read the review, note how the writer supports her evaluation with facts and details. Note also how her writing gives the impression that she is reasonably familiar with the topic of deaf culture and communication, adding to her credibility.

<u>Laurent Clerc:</u>

The Issue of Early Deaf Literacy

by Amy Braegelman

1   The preservation of a language, though the community that uses it may be small, is crucially important. Language is not just a

communicative amenity--it is a reflection of (and an influence on) a specific culture. Not only does a language allow a culture to flourish, but it allows the people within that culture to flourish. In some cases, a language is particularly well suited to a specific culture because it is all that allows its users to function in society. To allow or force a language so tailored to die is to leave the culture with no effective means of communication, only whatever its people have managed to acquire, usually by bare necessity, of the surrounding, dominant language.

2   Cathryn Carroll's book Laurent Clerc: The Story of His Early Years (Washington, D.C.: Kendall Green Publications, 1991) gives the reader a broader platform on which to base these convictions. Set in the early nineteenth century, Clerc examines the beliefs, stereotypes, and attitudes surrounding the deaf and their language. Like any culture that does not function within the mainstream, the deaf were heavily stigmatized historically; they were believed to be physically sick, mentally ill, or of low intelligence.

3   Of particular interest in Carroll's book is the account of Clerc's time at the Royal National Institute for the Deaf in Paris. The sadistic Dr. Itard, on the staff at the Institute during the first decades of the nineteenth century, dedicated all of his time and surgical background to the misguided endeavor of finding a cure for deafness. As Carroll points out, the school's students were the doctor's unfortunate subjects, and the consequences were "waste, folly, and pain" (86). Itard is a chilling representation of public sentiment at the time; the deaf were "sick" and needed to be cured. The cure, we know, was not available, and in Clerc we see how the deaf who were not used in experiments and were not part of the select few lucky enough to attend the Royal National Institute were treated: sent to live in filth in poorhouses, institutionalized in sanitariums, shunned as subhumans.

56b
arg

4   In this dramatic chronicle of deaf experience, Carroll goes on to show that even in the environment of the Royal National Institute, home and haven to men like Jean Massieu and Laurent Clerc--geniuses by any standards--the deaf were treated like an attraction. Presentations were given to influential politicians and heads of state to display the talents of these deaf men and gain funding for the school. Audiences were free to ask Massieu and Clerc, positioned on stage like performers, any questions they liked. "What is eternity?" they asked, as if to test the relationship between the ears and the mind. "What is hope?" "Does God reason?"

5   Carroll's portrayal shows that among themselves, where they could be natural and talk freely, the deaf students at the Institute showed an open-minded insight that the hearing, for the most part, lacked at the time. Sign language allowed these students to form a community and a web of support in the hearing world. As Clerc recounts, "I wasn't only alone, I was deficient" (35), but in the deaf world, he finds he is not alone. Clerc illustrates the principle of literacy as power and control. On a trip to England, for example, Massieu and Clerc are accompanied by a hearing person, Abbé Sicard. Clerc recounts that "surrounded by people who spoke a language very different from his, our dear Abbé was completely at a loss. Massieu and I had no trouble getting around [. . .] we know how to use our bodies to ask for things." Carroll describes Sicard as a pompous, self-important man who thrives on the control he feels he can exert over the deaf, always under the guise of helpfulness. In England, where he cannot use his own language, he is powerless and is reduced to petty criticisms of the English language. Massieu and Clerc are used to being surrounded by people who don't speak their language, and they adapt easily, feeling in control.

6   Carroll also devotes much of her book to explaining why the deaf were ostracized because of their lack of literacy and why it was

often priests who undertook their education. Greater society felt
that because the deaf could not learn about God, they were sinners
and savages--and were damned. As Clerc puts it, "Abbé Sicard said we
were savages. [. . .] He said we were children with no thoughts, no
feelings, no nothing. We were like statues until he, the great Abbé
Sicard, woke us in his classroom. [. . .] He said that deafness
doomed us to darkness and to hell" (75).

7   Carroll's fascinating book illustrates the folly of expecting
one mode of communication, one language, to suffice for every member
of society. Her book portrays the struggle of the deaf to gain equal
standing in a greater society that had so much trouble accepting
them. It is, finally, a grand illustration that not only does
literacy enable us to function in society, it shapes the way that
other people view us. The deaf students at the Royal National
Institute for the Deaf were intelligent children, fully capable of
functioning in society; many displayed potential to make valuable
contributions to science, art, and literature. However, because they
could not communicate with their mouths, it was socially acceptable
to confine them to asylums and poorhouses rather than giving their
language the status it deserved and elevating the deaf beyond the
realm of human silence.

56b
arg

2 Elements of a review

An effective review includes the following elements.

- It clearly describes the subject of the review at the start, providing all
the information a reader would need to share in the experience (if it is
repeatable) or to know when and where it happened (if it was a "one-
time" experience such as a one-night-only performance).
- It has a clear organization. Reviews of experiences and events (plays,
movies, and so on) are sometimes chronologically arranged, whereas
reviews of static objects such as books or art exhibits may focus on different aspects of the work in order of their importance.
- It offers a reasoned, supported evaluation of the subject's main elements. Movie reviews, for example, may evaluate the filming, acting,

costuming, directing, special effects, script, plot, casting, length, stunt work, or the adaptation of another work such as a novel.

- It is authoritative. A reviewer who discusses an actor's performance should probably know something about the actor's other work. A restaurant reviewer who judges the quality of the curry in an Indian restaurant should have some prior experience with Indian food.
- It is generally verifiable by its intended readers; that is, they should be able to see how one might arrive at the evaluation in the review, even though they may not entirely agree with that evaluation.

3 Commentary on Amy Braegelman's review

Amy's paper is a good example of a point-driven review, one that develops a thesis early on and then extends and supports that thesis with reference to the material found, in this case, in a nonfiction book. Her paper artfully treats the issue of deaf literacy, but its description of the book itself is sparse. Amy might have synthesized the book at the start or worked through its contents from beginning to end.

56.3

56c The point-driven essay exam

In many of your classes, teachers will use **essay exams** to evaluate your skills as a synthesizer of information and as a critical thinker, skills that cannot be seen from a true/false or multiple-choice test. Thus, merely listing information, facts, and quotes without discussing their significance or making connections among them is not acceptable. When you study for essay exams, you will need to move beyond memorization to thinking about what the information means and how it fits into a larger context. Writing these thoughts down in a journal will help you prepare. (See also 58h.)

When you begin the exam, *first read the question(s) carefully*. You have only a short time in which to write, even with a take-home exam. You need to write quickly and concisely, answering the question specifically and with as much support as possible. It is crucial to understand what kind of answer the teacher expects and to plan the essay before actually writing.

Next, decide what position you want to take or what point you will make in the essay. This will become your working thesis or proposition—a perspective or interpretation that you will support with evidence. Try creating a brief outline for your answer, even just a few lines or items listed on the facing page of the test booklet. Working from an outline will help you make your paper more focused, point-driven, and clearly organized.

1 Sample essay exam

This exam asked the student to identify and discuss a common theme running through a survey course in American literature and to show this theme in two stories. The students were allowed to use their books in class in order to find quotations. As you read selections from this answer, note how the writer focuses on one theme. Note, too, how he incorporates quotations to illustrate the theme.

Moral Perfection in "Young Goodman Brown" and

"The Birthmark"

by Ted Wolfe

1   Hawthorne's "Young Goodman Brown" explores the conflict between good and evil. Young Goodman Brown has his religious faith tested during a journey into the woods. In what may or may not have been a dream, he is shown by the devil that everyone he believed to be good is evil. [. . .] When the devil is about to baptize him, Brown calls out for Faith, his wife, telling her to resist the temptation. He is really calling out for faith, as in faith in God. When he does this, the hellish vision passes, and he is alone in the woods. From this, I think we can conclude that Hawthorne believes that people should try to resist temptation and live moral lives.

2   But Goodman Brown is never the same after the experience, be it dream or reality. He becomes "a stern, a sad, a darkly meditative, if not a desperate man." In his heart he doubts the goodness of Faith/faith, Deacon Gookin, Goody Cloyse, and everyone else. [. . .] Symbolically, the experience in the woods caused him to give up his faith. The overriding message that Hawthorne is trying to convey is that one should try to keep one's faith, to believe in others' inherent goodness, and to try to live morally. If one doesn't, life becomes as barren and miserable as it became for Goodman Brown.

3   Hawthorne's "The Birthmark" also addresses the issue of morality. [. . .]

[The answer continues with supporting detail from the second story.]

4   [. . .] Hawthorne's point is that one should not get so caught up in trying to be morally perfect that it ruins one's life. People must learn to "find the perfect future in the present."

**56c
arg**

2 Elements of a point-driven essay exam

Although the specific criteria for an effective essay exam will vary from teacher to teacher and from course to course, an effective essay exam that makes and defends a point includes the following general elements.

- It addresses the exam question directly, taking into account all parts of the question.
- It uses references—quotes, facts, and other information—efficiently, supplying enough to illustrate or back up the writer's point without overloading the essay.
- It synthesizes material, makes connections among references, and discusses the significance of the material; it does not merely list information but interprets it and uses it to illustrate or document a point.

3 Commentary on Ted Wolfe's essay exam

Although Wolfe titles his essay "Moral Perfection," he digresses slightly to the themes of good and evil, faith, and living morally. These themes are all related to "moral perfection," but Ted could make the relationship clearer. His use of quotes is effective and using specific phrases rather than long passages conserved his time.

CHAPTER 57

READING AND WRITING ABOUT LITERATURE

When you read a novel, see a play, or read (or listen to) a poem, you are encountering literature, or, more precisely, imaginative literature. The word *literature* has other meanings as well, some of them used in this book. The literature of a subject of academic study, for example, consists of all the things scholars have written about it. In addition, people often use the term *literature* to distinguish novels and plays that are well written, enjoyable, and worth taking seriously.

In most college courses, however, the term *literature* is applied to certain kinds of texts—fiction, poetry, and drama—that are meant to be read in a manner different from the way we read texts like biographies, histories, reports, scientific papers, or magazine articles. To read a work as literature means to pay attention both to the various meanings it conveys (its insights into human relationships, for example) and to the artistry with which these insights are conveyed (a lively and convincing portrait of a character, for example, or a passage whose vivid and original language evokes a strong emotional response or brings a scene to life in a reader's mind).

57.1

It is possible to read almost any kind of text with this dual attention. For instance, you might read a newspaper editorial with a simultaneous focus on the author's point of view and on the persuasive and artful way it is presented. Yet in those works regarded as imaginative literature, the author generally calls special attention to the techniques of presentation, techniques such as characterization, plot, symbolism, and figurative uses of language. In addition, imaginative literature often conveys its meanings through a fictional representation of some setting or human activity: the events of a story, a confrontation between characters, a monologue revealing thoughts and emotions, or a scene in which events take place. To understand the meaning of such texts, you need to read them with a different kind of attention than you give to other kinds of writing. Likewise, to present in writing your interpretation of and responses to literary texts, you need to employ some special strategies of explanation and support.

57a Reading literary texts

When you read a novel, short story, or poem or view a drama or a film, you need to pay attention to both meaning and artistic technique. In doing this, however, you should be aware that there are many different strategies for reading and interpreting such works. Your choice of a reading strategy can determine the way you interpret a work's meaning and the way you respond to the writer's forms of expression. Your focus in reading can also dictate the strategies you should use in presenting your responses to a work. Your goal as a reader and writer concerned with meaning is to develop and present interpretations that your readers will consider insightful and convincing.

1 Read for meaning

For many critics and students of literature, to read for meaning is to read for theme. You can view **theme** as an idea, perspective, insight, or cluster of feelings that a work conveys or that permeates a work, organizing the relationships among its parts. Or you can view theme as the responses and insights readers are likely to derive from their experience of reading a work. In reading for meaning, therefore, you need to pay attention to theme, both as it is developed in a work and as it develops in your responses to the work.

STRATEGY

As you read, write down any ideas, perspectives, insights, or clusters of feelings the work seems to focus on. Pay attention to the various techniques writers generally employ for conveying meaning (see 57a-2): characterization and dialogue, events and conflicts, descriptions or scenes, and discussions of ideas and emotions (either by characters, the speaker, or the writer addressing readers directly). Write down potentially important ideas or themes in the margins (if you own the book), on a sheet of paper, or in a journal you keep while you read. You need not explore potential themes in depth; for a first reading, at least, an informal list can be very valuable.

Look especially for repetition and contrast as a key to importance. Repeated words and ideas, contrasting characters or events, and patterns of images can signal themes worth noticing.

In the following marginal notes on Anson Gonzalez's short poem "Little Rosebud Girl," for example, Sevon Randolf, a college student, indicates some repetitions and contrasts that reveal an important cluster of feelings and ideas (a theme) that she thinks the poem conveys.

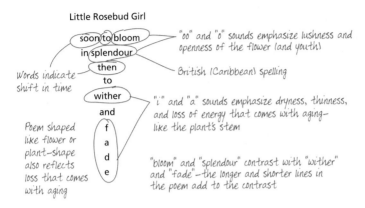

Little Rosebud Girl

soon to bloom
in splendour
then
to
wither
and
f
a
d
e

Words indicate shift in time

Poem shaped like flower or plant-shape also reflects loss that comes with aging

"oo" and "o" sounds emphasize lushness and openness of the flower (and youth)

British (Caribbean) spelling

"i" and "a" sounds emphasize dryness, thinness, and loss of energy that comes with aging— like the plant's stem

"bloom" and "splendour" contrast with "wither" and "fade"—the longer and shorter lines in the poem add to the contrast

—ANSON GONZALES, "Little Rosebud Girl" (1968)

The perspective you take as you read may suggest meanings and interpretations. If you know something about psychology, for instance, you might notice that the characters in a novel embody different psychological types or that the main character's actions can be explained as an attempt to overcome feelings of abandonment as a child. If you know something about history or political theory, you might be able to explain the events in a play as a reflection of an attempt to resolve contradictions affecting a particular society or culture. For example, you might be able to show that Shakespeare's plays *Macbeth* and *Henry IV* deal with questions of power and the proper form of government, major concerns in Elizabethan England. Finally, if you are familiar with contemporary feminist thought, you might note that the psychological and social portraits in a work seem to follow recognizable patterns of dominance and oppression and that the work seems to be designed as a commentary on the ways society has often distorted the lives of women. (Jennifer O'Berry's paper on "The Yellow Wallpaper" in 57c-2 draws on several such approaches.)

2 Read for technique

When you read for meaning, you inevitably read for technique. A writer cannot create events, portray characters, represent scenes, or elicit a reader's reactions without using techniques of characterization, plot, setting, or imaginative language. Nonetheless, because these techniques are such an important feature of every literary text, you may wish to focus on them as you read, either to understand a writer's artistry or to cite the writer's use of the techniques as evidence for your discussion of a work's meaning.

As you read, pay particular attention to the following elements of a novel, short story, poem, or drama and to the techniques the writer uses in creating these elements.

57a
lit

57a
lit

DID YOU KNOW?

> If you look to contemporary literary critics for ways to analyze texts, you may notice that their work follows one or more "schools" of criticism. Some critics emphasize the formal techniques in a work (new criticism); others look for the way a text contradicts or undermines its explicit purposes (deconstruction). Still others pay attention to the historical context, either to explain a work's meaning (historicism) or to interpret it as a product of a specific social formation (new historicism). Some critics look at the many ways readers respond to a text (reader-response criticism); others are more concerned with the writer's mind or the way a text probes human psychology (psychological criticism). And some pay special attention to the role of gender in the reading and writing of literary texts (feminist criticism).
>
> Steven Lynn, *Texts and Contexts: Writing About Literature with Critical Theory* (New York: HarperCollins, 1994).

Character. Identify the major and minor characters and their personality traits. Are they represented in depth with a variety of traits, even contradictions, or are they one-dimensional? Observe how the characters change and develop—or fail to change—in response to events. Note how self-aware the characters are. Which ones are presented positively, which negatively? Consider which characters, if any, represent values that the work (and the writer) seems to endorse.

Plot. Identify the order of events. Is it chronological, or have events been rearranged in some way? Decide what role conflicts play in developing the plot. Ask whether the events spring from the characters' personalities or serve primarily to reveal character traits. Is there a main conflict, a chain of conflicts, or a climax to which the work builds? Weigh the possibility that not all events are to be taken at face value. Watch for subplots alongside the main plot. Is the meaning of events clear to characters (and readers) from the start or only later? Pay attention to techniques of foreshadowing and suspense.

Setting. Note the time and place in which the events occur, along with any extended descriptions or background information relating to the place and time. Does the setting help explain the character's actions or reactions? Does it convey a mood that shapes the readers' reactions or the work's meaning? If the work is from an earlier period, check for elements in the setting that require historical explanation.

Point of view. For novels and stories, decide who is telling the story. Stories can be narrated in the first person (*I*) either by a character in the narrative or by a narrative voice (sometimes representing the author). They can also be told in the third person by a narrator who speaks of the characters as *he* and *she* but does not identify himself or herself as *I*. Narrators may be limited in what they know, be omniscient (knowing and seeing things the characters cannot), or combine both in some way. Narrators may be reliable and truthful, be unreliable and deceptive, or mix these and other traits. The speaker in a poem may be a character or may be a persona, a voice that speaks for the poet.

Language. Look for special uses of language: similes, metaphors, understatement, paradoxes, ironic comments, and the like. Pay attention to vivid descriptive language that creates scenes and images (sight, sound, and the like). Look for unusual word choice and striking or emphatic arrangements of words. Be alert for rhythms in the wording and for patterns of sound and rhyme.

57a
lit

Genre. Pay attention to **genre**—the specific form or kind of work: novel, short story, poem, drama, or film. Be especially alert to the techniques and conventions characteristic of each form, and note how writers use these conventions to convey meanings and shape readers' reactions. Note instances in which the writer varies or alters conventions, perhaps by undermining them or developing them in unusual directions.

STRATEGY

As you read a literary text, make notes on the large-scale techniques the writer uses to shape the work (genre, plot, and point of view, for example) and also on the smaller-scale techniques that appear to be important in a particular passage (language and character, for example). If you make your notes in the margins of your book, you can highlight passages you may wish to cite later in a paper. If you make notes in your journal, however, you will have more room to explore your responses and the ideas you may wish to develop in a paper. (Your journal entries also should note important passages for later use.)

Whenever possible, relate your observations on technique to your perceptions of a work's meaning. This will help you understand the purposes behind the techniques. It will also help you identify evidence for your interpretations of a work.

Note how T. J. Corini's marginal notes on the opening paragraph of John Edgar Wideman's novel *Philadelphia Fire* identify techniques and link them to meaning in a way that points toward a paper he might write.

first character—
a hero? an outlaw?

What's going on?

On a day like this the big toe of Zivanias had
failed him. Zivanias named for the moonshine his
grandfather cooked, best white lightning on the
island. Cudjoe had listened to the story of the name *2nd character*
many times. Was slightly envious. He would like to *Cudjoe uncertain*
be named for something his father or grandfather *of his manliness?*

The bones symbolize the contrast

had done well. A name celebrating a deed. A name *Admires 2?*
to stamp him, guide him. They'd shared a meal
once. Zivanias crunching fried fish like Rice
Krispies. Laughing at Cudjoe. Pointing to Cudjoe's *2. self-*

57b
lit

His actions make him seem verbal, self-assured

heap of cast-off crust and bones, his own clean *sufficient? Sure*
platter. Zivanias had lived up to his name. Deserted *of himself?*
a flock of goats, a wife and three sons up in the *Characterization*
hills, scavenged work on the waterfront till he talked *—2.'s actions*
himself onto one of the launches jitneying tourists *and attitudes*
around the island. A captain soon. Then captain *contrast w/C.'s*

Repetition and parallelism help emphasize his growing legend

of captains. Best pilot, lover, drinker, dancer, story- *contrast*
teller of them all. He said so. No one said different. On a day like this when nobody else dared *Contrast*
leave port, he drove a boatload of bootleg whiskey
to the bottom of the ocean. Never a trace. Not a
bottle or bone. *Whole ¶ presents contrasts of*
character, attitude, perspective, and detail

Exercise 1

A. Choose a short text or part of a text you are planning to write about.
Read it, making notes on the meaning and technique in the margins or
in a journal.

B. Ask a classmate to read the same text and make the same kind of
notes that you made in Exercise 1A. (Return the favor by reading and
annotating a text for your classmate.) Compare your notes, looking for
points of agreement. Discuss any annotations or interpretations that
need explanation or support.

57b Writing about literary texts

When you write about a literary text, you interpret and analyze an author's words and techniques. To do so, you must arrive at conclusions—judgments and observations—with which another reader may agree or disagree.
Consequently, you need to convince readers that your conclusions are both
reasonable and well founded. You can generally do this by offering evidence
from the text or from secondary sources.

1 Write about meaning

In writing about the meaning of a literary work, you may explain and support your conclusions about its theme. Or you may focus on insights you develop by applying a particular perspective to the work (a historical perspective or a feminist perspective, for example).

Developing a thesis. If you are writing about a work's theme, you need to make sure readers can easily identify your statement of the theme. Presenting your conclusion about the theme early in your paper in a thesis statement is a particularly effective strategy. In addition, if you develop a working thesis early in your drafting, you can revise it and use it to help focus your supporting paragraphs.

57b
lit

Selecting evidence. Suppose you developed the following working thesis for a paper.

> In "Young Goodman Brown," Hawthorne focuses on the dangers to human relationships and community posed by excessive concern with the self.

For supporting evidence, you can turn to passages in the text itself, either those that seem to state this theme or those you can analyze and explain in ways that support your conclusion. Simply quoting passages from the work is not enough. You need to discuss and analyze them in detail in order to show readers why the passages support your interpretation. You can also cite or summarize other elements of a work, such as events, characters, and symbols, analyzing them in detail to show that the text and the techniques it employs are consistent with your interpretation. Finally, you can turn to the writing of critics and scholars, using it to support your thesis and your view of specific parts of a work.

Organizing. Because a paper about meaning focuses on your view of a text's theme or on your interpretation of all or part of the work, you need to organize the paper to explain and defend your perspective. There are two general ways to do this (with many variations, of course). One way is to separate your thesis into parts and take up each part in a different section of your paper. In writing about Hawthorne's "Young Goodman Brown," for instance, you might first demonstrate that the story deals with a character obsessed with the self, then look at what the story says about the consequences of this behavior. The other way to organize your paper is to divide it into parts corresponding to different segments of the work (beginning, middle, end) or different elements (characters, language, symbols), then show in sections of your paper how the particular part or element supports your thesis.

> ## STRATEGY
>
> Follow these conventions for writing about literature.
>
> - Use the present tense when summarizing literary texts ("In the next section of the play, Falstaff *acts* in a manner that calls into question the kind of morality he represents").
> - Use the present tense for discussing what a writer does in a particular work or group of works ("Dickens *uses* descriptive passages in *Bleak House* to develop symbols that comment on the action and the characters").
> - Use the past tense for discussing a work in historical context ("During the Vietnam War, Levertov's poetry *took* on a distinctly political tone").

2 Write about technique

In writing about technique, you explain the choices the author has made from the resources available for creating fiction, poetry, or drama. You also try to highlight the author's variations on the techniques, if any. Finally, you draw conclusions about the roles the techniques play in shaping the work's meaning and the likely responses of readers.

Developing a thesis. Since your purpose in this kind of paper is to describe and analyze one or several techniques and then relate technique to meaning, your thesis statement should reflect this dual emphasis. In writing about the story "Young Goodman Brown," for example, you might say, "Hawthorne uses ambiguity in setting, symbolism, and characterization to suggest how excessive concern with the self can alter one's perception of everyday events."

Selecting evidence. The primary evidence in a paper about technique is the text itself, presented either through quotations or through paraphrase and summary. But details from a text are not enough on their own to support your conclusions. You need to discuss the evidence, explaining the particular ways a technique is used and pointing out how this use supports your conclusions about the text's meaning. (The work of critics and scholars can also provide supporting evidence.)

Organizing. If you are examining a single technique, consider dividing your essay into parts corresponding to different sections of the work, demonstrating how the technique is employed in each section and for what purpose. (For a short work such as a poem, you might examine the work line by line or sentence by sentence, creating an **explication**.) If you examine more than one technique, you can divide your paper into parts, each concerned with the way a different technique is employed. Or you can take up each section of a work in turn, looking at the various techniques used there.

A WORD ABOUT SPEAKING

When giving oral presentations about literature and literary analysis, it may be important for you to read lines from a work of literature aloud. The quality of your presentation will depend on the clarity and effectiveness of that reading. Because literature begs to be read in dramatic ways, think carefully about the literature you are quoting, and spend extra time practicing your reading of it.

57c
lit

Exercise 2

A. Choose a work you plan to write about. Read it, and write out a tentative thesis statement presenting your conclusions about the work's meaning and technique. Then prepare a list of particular passages or sections of the work you plan to use as evidence in your paper. Finally, create a rough outline or some other kind of plan for this paper.

B. Present your tentative thesis, list of evidence, and plan to a group of writers working on the same project. Discuss each writer's material, offering criticisms and suggestions to help each other prepare a draft. Draft your paper, and then share it with the same group for advice about revision. Take the group's advice into account as you revise and prepare the final draft.

57c The text analysis

57.2

A **text analysis** is a frequent assignment in many courses across the college curriculum. The first of the three examples here focuses on literary techniques in a poem. The second focuses on meaning in a short story. The third discusses visual strategies in a film.

1 Sample text analysis: Focus on technique

As you read the following paper, note how the writer goes through the poem line by line, accounting for nearly every image and phrase. This form of analysis is often called explication.

"Under Stars": A Portrait

by Chantele Giles

Under Stars

Tess Gallagher

The sleep of this night deepens
because I have walked coatless from the house
carrying the white envelope.
All night it will say one name
in its little tin house by the roadside.

I have raised the metal flag
so its shadow under the roadlamp
leaves an imprint on the rain-heavy bushes.
Now I will walk back
thinking of the few lights still on
in the town a mile away.

In the yellowed light of a kitchen
the millworker has finished his coffee,
his wife has laid out the white slices of bread
on the counter. Now while the bed they have left
is still warm, I will think of you, you
who are so far away
you have caused me to look up at stars.

Tonight they have not moved
from childhood, those games played after dark.
Again I walk into the wet grass
toward the starry voices. Again, I
am the found one, intimate, returned
by all I touch on the way.

1978

1   With the use of visual imagery in the poem "Under Stars," Tess
Gallagher paints a romantic, yet lonely portrait of the relationship
between the speaker of the poem and her long-distance lover. Although
the speaker's emotional state is plagued with images of loneliness,
she projects the long-distance romance as a positive relationship
that is warm and caring.

2   As Gallagher brushes "The sleep of this night deepens" of the
first stanza onto her canvas, her poetry begins to take shape. The
word "sleep" implies that the relationship with her lover is
peaceful. Since the "night" personifies the relationship, the phrase
implies further that the relationship is past the early stages and is
deepening with the "sleep" of the night. In the next lines the
speaker is walking "coatless from the house / carrying the white
envelope." She walks "coatless" because she does not need to cloak
the relationship; she is neither afraid nor ashamed. Since the "white
envelope" connotes purity, goodness, and truth, it symbolizes the
relationship as being true. The word "coatless" implies not only that
the speaker has nothing to hide, but that the affiliation is warm and
caring. If it were cold and dysfunctional, the speaker would not be
without a coat.

3   In the last two lines, Gallagher applies the final strokes to
the first stanza. The first of the two lines implies that the speaker
is consumed with thoughts of her lover. With the image of the "little
tin house by the roadside," Gallagher suggests that the speaker's
lover is some distance away, which implies that the speaker is trying
to bridge the distance between the two of them. She accomplishes this
by composing a letter and placing it in the "little tin house."

4   Since the second stanza exposes the inadequacies of the
relationship, Gallagher applies a darker paint to her canvas. The
"metal flag" suggests the cold reality of a long-distance
relationship, since metal is cold to the touch; the flag's "shadow"
implies that the relationship cannot be touched by the speaker. The

57c
lit

association with her lover leaves only a lonely "imprint" on the speaker's heart, which is symbolized by the "rain-heavy bushes." The final three lines are painted a lighter color. With these lines, the speaker implies that the "shadow" of loneliness is not permanent. Since the "town a mile away" symbolizes the future, the speaker implies that the future is close at hand. The "few lights" of the town suggest that there is hope in the near future.

57c
lit

5   Gallagher allows the readers into the realm of the speaker's fantasy, as she begins the third stanza. The "millworker" and "his wife" represent her fantasy relationship. The warm atmosphere created by the "yellowed light" implies that the speaker's fantasy is cheerful and bright. In this relationship, the couple reside and share their meals together. The "white slices of bread" connote food, nourishment, and sustenance. Since the "wife has laid out the white slices of bread" for the "millworker," the speaker implies that not only does she want to be her lover's sustenance, but she also wants to be consumed by him (the way the "millworker" will consume the "bread").

6   The last lines of the third stanza illustrate the speaker's need for closeness. Since the lover is "so far away" and the speaker looks "up at the stars," the speaker feels closer to her lover because of the possibility that the lover may be looking "up at the stars" also. This possibility creates a connection between the speaker and her lover. In the fourth stanza, Gallagher strokes onto her portrait "Tonight they have not moved / from childhood, those games played after dark." These lines suggest that the distance between the speaker and her lover has done little to change the affection she feels for her lover. "Those games played after dark" may refer to romantic liaisons; since these liaisons involve intense feelings, the speaker implies that the intensity of her feelings "[has] not moved from [the] childhood" of the relationship. Therefore, the speaker's connection to her lover is permanent.

7   With "Again I walk into the wet grass," Gallagher demonstrates
that the speaker looks "up at the stars" on a regular basis, thus
reinforcing the various images of the poem such as walking coatless
and the "rain-heavy bushes." The "starry voices" recall the images
set forth in the third stanza and the first part of the fourth
stanza. This line reinforces the images of the speaker's heavenly
fantasy, as well as the feelings of permanence.

8   In the last lines, Gallagher displays the speaker's final
analysis of the relationship. It is long-lasting and can survive the
long-distance barrier. Since she considers herself to be "the found
one," she implies that her lover is her one and only true love. She
says further that her love is "returned by all" she touches, implying
that their love is a powerful, all-encompassing natural force.

57c
lit

9   Tess Gallagher creates a gentle but stirring portrait of true
love. Although the images suggest that the speaker endures the
heartache of the separation, she does not succumb to the depression
usually associated with it. Instead, she embraces the negative
aspects of the situation and disempowers them through her fantasies
and stargazing.

2 Sample text analysis: Focus on meaning

As you read, note how the writer backs up her interpretation with
quotations from the story but does not let the quotations dominate the paper.
If you have read this short story, consider other ways it could be interpreted;
if you have not read the story, consider other ways the quotations used in this
sample could be interpreted.

Images of Self in "The Yellow Wallpaper"

by Jennifer O'Berry

1   During the 1800s the idea of the "new woman" was appearing.
Women began to realize that they were seen only as their husbands'
and society's "property." They began to pursue their independence and
create their own identities. In Charlotte Perkins Gilman's short
story "The Yellow Wallpaper," a nameless woman is searching for her

personal identity and freedom from the oppressive childlike treatment inflicted on her by her doctor/husband. Gilman presents an elaborate metaphor about the images seen by the woman within the wallpaper found in her nursery/bedroom. This metaphor and the images the woman finds in the wallpaper play a significant role in the woman's achievement of finding her true self. Her state of insanity at the end of the story serves as a safe mask for her newly found freedom from alienation and oppression.

2   Gilman presents the woman in her story as a somewhat unstable character who believes that she is sick, although John, her doctor/husband, believes that she is only suffering from a "slight hysterical tendency" (416). This characterization seems intentional on the part of Gilman because it makes the reader see clearly that the woman's ideas are oppressed, even from the beginning, by her husband. John thinks that all his wife needs is a strict rest schedule in which she is "absolutely forbidden to 'work'" (416) until she is "well" again. Gilman seems to suggest, by putting work in quotes, that the duties of the woman, and all women at that time, were not truly considered work. She was forbidden to write and to have visitors. Early in the story, when the "rules" for her recovery are stated, the woman begins to comment on her disagreement with her husband, but she stops abruptly, as if she does not dare to have such thoughts. She believes that she would more quickly recover if, instead of being quarantined and forbidden from such pleasures as her writing, she "had less opposition and more society and stimulus" (416).

3   The woman tells the reader that "Mary is so good with the baby" (417), implying that she herself does not want to spend time with the baby. The child is also never mentioned by the woman as being with her or spending time with her. This seems to suggest that she may actually be experiencing a type of postpartum depression, causing her

to want to abandon her child. The thoughts that lead her to feel that she may be ill may actually be due to her desire to abandon her role of wife and mother which was so rigidly demanded by society at that time. She gets "unreasonably angry" (416) about the condition of things sometimes, but she blames this anger on her "nervous condition" (416). She tries to dismiss these thoughts because she feels that they are not proper. Therefore, she feels that she must be ill.

4   Gilman uses many images to enlighten the reader about the childlike treatment of the woman by her husband. The woman is directed by her husband to rest in a bedroom that used to serve as a nursery. Gilman chooses this room to show how John thinks of his wife. When referring to his wife, John commonly chooses names such as "blessed little goose" (418), "blessed child" (420), and "little girl" (421). This shows that he does not see his wife as an equal but rather as a helpless child who is solely dependent on him. As the woman begins to realize that she has been a subject of this type of oppression, she begins to be "a little afraid of John" (422) and to "wish he would take another room" (424), which exhibits her awareness of this treatment and the desire to be free from it, and from him.

5   Because of her rigid rest schedule, the woman is forced to spend most of her time in her nursery/bedroom, where she begins to explore the "worst [wall]paper" (417) she has ever seen in her life. Since she is not allowed to do much else, she commits herself to "follow that pointless pattern to some sort of conclusion" (419). She finds many images in the pattern, all of which aid in her "improvement" (423) "because of the wallpaper" (423) out of her mother/wife roles. She describes the pattern as images that will "plunge off at outrageous angles, [and] destroy themselves in unheard-of contradiction" (417). These "contradictions" seem to be referring to the contradictory treatment of her by her husband and society's

57c
lit

contradictory expectations of her to be the perfect wife and mother. She becomes entranced by the wallpaper and "follows the pattern about by the hour" (419). With each second, the images become more numerous and complex. She begins to see "a broken neck and two bulbous eyes" (418), a woman behind the pattern in wallpaper. This woman "is all the time trying to climb through [. . .] but nobody could climb through [. . .] it strangles so" (424). She begins to identify with the woman and decides that she will stop at nothing until the woman is released from her entrapment.

6   At the end of the story, the woman is simultaneously on the brink of self-identity and insanity. On the last night she is to stay in the house, she is left alone in the room where she finally frees the woman in the wallpaper. When the woman in the wallpaper begins to "crawl and shake the pattern" (425), the main character "[runs] to help her" (425). Through the night, the two women pull and shake the bars and are able to "peel off yards of that paper" (425). She breaks down some of these cultural bars with the help from the woman in the wallpaper. When morning arrives, there is only one woman--the two have merged, and the woman's true identity has been found. In the remaining wallpaper are "many of those creeping women" (426). This symbolically represents the great number of women who also desire to be freed from the bars put up by society. She wonders if those women will ever "come out of the wallpaper as [she] did" (426). This shows her symbolic escape and her desire for other women to experience this personal freedom.

7   John returns at the end of the story to discover his wife in a state of insanity. When he sees her as the woman in the wallpaper, creeping around the room, he faints. She "had to creep over him" (426) because he was blocking her path. This strongly symbolizes the conquering of her husband because of her dominant position over him. She tells him that he cannot "put [her] back" (426) because she is finally free. Her creeping, which is like that of an infant, seems to

represent a birth of her new self. At the same time, she has become completely insane. It is rather ironic that she must move into this state in order to be free from oppression. This seems to represent society's view of a liberated and self-identified woman. John believes that his wife is not ill before she begins her pursuit of self-discovery. When this discovery is complete, he sees her as insane. The opposite is true for the woman herself. She sees herself as ill before her process of identification and fully healthy afterward.

57c
lit

8   The woman in Gilman's short story uses the yellow wallpaper as a tool to find her true self. The color of the wallpaper itself seems to represent the brightness and hope of a new horizon, yet at the same time, it is a reminder of the "old, foul, bad yellow things" (423), like a fungus that grows and decays. This is representative of the woman's life. She can never truly be free, because society's views and ideas will never acknowledge that a liberated woman can achieve her own identity.

3 Sample text analysis: Focus on technique (film)

As you read, notice how the writer organizes his paper and uses details from the film to illustrate and support his points.

Realism and Visual Effect in Educating Rita

by Jason Fester

1   Educating Rita is a realistic film. It depicts an older woman hairdresser who returns to college to become educated. As a realistic film it presents itself very conventionally with authentic sets, vernacular dialogue, and routine eye-level shots with conversations consisting of medium two-shots and close-ups. Since the film concentrates on language and the interaction of characters, the other elements of cinematic technique seem secondary, and as a realistic film, this seems appropriate. "Realists [. . .] try to preserve the illusion that their film world is unmanipulated; an objective mirror

of the actual world" (Giannetti 3). But the director inconspicuously uses color to parallel character development and contribute to the theme of his movie.

2   When Rita is first seen, she is light-skinned and has bleached blonde hair. She wears red lipstick, a thin white shirt, high heels, and a tight hot-pink skirt. The next time she is seen, she wears a white shirt, a bright red skirt, high heels, dangling silver earrings, and this time pink highlights adorning her hair. Rita is a vivacious, vivid woman, and the colors of her wardrobe reflect this. Her appearance presents her as sexual and corporeal.

3   The university, however, is a dull, colorless place. The building's walls are dirty white and gray stone. Frank's office is a dungeon of brown curtains, olive walls, and a drab red carpet, all bordered by a montage of tan, matte yellow, earth brown, and olive drab books. Everything associated with the university is plain, colorless, and somber. Frank's house continues the decorum of his office with brown curtains, muted yellow, and olive drab wallpaper. Frank wears suits exclusively in varying tones of tan; his friend exists in the same gray suit throughout the movie, and even Julia limits her wardrobe to red-browns. There is no vividness to any of these places or people. Everything, except Frank, is sober.

4   This is the world to which Rita commits herself, regardless of Frank's warning that she will have to "suppress, perhaps even abandon altogether, [her] uniqueness." Thus it is appropriate that at the stage of her development when she has chosen to commit to her education, saying "I want to change," she is wearing a tan jacket with a brown skirt.

5   With the advent of spring comes the next phase of Rita's transformation: summer school. Here her apparel consists of the light blues and greens of the fertile season, suggesting that Rita herself is flourishing and growing. Upon her return to Cambridge, she responds to a compliment on her appearance with "I got a whole new

wardrobe." Her appearance is now quite different from when she was first introduced. Her hair is now her natural brown; she is unadorned with jewelry or makeup; and she is clothed in a blue blazer, loose-fitting white pants, and a long white scarf. These neutral, asexual colors and styles continue throughout this period of her activities: light blues, greens, and soft grays cause her to blend with the garments of her student peers and the lusterlessness of the college.

6   Exceptions to this pattern are the retrogressive Roaring Twenties outfits Rita wears for the bistro. They consist of hot pinks, turquoise, pink and blue leopard skins, and lime greens arrayed in clashing ensembles. But these serve to mock her original style, for when she jokingly displays one outfit to Frank, he humourlessly replies, "Why can't you just be yourself?"

7   The end of the movie presents a Rita vastly different from the one introduced at the beginning. Rita is now merely Susan, a confused, unfulfilled woman. She is dressed in blue jeans, common and ordinary. She wears no makeup. Her long brown hair hangs limply on her shoulders. As she walks along, her blue clothes merge with the dreary blues and grays of the wet rained-on streets. She doesn't know where she's going; she doesn't know what she wants to do.

8   The director uses the colors of Rita's clothes contrasted against the colors of her environment to further express the character changes she undergoes. Even though this is a realistic film, the director surreptitiously manipulates one technique, color, in a way that affects the emotions and responses of the viewer.

57c
lit

Work Cited

Giannetti, Louis D. Understanding Movies. 6th ed. Englewood Cliffs: Prentice, 1993.

4 Elements of a text analysis

An effective text analysis includes the following elements.

- It presents a unified interpretation that attempts to convince its readers of one specific way of reading the text.
- It accounts for every idea, argument, image, or allusion; it does not overlook elements that don't fit into the interpretation.
- It does not try to hide behind a facade of objectivity, presenting opinions as absolute truths, but neither does it resort to the relativist plea that "one person's opinion is just as valid as another's."
- It attempts to add a new way of reading the text to the existing ways; it does not merely repeat what has already been written about the text.
- It assumes a dialogue with the reader.

5 Commentary on students' papers

Chantele Giles was faced with the problem typical of writing explications of poetry, that of making the explication as lively and as engaging as the poem itself. Knowing that she must account for every line and image of the poem, she starts at the beginning and moves line by line to the end. To add interest, she frames the explication with an analogy of the poet to a painter, but her prose still sounds too dry. She could enliven her paper by varying the organization, perhaps by using the analogy as a frame to begin and end the paper rather than to begin each paragraph. She could also alternate the line-by-line approach with an occasional comment on the overall meaning of the poem. And she could move beyond discussing the meaning of the poem to other ways of looking at it, such as analyzing its effect on her or other readers or comparing it to other poems.

Jennifer O'Berry uses quotations from the text well; she seems to have an intuitive sense of what is significant about them and how they relate to each other. She could improve the paper by discussing these quotations in more depth, explaining why they are significant in understanding how this story illustrates the ways women were oppressed. As the paper is now, the significance of the quotations is a bit unclear, mainly because Jennifer does not define the terms that she uses to explain their significance (terms such as *self-identity*, *true self*, *insanity*, and *oppression*). Defining these terms would help strengthen the connection between the quotations and the discussion.

Jason Fester assumes that readers will be familiar with the film he is discussing, and as a result, he does not adequately identify some of the characters, scenes, and relationships he discusses. At the same time, however, his discussion of Rita's appearance and its relationship to her character is especially clear. He organizes his discussion so that it follows the chronological order of the film. This is particularly appropriate not only because the organization aids him in demonstrating the pattern in Rita's changing dress but also because it allows him to draw parallels with Rita's changes in character and the themes developed through these changes. He also presents detailed evidence about the film's techniques so that he is able to show convincingly how the evidence supports his interpretations of the director's work.

CHAPTER 58

WRITING INFORMATIVE PAPERS ACROSS THE CURRICULUM

In many situations, your job as a writer may be primarily to convey information in a manner that is as clear, economical, and balanced as you can, serving the needs, interests, and curiosity of your readers. College writing assignments may ask you to gather and convey information—knowledge that you, as a student, have gained and are ready to convey to others. Unlike argument or other point-driven writing (see Chapter 55), **informative writing** doesn't aim primarily at supporting your opinion or your critical insights. Instead, informative writing asks you to adopt the stance of a careful reporter or an informed synthesizer.

Informative writing can describe a process or tell how to do something. It can report what others think about a topic or synthesize research findings. You can employ the strategies of informative writing to describe the components or structure of a natural object, to provide information that enables readers to arrive at informed judgments, or to record events.

Informative writing plays essential roles in business, government, research, and education. Most journalistic writing is also informative; reporters try to "tell it like it is" (or was). This chapter introduces some common uses for informative writing in college courses, and it outlines strategies you can employ in your informative writing in college and beyond.

58a Developing and presenting informative writing

58.1

Informative writing relies on thorough gathering of information, careful analysis and synthesis, and presentation shaped by both the subject matter and the readers' needs. Instead of thinking of readers as people to persuade, as in argumentative writing, you might think of them as clients who need information that you can supply in thoughtful, clear, and creative ways.

First, you need to offer your readers accurate information that is new, interesting, or useful to them. Your own values, attitudes, and opinions are less important than this information and its clarity and fairness. Though you,

809

as a writer, are present everywhere in the text, as a source of personal opinions you may move to the background to let your readers focus on the details, ideas, and events that are your subject. Explanations of complicated ideas and phenomena may challenge readers, but the reading experience itself should be free from complications such as poor organization, inappropriate wording, or hard-to-follow sentences.

1 Analyze your readers' needs

To provide an effective base for your informative writing, try to identify your readers and their purposes for wanting information. In academic settings, you can usually assume that you are providing a teacher and classmates with information related to the course work. Your classmates probably know relatively little about your topic; your teacher may have a fuller background but is reading both to learn something new and to discover what the presentation reveals about your knowledge and your insights.

58a
info

STRATEGY

Here are some ways to identify your readers' needs before you begin collecting and presenting information.

- In your journal or on a piece of paper, analyze your readers. How much background do they have in your subject? Are they experts, or do they represent a general, educated audience with no specialized knowledge? Are they merely curious about the topic, or will they do something with the knowledge (such as repair something, think differently about a subject, or seek more information)? (See also Chapter 5.)
- Find out what a friend or another trusted person would like to know about your topic, and list these questions or concerns.
- List information you already know about the topic. Then list questions you want to answer. If you ask and try to answer interesting questions, you are likely to share your involvement in the topic.

2 Collect information

Collecting expert material for an informative paper may involve probing your own memory or prior experiences; doing library research (see Chapters 45 and 46); doing field research through interviews, observations, surveys, or questionnaires; or collecting physical material for analysis. For a complex paper, you may need information from several different sources, organized in a sequence so that each stage of such work can inform the others.

Here are some planning tips for informative writing. (See Chapters 44–48 for important guidelines for library and field research.)

- Create a list of possible information sources, and then order the sources in different possible sequences. In each sequence, note what information will likely come from each source and how it might affect the use of the next source. Also include notes about any practical issues in the collection of information. Choose the possible sequence that seems the most practical. Here is a sequence one writer chose for a paper on recent biological research in the South American rain forests.

  1. Interview with Prof. James ⟶ help me focus on which Amazonian areas are most relevant for my paper, and suggest possible sources
  2. General library research ⟶ background on rain forest research
  3. Biology library research ⟶ information on medicinal discoveries from rain forest plants
  4. Interview with Susan Shoulder ⟶ what she felt when discovering plants that have never been classified

- Keep copious and accurate notes. If you are observing, write down only what you are sure you are seeing. If you are conducting an interview, take accurate notes or use a tape recorder. If you feel you are reaching a conclusion during the interview, don't mix your conclusions into the notes as if they came from the person being interviewed. Instead, ask your interviewee whether your conclusion is justified.

- Go back to your source, if possible, to verify or extend your data. If you *think* you saw a picture of a controversial activist on the office wall of the mayor you interviewed, see if you can verify its presence before mentioning it in your paper. You might even ask the mayor about its significance. If something in your library research is unclear, go back for more information to clarify the issue or fill the gap.

- Remember that your readers expect you to be fair to your subject and its various interpretations. Begin with what you know to be true, based on facts and evidence; don't leap to unsupported interpretations. Represent accurately what you *see* in your observations and what you *hear* in your interviews. If you cannot be balanced in your research or presentation, change subjects, or change to a kind of writing (argument, for instance) that allows you to take a position.

58a
info

3 Synthesize and "chunk" information

Informative writing relies on careful internal logic that helps readers to process and understand information. If you shift topics without an obvious plan, for example, readers will have trouble organizing information in their own minds and integrating it into their existing knowledge. In a paper about the relationship between diet and colon cancer in the United States, for instance, readers will be able to process the information more easily if you present it in logical categories rather than jumbling up disparate facts about colon cancer, the American diet, and the basic food groups.

58a
info

58.2

STRATEGY

To find an internal logic to your information, try some informal grouping and outlining techniques (see also Chapter 4).

- **Chunks.** List the main areas your paper will cover. All the information you have gathered should fit into these "chunks." If something does not fit, reconsider your list. Perhaps you can create an additional category for this item (and for others already listed elsewhere).

- **Patterns.** Look for patterns in your information. For example, if you are **comparing** or **contrasting** two objects or phenomena, then your work will involve two main groups of details or ideas—perhaps dividing your paper into two large sections or into a number of subtopics, each discussed in terms of your two main subjects. If you use **classification**, however, you will organize your information in terms of groups, categories, or parts, each presented in its own section. (See also 8b on patterns in paragraphs.)

- Also consider a **sequential order** (organizing information in a pattern within a particular perspective or focus) such as a *spatial sequence* (describing physical features in relationship to each other), a *chronological sequence* (describing events in a series to explain a history or the stages in a process), or a *hierarchical sequence* (describing relationships and the relative importance of a subject's features or parts).

In a complex paper, you may need to use more than one form of organization. A fairly long research paper about an artist might include chronological sequences about the artist's life and the development of his or her work, spatial sequences to describe and discuss specific works, and a hierarchical sequence in moving from least to most important works.

A WORD ABOUT SPEAKING

The same strategy for synthesizing and "chunking" information in writing applies to oral presentations. In most presentations, you can also choose to present certain kinds of information in visual form (on handouts, overhead transparencies, or *PowerPoint* slides), which allows you to sequence your information according to the suggestions in the Strategy box above. Think carefully about the relationship between what you want to *say* to your audience and what you want them to *see* or *read* during your presentation.

Exercise 1

58a
info

A. Choose a topic of interest to you. On the basis of your existing knowledge, select a potential organizing strategy to present some background information about the topic. Create a simple outline.

EXAMPLE

Topic: Building a deck
Organizing strategy: Sequential
Outline:
1. Planning the location and style
2. Determining and obtaining the materials
3. Setting concrete piers
4. Building a supporting frame
5. Laying deck boards
6. Building stairs and rails
7. Finishing and trimming the deck

B. Share your outlines in a small group. As you discuss the outlines, try to imagine an alternative organizing strategy based on the collective knowledge of the group.

4 Balance description with analysis or synthesis

In many kinds of informative writing, you will need to present information as a function of a careful **analysis** or **synthesis**. To analyze means to break a subject into its components and study the relationship among these parts—how they affect or relate to each other, how they work together, how they fit within a larger system, or how they are in turn divided into smaller systems. When you analyze, you look for connections, patterns, and relationships within the larger whole—for example, the "system" in a classroom rather than just the details describing it. On the other hand, synthesis involves combining separate elements into a unified whole, for example, bringing order to a "trend analysis" through an overview or general conclusion based on disparate studies or data.

STRATEGY

Try the following ways to find a balance, when appropriate, among analysis, synthesis, and description.

- Collect as much descriptive or factual information as you can. Then look for connections and relationships in the factual information. Such relationships may be *causal* (*A* causes *B*), *sequential* (*A* comes before *B*), or *hierarchical* (*A*, *B*, and *C* are really parts of *X*). (Try some of the Strategies in Chapter 4 to help you see beyond simple facts.)
- Ask yourself whether your description or facts alone are enough to give your readers insight into your subject. Recounting the events in a homicide may be enough for a newspaper report, but a simple list of facts about oil consumption in the United States may not interest readers as much as a careful, objective analysis of the likely consequences of these facts.

---

5 Check your stance

While conveying information fairly may seem like an easy task, don't be deceived; even journalists acknowledge that it is very difficult to report anything without subtly conveying a "point" or opinion. Consequently, it is important for you to think carefully about your own stance in relation to your subject, one in which you are not invested in a particular finding, conclusion, or set of facts. If you decide in advance that you can't write in a balanced way about your subject, don't deceive your readers into believing that you are being nonjudgmental in your treatment.

STRATEGY

- After writing a draft of an informative paper, ask yourself whether you are being true to the full range of information you discovered in your research. Ask yourself if you have left out information that might show your subject in a different and equally reasonable light. Responsible informative writing does not slant information but instead presents alternatives for readers to consider.
- Look carefully at any language in your draft that suggests an interpretation, such as *thus*, *therefore*, *as a result*, *consequently*, *it seems that*, or similar wording. Then ask whether that interpretation represents a fair conclusion in light of the information you gathered or whether it represents your particular opinion or bias.
- Locate and consider eliminating statements that carry strong personal opinions or judgments (such as *in my opinion*, *in my view*, *I believe*, or *I think*). Expletives like *it is clear that* and *there is evidence that*

can also help convey values and opinions (see 9c). You need not eliminate all of your conclusions or opinions, but make sure they are identifiable as your own and do not unfairly shape the information you present.

- The personal pronoun *I* is more commonly used now in informative writing than in the past but may signal a stance that is too subjective or biased. Look carefully at any personal pronouns, and ask whether they help give a personal touch to your writing without adding bias.

58a
info

Exercise 2

A. Indicate whether the following statements suggest a fair or biased stance on the topic. Write out a brief explanation of your conclusion.

EXAMPLE

After talking with about twenty mall shoppers, I am more convinced than ever that people who frequent malls are not avid readers.

Analysis: Suggests bias through the implication that the writer was convinced of the stated relationship before conducting the survey ("I am more convinced than ever").

1. These sixteen independent research reports indicate that people who live in the midst of suburban sprawl are just as likely to suffer from geographically related stress as people who live within city limits.

2. Although rural residents were not studied, I believe it is obvious that they are less stressed than urban and suburban residents.

3. Several studies showed conclusively that urban residents who spent at least one weekend a month at a rural retreat, such as a lakeside cabin, suffered from less stress than their counterparts who did not leave the city.

4. The results of most studies imply a lot about the relationship of stress to people's wealth. After all, if you're rich, you can afford to relieve your stress.

5. Three research studies also found that able people without jobs who lived in urban areas had less stress than their working counterparts. This fact shows that we must consider laziness when we think about stress.

B. In a small group, compare your responses to Exercise 2A. Collectively revise any sentences that the group agrees imply a biased treatment of the subject.

6 Present information clearly

Informative writing is highly sensitive to the ways readers understand and retain information. When you are working with many facts or statistics, for example, your readers may become confused, bored, or frustrated if you try to present all these in sentence form.

STRATEGY

To help your readers learn efficiently from your informative writing without confusion or frustration, try employing the following strategies if they are appropriate for your subject and your audience. For more information on these strategies, see Chapter 14.

- Use graphs, charts, tables, and figures. You can set off numerical data or words and short phrases elegantly in columns or boxes.
- Use section markers. Longer informative papers can benefit from sections organized by numbers or subtitles.
- Use graphic devices such as boldface, italics, or varied fonts (type styles) to help readers attend to specific terms or ideas that may be new. But be careful not to overuse such devices; too many different fonts, for example, can confuse readers more than help them.
- Use white space on the page. Too dense a text can tire your readers when you present a lot of information in long blocks. Break a discussion into shorter paragraphs, or use illustrations and tables.

Exercise 3

A. Examine a chapter from one of your textbooks in a course such as psychology or biology. Write a brief informal description of strategies used in the textbook to make the information easy to learn and retain. Look for section markers, graphic devices, tables and charts, illustrations, and the use of white space to help "chunk" the text. Make a photocopy of one page to attach to your description.

B. In a small group, compare textbook analyses. Observe any especially effective strategies for the presentation of information. Discuss how ineffective books or sections could be improved through the use of such strategies.

58b Developing an interview paper: Informative writing in progress

In his anthropology class, Brian Schwegler was assigned to write a paper about an interesting person, focusing particularly on the person's occupation. Examples his teacher offered were a mortician, a sky diver, and a female construction worker. The purpose of the assignment was to practice gathering information from sources other than library materials and to organize that information into an interesting, informative paper.

Brian remembered a performer at the boardwalk amusement area in a coastal resort town near his university campus. He decided that Dave "The Guesser" Glovsky would be a good subject. This person operated a guessing booth located near a striker hammer game. As a "guesser," Dave offers to guess people's ages, weights, occupations, and similar matters. When Dave agreed to give Brian an interview for his paper, Brian sketched this preliminary list of questions that could inform his final paper.

1. How do you guess? What do you do when you guess?
2. Do you do anything else besides guessing?
3. How did you get into this business?
4. What are some of your best guesses?
5. What types of people come to get guessed?

Arriving at the boardwalk armed with his questions and a tape recorder, Brian realized that he might be able to observe Dave at work as well as interview him. After spending about an hour with Dave doing both, Brian went home and began the long process of transcribing the tape-recorded session so he could accurately use quotations and details.

Below are the first few minutes of Brian's interview. Note how his list of preliminary questions helped to shape his interview without entirely controlling it. Also observe how accurately Brian created his transcript, even when other sounds on the tape drowned out a word or two.

Dave Glovsky

Palace Playland: Dave's Guessing Stand

July 8, 1999

Brian Schwegler

(Sound of game, "The Striker" hammer swing in background
for all of tape)

    First interchange between Brian Schwegler and Dave
Glovsky is inaudible, due to background noise.

BS: So, Dave, can you tell me a little something about
how you guess? Can you tell me how you guess?

DG: Ages? I read the lower lids. I read the lower lid. It
deteriorates as we get older. The more it gets darker,
they get older. Even children of sixteen can fool me with

the deterioration under the eyes. They can have beautiful skin, but I don't check the skin, I check the lower lid of their eyes.

BS: How about weight?

DG: Weight, well I just guess on the weight. You know, I feel the arm, I feel the stomach. Not women though, I don't touch the women. I just guess. . . .

[The interview continues until a customer arrives.]

DG: Hey come on in, have fun. What do you want me to guess?

Female cust: My age.

DG: All right, that's a dollar. (Holds up one-dollar bill) A hundred-dollar bill. Step into the office here. (Points to a patch of pavement) Are you going to tell me the truth?

Cust: Yeah.

DG: You wouldn't lie to me. You promise truly, yeah. Smile, is that your father here. (Points to male companion of similar age) I'm gonna say, look at the beautiful girl. Look at the face on her. Let's see if you are married. (Looks at hand to check for rings) Nope, not married. Holy Cow! (Writes 22 on pad) How old are you?

Cust: Eighteen.

DG: You got me, I got twenty-two.

Cust: Huh, yeah right.

DG: Well, the lower lid, the lower lid. What do you want me to guess on now? (To female companion of previous customer, who looks noticeably younger)

Cust 2: Age.

Cust: Twenty-two, I thought that you were going to say twelve.

DG: Can't get them all. Smile. [. . .]

At the end of the interview, Dave invited Brian to his home the next morning to talk further. Brian also wondered what other workers thought about Dave, so he returned to Palace Playland as well.

As he analyzed the transcript, it occurred to Brian that Dave's success as a guesser may depend on establishing the right social relationship with his customers, getting them to offer information or behave in a way that reveals something about their ages or other characteristics. Instead of making Dave's technique obvious to readers, Brian chose to present Dave's methods without detailed commentary. This approach would allow his paper to be true to the facts but point readers to an analysis of those facts without forcing them to accept any particular conclusion.

Brian decided to organize his essay in sequential order, using a "blended" chronological sequence that weaves details about Dave's life (past) with details of events occurring during the interview (present). Brian also planned to use some spatial sequences throughout the paper in describing Dave's surroundings. But as he wrote, Brian realized that he had three main sources of information—the original interview and observation, his brief interviews with other fair workers, and his visit to Dave's house. Not wanting to explain too much in his paper about the various interviews, he decided to "chunk" the two interviews with Dave into a single temporal sequence. Here is how he diagrammed the sequence in his planning notes.

Day 1:   *Interview and observation session ⟶ blend in workers'
          comments ⟶ Dave's invitation to come to his house*
Day 2:   *Dave's house*

Following are the first several pages of Brian's rough draft. Notice how Brian is able to maintain an objective, informative stance while still injecting some style and human interest into his account. Note also the artful balance of interview material and observational data, seamlessly blending information about Dave's life with the ongoing events in the present.

58b
info

First Draft: Dave the Guesser

by Brian Schwegler

1   "Come on in, have some fun with the famous guesser of Old
Orchard," says Dave "The Guesser" Glovsky. Relying on his voice and
personality to attract customers, he seems out of place in this
mechanized wonderland. Hand-painted signs covered with cramped
writing are his advertisement. I peer at them and try to decipher the
writing that is more anxious than able.

                         The Guesser Has Experience
                              Sex Appeal
                         Personality   Try him, you'll enjoy his
                                          humor and guessing skill.
               Palace Playland's World Famous Guess Station:
               Come in, fill up with fun--You'll be glad you did.

2   As I stand in front of his stand and read his signs, a young
woman approaches Dave.

3   "Hey, come on in, have fun. What do you want me to guess?" Dave
asks.

4   "My age," says the young woman.

5   "All right, that's a dollar." Holding up the dollar bill that
the woman gives him, Dave examines it the way a jeweler examines a
precious stone. "A hundred dollar bill." Pointing to a space on the
pavement, Dave says, "Step into the office here." Dave checks her out
from all angles, looking for the clue that will let him know her age
within two years, his margin of error. "Smile," he says while peering
into her face. Pointing to her boyfriend, Dave asks, "Is that your
father here?" Her face erupts into a smile, and Dave has gotten some
of the information he needs to make his guess. "Let's see if you are
married," he says, looking for a wedding ring. Seeing none, he smiles
and winks at me. He pulls a rumpled pad out of his pocket and a pen
out of nowhere and writes his guess on the paper. "How old are you?"

6   "Eighteen."

7   "You got me, I got twenty-two." Turning to her girlfriend, he
says, "Can't get them all. Smile. [. . .]"

8   Guessing is Dave's life, his living, his love. While at his
stand, he is an actor on a stage. He not only wants to take people's
money, he wants to entertain his customers. A former Portland
comedian, Dave once put on a show for Edwin Muskie while Muskie
was governor. Talking about the people that he guesses, Dave says,

"They like the fun that I give them. [. . .] I make them laugh."
There doesn't seem to be much of a difference to Dave between
being an actor and being a guesser. "I was a comedian anyways,"
he says with a shrug that tells me that is all that guessing
is about.

[The next two paragraphs further explain how Dave relates to people.]

11   Dave's guessing is a talent that he has worked on over the
years. He has a system worked out for guessing the person's age.
He relies on his knowledge of the human face, clinical knowledge
tempered by forty-five years of experience. He explains it to me
during a lull in our visit. I feel a kind of rush, excited to learn
the secrets of the trade.

12   "Well, the way I guess ages, they don't realize that I check
the lower lid of their eyes. And it's effective with eighty-five
percent of the people. The eyes on the bottom deteriorate as we
age. It gets darker and darker and wrinklier, and then at the
age of, beginning at the age of thirty-nine, it starts to get a,
getting a line up here, (on side of face). And then it gets deeper
and deeper and deeper, and when it gets way up here (at top of
cheeks), I really got to guess, fifty or sixty. And in the sixties,
they start getting these things (loose skin on neck). So, through
all of these years, I have accumulated all the knowledge of the
human face."

[The next four paragraphs explain Dave's other types of guesses and his impact on customers.]

17   Other workers at Palace Playland recognize the role that
Dave plays at the park. Chris McArthur, owner of Palace Groundz,
a coffee stand, says, "There's a lot of people that come in here
just to see him. And I've noticed people walk by and go, 'Oh my God,
he's still alive, he's still here. I remember him when I was a
little kid.'"

[The paper continues for five more pages.]

58c The short informative documented paper

In many courses, you may be asked to write an informative paper that draws on a few outside sources, most often those you have located in modest library research. Such papers do not argue a point but present information on a focused topic.

1 Sample short informative documented paper

As you read the following passages from David Aharonian's paper, note that even though it is informative, citing facts and statistics from four articles, it is not a paper without a thesis. Unlike an argumentative thesis (see 55c), however, David's thesis presents a conclusion based on his synthesis of research studies. Note, too, that his paper does not recommend a course of action, which would require taking a position; instead, it stops short of argument, allowing the reader to take the next step based on a considered response to the information David presents.

Desperate Times for Teachers

by David Aharonian

1   There is a major controversy regarding teacher salaries presently in this country. Many people feel that teachers are overpaid because they have summers off from work. They feel that teachers do not truly work year round and therefore are either getting a fair rate of pay or getting too much. Many teachers, however, disagree with this assessment. They feel that they are underpaid for the work that they do. Most teachers find it very difficult just to make ends meet on a teacher's salary, and often they resort to moonlighting.

2   Moonlighting means that a person holds another job in addition to his or her career. [. . .]

> [The next four paragraphs supply information and statistics on moonlighting teachers from two sources.]

7   But there really are no easy solutions to the problem. One obvious answer would be to increase teacher salaries (Alley 21). This would lead to less moonlighting and allow teachers to concentrate more on their primary occupation. But there are still plenty of

people who oppose raising teacher salaries. Many times teachers may go two or three years without any raise in their pay. Then when the teachers do get their raises, it may only be 2 or 4 percent. This certainly lowers the morale of the teachers and can cause the teacher to become frustrated (Henderson 12). As one teacher in Oklahoma put it, "It's hard to look across the hall and see a teacher who's taught 14 years, making only $4,000 more than you are" (Wisniewski and Kleine 1).

[This paper ends with a list of works cited.]

2 Elements of a short informative documented paper

An effective short informative documented paper includes the following elements.

- It concisely summarizes or synthesizes the views, research results, or positions of other writers.
- It presents information in the writer's own words but does so fairly, without bias.
- It may provide conclusions based on a reasoned consideration of the work it cites but usually allows the reader to decide what these conclusions mean for a course of action, set of beliefs, and the like.
- It is well organized and easy to read.

3 Commentary on David Aharonian's short informative documented paper

The writer does a good job of pulling together various research studies in an interesting short paper. His way of integrating the references into his own writing works nicely. If his paper had cited statistics more heavily, he could have presented them in a less narrative form, perhaps creating a box or chart. Although it ends with a direct quotation from a teacher, his paper seems to stop abruptly; he could have included a short paragraph summing up the material he cites. (For more information on research papers, see Chapters 44–48.)

58d The literature review

The **literature review**, also sometimes called a survey paper or a review of the literature, is usually one section of a longer paper but may be assigned as a paper in itself. In a psychology paper reporting the results of an experiment, for instance, the literature review is the first section after the introduction. The purpose of a literature review is to synthesize the existing research on your topic—to describe the main points of comparison and disagreement in others' studies. As the first section of a longer paper presenting your own research, it provides a backdrop for your study. Your study generally would not repeat what another study has already done but might test the hypothesis or the methods of an earlier study, examine an aspect overlooked by previous researchers, or study a related aspect of the topic in order to add to the accumulated knowledge. A literature review, then, establishes a context for your own research.

Most literature reviews try to present the findings of others in a fair and balanced manner. Two or more studies may reveal major disagreements in a field, but your job in a literature review is to document those disagreements without judging the studies themselves, at least initially. Some kinds of literature reviews do judge the works being summarized; for example, an author of a medical research article may present the findings of previous studies while criticizing their methods. Such a review tends to be more point-driven (see Chapter 56) because the writer is laying the groundwork for a claim that his or her own methods are superior. In most general college courses requiring a literature review, however, you will be asked to summarize the literature instead of critique it. Your reviews will be informative, aiming at summary and synthesis.

DID YOU KNOW?

College instructors often look for a thesis statement at the beginning of an academic paper as a guide to the line of reasoning and the kinds of evidence and arguments the student will present. Just as important for most instructors, however, are topic sentences and other statements in the body of a paper that guide readers through the steps in the reasoning and serve as reminders of the paper's overall purpose and direction. Students who do not include such reminders as they write may lose track of their own reasoning and produce disorganized papers. Even a well-organized paper can be hard to follow, however, if the writer does not provide readers with guidance throughout.

Linda K. Shamoon and Robert A. Schwegler, "Sociologists Reading Student Texts: Expectations and Perceptions," *Writing Instructor* 8 (Winter 1988): 71–84.

1 Sample literature review

Turn to the research paper in 52e for a sample literature review in the context of a longer paper. As you read this sample, note how the writer connects his sources to each other and to his own study.

2 Elements of a literature review

An effective literature review includes the following elements.

- It accurately and concisely summarizes the results of other researchers' work.
- It synthesizes these other studies, combining results where they overlap, while giving credit to each researcher.
- It includes major points of disagreement among the other studies.
- It establishes a context for your own study.

58e The lab report

If you take courses in subjects like biology, chemistry, physics, or engineering, you may find yourself writing lab reports. Your teacher will want to read, quickly, what you did in an experiment, and you will need to make your report as concise and as clear as possible. Although the format of a lab report can help you organize the information clearly, you will still need to avoid ambiguous language and unclear references.

The **lab report** represents a kind of informative writing in its sharp focus on the objective description of causes and effects. It requires just the right balance between too little and too much detail. If certain aspects of an experiment or procedure are irrelevant to the cause-effect relationship, you need not include them. However, it is important to describe very clearly just what was done in the experiment and what happened as a result. The color of the counter in the lab is irrelevant information, but the size of the beaker used may be important both to the replication of the experiment and to the nature of the processes involved.

Lab reports follow different formats, depending on the discipline in which they are written and even the requirements of individual teachers. Some teachers value conciseness and require all lab reports to be no longer than two double-spaced pages. Others expect more detail and may stretch the length to five or ten pages. Check with your teacher about the format, style, and other requirements of the report, such as specific section numbers and headings. A typical structure begins with an overview or *abstract* of the experiment, including its focus or goal (why it was done), an *introduction* to the problem or principles involved (what it shows), a description of the methods used (how it was done), an explanation of the *results* (what happened), a *discussion* of the outcomes (what the results mean), and a *conclusion* (what the experiment shows). See the sample paper in 52e for a similar presentation of research results in the social sciences.

1 Sample lab report

Speed of Sound in Water

by Michael Perry

I. <u>Abstract</u>. This experiment was designed to measure the speed of sound in water and determine how changes in the properties of the water affect the speed of sound. First, the speed of sound in water at room temperature was measured using a "time of flight" method. Then the speed of sound was measured at different temperatures to determine the change in the speed with varying temperature. The speed of sound from part 1 of the experiment was 1479.7 m/s. In part 2 the speed of sound was found to vary from 1419.75 m/s at 10.8°C to 1581.03 m/s at 33.10°C.

II. <u>Introduction</u>. A wave traveling through a material causes quick compressions and expansions of the material. The pressure and density oscillate where these compressions and expansions take place. The speed of the wave is determined by how much the density changes with a given pressure change. Water is a liquid and is therefore less compressible than a gas, for example, air. So it takes a greater pressure in water to change density a given amount. We can therefore expect the speed of sound in water to be greater than that in air. [. . .]

> [The paper continues with the following sections: III Experiment, IV Results, V Discussion, and VI Conclusion.]

2 Elements of a lab report

An effective lab report includes the following elements.

- It strictly follows the lab report format required by your teacher.
- It does not digress into unnecessary commentary on the experiment.
- It uses specific terminology and unambiguous language.
- It presents data and results accurately, without distortion.

3 Commentary on Michael Perry's lab report

Some of the terms are specialized for the field, but this report is written to an audience that understands the jargon. Perry's report is for the most part clear and concise; however, he could have explained why the time of flight method was not accurate.

58f The abstract

Teachers may often ask you to submit an abstract along with your lab report, study, or other research paper. An abstract is a concise summary of your paper. It is entirely objective, restating the content of the paper without extraneous commentary. An abstract for a scientific study must include, at a minimum, a summary of the hypothesis, the method, the results, and the discussion sections of your paper. An abstract of the review of the literature might be needed as well. The reader of your abstract, with no familiarity with your paper, should be able to understand not only the gist of the paper but your method, stance (your theory or opinion), and conclusions.

58g
info

1 Sample abstract

See the abstract in 58e, introducing a lab report, or in 50e, preceding a research study.

2 Elements of an abstract

An effective abstract includes the following elements.

- It summarizes all the important sections of your paper.
- It defines any key terms used in unique or unusual ways.
- It is concise; all unnecessary words and phrases are eliminated.

58g The annotated bibliography

An **annotated bibliography** is just like a regular bibliography (see Chapters 51–54) except that each entry includes an annotation describing the aim, purpose, or content of the work cited. Its purpose is to provide a useful resource for readers who want to find out what has been written about a topic or to consult specific works themselves. Annotated bibliographies are also commonly assigned in college courses either to help students to survey and report on a body of scholarship or to help them prepare for a longer research paper.

Usually you begin with a brief introduction to the topic, perhaps highlighting the kinds of works covered in your bibliography. You then cite each work and follow it with an annotation, usually in a short paragraph or two. Annotations sometimes employ an abbreviated sentence structure like this: Summarizes research on the development of the Cherokee syllabary.

1 Sample annotations

The annotation below has been taken from Ian Preston's annotated bibliography, which consisted of an introduction to the topic followed by twelve entries. He prepared his bibliography for a writing class focusing on language and bilingualism in the United States.

Annotated Bibliography on Bilingualism

by Ian Preston

Glazer, Nathan. "Where Is Multiculturalism Leading Us?" <u>Phi Delta</u>
    <u>Kappan</u> 75 (1993): 319-24. This article describes the Center for
the Study of Books in Spanish for Children and Adolescents, an
organization that promotes the positive aspects of bilingualism.
Unlike other organizations that portray their ethnic groups as
victims, the Center, Glazer argues, ought to be followed as a model
of a bilingual program.

2 Elements of an annotated bibliography

Effective annotated bibliographies usually include the following elements.

- An introduction that orients readers to the topic being covered, in several paragraphs or pages, depending upon the complexity of the topic or the range of the citations.
- A list of references to the literature cited, each followed by a clear précis or summary of the work that briefly but accurately represents the work.
- Accurate references that readers often use to locate the works listed. (See Chapters 51–54 for help with accurate bibliographical entries.)
- An emphasis on summary in order to provide readers with an accurate depiction of what the work says or does, without unnecessary detail.
- Alphabetical organization, generally by the authors' last names. Long or complex annotated bibliographies are often organized into sections, sometimes chronologically ("Nineteenth-Century Studies," "Twentieth-Century Studies"), sometimes by general topic or focus ("Studies Using Quantitative Research Methods," "Studies Using Qualitative Research Methods"), but still alphabetically within each section.

3 Commentary on Ian Preston's entry

Preston successfully captures the gist of the work cited. Notice how he includes both the topic of the article and its author's point of view.

58h The informative essay exam

Essay exams can be divided into those in which you illustrate and defend a claim or point (see 56c) and those in which you provide clear and objective information. The latter, the informative essay exam, can be relatively short—a paragraph or two describing a phenomenon, for example—or longer, involving more elaborate descriptions and data.

Informative essay exams must be carefully organized, clearly written, and detailed. After receiving your exam question, spend a few minutes developing a simple outline; even a three- to five-paragraph structure can help you to chunk your information and move from point to point logically so that a teacher can quickly see whether the essay reflects adequate knowledge of the subject.

1 Sample informative essay exam

The short informative essay exam that follows was written in a general biology course in response to this assignment: "Define the concept of natural selection, being sure to explain its main features and how it affects behavior." Students were given thirty minutes to craft their answers.

**58h
info**

Natural Selection Essay Exam

by Nicholas Branahan

Natural selection is a process in which the characteristics of an organism that best promote its ability to reproduce are selected and the characteristics which hinder it are weeded out. As random gene mutations form new characteristics, natural selection will select those that enhance the organism's ability to reproduce. Ability to reproduce depends on adaptability to the weather, ability to find food, avoidance of predators, and other aspects of survival.

[The answer continues in two more paragraphs.]

2 Elements of effective informative essay exams

An effective informative essay exam includes the following.

- It answers the question directly, without unnecessary padding.
- It is organized clearly and logically, with each paragraph focusing on a different aspect of the topic or question.
- It avoids obscure language or uninterpretable statements as a strategy for covering up an inability to answer the question.
- It includes, as possible, brief examples, cases, and references.

3 Commentary on Nicholas Branahan's informative essay exam

Branahan's essay shows that he understands the concept of natural selection. The first paragraph provides a general definition of the concept of natural selection. The second paragraph answers the question about the ways in which natural selection may affect behavior. The third paragraph extends the concept by considering what happens to the organism when the environment changes. The writing is clear, concise, and error-free, but adding one or two brief examples would make the answer less abstract.

CHAPTER 59

DEVELOPING BUSINESS WRITING

Enhanced by new technologies, communication between individuals and groups is a critical factor in virtually all business tasks. Your success in business depends largely on how you represent yourself through oral and written communication. Effective writers and speakers rapidly gain the respect and admiration of their colleagues; writing plays a major role in the adoption and implementation of new business strategies, projects, and practices; and demonstrated skills in writing and oral presentation are essential to professional advancement.

A complete discussion of business communication would take a book in itself. This chapter has more modest goals: to introduce you to some proven strategies that will help you achieve success in business writing, and to acquaint you with some standard business styles and practices. Think of it as a preliminary guide to successful business writing. As you become more familiar with the needs and expectations of the business community that you are entering, you should add a complete business writing guide to your personal library. These books offer sound advice on acceptable business writing styles and present models for a wide variety of business documents, in both hard copy and electronic form.

59a Using general strategies to learn the principles of successful business writing

Business writing is reader centered: you're writing to persuade, inform, or meet the needs and expectations of your audience. The strategies described in Chapter 1 and Chapter 5 of this handbook will help you enter the business community and make your writing and document design easily accessible to the reader. However, many businesses have a disciplinary foundation: community expectations are rigidly enforced. While most supervisors realize new employees need time to learn and adapt to the conventions of the business community, the following strategies will make this learning process quicker and less painful. And showing your employer you are actively seeking to learn local business writing practices demonstrates the kind of "take charge" attitude that is a marker of the successful businessperson.

1 Plan to meet your readers' needs

Your main focus while planning business writing will be the relationship between your information and your audience. Sometimes your audience will be made up of people working in different positions (for example, someone in the marketing department and someone else who handles shipments in the warehouse). Be sensitive to the needs and perspectives of your various intended readers.

59a
bus

Because your readers are likely to be busy and impatient—whether they are other people at work or members of the general public to whom you are writing in your professional capacity—you need to be especially careful in organizing your information.

Business documents should have a "friendly" design and layout, inviting the reader to read and to continue to read. Is there enough white space in your document to make it look uncluttered? Are your margins sufficient? What does the spacing of your document look like—are sections squeezed together, or have you left enough space to show blocks of information? Remember that a readable document is attractive and inviting, not tight and cluttered.

STRATEGY

Using the audience continuum in 6a, spend a few minutes writing about your intended readers. What do they know about the topic? How will they use the document? What do you know about their technical background, their level of education, their interest in the topic, and their need for what you have to offer?

STRATEGY

Write a precise outline of your information before you draft your document. In business writing, your reader should know what your document contains from the start, and its contents should have a logical and preconceived design. Outlines are especially effective (see Chapter 4).

2 Draft as clearly as possible

As you draft, remember to emphasize clarity. Effective business writing is easy to read—unambiguous, uncluttered, and direct.

> ## STRATEGY
>
> Instead of drafting with an eye to style, try to write the essential information as clearly and directly as you can. As you write, concentrate on exactly what you need to say. You can revise for a smoother and more appealing style after you've presented the main information directly.

3 Be sure to revise and edit

In some business settings you may be under pressure to write a document quickly—even more quickly than a paper due in two days for your composition class. Under these circumstances it's easy to skip the editing and revising process. Be especially careful not to fall into this trap. Reread *all* your documents. Plan your schedule so you have at least some time for revising and editing. Even a single badly chosen word, one garbled sentence, or a lone case of misinformation can be embarrassing.

In addition, set specific goals for your revising. Plan, for example, to eliminate wordy passages, extraneous information, and irrelevant facts. Or aim to avoid cliches, exaggeration, passive voice, and overly technical language. Try to choose vocabulary appropriate to your audience's level of expertise, and revise accordingly.

Business writing often makes use of graphics to present information clearly and concisely. When you use graphics, label them carefully, and mention them in the text of your document before they actually appear in the text. (See Chapter 14.)

59.1

59b Using specific strategies to learn the business writing process

As a new employee, one of your best resources is the fresh set of eyes you bring to the business. While observing the business writing process in your organization, look for answers to the following questions, which will accelerate your understanding of the ways in which the writing process is organized locally.

1 How are writing projects assigned?

Are assignments made by email, by memo, or by word of mouth? If your supervisor assigns projects orally, then be sure to take careful notes. However the assignment is made, be sure to check and double check that you have followed instructions exactly. If you have questions about the assignment, be sure to ask the supervisor, but don't pepper the boss with questions unless you have learned that she or he welcomes frequent discussions about work-in-progress.

2 Is most writing done individually, or in work groups?

If writing is done collaboratively, how is it done? Are individuals assigned to write sections of the project which are then assembled into a document, or do writers brainstorm and draft the document as a team, working around a conference table? Does collaboration occur electronically? If so, then it is important that you learn the conventions for electronic collaboration (see the section on email later in this chapter). Some companies use software packages, such as *Lotus Notes*, which provide an electronic environment for collaborative writing. Other companies simply use email but have conventions for file sharing and revision. Your co-workers are a good source of information regarding the ways in which your company approaches the invention and drafting process.

59b
bus

3 Does the company have a formal editing process?

Time is money is a mantra many businesses follow, and good editing takes time. Some companies have established formal levels of editing that will be assigned based on the type of document being produced. For example, an internal company memo might require only light editing for usage and clarity; a letter sent to an external supplier might require medium editing, which includes the elements of a light edit plus checking for passive construction, standard company formatting, and other stylistic issues; a proposal to win a competitive contract probably requires a heavy edit, which includes the elements of a medium edit, plus checking for organizational soundness, tone, coherence, and other more global issues. Regardless of the kind of editing process used by your company, it is important that you learn the expectations of your supervisor. Some supervisors want to see a draft quickly and care little about usage, mechanics, and style. Other supervisors want to see complete, well-edited drafts, regardless of the time constraints. Until you learn the needs and desires of your supervisor, careful self-editing is a must. Part Four of this handbook will be an invaluable aid to you in this process.

As you get feedback from your supervisor about your writing, start using that feedback to create a personal editing and revision checklist to ensure that you don't repeatedly make the same mistakes. This checklist can also help you better adapt to the stylistic preferences of your supervisor.

4 Does the company have a formalized set of writing genres?

Many companies have a set of document templates they expect writers to use. Other companies just direct their writers to a model document to follow. Many scientific and professional organizations publish style guides that resemble the MLA and APA styles you are familiar with. For example, a chemical company might expect its writers to conform to the style guide of the American Chemical Society. Some very large businesses and governmental organizations have created their own style guides. Again, your fellow writers can be a helpful source for this kind of information.

5 How are revisions to documents such as work procedures and technical specifications controlled?

Documents which are used to create a product, or that define the materials that go into the product, require careful control. It is important that companies have procedures to ensure that products are built to the plans and processes expected by their customers. Many manufacturing firms have a technical library or a document control office that controls the revision of such critical documents. Usually these offices are located within the engineering departments of manufacturing firms. If you are assigned to write this type of document for the first time, be sure to talk to the personnel who administer these systems to ensure that you meet the stylistic and administrative expectations of the manufacturing community.

Exercise 1

Interview a supervisor or a writer at a local company. Ask the person to describe how the editing and revision process is controlled in the company. Also ask which type of errors are most troubling. Prepare a short presentation to share what you learned about this local business community with the class or your collaborative group.

Exercise 2

In a small group, compare your findings from the interview you conducted for Exercise 1. Find common processes and themes, and note those processes and themes where interviewees differed. Prepare a short presentation to share what you learned with the class.

59c Writing business letters

Good business letters follow standard practices and established formats. Most business letters are written using **block format** on company letterhead, or a letterhead template where the company's name, postal address, phone and facsimile numbers, and Web address are centered at the top or bottom of the letter. All other paragraphs (including the inside address,

Acme Technical Products

3515 Lansing Road/Jackson, Michigan 49203
(517) 783-6651
www.acme.com

February 15, 2002

Ms. Janet Anderson
Purchasing Agent
Everett Batteries
15 Johnstown Boulevard
Westerly, RI 02891

Dear Ms. Anderson,

Thank you for using Acme products in your lithium-ion battery research and
development program. Acme is ready to support you with your future needs as
you transition from this developmental battery into a manufacturable consumer
product. We are ready to provide you with volume discounts and to work with
you to develop a "just-in-time" inventory control, which will save you
inventory and storage costs.

We also would like to provide you with information on our new separator
materials designed specifically for lithium-ion battery development. The
enclosed catalog provides you with pricing and technical data on a number of
different separator products designed for a variety of battery needs.

I look forward to working with you in the future.

Sincerely,

Steve Adams

Steve Adams
Sales Associate

Enclosure (1)

SA/rd
CC: Sales Manager

greeting, closing, and signature) are flush with the left margin. Some longer
business letters and many letters not printed on letterhead use a **modified
block format** in which the return address, greeting, closing, and signature
are centered on the page. In both styles, notations following the signature are
flush left along with the body of the letter, including initials for the writer and
typist (RL: gw), *Enc.* or *Enclosure*, or *cc: Nancy Harris* (the name of a person
sent a copy). Follow these additional guidelines for business correspondence.

- **Stationery.** The best is 25 percent or 50 percent white cotton bond paper at standard business weight (20 pound). Résumés and letters of application are often printed on a more durable weight paper (24 pound). Avoid colors and fancy paper styles.
- **Print quality and style.** Check that your printer, word processor, or typewriter is in good repair. While both laser and ink-jet printers will deliver high print quality, the laser printer has the advantage of delivering waterproof text. Avoid nonstandard or stylized fonts—they can be difficult to read and are often associated by readers with personal or nonprofessional correspondence.
- **Salutations.** Use the first name of your recipient only if you are already on a first name basis. Use the full name if you don't know the person's gender. Avoid gender-specific salutations such as "Dear Sir" or "Gentlemen"; they are not appropriate. If you do not know the name of the person to whom you are writing, use general salutations and titles such as "Dear Accounts Department" or "Dear Credit Manager."
- **Longer Letters.** Use plain paper of the same weight and color as the first page. Use letterhead stationery only for the first page.
- **Envelope.** Envelope paper should be the same color and weight as the letter, and the font should match that of the letter.

59d Writing memos

Although some companies still use pre-printed forms for memos on which a person can hand write or print a message, most companies use a corporate memo template or one of the standard templates for a memo found in word-processing programs. The organization's name and logo, or letterhead, may appear at the top of the memo, but no address information is needed since memos are internal company documents.

The words *To*, *From*, *Subject*, and *Date* appear on all memos, often in the order shown on the memo on page 837. Spacing, notations for enclosures, additional pages, and copies all follow the same pattern as in letters.

59.2

59e Writing email

The email message is replacing the memo as the preferred genre for internal communications within many organizations, and the phone call for communication outside the organization. Because the use of email is becoming such a commonplace part of business and personal communication, people have developed the habit of writing email without using the same composing processes they previously used for writing memos and letters. Yet a poorly composed email can damage a writer's credibility with readers in the same way a poorly composed letter or memo does. Developing the following habits when using electronic communication will help you avoid this pitfall.

Everett Batteries: Internal Memo

TO: Bob Rogers, Director of Battery Research and Development

FROM: Janet Anderson, Purchasing Agent

DATE: October 11, 2001

SUBJECT: Evaluation of Future Separator Needs

I recently received correspondence from Acme Technical Products with pricing information on their battery separator, as well as a catalog of new separator products. I am in the process of developing a purchasing plan detailing our separator needs for the next twelve months. Could you please provide me with a forecast of your department's projected use of Acme separator material on a month-by-month basis? I need this information by November 12 in order to meet MRP system deadlines.

I have enclosed a copy of the new catalog which contains technical specifications and pricing information for your use.

jck
Attachment

59e
bus

- **Choose your addressees carefully.** Organizational lore is full of stories of persons who inadvertently sent a personal response to a message sent by an electronic mailing list or to group of recipients. Such a response is thought of as *spam* (junk mail) within electronic communities and in some cases might inadvertently insult a reader *lurking* (silently reading messages) within the electronic community.
- **Proofread your message.** Use the same standards for grammar and punctuation you would use in a memo. Don't use abbreviations, acronyms, or jargon unless you are certain all recipients will understand them. Don't use all capital letters within an electronic message unless

you intend to strongly emphasize that point. Typing a message in all-capital letters is considered "shouting" by electronic communities.

- **Use a subject line.** Many recipients are overwhelmed with the volume of the email they receive. Most email programs index incoming messages by date, time, sender, and subject. A clear subject line will help the recipients to screen and identify those messages they need or wish to read immediately, and to delete unimportant messages.

59f   Writing résumés and letters of application

Résumés and the accompanying cover letter are among the most important sales documents you will write; the "product" is, after all, yourself and everything you have accomplished. There are countless "right" ways to prepare these documents. This section offers some guidelines for the content, design, and construction of a résumé and letter of application.

Your letter of application should be closely related to your résumé. The documents should work as a unit to convey the necessary information and to make you appear professional and organized. Letters of application offer you the chance to discuss or highlight skills or experiences mentioned in your résumé or to add information not in your résumé. These letters function best when the writer tailors the cover letter to connect skills and educational requirements found in the job advertisement or the description of the position to the résumé.

The purpose of the résumé package (résumé and letter of application) is to get an interview, not a job. Few employers hire using only the information contained in a résumé package. Many employers receive hundreds of résumé packages for every job position posted, so when constructing a résumé concentrate on trying to create a professional identity for yourself. Highlight your skills and achievements objectively and clearly, and be sure to proofread. Some employers look for grammar or punctuation errors in their résumé screening process.

Employers favor job candidates who are motivated, mature, and responsible. You can't simply state these things; your résumé package must exemplify these traits. For instance, employers like applicants who know how to start and finish a project independently and who are self-motivated, capable, and willing to face challenges confidently. Describe your experiences not only in terms of what you have actually done, but in terms of what you have learned from the experiences and how they will help you in the future.

1 Begin with a résumé preparation checklist

Before you start to prepare your résumé, you need to reflect about both your career goals and your own qualifications and background.

STRATEGY

Write informally in response to the following questions. Jot down your ideas and as many examples from your background as you can remember. Later you can select the best ideas and examples for your purposes.

1. What kind of work do you want to do? What kind of job do you want?
2. What are your career goals?
3. What jobs have you held?
4. What volunteer positions have you held?
5. What are your skills, abilities, or interests? (Include items even if you have not been formally educated in these things.)
6. What are the main features of your educational background? Consider the following points.
   a. College major, minor, and concentrations
   b. Special projects or research
   c. Honors and awards
   d. Memberships and offices in organizations
   e. Volunteer positions
   f. Special skills
   g. Grade-point average (overall, and within major field)
7. What other awards or special honors, if any, have you received (from work, volunteer efforts, or community organizations)?
8. Who might make a good reference for you? Try to identify at least one former or current professor, one former job supervisor or employer, and one personal reference.
9. What makes you different from other applicants? Why should a prospective employer interview you rather than someone else?

59f
bus

2 Use categories to construct your résumé

After you've collected the information for your résumé, your task is one of construction—placing the information into appropriate categories, phrasing it concisely, and arranging it in a visually appealing way that stresses your strongest traits first.

Career objective. When you write your career objective, be specific! Avoid empty phrases like *position of responsibility in a fast-growing firm*. Consider tailoring your objective to each type of position for which you apply.

Job experience. When you get ready to describe your job experience, list all the duties you had, and then choose the ones that are most similar to those of the job you want. If you have held many jobs, don't list them all in your résumé. List those jobs which you held the longest, the ones that are most similar to the job for which you are applying, or the ones that demonstrate your most employable characteristics. If you think that you have little specific experience that relates to the job you seek, highlight other job skills, such as the ability to work as part of a team, to handle responsibility, to supervise others, or to work with little or no supervision. When possible, don't simply state these skills; provide examples from your experience.

Volunteer experience. If you've held volunteer or unpaid internship positions that may be attractive to an employer, list them. They are often considered important experience. Note that the position was voluntary, but handle the rest of the information just as you would for any other job experience. Don't use an apologetic tone here; the fact that you were not paid for the job doesn't mean it was not serious work in which you developed valuable skills.

Sequence of experience. Typically, jobs are listed in reverse chronological order (with your most recent job first). If your most important job experience is not your most recent, however, list that one first, and then list the remaining jobs in reverse chronological order.

References. Unless the employer has specifically asked for references, use the general statement *References available upon request.* Few employers will want to look at your references unless they wish to interview you. You should bring a separate page listing the names, addresses, and phone numbers or email addresses of three or four references with you to the interview. (Always ask permission *before* you use someone as a reference.) Most colleges have placement services that will send out dossiers that include confidential reference lists or letters of reference.

A number of programs provide templates for creating a résumé on a computer. Most of these programs provide several different formats for a standard résumé. These programs allow you to spend your time focusing on the text of your résumé rather than spacing and layout.

Some companies may prefer that you submit your résumé electronically. If so, be sure to follow any instructions they may provide for formatting the electronic file. Frequently the résumé file will be attached to an email that will function as your letter of application. Another way of getting your résumé to a number of potential employers is to submit your electronic résumé to an Internet job service.

59.3

Many people are now creating résumés on the Web. Some advantages of Web-based résumés include the ability to "nest" information on subsequent pages without cluttering the main résumé page. For example, you might include links from the positions you have held to pages that describe

---

Carol E. Westermeyer

College Address: Home Address:
Apt. 22 College Park   7562 Galsworth Road
Greenville, Virginia 20205   Squires, Texas 30303
(804) 555-3345   (512) 555-7912
cwesr@school.edu

Objective Entry-level position as an electrical engineer

Education

• **B.S. Electrical Engineering, May 1999**
  Virginia Polytechnic Institute, Blacksburg, Virginia 24060
  G.P.A. 3.18/4.0 Minor: Economics

Experience

• **Technician/Assembler, May 1995–September 1995**
  Communication Technology, Inc., Fairview, Virginia 24059
  -Developed cost analysis and designed prototype wireless communication
  products for Masters Mountain Laboratories.
  -Built and tested various AF and RF products: transmitters, receivers,
  headsets, amplifiers, and antenna networks.
  -Served as company representative to demonstrate a new generation of
  wireless radios at Atlanta National Radio Conference.

• **Interoffice Administrator (part time), 1995–present**
  Bergland Technology Associates, Lakeview, Virginia 24051
  -Updated and reorganized shop inventory control using Microsoft Office
  software.

Project

• **Member, Design Team for Electric Vehicle**
  Department of Electrical Engineering, Virginia Polytechnic Institute,
  Blacksburg, Virginia 24060
  -Controller group duties included design and programming of a constant
  velocity transmission (CVT) controller.

Skills   Experienced with a variety of computer software programs, including
            Microsoft Office, Autocad, and Statistica.

Activities Vice-President, Student Senate, Virginia Polytechnic Institute

**59f
bus**

these positions and your accomplishments in them. If you choose to develop a Web-based résumé, however, be sure to pay special attention to issues of layout and design, and make navigation through the site easy and "user-friendly" for your readers. Like paper résumés, Web-based résumés need to present you and your work elegantly and without error.

GLOSSARY OF USAGE AND TERMS

Three kinds of entries are found in this glossary: grammatical terms (such as *irregular verb*), rhetorical terms (such as *freewriting*), and words that writers frequently find confusing or difficult (such as *farther* and *further*). The latter entries, which deal with matters of usage, are indicated by an arrow (→).

→**a, an** When the word that follows the article *a* or *an* begins with a vowel, use *an: an apple, an outrageous film.* Use *a* before consonants: *a banana, a shocking film.* (*See 16a.*)

abridged dictionary Any type of abbreviated dictionary that does not aim to be exhaustive in its treatment of English vocabulary. (*See 30a.*)

absolute phrase A phrase consisting of a noun, a pronoun, or a word group acting as a noun followed by a present or past participle and any modifiers; it is used to modify a noun or an entire clause. (*See 16c-2, 24d.*)

Their lungs burning from the acrid smoke, the firefighters pressed ahead into the burning building.

abstract A concise summary of a paper, sometimes used as an overview or preface at the beginning of the paper itself. (*See 58f.*)

academic community The interacting population of individuals involved in scholarly pursuits, from teachers to researchers to students, both within one institution and outside in the broader arena available through publication and the Internet. (*See 1a.*)

→**accept, except** Use *accept* to mean "to take or receive." Use *except* to mean "excluding."

She **accepted** the invitation.
Everyone finished the race **except** Larry.

acronym An abbreviation whose letters begin some or all of the words in the full version: *NASA* (National Aeronautics and Space Administration), *AIDS* (acquired immune deficiency syndrome). (*See 43a-2.*)

action statement In a writing assignment, the directions that specify the processes the writer should go through in completing the assignment.

action verb A verb that indicates an action or activity: *swim, analyze, dig, turn, negotiate.* (*See 16a-3; compare* **linking verb.**)

active voice The form of a verb in a sentence in which the doer (or agent) takes the position of the main subject, before the main verb. (*See 10c, 16a-3, 18d, 25c; compare* **passive voice.**)

ad hominem A **fallacy** in which an argument is based on personal attack rather than rational support and evidence. (*See 55f-5.*)

ad populum A **fallacy** in which an argument appeals to an audience's biases instead of using rational support. (*See 55f-5.*)

843

adaptation The principle of adjusting writing style, organization, and language to the expectations of readers in particular settings.

adjective A word that modifies a noun, pronoun, or word group acting as a noun by answering such questions as "How many?" "What kind?" or "Which one?" (*See 16a-5, 20a, 20b.*)

adjective clause (*See* **relative clause**.)

adjective phrase A phrase that modifies a noun. (*See 16c.*)

adverb A word that modifies a verb, an adjective, an adverb, or an entire sentence by answering such questions as "When?" "Where?" "Why?" "How often?" "Which direction?" "What conditions?" and "What degree?" (*See 16a-6, 20a, 20b.*)

adverb clause A clause that acts as an adverb. (*See 16c.*)

→**adverse, averse** Someone opposed to something is *averse* to it; if conditions stand in opposition to achieving a goal, they are *adverse*.

> Bill wasn't **averse** to going on the ski trip unless the warm temperature would be **adverse** to good skiing conditions.

→**advice, advise** *Advice* is a noun meaning "counsel" or "recommendations." *Advise* is a verb meaning "to give counsel or recommendations."

> Professor Raul wanted to **advise** his students, but they believed they needed no **advice**.

→**affect, effect** *Affect* is a verb meaning "to influence." *Effect* is a noun meaning "a result." More rarely, *effect* is a verb meaning "to cause something to happen."

> It is thought that CFCs **affect** the deterioration of the ozone layer. The **effect** of that deterioration on global warming is uncertain. Lawmakers need to **effect** changes in public attitudes toward our environment.

agenda A plan of action for a business meeting.

→**aggravate, irritate** *Aggravate* means "to worsen"; *irritate* means "to bother or pester."

> He was **irritated** that the hotel had no humidifiers because the dry air **aggravated** his skin condition.

agreement The correct matching, in **person**, **number**, and **gender**, of subjects and verbs or pronouns and their antecedents. (*See Chapter 19.*)

SUBJECT-VERB AGREEMENT	*The dog and the boy* **are running** in the field. *The dog* **is running** in the field.
PRONOUN-ANTECEDENT AGREEMENT	*A memo* should address the needs of **its** audience. *Memos* should address the needs of **their** audience.

→**ain't** Although widely used colloquially, *ain't* is inappropriate in formal writing. Use *am not, is not,* or *are not*; the contracted forms *aren't* and *isn't* are more acceptable than *ain't* but may still be too informal in some contexts.

all-purpose modifier A modifier that adds little or no meaning to a sentence and often can be cut: *very, totally, major, central* (*See 31a-1.*)

all-purpose word A filler word that carries little or no meaning and often can be cut: *factor, aspect, field, thing, kind.* (*See 31a-1.*)

→**all ready, already** *All ready* means "prepared for"; *already* means "by that time."

> Sam was **all ready** for the kickoff, but when he had climbed to his bleacher, the game had **already** started.

→**all right** This expression is always spelled as two words, not as *alright*.

→**all together, altogether** Use *all together* to mean "everyone"; use *altogether* to mean "completely."

> We were **all together** on our decision to climb the cliff, but it was **altogether** too hard for us to leave Jennie behind.

→**allude, elude** Use *allude* to mean "hint at" or "refer to indirectly"; use *elude* to mean "escape."

> Francis **alluded** to the time the refrigerator broke when he was on vacation; the rotten smell had **eluded** the house sitter, who never thought to open the refrigerator.

→**allusion, illusion** An *allusion* is a reference to something; an *illusion* is a vision or false belief.

> Peter found an interesting **allusion** to UFOs in a government document. It turned out that the UFOs were just an **illusion**.

→**a lot** This expression is always spelled as two words, not as *alot*. Even when spelled correctly, *a lot* may be too informal for some academic writing. Use *many*, *much*, or some other modifier instead.

→**a.m., p.m.** These abbreviations may be capital or lowercase letters. (*See 43a-3*.)

ambiguous reference A sentence in which a reader cannot identify a pronoun with its antecedent. (*See 23a-1*.)

→**among, between** Use *between* to describe something involving two people, things, or ideas; use *among* to refer to three or more people, things, or ideas.

> A fight broke out **between** the umpire and the catcher; then there was a discussion **among** the catcher, the umpire, and the team managers.

→**amount, number** Use *amount* to refer to a quantity of something that can't be divided into separate units. Use *number* when you want to refer to countable objects.

> A large **number** of spices may be used in Thai dishes. This recipe calls for a small **amount** of coconut milk.

→**an, a** (*See* **a, an.**)

analogy A comparison between two things, often on the basis of shared characteristics. (*See 55f-5, see also* **false analogy**.)

analysis Writing that analyzes or "takes apart" a topic, often looking at how the parts relate to one another. (*See 58a-4*.)

analytical reading Reading that identifies ideas and information presented in a text. (*See 2a*.)

analytical synthesis Bringing together summaries of several sources and pointing out their relationships in order to provide background information (*See 46c-d*.)

analyze To divide or break something up into its constituent parts to examine their relationships. (*See 5a-2*.)

gloss

→**and etc.** (*See* **etc.**)

→**and/or** Although widely used, *and/or* is usually imprecise and may distract your reader. Choose one of the words, or revise your sentence.

> IMPRECISE The police **and/or** the fire department will usually arrive first when someone calls 911.

> EDITED The police **or** the fire department will usually arrive first when someone calls 911.

anecdote A brief story or account of a personal experience, often used in an introductory paragraph to spark a reader's interest. (*See 9f-1.*)

annotated bibliography A bibliography that includes annotations (short descriptions of each entry, sometimes with accompanying evaluative comments). (*See 58g.*)

annotations Notes written about (or sometimes directly on) a draft or a published text. Annotations can include **interpretations**, questions, **counterarguments**, restatements, or **evaluations**. (*See 2a.*)

→**ante-, anti-** Use *ante-* as a prefix to mean "before" or "predating"; use *anti-* to mean "against" or "opposed."

> Some people experience strong **antiracist** feelings when touring the slave quarters of **antebellum** Southern plantations that survived the Civil War.

antecedent The noun or pronoun to which another word (usually a **pronoun**) refers. (*See 16a-2, 19c, Chapter 23.*)

> antecedent   pronoun
> **Jean** presented **her** proposal to the committee.

antithesis The use of parallelism to emphasize contrast within sentences. (*See 10d-4, 27a, 27b.*)

antonym A word opposite in meaning to another word: *hot* and *cold*. (*See 30a; see also* **thesaurus**.)

→**anyone, any one** *Anyone* as one word is an indefinite pronoun. Occasionally you may want to use *any* to modify *one*, in the sense of "any individual thing or person." (The same distinction applies to **everyone**, **every one**; *somebody, some body*; and *someone, some one*.)

> **Anyone** can learn to parachute without fear. But the instructors are told not to spend too much time with **any one** person.

→**anyplace** Avoid using this term in formal writing; instead, use *anywhere* or revise your sentence.

→**anyways, anywheres** Avoid these incorrect versions of *anyway* and *anywhere*.

APA documentation style The style of documentation suggested by the American Psychological Association and described in its guide. (*See Chapter 52.*)

application letter A brief letter of application for a job, usually accompanied by a **résumé**. (*See 59f.*)

appositive A noun or pronoun that renames or stands for a preceding noun (*See 33c-3.*)

appositive phrase A phrase consisting of an appositive (usually a noun) along with its modifiers, used to rename a noun in order to add information to a sentence. (*See 16c-3.*)

gloss

Ken Choi and Stephanie Almagno, **my classmates**, won an award for their innovative packaging design.

→**apt, likely, liable** Use *apt* to mean "a tendency to." Use *likely* to mean "probable." Use *liable* only to imply risk, or, in a legal context, obligation or responsibility.

Claude was **apt** to ski the most treacherous slopes when he was young, but he will **likely** keep to the moderate slopes now because he is **liable** to hurt himself again if he skis the expert slopes. The ski resort was **liable** for Claude's injuries because it did not mark the location of the cliff.

archaic word A word that is no longer in general use or is in the process of dropping from the language, such as *save* in the sense of "except." (*See 29b-4.*)

argue To prove a point or persuade a reader to accept or entertain a particular position. (*See 5a-1; see also* **argument**; **argumentative writing**.)

argument Not a disagreement, but the reasons, evidence, and explanations used in an attempt to resolve a disagreement by encouraging readers (listeners) to agree with the writer (speaker). (*See Chapter 55.*)

argumentative writing Writing that presents and defends a position or point of view. (*See Chapter 55.*)

article One of three words that precede a noun: *a, an,* or *the.* An *indefinite article* (*a* or *an*) precedes a general noun (one that does not refer to a specific thing). The *definite article the* precedes a specific noun. (*See 16a.*)

artifacts Material objects characteristic of a group or culture. (*See 50c.*)

→**as, like** Used as a preposition, *as* indicates a precise comparison. *Like* indicates a resemblance or similarity.

Remembered **as** a man of habit, Kant would take his walk at exactly the same time each day. He was **like** many other philosophers: brooding, thoughtful, and at times intense.

→**as to** *As to* is considered informal in many academic contexts and should be avoided.

INFORMAL	The media had many speculations **as to** the skater's involvement in the attack against her rival.
EDITED	The media had many speculations **about** the skater's involvement in the attack against her rival.

→**assure, ensure, insure** Use *assure* to imply a promise; use *ensure* to imply a certain outcome. Use *insure* only when you imply something legal or financial.

The surgeon **assured** the world-renowned pianist that his fingers would heal in time for the performance. To **ensure** that, the pianist could not practice for three weeks. In case of an even worse accident, the pianist had **insured** his hands with Lloyd's of London.

→**at** In any writing, avoid using *at* in direct and indirect questions.

COLLOQUIAL	Jones wondered where his attorney was **at**.
EDITED	Jones wondered where his attorney **was**.

atlas A book containing maps and related information.

gloss

audience The implied or intended readers for a particular piece of writing. (*See Chapters 6, 45.*)

audiovisual collection A library collection of videotapes, films, audio recordings, and similar resources. (*See 46b-4.*)

auxiliary verb (*See* **helping verb**.)

→**awful, awfully** Use *awful* as an adjective modifying a noun; use *awfully* as an adverb in verbal structures.

> Sanders played **awfully** at the U.S. Open Golf Tournament. On the sixth hole, an **awful** shot landed his ball in the pond.

→**awhile, a while** Awhile (as one word) functions as an adverb; it is not preceded by a preposition. *A while* functions as a noun (*while*) preceded by an article (*a*) and is often used in prepositional phrases.

> The shelter suggested that the homeless family stay **awhile**. It turned out that the children had not eaten for **a while**.

background information Information that helps readers understand the scope and substance of an issue, subject, or problem by providing knowledge of its history, context, or consequences.

→**bad, badly** Use *bad* as an adjective that modifies nouns or with a linking verb expressing feelings. Use *badly* as an adverb.

> The summit was scheduled at a **bad** time of year for some delegates. The British prime minister felt **bad** that some countries weren't represented. Several heads of state spoke **badly** of East–West relations.

balanced sentence A sentence built around pairs of parallel phrases and clauses, used to create emphasis. (*See 27b-4.*)

bandwagon argument A **fallacy** in argumentative writing in which the writer tries to convince the reader that everyone else feels a particular way about a topic and that the reader ought to as well. (*See 55f-5.*)

base form The present tense form of a verb. (*See* **tense**; *see 18a.*)

→**because, since** In general, avoid using *since* in place of *because*, which is more formal and precise. Use *since* to indicate time, not causality.

> INFORMAL **Since** the meeting was canceled, Sam gave his nonrefundable plane tickets to a friend.
>
> EDITED **Because** the meeting was canceled, Sam gave his nonrefundable plane tickets to a friend.
>
> CORRECT **Since** then, Sam has avoided buying nonrefundable tickets for meetings.

begging the question In argument, a **fallacy** in which assumptions are presented as facts, sometimes using words like *obviously* or *clearly*. (Also known as *overgeneralization* or *hasty generalization*.) (*See 55f-5.*)

→**being as, being that** Avoid using *being as* or *being that* in academic and other formal writing when you mean *because*.

→**beside, besides** Use *beside* as a preposition to mean "next to." Use *besides* as an adverb meaning "also" or an adjective meaning "except."

gloss

Betsy placed the documents **beside** Mr. Klein. **Besides** being the best lawyer at the firm, Klein was also the most cautious.

→**better, had better** Avoid using *better* or *had better* in place of *ought to* or *should* in formal writing.

> COLLOQUIAL   Fast-food chains **better** realize that Americans are more health-conscious today.

> EDITED   Fast-food chains **ought** to realize that Americans are more health-conscious today.

→**between, among** (*See* **among, between**.)

bibliographic sources Lists of resources you can consult in your research. **Bibliographies**, indexes, electronic databases, and catalogs all provide information about possible sources.

bibliographies Lists of library or other resources available in specific subject areas. (*See 46b-1*.)

bibliography A list of the sources used by the writer of a research paper, an article, or a book, prepared so that a reader can easily find the same materials. (*See, for instance, the formats in Chapters 51–54; see also* **annotated bibliography**.)

biographical sources Source materials that supply information about the lives and times of important people.

block format A format for short letters in which all the paragraphs are flush at the left margin. (*See 59c; compare* **modified block format**.)

block quotation A quotation of sufficient length to justify separating it from the body of a text in an indented block of prose. (*See 36b*.)

body The main section of a paper or written document. It is preceded by an **introduction** and followed by a **conclusion**. (*See 7a-2*.)

Boolean logic An electronic search strategy whereby you use *and, or*, and *not* to link terms in a subject you are searching for; usage selected will expand or limit your search. (*See 46c-1*.)

boundary statement A sentence at the start of a paragraph that acts as a bridge from the paragraph before. (*See 9d-2*.)

brainstorming A technique for generating material for possible use in a written document. Brainstorming involves concentrating on a topic, thinking associatively, and finding connections among different ideas.

→**bring, take** *Bring* implies a movement from somewhere else to close at hand; *take* implies a movement in the opposite direction.

> Please **bring** me a coffee refill, and **take** away these leftover muffins.

broad pronoun reference Using a pronoun to refer to an entire idea rather than a specific **antecedent**. (*See 23b*.)

→**broke** *Broke* is the past tense of *break*; avoid using it as the past participle.

> INCORRECT   The computer was **broke**.

> EDITED   The computer was **broken**.

browser A computer software program, such as *Netscape Navigator* or *Microsoft Internet Explorer*, allowing you access to Web sites. (*See 46c-1*.)

gloss

→**burst, bursted** *Burst* implies an outward explosion. Do not use the form *bursted* for the past tense.

CORRECT   The gang of boys **burst** the balloon.

→**bust, busted** Avoid the use of *bust* or *busted* to mean "broke."

COLLOQUIAL   The senator's limousine **bust** down on the trip to Washington.

EDITED   The senator's limousine **broke** down on the trip to Washington.

→**but however, but yet** These are **redundant pairs**; choose one word of each pair, not both.

INCORRECT   The medfly was a nuisance, **but yet** the state of California was finally able to control it.

EDITED   The medfly was a nuisance, **but** the state of California was finally able to control it.

→**calculate, figure, reckon** These three terms are sometimes used informally to mean "imagine" or "think." When in doubt, avoid them.

INFORMAL   John **figured** he had never seen such a large pike.

EDITED   John **thought** he had never seen such a large pike.

→**can, may** *Can* implies ability; *may* implies permission or uncertainty.

Bart **can** drive now, but his parents **may** not lend him their new car.

→**can't hardly, can't scarcely** Use these pairs positively, not negatively: *can hardly* and *can scarcely*, or simply *can't*.

→**capital, capitol** *Capital* refers to a government center or to money; *capitol* refers to a government building.

Madison is the **capital** of Wisconsin.

card catalog A file of printed cards listing a library's books and other holdings. An individual work usually has several cards that list it by author, title, and subject area(s). (*See* **online catalog**.)

case The grammatical role that a pronoun or noun plays in a sentence (as subject, object, direct object, and the like). *Subjective case* refers to the role played as the subject of a sentence. *Objective case* refers to the role played as the object of a sentence. *Possessive case* refers to the role played in a sentence to indicate possession or ownership. (*See* 17a.)

cause-effect paragraph A paragraph explaining why something has occurred and exploring consequences (*See* 9e.)

CBE/CSE documentation style The style of documentation suggested by the Council of Science Editors and described in its guide. (*See* Chapter 53.)

→**censor, censure** *Censor* means the act of shielding something from the public eye, such as a book or movie. *Censure* implies a punishment or critical labeling.

The school board **censored** *Catcher in the Rye*, but a group of parents **censured** the school by naming it on a list of "anti-intellectual" schools in the area.

gloss

→**center around** Something can't center *around* something else. Use *center on* or *focus on* instead, or reword as *revolve around*.

chain of reasoning In writing, the path a writer takes and asks others to follow. (*See 12c*.)

→**chairman, chairperson, chair** The use of *chairman* is now considered sexist. *Chairperson* is an awkward but acceptable substitute. *Chair* is now a common nonsexist alternative.

SEXIST	Gayle is now **chairman** of the provost's academic standards council.
EDITED	Gayle is now **chair** of the provost's academic standards council.

character Any person, usually fictional, in a work of literature. (*See 57a-2*.)

chat rooms Informal real-time communities hosted by private Internet services or available via the Internet Relay Chat (IRC) network. (*See 13c-3*.)

→**choose, chose** Incorrect use of these terms often has its source in a simple spelling error. Use *choose* for the present tense form of the verb; use *chose* for the past tense form.

chronological order A pattern for structuring writing in which elements of an event are presented in the order in which they happened. (*See also* **sequential order**.)

circular reasoning In argumentative writing, a fallacy in which an assertion is supported with the assertion itself. (Also known as *tautology*.) (*See 55f-5*.)

→**cite, site** *Cite* means to acknowledge someone else's work; *site* means a place or location.

Phil decided to **cite** Chomsky's theory of syntax as evidence for his thesis.
We chose the perfect **site** to pitch our tent.

claim (*See* **data-warrant-claim reasoning**.)

clarifying sentence (*See* **limiting sentence**.)

classification The organization of information into groups, categories, or parts.

classification paragraph A paragraph in which several subjects are sorted into groups based on their similarities or relationships. (*See 9e*.)

cliché An overused or trite word or expression: *startling discovery, today's modern world, turn you on*. (*See 31b-1*.)

→**climactic, climatic** *Climactic* refers to the culmination of something; *climatic* refers to the weather conditions.

climactic sentence order A sentence structured to build to a climax, often through the use of elements in a series. (*See 10c-2*.)

What every truly modern home has, she said, is a dishwasher, a gas grill, a Jacuzzi, and a divorce.

clustering A planning strategy in which groups of ideas are related graphically to a kernel topic. (*See 4b-1*.)

CMS documentation style The style of documentation described in *The Chicago Manual of Style*. (*See Chapter 54*.)

code shifting Adjusting language to meet the expectations of particular communities. (*See 1a-4*.)

gloss

coherence Writing in which each sentence or paragraph follows clearly from the one before and leads clearly to the next in a recognizable, easy-to-understand arrangement. (*See 9c, 9d.*)

collaborative revision The process of working with one or more people in order to revise writing drafts. (*See 8c.*)

collective noun A kind of noun that refers to a unit composed of more than one individual or thing: *group, board of directors, family.* Such nouns generally take a singular form even though they refer to more than one thing. (*See 16a, 19b-2, 19c-3; see also* **noun**; **count noun**; **mass noun**.)

colloquialism A word or expression that is used informally (often in specific regions or among specific groups) but is not usually considered appropriate in formal and academic prose. (*See 29a-1.*)

comma splice Two or more sentences (independent or main clauses) incorrectly joined with a comma. (*See Chapter 22, 33a; compare* **fused sentence**.)

COMMA SPLICE	The human eye is not like that of the cat, it has many more color-sensitive cells.
EDITED	The human eye is not like that of the cat; it has many more color-sensitive cells.

common adjective Any adjective that is not a **proper adjective**. (*See 39b-2.*)

common noun Any noun that is not a **proper noun**. (*See 16a-1, 39b-2.*)

comparative form One of three forms taken by an adjective or adverb to indicate whether the noun or verb modified is being compared to something else. The comparative form adds *-er* or *more* to the adjective or adverb. (*See 20c; compare* **positive form** and **superlative form**.)

ADJECTIVE	This oven is **cleaner** than mine. She is the **more imaginative** designer of the two.
ADVERB	Sometimes you can travel **faster** in Manhattan by foot than by car. Peggy designs **more imaginatively** than Horace.

→**compare to, compare with** Use *compare to* when you want to imply similarities between two things—the phrase is close in meaning to *liken to.* Use *compare with* when you want to imply both similarities and differences.

CORRECT	To help the child understand his virus, the doctor **compared** it **to** a tiny army in his body.
CORRECT	**Compared with** his last illness, this one was mild.

comparing and contrasting A technique for organizing an entire paper or for developing individual paragraphs or sentences. Opinions, characteristics, or objects are compared for similarities and differences, which often are presented in alternating form. (*See 9e; see 27b-3 on* **parallelism**; *see also* **point-by-point organization** and **subject-by-subject organization**.)

complement A word (noun, pronoun, or adjective) or phrase tied by a linking verb to a subject. (*See 16b-2, 17b-2, 20b-2.*) A *subject complement* "completes" the linking verb by describing the subject or renaming it. An *object complement* renames or describes the *direct object.*

→**complement, compliment** *Complement* means "an accompaniment"; *compliment* means "words of praise."

> The diplomats **complimented** the ambassador on her choice of opera.
> The theater's grand ceiling **complemented** the theme of the opera perfectly.

complete predicate (*See* **predicate**.)

complete sentence A sentence that contains both a subject and a complete predicate and is therefore grammatical. (*See Chapter 21; compare* **sentence fragment**.)

complete subject (*See* **subject**.)

complex sentence A sentence with one **main clause** and one or more **subordinate clauses**. (*See 16d, 28b-1; compare* **compound sentence**; **compound-complex sentence**; **simple sentence**.)

compound antecedent A group of words to which a pronoun or noun refers. (*See 23a; see also* **antecedent**.)

compound-complex sentence A sentence with two or more **main clauses** and one or more **subordinate clauses**. (*See 16d; compare* **compound sentence**; **complex sentence**; **simple sentence**.)

compound predicate A predicate that contains two or more complete verbs, usually connected with *and*.

> The car **struck and injured** the bystander.

compound sentence A sentence with two or more **main clauses** and no **subordinate clauses**. (*See 16d, 28a; compare* **complex sentence**; **compound-complex sentence**; **simple sentence**.)

compound subject Two or more subjects joined with *and* or *both . . . and*. (*See 17b, 19b-1*.)

> **Jim and the rest of the Boy Scouts** were responsible for the rescue.

conclusion The ending section of a paper, preceded by the **introduction** and **body** (*see 7a-2*), also the necessary consequence of a line of reasoning, especially in **deductive argument**. (*See 55d*.)

conditional statement A sentence that expresses something improbable or hypothetical, often beginning with *if*. Conditional statements use the *subjunctive* form of the verb. (*See 18g*.)

conjunction A word that joins two elements in a sentence. (*See 16a-8, 19b, 27b-2, 33a*.) *Coordinating conjunctions* (*and, but, or, nor, for, yet,* and *so*) link grammatically equal elements such as parts of compound subjects, verbs, objects, and modifiers.

> We analyzed **and** discussed the theory in class.
> Fresh orange juice **or** grapefruit juice contains citric acid.

Subordinating conjunctions (*because, although, while, if,* or *since*) create a **subordinate** (or *modifying*) **clause**.

> **Because** they were tired, they did not notice that the pot was boiling over.

conjunctive adverb An adverb such as *however, moreover, thus,* or *therefore* that joins sentences or elements within sentences and indicates a logical relationship between them. (*See 16a-6, 33b-3, 34a-2*.)

gloss

connotation The associative or affective "shades of meaning" conveyed by a word, as opposed to its literal meaning. If someone is said to have *retreated* from a gathering, the word connotes that the person was feeling attacked or bewildered. (*See 29b-2.*)

→**consensus of opinion** Avoid this redundancy by using *consensus*.

content The specific ideas or information presented in a piece of writing. (*See 6c.*)

→**continual, continuous** *Continual* implies that something is recurring; *continuous* implies that something is constant and unceasing.

> The **continual** noise of landing jets didn't bother the homeowners as much as the foul odor that drifted **continuously** from the landfill near the airport.

contraction A form in which two words are brought together, usually by eliminating one or more letters and adding an apostrophe to mark the omission(s): *it's, they're, can't.* (*See 35b-1.*)

controlling idea (*See* **thesis statement.**)

conversational speaking (*See* **extemporaneous speaking.**)

coordinate adjectives A pair of adjectives, each modifying a noun on its own and therefore separated by a comma. In *noncoordinate adjectives*, which are not separated by commas, the first adjective modifies the second, which modifies the noun. (*See 33f.*)

> COORDINATE   These drawings present a **quick, simple** solution to the drainage problem.

> NONCOORDINATE   We can use **flexible plastic** pipe to carry water away from the building.

coordinating conjunction (*See* **conjunction.**)

coordination A sentence structure that links and equally weights main clauses using *coordinating conjunctions.* (*See 28a; compare* **subordination**.)

correlative conjunctions Pairs of conjunctions (*not only . . . but also; either . . . or; neither . . . nor; both . . . and; whether . . . or*) that join sentence elements that are grammatically equal. (*See 16a-8, 27b-2 on* **parallelism**.)

→**could of, would of** These incorrect pairs are common because they are often pronounced as if they are spelled this way. Use the correct verb forms *could have* and *would have.*

> INCORRECT   I **could of** majored in psychology.

> EDITED   I **could have** majored in psychology.

count noun A type of noun that refers to individual ("countable") items: *chair, bean, cup.* Most count nouns can be made plural by the addition of an *-s.* (*See 16a-1; see also* **noun**; **collective noun**; **mass noun**.)

counterargument A claim or opinion opposed to the one being supported in an argumentative paper. (*See 55b, 55c, 55d.*)

→**couple, couple of** These terms are used colloquially; in formal writing, use *a few* or *two* instead.

> COLLOQUIAL   Watson took a **couple of** days to examine the data.

> EDITED   Watson took **a few** days to examine the data.

> EDITED   Watson took **two or three** days to examine the data.

criteria *Criteria* is the plural form of *criterion*. Make sure your verbs agree in number with this noun.

> SINGULAR   One **criterion** for winning the bonus <u>was</u> selling ten cars in two weeks.

> PLURAL   The **criteria** <u>were</u> too strict to follow.

critical notes Research notes that include comments, interpretations, or evaluations of a source.

critical reading Evaluating information and ideas presented by utilizing your own knowledge and insight, identifying unanswered questions, and interpreting sources. (*See Chapter 2, 47b*.)

critical synthesis Brings together perspectives, opinions, interpretations, and evidence from a variety of sources and explores their potential connections. (*See 47b-2*.)

critique A paper that summarizes and presents a critical reaction to a specific work, such as a speech or book. (*See 56a*.)

cumulative sentence A sentence that begins with the main clause and then adds details and statements in the form of modifying phrases, clauses, and words. (*See 10c*.)

→**curriculum** *Curriculum* is the singular form of this noun. For the plural, use either *curricula* or *curriculums*, but be consistent.

dangling modifier A sentence that contains no **headword** or **phrase** to which a modifier can be correctly linked. (*See Chapter 24; compare* **disruptive modifier** and **misplaced modifier**.)

> DANGLING   Staring from his study, **Paul's stomach** tied itself into knots.

> EDITED   Staring from his study, **Paul** felt his stomach tying itself into knots.

→**data** Although now widely used for both the singular and plural, *data* technically is a plural noun; *datum* refers to a single piece of data. If in doubt, use the more formal distinction between the two, and make sure your verbs agree in number.

> SINGULAR   This one **datum** is astonishing.

> PLURAL   These **data** are not very revealing.

data-warrant-claim reasoning A reasoning or argumentative strategy in which data (indisputable facts) lead to a claim (or conclusion) through a mental process involving probable facts and assertions (warrants). Also called Toulmin reasoning. (*See 55d-3*.)

database A computerized (CD-ROM or online) collection of resources available to researchers. Databases contain a wide variety of materials such as articles, graphics, bibliographies, and statistics and usually focus on a particular area of study or a particular topic. (*See 46b-2*.)

declarative sentence A type of sentence that makes a statement. (*See 16d; compare* **exclamatory sentence**; **imperative sentence**; **interrogative sentence**.)

> The motor is making a rattling noise.

decorum Proper conduct and behavior; in writing, style and tone that fit the expectations of a particular social context. (*See 11a*.)

gloss

deductive argument An argument that begins with an explicitly stated premise and goes on to support that premise, using **syllogism** as the basic logical format. (*See 55d-1; compare* **inductive argument**.)

definite article (*See* **article**.)

definition paragraph A paragraph designed to adequately introduce a term or concept to your readers. (*See 9e*.)

demonstrative adjective (*See* **demonstrative pronoun**.)

demonstrative pronoun A pronoun (*this, that, these,* or *those*) that points out or highlights an antecedent. (*See 17a-2, 19c-3*.)

dependent clause (*See* **subordinate clause**.)

description A kind of writing and a means of developing paragraphs that uses specific details to evoke images of places, objects, characters, or feelings. (*See also* **objective description** and **subjective description**.)

desk dictionary A midsized dictionary suitable for most professional and academic contexts. (*See 30a*.)

detailing list A prewriting and revision strategy for creating more detailed prose. (*See 4a-3*.)

dialogue journal A kind of collaborative **working journal** in which partners swap journal entries and respond to each other's ideas.

diction The choice of words and phrases in a piece of writing. (*See Chapter 29*.)

→**different from, different than** The subtle difference between these two phrases is marked by what follows them: use *different from* when an object follows, and use *different than* when an entire clause follows.

> Jack's quiche recipe is **different from** Marlene's, but his cooking method is **different** now **than** when he was an apprentice.

direct object (*See* **object**.)

direct quotation A quotation that presents a speaker's or writer's ideas and feelings in the same words the speaker used, set off by quotation marks. (*See 25d*.)

directions One type of process explanation in which the writer gives a step-by-step guide for assembling or creating something or for following a procedure.

→**discreet, discrete** *Discreet* means "reserved or cautious"; *discrete* means "distinctive, different, or explicit."

> Emmons was as **discreet** as an anthropologist could be, but he violated some of the **discrete** codes of research when he lived among the tribe.

discriminatory language Language that implies or reinforces racist or discriminatory views toward other cultures or groups. (*See 32b*.)

discuss To provide an intelligent, focused commentary in a paper. (*See 5a-2*.)

discussion list A type of electronic bulletin board with a specialized membership in a specific academic, work, or public community. (*See 44b-3*.)

→**disinterested, uninterested** *Uninterested* implies boredom or lack of interest; *disinterested* implies impartiality or objectivity.

> It wasn't that Reagan was **uninterested** in environmental issues; he was simply a **disinterested** party when it came to special-interest groups.

disruptive modifier A sentence in which two closely connected elements such as a noun and a verb are inappropriately disrupted by a modifier. (*See 24c; compare* **dangling modifier** and **misplaced modifier**.)

DISRUPTIVE	The engineer, **even though he could have lost his life if he had become trapped in the burning plant**, was able to shut off the gas valve and prevent millions of dollars in damage.
EDITED	**Even though he could have lost his life if he had become trapped in the burning plant**, the engineer was able to shut off the gas valve and prevent millions of dollars in damage.

division paragraph A paragraph in which a subject is split into its constituent parts so that the relationship between these parts can be highlighted or explained. (*See 9e-2.*)

documentation The process of citing the source or reference for an idea, sentence, passage, or text in a research paper. (*See Chapters 51–54.*)

domain name Locates an organization or other entity on the Internet. (*See 13b-2.*)

→**done** Avoid using *done* as a simple past tense; it is a *past participle.* (*See 18d.*)

INCORRECT	The skater **done** the best she could at the Olympics.
EDITED	The skater **did** the best she could at the Olympics.

→**don't, doesn't** These and other contractions may strike some academic readers as too informal. Check with your reader, or err on the side of formality (*do not, does not*) when in doubt.

double negative Avoid the incorrect use of two negative forms. (*See 20d.*)

INCORRECT	The state **hasn't** done **nothing** about it.
EDITED	The state **has** done **nothing** about it.
EDITED	The state **hasn't** done **anything** about it.

drafting The process of creating a preliminary but readable version of an essay or other text. (*See Chapter 7.*)

draft thesis statement (*See* **tentative thesis statement**.)

→**due to** When meaning "because," use *due to* only after some form of the verb *be*. Avoid *due to the fact that*, which is wordy.

INCORRECT	The mayor collapsed **due to** campaign fatigue.
EDITED	The mayor's collapse <u>was</u> **due to** campaign fatigue.
EDITED	The mayor collapsed **because** of campaign fatigue.

editing The process of fine tuning a rough draft for problems in grammar, wording, style, sentence rhythm or length, and other details. (*See Chapter 15; compare* **proofreading** *and* **revision**.)

→**effect, affect** (*See* **affect, effect**.)

→**e.g.** From a Latin term meaning "for example," this abbreviation is common in much writing but should be avoided when possible.

AWKWARD	Her positions on major issues, **e.g.,** gun control, abortion, and the death penalty, are very liberal.
EDITED	Her positions on major issues **such as** gun control, abortion, and the death penalty are very liberal.

gloss

either/or strategy In argumentative writing, a **fallacy** in which an issue is oversimplified, usually into two sides or positions. (*See 55f-5.*)

e-journals Scholarly journals published (or distributed) through electronic computer networks. (*See 46b.*)

electronic community Writers and readers who participate in one of the many clusters of related sites that form and re-form on the Internet and World Wide Web. (*See Chapter 1.*)

electronic indexes Computerized (CD-ROM or online) indexes to articles in magazines, newspapers, or scholarly journals. Indexes enable researchers to identify possible sources. (*See 46b; see also* **printed indexes***.*)

electronic mailing list The most common type of subscriber-based mailing list. (*See 13c.*)

electronic research Research conducted using electronic media or technology, such as CD-ROM databases, online resources, or electronic card catalogs. (*See 46b; see also* **research***.*)

ellipsis A series of three evenly spaced periods telling a reader that something has been left out of a quotation. (*See 38d.*)

> As Fielding describes it, Squire Allworthy's house had "an Air of Grandeur in it, that struck you with awe [. . .] and it was as commodious within, as venerable without."

elliptical construction The omission of an otherwise repeated element in a sentence; appropriate omissions are not misleading or confusing. (*See 26b-2.*)

LEFT IN	Some car owners invest lots of time caring for their cars; others **invest little time caring for their cars**.
OMITTED BUT CLEAR	Some car owners invest lots of time caring for their cars; **others invest little**.

email Mail exchanged through electronic computer networks. (*See 13b.*)

embedded quotation A quotation used within a sentence you have written, as contrasted to a **block quotation**.

→**emigrate from, immigrate to** Foreigners *emigrate from* one country and *immigrate to* another. *Migrate* implies moving around (as in *migrant workers*) or settling temporarily.

emoticons Faces drawn with keyboard characters. (*See 12b-2.*)

emotional strategy In argumentative writing, a focus on the values, attitudes, systems of beliefs, and emotions that guide people's lives and are central to most decision-making processes. (*See 55f-2.*)

empty phrase A phrase that adds little or no meaning to a sentence and can be cut or reduced: *at this point in time, due to the fact that, each and every*. (*See 31a-1.*)

e-newsletters Scholarly or professional newsletters containing current information and announcements, published (or distributed) through electronic computer networks. (*See 46b.*)

→**ensure, assure, insure** (*See* **assure, ensure, insure***.*)

→**enthused** Avoid *enthused* to mean *enthusiastic* in formal writing.

equivocation (*See* **misleading language/misleading evidence***.*)

→**especially, specially** *Especially* implies "in particular"; *specially* means "for a specific purpose."

> It was **especially** important that Nakita follow the workouts **specially** designed by her coach.

gloss

essay exam A test written out in essay form, either during a timed, in-class session or at home between class sessions. (*See 56c, 58h.*)

→**etc.** Avoid this abbreviation in formal writing by supplying a complete list of items or by using a phrase like *so forth.*

> INFORMAL   The Washington march was a disaster: it was cold and rainy, the protesters had no food, **etc.**

> EDITED   The Washington march was a disaster: the protesters were cold, wet, and hungry.

ethnographic research Research that interprets the practices, behaviors, language, and attitudes of particular groups that are tied together by their interests or ways of understanding and acting in the world. (*See 50c.*)

ethnography The written report of ethnographic research. (*See 50c.*)

etymological dictionary (*See* **etymology**.)

etymology The history of a word, including its source(s) and the changes it has undergone. (*See 30a.*)

evaluation The process of deciding the relative worth of a source, phenomenon, or opinion, including the credibility or authority of a researched source. (*See Chapter 47.*)

evaluative summary (*See* **summary**.)

→**eventually, ultimately** Use *eventually* to imply that an outcome follows a series of events or a lapse of events. Use *ultimately* to imply that a final or culminating act ends a series of events.

> **Eventually**, the rescue team managed to pull the last of the survivors from the wreck, and **ultimately** there were no casualties.

→**everyday, every day** *Everyday* is an adjective that modifies a noun. *Every day* is a noun modified by *every.*

> **Every day** in the Peace Corps, Monique faced the **everyday** task of boiling her drinking water.

→**everyone, every one** *Everyone* is a pronoun; *every one* is an adjective followed by a noun. (*See also* **anyone, any one**.)

> **Everyone** was tantalized by **every one** of the items on the dessert menu.

evidence Information that gives readers reasons for accepting the accuracy, value, or importance of conclusions. (*See 12c-3.*)

→**exam** In formal writing, some readers may be bothered by this abbreviation of the word *examination.*

→**except, accept** (*See* **accept, except**.)

exclamatory sentence A type of sentence that expresses something emphatically. (*See 10d-2, 16d-2; compare* **declarative sentence**; **imperative sentence**; **interrogative sentence**.)

> The car is on fire!

explanation A kind of writing that provides details on how a mechanism or procedure works.

expletive construction In indirect sentences, the use of opening expletives such as *there is, there are,* or *it is* to delay the actual subject until further into the sentence. (*See 10b, 31a-2.*)

> **This is** the case in which the man bit the dog.

gloss

explication A line-by-line analysis of a text. (*See 58b-2.*)

→**explicit, implicit** *Explicit* means that something is outwardly or openly stated; *implicit* means that it is implied or suggested.

> The conductors **explicitly** assured the passengers that they were traveling to a comfortable new life, but **implicit** in their voices was the Nazi menace that the Jews had come to recognize.

exploratory sources (*See* **preliminary sources**.)

extemporaneous speaking A style of oral presentation in which the speaker does not read a written text out loud but presents ideas from memory, using cues and notes.

extend In writing assignments, to take an idea or concept and apply it more extensively. (*See 5a-2.*)

fallacy Any flaw in reasoning, particularly in the context of persuasive or argumentative writing. (*See 55f-5.*)

false analogy A **fallacy** in which two things that are presented as comparable are actually not. (*See 55f-5.*)

→**farther, further** *Farther* implies a measurable distance; *further* implies something that cannot be measured.

> The **farther** they trekked into the wilderness, the **further** their relationship deteriorated.

faulty cause-effect relationship A **fallacy** in which one event is assumed or implied to have caused another event. (*See 55f-5.*)

faulty parallelism (*See* **parallelism**.)

faulty predication A sentence in which the second part comments on or names a topic different from the one announced in the first part. (*See 26a-1; see* **shift**.)

FAULTY	The **presence** of ozone in smog is **the chemical** that causes eye irritation.
EDITED	The **ozone** in smog is the **chemical** that causes eye irritation.

→**female, male** Use these terms only when you want to call attention to gender specifically, as in a research report. Otherwise, use the simpler *man* and *woman* or *boy* and *girl*, unless such usage is sexist. (*See Chapter 32.*)

→**fewer, less** Use *fewer* for things that can be counted, and use *less* for quantities that cannot be divided.

> Bush had **fewer** supporters for the bill than before, but there was much **less** media coverage this time.

field research (*See* **research**.)

field resources Original documents, interviews, surveys, questionnaires, and personal observations gathered during the process of **research**.

figure, calculate, reckon (*See* **calculate, figure, reckon**.)

→**finalize** Some readers object to adjectives and nouns that are turned into verbs ending in -*ize* (*finalize, prioritize, objectivize*). When in doubt, use *make final* or some other construction.

gloss

→**firstly** Use *first*, *second*, *third*, and so forth when enumerating points in writing.

INAPPROPRIATE	**Firstly**, I will compare Sartre's and Camus's versions of existentialism.
EDITED	**First**, I will compare Sartre's and Camus's versions of existentialism.

first person (*See* **person**.)

five-paragraph theme A kind of academic paper that has a simple, clearly defined structure including an **introduction**, a **body** of three paragraphs each starting with a **topic sentence**, and a **conclusion**.

focus-imagine-choose strategy A strategy for choosing the correct case of pronouns: focus on the pronoun, imagine each possible choice, and choose the correct form. (*See 17b-1*.)

focused freewriting Writing quickly, without stopping, about a particular idea or topic. (*See 4a-2*; *see also* **freewriting**.)

focused paragraph (*See* **paragraph**.)

format A general plan for the organization, such as length, level of formality, or the actual appearance of a document. (*See Chapter 14*.)

→**former, latter** *Former* means "the one before" and *latter* means "the one after." They can be used only when referring to two things.

fragment (*See* **sentence fragment**.)

freewriting A technique involving writing as quickly as possible without concern for style or grammar. Freewriting is often used to avoid writer's block, to "warm up" for more formal writing, or to generate ideas for a paper. (*See 4a-2*; *see also* **focused freewriting**.)

→**freshman, freshmen** Many readers consider these terms sexist and archaic. Unless you are citing an established term or group (such as the Freshman Colloquium at Midwest University), use *first-year student* instead.

further, farther (*See* **farther, further**.)

fused sentence Two or more complete sentences incorrectly joined without any punctuation. (*See Chapter 22*; *compare* **comma splice**.)

FUSED	Frank Lloyd Wright's Robie House is a good example of his architectural principles it embodies the idea of "space, not mass."
EDITED	Frank Lloyd Wright's Robie House is a good example of his architectural principles; it embodies the idea of "space, not mass."

future perfect tense (*See* **perfect tense**.)

future progressive tense (*See* **progressive tense**.)

future tense (*See* **tense**.)

gazetteer A dictionary of geographical places and cities.

gender Labeling of nouns and pronouns according to whether they are masculine, feminine, or neuter. Pronouns must agree in gender with the nouns to which they refer. (*See 16a-2, 17a*.)

Harry put on **his** shirt.

gloss

general academic writing Writing typically found in introductory courses across the college curriculum, including term papers, essay exams, short reports, abstracts, summaries, and argumentative analyses.

general-interest magazines Magazines that appear monthly or weekly, with each issue paginated separately. (*See 46b-2.*)

general pattern of development A type of paragraph development such as **narration**, **comparison**, or **cause-effect**, used to shape a paragraph's content and arrangement. (*See 9e-2.*)

general reference A reference to the main ideas in a source or to information presented throughout the work, not in a single place. (*See 51a; compare* **informational reference** and **specific reference**.)

general sources Books, indexes, databases, and nonspecialized periodicals used for background and to point the way to **specialized sources**. (*See 46a-3.*)

general-to-specific pattern (*See* **logical order**.)

generalizations Conclusions reached on the basis of facts (*see 12b-2*) and summing up their meaning or qualities, or broad conclusions about what your research has to say about your topic. (*See 47b-3.*)

genre The form, or category of discourse, to which a work conforms (e.g., poem, play, novel, novella, film). (*See 58a-2.*)

gerund An *-ing* form of a verb that acts as a noun. (*See 16a-4, 17b-6; see also* **verbal phrase**.)

> **Running** can be enjoyable.

gloss

→**get** Avoid imprecise or frequent use of *get* in formal writing; use more specific verbs instead.

INFORMAL   Martin Luther King had a premonition that he would **get** shot; his sermons and speeches before his death **got** nostalgic at times.

EDITED   Martin Luther King had a premonition that he would **be** shot; his sermons and speeches before his death **waxed** nostalgic at times.

→**goes, says** In very informal contexts, some speakers use *go* and *goes* colloquially to mean *say* and *says*. This usage is considered inappropriate in all writing.

INAPPROPRIATE   Hjalmar **goes** to Gregers, "I thought it best to make a clean break."

EDITED   Hjalmar **says** to Gregers, "I thought it best to make a clean break."

→**gone, went** Do not use *went* (the past tense of *go*) in place of the past participle form *gone*.

INCORRECT   The players **should have went** to their captain.

EDITED   The players **should have gone** to their captain.

→**good and** This is a colloquial term when used to mean "very" (*good and* tired; *good and* hot). Avoid it in formal writing.

→**good, well** *Good* is an adjective meaning "favorable" (a *good* trip). *Well* is an adverb meaning "done favorably." Avoid colloquial uses of *good* for *well*.

COLLOQUIAL	The Vikings played real **good** in the playoffs.
CORRECT	A **good** shot in the game of golf is not a hard-hit shot but a shot that is placed **well**.

→**got to** Avoid the colloquial use of *got* or *got to* in place of *must* or *have to*.

COLLOQUIAL	I **got to** improve my ratings in the opinion polls.
EDITED	I **must** improve my ratings in the opinion polls.

government documents Archives of congressional reports and documents issued by federal agencies as well as state and local governments. (*See 46b-2*.)

→**great** In formal writing, avoid using *great* as an adjective meaning "wonderful." Use *great* in the sense of "large" or "monumental."

INFORMAL	Our trip to Stone Mountain was **great**.
APPROPRIATE	As you approach Stone Mountain, **a great** carving appears on the rock face.

guessing Unsure of the correct spelling of a word, and guessing on the basis of reason or similar sounding words. (*See 44a-1*.)

guiding question In research, a specific question that helps to determine the kinds of sources to consult, the process of locating sources, and the possibilities for organizing the paper. (*See 45b-6*.)

→**hanged, hung** Although the distinction between these terms is disappearing, some readers may expect you to use *hanged* exclusively to mean execution by hanging and *hung* to refer to anything else.

The convict was **hanged** at dawn.
The farmer **hung** the dead pheasant upside down for a day before cooking it.

hasty generalization (*See* **begging the question**.)

→**have, got** (*See* **got to**.)

→**have, of** (*See* **could of, would of**.)

→**he, she, he or she, his/her** When you use gender-specific pronouns, be careful not to privilege the male versions. Look for ways to avoid awkward alternations of *he* and *she* or *his* and *her* by revising structures that require them. (*See 32a-3*.)

headword The word a modifier refers to. (*See Chapter 23*.)

helping verb The different forms of *be*, *do*, and *have* that link to main verbs and create complex verb forms. Helping verbs are sometimes called **auxiliary verbs** or **modal auxiliaries**. (*See 16a-3, 18b*.)

helping   main
verb   verb

The tourist agency is planning to make a video of the local attractions.

homophones Words that sound like each other but are spelled differently (*accept/ except; assent/ascent; principal/principle; stationary/stationery*). (*See 44b-4*.)

→**hopefully** Although the word is widely used to modify entire clauses (as in "Hopefully, her condition will improve"), some readers may object. When in doubt, use *hopefully* only to mean "feeling hopeful."

Bystanders watched **hopefully** as the workers dug their way to the trapped spelunkers.

gloss

→**however, yet, but** (*See* **but however, but yet**.)

→**hung, hanged** (*See* **hanged, hung**.)

hypercorrection The phenomenon in which speakers using nonmainstream dialect unwittingly create a new error in trying to "repair" their speech. (*See 11b-4*.)

hyphenated noun A single noun that consists of two or more words linked by hyphens: *father-in-law*. (*See 34a-3*.)

hypothesis A tentative assertion to be explored in an argument. (*See 55f-1*.)

idiom A common expression that typically means something different from its literal interpretation (e.g., *kick the bucket*). (*See 29b-5*.)

→**if, whether** Use *if* before a specific outcome (either stated or implied); use *whether* when you are considering alternatives.

> **If** holographic technology can be perfected, we may soon be watching three-dimensional television. But **whether** any of us will be able to afford it is another question.

illogical comparison (*See* **incomplete sentence**.)

→**illusion, allusion** (*See* **allusion, illusion**.)

→**immigrate to, emigrate from** (*See* **emigrate from, immigrate to**.)

imperative mood (*See* **mood**.)

imperative sentence A type of sentence that makes a request or command. (*See 10d-2, 16d; compare* **declarative sentence**; **exclamatory sentence**; **interrogative sentence**.)

> Do your chores immediately.

→**implicit, explicit** (*See* **explicit, implicit**.)

inattention Knowing the correct spelling of a word but failing to use it. (*See 44a-1*.)

incomplete comparison (*See* **incomplete sentence**.)

incomplete sentence A sentence that fails to complete an expected logical or grammatical pattern. An *incomplete comparison* leaves out the element to which something is being compared. An *illogical comparison* is worded so that it seems to be comparing things that cannot be reasonably compared. (*See 26b*.)

INCOMPLETE COMPARISON	The sound quality of the new digital audiotapes is much better.
EDITED	The sound quality of the new digital audiotapes is much better **than that of the old analog tapes**.

indefinite article (*See* **article**.)

indefinite pronoun A pronoun that refers to people, things, or ideas in general rather than to specific antecedents. Indefinite pronouns include *all*, *another*, *any*, *anybody*, *anyone*, *anything*, *both*, *each*, *every*, and *everyone*. (*See 16a-2, 17a*.)

independent clause (*See* **main clause**.)

indicative mood (*See* **mood**.)

indirect object (*See* **object**.)

indirect question A sentence whose main clause is a statement and whose embedded clause asks a question. Such sentences usually behave as statements, not as questions. (*See 37b-1*.)

> Phil wondered whether it would be too much work to take on an additional course.

gloss

indirect quotation A quotation in which a writer reports the substance of someone's words but not the exact words the person used. Quotation marks are not needed. (*See 25b-2, 25d.*)

inductive argument An argument that does not explicitly state a premise but leads the reader through an accumulating body of evidence to a conclusion. (*See 55f-1; compare* **deductive argument**.)

inferences Conclusions reached on the basis of facts. (*See 12c-2.*)

infinitive The "root," tenseless form of a verb. In English, infinitives are preceded by *to: to live, to perform, to abolish.* (*See 16a-4, 16c-4; see also* **split infinitive** and **verbal phrase**.)

infinitive phrase A phrase that uses the *to* form of a verbal. It can be used as an adjective, an adverb, or a noun. (*See 16c-4.*)

inform In a writing assignment, to tell the reader about some facts, views, or phenomena.

informants In field research, people interviewed or surveyed. (*See Chapter 50.*)

informational notes Research notes that record facts, details, concepts, interpretations, and quotations from sources.

informational reference A reference that provides background information or material potentially useful for readers but too cumbersome to include in the text itself. (*Compare* **general reference** and **specific reference**.)

informative writing Writing whose content and strategies are shaped by the purpose of conveying, explaining, or analyzing information (*See Chapter 58; see also* **point-driven writing**.)

→**in regard to** Although it may sound sophisticated, *in regard to* is wordy and unnecessary. Use *about* instead.

> WORDY   The cruise company was adamant **in regard to** its docking rights at Christiansted.

> EDITED   The cruise company was adamant **about** its docking rights at Christiansted.

→**inside of, outside of** When you use *inside* or *outside* to mark locations, do not pair them with *of.*

> INAPPROPRIATE   **Inside of** the hut was a large stock of rootwater.

> EDITED   **Inside** the hut was a large stock of rootwater.

→**insure, assure, ensure** (*See* **assure, ensure, insure**.)

intensifying phrase A phrase that is meant to make a sentence more forceful but carries little or no additional meaning; *for all intents and purposes, in my opinion, all things considered.* (*See 31a-1.*)

intensive drafting Creating a preliminary version of an essay in collaboration with a close friend or colleague. (*See 7c-3.*)

intensive pronoun A **reflexive pronoun** used to give emphasis to, or intensify, a sentence. (*See 16a-2, 17b-7.*)

> He was able to move the heavy refrigerator **himself**.
> She **herself** was responsible for the mismanagement of the firm.

intentional fragment (*See* **partial sentence**.)

interjection An emphatic word or phrase used to convey a strong reaction or emotion, such as surprise (*Hey!*) or disappointment (*Oh no!*). (*See 16a-9.*)

gloss

interlibrary loans Systems that allow for the exchange of books, articles, and other resources between libraries to serve users of a library that does not have an item in its own holdings.

Internet A network that links computers of all kinds through email, discussion groups, resource sites, and the World Wide Web. (*See 46c.*)

interpolation The introduction of your own words, marked with brackets, into a verbatim quotation from someone else. (*See 38b-1.*)

> Kent said, "Captain Sims **[the boat's owner]** has chosen a special place within two hours of Key West."

interpretation The process of reading into or adding your own understandings to a source, concept, or phenomenon. (*See 2b.*)

interpretive reading A kind of **analytical reading** to determine the meaning, perspective, and purposes, both explicit and implicit, of a text. (*See Chapter 2.*)

interrogative pronoun The pronouns *who* and *which* when these are used to introduce questions. (*See 16a.*)

interrogative sentence A type of sentence that poses a question. (*See 16d-2; compare* **declarative sentence**; **exclamatory sentence**; **imperative sentence**.)

interrupters Parenthetical remarks such as *in fact* or *more importantly*. (*See Chapter 31.*)

interviews Conversations, verbal or written, with a person in order to gather information or ideas. (*See Chapter 50.*)

in-text citation In research writing, a citation that is placed within the text of the paper rather than at the end in a works cited page or bibliography. (*See 49b.*)

intransitive verb A verb that is not followed by an **object** or **complement**. (*See 16b-2; compare* **transitive verb**.)

>   **verb**   **no object**
> The president **dreamed**.

introduction The first part of a paper or other document, often leading up to or containing a **thesis**. (*See 7a-2.*)

invention A term from classical rhetoric referring to the process of generating and exploring ideas before writing a draft. (*See Chapter 4; see also* **brainstorming**; **planning**; **prewriting strategies**.)

inverted sentence order A sentence in which the normal subject-verb-object/complement word order is shifted by placing a subsidiary element at the beginning of the sentence in order to call attention to it. (*See 10d-3.*)

> **NORMAL**   **The director's voice thundered** from the darkness near the rear of the auditorium with criticisms of our acting.
>
> **INVERTED**   **From the darkness near the rear of the auditorium thundered the director's voice** with criticisms of our acting.

→**irregardless** Avoid this erroneous form of the word *regardless*, commonly used because *regardless* and *irrespective* are often used synonymously.

→**irregular verb** A verb that does not follow the usual pattern for distinguishing forms for the present, past, and past participle. (*See 18a.*)

	PRESENT	PAST	PAST PARTICIPLE
REGULAR VERB	bake	baked	baked
IRREGULAR VERB	swim	swam	swum

gloss

→**irritate, aggravate** (*See* **aggravate, irritate**.)

issue A subject about which there are two (or more) clearly differing opinions. (*See 55a-1*.)

italic type Type that *slants to the right* and is the equivalent of <u>underlining</u> for emphasis or for some titles. (*See Chapter 40*.)

→**its, it's** Use *its* as a possessive pronoun and *it's* as a contraction of *it* and *is*. (Some readers may also object to *it's* for *it is* in formal writing.) (*See 35b*.)

The porcupine raised its quills threateningly. **It's** a shame that dogs must learn about porcupines the hard way.

→**-ize, -wise** Some readers object to the process of turning nouns or adjectives into verbs by adding *-ize* at the end (*finalize, itemize, computerize*). When in doubt, opt for different verbs. Also avoid adding the suffix *-wise* to words, as in "Weather*wise*, it will be a chilly night all over the region."

journalist's questions A set of questions (*who? what? when? where? why? how?*) used during the planning or prewriting process to generate or explore ideas or existing material.

keywords Most **database** resources and other electronic sources of information such as **online catalogs** or **electronic indexes** allow researchers to retrieve information and listings by typing in important (key) words identifying the subject or some important ideas or details related to the subject.

→**kind, sort, type** These words are singular nouns; precede them with *this*, not *these*. In general, use more precise words.

→**kind of, sort of** Considered by most readers to be informal, these phrases should be avoided in academic and professional writing.

gloss

lab report A paper that summarizes the methods and results of a laboratory experiment. (*See 58e*.)

→**latter, former** (*See* **former, latter**.)

→**lay, lie** *Lay* is a transitive verb requiring a direct object (but not the self). *Lie*, when used to mean "place in a resting position," refers to the self but takes the form *lay* in the past tense. (*See 18d*.)

| **INCORRECT** | I was going to **lay** down for a while. |
| **EDITED** | I was going to **lie** down for a while. |

→**less, fewer** (*See* **fewer, less**.)

→**liable** (*See* **apt, likely, liable**.)

library research (*See* **research**.)

→**lie, lay** (*See* **lay, lie**.)

→**like, as** (*See* **as, like**.)

→**likely, apt, liable** (*See* **apt, likely, liable**.)

limiting modifier A **modifier** such as *only, almost, hardly, just, scarcely, merely, simply, exactly,* or *even* that limits or qualifies a word, usually the one that follows it. (*See 24a-2*.)

limiting sentence A sentence that limits, or narrows, the focus of a **topic sentence**. (*See 9b-2*.)

link On a computer, a picture or icon or piece of text, usually shown in blue, that when clicked on takes you to another part of the Web page you are viewing, or to another site. (*See 4d-3*.)

linking verb Verbs that express a state of being or an occurrence: *is, seems, becomes, grows*. Also known as **state-of-being verbs**. (*See 16a-3, 16b-2*.)

listing A technique for exploring ideas by making a list of points, usually in preparation for writing a formal paper. (*See 4a-3*.)

listserv (*See **electronic mailing list**.)

→**literally** Avoid using *literally* in a figurative statement (one that is not true to fact). Even when used correctly, *literally* is redundant because the statement will be taken as fact anyway.

> **INCORRECT** The visiting scholars **literally** died when they saw their accommodations.
>
> **REDUNDANT** The visiting scholars **literally gasped** when they saw their accommodations.
>
> **EDITED** The visiting scholars gasped when they saw their accommodations.

literature review A paper or part of a paper that provides a **synthesis** of existing literature or research on a specific topic. (*See 58d*.)

logical order A pattern for paragraph development in which details and generalizations are arranged according to a *question-answer pattern*, a *problem-solution pattern*, a *general-to-specific pattern*, or a *specific-to-general pattern*, suggesting an internal logic to the flow of sentences and ideas.

logical strategies The arrangement of ideas and evidence in ways that correspond with patterns of thought that most people accept as reasonable and convincing. (*See 55f-1*.)

looping A technique involving successively **freewriting**, reviewing the material produced from freewriting in order to find new ideas or concepts, and then freewriting on those ideas or concepts.

→**loose, lose** Commonly misspelled, these words are pronounced differently. *Loose* (rhyming with *moose*) is an adjective meaning "not tight." *Lose* (rhyming with *snooze*) is a present tense verb meaning "to misplace."

> I was afraid that I would **lose** my ring because it was very **loose**.

→**lots, lots of, a lot of** (*See **a lot**.)

lurking Reading online without participating. (*See 13a-1*.)

main clause A word group that contains a subject and a verb and can act as a complete sentence. Also called an *independent clause*. (*See 16c; compare **phrase**.)

main conclusion The end point of a chain of reasoning. (*See 12c-1*.)

main verb The central or main verb (word showing action or state of being) in a sentence; it can stand alone or be accompanied by one or more **helping verbs**. (*See 16a-3*.)

major premise (*See **premise**.)

major revision (*See **revision**.)

→**man, mankind** For many readers, these terms represent sexist usage when they refer to all humans. Use *people, humans, humanity*, or some other substitute. (*See Chapter 32*.)

gloss

mass noun A kind of noun that refers to material that cannot be "counted," or divided into separate units to form a usual plural. (*See 16a-1; see also* **noun**; **collective noun**; **count noun**.)

| COUNT NOUNS | chair + *s*, cake + *s*, shadow + *s*, pea + *s* |
| NONCOUNT NOUNS | flour, rice, sugar, steel, sunlight, earth, water |

→**may, can** (*See* **can, may**.)

→**maybe, may be** *Maybe* means *possibly; may be* is part of a verb structure.

The President **may be** addressing the nation tonight, so **maybe** we should turn on the news.

→**media, medium** Technically, *media* is a plural noun requiring a verb that agrees in number. Many people now use *media* as a singular noun when referring to the press.

The **media** *is* not covering the story accurately.

Medium generally refers to a conduit or method of transmission.

The telephone was not a good **medium** for reviewing all the budget figures.

meeting minutes A report of the items discussed during a business meeting. (*See Chapter 59.*)

memo A short, usually internal, note between or among people working in a business. (*See 59d.*)

microfiche A flat sheet of **microfilm** on which printed materials have been placed to save space. (*See* **microform collection**.)

microfilm A type of film on which printed materials are recorded to save space. (*See* **microform collection**.)

microform collection A library collection containing books, **periodicals**, newspapers, and unpublished documents in the form of **microfilm** or **microfiche**. (*See 46b-4.*)

→**might of, may of** (*See* **could of, would of**.)

→**mighty** Avoid this adjective in formal writing.

| INFORMAL | It was a **mighty** proud moment for NASA. |
| EDITED | It was a **very** proud moment for NASA. |

minor premise (*See* **premise**.)

minor revision (*See* **revision**.)

minutes (*See* **meeting minutes**.)

misleading language/misleading evidence A **fallacy** in which a writer deceives a reader through the use of language or information. Using misleading language, the writer shifts the meaning of a term from one sense to another but still gives the erroneous impression of supporting the argument. Using misleading evidence, the writer uses faulty statistics, survey results, and other material slanted in favor of only one side of an argument. (*See 55f-5.*)

misplaced modifier A modifier incorrectly placed relative to its intended **headword**, giving the impression that it modifies something else. (*See Chapter 24; compare* **dangling modifier** and **disruptive modifier**.)

gloss

MISPLACED	In *Walden*, Thoreau describes how he **simply** lived, conserving his resources.
EDITED	In *Walden*, Thoreau describes how he lived **simply**, conserving his resources.

mixed sentence A sentence with mismatched topics or with a shifted grammatical structure. (*See 26a; see* **faulty predication**.)

MLA documentation style The style of **documentation** suggested by the Modern Language Association and described in its guide. (*See Chapter 51.*)

mnemonic An aid to memorization, for example, of correct spellings. (*See 44c-1.*)

modal auxiliary verbs (*See* **helping verbs**.)

moderator The person who decides which messages will be posted on an electronic mailing list. (*See 13c-1.*)

modified block format A format for longer letters in which the return address and the closing and signature are indented but paragraphs are not. (*See 59c; compare* **block format**.)

modifier A word or word group, functioning as an adjective or adverb, that qualifies or adds to a noun or verb. (*See Chapter 24.*)

mood The verb form that indicates the speaker's attitude in a sentence. *Indicative mood* characterizes statements intended as truthful or factual. *Imperative mood* characterizes statements that function as commands. *Subjunctive mood* characterizes statements expressing uncertainty. Many **conditional sentences** require the subjunctive mood. (*See 18, 5b.*)

INDICATIVE MOOD	It will rain today.
IMPERATIVE	Beware of lightning!
SUBJUNCTIVE MOOD	Were it to rain, we would not play golf.

→**Ms.** To avoid the sexist labeling of women as "married" or "unmarried" (a condition not marked in men's titles), use *Ms.* unless you have reason to use *Miss* or *Mrs.* (for example, when giving the name of a character such as *Mrs. Dalloway*). Use professional titles when appropriate (*Dr., Professor, Senator, Mayor*). (*See Chapter 32.*)

MUD (multi-user domain) A real-time venue used in academic and corporate settings, in which users learn a series of commands to communicate and move around in a carefully described text environment. (*See 13c-3.*)

multiple-word noun A noun consisting of two or more words that are treated as a single unit when marking plurality or possession. (*See 35a-3.*)

The **union leaders'** negotiations fell through.

→**must of, must have** (*See* **could of, would of**.)

narrative A type of writing, or **genre**, in which the writer usually traces events in the past, present, or imagined future. Narratives tell stories about people, places, or events, often from the writer's own experience.

narrowing The process of taking a more specific perspective on a chosen topic. (*See 5c-1.*)

neologism A word that has entered into general use very recently, sometimes not yet having been put into any dictionaries. (*See 29b-4.*)

netiquette Common sense guidelines that apply across nearly all Internet communities. (*See 13a-4.*)

newsgroups A format for online communities in which the user chooses which individual posts to read. (*See 13c-1.*)

nominalization A sentence in which a verb or adjective is (sometimes inappropriately) turned into a noun: *completion* (noun) from *complete* (verb), *happiness* (noun) from *happy* (adjective). (*See 10a-2, 31a-2.*)

noncoordinate adjectives (*See* **coordinate adjectives**.)

noncount noun (*See* **mass noun**.)

nonrestrictive clause (*See* **restrictive modifier**.)

nonrestrictive modifier (*See* **restrictive modifier**.)

→**nor, or** Use *nor* in negative constructions and *or* in positive ones.

> NEGATIVE   Neither rain **nor** snow will slow the team.
>
> POSITIVE   Either rain **or** snow may delay the game.

→**nothing like, nowhere near** These are considered informal phases when used to compare two things (as in "Gibbon's position is **nowhere near** as justified as Carlyle's"). Avoid them in formal writing.

noun A word that names a person, place, or thing and is often preceded by an **article** (*a*, *an*, or *the*). (*See 16a-1; see also* **collective noun**; **count noun**; **mass noun**.)

noun clause A clause that functions as a noun. (*See 16d.*)

noun string A string of nouns used as modifiers (usually adjectives) of a main noun. Such strings are grammatically correct but may seem overly abstract or technical. (*See 10a-4.*)

> The **area computer network downlink access program** failed.

→**nowheres** Use *nowhere* instead.

number A grammatical concept referring to whether a noun or pronoun is singular or plural. Pronouns must agree in number with the nouns they modify, and subjects and verbs must also agree in number. (*See 16a-2, 16a-3, 17a, 18b, 19a.*)

→**number, amount** (*See* **amount, number**.)

object A noun, pronoun, or group of words functioning as a noun to which the action of a verb applies. *Direct objects* receive the action of **transitive verbs**; *indirect objects* are affected indirectly by the action of a transitive verb. (*See 16b-2; see also* **complement**.)

object complement (*See* **complement**.)

object of a preposition The noun or pronoun that follows a preposition. (*See 16c-1.*)

object pronoun A pronoun that is the **object** of a verb. (*See 16c-1.*)

objective case (*See* **case**.)

objective description Description that emphasizes physical details. (*Compare* **subjective description**.)

objective summary (*See* **summary**.)

observation A kind of ethnographic research involving firsthand research (*onsite visiting and note taking*) of people, events, or settings. (*See 50c.*)

→**of, have** (*See* **could of, would of**.)

gloss

→**off of** Use simply *off* instead.

→**OK** When you write formally, use *OK* only in dialogue. If you mean "good" or "acceptable," use one of these terms.

→**on account of** Avoid this expression in formal writing. Use *because* instead.

online catalog A computerized listing of books, magazines, and other holdings in a library. A researcher can retrieve individual listings by author, title, or subject area. Many online catalogs list resources in more than one library and can be accessed through computer networks as well as by terminals in a library. (*See 46b-3; see also* **card catalog**.)

online (electronic) periodicals Periodicals available through the Internet, with past issues or selected articles sometimes available in electronic archives. (*See 46b-2*.)

outline A list, usually hierarchical, showing the main contents of a paper. (*See 4c-4*.) A *working outline* shows the general sequence of information in a paper and the relationships between the segments of information. (*See 48b*.)

→**outside of, inside of** (*See* **inside of, outside of**.)

overblown language **Diction** that is too formal or technical for the writer's purpose and audience, often used out of a misguided attempt to impress the reader. (*See 31b-2*.)

overgeneralization (*See* **begging the question**.)

paragraph A unit of prose marked by an indent at the left margin and consisting of a topic and its **development**. A *focused paragraph* is one in which the topic, main idea, or perspective is evident and is maintained throughout the paragraph. A *unified paragraph* contains sentences that are clearly and directly related to the main idea. (*See Chapter 9*.)

paragraph development The examples, facts, concrete details, explanatory statements, or supporting arguments that make a paragraph informative and give it a sense of structure. (*See Chapter 9*.)

parallel drafting Preparing a preliminary version of a document by having each member of a group responsible for a specific section. (*See 7c*.)

parallelism The expression of similar or related ideas in similar grammatical form. *Faulty parallelism* occurs when elements in parallel are given incorrect or unequal grammatical form.(*See Chapter 27*.) In paragraphs, parallelism refers to a technique in which grammatical structures are repeated in order to highlight similar or related ideas. (*See 9c*.)

paraphrase A rewriting of an original sentence or passage in your own words, preserving the essence and level of detail of the original. (*See 36a-2, 47a-2, 48c-1*.)

partial sentence An effective sentence fragment used for emphasis. (*See 21c*.)

participle The form a verb takes when it is linked to a helping verb. Verbs can take two participial forms, the *present participle* and the *past participle*. (*See 16b-4, 18b*.)

particle (*See* **phrasal verb**.)

passive voice The form of a verb in a sentence in which the doer (or agent) takes the position of the direct object. (*See 10c-3, 18e, 25c, 31a-2; compare* **active voice**.)

     subject   verb

    The ball was caught by the outfielder.

past participle (*See* **participle**.)

past perfect tense (*See* **perfect tense**.)

past progressive tense (*See* **progressive tense**.)
past tense (*See* **tense**.)
peer group A group of fellow writers, usually in a classroom, who participate in collaborative writing activities. (*See 6d-2.*)
→**per** Use *per* only to mean "by the," as in *per hour* or *per day.* Avoid using it to mean "according to," as in "per your instructions."
→**percent, percentage** Use *percent* only with numerical data. Use *percentage* to imply a statistical part of something.

INCORRECT	**A percentage** of my commute is through Tomkins State Park.
CORRECT	Ten **percent** of the sample returned the questionnaire.
CORRECT	A large **percentage** of the revenue from the parking meters was stolen.

perfect tense A tense used to indicate that something happens before something else happens. Three perfect tenses can be marked in verb phrases: present perfect, past perfect, and future perfect. (*See 18c.*)

PRESENT PERFECT	**I have reported** the fire already.
PAST PERFECT	The fires **had burned** for an hour before the brigade arrived.
FUTURE PERFECT	Nancy **will have finished** by the time the dentist is ready.

periodic sentence A sentence structured so that subsidiary phrases, clauses, or other elements are piled up at the beginning, delaying the sentence's main clause. (*See 10c-2.*)

> Because she knows that inspired designs often spring from hard work, because she loves perfection yet fears failure, and because she believes that risk-taking ought to be accompanied by attention to detail, Janelle is working up to eighteen hours a day on the clothing for her fall collection.

gloss

periodical A recurring publication that contains articles by different authors. Periodicals include magazines, scholarly journals, and newspapers. (*See 46b-2.*)
person The form that a noun or a pronoun takes to identify the subject of a sentence. *First person* is someone speaking (*I, we*); *second person* is someone spoken to (*you*); *third person* is someone being spoken about (*he, she, it, they*). Verbs must agree in person with their subjects. (*See 16a-3, 19a, 25a.*)
persona The way a writer chooses to characterize himself or herself through the choice of words and phrases, voice, and other devices. (*See 11b, 29a-3.*)
personal home page A category of Web page in which an individual author creates a personal space online. (*See 13d.*)
personal pronoun A pronoun that designates persons or things. (*See 16a-2.*)

SINGULAR	I, me, you, he, him, she, her, it
PLURAL	we, us, you, they, them

personal voice In writing, the use of stylistic devices (such as personal pronouns, narration, or the expression of beliefs and opinions) that convey a strong sense of the writer's self. (*See 2c-3.*)
phrasal verb A verb plus a closely associated word (**particle**) that looks like a preposition (*run down, burn up, call up, clear out*). Unlike prepositions, particles

can be moved from a position after the verb to a position after a direct object. (*See 16a-3.*)

BEFORE OBJECT   Mr. Sims **burned up** all the wood.

AFTER OBJECT   Mr. Sims **burned** all the wood **up**.

phrase A word group lacking one or more elements (such as a subject or predicate) that would make it a complete sentence. (*See 16c; compare* **main clause**.)

plagiarism The unethical practice of claiming that another writer's words or text are your own, or citing another person's words or text without credit, thereby giving the illusion that that person's words are your own. (*See 49c.*)

planning A set of writing strategies through which the writer generates material and makes decisions about the content, organization, and style of a piece of formal writing. (*See Chapter 4; see also* **brainstorming**; **prewriting**; **invention**.)

plot The chain of events in a work of fiction. (*See 57a-2.*)

→**plus** Avoid using *plus* as a conjunction joining two independent clauses.

INFORMAL   The school saved money through its "lights off" campaign, **plus** it generated income by recycling aluminum cans.

EDITED   The school saved money through its "lights off" campaign and also generated income by recycling aluminum cans.

Use *plus* only to mean "in addition to."

ACCEPTABLE   The wearisome reelection campaign, **plus** the pressures from the media, exhausted the senator.

→**p.m., a.m.** (*See* **a.m., p.m.**)

pocket dictionary An abbreviated or abridged dictionary useful for quick checks on spelling or definitions. (*See 30a.*)

point-by-point organization A strategy for arranging paragraphs that make use of **comparing and contrasting**. Comparable features of two different or opposed subjects are described one by one. (*See 9c-2; compare* **subject-by-subject organization**.)

point-driven writing Writing whose content and strategies are shaped by the purpose of explaining the writer's ideas, interpretations, and perspectives and providing support for them. (*See Chapter 56; see also* **informative writing**.)

point of view The perspective from which something (particularly a work of fiction) is told. (*See 57a; see also* **person** and **persona**.)

policy In argumentative writing, a position that a particular course of action is one that should be undertaken or avoided. (*See 55c.*)

poll In fieldwork, research gathered by questioning a representative sample of people to obtain information or opinion. (*See 50a.*)

position paper A short, often documented paper that defines an issue, considers an audience, and draws on evidence and logical strategies to make its point. (*See 55g.*)

positive form One of three forms taken by an adjective or adverb to indicate whether the noun or verb modified is being compared to something else. The positive form is used when no comparison is indicated. (*See 20c; compare* **comparative form** and **superlative form**.)

ADJECTIVE	This is a **clean** oven.
	She is an **imaginative** designer.
ADVERB	You can travel **fast** in Manhattan by foot.
	Peggy designs **imaginatively**.

possessive case (*See* **case**.)

possessive noun A noun that expresses ownership. Possession is usually marked with an apostrophe to distinguish the form from a plural. (*See 35a.*)

The bird's call is becoming fainter.

possessive pronoun A pronoun that shows ownership. (*See 16a-2.*)

SINGULAR	my, mine, your, yours, her, hers, his, its
PLURAL	our, ours, your, yours, their, theirs

post hoc **fallacy** (*See* **faulty cause-effect relationship**.)

PowerPoint Commercial software that produces slides and other visuals that can be projected from a computer onto a screen in oral presentations.

→**precede, proceed** *Precede* means "come before"; *proceed* means "go ahead."

The Mickey Mouse float **preceded** the mayor's car. The parade **proceeded** down Fifth Avenue.

predicate In a sentence, the word or words indicating an action, a relationship, consequences, or conditions. A predicate typically takes the form of a **verb phrase** preceded by the subject of the sentence. A *simple predicate* consists only of a verb or verb phrase; a *complete predicate* consists of a verb or verb phrase plus any modifiers and other words that receive action or complete the verb. (*See 16b-2.*)

prefix An affix, such as *un-* in *unforgiving*, placed before a word. (*See 44b-3.*)

preliminary sources Reference works (such as encyclopedias) or electronic sites (such as mail lists or bulletin boards) that you can consult early in a research project for background information or for issues and questions of current interest. Preliminary (or *exploratory*) sources help you explore broad topics and identify areas for further, more intensive research. (*See 46a-3.*)

premise A claim or assertion that serves as the foundation of an argument. **Syllogistic reasoning** includes both *major* and *minor premises*—assertions or claims on which conclusions can be based. (*See 55f-1.*)

preposition A word that indicates a location, direction, or time (for example, *to, from, with, under, in, over*). (*See 16a-6; see also* **object of a preposition**.)

prepositional phrase A phrase, created from a preposition plus a noun phrase, that can add information to a sentence or make it more precise or detailed. (*See 16a-6.*)

A faint smell **of grilled onions** came **through the window**.

prereading strategies A set of reading strategies in which the reader previews, skims, and samples a reading before working through it more formally. (*See 2a-1.*)

present participle (*See* **participle**.)

present perfect tense (*See* **perfect tense**.)

gloss

present progressive tense (*See* **progressive tense**.)

present tense (*See* **tense**.)

→**pretty** Avoid using *pretty* (as in *pretty good, pretty hungry, pretty sad*) to mean "somewhat" or "rather." Use *pretty* in the sense of "attractive."

prewriting strategies A set of writing strategies used to explore ideas and information in order to generate material for a formal paper. (*See* Chapter 4; *see also* **brainstorming**; **invention**; **planning**.)

primary sources (*See* **research**.)

→**principal, principle** *Principal* is a noun meaning "an authority" or "head of a school" or an adjective meaning "leading" ("a *principal* objection to the testimony"). *Principle* is a noun meaning "belief or conviction."

printed indexes Books listing articles that appear in magazines, newspapers, or scholarly journals. Indexes help researchers locate useful sources. (*See* 46b-2; *see also* **electronic indexes**.)

problem-solution grid A planning strategy through which a variety of hypothetical solutions are generated to solve a specific problem. (*See* 4c-2.)

problem-solution sequence A piece of writing in which a problem is presented followed by a proposal for one or more solutions, perhaps with their advantages and disadvantages. (*See* 4c-2.)

→**proceed, precede** (*See* **precede, proceed**.)

process Any kind of operation, mental or physical, including the specific steps and materials or mechanism involved in the operation. (*See* 9c-2.)

progressive tense A tense used to show an ongoing action in progress at some point in time. Verb forms can show three types of progressive tense: *present progressive, past progressive,* and *future progressive.* (*See* 18c.)

PRESENT PROGRESSIVE	The carousel **is turning** too quickly.
PAST PROGRESSIVE	The horses **were bobbing** up and down.
FUTURE PROGRESSIVE	The children **will be laughing**.

pronoun A word that takes the place of a noun, such as *them, his, she,* and *it.* Pronouns are often used to avoid repeating the nouns used in the sentence. (*See* 16a-2, 19c.)

Jim changed **his shirt** after spilling gravy on **it**.

pronoun-antecedent agreement (*See* **agreement**.)

pronoun reference The connection between a pronoun (*its, him, them,* etc.) and its antecedent, or the noun or person to which it refers. (*See* Chapter 23.)

proofreading The process of reading a draft in order to identify and correct distracting and usually minor errors in spelling, punctuation, incorrect hyphenation, and word division. (*See* 15d; *compare* **editing**.)

proper adjective An adjective derived from a proper noun, used to modify a noun: *Brazilian music, Dickensian portrait.* (*See* 39b-1.)

proper noun A noun that refers to specific people, places, titles, or things and is capitalized: *Miss America, New Orleans, Xerox Corporation.* (*See* 16a-1, 39b-1.)

proposition A **thesis statement** offering an opinion or conclusion that the writer wishes readers to accept or agree with. A proposition is supported or made convincing by an **argument**.

public community People linked by their interest in or participation in activities or organizations addressing the welfare or concerns of either the residents of a particular area or a clearly recognizable social group. A general, diverse population, rather than a specific one, such as a **work community**. (*See 1a.*)

purpose The writer's rhetorical goals or aim for a piece of writing. (*See Chapter 5, 29a-2, 55c.*)

purpose structure A series of statements briefly describing the function of each paragraph or section of a paper. (*See 5b.*)

quantifier A word like *each, one,* or *many* that indicates the quantity of a subject. (*See 19b.*)

query A question; more specifically, a string of words constructed to pose a "question" to the Internet, in a search. (*See 46c.*)

question-answer pattern (*See* **logical order**.)

questionnaire A printed set of questions used in a **survey** or often mailed to a large number of people, to extract information, possibly in-depth. (*See 50a.*)

→**quote, quotation** Formally, *quote* is a verb and *quotation* is a noun. *Quote* is sometimes used as a short version of the noun *quotation*, but this may bother some readers. Use *quotation* instead.

→**raise, rise** Raise is a transitive verb meaning "to lift up." *Rise* is an intransitive verb (it takes no object) meaning "to get up or move up."

He **raised** his head from the newspaper and watched the fog **rise** from the lake.

→**rarely ever** Use *rarely* alone, not paired with *ever*.

> REDUNDANT   He **rarely ever** spoke about the gulag.

> EDITED   He **rarely** spoke about the gulag.

reader The intended or imagined **audience** for a piece of writing. (*See Chapter 6.*)

→**real, really** Use *real* as an adjective modifying a noun; use *really* as an adverb.

Emmons drove **really** well in the race because for once she was in a **real** stock car.

real time Electronic discussions that take place without delay. (*See 13c-3.*)

→**reason is because, reason is that** Avoid these phrases in formal writing; they are wordy and awkward.

reciprocal pronoun A pronoun (*one another, each other*) that enables a writer to refer to individual parts of a plural antecedent. (*See 16a-2.*)

The two kinds of birds compete for territory by destroying **each other's** nests.

→**reckon, calculate, figure** (see **calculate, figure, reckon**.)

red herring A **fallacy** in which some fact or information distracts a reader from the real argument. (*See 55f-5.*)

redrafting Part of the revision process that involves writing unworkable material over again. (*See* **revision**.)

gloss

redundancy The use of unnecessary or repeated words and phrases that can be reduced through **editing**. (*See Chapter 15.*) *Redundant pairs* are two words used when only one is needed: *aid and abet, one and only, part and parcel, kith and kin.* *Redundant phrases* say the same thing twice: *each individual, fresh news, free gifts.* (*See 31a.*)

redundant pair (*See* **redundancy**.)

redundant phrase (*See* **redundancy**.)

reference chain A chain of pronouns whose antecedent is stated in the opening sentence of a passage. Reference chains can help to guide readers through a passage and remind them of the controlling topic. (*See 23a-4.*)

reference list List of sources found at the end of a document. (*See Chapter 52.*)

reflexive pronoun A pronoun that enables a subject or doer of an action also to be the receiver of the action. (*See 16a-2.*)

> **He** paid **himself** for the work.

→**regarding, in regard, with regard to** (*See* **in regard to**.)

→**regardless, irregardless** (*See* **irregardless**.)

register In communication, the form language takes in a particular context, showing variations in pronunciation, grammar, or word choice. (*See 11b.*)

relative clause An adjective-like clause that modifies a noun or pronoun and begins with a **relative pronoun**. (*See 16a, 16c, 17c-1.*)

> **Who** bought the new minivan?
> I reminisced about all the shellfish **that** I had bought in Seattle.

relative pronoun A pronoun (*who, whom, whose, which,* or *that*) introducing a subordinate clause that modifies or adds information to a main clause. (*See 16a-2, 16d, 17c-1, 28c.*)

remote reference Placing a **pronoun** at a distance from its **antecedent**. (*See 23a-2.*)

rereading The process of going back over a reading in order to review, summarize, or understand it. (*See 2a-2.*)

research The process of investigating a topic, either through *primary sources* such as interviews or observations or through *secondary sources* such as other writers' books and articles on the same topic. *Library research* is conducted primarily using the print and electronic materials in libraries; *field research* is conducted in settings where the subject of the research can be found in primary form. (*See Chapter 45, 46a.*)

research plan An anticipated sequence of activities that guides the work of a research paper. (*See 45d.*)

research thread Recurring ideas, issues, or keywords that act as links between research sources. (*See 45a.*)

→**respectfully, respectively** *Respectfully* means "with respect"; *respectively* implies a certain order for events or things.

> The senior class **respectfully** submitted the planning document. The administration considered items 3, 6, and 10, **respectively**.

restrictive clause (*See* **restrictive modifier**.)

restrictive modifier A midsentence clause that presents information essential to the meaning of a passage. In contrast, a *nonrestrictive modifier* adds information that is useful or interesting but not essential to the sentence's meaning. (*See 28c, 33c.*)

RESTRICTIVE MODIFIER	The charts **drawn by hand** were hard to read.
NONRESTRICTIVE MODIFIER	The charts, **drawn by hand**, were hard to read.

résumé A synthesis (in one or two pages) of one's education and employment history, usually prepared for the purpose of applying for a job. (*See 59f.*)

resumptive modifier A modifying clause or phrase used to extend a sentence that appears to have ended, adding new information or twists of thought. (*See 10d-4.*)

People who are careful about what they eat may lead healthier lives, **healthier, though not necessarily longer**.

review A critical appraisal of an event, object, or phenomenon, such as an art show, a concert, or a book. Most reviews are both descriptive and evaluative. (*See 56b.*)

revision The process of improving rough or preliminary versions of a document by making large-scale changes, additions, or deletions in the material. *Major revision* involves redrafting, reorganizing, adding, or deleting significant material; *minor revision* involves changes within paragraphs, often at the sentence level. (*See Chapter 8; see also* **editing** and **proofreading**.)

rhetorical purpose (*See* **purpose**.)

rhetorical question A question asked not in expectation of an answer but for the purpose of providing the answer. (*See 10d-2.*)

rhyming dictionary A dictionary that gives rhymes for words. (*See 30a.*)

→**rise, raise** (*See* **raise, rise**.)

Rogerian argument A strategy for argument that calls for acknowledging the reasonableness of the opposing point(s) of view rather than strong opposition to alternative perspectives. (*See 55f-4.*)

rough draft A preliminary version of a paper which will later undergo **revision**. (*See Chapter 7.*)

rough thesis A statement of the major ideas to be covered in a paper, used to guide further planning and drafting. A rough thesis often appears in a draft but is usually revised by the final version. (*See 5c-2.*)

run-in list A list whose items aren't placed on separate lines. Such lists can present items in full or partial sentences. (*See 39a-5; compare* **vertical list**.)

run-on sentence (*See* **fused sentence**.)

→**says, goes** (*See* **goes, says**.)

scholarly journals Journals that appear approximately four times a year, with the page numbering running continuously throughout the separate issues making up an annual volume. (*See 46b-2.*)

screen name A self-identifier the email user chooses. (*See 13b-2.*)

search engines Software dedicated to indexing and sorting Web pages for user convenience. (*See 13d.*)

search strategy A strategy for research papers in which you identify the type of research you are conducting, the sources you might consult, and the tasks you need to perform. (*See 46a.*)

second person (*See* **person**.)

secondary sources (*See* **research**.)

semidrafting While creating a **rough draft**, the process of writing out full sentences interspersed with *etc.* or other words indicating that something needs to be added later. (*See 7b-3.*)

gloss

sentence A group of words containing a complete subject and predicate. (*See also* **compound sentence**; **compound-complex sentence**; **declarative sentence**; **exclamatory sentence**; **imperative sentence**; **interrogative sentence**; **simple sentence**.)

sentence adverb An adverb used to modify an entire sentence. (*See16a.*)

sentence cluster A group of sentences that develop related ideas or information, often arranged using **parallelism**. (*See 27c-1.*)

sentence fragment A part of a sentence incorrectly treated as a complete sentence with a capital letter at the beginning and a period at the end. (*See Chapter 21.*)

>   FRAGMENT   They were able to get the pump started again. **By replacing the gas filter.**
>
>   EDITED   They were able to get the pump started again by replacing the gas filter.
>   By replacing the gas filter, they were able to get the pump started again.

→**set, sit** *Set* means "to place"; *sit* means "to place oneself."

>   The research assistant **set** the sample near the centrifuge and then **sat** down on the stool.

setting The physical and temporal context of a work of fiction. (*See Chapter 57.*)

sexist language Language that implies or reinforces unfair, misleading, or discriminatory stereotypes on the basis of gender. (*See Chapter 32.*)

shift An incorrect or inappropriate switch in **person**, **number**, **mood**, **tense**, or **topic**. (*See Chapter 25, 26a.*)

→**should of** (*See* **could of, would of**.)

show In a writing assignment, to demonstrate or provide evidence for something.

signal paragraph A type of transition paragraph used to alert readers to a major change in direction or the start of a new section of the discussion.

simple predicate (*See* **predicate**.)

simple sentence A sentence with one main (independent) clause and no subordinate (dependent) clauses. (*See 16d-1; compare* **complex sentence**; **compound sentence**; **compound-complex sentence**.)

simple subject (*See* **subject**.)

→**since, because** (*See* **because, since**.)

→**sit, set** (*See* **set, sit**.)

site, cite (*See* **cite, site**.)

slang New words not yet, possibly never to be, shared by the general population, but used by a limited social group. (*See 11b.*)

slanted statistics (*See* **misleading language/misleading evidence**.)

→**so** Some readers object to the use of *so* in place of *very*.

>   INFORMAL   The filmmaker is **so** thoughtful about giving his films distinct themes.
>
>   EDITED   The filmmaker is **very** thoughtful about giving his films distinct themes.

social context The social, cultural, generational, or economic circumstances of a writer; of an intended **audience**; or of a piece of writing. (*See 6b.*)

→**somebody, some body** (*See* **anybody, any body**.)

→**someone, some one** (*See* **anybody, any body**.)

→**sometime, some time, sometimes** *Sometime* refers to an indistinct time in the future; *sometimes* means "every once in a while." *Some time* is an adjective (*some*) modifying a noun (*time*).

> The probe will reach the nebula **sometime** in the next decade. **Sometimes** such probes fail to send back any data. It takes **some time** before images will come back to us from Neptune.

→**sort, kind** (*See* **kind, sort, type**.)

"sounding out" Trying to determine the correct spelling of a word by its sound. (*See 44a-1*.)

spamming Sending unsolicited email to large groups. (*See 13a-4*.)

spatial order In paragraph development, a pattern for arranging descriptive sentences based on the spatial or visual arrangement of a scene, work of art, person, mechanism, or phenomenon (left to right, top to bottom, and so on).

special collections Library collections that include rare books, manuscripts, and documents, including those of local historical interest. (*See 46b*.)

specialized dictionary Dictionary that lists terms from a particular field or about a specific topic.

specialized sources Focused, often complex or technical resources for research that provide detailed information on narrow topics and often include the latest scholarly findings. Sources of this kind include research reports, scholarly articles, specialized electronic databases, and interviews with experts.

→**specially, especially** (*See* **especially, specially**.)

specific pattern of development A preferred way of developing paragraphs reflecting reader and writer coming from a specific community; compare with **general pattern of development**. (*See 9e-2*.)

specific pronoun reference Using pronouns to clearly specify the relationships between statements. (*See 23b*.)

specific reference A reference that documents the exact location of a word, idea, or fact in a source (for example, on a specific page or in a chart or drawing). (*See 50a; compare* **general reference** *and* **informational reference**.)

specific-to-general pattern (*See* **logical order**.)

speculative writing Writing that explores and considers a topic without taking a position on it.

spelling dictionary A dictionary that gives the spellings of words but not their definitions or etymologies. (*See 30a*.)

split infinitive An **infinitive** in which a word separates *to* from the verb. Some readers object to split infinitives. (*See 24c-3*.)

SPLIT INFINITIVE	The office designer tried **to** respectively **address** each of the workers' concerns.
EDITED	The office designer tried **to address** each of the workers' concerns respectively.

squinting modifier A modifier that incorrectly appears to modify both the word or phrase that comes before it and the one that comes after it. (*See 24a-3*.)

gloss

SQUINTING	Those who smoke **seldom** seem concerned about the potential health hazards.
EDITED	Those who **seldom** smoke seem concerned about the potential health hazards.

state-of-being verb (*See* **linking verb**.)

→**stationary, stationery** *Stationary* means "standing still"; *stationery* refers to writing paper.

structure The arrangement of ideas, sections, or paragraphs in a paper or other text. (*See 6c; see also* **outline** and **purpose structure**.)

structured observation Carefully planned and focused observation of events, people, or situations intended to produce research data from which conclusions can be drawn. (*See Chapter 50*.)

style The distinctive choice of words (**diction**), sentence structures, and **persona** in a piece of writing. (*See 6c*.)

subject In a sentence, the doer or the thing talked about—typically the first noun phrase followed by a verb phrase. A *simple subject* consists of one or more nouns (or pronouns) naming the doer or the topic. A *complete subject* consists of the simple subject plus all its modifying words or phrases. (*See 16b-1*.)

subject-by-subject organization A strategy for arranging paragraphs that make use of **comparing and contrasting**. The writer considers one subject in its entirety and then the other, instead of presenting one point for both and then the next point. (*See 9e; compare* **point-by-point organization**.)

subject complement (*See* **complement**.)

subject pronoun A pronoun that is the subject of a clause. (*See 16d*.)

subjective case (*See* **case**.)

subjective description Description that emphasizes the emotional impact of events or phenomena. (*See 8e; compare* **objective description**.)

subject-verb agreement The verb agrees with the subject in grammatical form. (*See 19a*.)

subjunctive mood (*See* **mood**.)

subordinate clause A word group that contains both a subject and a predicate but cannot stand on its own as a sentence because it begins with a subordinating word such as *because, since, although, which,* or *that*. Also called a *dependent clause*. (*See 16c-5, 16d, 28c*.)

subordinating conjunction (*See* **conjunction**.)

subordination A sentence structure in which one clause modifies another, helping readers perceive the links between ideas and understand the relative importance of information. The **main clause** is accompanied by a **subordinate clause** that modifies, qualifies, or comments on the ideas or the information in the main clause. (*See 28c; compare* **coordination**.)

→**such** Some academic readers will expect you to avoid using *such* without *that*.

INFORMAL	Anne Frank had **such** a difficult time living the life of a normal young girl.
EDITED	Anne Frank had **such** a difficult time growing up **that** her diary writing became her only solace.

suffix An affix added to the end of a word in order to form a derived word (*bold + ness*) or to provide a grammatical inflection (*talk + ing*). (*See 44b*.)

summarize (*See* **summary**.)

summary A précis in your own words of an original passage, preserving the essence of the original but boiling it down to its essential points. An *objective summary* focuses on the content of the original passage, without any authorial judgment or commentary. An *evaluative summary* contains the author's opinions and comments on the passage. (*See 36a-2, 48c-1*.)

summary paragraph A transitional or concluding paragraph used to mark the end of a discussion or to help readers remember main points.

summative modifier A modifying phrase or clause that summarizes the preceding part of a sentence and then takes the sentence on a new course. (*See 10d-4*.)

> To protect your vegetables against harmful insects, you can use soap sprays, scatter insect-repelling plants among the beds, or introduce "friendly" insects like ladybugs and praying mantises—**three techniques** that will not leave a harmful chemical residue on the food you grow.

superlative form One of the three forms taken by adjectives and adverbs to indicate whether the noun or verb modified is being compared to something else. The superlative form adds *-est* or *-most* to the adjective or adverb and indicates a comparison of three or more objects or actions. (*See 19c; compare* **comparative form** and **positive form**.)

ADJECTIVE	This is the **cleanest** oven I've seen.
	She is the **most imaginative** designer of the three.
ADVERB	You can travel **fastest** in Manhattan if you ride a bicycle.
	Peggy designs **most imaginatively** of the three.

supporting conclusions The links in the chain of reasoning. (*See 12b-1*.)

supporting evidence Material that supports a central claim or **thesis**, including examples from personal experience, examples from other people's experience, quotations and ideas from recognized authorities, technical information and statistics, data from surveys and interviews, background and historical information, and comparisons to similar situations and problems. (*See 56d*.)

supporting idea Material that supports an assertion or **thesis**. (*See 5c; see also* **supporting evidence**.)

→**suppose to, supposed to** The correct form of this phrase is *supposed to*; the *-d* is sometimes mistakenly left off because it is not always heard in pronunciation.

→**sure, surely** In formal writing, use *sure* to mean "certain." *Surely* is an adverb; don't use *sure* in its place.

> He is **sure** to pass the exam.
> He has **surely** studied hard for the exam.

→**sure and, try and** *And* is sometimes used in place of *to* with *sure* and *try*. Write *sure to* and *try to* instead.

INCORRECT	We will be *sure and* bring our rackets.
CORRECT	Bob will *try to* win the match.

survey A research tool to obtain data for analysis, usually more complex than a **poll**. (*See 50a*.)

syllabification The correct division of words into their syllables. (*See 30a*.)

syllogism (*See* **syllogistic reasoning**.)

gloss

syllogistic reasoning A kind of logical reasoning that includes a *major premise*, a *minor premise*, and a conclusion. (*See 55f-1; see* **premise**.)

MAJOR PREMISE	All landowners in Clarksville must pay taxes.
MINOR PREMISE	Fred Hammil owns land in Clarksville.
CONCLUSION	Therefore, Fred Hammil must pay taxes.

synonym A word that is identical or nearly identical in meaning to another word: *ill* and *sick, large* and *big.* (*See 29b-2; see* **thesaurus**.)

synthesis The combining or distilling of separate elements into a single, unified entity. Synthesizing source material for a research paper involves combining concepts and details from a variety of sources to form a unified discussion of a topic. (*See 47a.*)

→**take, bring** (*See* **bring, take**.)

talking points Notes taken in advance of an oral presentation in which the presenter outlines major points and provides speaking cues and reminders for him- or herself.

tautology (*See* **circular reasoning**.)

team drafting A method of preparing a preliminary version of a document in which one member of a group begins, then turns it over to a second, and so on; drafts are recirculated before revision. (*See 7c.*)

tense The form a verb takes to indicate time—whether the verb's action occurred in the past (*past tense*) or the present (*present tense*). The present tense form is also called the **base form** of the verb. *Future tense* is marked with the use of **helping verbs**. (*See 16a, 18a, 18b, 25b.*)

PAST	Her grandmother **made** possum stew.
PRESENT	Her friends **stop** to pick up "road kill."
FUTURE	Her children **will find** these old customs offensive.

tense sequence The pattern of tenses in a piece of writing. Incorrect tense shifts can annoy a reader. (*See 18f.*)

tentative thesis statement A preliminary statement of your key ideas and purposes used to help focus planning for the drafting of a paper. (*See 48a-4.*)

text analysis A paper that provides a close, analytical reading of a particular text, often a work of literature. The analysis can focus on elements of the text such as technique or meaning. (*See 57c.*)

→**than, then** *Than* is a word used to compare something; *then* implies a sequence of events or a causal relationship.

Gregorian chants are more lugubrious **than** other vocal music from that period. As a result, we were lulled by the Gregorian chants, but **then** the organ recital started.

→**that, which** Although the distinction between *that* and *which* is weakening in many contexts, formal academic writing often requires you to know the difference. Use *that* in a clause that is essential to the meaning of a sentence (**restrictive modifier**); use *which* with a clause that does not provide essential information (*nonrestrictive modifier*).

THAT	He has the report **that** will vindicate Clareson.
WHICH	He has a penchant for emotionalism, **which** may help him win the jury's favor.

→**theirself, theirselves, themself** All these forms are incorrect; use *themselves* to refer to more than one person, *himself* or *herself* to refer to one person.

→**them** Avoid using *them* as a subject or to modify a subject, as in "*Them* are delicious" or "*Them* apples are very crisp."

theme In literary works, an idea, perspective, or cluster of feelings and insights conveyed to a reader through various fictional devices. (*See 57a-1.*)

→**then, than** (*See* **than, then.**)

→**there, their, they're** These forms are often confused in spelling because they all sound alike. *There* indicates location; *their* is a possessive pronoun; *they're* is a contraction of *they* and *are*.

THERE	Look over **there**.
THEIR	**Their** car ran out of gas.
THEY'RE	**They're** not eager to hike to the nearest gas station.

thesaurus A dictionary of **synonyms** and **antonyms**—words similar or opposite in meaning to each other. (*See 29c-2, 30a.*)

thesis or thesis statement A sentence, often at the conclusion of an essay's first paragraph, that establishes the point, main argument, or direction of a paper, giving the reader a sense of purpose and an understanding of the essay's contents. (*See 5c, 48a, 55c.*)

third person (*See* **person.**)

thread Continuing email discussion (*See 13b-2.*)

→**thusly** Avoid this term; use *thus* or *therefore* instead.

→**till, until, 'til** Some readers will find *'til* and *till* too informal; use *until*.

time sequence A planning strategy, particularly for papers involving chronological or temporal structures, in which events are labeled along a timeline. (*See 4b-3.*)

→**to, as** (*See* **as, to.**)

→**to, too, two** Because these words sound the same, they may be confused. *To* is a preposition indicating location. *Too* means "also." *Two* is a number.

The Birdsalls went **to** their lake cabin. They invited the Corbetts **too**. That made **two** trips so far this season.

topic The focus or subject of a piece of writing. (*See 5c-1.*)

topic sentence A sentence, usually located at the beginning of a paragraph, that announces its main idea or perspective. (*See 9b.*)

topic shift (*See* **faulty predication, shift.**)

→**toward, towards** Prefer *toward* in formal writing. (You may see *towards* used in England and Canada.)

trace In a writing assignment, mapping out a history or chronology or identifying the origins of something. (*See 5a-2.*)

transition (*See* **transitional expression.**)

transitional expression Words or phrases (*in addition to, on the other hand, therefore, without a doubt*) that link one idea, sentence, or paragraph to the next, helping readers to see relationships among ideas by connecting them logically. (*See 9d-2, 33b-3, 34a-2.*)

gloss

transitive verb A verb followed by an **object** or **complement**. (*See* 16b-2; *compare* **intransitive verb**.)

    transitive verb   **object**

The President **called** the British Prime Minister.

tree diagram A planning strategy in which a central idea (or trunk) generates many subsidiary or associative ideas (branches), which can branch off into even more subsidiary twigs. (*See* 4b-2; *compare* **clustering**.)

→**try and, try to, sure and** (*See* **sure and, try and**.)

→**ultimately, eventually** (*See* **eventually, ultimately**.)

unabridged dictionary A full-size reference dictionary, generally available in a library, that has not been abbreviated to save space. (*See* 30a.)

uncountable noun (*See* **noncount noun**.)

unified paragraph (*See* **paragraph**.)

→**uninterested, disinterested** (*See* **disinterested, uninterested**.)

→**unique** Use *unique* alone; don't write *most unique* or *more unique* since the word indicates an absolute condition.

→**until, till** (*See* **till, until, 'til**.)

URL Standing for Universal Resource Locator, a standardized notation specifying the address or location of files on the Internet. (*See* 46c-1.)

→**use to, used to** Like *supposed to*, this phrase may be mistakenly written as *use to* because the -d is not always clearly pronounced. Write *used to*.

usenet newsgroups Electronic bulletin boards tending to attract diverse membership from many geographic regions and professions. (*See* 45b-3.)

vague generalization A sentence or passage that offers so little specific information that it is not meaningful. (*See* 31b-1.)

vague pronoun reference Using pronouns that refer to antecedents that are implied rather than stated, or pronouns that are not connected explicitly to a specific antecedent. (*See* 23b.)

value judgment An argument that an activity, belief, or arrangement is desirable or undesirable. (*See* Chapter 55.)

verb The word in a sentence that indicates the action that has occurred, is occurring, or will occur. (*See* 16a-3.)

verb phrase A phrase that consists of a main verb plus a helping verb. (*See* 16a-3, 18b.)

verbal phrase A verbal plus its modifiers, object, or complements. (*See* 16c-4.)

verbals Verbs or parts of verb phrases that are used to function as nouns, adjectives, or adverbs. The three kinds of verbals are **infinitives**, **participles**, and **gerunds**. (*See* 16a-4, 16c-4.)

vertical file A library file of clippings, pamphlets, and other useful materials.

vertical list A list whose items are placed on separate lines. (*See* 39a-5; *compare* **run-in list**.)

visuals Drawings, photos, graphs, and other visual representations. (*See* 14, 48c-3, 55d.)

voice (*See* **active voice, passive voice**.)

→**wait for, wait on** Use *wait on* only to refer to a clerk's or server's job; use *wait for* to mean "to await someone's arrival."

Julie **waited on** the customers while she **waited for** Melissa to arrive.

warrant (*See* **data-warrant-claim reasoning**.)

Web sites Provide text and graphics with numerous links to related sites. (*See 46c*.)

→**well, good** (*See* **good, well**.)

→**went, gone** (*See* **gone, went**.)

→**were, we're** *Were* is the past plural form of the verb *was; we're* is a contraction of *we* and *are.*

> **We're** going to the ruins where the fiercest battles **were**.

→**where . . . at** (*See* **at**.)

→**whether, if** (*See* **if, whether**.)

→**which, that** (*See* **that, which**.)

→**who, whom** Although the distinction between these words is slowly disappearing from the language, many readers will expect you to use *whom* in the objective case. When in doubt, err on the side of formality. (Sometimes editing can eliminate the need to choose.) (*See 17c*.)

QUESTIONABLE	The person **who** we chose to be the next board president was Harland Clasgow.
EDITED	The person **whom** we chose to be the next board president was Harland Clasgow.
EDITED	We chose Harland Clasgow to be the next board president.

→**who's, whose** *Who's* is the contracted form of *who* and *is. Whose* indicates possession.

> The man **who's** going to Frankfurt tried to find the man **whose** bag he mistakenly took at the airport.

→**wise, -ize** (*See* **-ize, -wise**.)

wordiness Use of too many words. (*See Chapter 31*.)

work communities Groups of people or audiences that are involved in specific business or work environments, as well as governmental agencies. (*See 1a*.)

working bibliography An in-progress bibliography or list of references kept during the **research** process.

working journal A place to explore ideas, develop insights, experiment with prose, write rough drafts, and reflect on reading. (*See 2c*.)

working outline (*See* **outline**.)

working thesis (*See* **rough thesis**.)

works cited List of the works to which the writer makes reference in the body of a research paper, either through in-text (parenthetical) citations or through footnotes or endnotes. (*See 51d*.)

→**would of, could of** (*See* **could of, would of**.)

writer's commentary A writer's direct address of the reader or reference to himself or herself in prose that is not intended to convey personal feelings. (*See 31b-3*.)

writing and reading community People with similar goals, preferences, and uses for both verbal and visual texts. (*See 1a*.)

→**yet, however, but** (*See* **but however, but yet**.)

→**your, you're** *Your* is a possessive pronoun; *you're* is a contraction of *you* and *are.*

> If **you're** going to take physics, you'd better know **your** math.

gloss

CREDITS

*Anatomy of Anti-Comm*unism. New York: Hill and Wang, 1969, p. 118. The Holy Bible, Authorized King James Version. London: Oxford University Press, p. 397. "Bodybuilding" entry from *Info-Trac Academic Index*. Reprinted by permission of Information Access Co. Copyright © 1999 The Gale Group. "Bodybuilding" entry from *1991 Reader's Guide to Periodical Literature*, p. 271. Copyright © 1992. Reprinted by permission of H. W. Wilson Company. *The English Language*. London: Penguin Books, 1988, p. 69. "Exercise" entry from *1992 Reader's Guide to Periodical Literature*, p. 763. Copyright © 1993. Reprinted by permission of H. W. Wilson Company. "Exercise" entry from *1993 Social Sciences Index*, pp. 592–593. Copyright © 1993. Reprinted by permission of H. W. Wilson Company. *Merriam-Webster's Collegiate Dictionary*. Copyright © 1995 by Merriam-Webster Inc. By permission. "Sizing Up the Sexes" from *Time*, January 20, 1992. Copyright © 1992 by Time, Inc. Reprinted by permission. "The Stock Account" from *Prospectus*, College Retirement Equities Fund for Individual Retirement and Tax-Deferred Variable Annuity Certificates, March 1, 1990. Reprinted by permission. *Treasures of Tutankhamun*. National Gallery of Art, p. 13.

Edward Abbey, *Down the River* (New York: Dutton, 1982).

Edward Abbey, *The Journey Home* (New York: Plume, 1991).

Excerpt from "Editorial Policy and Manuscript Preparation Guidelines" *Journal of the Air & Waste Management Association*, Vol. 51, (May 2001). Copyright © 2002 Air & Waste Management Association. All rights reserved. Reprinted by permission.

Hanson W. Baldwin, "R. M. S. Titanic." *Harper's Magazine*, 1933.

H. G. Bissinger, *Friday Night Lights* (Reading, MA: Addison-Wesley, 1990).

Louise Bogan, excerpt from "Old Countryside" from *The Blue Estuaries: Poems 1923–1968* by Louise Bogan. Copyright © 1968 by Louise Bogan. Copyright renewed © 1996 by Ruth Limmer. Reprinted by permission of Farrar, Straus and Giroux, LLC.

Marcia Brown, from *Stone Soup* by Marcia Brown. Copyright © 1947 by Marcia Brown. Copyright © renewed 1975 by Marcia Brown. Reprinted with the permission of Atheneum Books for Young Readers, an imprint of Simon and Schuster Children's Publishing Division.

Maurice Broner, "Stand Up and Be Heard" *IEEE*, Trans. Eng. Writing Speech. Copyright © 1964 IEEE. Reprinted by permission.

Jacob Bronowski, The Ascent of Man (Boston, MA: Little, Brown, 1973).

Jimmy Buffett, "Where Is Joe Merchant" from *Tales from Margaritaville: Fictional Facts and Factual Fictions* (Orlando, FL: Harcourt Brace & Company, 1992).

Cathryn Carroll, *Laurent Clerc: The Story of His Early Years* (Washington, DC: Gallaudet University Press, 1991).

Colorado Division of Wildlife, "Tips" *The Denver Post*, July 30, 1998, p., 15 (A).

Wilkie Collins, *The Woman in White* (New York: Dutton, 1969).

"Fast-Track Recalls," *Consumer Product Safety Review*, Fall, 1998 Issue, Vol. 3, No. 1.

Stephanie Coontz, "The Way We Weren't." *National Forum: Phi Beta Kappa Phi Journal*, Vol. 75, No. 3 (Summer 1995). Copyright © Stephanie Coontz. By permission of the publisher.

Sharon R. Curtin, *Nobody Ever Died of Old Age* (Boston: MA, Little, Brown, 1972).

Mike Davis, "House of Cards," *Sierra*, 1995.

Joan Didion, from *After Henry* by Joan Didion. Copyright © 1992 by Joan Didion. Reprinted with the permission of Simon & Schuster, Inc.

Annie Dillard, *An American Childhood* (New York: HarperCollins, 1987).

A. H. Drummond, Jr., *The Complete Guide to Sailing* (New York: Simon and Schuster, 1986).

Brad Edmondson, from "Making Yourself at Home: The Baby Boom Generation Yearns to Settle Down." Reprinted by permission.

Barbara Ehrenreich, from *What I've Learned from Men: Lessons for a Full-Grown Feminist*. Reprinted by permission.

David Elkind, "The Family in the Postmodern World." *National Forum: Phi Beta Kappa Phi Journal*, Vol. 75, No. 3 (Summer 1995). Copyright © David Elkind. By permission of the publisher.

From "Fire Safety Tips for a Safe Holiday Season" http://www.sema.state.mo.us/firexmas.htm.

Tess Gallagher, "Under Stars" from *Amplitude* by Tess Gallagher. Copyright © 1987 by Tess Gallagher. Reprinted by permission of Graywolf Press, Saint Paul, Minnesota.

Laurie Garrett, *The Coming Plague* (New York: Penguin Books, 1994).

Clifford Geertz, The Interpretation of Cultures (New York: Basic Books, 1973).

Louis D. Giannetti, *Understanding Movies*, 6th ed., (Englewood Cliffs, NJ: Prentice Hall, 1993).

Nikki Giovanni, "Pioneers: A View of Home" from *Sacred Cows*. Copyright © 1988 by Nikki Giovanni. Reprinted by permission of William Morrow and Company, Inc.

Frank Goddio, "San Diego: An Account of Adventure, Deceit, and Intrigue," *National Geographic*, 1994.

Daniel Goleman, "Too Little, Too Late," *American Health*, 1992.

Anson Gonzalez, "Little Rosebud Girl." Copyright © 1972 by Anson Gonzalez. Reprinted by permission.

Ellen Goodman, "Religion in Textbooks." Copyright © 1994 The Boston Globe Newspaper Co./ Washington Post Writers Group. Reprinted with permission.

Google Logo and Search Code. Copyright © 2000 Google. The Google search code and Google logo used on the main page of this site are provided by and are used with the permission of: http://www.google.com.

Al Gore, *Earth in the Balance* (Boston, MA: Houghton Mifflin, 1992).

Rick Gore, "Dinosaurs," *National Geographic*, January 1993.

Beverly Green, "African American Families: A Legacy of Vulnerability and Resilience." *National Forum: Phi Beta Kappa Phi Journal*, Vol. 75, No. 3 (Summer 1995). Copyright © Beverly Green. By permission of the publisher.

Kenneth C. Green, Chart from *The Campus Computing Project*. Copyright © 1998 by Kenneth C. Green. Reprinted by permission.

Michael Gregor, "Milk . . . Help Yourself," *AnimaLife*, fall 1994, Vol. 5, No.1. http://liberator.enviroweb.org/ fall94/milk.html. Reprinted by permission of the publisher.

From "Gulf Ecosystem Monitoring and Research Plan," as it appeared on Exxon Valdez Oil Spill Trustee Council Website. http://www.oilspill.state.ak.us/restoration/index.html. Used by permission.

Donald Hall, "A Small Fig Tree," from *Old and New Poems*. Copyright © 1990 by Donald Hall. Reprinted by permission of Ticknor Fields/Houghton Mifflin Co. All rights reserved.

Thomas W. Harvey, *A New English Grammar for Schools* (New York: American Book Company, 1900).

Carl Haub: Figure 1. From "Population Reference Bureau estimates and UN (medium series) long-range projections of 1992" as it appeared in "Global and U.S. National Population Trends" by Carl Haub, *Consequences*, Vol. 1, No. 2 (1995). http://www.gcrio.org/CONSEQUENCES/summer95/fig1.html. Reprinted by permission of the author.

Nathaniel Hawthorne, *Young Goodman Brown* and *The Birthmark*.

Ernest Hemingway, *The Old Man and the Sea* (New York: Scribner, 1952).

J. N. Hook, *The Appropriate Word* (Reading, MA: Addison-Wesley, 1990).

"How Guns Move from Legal to Illegal Ownership," Figure 1 from *Gun Control in the United States*. Copyright © 2000 Open Society Institute. Reprinted by permission. http://www.soros.org/crime/figure1.htm.

Zora Neale Hurston, from *Their Eyes Were Watching God* by Zora Neale Hurston. Copyright © 1937 by Harper & Row, Publishers, Inc. Renewed 1965 by John C. Hurston and Joel Hurston. Reprinted by permission of HarperCollins Publishers, Inc.

Robert Jastrow, *The Enchanted Loom* (New York: Simon and Schuster, 1981).

Robert Jastrow, *Journey to the Stars* (New York: Bantam Books, 1989).

Maxine Hong Kingston, *The Woman Warrior* (New York: Alfred A. Knopf, 1976).

William Severini Kowinski, *The Malling of America* (New York: Morrow, 1985).

Robert Levine, from *A Geography of Time: The Temporal Misadventures of a Social Psychologist, or How Every Culture Keeps Time a Little Bit Differently* by Robert Levine. Copyright © 1997 Robert Levine. Reprinted by permission of Basic Books, a division of Perseus Books, LLC.

James Lundquist, *Chester Himes* (New York: Random House, 1988).

Ruth Macklin, *Mortal Choices* (Boston: Houghton Mifflin, 1987).

T. R. Mayers, from "(snap)shots." Reprinted by permission of the author.

Thomas R. McDonough, "Is Anyone Out There?" *Discover*, November 1992.

Bill McKibben, *The End of Nature* (New York: Random House, 1989).

Margaret Mead, *Male and Female* (New York: Morrow, 1949).

Barbara Mellix, "From Outside, In," *The Georgia Review*, Vol. 41 (Summer 1987).

From *Merriam Webster's Collegiate Dictionary* 9th Edition. Copyright © 1993 by Merriam-Webster Inc. Reprinted by permission.

Hugh Merrill, *The Blues Route* (New York: Morrow, 1990).

Desmond Morris, *Body Watching* (New York: Crown, 1985).

Paul Mungo and Bryan Clough, "The Bulgarian Connection," *Discover*, February 1993.

Edward R. Murrow, *In Search of Light* (New York: Alfred A. Knopf, 1967).

"Ninth Special Report on Alcohol and Health Marks Research Gains," National Institute on Alcohol Abuse and Alcoholism Website. http://www.niaaa.nih.gov/press/1997/ninthrep.htm.

Bill Neal, "How to Cure a Pig," Esquire, 1991.

Kesaya Noda, "Growing Up Asian in America," as it appeared in *Making Waves by Asian Women United*. Reprinted by permission of the author.

NCSU Libraries Website, Search results for "The UFO Invasion: The Roswell Incident, Alien Abductions, and Government Cover-ups." North Carolina State University Libraries, 2002. NCSU Libraries Website. Copyright © 2002. Used by permission of The Scholarly Communication Center, North Carolina State University.

Susan Orlean, *Saturday Night* (New York: Random House, 1990).

Alfonso Ortiz, "Some Concerns Central to the Writing of Indian History," *The Indian Historian*.

Parsons, Simmons, Shinhoster, and Kilburn, "A Test of the Grapevine: An Empirical Examination of Conspiracy Theories Among African Americans," *Sociological Spectrum*, 19.2 (1999).

Phil Patton, "How a Ridiculous Idea Mutated into a Marketing Star," *Smithsonian*, 1992.

Noel Perrin, "About Men: The Androgynous Man." *The New York Times Magazine,* February 5, 1984. Copyright © 1984 by The New York Times Company. Reprinted by permission.

David Popenoe, "The American Family Crisis." *National Forum: Phi Beta Kappa Phi Journal*, Vol. 75, No. 3 (Summer 1995). Copyright © David Popenoe. By permission of the publisher.

Neil Postman, *Amusing Ourselves to Death* (New York: Penguin, 1985).

Samuel J. Preeth, "Incident at Lake Nyos," *The Sciences*, 1992.

Richard Rodriguez, *Hunger of Memory* (Boston: David R. Godine, 1983).

Jay Sankey, from *Zen and the Art of Stand-Up Comedy*. Copyright © 1998. Reproduced by permission of Taylor & Francis /Routledge, Inc. http://www.routledge-ny.com.

Juliet B. Schor, *The Overworked American* (New York: HarperCollins, 1998).

Brian Schwegler, "Character Development Sketch: 'Dave the Guesser,'" *Salt Magazine*, August 1994. Reprinted by permission of the author and SALT Center for Documentary Field Studies.

Elsie Myers Stainton, *The Fine Art of Copyediting* (New York: Columbia University Press, 1991).

Judith Stacey, "The Family Values Fable." *National Forum: Phi Beta Kappa Phi Journal*, Vol. 75, No. 3 (Summer 1995). Copyright © Judith Stacey. By permission of the publisher.

"State Nonfiscal Survey: School Year 1993-94, US Department of Education, National Center for Education Statistics.

Jane Stern and Michael Stern, *Roadfood* (New York: HarperCollins, 1992).

Deborah Tannen, *You Just Don't Understand: Women and Men in Conversation* by Deborah Tannen (New York: Morrow, 1990).

Lewis Thomas, *Late Night Thoughts on Listening to Mahler's Ninth* (New York: Penguin, 1992).

"Sizing Up the Sexes," *Time,* January 20, 1992. Copyright © 1992 Time Inc. Reprinted by permission.

Treasures of Tutankhamun (Washington, DC: National Gallery of Art, 1976).

Richard H. Wagner, *Environment and Man* (New York: Norton, 1978).

"What research has been done on St. John's Wort?" http://www.athleticnutrition.com/Stjohns.html.

"Why Does Milk Bother Me?" National Digestive Diseases Information Clearinghouse, National Institutes of Health, http://www.niddk.gov/health/digest/pubs/whymilk/index.html. Reprinted with permission.

John Edgar Wideman, *Philadelphia Fire* (New York: Henry Holt, 1990).

Richard Wisniewski & Paul Kleine, "Teacher Moonlighting: An Unstudied Phenomenon," *ERIC* 1983.

Donna Woolfolk Cross, *Mediaspeak: How Television Makes Up Your Mind* (New York: Coward-McCann, 1983).

Carl Zimmer, "The Body Electric," *Discover*, February 1993.

We thank the following students for permission to reprint their work: David Aharonian, Summer Arrigo-Nelson, Amy K. Braegelman, Carey Braun, Sara Brilliant, Zachary Carter, Kimlee Cunningham, Jessica DiGregorio, Jenifer Figliozzi, Jason W. Fester, Chantele D. Giles, Shane Hand, Andrea K. Herrmann, Stephanie E. Lewis, Reid Nelson, Jenifer L. O'Berry, Michael Perry, Brian Schwegler, and Ted Wolfe.

credits

INDEX

index

index

index

index

index

index

Read, Recognize, and Revise
Ten Serious Errors

These ten errors are identified in our research as among those most likely to confuse or irritate readers in the academic community. Whether errors distort meaning or suggest carelessness, they distract readers from what you want to say. Too many errors can erode your relationship with your readers and diminish the success of your writing.

READ

Pay attention to potential problems as you revise and edit.	Consider the possible reactions of your community of readers.
1. The heavy rain turned the parking area to mud. *And stranded thousands of cars.* →	READER'S REACTION: **The second part seems disconnected. Now I've got to stop and figure out how it fits.** →
2. The promoters called *the insurance company they discovered* their coverage for accidents was limited. →	READER'S REACTION: **I'm confused. Is this** → **about some new insurance company that the promoters discovered?**
3. After talking with the groundskeeper, the security chief said *he* would not be responsible for the safety of the crowd. →	READER'S REACTION: **Who's *he*—the groundskeeper or the security chief?** →
4. The local authorities *hadn't scarcely* enough resources to cope with the flooding. →	READER'S REACTION: *Hadn't scarcely*— **this isn't the way a college graduate or a professional writes.** →
5. *After announcing the cancellation from the stage, the crowd* began complaining to the promoters. →	READER'S REACTION: **I know the crowd didn't announce the cancellation, but that's what this says!** →
6. Even the *promoters promise* to reschedule and honor tickets did little to stop the *crowds complaints.* →	READER'S REACTION: **I can't read this without feeling irritated that apostrophes are missing.** →
7. "The grounds are *slippery, the* mayor announced, "so please leave in an orderly manner." →	READER'S REACTION: **Here are more missing marks! Didn't this writer bother to proofread?** →
8. Away from the microphone, the mayor said, "I hope the security chief or the promoters *has* a plan to help everyone leave safely." →	READER'S REACTION: **Promoters *has*? This careless writer didn't even make the effort to fit subjects and verbs together.** →
9. If *people* left the amphitheater quickly, *you* could get to *your* car without standing long in the rain. →	READER'S REACTION: **Why is this sentence** → **mixing *people* with *you*? Is *you* supposed to mean *me*?**
10. *Although,* the muddy parking area caused problems, all the cars and *people, left* the grounds without incident. →	READER'S REACTION: **It looks as if the writer just tossed in some commas here—and they make the sentence hard to read.** →

USING THE "READ, RECOGNIZE, AND REVISE" APPROACH

Use the **read-recognize-revise pattern** to identify and edit errors. First, *read* the example provided (column 1). Consider the Reader's Reaction, showing how a reader might respond (column 2). Next use the handbook's advice, the Strategies suggested, or your own strategy to help you *recognize* the error (column 3). Finally, select a Strategy to *revise* or repair the error (column 4).

RECOGNIZE	REVISE
Try strategies for recognizing problems—or invent your own.	**Use strategies to edit, repair, or replace errors or problems.**
Fragment: Ask questions. Who (or what) does? Who (or what) is? (**21a**) →	The heavy rain turned the parking area to mud and stranded thousands of cars. (**21b**)
Fused Sentence: Look for a long sentence without internal punctuation; count the separate statements it contains. (**22a**) →	The promoters called the insurance company, and they discovered their coverage for accidents was limited. (**22b**)
Unclear Pronoun Reference: See whether → your sentence contains two or more words to which a pronoun might refer. (**20d**)	After talking with the groundskeeper, the security chief said, "I will not be responsible for the safety of the crowd." (**20d**)
Double Negative: Check for combinations → of negative words like *no, not, scarcely,* or *don't.* (**24b**)	The local authorities had scarcely enough resources to cope with the flooding. (**24b**)
Dangling Modifier: When a modifier begins a sentence, consider whether the person or thing modified is the subject of the main clause. (**35a**) →	After the promoters announced the cancellation from the stage, the crowd began complaining about the decision. (**35a**)
Missing Possessive Apostrophe: Test for → possession by trying to turn a noun ending in *-s* into an *of* phrase. (**36a**)	Even the promoters' promise to reschedule and honor tickets did little to stop the crowd's complaints. (**36b**)
Missing Marks: Look for marks often used → in pairs such as quotation marks (**36a**) and commas. (**34d, 34j, 36a**)	"The grounds are slippery," the mayor announced, "so please leave in an orderly manner." (**34c**)
Lack of Subject-Verb Agreement: Find → the subject (especially if separated, plural, or compound); match the verb. (**19a–b**)	Away from the microphone, the mayor said, "I hope the security chief or the promoters have a plan to help everyone leave safely." (**19a–b**)
Shift: Hunt for illogical or inconsistent shifts → among *I, we, you, he, she, it,* or *they.* (**25a**)	If people left the amphitheater quickly, they could get to their cars without standing long in the rain. (**25a**)
Unnecessary Commas: Check for un- → needed commas after words like *although* or between subject and verb. (**35j**)	Although the muddy parking area caused problems, all the cars and people left the grounds without incident. (**35j**)

Revision and Editing Symbols

abbrev	incorrect abbreviation, **43**	**no ¶**	no new paragraph, **9**
agr	error in subject-verb or pronoun-antecedent agreement, **19**	**p**	error in punctuation, **33–38**
		punc	error in punctuation, **33–38**
		$\hat{,}$	comma, **33a–j**
apos	lack of (or incorrect) possessive apostrophe, **35**	**no** $\hat{,}$	no comma, **33j**
art	article used incorrectly, **16**	**;**	semicolon, **34a**
awk	awkward construction, **10a–b**	**:**	colon, **34b**
		$\overset{\vee}{,}$	apostrophe, **35**
cap	capital letter needed, **39**	" "	quotation marks, **36**
case	incorrect pronoun case, **17**	**.**	period, **37a**
clear	clearer sentence needed, **10a**	**?**	question mark, **37b**
coh	paragraph or essay coherence needed, **9c**	**!**	exclamation point, **37c**
		( ) [ ] —	parentheses, brackets, dashes, **38a–e**
cs	comma splice, **22**	**. . . /**	ellipses, slashes, **38d**
coord	faulty coordination, **28a–b**	**prep**	preposition error, **16a**
dev	paragraph or essay development needed, **9e**	**pr ref**	pronoun reference error, **23**
		ref	pronoun reference error, **23**
discrm	sexist or discriminatory language, **32**	**rep**	repetitious, **31**
dm	dangling modifier, **24b**	**sent**	sentence revision needed, **10**
dneg	double negative, **20d**	**shift**	shift, **25**
emph	emphasis needed, **10c**	**sp**	word spelled incorrectly, **44**
foc	paragraph or essay focus needed, **9a–b**	**spell**	word spelled incorrectly, **44**
		sub	faulty subordination, **28c**
frag	sentence fragment, **21**	**t**	wrong verb tense, **18a–c**
fs	fused sentence, **22**	**tense**	wrong verb tense, **18a–c**
hyph	hyphen (-) needed, **41**	**trans**	transition needed, **9c–d**
inc	incomplete sentence, **26b**	**und**	underlining (italics), **40**
ital	italics (underlining), **40**	**us**	error in usage, **Glossary**
lc	lowercase letter needed, **39**	**var**	sentence variety needed, **10d**
link	paragraph linkage needed, **9d**	**verb**	incorrect verb form, **18**
log	faulty reasoning, **12c–d, 55f**	**wc**	faulty word choice, **29a**
mixed	grammatically mixed sentence, **26a**	**wordy**	too many words, **31**
		ww	wrong word, **29**
mm	misplaced modifier, **24a**	^	insert
modif	incorrect adjective or adverb, **20a–b**	℘	delete
		◠	close up space
num	incorrect number, **42**	∿	transpose letters or words
//	parallel elements needed, **27**	**#**	add a space
¶	new paragraph, **9**	**X**	obvious error